Measuring and Promoting Wellbeing

How Important is Economic Growth?

Essays in honour of Ian Castles AO and a selection of Castles' papers

Measuring and Promoting Wellbeing

How Important is Economic Growth?

Essays in honour of Ian Castles AO and a selection of Castles' papers

Edited by

Andrew Podger and Dennis Trewin for the Academy of Social Sciences in Australia.

Australian National University

PRESS

Published by ANU Press
The Australian National University
Canberra ACT 0200, Australia
Email: anupress@anu.edu.au
This title is also available online at http://press.anu.edu.au

National Library of Australia Cataloguing-in-Publication entry

Author: Podger, A. S. (Andrew Stuart), author.

Title Measuring and promoting wellbeing : how important is economic growth? : essays in honour of Ian Castles AO and a selection of Castle's papers / Andrew Podger and Dennis Trewin.

ISBN: 9781925021318 (paperback) 9781925021325 (ebook)

Series: Australia and New Zealand School of Government monograph.

Subjects: Castles, Ian.
Festschriften--Australia.
Economic development--Social aspects.
Economic development--Sociological aspects.
Quality of life--Economic aspects.
Well-being--Economic aspects.

Other Authors/Contributors:
Trewin, D. J. (Dennis John), 1946- author.

Dewey Number: 306.3

Cover design by Nic Welbourn and layout by ANU Press

Printed by Griffin Press

Contents

Part Three: Measuring Inequality

Part Four: Climate Change and Limits to Growth

Preface

Andrew Podger and Dennis Trewin

The underlying theme of the symposium held by the Academy of Social Sciences in Australia (ASSA) and the ANU Crawford School of Public Policy on 21/22 November 2012 was whether economic growth was worth having. Ian Castles argued throughout his illustrious career that economic growth should be an outcome of good policy not a policy objective in its own right. A second theme was the role that broader wellbeing indicators play in informing and shaping public policy. The event brought together a number of distinguished former public servants, politicians and academics as well as current policy advisers including departmental officials from Treasury and the ABS and several eminent Australian economists and other social scientists. The objective was to review contemporary developments in measuring and promoting economic growth and society wellbeing, and the role of economic growth, whilst reflecting upon the work in these fields by Ian Castles AO.

This symposium was held in memory of Ian Castles, who passed away in 2010. As a long-time senior member of the public service, including as Secretary of the Department of Finance, Australian Statistician and Under Secretary in the Department of Prime Minister and Cabinet, and subsequently as an academic at ANU and Deputy President of ASSA, Ian dedicated much of his professional career to pursuing a rigorous appraisal of measures and drivers of economic growth and wellbeing. He was also an important advocate for the social sciences, particularly economics and official statistics. Despite the constraints of public service, Ian's contributions over 40 years include an impressive array of fine writings and publications available to the public, a selection of which are included in this collection and were provided as background to the symposium. An overview of Ian's work is provided in Michael Keating's chapter in this book, a speech he gave at the opening dinner.

The context of the symposium and this book is the more recent developments both in Australia and overseas in the measurement of wellbeing and the use of such measures in public policy, and also the renewed debates about 'sustainability' and whether continued economic growth might present unacceptable social and environmental costs for future generations.

To facilitate careful examination of these developments and debates, the symposium and this book explore in some detail three dimensions of the issues involved:

- measuring real income and wellbeing;
- measuring inequality; and
- the possibility of limits to growth, particularly because of climate change, if the wellbeing of future generations is to be protected.

Before coming to these matters, however, the book commences with an overview of the symposium, followed by some broader reflections on the role of economics in defining and promoting wellbeing, including Mike Keating's appreciation of the contributions made by Ian Castles. We have included here two of Ian Castles' most significant contributions not well known beyond close colleagues or not known to be his work. The first, *Economics and Anti-Economics,* was a paper he presented in 1984 to an ANZAAS conference but never published. The second, *Economic Growth: Is it Worth Having?,* was published as Treasury Economic Paper No 2 in 1973 without attribution to Castles, but known to have been written by a small team Castles led at the time. Central to both papers was Ian's conviction that economics as part of the social sciences can and should be used to improve the wellbeing of people however wellbeing is defined by individuals and collective public policy.

While firmly supporting wider concepts of wellbeing, there was almost unanimous agreement among the symposium participants that economic growth is worth having as it is closely linked to improvements in most other aspects of wellbeing and provides opportunities for further action to improve society wellbeing.

We hope this book will promote better understanding of the concepts and measurement of economic growth and wellbeing, support further improvements to the contribution of the social sciences to wellbeing in its broadest sense, and encourage further research.

Andrew Podger

Dennis Trewin

(Editors)

Contributors

Jeff Bennett, FASSA, is Professor in the Crawford School of Public Policy at The Australian National University. He is also a Distinguished Fellow of the Australian Agricultural and Resource Economics Society. Professor Bennett has published widely in the economics of environmental, natural resource and agricultural issues. In particular his research focuses on the estimation of non-marketed environmental values for policy analysis and the role of the private sector in the provision of environmental management services. He has a PhD from The Australian National University.

Rob Bray is a research fellow in the Social Policy, Evaluation, Analysis and Research Centre at the Research School of Economics at The Australian National University. He took up this position in 2010 after a long public service career which encompassed policy development, program management and research across a wide spectrum of social and related policies including income support, housing and urban development, labour market programs and residential care. His current research interests include income distribution and the impact of taxes and transfers and labour market outcomes including minimum wages. In addition he is involved in undertaking a range of projects relating to the evaluation of Australian government social policies.

Ian Castles, AO OBE FASSA, was Secretary of the Department of Finance (1979-86) and the Australian Statistician (1986-94) as well as holding senior positions in the Departments of Prime Minister and Cabinet and Treasury. He was also Executive Director and Vice President of the Academy of the Social Sciences in Australia (1995–2000) and President of the International Association of Official Statistics. His interests included research into the information requirements for public policy (especially at the international level) and the history of economic thought. He was a strong critic where he thought public policy was misinformed by poor statistics or poor statistical analysis. Ian Castles died on 2 August 2010, aged 75.

William Coleman is a Reader at the Research School of Economics of The Australian National University. He has written extensively upon inflation, the history of economic thought and the contested position of economics in society. He is currently the editor of *Agenda: A Journal of Policy Analysis and Reform*, and has authored, or co-authored, several books, including *Giblin's Platoon: The Trials and Triumph of the Economist in Australian Public Life*. He has a PhD from the London School of Economics.

Richard Eckersley, AM, is an independent researcher and a founding director of Australia 21, a non-profit, strategic research company. His work explores progress and wellbeing, and includes: measures of national progress; the relationships between economic growth, quality of life and sustainability; the social and cultural determinants of health and happiness; visions of the future; and young people and their world. His work has been published in leading international scientific journals and major Australian newspapers, and brought together in a book. He has held positions with *The Sydney Morning Herald*, CSIRO Australia, the Commission for the Future, the Australian Government and The Australian National University.

Henry Ergas is Senior Economic Adviser, Deloitte Access Economics, and Professor of Infrastructure Economics, University of Wollongong, as well as a columnist for *The Australian*. He spent many years as an economist at the OECD in Paris, and has taught at a number of universities. He has a Master of Economic Studies from the University of Queensland.

Will Gort is currently enrolled at the ANU, completing a Bachelor of Economics with Honours, graduating at the end of 2013. Since 2012 he has been employed as a tutor at the Research School of Economics at the ANU and in 2012 was president of Burton and Garran Hall. In 2014 he will begin a role as a graduate economist with Deloitte Access Economics in Melbourne.

David Gruen is the Executive Director of Macroeconomic Group at Australian Treasury. He joined the Treasury in January 2003. Before that, he was Head of Economic Research Department at the Reserve Bank of Australia from May 1998 to December 2002. Before joining the Reserve Bank, he worked as a research scientist in the Research School of Physical Sciences at The Australian National University. He holds PhD degrees in physiology from Cambridge University, England and in economics from The Australian National University.

Mark Harrison is Senior Research Fellow at the SMART Infrastructure Facility, University of Wollongong and a free-lance economic consultant. He has 30 years experience in undertaking applied economic research and providing policy advice as a public servant, academic and consultant, including a stint as a visiting researcher at the Productivity Commission. He has a PhD in economics from the University of Chicago.

John Hawkins is a PhD student at The Australian National University. He holds masters degrees in economics and politics from the London School of Economics and Macquarie University. He has worked in the Reserve Bank of Australia, Hong Kong Monetary Authority, the Bank for International Settlements and the Australian Treasury. He was formerly the secretary of the Senate Economics Committee and senior economics adviser to the Australian Greens.

David Henderson, CMG, is a British economist, now based in London, who is currently Chairman of the Academic Advisory Council of the Global Warming

Policy Foundation. He was Head of the Economics and Statistics Department of the OECD in Paris from 1984 to 1992, having previously worked at Oxford University, Whitehall, the World Bank and University College London.

Michael Keating, AC FASSA FIPAA, was the Head of three Australian Government Departments from 1983 to 1996 including the Department of Prime Minister and Cabinet. Since then he has held positions at The Australian National University and Griffith University. He has also been a member of various private and government boards, and has continued to work as a consultant to major companies and governments on corporate and government strategy and policy development. Michael Keating has always had strong research interests and has published various economic and employment related articles and co-authored a book on Australian economic policy. He has also published extensively in Australia and overseas on the capacity of our system of governance and public sector management reform. He has a PhD from Duke University.

Jonathan Pincus, FASSA, returned in 2008 to Adelaide University as Visiting Professor of Economics, from his position as Principal Adviser Research at the Productivity Commission. His current research interests are fiscal federalism, mining royalties and nineteenth century Australian infrastructure. He has a PhD from Stanford University.

Brian Pink has been the Australian Statistician since March 2007. Mr Pink's career in official statistics in Australia started with the then Commonwealth Bureau of Census and Statistics in 1966. He has also served as Government Statistician and Chief Executive of Statistics New Zealand from October 2000 until his current appointment. Brian Pink is Chairman of the Organisation for Economic Co-operation and Development Committee on Statistics, Chair of the Statistics Committee of ESCAP and Vice Chair of the United Nations Statistical Commission. Back home he is an ex officio member of the Australian Statistics Advisory Council and an Australian Electoral Commissioner.

Andrew Podger, AO FASSA FIPAA, is Professor of Public Policy at ANU. He was previously a career public servant having started as a cadet with the Australian Bureau of Statistics and becoming Secretary of various Commonwealth departments and the Public Service Commissioner. His research interests include public management and social policy. Before leaving the Australian Public Service in 2005, he chaired a review of the delivery of health and aged care services.

Duncan Spender is a Senior Adviser in the Macroeconomic Group at Australian Treasury. He has worked in various parts of Australian Treasury since September

1999, apart from a period in New Zealand Treasury from 2004 to 2006. Before coming to Australian Treasury, he worked as a research officer for the Local Government Association of Queensland.

Sue Taylor is currently Director in the 2016 Census program. She was formerly Director of the Social and Progress Reporting section of the Australian Bureau of Statistics with responsibility for reporting on wellbeing in Australia, through Australian Social Trends, and for Measures of Australia's Progress. Prior to her move to Australia in 1986 she worked as teacher and part-time lecturer in Nigeria and Botswana.

Dennis Trewin, AO FASSA, was the Australian Statistician and head of the Australian Bureau of Statistics from July 2000 until January 2007. Prior to that he was Deputy Australian Statistician and Deputy Government Statistician in New Zealand. He has also been a Trustee and Board member for the Australian Reward and Investment Alliance, an Associate Commissioner at the Productivity Commission for the Study into the Not for Profit Sector and an Australian Electoral Commissioner. He has been the President of the International Statistical Institute. He has recently been working as a statistical consultant mostly on international assignments.

Hannah Wetzler is a social data analyst at the Australian Bureau of Statistics. She currently works in the Social and Progress Reporting Section, reporting on Australia's progress and wellbeing through Measures of Australia's Progress and Australian Social Trends. She achieved first class honours and the University medal at the University of Newcastle for her honours thesis, which focused on young Australians' engagement with international poverty.

Peter Whiteford is a Professor in the Crawford School of Public Policy at The Australian National University, Canberra. Between 2008 and 2012 he worked at the Social Policy Research Centre at the University of New South Wales (UNSW) in Sydney. He previously worked as a Principal Administrator in the Directorate of Employment, Labour and Social Affairs of the Organisation for Economic Co-operation and Development in Paris. Professor Whiteford's work at the OECD encompassed pension and welfare policies in OECD countries, Eastern Europe and China. He also worked on child poverty, family assistance policies, welfare reform, and other aspects of social policy, particularly ways of supporting the balance between work and family life.

1. Economic Growth, Wellbeing and Protecting the Future: An Overview of the Castles Symposium

Andrew Podger, Dennis Trewin, William Gort

The symposium context

Australia has for many decades been at the forefront of efforts to improve measurement of wellbeing, and is investing significantly in continuing this work. There is increasing international interest in the field highlighted by such contributions as Bhutan's famous 'Happiness Index' and the 2009 Stiglitz, Sen and Fittoussi report commissioned by French Prime Minister Sarkozy which has heavily influenced work by the OECD. Australia has also been exploring ways to make use of such measures and their underpinning concepts of wellbeing in advising on public policy. Behind all these efforts has been widespread criticism of the use of GDP and GDP per capita as indicators of wellbeing, some critics renewing past debates about whether the pursuit of economic growth may involve significant social costs including unacceptable inequality and/or may undermine the wellbeing of future generations because of the environmental costs involved. At the same time, while Australians are currently experiencing unprecedented levels of wealth and living standards with relatively low unemployment, inflation and interest rates, the political debate is dominated by talk of increasing cost of living pressures, poor international economic conditions, sluggish growth and structural budget deficits, and whether measures to address climate change and other environmental concerns might be imposing unreasonable costs now.

What do we mean by 'wellbeing' and 'economic growth', and what have we learned about measuring them? How does inequality impact on overall wellbeing? Is economic growth a 'good' or a 'bad'? How should we balance concerns for the present with considerations for future generations? These are the main issues explored in this symposium.

The issues are certainly highly relevant to contemporary policy debates, and are usefully informed by the substantial body of recent research and development. But they are also hardly new as Ian Castles' work over four decades illustrates.

The role of economics in defining and promoting wellbeing

Castles' work remains highly relevant, particularly in highlighting how economics and the social sciences more generally can help people and governments to manage the trade-offs necessarily involved in these issues.

Michael Keating draws attention to Castles' deep concern for facts and their proper interpretation, noting his anguish when facts were distorted or numbers manipulated in the pursuit of some predetermined objective, no matter how worthy (or not). Castles himself was in no sense political, says Keating, but committed to good policy process, acutely aware that good policy advice must address the inevitable trade-offs involved and that in this respect economics is, or at least should be, especially useful.

William Coleman focuses on Castles' 1984 paper, 'Economics and Anti-Economics', 'a *tour de force'* says Coleman. In this paper, Castles shows with devastating evidence that it was the classical economists of the nineteenth century – Smith, Ricardo, Mill, Malthus *et al* - who demonstrated real concern for the poor and disadvantaged, support for universal education and opposition to slavery, in direct contrast to their critics of the time – Coleridge, Carlisle, Ruskin *et al*. Castles takes on three contemporary celebrity intellectuals – CP Snow, JK Galbraith and Kenneth Clarke – showing how their portrayal of the classical economists represented the reverse of the truth. In discussing Castles' paper, Coleman highlights the different motivations of the professional commentators today and the classical economists of the past, that they 'make a profession of saying with elegance and unction what their audience finds most acceptable' to quote Galbraith himself (as Castles mentions with some disdain).

The question is why did Castles, being Secretary of the Finance Department at the time, put so much time and effort into this 30,000-word treatise? We do not know for sure, but suspect the context was critical: 1984 was in the early days of the Hawke-Keating Government as it began its agenda of social and economic reform, an agenda Castles and his department contributed to greatly. By showing so convincingly the role of the nineteenth century economists in reforms that not only increased efficiency and fed the industrial revolution, but also improved the condition of people and their rights and opportunities, and by demonstrating that their opponents were not fighting for the poor and oppressed but for the preservation of the privileges of the rich and powerful, Castles provided the reformers of the 1980s reason to believe economics could successfully assist them, whatever their social policy priorities might be. In this and other papers he wrote in the 1980s (such as 'Facts and Fancies of Bureaucracy' in 1986), Castles challenged populist critics of the economics profession (and the public service) in their portrayal of economists as conservative protectors of the status quo and supporters of inequality. He may also have had concerns that some critics of the government on the right were cloaking themselves in the mantle of economics as if the discipline necessarily supported their political preferences.

The 1984 paper is also illustrative of Castles' views of the need for a broad definition of wellbeing. This appreciation that wellbeing involves far more than GDP per capita was most clearly set out in the 1973 Treasury paper, *Economic Growth: Is It Worth Having?,* which we understand Castles was responsible for putting together. The paper in fact provides fascinating background to the whole symposium, touching on each of the issues discussed.

The paper addresses the common misconception that economists have a pre-occupation with a narrow concept of economic growth based on GDP and GDP per capita. Economists have never claimed that GDP covers all aspects of welfare or wellbeing. Indeed, the rate of growth in GDP is never the objective: the objective is the efficient use of available resources to establish and maintain those patterns of production and distribution which conform most closely to the preferences of the community. One of the consequences of policies that achieve this objective is, in most but not all cases, increases in measured GDP and GDP per capita. That is, economic growth 'is best regarded not as a goal or a target but rather as a *result'* of good policies.

Interestingly for people today, this 40-year-old paper not only promotes a wide concept of wellbeing but includes many references to environmental concerns including 'the possible "greenhouse" effect of increased carbon dioxide in the atmosphere'. It acknowledges the need for pollution abatement (not specifically for carbon pollution, the paper noting the 'uncertainty and dissension amongst scientists' at the time), but not by dampening economic growth. The deficiency that causes excessive pollution is inherent in the unregulated working of the market which allows the 'wrong' market price, a deficiency which 'occurs independently of the rate at which the economy which that system regulates is growing'.

This distinction between economic growth and measures that might address broader concepts of wellbeing, including 'sustainable' wellbeing, remains important. The concept of 'growth' suggested in the 1973 paper – 'expanding the options available to realise society's priorities' – leaves no real room for opposition to growth. It allows for consideration of wellbeing factors not included in standard measures of the economy, it allows consideration of the distribution of wellbeing, and it allows consideration of balancing future and current wellbeing.

A danger is that, for some, this might seem to be sophistry, providing an all-too-easy escape route for economists from criticism that their tools of analysis are not value-free. The points so clearly exemplified by Castles himself are to allow both governments and individuals to set their values, objectives and priorities, for economists to focus on the tools and related evidence that support governments and individuals to do so acknowledging when they themselves are advocating a particular value, objective or priority, and for continuing effort to improve the tools and related evidence.

Session 1: Measuring real income and wellbeing

Brian Pink (the Australian Statistician), *Sue Taylor and Hannah Wetzler*, provide a brief history of the development of measures of social and economic progress over the last fifty years, highlighting how the focus has shifted from economic development, towards societal wellbeing and environmental sustainability. The ABS has long contributed to this, from its social indicators work in the 1970s followed by the Australian Social Trends series introduced by Ian Castles in 1994. Pink *et al* describe how the Australian initiatives paralleled international efforts including through the United Nations, aimed to promote 'social progress and development' and, later, to address progress against the UN's Millennium Development Goals.

Pink *et al* describe in some detail more recent work both in Australia and overseas to develop broader overarching ways to view and measure progress and wellbeing. The ABS Measuring Australia's Progress (MAP) was a watershed when first introduced in 2002, the first national statistical agency effort to produce a broadly focused measuring tool for assessing national progress. Importantly, MAP offers instead of some aggregate index, a 'dashboard' of progress indicators across three dimensions – society, economy and environment – allowing people to weigh the different elements as they see fit. MAP has also been refined over the years and, most recently, has been subject to a very extensive consultation process with a wide range of stakeholders and the general public to identify Australians' 'aspirations' for future progress. These developments have contributed to, and been influenced by, international work such as the UK's Measuring National Wellbeing initiative, the EU's Beyond GDP and even Bhutan's famous 'happiness index'. A key international development came with the 2009 Stiglitz-Sen-Fitoussi report on the Measurement of Economic Performance and Social Progress. Like MAP, this report avoids any aggregate indicator instead offering a range of measures - of both averages and distributions - in three fields, allowing people to set their own weights for the different aspects of wellbeing. The report also suggests the use of both subjective and objective measures. The subsequent OECD 'How's Life' framework uses indicators in the three fields identified – quality of life, material living conditions and (not yet completed) sustainability of wellbeing over time – and also incorporates subjective data based on survey information.

Looking to the future, Pink *et al* mention the ABS work now on a fourth dimension for MAP on governance, and on improving measures of family and community wellbeing, the built environment and the distribution of wellbeing. They also describe the next stage of international work, referring to the OECD's desire for an international agenda on progress goals to bring together work on wellbeing, the post-2015 development agenda (involving the review and update of the Millennium Development Goals) and the Sustainable Development Goals to create a more holistic understanding of progress. The challenge for Australia and for the world will be to harmonise and link consistent information on the state of individual households to macro-measures of wellbeing and to come up with a consistent approach to subjective wellbeing measures in order to allow for some level of international comparison.

Pink *et al* note the important contribution Castles made both to Australian developments and internationally. Castles' papers included in this volume illustrate aspects of this contribution. The first paper included in this section, 'Measuring Economic Progress: From Political Arithmetick to Social Accounts', demonstrates his deep understanding of economic history (and his appreciation of the work of Colin Clark and other Australian economic pioneers) and the long-standing challenge to measure progress. In papers included in other sections of this volume, Castles shows just how misleading the focus on GDP and GDP per capita can be when trying to assess and compare wellbeing in different societies, revealing Australians benefit in many ways from things not incorporated into GDP. At the same time, Castles was fascinated by the strong correlation between GDP per capita and many other indicators of wellbeing including those relating to health, education and the environment.

Furthermore, Castles had a long interest in measuring wellbeing as demonstrated by the five papers in this part of the book. There are at least two aspects to this interest – (1) that wellbeing encompassed much more than economic growth and how do you measure it and (2) that reliable international comparisons could provide valuable insights.

On the first issue, Castles was sceptical of composite indices which involved value judgements on the relative importance of the variables involved in the index. In his 1999 paper, 'Reporting on Human Development: Lies, Damned Lies and Statistics' he was particularly critical of the Human Development Index bemoaning that 'Packaged information has replaced scholarship as the source of knowledge about the world in which we live'. He was also critical of the lack of recognition of social sciences including by bodies such as UNESCO which have a responsibility for the advancement of science.

On the second issue, Castles was often horrified by the lack of concern given to good quality data and appropriate methods when making international comparisons. On a number of occasions he intervened and the papers provide several examples of his interventions. His motives were often misunderstood. He had no ideological agenda. He was driven purely by the desire that analyses, that can influence policy, be done properly. In particular with international comparisons, he wanted to ensure that like was compared with like as far as possible especially with the underlying statistical data.

The papers provide several important examples.

- The poor quality data used in the Human Development Index led to many results lacking any credibility.
- The use initially of exchange rates rather than purchasing power parities resulted in grossly exaggerated estimates of global inequalities of incomes in the UNDP's Human Development Report. As a consequence of this flaw, the UNDP had concluded that developed countries were getting richer and that developing countries were getting poorer despite much higher average growth rates in developing countries. There were riots in places like Seattle based on this false premise.
- The initial failure by the International Panel of Climate Change to use purchasing power parities when estimating the size of countries' economies for input into its then climate change model resulted in unrealistic estimates of future economic growth – and consequential growth in carbon emissions - because the starting points in the model for developing countries were far too low.
- The failure also by the World Bank to use purchasing power parities when estimating energy intensities led them also to exaggerate the extent of energy inefficiency in developing countries.

While the UNDP did finally accept Castles' suggestions, this was only after vigorous debate in which Castles' tenacity finally won through as is clear from the papers included here (particularly 'The Mismeasure of Nations: A Review Essay on the Human Development Report' and 'Lies, Damned Lies and Statistics'). Not only did the errors Castles identified greatly exaggerate inequality across nations but, more importantly, the false data were being used to suggest entirely inappropriate countries as models for development success. Castles objected strongly to the political advocacy involved and the failure to let policy respond to the facts rather than to mould 'facts' to a pre-established policy. Whilst immensely pleased that his efforts resulted in significant improvements to the HDI, Castles was still not a supporter. He did not believe a single number could ever accurately represent a complex phenomenon like development.

John Hawkin's contribution is to summarise four different approaches to measuring wellbeing: adjusted GDP, a dashboard of indicators (e.g. ABS's Measures of Progress), composite indices (e.g. HDI), and subjective happiness indicators.

While Pink focuses on the measurement of wellbeing, *David Gruen* and *Duncan Spender* examine how a wellbeing focus might improve the process of policy advising. Their paper explains the Treasury Wellbeing Framework (TWF) and the rationale behind its introduction: to help Treasury in its role to advise and assist ministers on the trade-offs involved in promoting wellbeing. The TWF starts with a statement that wellbeing primarily reflects people's substantive freedom to live the life they want, a pluralistic concept drawing on Amartya Sen's capabilities approach emphasising opportunities. While acknowledging the conceptual and measurement challenges involved in using 'wellbeing' as the focus, Gruen and Spender highlight the pragmatic nature of the TWF and that its application draws upon rather than replaces the many analytical tools traditionally used by Treasury.

Gruen and Spender also emphasise that the TWF is used to help ministers and cabinet make their choices on policy and the trade-offs involved, not to establish any Treasury value judgements. This emphasis on Australia's democratic process is not only in line with the apolitical role of the public service but is also consistent with evidence of a positive relationship between democracy and societal wellbeing.

The TWF uses five dimensions of wellbeing: opportunities, distribution, sustainability, allocation of risk, and complexity of choices facing people. In response to a particular public policy issue, the TWF guides Treasury officers to identify options and their impacts on these five dimensions, and to assist ministers to make value judgements on the balance between them (or within them such as the distributional impact), taking into account their assessment of community preferences and hence wellbeing.

Jonathan Pincus provides a critique of the Treasury Wellbeing Framework at a number of levels. At one level, he questions whether we actually want Treasury to worry about the wide range of issues Australian society worries about or whether it should concentrate on its primary role as economic adviser to government In this context, perhaps TWF is symptomatic of a principal-agent problem, where Treasury in fact has incentives that differ markedly from those (ministers and cabinet) its framework proposes to support. Pincus also questions whether the TWF can possible guide Treasury or the government consistently across time and across policy decisions without identifying any ranking or weighting of its component parts. TWF may, as Treasury asserts, reinforce the importance of trade-offs both between and within the dimensions, but without any lexicographical ordering or without using weights explicitly or implicitly it can do no more than this. It may even allow Treasury officers to pursue any bee they may have in their bonnets. Pincus asks for some evidence of how in practice Treasury has used TWF and whether it has been subject to review. At a more detailed level, Pincus comments on each of the five dimensions of TWF, criticising the lack of precision in much of the language and the limited application of relevant economic theory and research; again he questions how the TWF can be made operational and help with consistency and transparency. Pincus concludes that the TWF needs far more work and, in its current form, could do more harm than good.

Richard Eckersley pays tribute to Castles, while noting that they had been sparring partners over many years. He continues to challenge the Castles' view that 'GDP is a valuable and necessary, but not sufficient, measure of material progress', notwithstanding that Castles acknowledged a much wider understanding of wellbeing than economic development or money and was willing to incorporate subjective measures. Eckersley is concerned that such models of wellbeing still focus on material progress, usually measured by GDP, in the face of growing evidence that such progress is not making life better, quite apart from its limitations in terms of sustainability. His argument is that GDP, and more recent wider measures incorporating subjective wellbeing, measure westernisation or modernisation and do not capture the sense of disquiet and pessimism western people feel about their societies. He draws attention to research findings that reveal a stark difference between people's assessment of their own personal happiness and life satisfaction and their assessment of life in general or the lives of others. The more pessimistic views of society wellbeing are also reflected in recorded views that emotional wellbeing of Australians has been declining even though most said their material standard of living was higher.

Eckersley is also concerned about the 'paradox of freedom'. Modernisation may have shifted people's concerns from simply having enough of life's basic necessities to a desire for free choice in how to live their lives, but such freedom is not without its downsides. It may create new opportunities for personal experience and growth but it also carries risks of social dislocation and isolation. Social wellbeing measures, he believes, have a bias in favour of individualistic societies and are still missing a critical dimension of human wellbeing – the more intangible, cultural, moral and existential aspects of life.

There was a rich debate at the symposium about the TWF and Pincus's criticism of it. While some agreed with Pincus, expressing concern that the TWF could dilute Treasury's particular contribution to government decision-making including its devil's advocate role, others welcomed Treasury taking a broader view, noting that in the past a narrower perspective had limited the Treasury's influence in government and also that a broader view can help in attracting and retaining high quality staff. A critical dilemma was also highlighted: who should rank the TWF dimensions or place weights within and between them? While such weighting may be essential for applying the framework to determine a particular policy and to ensure consistency, surely this is the role of the elected government not officials.

Nonetheless, suggestions were made to make TWF more robust and intellectually more rigorous, including by explaining in more detail each of the five dimensions. One possibility raised was whether the five dimensions might be mapped in some way to traditional public finance theory on the role of government in a market economy. Musgrave and Musgrave[1] identify three functions of government: allocation, distribution and stabilisation. Perhaps the 'opportunities' dimension could be mapped to the 'allocation' function, delivering public goods and addressing market failures; the 'distribution' dimension is presumably the same as the traditional 'distribution' function; and the 'sustainability', 'allocation of risk' and 'complexity' dimensions may all relate to the 'stabilisation' function (though the Musgraves focus on full employment and inflation rather than broader concerns about risks the market may not be able to handle). Such consideration might also stimulate more careful study of the contribution the TWF does or could make in responding to developments in economics and the social sciences and understanding of the role of government. For example, more might be made of how the TWF emphasis on 'opportunities' reflects Amartya Sen's work (interestingly, it also resonates with the 1973 Treasury paper's definition of 'growth' as 'expanding opportunities'). Greater clarity is also needed about the application of the 'complexity' dimension, noting its obvious and direct relevance to concerns about the complexity of tax and social security laws and many areas of regulation, but also the more ambiguous role of government in addressing complexity outside of government such as in international financial markets. TWF might also be enhanced if it were subject to independent expert review including examination of its application in a range of cases of policy advising.

Eckersley's concerns, of course, come from the other direction: that the concept of 'wellbeing' is still not broad enough. What remains unclear is whether the foreshadowed further work by the ABS and the OECD and others, on governance, family and community, will or even could address the claimed limitations of the current individualistic approach. Will the even broader approaches mooted by these organisations still reflect values of modern western society that may have unacknowledged negative impacts?

1 Musgrave, Richard A and Musgrave, Peggy B (1980). *Public Finance in Theory and Practice*, (Third Edition), McGraw-Hill Kogakusha, Ltd, Tokyo.

Session 2: Measuring inequality

Henry Ergas concludes provocatively that inequality is good for you, albeit unequally so, and hence that not all problems are as bad as they seem, and not all solutions as wise. He bases this conclusion on four propositions: firstly, that not all increases in inequality are bad; secondly, that not all reductions in inequality are good; thirdly, that some changes to reduce inequality can be bad; and, finally, that fashionable policy responses could do more harm than good. Ergas draws on both Australian and international data to support each of these propositions, noting for example the dominant role of widening market incomes in recent increases in inequality internationally and the contribution to this of such positive factors as increasing workforce participation by women and an ageing but better skilled workforce. He also questions concern about increased inequality if those on low incomes also experience increased real incomes from economic growth: if more redistributive policies reduced overall economic growth, the poor as well as the rich might be worse off. Moreover, increasing taxes for the rich may not raise the expected additional revenue given the likely elasticity of taxable incomes. Ergas also notes that there has been little change in recent years in the distribution of disposable incomes (after tax and including transfers) in Australia in contrast to much overseas experience, in part due to some compression of real wages here offsetting the impact of reduced working hours of those on low incomes (which has also occurred elsewhere) and of increased working hours of those on higher incomes (but with relatively lower incomes given the compression of wages). The forces driving this result, Ergas suggests, include many positive features.

Ergas highlights the importance of the dynamics involved in income distributions: he refers to Australia's relatively high rates of transition out of poverty and also to evidence that the share of income by the top few per cent of Australians has not changed much, but that the turnover of people in that group is very high – 'the top floor is full, but with different people every night'. He implies that the focus of policy should be on those with multiple disadvantages and who suffer persistent disadvantage, and on equality of opportunity, rather than inequality *per se*. He suggests that, just as Castles argued that growth in GDP should not be the objective but may be the result of good policy, no particular income distribution should be set as a target: the distribution (quoting Castles on GDP) 'come(s) out of the complex of decisions made by governments, institutions and individuals ... (and is) to be neither pursued nor shunned'.

Ergas refers frequently to Castles' work, highlighting the care Castles took to rest his assessments on a sound analytical base. This is demonstrated in the two Castles papers included in this section of the book. In comparing living standards in Australia and Japan in his 1990 paper, Castles not only examined factors such as population density, the use of time (including the work time required to purchase necessary supplies of food and power), housing conditions and land use, going well beyond prevailing measures of wellbeing that suggested that Japanese living standards were higher on average than in Australia, but he also explored the living standards of low and high income households. Not only did he find Australian living standards higher on average but also that low-income households were more affluent than their Japanese counterparts. Low-income households in Sydney were smaller, had fewer earners and spent less of their income on essential food and utilities.

Castles focused even more closely on distribution issues in his 1987 paper comparing Australia, Sweden and the United States. In this study, Castles examined both income distributions and distributions of consumption power, carefully working through the demographic and tax and social security differences across the countries and applying consistent definitions of income and household types. The data strongly suggest that the distribution of household incomes in Australia was less equal than in Sweden in 1984, and more equal than in the US, that the purchasing power of money incomes in Australia was lower on average than in the US and higher on average than in Sweden, and that the real value of low household income in Australia was higher than in the US and lower than in Sweden. These findings however encompass much more complex differences across different household types and different sources of income.

Rob Bray examines changes in income inequality in Australia and the re-distributional impacts of taxes and government benefits. Rather like Ergas, Bray suggests that it is frequently not changes in inequality itself which matter but rather the causes and the consequences. Bray also cautions about relying on income when examining inequality, noting that wellbeing involves more than income and that the other factors may not always correlate well. He demonstrates this by revealing the differences in the distribution of income, consumption and wealth (noting for example that only 3.2 per cent of the population are in the lowest deciles of both income and consumption despite a degree of correlation between the two, and that the correlations of income and consumption with wealth are much lower).

Bray disaggregates the main factors which impact on income inequality – earnings, workforce participation, government transfers and income tax – noting that increased income inequality can be caused by greater workforce participation and more two-job households, higher levels of retirement, falling reliance on income support and lower tax rates, all of which are arguably good things for individuals. Overall, Bray identifies a small increase in income inequality since 1990, based on Gini coefficients and a range of data sources, though he notes some inconsistency between different data series and some volatility. He also notes that there have been significant real increases in income at all levels over this period. The main contributors to the increase in inequality include, in particular, changes in the market incomes of both first and second household earners, and from investments and superannuation; interestingly, income tax has also contributed to the increased inequality over the last two decades not because of any less progressive a scale but because of a lower average tax. Bray suggests the changes in inequality should be split between two periods. Between 1984 and 1999 the spreading of wages and growth in employment increased inequality while increased family benefits worked in the opposite direction; between 1999 and 2008 wage dispersion decreased but family payments changes contributed to higher levels of inequality even after allowing for taxes and transfers. In sum, incomes are less equally distributed across households than at some points in the past; more recent changes indicate a somewhat reduced role for income support payments and income tax in redistributing income, though this may be due to the way these interact with other changes in society rather any changes in policy.

Peter Whiteford uses international comparisons across the OECD to assess income distribution especially the re-distributional impact of taxes and government transfers. Many of Whiteford's findings are contrary to conventional wisdom in Australia. These include findings that, compared with other OECD countries, Australia (a) has a relatively low level of inequality, (b) has one of the most progressive tax systems essentially because of the low direct tax paid by low-income households, (c) has a welfare system that is the most targeted in the OECD, and (d) has a relatively low level of middle class welfare compared to other OECD countries.

Despite these findings the reduction in inequality from government income transfers is not as great as might be expected. Redistribution is a product of both the progressivity of spending and the level of spending. As the overall level of government transfers is relatively low (18.7 per cent of GDP in 2012 compared with an OECD average of 21.7 per cent), the impact of Australia's tax and transfer system on reducing inequality is not as great as it might otherwise be. If a further reduction in inequality were desired it would probably require an increase in government taxes and benefits. On the other hand, an implication of Australia's strong targeting is that a relatively small cut in transfer spending would increase income inequality in Australia to a larger extent than in any other OECD country.

Whiteford highlights that although inequality is relatively low in Australia, there are important areas of inequality that need addressing with Indigenous people being a particularly important group.

One of Whiteford's important contributions is his analysis of the measurement challenges involved in analysing and comparing income distributions and the impact of government taxing and spending. Apart from the impact of tax and transfer systems, he also looks at the redistribution effects of non-cash benefits building on the pioneering methodology first introduced by Ian Castles in 1987 for the fiscal incidence studies he led during his time at the ABS.

What is clear from all the papers and the symposium discussion is how complex is the issue of inequality. Inequality of what – income, consumption, 'wellbeing'? Inequality amongst whom – individuals, families, households, different types of households? What measures of distribution should be used? How to take into account mobility within a distribution. Over what period should distribution be measured and changes identified? What is contributing to inequality and changes in inequality?

Secondly, there is the issue of where the focus of policy should be in addressing inequality. Most participants accepted that inequality *per se* is not generally the problem, and that the main focus should be on multiple disadvantage and persistent poverty (including inter-generational poverty), and on ensuring equality of opportunity. Recent ABS consultations associated with future development of MAP revealed that equality of opportunity was widely identified as critical to society wellbeing.

This considerable degree of consensus should not be mistaken for agreement that the current level of inequality does not represent a problem deserving serious attention. There remain important areas for debate, some related to the issues debated more vigorously in the previous session of the symposium. Is it true that increased inequality is of no concern if all incomes are increasing, or is there a limit to inequality in order to protect social solidarity? Also, some expressed concern that inequality within families and households needs to remain on the agenda, and that the current emphasis on family-based means testing is disadvantaging women.

Session 3: Climate change and limits to growth

David Henderson provides a fascinating and highly personal account of how he and Ian Castles became involved in the debates over climate change. Castles' involvement was, he says, 'entirely unplanned and fortuitous', arising from a meeting he attended in 2002 with the newly appointed Chair of the Intergovernmental Panel on Climate Change (IPCC), Dr RK Pachauri. Pachauri invited Castles to write to him about the concerns he had raised at the meeting about technical faults in handling of international comparisons of GDP in the Special Report on Emissions Scenarios that had been prepared as input to the IPCC's Third Assessment Report in 2000. Castles' concerns were essentially the same as those he had raised previously with the UNDP about its original Human Development Index: that they had used exchange-rate-based comparisons of GDP rather than PPP-based comparisons thereby drawing inaccurate conclusions. Castles duly wrote to Pachauri, and then suggested to Henderson that he also write in support, Henderson having become a collaborator with Castles over the previous seven years since they first met, particularly in commenting on the HDI. The technical issue raised by Castles and Henderson seemed in fact very material to the scenarios the IPCC was then highlighting. Exaggerating the differences in GDP between developed and developing countries at the beginning of the forecast period, together with assumptions of convergence in GDP across countries, meant that assumed global growth rates in GDP were also exaggerated. This implies important concerns about the reliability of climate change predictions. This flaw also resulted in exaggerated differences in energy and emissions intensities and meant that bridging those differences (which the scenarios assumed would occur) may represent a far greater task involving a much bigger and faster growth in global carbon emissions than would be revealed if appropriate comparisons of GDP had been made.

Pachauri not only rejected the Castles and Henderson critique but made a personal attack on the two. Subsequently, they began to question the whole IPCC process, observing the poor quality of many papers prepared by IPCC Experts and concluding that there were disturbing signs that the IPCC's role in the assessment of climate change had become subservient to its role in advocating a specific policy agenda. The two of them pressed for wider official participation in the process including by national statistical offices and the International Statistical Institute. Their comments to this time had focused on economic and statistical aspects of IPCC work, but concerns about the process as a whole drew them to engage with others who were criticising the professional conduct of some of the IPCC-related work on climate science. This led them to call for a broadening of the IPCC peer review process.

As Henderson explains, however, the extension of Castles' involvement beyond the original technical issue was not at all surprising. He had long been concerned about resource and environmental pessimism. However, to their surprise, as (eventually) economists were brought into the process, there was a marked division of opinion amongst them. Moreover, most were not willing to challenge the generally received opinion about 'the science' of climate change, including most of those who like Castles and Henderson were critical of the 2007 Stern Report. Henderson describes himself and Castles as amongst the 'dissenters' and sets out the three failings they saw in the wide array of material on climate change including from the World Bank and the IMF: over-presumption, credulity and inadvertence.

The *Castles* papers included in this section of the book include a criticism co-authored with Henderson (and others) of the Stern Review into the Economics of Climate Change. They are highly critical believing that the Review systematically over-states the costs of climate change by largely ignoring the scope for adaptation, underestimates the likely cost of the mitigation program that is called for, and proposes worldwide adoption of a specifically low rate of interest for discounting the costs and benefits of mitigation. This latter point is addressed by Mark Harrison's paper in this volume.

The other paper, 'Scientists, Statisticians and the Prophets of Doom' takes to task those in the science community who are more strongly committed to implementing their priorities than to the value of scientific enterprise. To achieve this he expresses special concern about a tendency to abuse critics (possibly with his personal experience of the IPCC in mind) and argues that if contrary views are unsound on scientific grounds, it should not be beyond the capacity of scientists to demonstrate this in free, critical and civil discussion. He also points out the tendency of some scientists to be prophets of doom with a prime example being the Club of Rome and their prediction that the world would not be able to feed itself. Castles highlights that economic growth and good environmental outcomes are not necessarily opposites. For example, the former may facilitate technological advances as well as allowing more funds to be diverted to environmental concerns.

Mark Harrison explores in some depth the challenge of balancing wellbeing over time, which is central to the climate change and other environmental debates. Harrison focuses in particular on discount rates and their crucial role in setting any carbon prices today in order to limit the costs of carbon pollution and climate change in the future. Given the many decades involved over which the impact of carbon pollution is suggested will occur, he demonstrates how much the choice of the discount rate matters – over 100 years, Stern's discount rate of 1.4 per cent a year leads to a carbon price today fifty times as high as Nordhaus's discount rate of 5.5 per cent. In his highly technical paper drawing on a wide range of economic theory, Harrison describes both a social welfare function approach to policy evaluation and an efficiency approach. The former requires normative value judgements or ethical considerations about the distribution of welfare within society while the latter is perhaps easier to apply in practice ignoring distributional issues and using cost-benefit analysis where willingness to pay measures the benefits and opportunity cost measures the costs. He then analyses how a range of climate change modellers determined their preferred discount rates and finds that they implicitly use the social welfare function approach, but mix ethical and empirical parameters and conceal assumptions. Harrison argues that the cost-benefit approach is to be preferred, where discounting is about opportunity cost and not about an ethical choice of the correct weight to apply to future generations' welfare, an approach he describes as 'prescriptive'. Harrison examines and rejects four 'myths' about discounting that have been used by the 'prescriptive' climate change modellers: that market discount rates imply sacrificing our grandchildren for a few dollars, that life should not be discounted, that high private sector discount rates are specific to the share market only, and that governments should discount with a risk-free rate of return. The low discount rates chosen by the modellers ignores the opportunity costs involved, directing resources away from projects known to have higher returns. Harrison considers that, if anything, efficiency analysis is more, not less, useful in an inter-generational context.

Jeff Bennett focuses on issues of sustainability and limits to growth, referring in particular to the 1973 Treasury paper largely credited to Ian Castles. He argues that concerns about 'sustainability' frequently fail to recognise the capacity of society to adapt. He discusses the concept of human adaptation and the wide range of ways in which humanity has demonstrated its 'amazing ability' to change to new circumstances. Adapting markets, prices, innovative substitutions and the discovery of new energy sources are all possible forms of adaptation to climate change. Bennett notes environmental improvement may, over time, follow economic growth, but that this relies upon an institutional framework that facilitates adaptation, including decentralised market processes and collective arrangements through government. Bennett supports the use of cost/benefit analysis applied by politically independent analysts to counter the dangers of collective arrangements being captured by sectional interests or being ill-informed, and to support appropriate adaptation. In this context, Bennett rejects the 'costs of inaction' argument often used to support immediate and substantial collective action because he fears it provides too many opportunities for rent-seeking behaviour. He suggests that many climate change policies will have negative impacts on growth without achieving their initial purpose, imposing an opportunity cost including by limiting opportunities to pursue policies more suited to effective adaptation.

The concerns Henderson highlighted that he and Castles shared about the quality of the received opinion on 'the science' of climate change was not explored further at the symposium, perhaps to the disappointment of Henderson but not entirely surprising given the absence of scientific experts. Nor was this a symposium of 'climate change sceptics' (and, as Mike Keating said in his speech, Castles should not be described as a 'climate change sceptic' either – another participant suggested he be described as 'agnostic' rather than as a 'sceptic'). The symposium comprised expert social science academics and practitioners most of whom felt more comfortable focusing on economic and social aspects of the climate change debate and the issue of how best to balance wellbeing over time including between generations. They focused therefore more on Henderson's concern that climate change policy should be based on proper economic and statistical analysis, whatever 'the science' of climate change suggested. There was certainly no disagreement with Castles' original criticisms of the IPCC and every sympathy about the extraordinary way in which his criticism had been treated, which left a continuing bad taste and unease about the IPCC's work.

The main focus of discussion was on the issue of discount rates, one of the core criticisms Castles and his co-authors had made about the Stern Report, criticisms equally relevant to the Garnaut Report. Harrison and Bennett's call for a cost-benefit approach was widely shared, with the implication that a higher discount rate than applied by Stern and Garnaut was required. Given the level of uncertainty, however, focusing solely on the discount rate might not be particularly helpful. A more practical approach might be to unpack the problem and consider a range of options against a range of possibilities. The options might include deferral of action other than investing money (with returns much higher than the Stern/Garnaut discount rates) for later mitigation and adaptation effort, or some modest effort now, perhaps involving more effort on research and on capacity for adaptation and less on setting a price for carbon. The emphasis should be on, as Castles often argued, a measured response to claims of impending crisis or doom, with a degree of optimism about society's capacity to manage future challenges. Whether current government policy is 'modest' or not was not discussed.

Certainly, there was wide agreement that restricting economic growth was not a sensible objective, though no doubt there remained different views on how to pursue growth and how to use the opportunities growth offered.

A critical issue for the academic community is the continuing lack of appreciation of the different perspectives and expertise offered by social scientists and natural scientists. The debates over the last decade indicate not only a lack of genuine engagement but also a lack of mutual respect. Castles had tried to address this as Vice President of ASSA. The recent initiative of the Council of Learned Academies to promote cross-sectoral research and multi-disciplinary approaches is therefore welcome.

Concluding remarks

There is still a perception in some quarters that economists push for economic growth without any appreciation of broader concepts of personal and society wellbeing, or the importance of future sustainability. This perception also leads some to typecast economists as social conservatives determined to maintain the status quo.

Castles constantly tried to change these perceptions, not by public campaigning but by careful analysis and scholarly exposition. He focused in particular on exploring and measuring broad concepts of wellbeing, examining whether and how economic growth can contribute to wellbeing, demonstrating how economists in the past have led many of the social reforms that underpin a more inclusive and free society, and showing by his own efforts as a professional public servant that economists can help governments of any political persuasion to achieve their particular political objectives more effectively and efficiently.

The Castles Symposium was, however, much more than a nostalgic *déjà vu* reflection on Castles' contribution. Participants certainly did, on the whole, endorse the majority of Castles' lifetime views, sharing his quiet passion for economics as a social *science* that can contribute much to good policy. But the symposium also brought past debates up to date and allowed participants to explore contemporary developments and challenges. In doing so, it drew out some substantial debates that need to be properly aired, as distinct from the shallow arguments based on common and continuing misconceptions of the role of economics and economists.

Hopefully, this book will help to disseminate a clearer picture of what economics can contribute, and promote more constructive debate of contemporary issues and policies that might advance society wellbeing now and into the future.

Perhaps, most importantly, the symposium re-affirmed the criticality of 'evidence-based policy' and the real dangers of 'policy-based evidence', celebrating Castles' constant emphasis on rigorous analysis of facts.

Part One: The Role of Economics in Defining and Promoting Wellbeing

2. Economic Growth and Wellbeing: Ian Castles' Contribution

Michael Keating

Personal connections and reflections

Ian's path and mine first crossed almost 50 years ago in the early 1960s. I had been seconded from the then Bureau of Census and Statistics to work on some of the Treasury submissions to the Vernon Committee. This committee had been established to advise on the future development of economic policy, following the almost defeat of the Menzies government in 1961. At the time all of Treasury, which then included today's Finance Department, the Tax Head Office, and most of the Statistics Bureau, was located in West Block. Clearly government was smaller then. Now each of these agencies and departments occupy much bigger buildings on their own.

Part of the reason for the increase in the size of the bureaucracy, especially in Canberra, is the increase in the amount of information and the analysis of that information. Perhaps in our discussions we should take time to consider whether all this information and analysis has made government more effective or efficient; or perhaps more pertinently, what changes are needed to ensure that the information contributes to more effective and efficient government?

The small size of government in those days made it easier to know people across different but related agencies. Also, junior officers, such as I then was, could participate in drafting quite important papers, and work almost directly to very senior people. I don't recall that Ian was working on the Treasury submissions for the Vernon Committee, or at least not on the same ones as me, but I think he was asked to comment on the submissions I was engaged upon. I remember at the time taking this as an indication of the very high regard in which Ian was held.

A decade or so later Ian and I first started working directly together when, after the demise of the Whitlam Government, he asked me to join the Income Security Review, which he was chairing, as his deputy. Andrew Podger spoke at some length about the work of this review at a similar function last year, and I will not repeat what he had to say then, especially as, unlike Andrew, I did not stay long with the review but instead returned to Paris.

However, a bit over two years later Ian was instrumental in my decision to return to Australia and to take up a position in PM&C where Ian was a deputy secretary. Shortly after Ian left PM&C to become secretary of the Department of Finance. However, we kept in close touch and I joined Ian three years later as his deputy in Finance in early 1982. In short I believe I owe Ian an enormous debt, as he effectively had a very considerable influence over my career at certain critical points.

All of us who worked with Ian will remember his considerable intellect. Ian was one of the most clear-thinking and logical people I have ever met, with a deep concern for the facts and their proper interpretation. As became even clearer after he left the public service, Ian anguished when facts were distorted or numbers were manipulated in the pursuit of some pre-determined objective, no matter how worthy.

Perhaps equally important during Ian's time as a policy adviser, were his outstanding communication skills, and his ability to engage with ministers. But while Ian was a highly influential public servant, he was in no sense a political public servant. On all the issues on which I worked closely with Ian, I never had any sense that he was committed to achieving a particular policy agenda. Rather he was committed to good policy process where information was properly assessed. What concerned Ian was the misuse of information, and the failure to recognise and address competing objectives. Ian was acutely aware that good policy advice must address the inevitable trade-offs involved, and in this respect the intellectual tradition of economics is or at least should be especially useful.

I believe it was for these reasons that Ian was held in such high regard by governments of both political persuasions. It was also because of these attitudes, combined with his previous experience, that Ian was able to make such an important contribution to the work of the Australian Bureau of Statistics (ABS) as chief statistician.

What I would now like to do is to spend a little time outlining some of the contributions Ian made to our understanding of economic growth and wellbeing. My hope is that this will provide a useful background for our discussions, and accordingly I have grouped my remarks to correspond roughly with the program sessions.

Economic growth – is it important?

A large part of Ian's professional career was spent thinking and writing about economic growth and its measurement. The first significant piece that I am aware of was the Treasury Economic Paper, published in 1973, titled *Economic Growth: Is it Worth Having?*, and I believe that Ian was the principal author.

At that time economic growth was under challenge with concerns about exponential population growth, that the world would run out of non-renewable resources, and that the 'blind pursuit of growth' would cause environmental crises – sound familiar? A widely publicised report, *The Limits to Growth,* had been published a year earlier in 1972 by an organisation called The Club of Rome, and that report concluded that there was an urgent need to bring about a deliberate, controlled end to growth.

I think it is fair to say that Ian's Treasury paper was partly a response, directed to reassessing the objective of economic growth in the light of these changes in attitudes and criticisms. Having regard to our discussions there are a number of key points in the paper that I would like to highlight.

First, as Ian frequently emphasised, economists have never claimed that the measure of GDP covered all aspects of welfare or wellbeing. Nor have they ever urged that economic growth should be pursued for its own sake. Rather the Treasury paper concludes that economic growth 'is best conceived of not as an objective in its own right but as the likely *result* of policies directed to improving the lot of the community without using resources wastefully'. The paper then goes on to argue that the objective of economic and social policies should not be the achievement of any particular statistical rate of economic growth in the longer-run, but rather the efficient use of available resources to establish and maintain those patterns of production and distribution which conform most closely to the preferences of the community.

The Treasury paper suggests that much of the negative debate about economic growth originates in a confusion between economic growth and its statistical indicator – the increase in GDP at constant prices. The paper freely acknowledges that 'The trend in GDP at constant prices is not ... a comprehensive measure of changes in national wellbeing, or in progress (if any) towards the '"good life"'. Furthermore, the Treasury paper then goes on to discuss alternative ways for developing more comprehensive information which can supplement the consideration of wellbeing.

Nevertheless the Treasury paper does contend – correctly in my view – that 'estimates of 'real' GDP, are valuable – indeed essential – for some types of economic analysis'. Most importantly we need these estimates of economic activity if the authorities are to successfully intervene to ensure full employment and low inflation. In addition, the paper 'suggests that some of the objections which are said to be to economic growth are, in fact, objections to the prevailing pattern of growth – that is they are really arguments about priorities'.

While not all things can be valued by a market, in practice we ourselves and our governments do have to take account of such things as personal security, work satisfaction, good health, pleasant surroundings, recreation opportunities and so on when making our decisions. There are costs and benefits in each case, irrespective of whether the values are economic or non-economic, tangible or intangible, social, strategic, aesthetic or even environmental. As the Treasury paper puts it, 'all decisions *imply* a valuation of those effects which are difficult to quantify'. And in a sentence which very much reflects Ian's views, the paper suggests that 'The greater the effort to quantify and to make such judgements explicit, the more rational and consistent will the decision-making process become'.

Finally the Treasury paper concludes by putting forward 'the view that if what economic growth is all about is carefully examined, it seems to constitute the key to achieving many of the things going to make up the national wellbeing'. In this regard it is also of some interest that the OECD much more recently found that cross-country rankings of GDP per capita were generally similar to when GDP is extended to include leisure time, the sharing of income within households, and the effect of income distribution. Indeed, this has led to some to conclude that GDP per capita can serve as a reasonable proxy of overall wellbeing. But I think Ian would perhaps have been more cautious; he might have reminded us that there are other dimensions of wellbeing, and that more work would need to be done to fully establish this conclusion. Indeed the OECD study did not find any strong relation between survey-based data on happiness and life satisfaction and levels of GDP per capita across countries. Instead happiness and life satisfaction may depend more upon one's present living standard relative to the past and relative to one's neighbours.

Equality

I would now like to say a few words about equality, which is one dimension of wellbeing to which Ian contributed a lot both in terms of policy and our understanding.

Ian's approach to equality was perhaps distinctive by today's standards, as he insisted that there are in fact two dimensions to equality – there is both horizontal and vertical equality. Horizontal equity requires that individuals in similar positions be treated consistently in a similar manner, while vertical equity requires that individuals in different positions be treated in a consistently different manner so as to reduce the differences in their positions. There can be tensions between these two dimensions and one dimension is not necessarily more important than the other.

Last year Andrew Podger recalled how the Department of Finance never supported the means testing of family allowances while Ian was head of that Department. Ian had previously led the Income Security Review that persuaded the Fraser Government to adopt the system of family allowances, and he was very aware of that system's antecedents and rationale. I believe that Ian's opposition to means testing stemmed from his view that family allowances were derived from the tax system and should be considered as part of that tax system. In Ian's view income tax should be levied according to capacity to pay, and family allowances were a recognition that families with children had a lower capacity to pay than other taxpayers without children. In effect there would be a reduction in horizontal equity if family allowances, which were an offset to tax in recognition of reduced taxable capacity, were subsequently subject to taxation in the form of a means test.

Ian was also involved in many other policy changes that contributed to greater equity, but time does not permit me to go into detail tonight. I would, however, like to draw your attention to some of Ian's work as the head of the ABS, and how this led to improved understanding of distribution issues. In particular Ian pioneered fiscal incidence studies showing the distributional impact of taxes and government expenditure on household incomes. These studies helped inform policy about the effectiveness of government intervention to reduce the inequality of income distribution. Under Ian's direction the ABS also expanded the range of its social surveys and we now have a much better appreciation of how to interpret income distribution statistics and the variety of possible factors leading to inequality.

For example, in a paper that he wrote comparing the distribution of money incomes in Sweden and Australia, Ian showed that the proportion of aged income units was much higher in Sweden than in Australia at that time. As a consequence, for Sweden to achieve the same relative level of income support per aged person unit as in Australia the aggregate of net cash transfers to the Swedish aged population would need to have been almost twice as great relative to GDP. On the other hand Ian showed that the proportion of 'dependent' units in the working age population was much higher in Australia than in Sweden. Furthermore, 80 per cent of this much smaller dependent population of working age in Sweden were single people, whereas most of the dependent units in Australia were couples with or without children and single parents. This relatively high rate of dependency is probably one of the reasons why income distribution is less equal in Australia than in Sweden, and arguably those who want greater equality in Australia should focus on trying to improve employment participation rather than increasing the amount of welfare transfers.

In short, what Ian effectively did in this paper was to remind us of the sort of information that is relevant if we want to make meaningful international comparisons of welfare expenditure and the amount of income redistribution achieved.

Economic growth and the environment

A large part of Ian's work in his last years was directed towards trying to correct the distortions in much of the advocacy in favour of increased action to combat climate change. Personally I never had any sense that Ian was by conviction a climate change sceptic – that would have been completely out of character; Ian reached his conclusions by examining the evidence, not by conviction.

Indeed, Ian's original Treasury paper on economic growth, to which I referred earlier, clearly accepted some 40 years ago that economic growth has led to increasing pollution that 'could wreak death and destruction on a global scale'. The paper, however, argues that 'Pollution problems are mainly attributable not to economic growth *per se*, but to the economic conditions under which growth has been allowed to take place'. The paper acknowledges that 'the price charged for using environmental resources has been too low – in many cases zero. What is needed, therefore, is to equate the price charged for use of environmental resources with the cost of damage inflicted on society by using them'. In other words society needs to achieve a trade-off between legitimate, but competing objectives, using pricing and based on the best statistical information available.

What I believe upset Ian, however, was that too often the advocates of action to combat climate change did not use the best statistical information available. Instead, their analysis has too often manipulated the statistical evidence to achieve what seems to be a pre-determined conclusion. Ian's work was dedicated to trying to correct these mistakes.

Others here tonight are more qualified than I am to enlarge on Ian's criticisms, but I will try briefly to outline the main points that Ian sought to make.

First, and probably most importantly, Ian thought the projections by the Intergovernmental Panel on Climate Change (IPCC) of future world economic growth were way too high, and therefore their projections of future carbon emissions were correspondingly too high. Ian pointed out on numerous occasions that the IPCC economic projections have been derived by converting national GDPs in nominal values into a common currency using exchange rates. Instead, in line with international statistical practice, which Ian had played a major role in developing, the conversion to a common currency should have been done using estimates of purchasing power parity for different countries.

The use of exchange rates greatly exaggerated the gap between the per capita incomes in the rich countries relative to the developing countries. Thus as Ian pointed out, the IPCC found that in 1990 the relative average incomes in the rich countries were 40 times higher than in Asian developing countries and 12 times higher than the average of developing countries elsewhere. Whereas in fact Ian showed that, using PPPs, average incomes in developing countries are three or four times higher than the IPCC assumed.

Because this initial gap between the developed and developing countries was exaggerated this led the IPCC to project extraordinarily high rates of growth in the developing countries as part of their expected convergence towards the living standards in the rich countries over time. Indeed Ian showed that the IPCC projections reflected increases in per capita output by 2100 for most of the world's population of between 30 and 70 times the 1990 levels – rates of increase that are ridiculously high by any historical standards.

Second, by underestimating the present levels of per capita output in the developing countries the IPCC has grossly under-estimated their present energy efficiency. The high levels of energy consumption implied by the IPCC per each under-valued unit of consumption in the base year leads to further overestimation of future energy consumption in response to further economic growth. Indeed, Ian calculated that the ratio of energy use per unit of GDP in non-OECD countries to that in OECD countries was not the 3.8:1 found when using exchange rates as the conversion factor but instead only 1.2:1 using PPPs. In other words the non-OECD countries are three times more energy efficient relative to the OECD than the IPCC estimates suggest. Furthermore other estimates cited by Ian suggest that energy efficiency has been rapidly improving; thus in China, for example, emissions per unit of output by 2000 were less than half their levels of twenty years before.

As Ian described himself in his presentation to an IPCC expert meeting in Amsterdam in 2003, he was 'someone who is strongly committed to the application of sound scientific method in the social sciences no less than in the natural sciences'. What I think most upset Ian about his experience with the IPCC was the unwillingness to make the corrections that he was asking for, especially when he was led to believe that they would. Furthermore he had previously made the same criticisms of the UNDP's Human Development Index, and the UNDP had changed its procedures in response.

A third principal criticism that Ian had of the work of the IPCC was that instead of referring to their findings as projections, and conditional projections at that, the IPCC readily slipped into referring to these projections as predictions. This shift in language has helped to endow the IPCC findings with an authority that they really don't have; an authority that is further endorsed by the practice of referring all IPCC research to peer groups. In principle, peer-group review of research is most welcome and necessary, but in this case too many of the peer reviews seem to be drawn from the same disciplines as the researchers. Thus these peer reviews were not competent to review the work by Ian and his fellow economists, and appear not to have understood the devastating nature of Ian's criticisms for the overall standing of the IPCC. Instead of carefully responding to Ian and other like criticisms, the IPCC sought to dismiss the critics by labelling them as the 'originators of some disinformation'. I think these manifold faults with the IPCC process led Ian to the sad conclusion that 'the Panel's role in the assessment of the science of climate change has now become subservient to its role in supporting a specific policy agenda'.

Economists and anti-economists

Finally before concluding my remarks tonight I did want to say a few words about Ian's reverence for the intellectual forebears of economics. Ian was a willing biographer and I think it was no accident that much of his writing has provided us with a better appreciation of our intellectual inheritance – especially how our forebears formed their judgements and the nature of the problems they faced.

In the papers for the last session of this meeting you have been provided with copies of pen portraits by Ian describing the early efforts to compile summary statistics, the role of particular pioneers such as Colin Clark and Jevons, the leading people who contributed to the population debate which ran for most of 100 years, and the gradual shift towards a more scientific approach to economic analysis, first in universities in the inter-war years, but after the war led by Sir Roland Wilson in the Treasury. I am sure that Ian was proud of this Australian intellectual tradition, and he certainly played his part in keeping it alive and adding to it further.

Although Ian did not live long into the twenty-first century he was a model for twenty-first century man. Ian had a wide range of interests, a passion for libraries and was very well read. Above all he was committed to the role of economics in particular, and the social sciences more generally in improving policy discussions and analysis. But he fervently believed that this dialogue could be and must be based on a respect for scientific method. I consider myself fortunate to have worked closely with Ian, and I believe he very much provided a role model, both as an intellectual and as a senior adviser to governments.

3. Ian Castles: Scholar as Truth Teller

William Coleman

Ian Castles possessed a rare suite of talents. Not many people have the requisites to become successful agency heads. Only a few of those will succeed in careers of public advocacy after their formal retirement. And still fewer will additionally contribute to scholarship. Castles did all three.

This chapter shines a light on the scholarly dimension of Castles by examining his 1984 paper 'Economics and Anti-Economics'.[1] This paper is equally remarkable and neglected. It is neglected: until this volume was published the paper was almost impossible to obtain. And it is remarkable: we may wonder how could a senior public servant, engrossed in the cares of administration, produce an incisive tract begotten by the careful scrutiny of recondite texts?

The subject of 'Economics and Anti-Economics' is the so-called 'moral critics of political economy' of the nineteenth century. Castles' thesis is that that these men were, in truth, *immoral* critics of political economy. Indeed, in reading Castles paper, I wonder if even 'immoral' is an understatement; 'appalling, atrocious, indecent to the point of villainy' might be a truer indictment.

Castles' case for his judgement is a careful 30,000 word long examination of *the actual*; what was actually said by the economists, as distinct from what they were said to have said. And of what was actually believed by anti-economists. In detailing the gulf between these two actuals, Castles' paper amounts to a crushing piece of table-turning upon these supposed 'moral critics' of political economy.

But for all its brilliance 'Economics and Anti-Economics' surely did not succeed in all the ways that Castles may have hoped it would. This chapter seeks to capture in a few strokes the character of Castle's paper, to speculate on its origin, and to ponder its fate.

The character of Castles' paper

At the very outset Castles groups his protagonists. On one side Castles places the 'economists'; by which he means the classical economists. On the other side are 'anti-economists'. These include ST Coleridge, Thomas Carlyle and

1 Another scholarly interest of Castles lay in the Australian sojourn of WS Jevons. One fruit of this is a display in the Power House Museum devoted to Jevons.

John Ruskin. These are sometimes known to historians of ideas as the 'sages' of nineteenth century Britain, but could be better described as the rhapsodists, the Savonarolas, the berserks of that society: three men who, over two generations, personified a blazing seam of social and political reaction in British intellectual life; and exhaled cyanide gas against the 'dismal science', as Carlyle so enduringly branded it.

But, critically, Castles adds to his enumeration of 'anti-economists' a second trio of persons; very different in character and station from the first but who, under the mantle of progressivism, broadcast in the twentieth century the same travesty of economics promulgated by reactionaries of the nineteenth. These are three 'teledons' or celebrity intellectuals of the 1960s and 70s; CP Snow, JK Galbraith, and Kenneth Clarke; the authors of *The Two Cultures and the Scientific Revolution*; *The Age of Uncertainty*; and *Civilisation: A Personal View*, respectively.

The case against classical economics which these three disseminate amounted to insinuating a responsibility of classical economics for the banes of nineteenth century 'industrialism': the Dark Satanic Mills, 'the condition of the working class', poverty amidst plenty, the Poor House *vs* Ascott House. The classical economists, at the very least, bestowed a self-satisfied benediction on this awfulness. They were therefore culpable of moral delinquency; or 'inhuman[ity]' in the words of Kenneth Clark, the art critic who Castles rightly identifies as the leading twentieth century disciple of Ruskin's 'devastating'[2] anti-economics.

Ian Castles contends that the truth about the economists and the anti-economists is much closer to the very opposite: that classical economists possessed a feeling of humanity, and a sympathy for it; while it was the anti-economists who were gripped by a loathing for much of their fellow species.

Castles sustains that claim by contrasting the positions of the two groups on various heads of social and economic policy of the day. Let me go through them.

Education

Castles points out that 'probably the first serious proposal ever' for universal [publicly funded] education' was made by Adam Smith, in the *Wealth of Nations*.[3] In his lead on education Smith was followed by virtually every political economist. By contrast, Coleridge was roughly contemptuous of such programs of universal education, and Ruskin maintained it was best if not all children were required to learn to read.

2 Clark's judgement, taken from Clark (1950).

3 Barthelemi-Gabriel Rolland is recorded by historians of education to be the author, in 1768, of the very first such proposal (see Coleman: 2004: 257).

Ireland

Castles bears evidence of a leniency of the classical economists to perpetually troubled Ireland. Ricardo recommended that to Ireland be applied a 'system, of kindness, indulgence and conciliation'. And Nassau Senior, no soft touch in these matters, contended that 'the erection, regulation and support of fever hospitals, infirmaries and dispensaries [in Ireland] should be fully and immediately attended to' (Senior: 1831).[4] It was the anti-economists who, as Castles documents, felt an irritated, resentful impatience at such solicitation for Ireland's wants, and repeatedly insisted that the Lord would provide whatever necessaries Ireland might require.[5]

The New Poor Law

The 'New' Poor Law of 1834 provides one of the landmarks of the Dickensian vision of the Industrial Revolution.

But however severe the New Poor Law, it needs to be registered that it was the express position of Political Economists who favoured the Law (such as JS Mill) that the Law was warranted by an obligation of society to relieve the destitution of the destitute. However qualified that obligation was in the minds of Mill and the like, they held that the destitute had a rightful claim on society, and the New Poor Law was to meet that claim.[6] If they significantly underestimated the size of that claim, it does well to keep in mind that no country in the world (of comparable size) at the time had a national (i.e. state) based system of assistance that the Poor Law provided. Indeed, the political economists most associated with the Poor Law were convinced that it was the relief provided by that Law that had preserved Great Britain in 1848 from the revolution suffered by France, which had no such law (see Senior: 1872).

Political Economists could also be friends of private charity, and the greatest of them was the greatest friend: Ricardo. On his estate Ricardo established a dispensary, an alms house, and a school; he was a prolific subscriber to various charities: for example, the Poor of the Parish of Hanovers Square, Extreme Distress at Spitalsfield and Persons Confined for Small Debts (the list is extensive).

4 James McCulloch, the Ricardian economist, believed that in Ireland 'the poor should have a *claim*, a *right* to support'. Senior opposed any right to such a claim (Senior: 1831: 30).

5 'What are the great causes of Irish misery?' asked John Wilson (anti-economist and friend of ST Coleridge) ... Without hesitation we reply ... he is the author of his own misery ... in the qualities of disposition for national prosperity, he stands at the lowest of civilised men' (see Castles: 1984: 34).

6 Some of the more obnoxious provisions of the administration of these Laws – such as the enforcement of silence during the meals of the inmates of the workhouses – were the coinage of Edwin Chadwick, and bespeak a rationalist confidence in the power of social design that is alien to political economy. I venture no such specific measures were recommended by any political economist of significance.

As Castles stresses, it was Carlyle who considered all this provision for the poor (be it public or private) an absurdity.

> Why not regiment these unfortunate wretches, put colonels and corporals over them and thrash them, if it proved needful, into habits of industry ...Try them for a couple of years and if they could not feed themselves ... they ought to be put out into the world' .... Sell them in Brazil as niggers.

Slavery

Smith, Ricardo, Mill, Senior, were strenuous anti-slavers. The anti-economists, by contrast, were almost always slavers.

Coleridge snarled that the Empire was being subverted by abolitionism. In *Unto This Last* – the frenzy anti-economics so praised by Clarke – Ruskin announced that slavery is 'an inherent, natural and eternal inheritance of much of the human race. It was Carlyle's fury at abolitionism that was the very occasion of his coinage the 'Dismal Science'; in his paper the 'Nigger Question' of 1849, amidst fantasies of firing squads for political economists, he champions slavery as 'the answer' to that 'question'.

There is an historical epilogue here: 'the Eyre Controversy'. In October 1865 a rioting mob in Jamaica killed 18 people. At the behest of the Governor, Edward James Eyre, British troops executed, or lawlessly killed, 586 blacks, and flogged another six hundred. Scandalised, JS Mill formed a Jamaica Committee to bring Eyre to account. But Carlyle felt 'heartily sorry for Eyre', and with Ruskin formed an Eyre Defence Committee to rebut the 'nigger philanthropists' of Mill and Henry Fawcett.

Let me pause to insert a speculation. I put to you that all three of these 'moral critics' of political economy adopted – presumably as a model for British public – the persona of *tyrant*. In the conduct of Eyre we have sinister possibility of Life imitating Art. Thus there is a more than personal significance in the character – the bad character – of the anti-economists; and there is a broader significance in the *good character* of Ricardo and Malthus. The evidence on that score, that Ian Castles carefully plots, is that these most vilified of men were equable, amicable, and affectionate.

Castles also assembles a fund of personal testimony as to the intellectual honesty of the classical economists. This evidence, too, has a broader significance. For the insinuation of JK Galbraith in the *Age of Uncertainty* is that the classical economists were not so. Certainly, Galbraith's implicit message is that the only significance in their thought lies in whatever propaganda purpose to which it might be put. Galbraith's imputation of *logical* insignificance to the theories of classical economics is doubtless rooted in the position (so congenial to the adversaries of classical economics) that reality is plastic; that it can be pushed into any desired shape; that we have a kind of play-doh economy free of constraints, trade-offs, costs etc. The upshot of this line of thinking is that there is no hidden mechanism to trouble over, there is no economic law to be uncovered; only political power to be obtained

Very different was the outlook of the political economists: they believed that a powerful but complex mechanism underlay economic events; a mechanism that was hidden from a careless observer but yet could be found. It was on account of this outlook that, as Maria Edgeworth records, '[Ricardo and Malthus] hunted in search of truth and huzzaed wherever they found her ...'. I suspect it was partly that naïve sense of discovery that impelled Ricardo to unabashedly advance his doctrines in the form of motions to the House of Commons, that were lost by vast majorities; provoking even one of his parliamentary allies to rise from the bench and declare that the Member for Portarlington must have 'descended from Jupiter'.

How *un*worldly the 'worldly philosophers' seem in contrast to Clark, Galbraith and Snow, those three sleek greyhounds of various mid-twentieth century 'corridors of power'. The ambassador's residence, the division lobby of the House of Lords, the weekend party at Windsor castle: such were their natural habitats.

And it is on account of their unworldliness that the classical economists were very differently motivated to write than Galbraith, etc. On this difference Castles tellingly quotes Galbraith from his *Affluent Society*:

> Audiences of all kinds applaud what they like best ... the great television and radio commentators make a profession of ... saying with elegance and unction what their audience[s] find most acceptable.

Indeed.

The conflict between the wish to be something in the world and the wish for other things brings me to Castles' treatment of CP Snow.

What provokes Castle's ire in Snow's *Two Cultures* is Snow's light-minded pairing – in a single phrase – of Napoleon with Adam Smith. One might give some quarter to Snow for this apparent fatuity; was Snow as a self-identified 'democratic socialist' seeking some epitomisation of 'autocratic capitalism' and in failing to find one settled for epitomisation of autocracy (Napoleon) and epitomisation of capitalism (Smith)? But, however that may be, Castles does not hesitate to pounce, and stresses the perfect antipathy between the world views of the Emperor and the professor; the one with a philosophy of conquest, and the other a philosophy of exchange; an antithesis exemplified in their stance to empire: the one the supreme imperialist, the other an emphatic anti-imperialist, who saw empire as corrupt and based on costly methods of Mercantilism, and who would have found every corroboration for this thesis in the 'Continental System' introduced by Napoleon. This last policy provoked some forward opposition by some economists in France, which Napoleon dismissed as 'the twaddle of economists'. As T B McCauley said, Napoleon 'hated political economy'.

We can detect in the Napoleonic Empire a prefiguring of the totalitarian state. We see it, among other places, in Napoleon's sensitivity to (and anxiety about) social ideas, including economic ideas. Napoleon once complained if there were a monarchy made of granite, the abstractions of the economists would be enough to grind it into dust. Napoleon was resolved to subvert any such subversion by abstract thought: thus J-B Say, having refused the importunate overtures of the Emperor, was dismissed from the Legislature, and publication of his *Treatise of Political Economy* forbidden; thus Napoleon abolished the *Institut* concerned with social sciences, amidst much fuming about 'ideologists' (while preserving the Institut of natural sciences and humanities).

Warp it, break it; make it teach that black is white. This is how totalitarian societies deal with social thought. War is Peace, Freedom is Slavery, Ignorance is Strength.

In 'Economics and Anti-Economics', written in 1984, Castles makes effective rhetorical reference to Orwellian oxymorons to underline the perverse rewriting of history of economics by Clark and Galbraith. 'Inhumanity is Humanity' is the double-speak slogan under which they stand. And yet Castles' references to Orwell's *1984* in some respects miss the mark. For we don't live in a totalitarian state; and the perversely false mythologies of Clark and Galbraith flourish without the terroristic negative incentives of such a state. A free society evidently contains *positive* incentives that powerfully nourish such mythologies. Pondering what those positive incentives are brings me back to the unwitting (or shameless) admission of Galbraith that Castles highlighted:

> Commentators make a profession of saying with elegance and unction what their audience[s] find most acceptable.

The looming reference is the corruption to thought that lies in the temptations to celebrity. To put the reference another way, unpopularity and obscurity can be a price of integrity. An indifference to those prices can be a source of integrity.

Gladly, considerations of celebrity did not figure in Ian Castles' motivations to write 'Economics and Anti-Economics'. It was not his lot to deliver his economics by Reith Lecture; he did not have a BBC microphone or camera. Instead he gave his paper to a session in Canberra of the (soon to expire) ANZAAS Conference; no place at all for any 'great radio and television commentator'. Ian Castles had the worldly unworldliness of Ricardo, and regardless of the presence or absence of the television camera, he 'hunted in search of truth and huzzaed wherever he found her'.

Castles' audience then and now

Yet perhaps we should also regret Castles' apparent unconcern about the size of his audience. For I am conscious that Ian's apparently vanquishing riposte to anti-economics appeared not long before an eruption of anti-economics in Australia of which in its ignorance, frenzy and indecency would almost match that of the nineteenth century originals (see Coleman and Hagger: 2001 for an account of this episode).

The proximity of Castles paper to the eruption of anti-economics also invites questions about what occasioned Castles, then secretary of the Department of Finance, to devote considerable hours to making such a foray.[7]

Perhaps a clue lies in the fact that in 1984 Australia had a new government, the Hawke Labor government. The earlier Whitlam Labor government had, of course, experienced tortured relations with Treasury and the Reserve Bank. The apparent tension between 'economists' and Labor were reinforced by the almost simultaneous collapse of the Keynesian consensus, and the cordial reception by Thatcher and Reagan of the monetarism of Milton Friedman. The potential for a renewed division with 'economists' on one side and 'labour' on the other was brought out by Friedman's 1981 visit to Canberra. This concluded with a dinner with a group of Labor members including what Friedman classified as 'real socialists'. In this 'acrimonious' encounter, Friedman later recalled, Bob Hawke 'made a long and involved statement out of which I could make neither hide nor hair' (Friedman and Friedman: 1999: 432).

In 1984 the new Hawke government was finding its way towards a program of deregulation and privatisation, and Hawke himself had excellent relations with his chief economic advisor, Ross Garnaut. But was it not also true that Hawke had a history of a conflicted response to economics? He had majored in economics in his undergraduate degree, but in Oxford his undertaking to complete a dissertation under the rubric of economics was derailed by an

7 He is recalled in this period as a visitor the National Library of Australia. Doubtless he became acquainted with its valuable records of political tracts in his employment in the archives division of the National Library in the mid 1950s.

'almighty row' with his supervisor, Colin Clarke, who was disdainful of Hawkes 'ability with economics'. For all that, Hawke formed on his return to Australia an 'inseparable trio' with two economists Max Newton and Ron Hieser, and an ANU professor of economics, Horrie Brown, became his 'mentor'. It was through Brown that Hawke gained an introduction to the ACTU, which employed him from 1957. But in 1950s 'national wage cases' economics seemed to be the possession of employers. Their counsel was Sir Richard Eggleston who had a 'knowledge of economics ... unique in the [legal] profession', and he would call economists as witnesses. But Hawke had the economists Wilfred Salter and Eric Russell coach him in the economics of index numbers. He successfully called DB Copland as a favourable witness, and successfully daunted JON Perkins, later a professor of economics, into withdrawing as witness for employers. All in all, the encounter of Hawke with economists was a chequered one.And in 1984 Hawke was Prime Minister. Was Castles paper an attempt to replace the motif of 'economists versus socialism' with 'economists versus reaction'? Possibly. What is certain is that the paper did not prevent that eruption of anti-economics that followed from around 1990; we may suspect it did little to temper its frenzy. During that ghastly episode Castles paper would have given some heart to the few who knew of it.[8] But by its nature it could not supply the logical tools that might provide a logical antidote to the distemper. For while Castles paper is a *tour de force*, the very source of its force also constitutes a frailty: its *ad hominem* aspect. When I say *ad hominem* I need hardly say that Castles does not proceed by denigrating the personal attributes of his targets; he did not describe any of them as an 'ill-bred, half witted Scotchman with a damned soul'; that is John Ruskin's own well-bred caption for Adam Smith. When I say *ad hominem* I mean that Castles' strategy is to show that the positive positions of anti-economists were ignorant and ludicrous, and their normative positions were sometimes abhorrent. There is both a strength in this, and a frailty: for to show that someone has misrepresented (besmirched, calumnied) a corps of doctrine is clearly not to show the doctrine is true, or even an advance towards truth. And to demonstrate that the persons who have censured some tendency are far more censurable themselves, is not to demonstrate the tendency itself is beyond any censure. Thus while Castles' paper establishes that the 'moral critics' offended justice, it leaves unidentified, unexamined and unresolved the issues that were the background of that act of injustice. And his method of 'personal critique' leaves open a method of 'personal defence'; whereby the modern day anti-economist sheds the burden of their predecessors' follies with the remark, 'we all know that Ruskin was barking mad, but still... '.

---

8 Peter Walsh, the Minister of Finance 1984-1990, knew and appreciated the paper. In the mid 1990s the Secretary of the Australian Department of Housing and Regional Development distributed it amongst senior people in the department. 'My impression was that the minister [Brian Howe] and his advisers (then including Jenny Macklin) were a bit bemused, perhaps even wary of what this might mean given their emphasis on planning and government intervention!' (Communication to author).

But to say Castles' paper left 'unresolved the issues' is only to say he left unresolved what no one else has yet resolved. What he did do in 'Economics and Anti-Economics' is to use the scholar's pen to slay a mythology; and not a harmless mythology but one that has been an adversary of improvement. Ian Castles the scholar was at one with Ian Castles the servant of the public.

References

Castles, Ian (1984). 'Economics and Anti-Economics', 54th ANZAAS Congress, 18 May 1984.

Clark, Kenneth (1950). *The Gothic Revival: an Essay in the History of Taste*, London, Constable.

Coleman, William (2004). *Economics and Its Enemies: Two Centuries of Anti-Economics*, Palgrave Macmillan.

Coleman, William and Alf Hagger (2001). Exasperating Calculators: the Rage Against Economic Rationalism and the Campaign against Australian Economists, Macleay Press.

D'Alpuget, Blanche (1982) . *Robert J Hawke, a biography*, Lansdowne Press.

Friedman, Milton and Rose D (1999). *Two Lucky People. Memoirs*, Chicago: University of Chicago Press.

Senior, Nassau (1831). *Letter to Lord Howick on a Legal Provision for the Irish Poor*.

Senior, Nassau (1872). *Correspondence and Conversations of Alexis de Tocqueville with Nassua William Senior From 1834 to 1859*, London: Henry S King.

4. Economics and Anti-Economics[1]

Ian Castles

Synopsis

The paper traces the development of mainstream British economics during the century following the publication of *The Wealth of Nations* in 1776. The emphasis is not on the economists' formal statements of principles and doctrines, but on the policy prescriptions and social attitudes which they inferred from them.

It is suggested that the economists saw a clear connection between their economic principles and their attitudes to other controversial questions, including issues related to civil liberties, public education and the role of women; and that the economists' opponents – the anti-economists – also saw the connection.

The paper shows that the attitudes of the leading economists on these issues were well in advance of their time. This is true even of those who have subsequently been regarded as arch conservatives.

The economists' views on many social and national issues were, indeed, so radical as to lead to a continuing conflict in their minds as to how far they should express or publicise them – thereby prejudicing their capacity to influence the course of policy on economic issues which were themselves the subject of bitter controversy.

All of the economists whose views are discussed here were subjected to strong criticism, and most of them to venomous verbal attacks. Ironically, they are commonly represented in the late-twentieth-century conventional wisdom as having themselves held the false opinions against which they were arguing.

It is shown that television series such as Kenneth Clark's *Civilisation* and John Kenneth Galbraith's *The Age of Uncertainty* have grossly misrepresented the economists' position and understated their contribution. Such popularisations have amounted, in effect, to Newspeak versions of the classical economic texts; and in fact accord with Orwell's definition of Newspeak versions in that they have 'not merely changed into something different, but actually changed into something contradictory to what they used to be'.

1 Paper presented by Ian Castles, President, ANZAAS Economics Section on 18 May 1984 at the 54th ANZAAS Congress. Except where otherwise indicated, all figures and tables in this chapter are Castles' own.

The economists	The anti-economists
Adam Smith, 1723-90	Napolean Bonaparte, 1769-1821
Dugald Stewart, 1753-1828	Samuel Taylor Coleridge, 1772-1834
Thomas Robert Malthus 1766-1834	Robert Southey, 1774-1843
David Ricardo, 1772-1823	Michael Thomas Sadler, 1780-1835
James Mill, 1773-1836	John Wilson, 1785-1854
John Ramsay McCulloch 1789-1864	Frederick Engels, 1820-1895
Nassau William Senior, 1790-1864	Thomas Carlyle, 1795-1881
John Stuart Mill, 1806-1873	John Ruskin, 1819-1900

> *The ingratitude of mankind towards their benefactors has been notorious. It is not indeed universal ... But in general it will be found that those whose merits have been promptly and adequately recognised have been men who have participated in the opinions and the passions of those around them. They have been statesmen or soldiers or demagogues, whose objects have been the same as those of their contemporaries and who have differed from them only by perceiving more clearly or employing more unscrupulously the readiest means of attaining them. Men of a higher moral and intellectual character – men who are unaffected by the prejudice of their age and country – who refuse to aid in gratifying irrational desires or in maintaining irrational opinions, must not expect power or even popularity ... This is peculiarly the case where the services rendered have been those rather of a teacher than of a legislator, where they have consisted in exposing fallacies, softening prejudices, stigmatising selfishness, and preparing in one generation the way for measures which are to be adopted by another.*
>
> – Nassau W Senior, in *Biographical Sketches* (London 1863)

I

In George Orwell's *Nineteen Eighty-Four*, Syme, the philologist, explains to Winston Smith that

> By 2050 – earlier probably – all real knowledge of Oldspeak will have disappeared ... Chaucer, Shakespeare, Milton, Byron – they'll exist only in Newspeak versions, not merely changed into something different, but actually changed into something contradictory to what they used to be.

The creation of Newspeak versions was not to be confined to works of the imagination:

> Considerations of prestige made it desirable to preserve the memory of certain historical figures. Various writers, such as Shakespeare, Milton

> (and) Swift...were therefore in process of translation...There were also large quantities of merely utilitarian literature...that had to be treated in the same way.

Orwell's book was written in 1948. It soon became apparent that the classics of utilitarian literature were already being changed 'into something contradictory to what they used to be'.

The early chapters of John Kenneth Galbraith's *The Affluent Society,* which was published in 1958, provided summary translations of Adam Smith's *Wealth of Nations,* Malthus' *Essay on Population* and Ricardo's *Principles of Political Economy and Taxation.* These were Newspeak versions: their purpose was to support the arguments in later chapters of Galbraith's book, not to reproduce the sense of the Oldspeak originals. Indeed, Professor Galbraith provided a remarkably frank justification for his approach:

> Within a considerable range, (the individual) is permitted to believe what he pleases. He may hold whatever view of the world he finds most agreeable or acceptable to his taste...Audiences of all kinds applaud what they like best. And in social comment the test of audience approval, far more than the test of truth, comes to influence comment... Individuals, most notably the great television and radio commentators, make a profession of knowing and saying with elegance and unction what their audience will find most acceptable.

The *Affluent Society* passed the test of audience approval with honours. Within five years one of Galbraith's professional colleagues had expressed 'shock' that it had been read by many more Americans than *The Wealth of Nations.* And in 1973 Professor Galbraith was chosen by the BBC to 'do a television series on some aspect of the history of economic or social ideas'. *Teledep* within Orwell's Ministry of Truth could not have chosen better. The series attracted millions of viewers all over the world. It was entitled *The Age of Uncertainty* because, Professor Galbraith explained,

> It sounded well; it did not confine thought; and it suggested the basic theme: we would contrast the great certainties in economic thought in the last century with the great uncertainty with which problems are faced in our time.

The great certainties were proclaimed 'with elegance and unction' and the audiences found it most acceptable.

II

In the same year as *The Affluent Society* was published, CP Snow suggested an alternative formula for writing the history of modern times:

> What is needed is that in the general history books the development of science should take its place along with political and economic developments. It is only just that this should be done even from the historian's point of view, for the world we live in is as much the produce of science as of politics and economics. The steam engine helped shape the modern world at least as much as Napoleon and Adam Smith, but only rarely do the historians admit the fact...this is one way in which history must be written if the worlds of science and the humanities are not to drift still farther apart.

The underlying assumption, developed at length in Snow's famous lecture in the following year, was that it was sensible to conceive of the modern world as having been shaped by two non-communicating cultures – science, which included the steam engine; and the humanities, which included Napoleon and Adam Smith.

It is difficult to think of two figures from the same era of whom it could more certainly be said that they represented *different* cultures than Napoleon and Adam Smith. As was pointed out within five years of Napoleon's death, by Oxford's first professor of political economy:

> Napoleon...had an utter horror of political economy; the principles of which...he said, if an empire were built of granite, would grind it to powder. On such subjects he trusted to commonsense. And his commonsense was an undistinguishing acceptance of the whole theory of the mercantile system. It appears, from his conversations at St Helena, that he fully believed that the continent must be a loser by its commerce with England, and that it must be so on account of the excellence and cheapness of English commodities. These abominable qualities must, he thought, enable us...to undersell the continent in its own market, and ultimately produce its ruin...He thought that he could put an end to this trade by his continental system. Without doubt the principal object of that system was to ruin England; but he appears to have implicitly believed that it was also a blessing to the continent. The murmurs of his subjects and allies he treated like the complaints of spoiled children, who do not know what is for their own good and who, when experience has made them wiser, will embrace from choice what they have submitted to from necessity. There can be no doubt, I think, that these opinions and the obstinancy into which they led him, were the ultimate causes of his downfall.

Thus Adam Smith's culture was the antithesis of Napoleon's. It was in fact, the scientific culture. Nothing could have been more foreign to his habits of thought than the dichotomy perceived by Snow. Adam Smith wrote *A History of Astronomical Systems* and planned a 'connected history of liberal sciences and elegant arts'; he was an enthusiastic botanist; and the two greatest Scottish natural scientists of his day – the chemist Joseph Black and the geologist James Hulton – were his lifelong friends and his literary executors.

By suggesting that historians should write about the history of the steam engine as well as about Adam Smith, Snow revealed his ignorance of what they had written about both. Here is an historian writing over a century ago:

> It was in Glasgow that Adam Smith saw a most startling proof of the obstacles thrown in the way of industrial originality by the old regulations of industry. Whilst he was Professor at the University, there came to Glasgow James Watt, the inventor of the condensing steam-engine, anxious to set up as a mathematical instrument-maker; but the Corporation of Hammermen refused him permission, on the ground that he was neither a burgess of the town nor had served an apprenticeship to the trade. Fortunately, however, for Watt, he had a friend among the Professors, by whose influence he was allowed to establish his workshop within the University buildings, where the power of the corporation could not penetrate...The world was on the eve of an industrial revolution; and...the two men who did most to bring it about...met... in Glasgow, when one was dreaming of the book, and the other of the invention, which were to introduce a new industrial age.

Adam Smith enjoyed visiting Watt's workshop and Watt, for his part, later recalled with gratitude that it was to the conversation at this time with Adam Smith, Joseph Black and others that 'my mind owed its first bias towards... subjects in which they were all my superiors, I never having attended a college, and being then but a mechanic'. And when Watt was 'amusing the leisure of his old age...with his new invention of the sculpture machine, and presenting his works to his friends as "the productions of a young artist just entering his eighty-third year", one of the first works he executed with the machine was a small head of Adam Smith in ivory'.

From experiences such as the initial Watt episode and his subsequent friendship with Watt, Smith drew two of the most important conclusions of *The Wealth of Nations*. In the first place

> The property which every man has in his own labour, as it is the original foundation of all other property, so it is the most sacred and inviolable. The patrimony of a poor man lies in the strength and dexterity of his

> hands; and to hinder him from employing this strength and dexterity in what manner he thinks proper without injury to his neighbour, is a plain violation of this most sacred property.

And secondly

> Though the interest of the labourer is strictly connected with that of the society, he is incapable either of comprehending that interest, or of understanding its connexion with his own. His condition leaves him no time to receive the necessary information and his education and habits are commonly such as to render him unfit to judge even though he was fully informed. In the public deliberations, therefore, his voice is little heard and less regarded, except upon some particular occasions, when his clamour is animated, set on, and supported by his employers, not for his, but for their own particular purposes.

A policy prescription of the greatest significance followed. The public should 'establish, in every parish and district, a little school' and should 'impose upon' almost the whole body of the people the necessity of acquiring those most essential parts of education'; and these essential parts were not just 'the three R's' but elementary science:

> There is scarce a common trade which does not afford some opportunities of applying to it the principles of geometry and mechanics, and which would not, therefore, gradually exercise and improve the common people in those principles, the necessary introduction to the most sublime, as well as to the most useful, sciences.

This was probably the first serious proposal ever made for universal formal education of the young in elementary science; and it was supported not only on vocational grounds but because it would help students to fulfil themselves as human beings and citizens. 'Science', said Adam Smith, 'is the great antidote to the poison of enthusiasm and superstition'.

One immediate reaction from the scientific establishment to *The Wealth of Nations* is recorded by Boswell. Within days of publication, Sir John Pringle, President of the Royal Society, observed to him

> that Dr Smith, who had never been in trade, could not be expected to write well on that subject any more than a lawyer upon physick.

Thirty years later Davies Giddy, who was to succeed his friend Sir Humphry Davy as President of the Royal Society, vigorously opposed legislation to have all children taught:

> However specious in theory the project might be, of giving education to the labouring classes of the poor, it would in effect be found to be

> prejudicial to their morals and happiness; it would teach them to despise their lot in life, instead of making them good servants in agriculture, and other laborious employments to which their rank in society had destined them; instead of teaching them subordination, it would render them factious and refractory, as was evident in the manufacturing countries; it would enable them to read seditious pamphlets, vicious books, and publications against Christianity; it would render them insolent to their superiors; and in a few years the result would be that the legislature would find it necessary to direct the strong arm of power towards them, and to furnish the executive magistrate with much more vigorous laws than were now in force.

Fifty years after *The Wealth of Nations* appeared, Coleridge, who has been praised in the twentieth century for his unique understanding of the scientific as well as the literary culture, wrote:

> The whole pretended sciences (of political economy) is but a humbug. I have attentively read...Adam Smith...Malthus and Ricardo and found (i.e. believe myself to have found) a multitude of sophisms but not a single just and important result which might not more convincingly be deduced from the simplest principles of morality and common sense.

Among the sophisms that Adam Smith, Malthus and Ricardo had all produced were strong statements in support of universal education. But Coleridge had other ideas:

> The breaking-up of the cottage home education...(is) one of the most miserable mistakes which the well-intentioned people of the day have yet made; and they have made, and are making, a great many, God knows.

As for the school curriculum, here is Coleridge in 1833:

> I more than doubt the expedience of making even elementary mathematics as part of the routine in the system of the great schools.

In 1955 Dr Jacob Bronowski addressed the Education Section of the British Association for the Advancement of Science meeting. His subject was *The Educated Man* in 1984 and his conclusion was

> My program...(is) to make the language of science part of the education, the cultural education, of the young who will have either to make or to suffer 1984.

No mention was made of Adam Smith's earlier program to make the language of science part of the cultural education of the young. In fact, Bronowski had claimed that economics

> has never become an empirical science, because it has never recovered from the fatal reasonableness of Adam Smith's *The Wealth of Nations.*

In 1960 Bronowski was the joint author of a book which referred to Adam Smith's proposal to have 'the government intervene and educate the labouring poor' and commented that this was 'strange doctrine for a supposed free enterpriser'.

The wheel had now turned full circle. In 1776 the President of the Royal Society thought that Smith, being a philosopher, could not know about trade; and in 1960 one of the greatest science popularisers thought that Smith, being a free trader, could not know about anything else.

Bronowski later achieved world-wide fame with *The Ascent of Man* – the BBC television series on the history of science. He did it well, but he never mentioned Adam Smith or *The Wealth of Nations.*

III

The model for the BBC's Bronowski and Galbraith television serialisations had been Kenneth Clark's *Civilisation.* The subtitle of this series was *A Personal View,* and Lord Clark's personal view of the contribution of *The Wealth of Nations* to civilisation was an idiosyncratic one. This is the only reference:

> In *The Wealth of Nations* Adam Smith invented the study of political economy, and created a social science that lasted up to the time of Karl Marx, and beyond.

Earlier historians of civilisation had taken a different view. Henry Buckle, the champion chess player who spoke 19 languages and acquired 22,000 books, declared in his *History of Civilisation in England* that *The Wealth of Nations* was

> in its ultimate results probably the most important book that has ever been written; (it has) done more towards the happiness of man than has been effected by the united abilities of all the statesmen and legislators of whom history has preserved an authentic account.

The two great reformers of the criminal law in the early nineteenth century – Sir Samuel Romilly and Sir James Mackintosh – had both known Adam Smith personally. Their recorded opinions about the influence of Adam Smith and his book are also in striking contrast to Kenneth Clark's.

Romilly, who was to be the Solicitor-General in the 'Ministry of All the Talents' wrote a letter to France about a month after Smith's death in which he said:

> I have been surprised and, I own, a little indignant to observe how little impression (Adam Smith's) death has made here. Scarce any notice has been taken of it, while for over a year together after the death of Dr Johnson nothing was to be heard of but panegyrics of him...

Mackintosh was a member of the House of Commons for twenty years, and a professor of law and politics for seven. As parliamentarian, academic, advocate, historian and philosopher, he was one of the most prominent figures in British life during the first turbulent half century of the Smithian revolution. This was his assessment:

> The great name of Adam Smith rests upon...*The Wealth of Nations*; perhaps the only book which produced an immediate, general and irrevocable change in some of the most important parts of the legislation of all civilised nations...In a few years it began to alter laws and treaties; and has made its way through the convulsions of revolution and conquest to a due ascendant over the minds of men...

Another prominent figure in politics, literature and the law during the first half of the nineteenth century was Lord Brougham, a key figure in securing the passage of the great Reform Bill of 1832. Here is Brougham's comment on the literary merit of *The Wealth of Nations:*

> There is not a book of better English to be anywhere found. The language is simple, clear...homely...idiomatic...Besides its other perfections, it is one of the most entertaining of books. There is no laying it down after you begin to read. You are drawn on...by the strong current of the arguments...the fulness and force of the illustrations, the thickly strewed and happily selected facts.

In *Civilisation,* Clark makes frequent reference to Smith's compatriot and contemporary Robert Burns. In one such reference he notes that

> The only people who saw through industrialism (in the late eighteenth century) were the poets...Burns, passing the Carron Iron Works in 1787, scratched these lines on a window pane:
>
> *We cam na here to view your works,*
>
> *In hopes to be mair wise,*
>
> *But only, lest we gang to hell,*
>
> *It may be nae surprise.*

Such graffiti are slender evidence that Burns 'saw through industrialism' (whatever that means). But we know that, soon afterwards, Burns read the great book by industrialism's 'patron saint'. Perhaps he enjoyed Adam Smith's non-sexist version of 'A man's a man for a'that':

> By nature a philosopher is not in genius and disposition half so different from a street porter, as a mastiff is from a greyhound...

Or perhaps the author of *Ye banks and braes* enjoyed the economist's praise of country living:

> The beauty of the country besides, the pleasures of a country life, the tranquility of mind which it promises and, whenever the injustice of human laws does not disturb it, the independency which it really affords, have charms which more or less attract everybody.

Or perhaps it was the impact of the whole which led him to write to a friend:

> That extraordinary man, Smith, in his *Wealth of Nations*, finds me leisure employment enough. I could not have given any man credit for half the intelligence Mr Smith uncovers in his book. I would covet much to have his ideas respecting the present state of some quarters of the world that are or have been the scenes of considerable revolutions since his book was written.
>
> *The pith o'sense, and pride o'worth,*
> *Are higher rank than a'that'.*

IV

We now turn to Galbraith's views. In *The Wealth of Nations,* he says,

> Private vice became public virtue, which has been considered ever since a most convenient thing.

Here Professor Galbraith appears to have confused *The Wealth of Nations* with Mandeville's satire *Fable of the Bees or Private Vices made Public Benefits* which was written 70 years earlier. A major theme of *The Wealth of Nations* is that private vice becomes a public vice – for example, the greed of private manufacturers leads to 'the most infamous abuse and detraction,...personal insults (and) sometimes...real danger' to Members of Parliament; and only statesmen who are excessively under the influence of private shopkeepers could employ 'the blood and treasure of their fellow citizens to found and maintain... an empire'.

Another Galbraith line is that Adam Smith, in his 'greatest phrase', said that the individual is 'guided as though by an unseen hand' to serve the public interest in serving his own. The Oldspeak text is considerably less sweeping,

> By directing (his) industry in such a manner as its produce may be of the greatest value, (the individual) intends only his own gain, and he is in this, as in *many* other cases, led by an invisible hand to promote an end which was no part of his intention. *Nor is it always* the worse for society that it was no part of it. By pursuing his own interest he *frequently* promotes that of the society more effectually than when he really intends to promote it (emphasis added).

Then there is Adam Smith's 'great thought', which as presented by Professor Galbraith is an eighteenth century version of 'What's good for General Motors is good for the USA':

> The wealth of a nation results from the diligent pursuit of each of its citizens of his own interests...In serving his own interests, the individual serves the public interest.

This is Newspeak again. *The Wealth of Nations* says almost the opposite – that the interest of merchants and manufacturers 'is always in same respects different from, and even opposite to, that of the public'; and so their proposals required 'the most suspicious attention' because they

> had generally an interest to deceive and even to oppress the public, and (they) accordingly have, upon many occasions, both deceived and oppressed the public.

Finally, Galbraith categorises Adam Smith as a 'conservative' (though he is 'far too wise and amusing to be left to the conservatives'). But, Smith himself regarded his book as radical – as a 'very violent attack...upon the whole commercial system of Great Britain'. It was, in fact, an attack on more than the commercial system: it was one of the most comprehensive assaults on 'sacred cows' in the history of literature. Among the targets were:

- *the universities* – 'sanctuaries in which exploded systems and obsolete prejudices found shelter and protection, after they had been hunted out of every other corner of the world';
- *the professors at Oxford* – most of them had 'given up altogether even the pretence of teaching';
- *the established Church* – 'philosophical good temper and moderation' are promoted when the law 'favours no one sect more than another';
- *parochial schools* – they taught a useless smattering of Latin while failing to teach science;

- *the electoral system* – the representation of the people in the House of Commons was very unequal;
- *the East India Company* – it 'oppresses and domineers';
- *slavery* – it was harsher in the West Indies than in medieval Europe, and was only maintained because 'the pride of man makes him love to domineer, and nothing mortifies him so much as to have to condescend to persuade his inferiors';
- *laws against forestalling* – they appealed to the same fears as laws against witchcraft;
- *customs policy* – 'the sneaking arts of underling tradesmen are...erected into political maxims for the conduct of a great empire'; and
- *taxation policy* – 'there is no art which one government sooner learns from another than that of draining money from the pockets of the people'.

The radical influence *of The Wealth of Nations* is apparent in the hatred and fear of those who deplored that influence. Galbraith says that 'the acclaim (for the book) was immediate' and notes that it was praised by Hume and Gibbon – but at that time Hume, Gibbon and Smith were all being reviled by respectable opinion for their 'infidelity'. Fourteen years after *The Wealth of Nations* was published, *The Times* concluded its obituary notice for Adam Smith with:

> he deserves the chief praise, or the chief blame, of propagating a system which tends to confound National Wealth with National Prosperity.

The meaning of the phrase is not clear, but it was not intended as a compliment. Robert Southey, the reactionary and bigoted Poet Laureate, described *The Wealth of Nations* as 'a tedious and hard-hearted book, greatly over-valued even on the score of ability' – but it is significant that, writing in 1816, Southey saw all of the ills of modern times as beginning *40 years* earlier (that is, in 1776, not in 1766 or 1786).

The peak of hostility to the revolutionary doctrines of T*he Wealth of Nations* was reached in the immediate aftermath of the French revolution. On February 1 1793, the day that Britain went to war with France, the Marquis of Lansdowne, former Prime Minister and former friend of the new-dead Adam Smith, had told the House of Lords that the so-called 'French principles'

> had been exported from us to France and cannot be said to have originated among the people of the latter country. The new principles of government founded on the abolition of the old feudal system... have...been inculcated by Dr Adam Smith in his work on *The Wealth of Nations*, which has been recommended as a book necessary for the information of youth by Mr Dugald Stewart...

Mr Dugald Stewart would have known that only eighteen months earlier the church, house and laboratory of Joseph Priestly, the discoverer of oxygen, had been wrecked and burned by the 'Church and King' mob in Birmingham; and that Priestly had also, in happier days, been a friend of Lord Lansdowne's.

And so, not far from where Galbraith joked in 1973 that 'Adam Smith is far too wise and amusing to be left to the conservatives', Professor Stewart decided to abandon his intention of giving a long account of Adam Smith's opinions, in an address he was about to give to the Royal Society of Edinburgh; because at that period, as he was to explain nearly 20 years later,

> the doctrine of a Free Trade was itself represented as a revolutionary tendency, and some who had formerly prided themselves on their intimacy with Mr Smith, and on their zeal for the propagation of his liberal system, began to call in question the expediency of subjecting to the disputation of philosophers the arcana of State policy and the unfathomable wisdom of the feudal ages.

In 1801-02, when Stewart first began to give a course of lectures on political economy at the University of Edinburgh, the mere term 'political economy' made people start. 'They thought it included questions touching the constitution of governments', said Lord Cockburn, 'and not a few hoped to catch Stewart in dangerous propositions'. By this time, however, political economy had produced a book whose basic proposition was seen by many as far more dangerous than any in *The Wealth of Nations*.

V

No book in history has evoked such contrary reactions, from the highest praise to the most violent condemnation, as Malthus' *Essay on Population*. As an example of the hostile assessments, Coleridge lamented the acceptance of 'the monstrous practical sophism of Malthus' and went on:

> I solemnly declare that I do not believe that all the heresies and sects and factions which the ignorance and the weakness and the wickedness of man have ever given birth to, were altogether so disgraceful to man as a Christian, a philosopher, a statesman, or citizen, as this abominable tenet.

That was said in 1832, still in Malthus' lifetime. Here is Keynes' assessment, exactly 100 years later:

> Malthus's *Essay* is a work of youthful genius. The author was fully conscious of the ideas he was expressing. He believed that he had found the clue to human misery. The importance of the *Essay* consisted not

> in the novelty of his facts but in the smashing emphasis he placed on a simple generalisation arising out of them...The book can claim a place amongst those which have had great influence on the progress of thought. It is profoundly...in that tradition of Scotch and English thought... the tradition which is suggested by the names of Locke, Hume, Adam Smith, Paley, Bentham, Darwin and Mill, a tradition marked by a love of truth and most noble lucidity, by a prosaic sanity free from sentiment or metaphysic, and by an immense disinterestedness and public spirit...It is in this company that Malthus belongs.

Many in that company were reviled by their contemporaries. Boswell 'talked with indignation and contempt of the poisonous productions with which (his) age (was) infested' and asked Johnson to 'knock Hume's and (Adam) Smith's heads together'. Paley was regarded by George III as a 'dangerous revolutionary'. Bentham, Darwin and Mill were all to suffer vicious verbal assaults. But only Malthus was ferociously assailed for decades by the most pious, respectable and worthy people of his time.

'Mr Malthus is cast in his action against God Almighty', wrote the pious Robert Southey. 'The insults the theory of Malthus levels at God,' wrote the pious Michael Sadler, 'and the injuries it meditates inflicting upon man, will be endured by neither'. 'Instead of distrusting his own conclusions,' complained RB Seeley, Sadler's pious biographer, Malthus 'boldly puts forward a system...wholly opposed to the whole tenor of Scripture'. And to the pious Hudson Gurney, heir to an enormous banking fortune, a bill before the House of Commons was 'an attempt to bring the detestable system of Mr Malthus to bear upon the legislation of the country – a system which every chapter of sacred history condemns, every page of civil history confutes and every map of a half-unpeopled world, after a duration of nearly 6000 years, proves the absurdity of'.

In the late-twentieth-century Newspeak versions of history, these attacks have been expunged from the record. Malthus is portrayed as a great ally of the pious and the respectable. Here is Lord Clark in *Civilisation*:

> When I call (the works of Malthus and Ricardo) sacred books I am not joking. (They) were taken up as gospel by the most serious and even pious men, who used them to justify actions they would never have thought of defending on human grounds...the very words 'pious', 'respectable', 'worthy', have become joke words, used only ironically.

Presumably Clark is still not joking when he goes on to say that 'one hates the inhuman way in which the doctrines of Malthus were accepted'. This is Newspeak again: what one hates, if one studies the Oldspeak documents, is the inhuman way in which the doctrines of Malthus were for so long *rejected*.

At first Malthus' assailants expected that he would be a 'pushover'. In 1803 Southey reminded John Rickman of the Census Office:

> Do not forget Malthus's rascally metaphysics. Break him on the wheel. I will see the sentence registered. You ought to set our foot on such a mischievous reptile and crush him.

Seven years later Southey wrote to Sir Walter Scott that he was 'making ready to come upon that precious philosophist, or philosophicide, with a thunder clap'; and to Walter Savage Landor that 'I meditate a mortal blow at Malthus, who is the special object of my contempt and abhorrence'.

Malthus made no reply to the vicious personal attacks, corresponded prolifically with those who addressed issues in a scientific spirit and prepared successive new editions of the *Essay*. In these he readily modified his position in the light of sound argument and evidence but not otherwise. By 1815, Coleridge was scandalised

> to hear Malthus quoted in a British Senate! Stupid, hard-hearted blunders ingrafted on pedantically disguised, and yet falsely worded, truisms...Were the Prince to knight him, he would smell no worse to my nostrils.

This letter of Coleridge's also referred offensively to Malthus in German and Greek. It was a particular cause of outrage among Malthus' critics that he had written the *Essay* in English, thus risking the possibility that its contents might be read by those who should be protected from such blasphemy: the working classes and perhaps even women. Southey protested in 1816 that the book was

> written in the vulgar tongue, and sent into the world for the edification of all dabblers in metaphysics, male and female! One might have thought that such an argument could never have been advanced 'by one of women born'; that it would never have been heard without indignation by one who had a wife, a sister or a daughter.

In another essay the Poet Laureate was more specific:

> A book necessarily leading to such topics of discussion as Mr. Malthus's ought not to have been written in English. The main point upon which his argument turns, and the necessity of *vice* for the preservation of *good order,* were not subjects to be sent into circulating libraries and book-societies, and to be canvassed at tea-tables.

Such prudish attitudes imposed costs in human suffering which are beyond calculation. As John Stuart Mill was to point out in his *Principles of Economics,* published 50 years after Malthus' *Essay:*

> Religion, morality and statesmanship have vied with one another in incitements to marriage, and to the multiplication of the species...the rich, provided the consequences do not touch themselves, think it impugns the wisdom of Providence to suppose that misery can result from the operation of a natural propensity; the poor think that 'God never sends mouths but he sends meat'. No one would guess from the language of either, that man had any voice or choice in the matter. So complete is the confusion of ideas on the whole subject, owing in a great degree to the mystery in which it is shrouded by a spurious delicacy, which prefers that right and wrong should be mismeasured and confounded on one of the subjects most momentous to human welfare, rather than that the subject should be freely spoken of and discussed. People are little aware of the cost to mankind of this scrupulousity of speech. The disease of society can, no more than corporal maladies, be prevented or cured without being spoken about in plain language...One would imagine that children were rained down upon married people, direct from heaven, without their being art or part in the matter; that it was really, as the common phrases have it, God's will, and not their own, which decided the numbers of their offspring.

Mill went on to suspect that an important reason for the slow acceptance of Malthus' principle of population was that it was true:

> One may be permitted to doubt whether, except among the poor themselves (for whose prejudices on this subject there is no difficulty in accounting) there has ever yet been, in any class of society, a sincere and earnest desire that wages should be high...Nearly all who are not laborers themselves, are employers of labor, and are not sorry to get the commodity cheap.

And he also pointed out that, if given the chance it would be the wives, sisters and daughters who would welcome the Malthusian doctrine most warmly:

> It is never by the choice of the wife that families are too numerous; on her devolves (along with all the physical suffering and at least a full share of the privations) the whole of the intolerable domestic drudgery resulting from the excess. To be relieved from it would be hailed as a blessing by multitudes of women who now never venture to urge such a claim, but who would urge it, if supported by the moral feelings of the community. Among the barbarisms which law and morals have not yet

> ceased to sanction, the most disgusting surely is, that any human being should be permitted to consider himself as having a *right* to the person of another.

Mill regarded Malthus' *Essay* as the 'fountain-head' from which 'the permanent place now occupied in the minds of thinking men by the question of improving the condition of the labouring classes may be dated', because it

> furnished a sufficient explanation of the state of extreme poverty in which the majority of mankind had almost everywhere been found, without supposing any inherent necessity in the case...And the explanation afforded a sure hope...Whatever raises the civilization of the people at large – whatever accustoms them to require a higher standard of subsistence, comfort, taste, and enjoyment, affords itself... the means of satisfying the wants which it engenders...these are the prospects which the vilified population principle has opened to mankind. True, indeed the doctrine teaches this further lesson, that any attempt to produce the same result by other means...might, for any *general* effect of a beneficial kind which it can produce, as well be let alone. And, the doctrine being brought thus into conflict with those plans of easy beneficence which accord so well with the inclinations of man, but so ill with the arrangements of nature, we need not wonder that the epithets of 'Malthusians' and 'Political Economists' are so often considered equivalent to hard-hearted, unfeeling, and enemies of the poor – accusations so far from being true, that no thinkers, of any pretensions to sobriety, cherish such hopeful views of the future social position of labour, or have so long made the permanent increase of its remuneration the turning-point of their political speculations, as those who most broadly acknowledge the doctrine of Malthus.

The late twentieth century conventional wisdom finds such opinions disagreeable and has suppressed them. In *The Affluent Society* Galbraith described John Stuart Mill as 'conscientious and immeasurably learned' but titled the chapter 'Economics and the Tradition of Despair' – which presumably means that Mill was also, in Galbraith's view, immeasurably wrong; and in *The Age of Uncertainty,* Mill was described 'prodigious and luminous' in the same episode as viewers were told that 'It was with Malthus and Ricardo that economics became the dismal science'.

In *Civilisation* Kenneth Clark did not mention Mill at all; but his comments on Malthus and the population principle were classical specimens of Newspeak, reminiscent of the slogans in bold letters on the wall of the Ministry of Truth. The crusade of the pious and respectable against Malthusianism disappeared and their enthusiastic acceptance of Malthus' gospel was substituted: WAR IS PEACE. The costs to welfare which Mill attributed to confusion of ideas and spurious delicacy were attributed by Clark to politicians being 'held in the intellectual prison of classical economics': FREEDOM IS SLAVERY. And children apparently *did* rain down direct from heaven – 'the squalid disorder of industrial society', said Clark, had arisen 'because of unpredictables, and in this case the unpredictable was the growth of population': IGNORANCE IS STRENGTH.

VI

In the Newspeak histories, Ricardo's image is even more tarnished than that of Malthus. In *Civilisation* he was portrayed as a prophet of the 'new religion of gain...a most earnest man...but inexorable'. Galbraith filled out the portrait in *The Age of Uncertainty:*

> Nor was Ricardo ever thought an optimist. In the Ricardian world workers would receive the minimum necessary for life, never more. This was the iron law of wages. It led...to the conclusion that not only was compassion wasted on the working man but it was damaging...The more numerous the people, the richer were the landlords. They fattened, the people starved. And...nothing could be done about it...David Ricardo was not, by his own lights a cruel man. In a naturally cruel world he merely urged against contending in a futile way with the inevitable...He did provide the rich with a very satisfactory formula for suffering the misfortunes of the poor.

CP Snow presented Ricardo as an example – indeed the example – of moral blindness in an 'intelligent man'. Two years after his 'put science into history' proposal, he told the American Association for the Advancement of Science:

> the scientists who want to contract out say, *we* produce the tools. *We* stop there. It is for the rest of *you* – the rest of the world, the politicians – to say how the tools are used. (This) is one of the easier methods of letting the conscience rust. It is exactly what the early nineteenth-century economists, such as Ricardo, did in the face of the facts of the first industrial revolution. We wonder now how men, intelligent men, can have been so morally blind.

Thus has Ricardo been portrayed in the Newspeak texts: priggish, inflexible, solemn, pessimistic, gutless, hard-hearted, unfeeling, aloof, humourless, impotent and unprincipled. But the Oldspeak records paint him differently.

Two years before Ricardo died suddenly at the age of 51, at a time when he was at the height of his fame as an economist and as an active member of the House of Commons, Maria Edgeworth spent several days at his home. She was an intelligent and acute observer – the foremost woman novelist of the day and the co-author of the first modern book on the education of children; and her observations of Ricardo survive in letters sent to friends during her visit. Here are some extracts:

> Mr Ricardo is altogether one of the most agreeable persons as well as the best informed and most clever I ever knew.
>
> I did not know how much I wanted better conversation and more warmth of character till I came here...I never argued or discussed a question with any person who argues more fairly or less for victory and more for *truth* (than Ricardo). He gives full thought to every argument brought against him and seems not to be on any side of any question for one instant longer than the conviction of his mind is on that side. It seems quite indifferent to him whether *you* find the truth or *he* finds it provided it be found.
>
> You have no idea how easily grave Mr Ricardo is amused. He delights so in Mr Smith's acting that he cannot help laughing and forgetting his own part when he is acting with him.

Maria Edgeworth visited 'Mr Smith's' household several days later. From there she wrote of being disturbed before breakfast:

> 'Mr Ricardo is come! Has ridden 9 miles to breakfast with us!' Joy – down went pen and Maria – delightful conversation at breakfast – all laughing and openhearted – mixed with placid deep philosophy now and then from Ricardo...

Ricardo returned to his London house after Parliament resumed, and Maria Edgeworth's letters during the session provide a revealing commentary on Snow's charge that Ricardo 'contracted out':

> All who have any sense themselves or any taste for sense in others are ambitious of knowing Mr Ricardo, and his kind permission to me to bring who I please to breakfast with him has put it in my power to oblige several...especially our young American friend Mr Ralston and young John le Favre...It has now become high fashion with blue ladies to talk political economy. There is a certain Lady Mary Shepherd who makes a great jabbering on this subject while others who have more sense like Mrs Marcet hold their tongues and listen.

Miss Edgeworth also reported that the President of the Royal Society was not so free with his invitations as was Ricardo:

> With Sir Humphry Davy's grand Academical Conversaziones...we can have nothing to do as no ladies are admitted.

One of Maria Edgeworth's letters from this period reported Ricardo's account of his childhood:

> Mr Ricardo began to tell me a part of his history when we were out walking the other day through a charming wood. 'We were 15 children. My father gave me but little education. He thought reading writing and arithmetic sufficient because he doomed me to be nothing but a man of business. He sent me at eleven to Amsterdam to learn Dutch, French, Spanish but I was so unhappy at being separated from my brothers and sisters and family that I learned nothing in two years but Dutch which I could not help learning.'

Some years after entering his father's stockbroking firms, Ricardo outraged his family by becoming a Unitarian and marrying a Quaker. Expelled and disinherited, he rapidly established in business on his own account and prospered. He took up geology as a pastime, setting up his own laboratory and mineral collection. A chance reading of *The Wealth of Nations* led him to economics and thence to James Mill. Maria Edgeworth wrote of this too:

> He (Ricardo) told me another time that Mr Mill...was the person who encouraged him to educate himself and pursue his studies after he made a fortune. He dotes upon Mr Mill – says he could never find a blemish in him...

At 42, Ricardo retired from business in order to devote himself exclusively to public service in the broader sense. His *Principles of Political Economy and Taxation* appeared in 1817 and he entered Parliament soon afterwards.

Some brief extracts from his speeches and writings must now be quoted in order to demonstrate the absurdity of the accounts of his views and attitudes which are given by Galbraith, Clark and Snow.

According to Professor Galbraith, Ricardo was never thought an optimist. Some must have thought he was, when he told the House of Commons that:

> If corn were exported and imported, as in other countries, without restraint, this country, possessing the greatest skill, the greatest industry, the best machinery and every other advantage in the highest degree, its prosperity and happiness would be incomparably, and almost inconceivably, great.

Ricardo thought compassion was wasted on the working man, Galbraith told his viewers. Not when he was writing to Malthus, commenting on the draft of a book by the radical leader Francis Place:

> He (Place) has stated the case of the poor with great force, and I think in many respects with great justice. He tells you what their complaints

> are against the rich, the chief of which is a want of sympathy with their distress, and oppressive laws – such as combination laws, corn laws, restraints on commerce and many others.

According to Galbraith, Ricardo thought it was futile to contend against a naturally cruel world. In fact Ricardo was convinced it was *not* futile – that is why he went into Parliament; and the Hansard records of his speeches – abbreviated and rough as they are – show that he constantly implored his colleagues *not* to take this defeatist line:

> If the argument of the honourable member were to be considered as valid, there was an end to all hopes of future improvement. The present generation had invented steam-engines and gas lights and...other useful and beneficial discoveries, and he trusted that they would never be stopped in their progress by being told of the wisdom of their ancestors...

Galbraith's sarcastic remark that Ricardo provided the rich with a very satisfactory formula for suffering the burdens of the poor is yet another reversal of the reality preserved in the Oldspeak records. It was Ricardo who robbed the rich landlords of their mercantilist rationalisations, by throwing the weight of his authority against the corn laws and high food prices:

> Let him implore (his colleagues) to recollect that they were legislating for the happiness of millions, and that there was no evil so intolerable as the high price of human food. He was astonished to hear the honourable member...declare that it was a matter of indifference to him whether (these) prices were high or not.

Ricardo was wealthy ('In this house all the luxuries that riches can give without the ostentation', wrote Maria Edgeworth) but so were many of his parliamentary colleagues; and at the time of life when most of them had been living in Oxford or Cambridge colleges, the young Ricardo had been observing the misery of London's poor from 'Jews' walk'. He did not need to wait for the statistical demonstrations to know that the death rate was positively correlated with the price of food.

During his parliamentary career, Ricardo was the object of some offensive personal comment, usually of an anti-semitic character. William Cobbett wrote:

> I see that they have adopted a scheme of one Ricardo (I wonder what countryman he is)...Faith! they are now become *every thing. Baring* assisted at the Congress of Sovereigns and Ricardo regulates things at home. The Muckworm is no longer a creeping thing; it rears its head aloft...This Ricardo says, that the country is happy in the discovery of a paper money; that it is an *improvement* in political science.

But Ricardo's alleged moral blindness, which to CP Snow was so obvious as not to require explanation or elaboration before an audience of American scientists, was not observed by his contemporaries. A memoir published soon after his death referred to the 'disinterestedness which made him always regardless of his own personal benefit, in the maintenance of general principles':

> When a Bank proprietor, he argued strenuously and warmly against the inordinate gains of that body; he defended the cause of the fund-holders when he had ceased to be one; he was accused of an attempt to ruin the landed interest after he became a large landed proprietor; and while a member of parliament, he advocated the cause of reform, which, if adopted, would have deprived him of his seat. Superior to the misleading power of self-interest, his aim was the dissipation of erroneous, and the promulgation of true and correct principles, the adoption of which should tend to the amelioration of mankind, and the production of the greatest possible good.

The posthumous tributes from both sides of politics were not of the kind usually paid to the possessor of a rusty conscience. Henry Lord Brougham, the Whig statesman who was a member of The Commons throughout the Ricardo period, wrote 16 years later:

> His speaking, his conduct, his manner, were all unexceptionable, and all suited to the man, his high station among philosophers, his known opinions on political affairs, his kindly nature, and his genuine modesty. There was something about him, chiefly a want of all affectation as well as pretension in everything he said or did, that won the respect of every party. His matter was ever of high value. Whether you agreed or differed with him, you were well pleased to have it brought out and made to bear upon the question, if indeed the pursuit of right and truth was your object...He was uniformly and universally respected for the sterling qualities of his capacity and his character, which were acknowledged by all...Few men have...had more weight in Parliament; certainly none who, finding but a very small body of his fellow-members to agree with his leading opinions...ever commanded a more patient and even favourable hearing; this...might be regarded as the triumph of reason, intelligence and integrity over untoward circumstances and alien natures.

Thomas de Quincy, author of *The Confessions of an Opium Eater,* was a Tory. In an article published six months after Ricardo's death in which he regretted never having met Ricardo, de Quincy wrote:

> I do not remember that any public event of our own times has touched me so nearly, or so much with the feelings of a private affliction, as the death of Mr Ricardo. To me in some sense it *was* a private affliction –

> and no doubt to all others who knew and honoured his extraordinary talents...His privilege of intellect has a comprehensive sanction from all the purposes to which he applied it in the course of his public life: in or out of Parliament...he was known and honoured as a public benefactor. Though connected myself with persons of the political party hostile to his, I heard amongst them all but one language of respect for his public conduct.

Ricardo's speeches were not confined to explaining to 'the rest of the world, the politicians' how the principles of political economy should be applied in the real world. He also spoke out, with courage and eloquence on behalf of civil liberties and freedom of expression. On 19 March, 1823, at the General Court of the East India Company, he attacked 'the infamous custom, the shocking system' of slavery

> for surely it was impossible that any man could, for a moment, reflect on the treatment and punishment of slaves without shuddering...On this day, he believed, a petition would be presented to parliament by a most benevolent individual (Mr Wilberforce) in favour of that unfortunate race of men who were subject to the horrors of slavery. He hoped the application would produce its just effect...

It did not do so, because there were many who apparently contemplated the treatment of slaves with greater equanimity than Ricardo. Among them was Coleridge, who asked ten years later:

> Have you been able to discover any principle in this Emancipation Bill for the slaves, except a principle of fear of the abolition party struggling with a dread of causing some monstrous calamity to the empire at large?

Ricardo, who could not think of slaves without a shudder, was described by Kenneth Clark as 'inexorable'; whilst Coleridge, who could not see any point in freeing them, was praised because he 'looked at nature in the high mystical manner'. And Wilberforce, whom Clark ranked first in 'the greatest civilising achievement of the nineteenth century: humanitarianism' had a poor record on civil rights issues by comparison with Ricardo.

It had been Wilberforce who had persuaded the Parliament to impose, 25 years earlier, the laws against trade unions that Ricardo and his colleagues were fighting to remove: it had been Wilberforce who had, throughout this period, been a leading figure in the Society for the Suppression of Vice, which directed itself mainly towards ensuring that the harsh laws against blasphemy and sedition were rigidly enforced; it had been Wilberforce who had been on the secret committee which had recommended severe repressive legislation in 1818; and it was Wilberforce who, only one week after the speech in which Ricardo had described him as a 'most benevolent individual' attacked Ricardo strongly because he 'seemed to carry into more weighty matters those principles of free trade which he had so successfully expounded'. Ricardo had dared to advocate that 'fair and free discussions...be allowed on all religious topics', and had stated his view that 'prosecutions ought never to be instituted for religious opinions... however absurd and extravagant'. Richard Carlile, the free thinker, was in prison for expressing his religious opinions and Wilberforce was certainly not in favour of emancipating *him*. He wrote bitterly in his diary:

> I had hoped that Ricardo had become a Christian: I see now that he has only ceased to be a Jew.

So in his lifetime Ricardo was blamed by the most famous humanitarian of the age for giving his views on 'weighty matters' to the parliament; and 140 years after his death the future parliamentary under-secretary for science chose him as *the* example of the scientist who had 'contracted out'.

As Brougham said, the career of the historical Ricardo epitomised 'the triumph of reason, intelligence and integrity'. Nothing demonstrates more surely the subsequent triumph of prejudice, ignorance and superstition than the fact that the same career could be pointed to in 1960 as epitomising moral irresponsibility in science.

Throughout his busy parliamentary years David Ricardo maintained close friendships and an unceasing correspondence with his professional peers – with Malthus, James Mill and McCulloch. That he had their unreserved affection and unfeigned respect is evident both from their later comments ('I have never loved anybody out of my own family so much', said Malthus), and from the hundreds of letters which survive. Maria Edgeworth's lines, penned 20 years later, celebrate the true spirit of science which shines from every letter between the two greatest economists of the day:

> Malthus and Ricardo...hunted together delightfully in search of truth, and huzzaed when they found her on whichever side she was and without caring who found her first; and indeed I have seen them put both their able hands to the windlass and drag her up from the bottom of the well in which she so strangely loves to dwell...

VII

The boy whose father thought reading, writing and arithmetic sufficient education for a career in business became a remarkably effective correspondent, and not only on economics. Ricardo's penultimate letter to James Mill included a long paragraph commenting on the correspondence between Voltaire and

D'Alembert ('nothing surprises me more than the fire and activity of Voltaire's mind, when borne down by age and infirmities'); chided Mill for delaying and unreasonably shortening a forthcoming visit; and reflected on the progress of the nation:

> The grand cause, good government, is always present to my mind, but I hope it will have a better champion in the House of Commons...I am quite sure that the good cause is advancing, though at a very moderate step, and all we can do in our time is to help it a little forward.

In his last letter to Mill, Ricardo made no mention of his condition although he was now suffering from acute pains in his head. This letter was devoted exclusively to comments on a paper, now lost, by Mill's brilliant 17-year-old son John Stuart. Less than a fortnight later, the desolate elder Mill wrote to McCulloch:

> You and I need not tell to one another how much we grieve on this deplorable occasion. (I have) an estimate of his value in the cause of mankind which to most men would appear to be mere extravagance...His memory must be a bond of connection between us. In your friendship I look for a compensation for the loss of his.

The following issue of *The Republican,* a journal which was being produced by those of Richard Carlile's associates who were not in jail, published the text of a letter which had been sent to Ricardo two months earlier. The writer was not one of the pious and respectable people whom Kenneth Clark supposed were Ricardo's warmest supporters. On the contrary, he was 'one of the numerous body of men who profess republican principles'. He had been pleased to see 'gentlemen of talents, fortune and integrity, standing up and holding...just and liberal sentiments, undismayed by the taunts of the bigot and the frowns of the interested'; and he had gone on to express to Ricardo his

> admiration of your conduct with respect to that much injured... calumniated and misrepresented individual Mr Carlile...It is in pursuing such a course as this...that you secure the affections of all honest and well-meaning men...

Young John Stuart Mill had also been active in Carlile's support, having just written a series of letters to the *Morning Chronicle* on the subject of Carlile's persecution and on freedom of expression. It was probably at about the same time that young Mill and several of his friends had been arrested for distributing the 'abominable handbills' – a series of pamphlets outlining contraceptive techniques. Though he made no mention of the incident in his autobiography, Mill did say that, among his contemporaries,

> Malthus's population principle was quite as much a banner, and a point of union among us, as any opinion specially belonging to Bentham.

> This great doctrine, originally brought forward as an argument against the indefinite improvability of human affairs, we took up with ardent zeal in the contrary sense, as indicating the sole means of realising that improvability by securing full employment at high wages to the whole labouring population through a voluntary restriction of the increase of their numbers.

The population principle of Malthus was also a 'point of union' among the older generation of economists. James Mill, in his *Elements of Political Economy*, wrote that:

> The limitation of the number of births by raising wages will accomplish everything that we desire, without trouble or interference...The limitation of the numbers...may be carried so far as...to raise the condition of the labourer to any state of comfort or enjoyment which may be desired.

And McCulloch wrote in his *Lectures*

> the well-being and happiness of society must ever necessarily depend on the degree in which the principle of increase is subjected to prudential control and regulation.

By this time, Malthus had brought about a revolution in economic thought. Even the concept that the birth rate might be influenced by the knowledge and will of individuals was revolutionary. Coleridge, as we have seen, thought that political economy was humbug, and he had sneered at Malthus for writing a volume to prove that man could not live without eating. In an article published in the month after Ricardo's death, de Quincy took him to task:

> I must assure Mr Coleridge that there is something more to it than *that*... Is it nothing for lawgivers and the governors of the world to treat with contempt the pernicious counsels of political economists from Athenian days down to our own – clamouring for direct encouragements to population? Is it nothing for England that he first has exposed the fundamental vice of our Poor Laws (viz. that they act as a bounty on population), and placed a lighthouse upon the rocks to which our course was rapidly carrying us in darkness? Is it nothing for science and the whole world that, by unfolding the laws which govern population, he has given to political economy its complement and sole desideratum?

There is ample evidence from the literature of the day that contraception must have been widely discussed and practised in the mid 1820s. John Stuart Mill's brush with the law was alluded to in a verse which was published in *The Times* in February 1826:

> There are two Mr M-'s, too, whom those that like reading

> Through all that's unreadable, call very clever;
> And, whereas M- Senior makes war on *good* breeding
> M- Junior makes war on all breeding whatever!

Several months later Francis Place – who had been responsible for the printing and distribution of the pamphlets which Mill junior and his friends handed out 'at market time among the wives and daughters of mechanics and tradesmen' – wrote an article in *The Trades Newspaper and the Mechanics Weekly Journal*. One paragraph is interesting both for its general sense and for the unmistakable implication of one phrase:

> The political economists are the great enlighteners of the people. Look at their works from the time of the great man Adam Smith to the *Essay on Wages* just published by Mr McCulloch, and see if they have not, all along, deprecated everything which was in any way calculated to do injury to the people; see if they have not been pre-eminently the advocates for increasing the knowledge of the working classes *in every possible way* and then let any man say, if he can, that they have not been pre-eminently the best friends of these classes (emphasis added).

Francis Place was at this time corresponding with Richard Carlile who, during or between his prison terms, wrote the pamphlet *What is Love*? This pamphlet included descriptions of contraceptive techniques and this revealing paragraph:

> *It is better to prevent than cure, and here prevention is most simply practicable, a means within the reach of all.* The best and wisest of men labour with zeal to promulgate secretly or covertly a knowledge of this plan. Women are also secretly engaged in it, after having got over the prejudice of the old customs by giving it a full consideration. It is alluded to in Mill's *Elements of Political Economy*. And still more plainly in the article *Colonies* in the supplement to the *Encyclopedia Brittanica*, from the pen of the same gentleman. It is clearly alluded to in Place's *Illustrations of the Principle of Population*. It has been broached somewhat disguisedly in several newspapers, and preached in lectures to the working people by a most benevolent gentleman at Leeds; it has been circulated by thousands of handbills through the populous districts of the north, and is the hinted inference, as the only remedy, for all that is said in the House of Commons or elsewhere upon the subject of the unemployed and badly paid surplus population.

In addition to supporting measures to reduce the birth rate, the economists advocated schemes of assisted emigration to the colonies and a method of raising wage levels and relieving poverty. Torrens had put forward such a scheme in 1817 as a means of 'affording effectual and permanent relief of the labouring classes'; and early in 1823 Ricardo had written to Wilmot Horton, the Under-Secretary for Colonies, endorsing a *Plan of Emigration to Upper Canada*:

> The plan would be economical; it would enable us to get rid of the most objectionable part of the poor laws, the relieving able bodied men; and what is to me by far the most important consideration, it could not fail to make the wages of labour more adequate to the support of the labourer and his family, besides giving him that as wages which is now given to him as charity.

Wilmot Horton took this as a clear statement of Ricardo's support for assisted emigration as an anti–poverty measure, and reproduced the letter in his pamphlet *Causes and Remedies of Pauperism*. Professor Galbraith – having attributed to Ricardo the views that there were *no* remedies for poverty, that workers must *always* be in misery and starving and that it was futile to contend against fate and the iron law of wages – could not accept such a simple interpretation. There was another possible explanation:

> Ricardo's reputation as a bad writer is greatly deserved...his prose was awkward, uncertain and unpredictable as to meaning conveyed...It is bad writing based on incomplete thought.

The belief that Ricardo could not say what he meant certainly made it easier for Galbraith to believe what he pleased about Ricardo's views. But the obscurity that Galbraith discovered does not appear to have been perceived by Ricardo's contemporaries and near-contemporaries. John Stuart Mill, who has not been thought to be notably clumsy in thought or expression, wrote much later that Ricardo was

> the time founder of the abstract science of political economy (and his) writings are still, after all that has been written, its purest source. What had been added to the science since Ricardo does not need to be substituted for his doctrines, but to be incorporated with them. They do not require alteration or correction, so much as fuller exposition or comment.

Four years after receiving Ricardo's letter, Mr Wilmot Horton received unambiguous support for his emigration proposals from the greatest economist then living. Malthus appeared as a witness before the Select Committee on Emigration from the United Kingdom, which was chaired by Wilmot Horton. Before summarising Malthus' evidence, we must recall Kenneth Clark's statement that Malthus' doctrines were used by pious and respectable people 'to justify actions that they would never have thought of defending on human grounds'; and Galbraith's statements that 'Thomas Robert Malthus, going a step further (than the iron law of wages) adduced his immortal conclusion that people everywhere would proliferate to the point of starvation' and that 'Malthus was on the whole unperturbed by his conclusions and...did not feel called upon to produce any remedy'.

In the course of his evidence, Malthus answered about 250 questions. The following extracts from the transcript indicate his general line:

> *Is not the tendency of a redundant supply of labour, ready at all times to fill up the decrease of the labouring population by want and disease, beneficial to the manufacturing and commercial interest – inasmuch as it lowers wages and raises profits, and renders possible a successful competition with foreign capitalists?*
>
> I should think that, even if it did so, no person could possibly bring themselves to encourage such a system with that view.
>
> *Compassion for the labouring poor and regard to the public peace may render the diminution of the supply of labour desirable, but a redundancy is favourable to trade and commerce, is it not?*
>
> In one respect it is, and in one respect not; it may enable the capitalist to work up his commodities cheaper, and to extend his foreign trade, but it certainly will have a tendency to diminish the home trade and I think the home trade much more important than the foreign...
>
> *Although the redundancy in the supply of labour should tend to impoverish the condition of the labouring classes generally, yet is it not possible that the demand in the home market for the gross amount of produce might be fully as great as if the labouring classes were fewer in number and in more prosperous condition?*
>
> The difference in the demand of the labouring classes, living well and comfortably, would in my opinion be such as to more than balance the numbers...I should say there is a great difference in the manner in which the labouring classes live, as to clothing, houses and other domestic comforts and conveniences, and that habits of that kind must create a great demand for commodities and labour, a great home demand...
>
> *(The) proposition involves on the one hand the happiness of the labouring classes, and on the other their misery?*
>
> Yes; which I hold to be the most important of all considerations, the one to which all others should give way...
>
> *Does not the rate of increase of population in different countries depend very much on the different habits of the people?*
>
> Very much.
>
> *With reference to Ireland, what is your opinion of the habits of the people...?*

The habits are very unfavourable in regard to their own condition, because they are inclined to be satisfied with the very lowest degree of comfort, and to marry with little other prospect than that of being able to get potatoes for themselves and their children.

Do you think that any combination of circumstances could effect (a removal of those habits, unless there is emigration)?

It would be a work of great time, and probably of great suffering, if it *were* accomplished, but I should not expect it to be accomplished without emigration; and one of the cases in which...a government is called upon to make a great pecuniary sacrifice is where there is a prospect of some great and beneficial change, which change cannot take place without such sacrifice unless you are disposed to overlook the greatest possible degree of misery...

If cheap tracts were written and given to the poor, and in some instances taught in the schools, explaining the doctrines you have just laid down with respect to the condition of the poor, do you imagine they would be able to understand them, and that they would apply what they learned to their own case?

I think they are not very difficult to be understood, but they are perhaps rather difficult to apply. I believe some tracts of that kind have been occasionally circulated.

Have you any knowledge of the effects produced?

I have understood that many of the labouring classes, particularly the artisans, acknowledge the doctrines that have been laid down on the subject of population...

To which do you think the principles of emigration is of most importance at present, to England, to Scotland or to Ireland?

Unquestionably to Ireland...

What is your opinion of the capability of Ireland to become a rich and flourishing country?

My opinion is that it has very great capabilities, that it might be a very rich and very prosperous country...

Do you think any one circumstance would more tend to accelerate that state of things, than a judicious system of emigration put into force in that country?

> I think that a judicious system of emigration is one of the most powerful means to accomplish that object.

The Committee received this evidence with the greatest satisfaction. Its final report quoted Malthus' evidence at length in rebuttal of the argument that 'redundancy of labourers is calculated to promote the interests of the proprietors and capitalists', and noted that:

> The testimony which was uniformly given by the *practical witnesses* has been confirmed in the most absolute manner by that of Mr Malthus;... the experience of facts is thus strengthened throughout by general reasoning and scientific principles.

VIII

According to Kenneth Clark in *Civilisations:*

> Poverty, hunger, plagues, disease: they were the background of history right up to the end of the nineteenth century, and most people regarded them as invevitable – like bad weather. Nobody thought they could be cured...The old Poor Laws were not designed to abolish poverty but to prevent the poor from becoming a nuisance. All that was required was an occasional act of charity...

This was the environment in which the business and landed establishment reacted to the report of Mr Wilmot Horton's Emigration Committee. From their standpoint, an occasional act of charity was one thing; but having to make a 'great pecuniary sacrifice' in the hope of bringing about 'some great and beneficial change' was another. It was high time that the practitioners of the pseudo-science of political economy, and their fellow travellers, were put firmly in their place. In a pamphlet published in the same year as the Committee's report, Richard Carlile forecast the reaction precisely:

> All pretend to desire the improvement of the condition of the working people; but the moment that any attempts are practically made toward the improvement an outcry, founded upon the most contemptible prejudices, is raised, and the effort has no encouragement. The truth is, that the aristocracy which forms the legislature of this country flourishes upon the vices and miseries of the working people...

Southey, the Poet Laureate, was quickly into the attack. It was now 25 years since he had urged John Rickman to 'break (Malthus) on the wheel'. And over 10 years since he had publicly described Malthus' population principle as 'too foolish, as well as too wicked, ever to become permanently prevalent; the temporary reputation which Mr Malthus obtained by renewing it is disgraceful to the age'. Time had not improved Southey's temper:

> We may shudder at the application of Mr Malthus's doctrines, made by certain wretches of the radical school, for whose writings the pillory and a pelting shower of popular indignation would have been the deserved and proper punishment, if there were not some offences of such a nature that it is better that they go unpunished in this world, than be brought to light and notice. The poor will continue to increase and multiply, notwithstanding the schemes of madmen and the devices of men who are the opprobrium of humanity...The poor are the prolific portion of the community. Increase and multiply they will and must; it is in the order of nature, whose institutions should strive against that order.

A more comprehensive attack on the Committee and its report was mounted by Michael Thomas Sadler, MP in a book of over 400 pages entitled *Ireland: Its Evils and Their Remedies: Being a Refutation of the Errors of the Emigration Committee.* The theme of the book was outlined in a critical notice in the *Edinburgh Review*:

> The leading object of the work is to show that the theory of population, as laid down by Mr Malthus and others, is entirely false; that those who maintain (it) impeach the goodness and power of the Deity; and that the true law of population, by which the increases of mankind has been, and still is, in all cases, regulated is simply this, '*The fecundity of human beings, under equal circumstances, varies inversely as their numbers on a given space*'.

Mr Sadler explained that the book was written as a supplement to a work which he was still preparing, which would contain the proof of this proposition; but he did outline the key argument in relation to Ireland, which was summarised thus in the *Edinburgh Review*.

> In the days of...Sir William Petty, the population of Ireland was under a million and half; and 'yet the wretchedness of the inhabitants was more conspicuous than it is even at present' when it exceeds *seven* millions. This, according to Mr Sadler, is an irrefragable proof of the hollowness of the modern theory of population; and of the 'ignorance and folly' of those who represent the miseries of Ireland as resulting from the increased number of her inhabitants.

The experience of thousands of years, Sadler went on, had taught the world that obedience to the divine command to 'Multiply – *replenish* the earth' was the only certain road to national prosperity and individual happiness'. Ireland was, he said, grossly underpopulated:

> Its surface might, on the very lowest calculations which our practical agriculturalists have ever made, sustain in plenty far above ten times the number of inhabitants that it now nearly starves; while 'the wastes of the sea'...remain almost totally untouched.

The members of the Emigration Committee were labelled 'political quacks', whom 'it is hard to acquit...of either ignorance or cruelty'. The *Edinburgh Review* commented:

> When the non-employment, squalid poverty and wretchedness of the Irish poor are universally admitted, it is really farcical to talk of the 'cruelty' and 'atrocity' of encouraging their emigration to Canada and the United States...If there be inhumanity in the case, it is fairly chargeable on those who endeavour to prevail on the poor to continue where there are no means of providing for their comfortable support, and who, by misrepresenting the objects and motives of those who would improve their condition...make them cling to the very poverty of which they are at once the victims and the source.

Sadler's attack on Malthus and the Committee gained much attention, the *Edinburgh Review* article noting that:

> The speech and the book of the member for Newark were for three long months the subjects of eternal eulogy with the writers and readers of the *Morning Journal* and *Standard*; and Mr Sadler...was declared to be the only statesman in the House of Commons.

When Wilmot Horton spoke in defence of the Emigration Committee in May 1829, he complained that there were few in the House to hear him. He praised Malthus and the other expert witnesses, and reiterated the view that emigration was the only remedy for the immediate problem that could be applied with a prospect of success. Sadler replied, strongly objecting 'to the principle of public and national emigration as unnecessary, impolitic and productive of much individual suffering', and to wasting the country's resources 'in so fruitless and anti-national and... cruel an attempt as that of lessening the population'.

Four months later Sadler received a request, signed – in the words of his biographer – 'by nearly all the wealth and respectability' of the town of Whitby, 'that he would accept the honour of a public dinner'. The peroration of the speech Sadler made at the dinner ran thus:

> It was the province of God, saving the presence of our political economists, to decide (the numbers of our countrymen); and He has decided it, in the superabundance of the means of human subsistence which, as a nation, He has lavished upon us...Short indeed, and infernal, would be the remedy were (Malthus') revolting notion true. Deportation...(and) murder...would be obvious and general benefits...

> Rather than on the dogmas of political economists, we will still rest, as to this matter, upon the assurances of Him who giveth food to all flesh; for His mercy endureth forever.

Soon after, Sadler, a Wesleyan linen manufacturer, had provided this illuminating indication of 'the inhuman way in which the doctrines of Malthus were accepted' by himself and by the wealth and respectability of a provincial city, the book of which his *Ireland* had been the supplement, appeared. Entitled *The Law of Population, and Disproof of Human Superfecundity,* Sadler's treatise ran to 1300 pages. His biographer was to describe it as 'the greatest gift bestowed on mankind by any secular writer of modern times'.

It is of interest to note Sadler's connections. His book was dedicated to his patron, the Duke of Newcastle, of whom the *Dictionary of National Biography* makes the following comments:

> He was a rigid conservative, and violently opposed the claims of the protestant dissenters, catholic emancipation and parliamentary reform...For more than twenty years the general public censured the duke's motives as a landlord and member of the House of Lords, and his appetite for jobbery was declared to be insatiable.

The copy of Sadler's book in the National Library of Australia is inscribed, in the author's hand, to 'The Right Honourable Lord Wynford, with the author's respectful compliments'. It was Lord Wynford who, as Mr Justice Best, had told Richard Carlile at one of his trials that 'Persons were at liberty to put their own construction upon texts of Scripture, but they must not dispute the truths of Scripture'. *The Dictionary of National Biography* entry on Best states that

> He was a vehement supporter of the Tory party, and strenuously opposed the Reform Bill at every stage...As a judge he was unfortunately far from free of bias of temper, and sometimes even of political prejudice.

In essence, Sadler's book was an expression of the thesis that he had already propounded. Indeed there was another attack on the Emigration Committee:

> I deny that general deportations of our countrymen are necessary; ...they are...unnatural in themselves, and cruel in their consequences...the main instrument in...colonizing migrations was barbarism...Those purposes accomplished, that veil of ignorance which seemed as effectually to conceal the inexhaustible bounties of Providence from their benighted eyes as it does from those of some of our political economists, was drawn aside...In the Divine economy, no such remedy is contemplated... As the population of the nations has increased, the necessity of these

> wanderings has diminished. I speak thus, advisedly, and in defiance of the information, or, I would rather say, the more formidable ignorance, of all the emigration committees on earth.

In his chapter on 'The Preventive Check', Sadler claimed that

> The restraining of marriage, under whatever pretence, is never, in any part of the Scriptures, for one moment sanctioned. On the contrary, the primary command and blessing of the Deity are 'INCREASE AND MULTIPLY'.

Morerover, the postponement of marriage 'would...counteract the plain desire of Nature' and lead, because of the ages of the parents, to 'a fatherless or motherless child to every labouring family in the empire'. Nor could there by any attempt at family planning:

> Some of the converts and advocates of (the Malthusian theory of population) have already begun to act upon it by explaining and recommending, in a scientific form, and in plain and unequivocal language, the means by which the passions may be in some sort gratified, and the consequences – human increase – prevented or evaded. Some of these passages I have selected and had meant to give them in another language, but I forbear; in the words of the act of Parliament...they 'are not to be rehearsed'. Such are the auxiliaries, 'most foul, strange and unnatural', of the modern theory of population; such are the assistants of the 'preventive check'...(Human) increase is equally commanded by the Deity, prompted by Nature and required for the promotion of the happiness and prosperity of the species. Inexpressibly sinful, as well as presumptuous, is...any systematic and premeditated attempt to repress the natural numbers of mankind.

So far as Sadler could see, there was little difference between birth control and infanticide;

> There is a broad distinction made, it is true, between preventing beings from living which would otherwise emerge into existence, and depriving them of life when they have obtained it...But, believing in the immortality of the soul, the perpetual happiness of the innocent after death (and) that religion which has 'brought life and immortality to light', I confess I cannot fully comprehend the distinction...(This) argument will have little weight with the political economists who, as it regards this question, reject all consideration of a future state...

IX

To the pious and respectable middle-class, the publication of Sadler's massive book marked the end of a bad dream. Sadler's biographer, RB Seeley, was to write twelve years later:

> The Malthusian theory received its death-wound on the day when Mr Sadler's work appeared; its dying struggles were decently concealed by the mantle cast over them by its friends; but the whole system has now passed away...We might apply to it the expressive words of the Psalmist – 'I sought for it, but lo, it could nowhere be found'.

The 'mortal blow' that Southey had planned twenty years earlier had at last been delivered: another writer had come upon 'that precious philosophist... with a thunder clap' but Southey was as pleased as if he had achieved the great work himself:

> You have demonstrated that Malthus's theory is as absurd, as the consequences to which it necessarily leads are execrable...Hereafter the truth will be universally acknowledged: but...the present generation of political economists (who are the pests, and bid fair to be the ruin of the country)...will not be persuaded, though one rose from the dead!

Sharon Turner, the author of the best-selling *Sacred History of the World* pointed out that Mr Sadler's work has

> rescued us from that chimerical dread of the superabundant population of the earth under which we have been labouring for the last thirty years.

John Wilson of *Blackwood's Magazine* joined the chorus of praise:

> Our business is not now with this distinguished man as a member of Parliament – he comes before the public as the author of one of the most ingenious, able, and learned works, on perhaps the most difficult and important part of Political Economy, that has been given to the world since Political Economy deserved the name of a mixed Science...The work was a good deal abused before it was published by some ingenious persons who, since its publication, have been mum; nor, as far as we have seen, have any of the Malthusians yet made upon it any formidable attack.

And Wilson doubted whether any of them could do so:

> How arid are the writings of the economists! Reading their works is like toiling across a flat desert ankle-deep in sand – no well, no oasis, all dry

> dust and not a single tree. No wonder so many travellers sink and are seen no more; and that they are now shy of joining even the caravan under Mr McCulloch...

But the bad dream was now over. The economists had been routed by the shining knight, Sadler. God was in his heaven and all was right with the world. The Cinderellas from the slums could get married, have lots of children, and live happily ever after:

> The admirable old Public, God bless her! – nay, say not old – the admirable young, bold, bright, and buxom Public – just like Miss in her teens running off to Gretna-Green with her own chosen suitor, out of a score of sailors, and soldiers, and civilians – selects such a man, for example, as the member of Newark, places her colours in his cap; and on his return from routing all his foes, flings her arms round his neck, and absolutely smothers him with kisses. The rejected slanderers sneak into corners and bite their thumbs – the nails whereof have already been nibbled to the quick in a habit unconsciously acquired by thirst and hunger.

There were some who were not prepared to put their colours in Mr Sadler's cap, and who even preferred the rejected slanderers skulking in the corners. The young Thomas Babington Macaulay told the readers of the *Edinburgh Review* that

> The spirit of the work is as bad as its style. We never met with a book which so strongly indicated that the writer was in a good humour with himself, and in a bad humour with everyone else...Mr Malthus is attacked in language which it would be scarcely decent to employ respecting Titus Oates. 'Atrocious', 'execrable', 'blasphemous' and other epithets of the same kind are poured forth against that able, excellent and honourable man with a profusion which in the early part of the work excites indignation, but after the first hundred pages produces mere weariness and nausea.

And Macaulay was less than impressed with the scientific merit of the work:

> We have shown that Mr Sadler is careless in the collection of facts; that he is incapable of reasoning on facts when he has collected them; that he does not understand the simplest terms of science; that he has enounced a proposition of which he does not know the meaning; that the proposition which he means to enounce, and which he tries to prove, leads to all those consequences which he represents as impious and immoral; and that, from the very documents to which he has himself appealed, it may be demonstrated that this theory is false.

This article provoked Sadler to write another book entitled *Refutation of an Article in the Edinburgh Review;* Macaulay responded in the *Edinburgh* with *'Sadler's Refutation Refuted';* and *Blackwood's* began to publish 'Mr Sadler and the *Edinburgh Reviewer*: A Prolusion in Three Chapters'.

The author of these last articles was John Wilson, who had succeeded Dugald Stewart as professor of moral philosophy at Edinburgh. Although no one had succeeded in catching Stewart in dangerous propositions, his lectures on political economy had been a continuing irritant to the conventionally wise (an 1817 essay by Southey referred to 'critics of all dimensions, from the undergraduate in the ungentle craft...to the Scotch professor who for fifteen years has been discharging his blunderbuss against a shield from whence the leaden shot falls flattened'); and the establishment was relieved when in 1820 the economist retired and an anti-economist was installed in his place.

Just before Sadler's *Law of Population* appeared, Wilson had written an article on 'Education of the People' which showed that he was free of the unsound views on that subject which had been expounded by an earlier Scottish professor of moral philosophy in *The Wealth of Nations*. Here is an extract:

> To the lower orders, knowledge is not their business – that is, not to the great lower order, those who render the daily labour of their hands to the use of others. Their business is to render a prescribed and taught, and, for the most part, a very simple, and uniformly recurring labour. Their calling, then, is in a great measure independent of knowledge, except what is communicated to them in it.

In his 'Prolusion' on Sadler and the Edinburgh Reviewer, Wilson said that Malthus' population principle had been 'hanging like a deadweight on the hopes of all who hoped highly of the future happiness and virtue of man'. In fact:

> This doctrine of a supposed great Master in Political Economy revolted not only the feelings, but the reason, of men who studied the nature and condition of their own race in the schools of common humanity; and was thought by them irreconcilable with much of what they humbly believed it had been permitted them to know of the attributes and providence of God.

Wilson followed up with an attack on Francis Place, who was a tailor by profession:

> We have seen in bad Latin, schemes proposed to thwart the principle of population, which, as they were disgraceful to manhood, it was satisfactory to know originated out of the pale of humanity – *measures* which, as they were addressed, we believe, so could they only have

> had any temptation, to a tailor. Others, again, who did not directly recommend men to become monkeys or monsters, aimed abuse – in words to us unintelligible – against marriage.

Then there was an attack on the political economists as a group – including on Nassau Senior, who had just lost his chair at Oxford because he had put forward a proposal on policy towards Ireland which displeased the Tories:

> Men are not naturally the brute beasts these writers have insultingly represented them to be...That egregious wiseacre, ex-Professor Senior, seems to have lately felt this – and, with all the pomposity and pedantry of the school and the schools, has dedicated some pages of a lecture to prove that human beings have reason as well as passions. When it is a duty to marry, and what are the duties of marriage, Nature herself dictates; nor have there ever been wanting in this long-enlightened land, moral and religious teachers to expound such duties, not out of such books as these pragmatical coxcombs and Cockney political economists have produced or studied, but out of a book which few of them know much about, and many of them nothing – THE BIBLE. With regard to that mighty class, which we have higher authority than that of the political economists for believing never shall cease out of the land – the Poor – the deductions drawn from the Malthusian law of population were impious and cruel.

Sadler had also realised that the economists were defying Christian teaching in supposing that they could abolish poverty; and without the fear of poverty, he pointed out, people could not be induced to work. Here is how the member for Newark developed this theme in the House of Commons on June 3, 1830:

> It is not possible to rid any country of what too many consider as its nuisance and disgrace; nor is it perhaps desirable, were it even possible. Not only does the condition in which poverty stands in relation to wealth call into existence the best feelings and noblest virtues of the human heart; poverty, or rather the fear of poverty, which could only be inspired by its actual existence, calls forth all that activity, and animates all those exertions by which...the independence of the individual is secured (and) the public prosperity enlarged...Yes, sir, the poverty we seek to relieve will never cease; poverty of too deep and distressing a character to be tickled into mirth and ecstasy by the ready but empty hand of wealth and affluence....–the 'be thou warmed and be thou clothed' schemes of recent economists. 'The poor ye have always with you' says the author of our religion...

Political economy had now become a difficult science indeed. Only three years earlier, Nassau Senior had devoted a significant part of his introductory lecture at Oxford to the problem of poverty in civilised societies. He had said that

> the misery of those upon whom actual want does fall...is too painful to be steadfastly contemplated, and forms only a small part of the evil. The great evil is the general feeling of insecurity; the fear which must beset every man whose labour produces him only a subsistence...that at some period, how near he cannot tell, the want under which he has seen others sink may reach himself.

Senior went on to cite recent English actuarial data which demonstrated that any material reduction in the price of wheat was almost always accompanied by a decrease in the number of burials. From this he deduced that 'there must be almost always in this country a considerable number of persons just vibrating between the possession and the want of mere food'. He pointed out that, while he was speaking, there were 'tens of thousands of families of hand weavers... who are working fourteen hours a day for what will scarcely support animal existence'. He quoted at length from the evidence of witnesses before Wilmot Horton's Committee, demonstrating the desperate plight of millions of people in England and Ireland. And he concluded that his hope for the future was:

> founded solely on the expectation that the diffusion of sound principles of political economy will aid our enlightened ministers with the whole strength of public opinion, and enable them to conquer the ignorance, prejudice and individual interest which have always been opposed to every improvement.

Senior would have expected that there would be disputes about whether or not the key principles of political economy were sound; but he would not have contemplated for a moment the possibility that a leading politician would soon win wide acclaim by asserting that the *objective* of removing want was unsound.

Malthus himself was the leading proponent of the '"be thou warmed, be thou clothed" scheme of recent economists': he had told the Emigration Committee of the advantages of the labouring classes 'living well and comfortably...with clothing, houses and other domestic comforts and conveniences'. Ten years earlier Ricardo, in his *Principles*, had written that

> The friends of humanity cannot but wish that in all countries the labouring classes should have a taste for comforts and enjoyments, and that they should be stimulated by all legal means in their exertions to procure them.

These aspirations were now being challenged. The Creator's commands, said Sadler, were to increase and multiply, and replenish the earth and subdue it: there were no commands to live well and comfortably, and develop a taste for enjoyment. 'By the sweat of thy brow shalt thou eat bread', said the Scriptures: there was nothing about sweating to produce domestic comforts and conveniences. 'If man will live, he must eat: and if he will eat, he must labour', Lord Hale had said nearly two centuries earlier; and the great economist of Hale's day had insights to which all of the modern economists were blind:

> The fact is, as Sir William Petty observed long ago, nothing but necessity makes man labour at all, and the bulk of mankind will never labour beyond what is adequate to supply their habitual necessities.

So Mr Sadler told the House of Commons in 1830, and the conventional wisdom was as powerful then as it is now. Within a considerable range the worthy politicians and upright middle class gentlemen were permitted to believe what they pleased; and most of them found it agreeable to believe that Sadler the rising politician had demolished Malthus the ageing academic. Sadler's 2000 pages of abusive refutation were being lauded by most of the respectable journals, and his scientific achievements had earned him a Fellowship of the Royal Society.

We have two significant measures of the attitude of the establishment to Malthus at the time of his death.

One of them is the market price of his *Essay,* it dropped (according to Seeley, who was a publisher and bookseller) from 24/- in 1830 to 5/9 in 1835.

The other indication of Malthus' standing with the establishment was the obituary notice in *The Times*. It consisted of one sentence:

> We see with regret the announcement of the death of Mr Malthus, the eminent writer – a man whose private virtues were not, and could not be, disputed by those who were most hostile to his views on political economy.

The deaths of those who were most hostile to Malthus' views on political economy were treated with less circumspection. The notice for Coleridge, who had died five months earlier, began:

> We have this week to record the departure of another mighty spirit from among us – the quenching in the darkness of the grave of another of the few bright stars which yet remained to us...

And that for Sadler, who died six months later, included the following:

> Men unaccustomed to witness such devoted reverence for truth cannot conceive the toil with which Mr Sadler was accustomed to verify the most minute and apparently unimportant fact employed in the course of his argument. Never will the poor have such an advocate; his whole heart and conversation were in their cause; and his deepest regret during his illness referred to the incompleteness of his work on population – an incompleteness that lost to the poor the advantage that a full confirmation of his system by the recent censuses would have conferred upon them.

There was no possibility that apparently unimportant facts and census results could have *destroyed* Sadler's system – he was too devout for that. As Seeley was to write in his massive biography of Sadler seven years later:

> Mr Malthus's criminality lay here...Instead of distrusting his own conclusions, he boldly puts forward a system...wholly opposed to the whole tenor of Scripture...Had his facts been as clearly established as the rotation of the earth, or the mortality of man, still a proper reverence for the All-wise should have held his judgement suspended.

A tribute to Malthus by William Empson, who had been professor of politics and law at the college where Malthus held the chair of political economy, confirmed that he had indeed followed this criminally scientific approach:

> If popular declaimers ever put themselves in the way of learning humility and charity, it might do something towards teaching them these virtues to be informed that when Mr Malthus first entered upon (his) inquiries...he entertained most of the erroneous opinions in which they are immersed at present. He had to do what they refuse to do – to unlearn false knowledge, and to master the prejudices of his age and country. This made him frequently remark that there was no science in which first impressions were so generally wrong as political economy.

X

'Adam Smith and Malthus and Ricardo! There is something about these three figures to evoke more than ordinary sentiments from us their children in the spirit'. So wrote Keynes in 1933, and he may well have had in mind a passage from the article by Empson which has just been quoted:

> Political economy – the science of civilisation – is sought to be discredited by the help of private slander, and the name of one of the best of men is made an ignominous by-word for inflaming the passions of the poor...Political economy is charged with hardness of heart. The science can appear and call witnesses to character only in the persons of its professors. We remember Sir James Mackintosh saying that he had known Adam Smith slightly, Ricardo well, Malthus intimately. He added 'Is it not something to say for a science that its three great masters were about the three best men I ever knew?'

The testimony of many other witnesses to Malthus' character is recorded in Oldspeak literature.

Malthus and his doctrines provided splendid opportunities for the wit of Rev. Sydney Smith – the famous Dean of St Paul's whose conversation frequently reduced his audience to helpless mirth. There are numerous stories of servants having to flee in uncontrollable laughter from the dining rooms of his hosts. To one of his correspondents Smith wrote:

> Philosopher Malthus was here last week. I got an agreeable party for him of unmarried people. There was only one lady who had had a child; but he is a good-natured man and, if there are no appearances of approaching fertility, is civil to every lady...

Soon after Malthus' death, Smith wrote to Wilmot Horton, who was now Governor of Ceylon:

> Poor Malthus! everybody regrets him; – in science and in conduct equally a philosopher, one of the most practically wise men I ever met, shamefully mistaken and unjustly calumniated, and receiving no mark of favour from a Liberal Government, who ought to have interested themselves in the fortunes of such a virtuous martyr to truth.

Four years later, Sydney Smith was editing for publication his numerous contributions to the *Edinburgh Review,* the great journal of which he had been co-founder. Coming across a reference he had made to Malthus in an article written nearly forty years earlier, Smith wrote a footnote which is unlike anything else in the book:

> I cannot read the name of Malthus without adding my tribute of affection for the memory of one of the best men that ever lived. He loved philosophical truth more than any man I ever knew, was full of practical wisdom and never indulged in contemptuous feelings against his inferiors in understanding.

Another witness for Malthus is Maria Edgeworth, the Irish novelist who for many years was attacked for her attitude to Christianity in every review of her books, even of those where religion was not touched on. In a letter of 1822, she wrote to her father's widow of her 'love and admiration and *gratitude* to Mr Malthus' who was

> a most amiable man – of strict truth, perfect integrity and rational benevolence as all who know him declare – and this is the man whom party represents as a bloodthirsty monster – An Ogre! Cobbett began one of his papers lately with these words 'I have hated many men but I *never* hated any man as much as I hated Malthus'.

Yet another witness for Malthus who was not pious in the conventional sense is Harriet Martineau, the journalist and social critic who inspired the famous line 'There is no God, and Harriet is his prophet'. In her *Autobiography* she wrote:

> Mr Malthus, who did more for social ease and virtue than perhaps any other man of his time, was the 'best-abused man' of the age. I was aware of this; and I saw in him, when I afterwards knew him, one of the serenest and most cheerful men that society can produce. When I became intimate enough with the family to talk over such matters, I asked Mr Malthus one day whether he had suffered in spirits from the abuse lavished on him. 'Only just at first,' he answered. - 'I wonder whether it ever kept you awake a minute' – 'Never after the first fortnight,' was his reply. The spectacle of the good man in his daily life, in contrast with the representations of him in the periodical literature of the time, impressed upon me, more forcibly than any other thing in my own experience, the everlasting fact that the reformers of morality, personal and social, are always subject at the outset to the imputation of immorality from those interested in the continuance of corruption.

All of these comments were made about an economist whom Clark's television series noticed only as 'a clergyman named Malthus' whose 'sacred book' provided Victorian hypocrisy with one of its chief supports; and whom Galbraith's series lampooned because his 'Principle on Population' referred to

> 'the passion between the sexes' (a most damaging thing that he sometimes thought might be subject to 'moral restraint' and against which he suggested ministers might warn at marriage)...

– a sensible and indeed courageous suggestion in the social environment in which it was made.

The remarks of Professor WS Jevons, in his presidential address to the Economic Science and Statistics Section of the British Association for the Advancement of Science meeting in 1870, are as pertinent today as they were 114 years ago:

> There is no one who occupies a less enviable position than the political economist. Cultivating the frontier regions between certain knowledge and conjecture, his efforts and advice are scorned and rejected on all hands. If he arrives at a sure law of human nature, and points out the evils which arise from its neglect, he is fallen upon the large classes of people who think their own common-sense sufficient; he is charged with being too abstract in his speculations; with overlooking the windings of the human heart; with under-valuing the affections. However humane his motives, he is lucky if he escapes being set down on all sides as a heartless misanthrope. Such was actually the fate of one of the most humane and excellent of men, the late Mr Malthus.

XI

The theme of Galbraith's *The Age of Uncertainty* was, as noted earlier, to 'contrast the great certainties in economic thought in the last century with the great uncertainty with which problems are faced in our time'. It will be clear by now that the great certainties in economic thought did not in fact *exist* in the last century, but only in the minds of Galbraith and his viewers as they *contemplated* the last century.

It was also noted earlier that all of Galbraith's certainties about Ricardo were wrong – that Galbraith believed Ricardo was very pessimistic when in fact he was very optimistic; that Galbraith believed that Ricardo regarded compassion on the working man as wasted when in fact he contended that it was not; that Galbraith believed that Ricardo regarded it as futile to seek remedies for poverty, when in fact his concern was that the available remedies were not being applied; and so on.

Professor Galbraith was not content with being certain about what Ricardo said and wrote in his lifetime. He was equally certain about what he would have expected and recommended after he was gone. Here is Galbraith's account of the great potato blight of the late 1840s which occurred a quarter of a century after Ricardo's death:

> Not only were the circumstances as Ricardo and Malthus foretold; the response of Westminster to the Irish disaster was as Ricardo would have recommended. As now would be said, it was from the book. The Corn Laws were repealed to allow the free import of grain. Though excellent in principle, this did not help those without money to buy grain, a category that included the entire starving population...Corn was imported not for the purpose of feeding the hungry but of keeping down prices. Low prices were also not helpful to people who had no money at all. In 1845, a program of public works was inaugurated. This was in conflict with the principle that the poor should never be helped and in the following year, when it was greatly needed, it was abandoned.

Presumably Ricardo had sent a message of protest. Perhaps he was shown sanctimoniously holding 'the Ricardian Tablets' while the greater part of the television screen represented several hundreds of thousands of people starving to death. It was of course futile to contend against a cruel world:

> There is (a) tendency...for the consequences of principled action, if they are very unpleasant, to be given divine sanction. Smith's unseen hand had become the hand of God – the hand of a rather ruthless God who couldn't have had much liking for the Irish.

The ratings of *The Age of Uncertainty* among Irish Americans would have been wonderfully boosted by these reflections, thus confirming in striking fashion Galbraith's dictum that, in such matters, the test of audience approval invariably triumphs over the test of truth.

Living in the middle of the real Ireland throughout the years of the real famine was Maria Edgeworth. She turned 80 in 1847, the worst year. She no longer managed the Edgeworthstown family property – though she had done so with considerable skill for 15 years, until she was well into her 70s. Though stunned by the misery which surrounded her on every side, she worked tirelessly to relieve distress; and through it all she thought often of David Ricardo, and of what he would have said and done if he had lived.

This is not a speculation, but a fact which is proved by surviving Oldspeak records. Maria Edgeworth wrote regularly to Richard Jones, who was Malthus' successor in the political economy chair at Haileybury College. In one letter written in 1847 she concluded a discussion about the potato as a staple food with:

> ...and it brings in the lowest price, affording nothing to fall back upon in case of failure. I have letters of Ricardo's in which all the *requisites* for a safe national food are ably stated and the potato is lowest in his scale.

And in April 1849, the month before she died, she wondered in another letter what 'our dear deceased friend Mr Ricardo' would have said about the discussion of Irish problems in Berkeley's *Querist*.

The letters in which Ricardo and Edgeworth discussed the potato also survive. They begin with Maria Edgeworth asking a question:

> which is one of *vital* consequence to this country – the question *for* and *against* the potato, which has for some hundred years past been alternatively cried up as the blessing and cried down as the bane of Ireland.

She went on to discuss McCulloch's article on *Cottagers* in the *Encyclopedia Brittanica*. She contested the view that potatoes were not storable and enclosed with her letter a sample of storable flour which had been converted from potatoes twenty years before. She then asked whether

> You in England who do not live upon potatoes and who have gone through all the prosperity and adversity of manufactures, are you better off? – are you happier? – I don't ask whether you are richer than we are in Ireland. Take an average of years – don't fix your eye upon this dreadful time of famine. I wish my dear Sir that after your intended excursion to France you would come to poor little Ireland and see and judge it for yourself...

Ricardo's reply ran to more than six pages. He made clear, though politely, that it was wrong to 'take an average of years':

> The argument that the failure of the potato crop is only occasional... appears to me defective. Judging by my own feelings, if for five six or seven years of easy competency with respect to food, I had to endure one year of famine and to witness the sufferings of my family and friends for that one dreadful year, I would rather that I had never been born; no happiness can compensate perpetual hunger for one year; much less can it compensate for the dreadful suffering of starvation...

Ricardo went on to ask the obvious questions – you say that potatoes are storable but what is the cost of preparation and storage? Will people be able to afford them in famine years? Do you have some of those 'patient, plodding, calculating merchants' who can wait that long for their return? 'I think we are not only richer but happier in England', he concluded. 'We are never so near actual famine as you are; what can you put in the scale against this dreadful evil?'

Quickly Miss Edgeworth wrote another long letter back to the inexorable lawgiver, the arch-hypocrite who had engraved on tablets of stone the principle that the poor should never be helped. It began:

> Welcome dear Sir most welcome you and your family back to England – I feel as if I had warm friends nearer to me – and...I feel assured that at some future time you and yours will be in the midst of us at Edgeworths town – by the time we have done quarrelling about decking King William's statue with orange ribbons, and...throw no more bottles or rattles at our Lord Lieutenants.

In this letter Maria Edgeworth supported her argument for potatoes with the answers to a number of questions she had asked of one of the more experienced tenant-farmers on the Edgeworth estate. Ricardo's response acknowledged the force of some of the answers but pointed out that what was a *profitable* crop to the farmer might not be the crop which would secure an abundant supply of food to the people: 'what you state respecting the want of money to purchase food among the lower classes last year is precisely the evil which will accompany every failure of the potato crop in Ireland'.

The viewers of Galbraith's series were told, in effect, that Ricardo and his colleagues were simple-minded. They were incapable of seeing that people without money could not buy corn; they thought that the repeal of the Corn Laws would be a panacea for all ills; and they were unmoved by evidence. It was all pure Newspeak.

XII

In his last letter to Maria Edgeworth, Ricardo wrote that:

> Your restless nation gives us a great deal of trouble in Parliament. The best amongst us do not know how to manage you, nor what course to take to give you the blessings of peace, order, and good government. You have been so long subjected to misrule as hardly to be in a fit state to be reclaimed by common means. Coercion and severity have proved of little use, and I hope the system of indulgence, kindness, and conciliation will now be tried. If that system will not succeed I hope we shall get rid of you altogether; – we could do very well without you.

But the system of indulgence, kindness and conciliation was not to be tried; nor was the option of separation or home rule which Ricardo canvassed in his letter to Maria Edgeworth and also, without doubt, in the discussions of the Committee on Ireland of which he was an active member.

In the same issue of *Blackwood's* as one of the chapters in his *Prolusion* on Sadler was appearing in 1831, John Wilson contributed an article on *The State of Ireland*.

He lamented that 'the existence of the Church is endangered, the separation of Ireland from Britain is made a matter of open attempt and probability and sufferings of the former are increased'; and he knew who to blame:

> Catholic Emancipation is confessed by those who advocated it to be a total failure – a failure as complete and destructive as Free-Trade, and the other nostrums which have filled the empire with calamity and convulsion.

As for indulgence, kindness and conciliation:

> The time has come when the truth, and the whole truth, must be spoken to the Irish people...they must be told strongly and unsparingly of their defects and infirmities, not to insult and upbraid, but to reform and instruct them. What, then, are the great causes of Irish penury and misery? Without hesitation, we reply – the individual deficiencies and misconduct of the Irish people. It is self-evident that the very best laws and institutions cannot preserve the individual from want and barbarism, who is improvident, incapable, vicious and turbulent – that he is the cause of his own suffering...In the more shewy kinds of natural ability, the Irishman has no superior; in the more solid kinds, and the qualities of disposition essential for producing national prosperity, he stands the lowest of civilised men.

It was in this same year that 'that egregious wiseacre ex-Professor Senior' wrote his *Letter to Lord Howick on a legal provision for the Irish poor.* Senior, who has been pilloried by anti-economists for a century and a half as the arch-priest of doctrinaire *laissez-faire,* summarised his recommendations as follows:

> I am anxious that these provisions should be made as ample as possible: that public money should be advanced to facilitate emigration, and for the formation of roads, canals and harbours; that the Irish should be relieved from one of the worst relics of feudal barbarism, the local taxation imposed on fairs and markets; that they should also be relieved from the absurd duties on timber...and above all I am anxious that they should be relieved from the expense of supporting the Catholic Church.

The major recommendations were anathema to the establishment, and were never seriously considered.

Through the 1830s and early 1840s the population of Ireland continued to rise, and so did its prosperity. The anti-economists had no doubt that these developments were connected, and that the absurdity of the Malthusian doctrine so ruthlessly exposed by Sadler was being confirmed with every passing year. Their confidence was fortified by the publication in 1841 of a book by one G Tradescant Lay entitled *The Chinese as they are: their moral, social and literary characte*r. Mr Lay explained that

> The prosperity of the Chinese tempts me to frame a system of political economy, which lays population as the foundation whereon everything in the way of social comfort and personal affluence is reared...I look upon man as the great capital of a nation – a view which is based on what I see in China, where a *swarming people are encircled by a swarm of comforts.* In no country do the inhabitants crowd every habitable spot as in China; in no country do the poor people abound with so many of the elegancies and luxuries of life. Early marriage encourages fertility and augments the population...and...consequently, the means of living...In China, the natives throng all those parts which are susceptible to tillage, till there is not enough room to hold them. Here we behold an assortment of comforts for the poor, such as no other country can parallel...

The reaction against Malthusianism received further support in Frederick Engels' *Outlines of a Critique of Political Economy* which was first published in 1844. According to Engels:

> The productive power at mankind's disposal is immeasurable... According to the most able economists and statisticians...'over populated' Great Britain can be brought within ten years to produce a corn yield sufficient for a population six times its present size... Malthus...maintains that population is always pressing on the means of

> subsistence...If we want to be consistent, we must admit that *the earth was already over-populated when only one man existed*...Am I to go on any longer elaborating this vile, infamous theory, this hideous blasphemy against nature and mankind?...Here at last we have the immorality of the economist brought to the highest pitch...It is just this theory which is the keystone of the liberal system of free trade...If it is a fact that every adult produces more than he himself can consume...then it must be assumed that each worker ought to be able to produce far more than he needs...One must consider a large family to be a very welcome gift for the community. But the economist...is so firmly set in his antithesis that the most striking facts are of as little concern to him as the most scientific principles...It is absurd to talk of over-population so long as there is enough waste land in the valley of the Mississippi for the whole population of Europe to be transplanted there.

If a large family was a very welcome gift to the community, the Irish problem was near to being solved. But the economists, as impervious to the most striking facts as to the most scientific principles, continued their immoral search for other solutions. In the same year as Engels' *Outlines of a Critique*...appeared the *Edinburgh Review* published an article by Nassau Senior entitled 'Ireland in 1843'. Sydney Smith, who had been one of the founders of the *Edinburgh* 40 years earlier, said of this article that 'nothing could be wiser or better'. Lord Jeffrey, another of the founders, wrote to the editor:

> I have just finished that great paper on Ireland, and am so full of admiration and gratitude to the author, that I cannot help telling you of it. Nothing so wise, so impressive, so bold, so temperate, nothing, in short, so powerful and so practical, has appeared in our pages, since the time when we battered in breach in the minor causes of catholic emancipation and slavery abolition. The truth and justice of the leading doctrines are sustained with clearness and force, and urged in a tone of calm confidence and authority that must command attention, and lead to conviction in many unwilling quarters. I have never read any publication which is so sure to produce an impression, so certain not to be overlooked, so secure against all answer, and so likely to have beneficial effects.

Though Sydney Smith and Francis Jeffrey had been leaders in every liberal movement for almost half a century, Lord Clark presumably regarded them as locked up with the politicians in the intellectual prison of classical economics. Engels had escaped. In *Civilisation,* Clark said that his *Conditions of the Working Classes in England*, published in the same year as the *Outlines of a Critique*...was

> presented as documentation, but is in fact the passionate cry of a young social worker, and as such it provided, and has continued to provide, the emotional dynamo of Marxism. Marx read Engels – I don't know who else did: that was enough.

The condition of the working classes revealed by Engels' book was not more shocking than their condition as revealed in Malthus' *Essay* nearly half a century earlier. Harriet Martineau pointed out in her *Autobiography* that:

> (Malthus) found, in his day, that a portion of the people were underfed; and that one consequence of this was a fearful mortality among infants; and another consequence, the growth of a recklessness among the destitute which caused infanticide, corruption of morals, and, at best, marriage between pauper boys and girls.

Kenneth Clark's statement that nobody up to the end of the nineteenth century thought that these evils could be cured was wrong. The belief that they could be cured was the primary motivation of all of the great nineteenth-century economists, as well as some of the anti-economists such as Engels. The difference was that the economists' remedies were based, as the Emigration Committee of 1827 recognised, on general reasoning and scientific principles; whereas Engels' remedies were based on false reasoning and ignorant prejudice.

Engels' belief that a large family was a very welcome gift for the community was just as wrong as (and far more dangerous than) the belief of many of his contemporaries that the world was only 6000 years old. This should have been abundantly plain to John Kenneth Galbraith, a professor of economics and a former ambassador to India. It is a telling indication of the potency of the conventional wisdom that it was not.

XIII

Several weeks after Maria Edgeworth's death, the historian and philosopher Thomas Carlyle made his first visit to Ireland. Carlyle was at the height of his fame, the author of *Sartor Resartus*, *The French Revolution*, and *Chartism*. Frederick Engels had lavished praise on his *Past and Present*.

> This much is certain: a Whig would never have been able to write a book that was half so humane as *Past and Present*.

Carlyle's companion on his visit was Charles Gavan Duffy – then a leading Irish politician, later to be a prominent figure in Australian politics. In his *Conversations with Carlyle*, published over 40 years later, Duffy told of their discussions. One day, Duffy asked Carlyle for his view of Dickens, whose *David Copperfield* was then appearing in serial form. 'His theory of life was entirely wrong', said Carlyle:

> He thought men ought to be buttered up, and the world made soft and accommodating for them and all sorts of fellows having turkey for their Christmas dinner. Commanding and controlling and punishing them he would give up without any misgivings in order to coax and soothe and delude them into doing right. But it was not in this manner the eternal laws operated, but quite otherwise.

The philosopher and the politician visited a workhouse, and Carlyle was scandalised:

> Consider the absurdity of shutting up thousands of forlorn creatures to be fed at the cost of beggars like themselves. Why not regiment these unfortunate wretches, put colonels and captains, sergeants and corporals, over them and thrash them, if it proved needful, into habits of industry on some lands at home or in the colonies? Try them for a couple of years, he would say, and if they could not feed and clothe themselves, they ought to be put out of the world.

This was a more ambitious emigration scheme than that recommended by the inhumane Whigs such as Malthus and Senior, and it incorporated a more clearly specified incentive structure.

On his return to England, Carlyle wrote to his friend Emerson in the United States that the chaotic ruin he had seen everywhere was

> the general fruit of long-continued falsity and folly...the gospels of political economy, of *laissez-faire*, no-government (and) paradise to all comers...will first have to be tried, and found wanting...What is to be done? asks everyone...'*Blacklead* these two million idle beggars,' I sometimes advised, 'and sell them in Brazil as niggers – perhaps parliament...will allow you to advance them to be niggers?'

Carlyle immediately wrote the essay which *Fraser's Magazine* published as 'The Negro Question'; but which he entitled – when he published it in his own name three years later – 'the Nigger Question'.

It was in this article that Carlyle gave economics its name – the most quoted description that any science has ever had. He referred to

> the social science...which finds the secret of this universe in 'supply and demand', and reduces the duty of human governors to that of letting men alone...Not a 'gay science' (but) a dreary, desolate and indeed quite abject and distressing one; what we might call the *dismal Science*.

According to Carlyle, the 'unhappy wedlock of philosophical liberalism and the dismal science' had produced a 'wide-weltering deluge of benevolent twaddle and revolutionary grapeshot'. The human species had been 'reduced to believe in rosepink sentimentalism alone' and was

> sunk in deep froth-oceans of 'benevolence', 'fraternity', 'emancipation-principle', 'Christian philanthrophy' and other most amiable-looking but most baseless...baleful and all-bewildering jargon...the flunky-world... descends, manipulating its ballot-boxes...and divine constitutional apparatus; quoting its dismal sciences, statistics and other satisfactory gospels and Talmuds...

There were however 'fixed headlands' where 'fact and nature...say a few words to us':

> The everlasting duty of all men, black or white, who are born into this world (is) to do competent work...; for that and for no other purpose was each of us sent into this world...If it be (a man's) own indolence that prevents and prohibits him (from working), then his own indulgence is the enemy he must be delivered from: and the first 'right' he has – poor indolent blockhead...is that every unprohibited man...shall endeavour to 'emancipate' him from his indolence, and by some wise means... compel him, since inducing will not serve, to do the work he is fit for.

Since the 'indolent two-legged cattle' in the West Indies would not work for money, Carlyle considered that they should be compelled to work 'with beneficent whip'. (It was 75 years since Adam Smith had said that slavery was maintained in the West Indies only because 'the pride of man makes him love to domineer, and nothing mortifies him so much as to have to condescend to persuade his inferiors').

Carlyle went on to point out that 'in other places than Demerara, and in regard to other interests than those of sugar-making', the same problems existed:

> I have to complain that, in these days, the relation of master to servant, and of superior to inferior...is fallen sadly out of joint...Austere philosophers...have talked to me about the possibility of doing without servants; of trying somehow to serve yourself (boot cleaning, etc., done by contract). The Duke of Trumps (told me) that the state of his domestic service was by no means satisfactory...'Five-and-forty of them', said his Grace; 'really, I suppose, the cleverest in the market, for there is no limit to the wages...An iron law presses on us all here...It is I that am a slave; and often I think of packing the whole brotherhood of them out of doors one good day.'

XIV

This essay of Carlyle's produced one good outcome. John Stuart Mill, whose *Principles of Political Economy* had recently been published, replied in the following issue of *Fraser's*. He did not mention the 'dismal science' jibe, but he vigorously defended the humanitarians; and he angrily criticised Carlyle for strengthening the forces of tyranny:

> At this crisis of American slavery, when the decisive conflict between right and iniquity seems about to commence, your contributor steps in, and flings this missile, loaded with the weight of his reputation, into the abolitionist camp. The words of English writers of celebrity are words of power on the other side of the ocean; and the owners of human flesh...will welcome such an auxiliary. Circulated as his dissertation will probably be, by those whose interests profit by it, from one end of the American Union to the other, I hardly know of any act by which one person could have done so much mischief as this may possibly do...

More importantly, Mill severely criticised Carlyle for his 'gospel of work', and cogently stated his own attitude:

> This 'gospel of work'...as justly deserves the name of a cant as any of those which (your contributor) has opposed...To give it a rational meaning, it must first be known what he means by work. Does work mean every thing which people *do*? No; or he would not reproach people with doing no work. Does it mean laborious exertion? No; for many a day spent in killing game includes more muscular fatigue than a day's ploughing. Does it mean useful exertion? But your contributor always scoffs at the idea of utility. Does he mean that all persons ought to earn their living? But some earn their living by doing nothing, and some by doing mischief; and the negroes, whom he despises, still do earn by labour the 'pumpkins' they consume and the finery they wear...
>
> There is nothing laudable in work for work's sake. To work voluntarily for a worthy object is laudable; but what constitutes a worthy object? On this matter the oracle of which your contributor is the prophet has never yet been prevailed on to declare itself. He revolves in an eternal circle round the idea of work, as if turning up the earth, or driving a shuttle or a quill, were...the ends of human existence...
>
> The worth of work does not surely consist in its leading to other work, and so on to work upon work without end. On the contrary, the multiplication of work, for purposes not worth caring about, is one of the evils of our present condition...The beautifying of existence is as

> worthy and useful an object as the sustaining of it; but only a vitiated taste can see any such result in those fopperies of so-called civilization, which myriads of hands are now occupied and lives wasted in providing.
>
> In opposition to the 'gospel of work', I would assert the gospel of leisure, and maintain that human beings *cannot* rise to the finer attributes of their nature compatibly with a life filled with labour. I do not include under the name labour such work...as is done by writers and afforders of 'guidance', an occupation which, let alone the vanity of the thing, cannot be called by the same name with the real labour, the exhausting, stiffening, stupefying toil of...agricultural and manufacturing labourers. To reduce very greatly the quantity of work required to carry on existence is as needful as to distribute it more equally; and the progress of science, and the increasing ascendancy of justice and good sense, tend to this result.

The future of work and of leisure is the subject of an extensive literature in recent times. It is often held that the traditional structure of economic theory does not provide a satisfactory framework within which to examine the matter. Few who have made this claim could set down the key issues as clearly and as forcefully as did the foremost classical economist of the day in this article published in 1850.

Carlyle regarded Mill's response as pathetic. In his *Journal* on February 7, 1850 he wrote:

> Nigger article has roused the ire of all philanthropists to a quite unexpected pitch. Among other very poor attacks on it was one in 'Fraser'; most shrill, thin, poor and insignificant, which I was surprised to learn proceeded from John Mill...No use in writing that kind of criticism.

XV

'With Ricardo and Malthus the notion of massive privation and great inequality became a basic premise' – so Galbraith wrote in *The Affluent Society*. As we have seen, the statement is absurd. 'It was to Ricardo and Malthus that Carlyle alluded', Galbraith went on, 'when he spoke in 1850 of the "Respectable Professors of the Dismal Science" and gave to economics a name that it has never quite escaped because it was never quite undeserved'.

It is clear that Professor Galbraith had never looked at the Carlyle essay in which 'the dismal science' appeared, or the subsequent *Latter-day Pamphlets* in which the 'respectable professors' were added. If he had done so, he would have realised immediately that Carlyle's complaint was that the economists were soft-hearted, warm and sentimental – and not (as Galbraith assumes) that they were hard-hearted, cold and ruthless.

He would also have realised that it was *not* to Ricardo and Malthus that Carlyle was alluding: the attack was on living professors, not dead ones. The name McCroudy appears frequently in the *Latter-day Pamphlets* and refers to McCulloch; and Nassau Senior, who had been professor of political economy at Oxford at 35 and was now back in his old Chair at the age of 60, is featured in the first of the *Latter-day Pamphlets:*

> Never till now did young men, and almost children, take such a command in human affairs. A changed time since the word Senior (Seigneur, or Elder) was first devised to signify 'lord,' or superior; as in all languages of men we find it to have been!...In times when men love wisdom, the old man will ever be venerable, and be venerated, and reckoned noble: in times that love something else than wisdom, and indeed have little or no wisdom, and see little or none to love, the old man will cease to be venerated: – and looking more closely, also, you will find that in fact he has ceased to be venerable, and has begun to be contemptible; a foolish *boy* still, a boy without the graces, generosities, and opulent strength of young boys. In these days, what of *lordship* or leadership is still to be done, the youth must do it, not the mature or aged man; the mature man, hardened into sceptical egoism, knows no monition but that of his own frigid cautions, avarices, mean timidities...

These sentences would have been grossly offensive even if it had been the case that Professor Senior lacked maturity and wisdom. In fact, he had an abundance of both. In 1841 Sir James Stephen wrote to McVey Napier, editor of the *Edinburgh Review,* 'you cannot rate Senior too highly in his own peculiar walk, which is that of comprehensive, mature and luminous thinking about permanent national interests'.

Twenty years earlier, when Senior was putting forward the sane and forthright remedies for dealing with the Irish problem which we noted earlier, Carlyle had written:

> Never since the beginning of time was there...so intensely self-conscious a society. Our whole relations to the universe and to our fellow-man have become an inquiry, a doubt; nothing will go on of its own accord, and do its function quietly; but all things must be probed into, the whole working of man's world be anatomically studied...Till at length indeed, we have come to such a pass that except in this same *medicine,* with its artifices and appliances, few can so much as imagine any strength or hope to remain for us. The whole Life of Society must now be carried on

> by drugs: doctor after doctor appears with his nostrum of cooperative societies, universal suffrage, cottage-and-cow systems, repression of population, vote by ballot.

With respect to Senior's work as Royal Commissioner on the Poor Law Inquiry in the 1830's, the *Economist* was to remark many years later:

> It rarely falls to the lot of any individual to do so much permanent good to his country by the labours of a whole life as Mr Senior effected on this occasion by the well-directed exertions of a few brief years.

While Senior was engaged in these 'well-directed exertions', and working to use the mass of data available to maximum advantage, Carlyle scoffed at a publication which drew together the available actuarial data on the expectation of life in Britain ('Is it not as if some zealous scientific son of Adam had proved the deepening of the ocean by survey...of two mud-plashes on the coast of the Isle of Dogs?')

The Report of the Royal Commission on the Handloom Weavers, which was written by Senior, included a reference to the 'wage' system applying before the Poor Law Amendment Act:

> Under the unhappy system prevalent during the forty years immediately preceding the Poor Law Amendment Act, a large portion of the labourers of England were treated not as freemen but as slaves or domestic animals, and received not strictly speaking wages, regulated by the value of their labour, but rations proportioned to their supposed wants...Under such circumstances wages, if we can apply the term to payments so regulated, rose and fell with the price of bread, just as the keep of a horse rises or falls with the price of oats.

In the first of the *Latter-day Pamphlets,* Carlyle argued that the old system was not an unhappy one:

> In the progress of Emancipation, are we to look for a time when all the horses also are to be emancipated, and brought to the supply-and-demand principle? Horses too have 'motives'; are acted-on by hunger, fear, hope, love of oats, terror of plaited leather; nay, they have vanity, ambition, emulation, thankfulness, vindictiveness; some rude outline of all our human spiritualities, – a rude resemblance to us in mind and intelligence even as they have in bodily frame...Small kindness to Hodge's horses to emancipate them! The fate of all emancipated horses is, sooner or later, inevitable. To have in this habitable Earth no grass to eat...

While Carlyle argued for government action so that the unwilling could be compelled to work with 'beneficent whip', and jeered at the 'dismal science' for reducing the duty of human governors to that of letting men alone, Senior was telling his students in his lectures at Oxford that government

> cannot of course enact that every family shall have five well-built, well-ventilated rooms, any more than it can enact that every family shall live on roast beef, but it can prohibit the erection of houses without drainage, or in courts, or back to back. It can require the streets to be paved, it can regulate their width and the thickness of the walls. In short, it can provide prospectively against the creation of new seats of disease and vice.

While Carlyle argued in another of the *Latter-day Pamphlets* that 'the grammar of nature, which he learned from his mother...was, as it still is, the grand education of the working man', Senior worked tirelessly for compulsory state-supported education. In his seventies he was to be Chairman of the Royal Commission which recommended such a system. As one of his biographers commented;

> It is sometimes maintained that the progressive spirit deteriorates with age. In this instance, however, the record shows that the septuagenarian economist was the most vehement protagonist of the majority opinion; whereas the old-fashioned view of the minority was zealously supported by the youthful Goldwin Smith.

Finally, and remembering Engels' comment about Carlyle's humanity and the Whigs' lack of it, we may compare this extract from one of the *Latter-day Pamphlets* –

> They are wont, here in England for some time back, to proclaim in the gross, as if it had become credible lately, all two-legged animals without feathers to be 'free'. 'Here is a distressed Nigger,' they proclaim, 'who much prefers idleness to work – should not he be free to choose which? Is not he a man and brother?'...My friends, I grieve to remind you, but it is eternally the fact: Whom Heaven has made a slave, no parliament of men nor power that exists on earth can render free. No; he is chained by fetters which parliaments with their millions cannot reach...The bigger candle you light within the slave-image of him, it will but show his slave-features on the larger and more hideous scale...Him the Supreme Powers marked in the making of him, *slave*; appointed him at his and our peril, not to command but to obey...

with this passage, also on the subject of slavery, in Senior's review of *Uncle Tom's Cabin*:

> The civilised Virginian, who can never go from his cabin with the certainty of spending another night in it;...the Virginian wife, who sees

> her husband handcuffed and carried off, because his good conduct, industry and skill have made him so valuable that his master thinks that he cannot afford to keep him; the Virginian mother, who finds that her children, one after another, disappear, as each attains the age of sale;... all these feel their sense of suffering sharpened by their sense of wrong. All around them are whites, their fellow-countrymen...whose homes are inviolable, among whom the child belongs to its parents, husbands and wives to one another, and a man to himself. To the black race alone... all family ties and security are denied; domestic affections, the greatest source of happiness to the rich, almost the only source of happiness to the poor, are to them converted into instruments of torture (and) the causes of constant anxious terror.

XVI

Nassau Senior was a major contributor to Britain's academic public life for 40 years. He was also, contrary to the popular image, a progressive and creative contributor. He believed that there should be no legal or economic discrimination against the female sex, saying that 'I believe women to have as clear a perception of their own interest and as much determination and as much power to follow it as belong to their brothers or to their fathers'. His *Lectures* at Oxford were frequently critical of the attitudes of governments to the disadvantaged:

> I ought perhaps to include among the evils of poverty, the carelessness with which the individual interests of the poor are dealt with by the legislature, and particularly...by those who profess peculiar humanity.

It was in recognition of such attitudes, and of Senior's remarkable intellectual powers, that Count Cavour, the father of modern Italy, described him as 'the most enlightened thinker in Great Britain'.

When Senior died in 1864 he was, without question, the most significant economist to have died since Malthus 30 years earlier. As we have seen, *The Times* noticed Malthus' death in a single sentence; for Senior there was no obituary notice at all.

When Carlyle died nearly 20 years later, the obituary notice covered the whole of the leading page and the greater part of another. It began by claiming that

> No recent man of letters has held in England a place comparable to that which for at least a quarter of a century has been his without dispute...A great man of letters, quite as heroic as any of those whom he depicted, has passed away amid universal regret.

and went on to celebrate his massive triumph over the economists and their fellow travellers:

> The political economists mumbling barren truisms or equally unfruitful paradoxes about supply and demand; Malthusians preaching...the most unacceptable of gospels; so-called statesmen collecting with impotent hands information about the 'condition of England' question;`...the helpless babbling of Parliament' and liberty made a pretext, in the West Indies, and elsewhere, for flying in the face of the great law that, if a man work not, neither shall he eat – these were some of the butts of his scorn and contempt...It is astonishing to note how, under uncouth, rhapsodical phraseology, lie many ideas which are now the common property of most educated men. The novelties and paradoxes of 1840 are, to a large extent, nothing but the good sense of 1881. Who would not now echo Mr Carlyle's protests against the supposed omnipotence of Parliament or the possibility of saving nations by the use of the ballot box? Who now believes...that human nature can be reformed by any order of the Poor Law Commissioners? Who does not own that the change in our colonies from servitude to idleness and squalor...was not an unmixed blessing to those most concerned?...It is enough to say that again and again he reminded...his generation of stern truths it was in danger of forgetting.

Audiences were applauding what they liked best long before the days of television.

XVII

In *Civilisation*, Kenneth Clark wrote that:

> The strange thing is that none of these mid-nineteenth century writers *(except for Carlyle and Ruskin)* seemed to notice that the triumph of rational philosophy had resulted in a new form of barbarism (emphasis added).

The way in which Carlyle noticed the new form of barbarism has already been illustrated. We must now turn to the other figure with whom his name is so often bracketed – John Ruskin.

In his autobiography, Kenneth Clark tells how

> for many years, Ruskin became the greatest single influence on my mind. My chapter on Ruskin in *The Gothic Revival* must have been the first attempt to do him justice since his obituaries...

Ruskin's influence was not confined to art. Clark also explained how he had, as an undergraduate, been deeply influenced by 'Ruskin's beautifully simple and candid examination of the basic truths of economics':

> My economics tutor, Freddie Ogilvie, who was to become Reith's successor at the BBC, was trying gently to persuade me of the reasonableness of classical economic theory. Ruskin made me entirely unresponsive.

The implied assumption is interesting. If Ogilvie had suggested that Landseer was a finer painter than Rembrandt, Clark the art critic could have told him that he was wrong. He might have offered to help Ogilvie appreciate Rembrandt's genius, but any failure to respond would have been Ogilvie's problem – not Clark's. It does not seem to have occurred to Lord Clark that his opinion that Ricardo was inferior to Ruskin reflected on *him* – not on Ricardo's genius or Ogilvie's powers of persuasion.

XVIII

Ruskin was already famous as the author of *The Seven Lamps of Architecture, Modern Painters* and *The Stones of Venice* before he took up political economy. His change of interests dates from about the year 1854, when he was 35. In that year Ruskin's wife left him and he went back to live in his parents' house. To understand the personal background on which his approach to political economy was based, it is necessary to know that this was 'a large house with seven acres of gardens, and a troop of servants, each with his or her appointed station and appointed work'.

During the following year, Ruskin began to read the main texts on political economy and was not impressed. He wrote to Mrs. Carlyle:

> My studies of political economy have induced me to think...that nobody knows anything about that, and I am at present engaged on an investigation, on independent principles, of the natures of money, rent and taxes...

The outcome of these reflections was a series of lectures called *The Political Economy of Art,* which were delivered at Manchester in 1857. In the first of these lectures, Ruskin expressed the anti-Malthusian view that over-population was impossible:

> The world is so regulated with the laws of Providence that a man's labour, well applied, is always amply sufficient to provide him during his life with all things needful to him, and not only with those, but with many pleasant objects of luxury; and yet farther, to procure him with large intervals of healthful rest and serviceable leisure. And a nation's labour,

> well applied, is in like manner, amply sufficient to provide its whole population with good food and comfortable habitation; and not with those only, but with good education besides, and objects of luxury...

He recognised that there *were* people who were in want or misery or degradation, but this was because industry had been wanting or was in error:

> When there should have been providence, there has been waste;
> when there should have been labour, there has been lasciviousness;
> and wilfulness, where there should have been subordination.

And he quoted from Proverbs, chapter 13, verse 23:

> Much food is in the tillage of the poor, but there is that is destroyed for want of judgement.

Ruskin's 'beautifully simple and candid examination of the basic truths of economics' was that economy meant '*applying* your labour rationally...*preserving* its produce carefully...*distributing* its produce seasonably'. Applying labour rationally meant 'not growing oats in land where you can grow wheat'; preserving its produce carefully meant 'laying up your wheat wisely in storehouses for the time of famine'; and distributing its produce seasonably meant 'being able to carry your corn at once to the place where the people are hungry'.

This was a fair description of the *problems* which political economists and legislators had been addressing during the previous century. Ruskin offered no solutions. Indeed, there was no sign that he perceived that his exposition had begged all of the significant questions.

The argument in this and other lectures during the succeeding years suggests that Ruskin had not read the works of political economy which he criticised, other than to ferret out debating points.

'Economists usually speak as if there were no good in consumption absolute', he claimed. 'So far from this being so, consumption absolute is the end, crown and purpose of all production'. So far from economists speaking as if there were no good in consumption absolute (that is, as distinct from consumption as a means to sustain production and investment) this was what modern economics was about – the key difference between the system of Adam Smith and the system on which he mounted his 'very violent attack'. In *The Wealth of Nations,* Smith had written:

> Consumption is the sole end and purpose of all production; and the interest of the producer ought to be attended to, only so far as it may be necessary for promoting that of the consumer. The maxim is so perfectly self-evident, that it would be absurd to attempt to prove it. But in the mercantile system, the interest of the consumer is almost constantly

> sacrificed to that of the producer; and it seems to consider production, and not consumption, as the ultimate end and object of all industry and commerce.

In another lecture, Ruskin presented as the current thinking of economists a theory which was close to what Malthus had put forward in the first edition of his *Essay* in 1798, but which he had already abandoned in the 1803 edition:

> In all the ranges of human thought I know none so melancholy as the speculations of political economists on the population question. It is proposed to better the condition of the labourer by giving him higher wages. 'Nay,' says the economist, – 'if you raise his wages, he will either people down to the same point of misery at which you found him, or drink your wages away'.

Ruskin went on to attribute to political economists the view that labourers 'cannot receive education' (which was, of course, a ludicrous misrepresentation), and then asked 'Why not? That is precisely the point at issue'. It was not the economists that Ruskin was here attacking but the anti-economists – including himself; because in evidence to a House of Commons Committee at about this time Ruskin had said of his art lectures

> In my class, workmen are especially tempted to think of rising above their own rank...– becoming something better than workmen, and that effect I particularly dread...I think that the moment a man desires to rise out of his own class, he does his work badly in it;...they wish to become something better than workmen, and I want to keep them in that class; I want to teach every man to rest contented in his station...

And Ruskin went on to tell the Committee that 'Nothing assists the working man so much as having the moral disposition developed rather than the intellectual...'– which was precisely the attitude to education which Adam Smith and his successors had criticised.

In another lecture, Ruskin criticised political economy because it was 'founded on self-interest'. He quoted in support of this view a sentence from Mill's *Principles:*

> In all reasoning about prices, the proviso must be understood, 'supposing all parties to take care of their own interest'.

Ruskin could with equal validity have criticised medical science for being 'founded on self interest'; because much of its reasoning supposes that 'all parties...take care of their own interest'.

Like many of the other anti-economists, Ruskin asserted that the greatest good for a country *was* in having the greatest number of people: 'that country is the richest', he said, 'which nourishes the greatest number of noble and happy human beings'. The underlying assumption that the greatest number is conducive to the greatest good is the doctrine that de Quincy had described in 1823 as the 'pernicious...counsels from Athenian days to our own clamouring for direct encouragements to population'.

The most famous of Ruskin's anti-Malthusian statements was in the chapter on the 'veins of wealth' in *Unto this Last*:

> It may be discovered that the true veins of wealth are purple – and not in Rock, but in Flesh – perhaps even that the final outcome and consumation of all wealth is in the producing as many as possible full-breathed, bright-eyed and happy-hearted human creatures. Our modern world, I think, has rather a tendency the other way; – most political economists appearing to consider multitudes of human creatures not conducive to wealth, or at best conducive to it only by remaining in a dim-eyed and narrow-chested state of being.

The first of these two sentences was quoted with enthusiasm by Sir Oliver Lodge, who had ten children, in his Introduction to the *Everyman* edition of *Unto this Last* in 1907. It showed, said Lodge, the contrast between real and spurious national wealth. Seven years later Lodge, as President of the British Association for the Advancement of Science, delivered a public lecture in Adelaide in the course of the Association's only meeting in Australia. Sir Oliver's discourse was entitled 'the Ether of Space'. He

> described the properties of the ether of space as the omnipresent connecting medium, and maintained its complete reality, in spite of its intangible and generally insensible character. He discussed the relation between ether and matter, and urged that the experimental elusiveness of the ether was a natural consequence of its uniformity and of the universality of its functions.

But by now the ether had no functions, universal or otherwise; because, as many of the scientists present must have known, Einstein's work had made the ether obsolete. Lodge continued to believe in the 'complete reality' of the ether until his death in 1940: to the end, he remained as impervious to the findings of natural science at the outset of the twentieth century as to the findings of economic science at the outset of the nineteenth.

XIX

John Ruskin was a friend and dedicated disciple of Thomas Carlyle, and a strong advocate of his 'gospel of work'; and, as the years went by, he became increasingly bitter in his attacks on the economists and their (as he saw it) distorted attitudes to work and to life.

In 1870 – the same year as Jevons complained about the treatment of economists in his Presidential Address to the British Association – Ruskin began the famous series of letters to the working men of England which he entitled *Fors Clavigera*. The tenth of these letters contained a savage attack on the economics profession. In order to understand the nature and force of the attack, it is necessary to know that, at this stage and for the preceding thirty years, John Stuart Mill was afflicted by a continuous twitch in one eye. This is what Ruskin wrote to the workers of England:

> Now I tell you once for all, Carlyle is the only living writer who has spoken the absolute and perpetual truth about yourselves and your business; and exactly in proportion to the inherent weakness of brain in your lying guides, will be their animosity against Carlyle...For in the modern liberal there is a new and wonderful form of misguidance. Of old, it was bad enough that the blind should lead the blind;...but now a worse disorder is upon you, that the squinting should lead the squinting...The modern liberal politico-economist of the Stuart Mill school is essentially of the type of a flat-fish – one eyeless side of him always in the mud, and one eye, on the side that *has* eyes, down in the corner of his mouth...Read your Carlyle, then, with all your heart,... and you will learn from him...that every man shall do good work for his bread...If you are resolved that the work shall be good, the bread will be sure; if not – believe me, there is neither steam plough nor steam mill, go they never so glibly, that will win it from the earth long.

When John Stuart Mill died less than two years after this letter was published, the short obituary notice in *The Times* was almost sneering in its tone. Whilst acknowledging that it was from Mill's *Principles of Political Economy* that 'the existing state of the *so-called* science may be learnt' (emphasis added) *The Times* went on

> But in this work, instead of confining himself to the collection of known and recognised theories or facts, he had propounded sundry doctrines of dangerous tendency and doubtful soundness...We need hardly add that many of his opinions on society and government have been generally and justly condemned...He was often a wrong-headed, but always a kind-hearted man...Of late years Mill has not come before the world with advantage. When he appeared in public it was to advocate

> the fanciful rights of women, or to propound some impracticable reform or revolutionary change in the laws relating to the land; but, with all his errors and paradoxes, he will be long remembered as a thinker and reasoner who has largely contributed to the intellectual progress of the age.

The respectable public figures of mid-Victorian England did not want to remember Mill unless they could do it discreetly. Five days after his death *The Times* carried a notice that Lord Derby

> 'will, with pleasure, join in any mark of respect to the late Mr Mill which does not take such a form as to imply on the part of the contributors or promoters an agreement in Mr Mill's political opinions.' It is understood that the movement will be organised on this basis.

Mr Gladstone initially joined the organising committee, but then withdrew.

In the same year as *The Times* was inveighing against Mill's advocacy of 'the fanciful rights of women' the name of Alfred Marshall – who was to be the dominant figure in British economics for the next 50 years – appeared in print for the first time as the author of an essay entitled 'The Future of the Working Classes'. The opening passage of the essay was an eloquent endorsement of Mill's position on 'the fanciful rights of women'. All Mill's instances, he wrote

> tend to show how our progress could be accelerated if we would unwrap the swaddling-clothes in which artificial customs have enfolded woman's mind and would give her free scope womanfully to discharge her duties to the world.

Several years later, Mill's attitude to the emancipation of women again came under public notice. One of John Ruskin's letters published as *Arrows of the Chace* included the following sentence:

> My friend, while you still teach in Oxford the 'philosophy'...of that poor cretinous wretch, Stuart Mill, and are endeavouring to open other 'careers' to English women than that of the Wife and the Mother, you won't make your men chaste by recommending them to leave off tea.

But by now, Ruskin's interests had taken a new turn. In his address to the students of Oxford on taking up his professorship there, he said:

> There is a destiny now possible for us, the highest ever set before a nation to be accepted or refused. We are still undegenerate in race; a race mingled of the best northern blood...This is what England must either do, or perish; she must found colonies as fast and as far as she is able, formed of her most energetic and worthiest men; seizing every piece of

> fruitful waste ground she can set her foot on, and there teaching these her colonists, that their chief virtue is to be fidelity to their country, and that their first aim is to be to advance the power of England by land and sea...

Cecil Rhodes was in the audience. As one of Rhode's biographers wrote, John Ruskin had

> supplied the philosophic jumping-board from which Cecil Rhodes was to plunge into the African continent to paint its map red with the colour of Britain and the blood of thousands.

Ruskin was to live on for more than a quarter of a century. As the 1960's editions of the *Encyclopedia Brittanica* stated:

> The close of his life was one of entire peace and honour. He was loaded with the degrees of universities and membership in numerous societies and academies. 'Ruskin Societies' were founded in many parts of the kingdom...

On Ruskin's death in 1900, *The Times* produced one of its most fulsome eulogies. The *litterateur* who had referred to John Stuart Mill as a squinting flat-fish had many virtues, but one above all deserved special mention:

> Never was any man so sympathetic, so winning, so uniformly and invariably courteous;...it was the same at all times, and to all men.

5. Economic Growth: Is it Worth Having?[1]

Ian Castles and Treasury

Foreword

This paper re-assesses economic growth in the light of questions that have been raised about its desirability in recent years. It pursues five main themes.

First, the paper recognises that economic growth is not to be pursued for its own sake. It is best conceived of not as an objective in its own right but as the likely *result* of policies directed to improving the welfare of the community without using resources wastefully. Secondly, and that observation notwithstanding, it suggests that those who question economic growth on the grounds that it means increasing pollution are attacking growth rather than pollution itself. Thirdly, and generalising that particular theme, the paper suggests that much of the debate on the relationships between growth and the environment originates in a confusion between economic growth and its conventional statistical indicator – the increase in gross domestic product at constant prices. Fourthly, the paper takes issue with the view put forward by some commentators that economic growth should be slowed or brought to a halt because, in their opinion, the world is running out of resources. Finally, the paper suggests that some of the objections which are said to be to 'growth' are, in fact, objections to the prevailing pattern of growth – that is, they are really arguments over priorities.

The paper, in concluding, puts forward the view that if what 'economic growth' is all about is carefully examined, it seems to constitute the key to achieving many of the things going to make up the national wellbeing.

Part 1: Growth under challenge

> No one can doubt that there are differences in social attitudes among countries – in the relative value placed on work and leisure, on money making, on duty and discipline – which cannot help but affect the rate

1 First published in June 1973 as Treasury Economic Paper 2. The editors of this volume have taken the liberty of re-publishing the paper with Castles identified as the main author as Ian Castles is known to have led the Australian Treasury team which prepared it. Except where otherwise indicated, all figures and tables in this chapter are Castles' own.

> of economic growth. Australians, though no more consistent in their demands on life than other people, have for long leaned towards the view which has recently found increasing favour also in other countries, that economic growth is not everything. (OECD Economic Surveys: Australia, December 1972: 28.)

I

All over the world, in developed and developing countries, alike, there was by the middle of the 1960s an intensive concern with rates of increase in the gross national product at constant prices. Differences in this measure, over time and between countries, were subject to the most minute examination.

No single statistic had ever claimed such attention. It became a standard against which almost all aspects of economic performance were judged. A low ranking on the international growth 'league ladder' was regarded as a sign of national failure, reflecting not only upon the performance of a country's economy but on the whole condition of its society. A high place, by contrast, connoted not merely enlightened economic management and a rapid rate of improvement in overall efficiency; it demonstrated a progress towards a higher destiny. It was the heyday of what came to be called 'growthmanship'.

In the 1970s a different view has increasingly been heard. Though economic growth remains an important object of concern of national governments in all countries, and in its broadest sense retains much of its 'grass roots' support among people generally, it is under increasingly strong attack by articulate and influential minorities. It is held to be responsible for many of the ills of modern industrial society – for the increasing pace and pressure of urban living and for the co-existence of 'private affluence and public squalor'; for the creation of 'imagined' wants rather than the satisfaction of 'real' needs; for the relentless exploitation of the earth's non-renewable resources; for poisoning of the air and waters; for despoliation of the environment and threats to the biosphere; for ugliness, materialism and acquisitiveness; for crime, violence and drug addiction; and for a variety of other problems and failings.

As discussion has proceeded those who see problems (and solutions) in over-simple terms have gained a good deal of attention. The persuasive effect of such opinions is magnified by the dire consequences that are foretold if they are not heeded. There is irony in the fact that a decade ago a very different viewpoint held sway.

Ten years ago there was a view that if a country failed to keep up with the international Jones' in the growth league tables, there was clearly something amiss. 'Projections showed' that by the end of the century – perhaps earlier – it would be an object of international derision, dependent on the favours of the pace-maker countries which would increasingly dominate the world economy. To avoid such humiliation, it was necessary to push up savings, force-feed investment, subsidise exports and steer resources towards those industries in which statistically measured productivity growth was higher.

Now, however, measures to the contrary are urged by many. Their claim is that the rations on 'spaceship Earth' will soon be running low and that only urgent and drastic action can avert ecological catastrophe. Internationally, the most widely publicised of such predictions have been those contained in '*The Limits to Growth*', a study sponsored by the Club of Rome and conducted by a team at the Massachusetts Institute of Technology which was published in March 1972.[2] This concluded that there was an urgent need to bring about a deliberate, controlled end to growth; the Executive Committee of the Club of Rome commented that '...only the conviction that there is no other avenue to survival can liberate the moral, intellectual, and creative forces required to initiate this unprecedented human undertaking'.[3]

'*The Limits to Growth*' has aroused widespread controversy and many aspects of the study and, more importantly, its basic thesis have been subjected to exceedingly damaging criticism.[4] But that criticism has been little publicised. Certainly, it has received nothing like the attention that was aroused in the dramatic predictions and prescriptions of the original study, or by other writings claiming that an early end to growth is imperative if mankind is to survive.[5]

The purpose of this paper is to reassess the objective of economic growth in the light of these changes in attitudes. Eight years ago, an earlier Treasury paper discussed the meaning and measurement of economic growth and, in the process of doing so, sought to point out some of the cruder fallacies of the 'growthmanship' school with a view to clarifying debate.[6] Now that the intellectual pendulum has swung so far in the other direction, it may be no more than timely to examine whether indeed the swing may not have carried too far.

Accordingly, this paper is primarily concerned with the worth of growth. It discusses such questions as: Is continuing economic growth a curse rather than a blessing, as the more extreme of its latter-day critics would claim? Would some cutback in the growth in output per head be desirable? Is there a necessary conflict between increases in output and improvements in what is often termed

2 DH Meadows and others, *The Limits to Growth: A Report for the Club of Rome's Project on the Predicament of Mankind*, (New York, 1972).

3 *Ibid*: 196.

4 See, for example, Report on *The Limits to Growth: A Study by a Special Task Force of the World Bank* (Washington, September 1972) and W Beckerman 'Economists, Scientists and Environmental Catastrophe' *Oxford Economic Papers*, November 1972: 327-344.

5 For example, 'A Blueprint for Survival', the *Ecologist*, London, January 1972, now available in paperback, has also attracted great attention.

6 *Supplement to the Treasury Information Bulletin: the Meaning and Measurement of Economic Growth*, (November 1964).

the 'quality of life'? Does *measured* economic growth (output at constant prices) provide a policy guide to increased efficiency in meeting the wants of the community? Given that the world's resources are finite, is not the real question one of the practicability of continued growth, rather than of its desirability? To the extent that the pursuit of growth conflicts with other national goals, what should guide decisions involving priorities between competing goals, and by whom should such decisions be made?

II

If the extreme differences in attitude commented on in the preceding pages resulted entirely from differing value judgements about the end purposes of society, the prospects of achieving consensus on community goals would appear slim. The very thing which to many represents 'progress' would be contested by many others as 'regress'.[7]

Fortunately there is a less depressing possibility. The differing attitudes to growth may arise in part – perhaps in large part – from differing beliefs or judgements on matters of *fact*, including the casual relationships which exist between economic growth and the results which it is desired either to avoid or achieve. If so, there is scope for discussion of the kind attempted here.

In short, there will always be differences of opinion on such basic questions as the emphasis to be assigned to economic growth; but it is worthwhile seeking to narrow the areas of disagreement to those that necessarily arise from fundamental differences of philosophical outlook about the proper pursuits of society.

III

The overall growth in economic activity is, of course, the compounded outcome of growth in population and the growth of economic activity *per capita*. This paper is concerned with economic growth as a *per capita* concept. Growth in total is a related concern to the degree that it may affect *per capita* output, directly or indirectly.[8]

Policies antagonistic to *per capita* economic growth are often linked with policies of population control. For an advanced economy such as Australia, the relationship of population growth to growth in output *per capita* is complex and

---

7 'Consensus' can never be more than approximate, and opinions will inevitably differ as to the desirability of particular objectives and courses of action. But the difficulties are moderated in most areas by the fact that disagreements are relative rather than absolute – e.g. should *more* or *fewer* resources be devoted to defence, education, environmental protection, etc?

8 Economic activities, whether industrial or social (e.g. engineering or education), may gain economies from the expansion of the domestic market and, thereby, tend to raise living standards.

by no means clear. For the 'third world', by contrast, the relevant relationship is all too simple; declining death rates are an almost certain consequence of growth, but corresponding declines in birth rates are far from certain and in any case tend to occur after a long time lag. Experience in the advanced economies does suggest that eventually the processes of industrialisation, organisation and education that are associated with growth tend to bring reproduction rates down to (or close to) replacement levels.[9] But even if this were certain to happen ultimately in the developing countries, their populations would continue to increase rapidly for many decades. Those governments in the 'third world' who strongly favour positive population policies also strongly favour *per capita* economic growth. Indeed the rationale of the first is to assist in the achievement of the second. It is only in some advanced economies that both population growth *and* economic growth *per capita* are under challenge.

In some advanced economies which (unlike Australia) have very high population densities, there is rising concern about rates of increase in population which are in reality quite slow. Other natural resources can be imported, and even water can be obtained (at an extra cost) from the sea. But *space* is a resource which many see as ultimately imposing limits on more intensive use. 'Crowding' comes not only from increased numbers but also from increased mobility and the use of space that goes with that. In these countries, policies of zero population growth are attracting increasing attention, and are sometimes supplemented by proposals to restrict 'economic growth' *per capita* because of the space-consuming pattern of growth.[10]

But what has changed the flavour of debate of these matters is the series of predictions of global disaster, of which last year's report for the Club of Rome has merely been the most conspicuous example. These predictions see continuing economic growth (whether from population growth or growth in output *per capita*) coming up against constraints such as an inexorable increase in pollution or rapid depletion of non-renewable resources.

Such views implicitly involve assumptions about the capacity of communities to change the pattern of economic growth and about the predictability of resource availability and technology.[11] It is to the substance of these assumptions that this paper addresses itself.

---

9 For example, reproduction rates are at present roughly equivalent to replacement levels in the United States, Britain and a number of countries in Western Europe. If the current rates were to be sustained over a prolonged period, natural increase in these countries would ultimately decline to zero.

10 The relationship between economic growth and the consumption of space is a flexible one. However, the assumption that it cannot be flexible sometimes appears to underlie discussion and is analogous to an assumption about the relationship between economic growth and pollution which is considered in Part 2. Various interest groups have very different views about the way in which space should be utilised, and these differences in desired purposes have a large bearing on the relative 'supply' of space.

11 Predictability of resource availability and technology must underlie questions about the possibility of determining an 'optimum' population.

The first subject considered is the relationship between economic growth and environmental problems. It is often supposed that there is an inexorable connection between growth in economic activity and in environmental pollution. On this view, further economic growth will necessarily lead to more and more pollution and, eventually, to environmental catastrophe. Even some of those who take a less apocalyptic view have real doubts whether further rises in *per capita* output of goods and services will improve the community's wellbeing. Is there any point, they ask, in winning more goods and services when the process which makes this possible destroys the pleasant conditions of life which are essential for their enjoyment?

It will be suggested in Part 2 that the premise that increases in output of goods and services must *necessarily* be accompanied by corresponding increases in pollution is mistaken. Relationships between output and pollution can readily be changed if society has the will to do so. Such changes can make a far greater contribution to reducing pollution than measures designed to halt or slow down the rate of economic growth.

Part 3 explores the relationships between economic growth and national 'wellbeing'. It points out that the most commonly used indicator of economic growth – the rate of increase in the gross domestic product (GDP) at constant prices[12] – is not a comprehensive measure of changes in the welfare or wellbeing of the community. Hence, some of the alleged conflicts between economic growth and other goals only arise if the substance of growth is identified with its conventional statistical shadow. The fact that such an identification has frequently been made has confused discussion.

Part 3 suggests that economic and social policies should not be directed towards achieving any particular statistical rate of growth in the longer-run, but rather to the efficient use of available resources to establish and maintain those patterns of production and distribution which conform most closely to the preferences of the community. This is a simple statement which begs some important questions; and, however carefully the objective is defined, it could never be achieved except in the most approximate and by and large fashion. But the important point in the present context is that to set up a longer-term target rate of growth in GDP – whether that rate be a high one or, as some are now advocating, a 'zero' rate – is to miss the point. The criteria for decision-making must be related not to the achievement of a pre-ordained statistical result but to the desires of the community, as expressed by people in their capacities as consumers, workers and electors.

12 The more familiar term, which has been used until recently in the Australian National Accounts, is the gross national product (GNP) at constant prices. The change in terminology is part of a restructuring by the Commonwealth Statistician to place the Australian national accounting system on a broadly similar basis to the United Nations System of National Accounts (SNA).

The third and last of the particular problems to be discussed is that of the depletion of non-renewable (i.e. mineral) resources. The report for the Club of Rome, to which reference has already been made, has intensified concern about this topic. Predictions that the availability of mineral resources to sustain growth is limited to a few decades are being made with increasing frequency. If there were strong grounds for believing such predictions, many would doubtless agree that the present generation should put a stop to growth and delay a global crisis as long as possible. Again, the main dispute is not on the value judgement about what should be done if resources are running out, but on the question of fact. Is there a danger that non-renewable resources will be seriously depleted in the foreseeable future?

It will be suggested in Part 4 that there is no way of defining practicable physical limits to non-renewable resources. Availability of resources in the long-term future depends rather on the overall *demands* on resources and the technical responses induced by those demands. Such responses are an integral part of the growth process. In a real sense, technical progress 'creates' resources, so that the faster and further growth continues, the greater the availability of resources (at a given real cost) will be. If this overall view were accepted, it would obviously be wrong to advocate checking economic growth in order to conserve resources for future generations.

The concluding Part reflects on certain fundamental issues, such as the social forces underpinning economic growth, which are suggested by the more technical discussions earlier in the paper. Its purpose is to shed light on certain basic national questions, not to attempt definitive answers to those questions.

IV

Before turning to the specific growth-related issues to be discussed in the succeeding Parts of this paper, it may be useful to make some preliminary observations about the place of economic growth in relation to the objectives of society generally.

Economic growth is a stated objective of national policy in most countries. But, there are dangers of misinterpretation in the description of growth as an 'objective' or a 'goal'.

> ...we might go so far as to suggest that economic growth *per se* should be jettisoned as an independent goal of policy. For if we are concerned primarily with social welfare, those forms of economic growth that meet our welfare criteria will in any case be approved and adopted, the remainder being rejected: thus, sources of worthwhile economic growth will continue to be sought after.[13]

13 EJ Misham, *The Costs of Economic Growth*, (London 1969) paperback edition: 65.

Whether economic growth should properly be described as a goal appears to be basically a question of presentation rather than of substance. To describe growth in this way can often be a convenient abstraction, an aid to exposition. Nevertheless, what ought to be an intellectual tool can sometimes become identified with reality in the course of debate. In the process, there is a risk that the *interdependence* of economic, social and technological goals will be disregarded.

Obviously the pursuit of growth for its own sake misses the point: the aim must be to improve the welfare of the community. Policies directed to this latter end are likely in fact to lead to increases in the real output of the economic system per head of population and can thus fairly be described – without abuse of language – as policies for economic growth. But there are obvious possibilities for confusion and misunderstanding here, particularly when economic growth is identified with growth in statistical measures of output such as the gross domestic product at constant prices. More will be said about this in Part 3.

V

This leads to another important distinction which should be made at this stage, though its full significance will only become apparent later. This is that the boundaries of the 'economic problem' – the problem of allocating scarce means to plentiful but competing ends – coincide neither with the market economy nor with that part of the output of the economic system which GDP seeks to measure. Economic decisions cover a wider area than either.

The truth of this has been obscured for various reasons. Not least of these has been the tendency for the phrase 'quality of life' to be used very loosely.[14] In current usage the phrase appears to cover a miscellany of desirable things not recognised, or not adequately recognised, in the marketplace. It compounds at least two sorts of things. First, there are such things as personal and family relationships, civil liberties, compassion, justice, freedom, fair play – all the qualities of a civilised society which cannot readily be valued or measured. Secondly, there are such things as the enjoyment of wilderness, wildlife, clean air and water, recreation, health and education – desirable 'goods' which are the resources of the community. Often the term 'quality of life' gives to the second category of things an aura that more properly belongs to the first.

The discussion which follows will emphasise the importance of evaluating environmental and other social 'goods' so that they can be properly related to other goods and services which make demands upon resources. To attempt to

14 The same thing had, of course, happened to the term 'economic growth'. Professor James Tobin wrote in 1964: 'Growth has become a good word. And the better a word becomes, the more it is invoked to bless a variety of causes and the more it loses specific meaning'. 'Economic Growth as an Objective of Government Policy', *American Economic Review, Papers and Proceedings (1964): 1.*

quantify the worth of social goods in this way is not to 'commercialise' them or to scrutinise them by the standards of a 'production ethic'. It is simply to acknowledge that there are competing ends for resources, and that some way has to be found of sorting out how worthwhile any one aim is in terms of its competitors.

VI

Assessment of the feasibility and desirability of public projects or programs, or government decisions following such assessments should, in principle, take into account the whole spectrum of effects on the community. Individuals do not, of course, only look to income return on their work efforts but to such things as personal security, work satisfaction, good health, pleasant surroundings recreational opportunities, and so on. In a similar way governments will attempt to take social valuations into account in the appraisal of projects. The effects of some of these things are difficult to quantify or incorporate formally in analyses, though there is no dispute about the desirability of doing so to the greatest extent possible. 'Environmental impact' statements have an important potential role to play in this respect.[15] Much of the effort being made in many countries to develop and refine techniques to aid the decision-making process in the public sector (cost-benefit analysis, cost effectiveness evaluations, etc.) is directed to devising means of bringing into account *all* of the costs and benefits of decisions – whether economic or non-economic, tangible or intangible, social, strategic, aesthetic or environmental.

> ...there will be some cases in which non-economic considerations are indisputably relevant, in which case, however, the weight to be attached to them is a matter for the decision-maker. To take a highly simplified example, it would obviously be difficult in a benefit-cost study to weight the marring of a scenic reserve, an increase in national product by a given amount, and a reduction of two road deaths per year, all of which are expected to result from the construction of a highway. The function of benefit-cost studies in such circumstances is to illuminate the choices underlying the decisions to be taken, by highlighting the cost of one objective in terms of others or possibly, in some cases, pointing towards the desirability of redesigning the projects.[16]

The key point is that all decisions *imply* a valuation of those effects which are difficult to quantify. If such effects have been ignored entirely, their implied

15 The Australian Government has decided that such statements will be mandatory from 1 January 1974 in respect of proposals having significant environmental consequences and where Commonwealth funds are involved and/or where Commonwealth constitutional power is involved.

16 *Supplement to the Treasury Information Bulletin: Investment Analysis*, (July 1966): 16.

value is nil (which would almost certainly be wrong). If a decision is made to proceed with a project which would not otherwise be regarded as viable because, for example, there are strategic benefits, a value has been placed – explicitly or implicitly – on those benefits. Conversely, if a decision is made *not* to proceed with a project because of its undesirable environmental effects, a judgement has been made – explicitly or implicitly – *about* the value to be gained from avoiding those effects. The greater the effort to quantify and to make such judgements explicit, the more rational and consistent will the decision-making process become.[17] The same broad approach is required when the object of investigation is a private sector activity which is imposing costs upon others, through pollution for example.

In short, the level, pattern and rate of growth of national economic activity reflect the outcome of decisions, by individuals and by governments which take into account a great variety of goals. Of course, depending on the prevailing national ethos, some objectives will be pursued more actively and visibly than others. As the ethos changes so will the various valuations – the weight which is effectively given to each of the objectives. In particular, as levels of income rise beyond that needed to satisfy basic needs such as food, clothing and shelter, attention turns increasingly towards less immediately material components of human wants.

An obvious example of this phenomenon is the current concern with the effect of pollution in its various forms on human life and on the environment. It is to this subject that we now turn.

Part 2: Growth and the environment

> ...and most importantly, the elimination of 'bads' contributes to economic growth just as does the production of goods, and both activities require the utilization of human and material resources. The choice is not between economic growth and a pleasant environment, but between the various ends to which economic growth – which, fundamentally, means greater capacity to do what we would wish to do – can be directed.[18]

---

17 The criticism is sometimes made – and not without justification – that there is a tendency in analytical evaluation to give too much weight to those effects that are more easily quantified. On the other hand inability or failure to quantify some effects at the analytical stage can often mean that those effects are *over*-weighted in the decision-making process. These are not so much criticisms of the techniques themselves, but rather of how they may be applied in practice.

18 RM Parish: 'Economic Aspects of Pollution Control', 1971 Autumn Forum, Economic Society of Australia and New Zealand, Reprinted in *The Australian Economy*, HW Arndt and AH Boxer, (eds), (Melbourne 1972): 535.

I

Pollution and environmental damage are seen by many as a relentless consequence of economic growth. Though material progress has brought improvements in standards of hygiene and the removal of pollution in its grosser and more obvious forms, it has also been associated with subtler and more insidious types of environmental damage. In the most advanced economies, the engines of industrialism fog the air with irritant gases, and make lakes moribund with decaying wastes; ears are assaulted by lawnmowers, cars, motor cycles, aeroplanes and construction equipment; and farmers may disperse poisons which cumulate potently in the bodies of animals, including Man. It is scarcely a matter for surprise that there is increasing support for action to proscribe activities that degrade the environment and – at the extreme – for action to put a stop to the process of growth that some see as the root cause of the damage.

Yet most people still want to be better off, even in relatively wealthy countries such as Australia. They have many pressing wants, of which the desire for a cleaner and quieter environment is only one, and one the relative importance of which differs greatly from one person to another. It would be a grim choice if hopes for improvement in all other directions had to be sacrificed to this one end – especially as a complete halt to growth would not itself be a remedy for pollution, but at best a palliative that might prevent the problem getting any worse.[19] But is the demand for a better environment necessarily in conflict with continuing economic growth? Or can further growth play a part in satisfying the totality of the material desires of society, including the desire for a healthier and more pleasing environment in which people can live, work and play?

II

It was mentioned in the first Part that the goals of an advancing community are not solely pecuniary. This is shown in such historical trends as the taking out of some part of the benefits of rising productivity in increased leisure. Why then, it may be asked, has there been so little apparent interest – at least until very recently – in taking out more of the benefits of economic growth in environmental improvement or, at the least, in minimising the environmental damage attributable to economic activity?

This is a difficult question to answer fully but some contributory factors can be identified readily enough.

First, there has been a lack of knowledge and appreciation of the complexity and seriousness of environmental problems. Few have recognised the intricacies

19 Some problems would in fact continue to grow even if output remained constant, because of the long-delayed cumulative effects of many pollutants.

of ecological balance: for example, that bacteria which decompose sewage disposed into rivers may make such demands on available oxygen as to kill off their aquatic life. With greater knowledge of such problems has come a widespread belief that they cannot be ignored.

Secondly, it is only the increasing scale and concentration of economic activity that make some types of pollution a matter for concern. The assimilative capacity of the environment is not taxed by sparse development over large areas, but by intensive and concentrated development. That is why the most acute problems have arisen in and around the huge 'megalopolises' of Europe, North America and Japan; and why Australia's pollution problems have first shown up around our largest cities.

Thirdly, the quality of the environment naturally acquires a higher priority as a society becomes more affluent. It still has a low place in most developing countries, where resources for pollution abatement could only be found at the expense of people's most basic needs for food, clothing and shelter. Moreover, in those countries the grosser and more direct forms of pollution which material progress has removed in the more affluent countries, persist in some degree and it is to material progress that such countries have to look for improvement.

Finally, there is a key point which largely follows from the three already mentioned. The lack of knowledge of many environmental problems in the past, the relatively limited adverse impact of pollutant emissions when they were within the environment's assimilative capacity and the pre-occupation of governments with more pressing economic and social problems, have meant that most governments have not created the conditions in which community preferences for a clean environment could be properly taken into account when consumers and producers were making decisions affecting the composition of output and the techniques of production. Polluters 'use up' the community's resources of pure air, clean water, etc., but in general they have not had to pay for these resources. Unless polluters are induced to take into account the harm they do to society by being obliged to bear the *full* costs of their actions and not just the 'private' costs, insufficient resources will continue to be devoted to avoiding or remedying pollution.[20]

This is a matter of central significance to the argument of this Part of the paper and, indeed, to the subject of this paper as a whole. Efficient economic growth requires that available resources, which include air, water and the natural environment generally, be put to their 'best' use, which means - to anticipate discussion - the use which enables people to have most of what they want.

20 This is not of course, a proposition that economists have suddenly discovered in an effort to rationalise pursuit of economic growth. The approach briefly outlined here (including its application to pollution problems) was outlined by AC Pigou in *The Economics of Welfare,* first published in 1920. A basic thesis of that book was that the private and social costs of any productive process may differ and that, where this is so, they should be brought into equality by Government action (e.g. taxation).

Since resources are not unlimited, their use must be regulated either by the resource-user paying a price or by direct regulation. The services of labour, for example, are not available to employers except at costs which reflect both market conditions and the regulatory activities of governments and their authorities. Similarly, the services of land and other productive facilities must be bought from those in whom the property rights are vested by law. But no charge is customarily made for the use of environmental resources - of the air and of rivers, lakes and oceans. Wastes can be ejected into the environment at no cost to the waste-maker. It is hardly to be wondered at that the result has been escessive levels of pollution. *Any resource will be grossly over-used if its use is unrestricted and no charge is made for it.*[21]

This is the crux of the matter. Pollution problems are mainly attributable not to economic growth *per se*, but to the economic conditions under which growth has been allowed to take place. It follows that the proper *remedy for pollution problems is not to halt growth or slow it down, but to change the conditions under which producers and consumers are allowed free and unrestricted use of the 'shared resources' of the environment*. It will be shown that this is by no means a simple matter, either in principle or in application. But first it is necessary to consider the alternative prescription for environment problems - to curb future rises in output, or at the least to prevent rises in output having anything like the composition that has prevailed in the past.

III

Probably the most extreme opponents of growth are those who accept the tentative suggestions by some scientists that certain almost inescapable by–products of economic activity – notably heat and carbon dioxide – have pollutive effects that could wreak death and destruction on a global scale. There is, for example, the possible 'greenhouse' effect of increased carbon dioxide in the atmosphere: the sun's rays penetrate such a polluted atmosphere, but heat radiation from the earth is less able to. The theory is that as the volume of fossil fuels consumed goes up and deforestation spreads, by the early decades of next century there might be such a rise in world temperature as to melt the polar ice caps and inundate the world's great coastal cities. In the past thirty years the world's temperature has been falling but this appears to be due to other atmospheric pollutants – dust, soot and gas: and it is argued that in certain circumstances this thickening of the atmosphere could reinforce the 'greenhouse' effect.

21 Unless the resources concerned are available in virtually unlimited quantities. This is not true of environmental resources, though it could be said to have been approximately true when the total use of such resources did not tax assimilative capacities.

These theories and predictions cannot be evaluated here; they are a subject of uncertainty and dissension amongst scientists.[22] Probably the main point to be made is that the prospective scale of man's economic activities is so great that the atmosphere might some day be polluted sufficiently to produce major climatic changes. But until the relationship between pollution and climates can be further clarified, there can scarcely be said to be a case for checking economic growth on these uncertain grounds. Moreover, were the 'greenhouse' or some other effect found to be established, the change in temperature would presumably be slow enough to enable a major switch in resources – for example, from the combustion of fossil fuels to the use of nuclear or solar energy – without undue disruption to the path of growth. It is possible or even likely, in fact, that changes of the kind required will be made in any case, for other reasons than the need to avoid the possibility of global climatic disruption.[23]

Scientific speculations of this kind about possible distant catastrophes do however appear to reinforce viewpoints already hostile to continued growth on other grounds relating to its alleged pollutive effects. A number of arguments are advanced for such views.

First, it is said that higher levels of economic activity might transform an otherwise controllable problem into one that is quite unmanageable. If increased economic activity increases the concentration of pollutants within a given space, higher pollution control standards may be required and at more than proportional cost. There is an implicit assumption that technical advances will not counter any such trend. Secondly, there is the idea that the inter-relations of events (particularly organic events) is such that the 'solution' of one problem only leads on to the generation of another. For example, mercurial compounds were developed to protect seed from fungi, and were thought to be disposable into rivers and lakes without harm but mud bacteria unexpectedly converted the supposedly inert compounds to lethal and persistent methyl mercury, which increases in concentration as it passes up the food chain to man. Such examples can lead to a distrust of technical progress and the growth in output which such progress makes possible. Thirdly, there is the belief that nothing effective

---

22 The United Kingdom Royal Commission on Environmental Pollution, in its *First Report* (HMSO, February 1971) considered that, on plausible assumptions, the 'greenhouse effect' might cause a warming of the atmosphere at the earth's surface by about 0.1 to 0.2 degrees centigrade in thirty years time. The Commission added 'such a rise in temperature is unlikely to be significant. These figures are tentative, and cannot become more precise until more advanced mathematical models of the problem have been developed' (37).

23 There is a further side-effect of energy use which arises from the fact that all energy generated must ultimately be dissipated as heat. If the source is something other than solar energy – potentially an important qualification in the very long-run – that heat will warm the atmosphere, directly or indirectly. But the *global* effect is very slight indeed, and the *First Report of the (UK) Royal Commission on Environmental Pollution* stated that 'it seems clear that it will be a very long time before direct thermal pollution of the environment reaches the point at which it could have a detectable effect on world climate' *(op cit.*: 41). Local climatic effects would be more significant, a factor that might eventually need to be taken into account in decisions affecting industrial location.

will be done about pollution – that industrialists will resist the imposition by governments of effective standards, and that the man in the street is not prepared to pay up either as consumer or taxpayer. Fourthly, there is an attitude that seems to be merely a semantic confusion, but is influential nevertheless; it identifies 'economic growth' with the growth of the composite measure known as Gross Domestic Product (GDP). Because environmental quality does not enter into the calculation of that composite – as to the significance of which, see the next Part – it is supposed that there is an inevitable conflict between the two.

These views on the environment are often associated with a more fundamental attitude: that which puts a low value on the products of an industrial society as such. Industrial society is seen not only as satisfying man's wants but also as shaping them. Defenders of industrialisation have seen economic advancement as the means whereby men may escape from the thrall of a life 'nasty, brutish and short', and as holding out the possibility of a high civilisation participated in by all. But the more critical view referred to sees the process of advancement as forever frustrating such an achievement by becoming an end in itself and leading onto the compulsive acquisition of 'things' –fanciful substitutes and elaborate junk that are usually trivial and often ludicrous. Whatever the validity of this view more will be said about it later – it would explain why some critics are undismayed by the costs of slowing or halting economic growth as methods of checking pollution or preserving natural features.

This radical revaluation of industrial society aside, it is important to see that there is no logical inevitability about the connection between continued economic growth and the effects that the opponents of further growth are seeking to avoid. Implicit in the other views noted are all kinds of challengeable judgements. Does pollution abatement require that cars need to be equipped with several hundred dollars worth of extra equipment or abolished altogether? Are the risks of *possible* unanticipated consequences arising from particular technical advances significant enough to justify forgoing the *certain* benefits? Would the large-scale re-organisation of society required to curb growth encounter less resistance than specific measures to counter pollution?

These are large questions, and there are (and will continue to be) differing opinions about the answers. For the present purpose it is sufficient to note that it is possible to take up a position – which is the position of this paper – that fully acknowledges the technical relations between events (for example, inorganic fertilisers boosting productivity on farms, but running off into rivers and atrophying them), but which sees pollution abatement as involving a modest – even small – redistribution of resources, and relatively minor changes in the prevailing pattern of production. It is to the means of achieving these required changes that we now turn.

IV

Contemporary environmental deterioration takes a bewildering variety of forms, but noise may be taken – for various reasons – as symbolic of the problem as a whole. It has required high technological advance in order to produce it on the current scale; its effects on hearing, nervous tension and physical vigour, especially over a long period, have only recently come to be appreciated; it is pervasive and difficult to escape; and its creators, whether they be operators of jet airliners or jackhammers, will not take on the extra cost of suppressing their screechings and bangings as long as there is no charge for perpetrating them.

Let us assume, for the sake of illustration, that the noise of compressors used in construction can be reduced to about one per cent of its present intensity by the use of equipment that costs about ten to 15 per cent more.[24] It will be assumed that there are not laws governing permissible levels of noise from construction equipment. Then a normally profit conscious operator, confronted with the choice between two compressors of equal specifications except that one is noisier but cheaper than the other, will obviously buy the equipment that costs him less. He will not take into his reckoning the cost which the noisier compressor imposes, on others, but only the costs which he must bear. He will justify his decision by pointing to the lower cost (of the work involved) which his decision has made possible and, of course, his need to match the tender prices of his competitors who are making their decisions on the same basis.

This is the key point for those who do not see growth of output, of itself, as the cause of pollution problems. Individual decision-makers, be they producers or consumers, do not necessarily have to pay a price for what they buy which reflects the full costs (the costs to society) of the action they have taken. The market prices are 'wrong'. Moreover the deficiency, being inherent in the unregulated working of the market system itself, *occurs independently of the rate at which the economy which that system regulates is growing*.[25]

Thus the cure to the conflict which some see between growth and pollution control lies not in restricting growth but in eliminating divergences between the private costs and full (i.e. social) costs arising from particular decisions. This may not be easy – indeed it may not be possible in any precise way – but it is clearly the right approach.

If laws (with appropriate penalties) are introduced regulating levels of noise from construction equipment, the operator of a compressor would have to take

24 This is stated to be the case in the *Second Annual Report* of the (US) *Council on Environmental Quality* (Washington 1971): 102.

25 That is, a stationary or 'no growth' economy will generate excessive pollution just as a growing economy will, unless action has been taken to eliminate divergences between private and social costs. The proportion of resources devoted to pollution control will be too small in both cases.

account of those laws in the choice of his equipment.[26] The 'right' level of noise pollution to be permitted would of course be a matter of `judgement', to be based on study of the social costs involved at various levels. Depending upon the level chosen and the additional cost of providing equipment to conform to that specification, there would, of course, be a rise in building costs and probably a slowing effect on economic growth as conventionally conceived. The rate of improvement in welfare, however, would not be slowed – the increased cost of building would be offset by the decreased 'cost' of noise. Note, however, that had the attack been on economic growth as such rather than its pollution effects, the noise would have been done away with only by not constructing the building at all – a classic example of throwing out the baby with the bathwater.

V

To some the notion that there is a 'right' level of pollution other than zero may seem repugnant. Should not the aim be the *elimination* of pollution, rather than its controlled reduction?

Superficially, such an objective may appear attractive. In fact, it involves the implicit assumption that the most productive use of resources for any purpose other than pollution reduction could never yield as great a return as the least productive use of resources in reducing pollution. Such an assumption needs only to be spelled out for its unacceptability to be clearly evident. The problem of applying available resources to best meet society's needs cannot be avoided by setting up absolutes to which unlimited resources must be directed irrespective of the return on those resources.

To return to the compressor illustration, it might be technically possible to develop a machine that reduced the noise level further – from one per cent of the present level to one-hundredth of one per cent. But the additional cost of compressors, and therefore of construction activities, would be substantial, while the additional benefits of being closer to total silence would be negligible. The community would be better off if resources were applied to some other purpose than the replacement of very quiet compressors by silent ones.

The point still applies even to those forms of pollution which more obviously affect human health. In such cases governments have been more active over a long period, and have understandably insisted that no one has the right to take actions which impose *undue* risks on the health (sometimes the lives) of others. Yet the very presence of the word 'undue' exposes the fact that the problem is still implicitly a cost/benefit one – the balancing of risks against the costs of reducing or eliminating them. There is always a gap between what is desirable

---

26 Regulation is not the only form of pollution control, nor is it necessarily preferable to measures which utilise the market. See pages 126-128.

and what is possible, and it arises because, at any point in time, resources are not unlimited. There must be some limitation since damage to life and health from other causes can also be reduced (at cost), and there is also the alternative of using the resources to provide a more satisfying existence in other ways. It may not, of course, be human life itself that is at stake but the refreshment of the human spirit that comes from close contact with nature. However, the preservation of a piece of woodland of moving natural beauty, 'priceless' though it appears, must contend for its claim on resources with alternative uses: on hospitals, schools or even less honorific avenues. Skies unsmudged by smoke and waters sparklingly pure are desiderata but their achievement may frustrate other aims.[27]

If degradation of the environment is to be prevented some of society's resources must be diverted from other tasks. Whether these resources are applied in ways known under existing technology or to solve hitherto unsolved problems, they could have been used for some other purpose. In the language of economics, their use to improve the environment incurs a cost to society which is equal to the good which those same resources could have achieved in their most beneficial alternative employment; but there is also, of course, a *benefit* to society represented by the greater enjoyment which people will derive from an environment of higher quality. The principles of resource allocation are no less applicable to environmental improvement than to any other aspect of the economic problem. Those principles decree that society will be best served if resources are applied to pollution abatement to, but not beyond, the point where the costs of doing so are covered by the benefits derived.

That is a technical and very general proposition, and it is scarcely necessary to add that, like most sound advice, it is more easily stated than applied. In fact, the application is so much more difficult than the theory that some might doubt whether the theory has any practical value at all.

It may therefore be worth recalling what was said in the previous Part I about the proper basis of decision-making: all decisions imply a valuation of those effects which are difficult to quantify, so that there is point in exposing implicit valuations and distinguishing objective factors from value judgements. It is true that many of the benefits to be derived from devoting more resources to environmental improvement defy valuation at all, let alone any precise measurement. How can a value be placed upon clean air and streams, upon unspoiled countryside and the preservation of natural systems? The problems

27 'To listen to some scientists on the question of water pollution, for example, one gets the firm impression that they regard the proper object of policy as being to eliminate pollution entirely, and the costs side of the story enters into it only in so far as it means that they have difficulty in achieving this objective. But even if the funds were to be made available, I, for one, have no wish to spend thousands of millions of pounds on what would be, in effect, the conversion of all our rivers into beautiful open-air swimming pools for fish. I live in a town where there are not even adequate swimming pool facilities for humans' Beckerman, *op cit*: 331.

are compounded by other facts: that individual valuations will differ greatly,[28] that the effects of many actions only come to light after a long time lag, and that many decisions once made are irrevocable – what is lost is lost for all time.

Yet, for all that, the difficulties are not obviously more daunting than those which face governments in other areas. What values are to be placed on improving preschool education, seeking a cure for cancer, developing the national opera? Decisions must be made, however arguable their basis may be; and, having been made, there is much to be gained from ensuring that resources are not used wastefully for the achievement of these purposes. In the use of resources there can be no absolutes: *every purpose, no matter how over-riding it may appear to be, is ultimately in competition with every other*.

VI

The question of how the use of resources to protect and improve the environment is to be reconciled with the competing demands on resources to satisfy people's other desires – for food, clothing, entertainment, defence, health services and so on – raises complex technical issues. The general nature of these issues will be indicated briefly in this section, but it is worth mentioning at the outset that the discussion is concerned essentially with matters of *technique*. Those who are content to accept that there are devices to facilitate decision-making processes in this area may prefer to move straight on to the next section.

So far as public sector projects are concerned, the key point is that the framework of evaluation of such projects or programs must incorporate environmental factors, whether or not it is possible to quantify these factors and charge or credit them to the project. Reference has already been made to the role of 'environmental impact' statements in this respect. There are many non-environmental considerations entering into the assessment of public expenditure proposals which involve large subjective judgements – judgements about relative prices in the long-term future, about the directions of technological change, or about the value to be placed on leisure time or on reducing accidents.[29] That there are formidable problems in measuring or quantifying environmental factors is not a reason for abandoning or ignoring the techniques which have been developed to evaluate public sector decisions.[30]

---

28 There are clean air, clear streams and unspoiled natural environment to be found in Australia – most people, however, prefer to live in urban areas. That is, they value the higher incomes and social amenities to be found in those areas above the life of 'the noble savage'.

29 This arises in the evaluation of road projects, for example.

30 '...the difficulties of obtaining precise scientific measures of the relationship between the costs and the benefits must not provide a pretext for failure to analyse individual pollution problems as carefully and quantitatively as possible. The fact that no simple or mechanical cost-benefit exercise will provide all the answers does not mean that such analysis is not an important ingredient in the decision-making process. It is often the only way to ensure that all the main relevant variables are brought to light and to demonstrate the consequences, both direct and indirect, of alternative measures to deal with pollution. Moreover, the

In the private sector of the economy the objective should also be to ensure that decision-makers take into account all of the costs (i.e. the costs to society) of their decisions.

In general, this already happens with respect to most non-environmental aspects of proposed actions: prices charged for using resources reflect (or should reflect) the costs of using them. A 'go ahead' decision by a producer implies that his assessment of the benefits (or revenue) from the use of these resources exceeds costs. As previously noted, the cause of excessive pollution has been that the price charged for using environmental resources (water, landscape, air) has been too low – in many cases zero. What is needed, therefore, is to equate the price charged for use of environmental resources with the cost of damage inflicted on society by using them.

This approach via the price structure may be applied in any of a number of ways, with implications for the ultimate bearer of such costs. The price charged might be levied directly – for example, as taxes on the process which generates pollution or as the purchase price of licences which entitle the holder to generate specific quantities of pollutants. Such charges make it more expensive to produce (and therefore, indirectly, to consume) a polluting good than before. If a producer or consumer can avoid the extra expense, he will tend to do so: there is, therefore, an incentive to refrain from using the polluting good or to change consumption patterns or production processes in ways which mitigate pollution.[31]

In contrast to measures of this kind in which the 'polluter pays' principle applies, are measures in the form of direct payments from the 'public purse', most notably in the form of subsidies to polluters not to pollute. Such subsidies have the pattern of final demand unchanged – that is, the same as it would have been in the absence of pollution abatement measures. The act of pollution entails a cost to the producer only as much as the subsidy must be foregone.

The difficulty with market procedures lies in deciding the 'right' price to charge for those uses of environmental resources that generate pollution, or the 'right' subsidy to pay for not polluting. For most other resources prices can be ascertained or inferred from market behaviour. But as the 'market' for a clean

---

difficulties, formidable as they are, should not prevent us from reaching decisions about the scale of abatement of pollution which is socially desirable.' *First Report of (UK) Royal Commission on Environmental Pollution, op cit*: 7-8.

31 In the nature of things some techniques to avoid pollution will be readily at hand, others will have to be searched out. If the decision-maker concludes that it would be more expensive to employ known or new procedures to avoid pollution than to bear the pollution expenses himself, then, provided the charge equals society's valuation of damage suffered (a big proviso), the cost-benefit calculation has come down against pollution abatement with respect to this activity. Other uses of available resources would yield greater benefit to the community than this act of pollution abatement.

environment is yet to be established, this approach is not available. Inevitably indirect means of assessment must be used (such as seeking to identify the extra price that people appear to be prepared to pay to live in a clean environment). It is this difficulty of obtaining or interpreting necessary information that often prompts the exploration of an alternative group of direct measures – namely, non-market techniques.[32]

Non-market techniques of pollution control may also be differentiated according to whether the polluter or the public purse pays. Under the 'polluter pays' principle, non-market measures encompass the promulgation of regulations governing the permissible emission of pollution (such as the maximum noise regulations referred to earlier).

Regulations to curb pollution tend to lead to rigidities and inefficiencies. For example, depending upon how such regulations are framed, they may stifle research into cheaper forms of total pollution control and mitigate against efforts to do better than the regulations stipulate. But the regulatory approach also has some advantages over market approaches to pollution control. Provided that achieving the improved environmental quality is not more costly than the benefits from doing so, and that the regulations can be closely attuned to the community's own assessment of tolerable pollution levels, regulations eliminate some of the uncertainty which is inherent in market approaches.

Non-market intervention may also be undertaken directly by government; such intervention often involves cleaning up pollution which has been generated, rather than changing the form of production and consumption in the first place.[33] Under this approach society may sacrifice more than is necessary for the sake of a given improvement in wellbeing due to pollution control.

Whether the best approach to pollution control is via market measures, non market measures or some combination of the two is thus essentially a question

---

32 There are market and non-market approaches to indirect measures also. The difference between direct and indirect lies not with the instruments employed (taxes, regulations, etc) but with the point at which they are applied. Direct measures are those applied to the *actual* pollution generated; for example, a charge per unit of sulphur dioxide emitted from a plant. Indirect measures are those applied to the *potential* for consumption or production to cause pollution; for example, inputs which might be highly pollutive are discouraged, or certain methods of production or consumption are prohibited or particular goods banned outright. Because indirect measures will apply regardless of whether this potential pollution occurs or not, they provide no incentive to find other ways of reducing the actual level of pollution. There will be occasions when these other means of curbing pollution are cheaper than those encouraged by the indirect measures. But if indirect measures are employed, the cheaper alternatives will be overlooked and the community will incur a higher cost for pollution control than necessary. Since direct measures operate on actual pollution generated they provide the needed incentive and avoid this problem.

33 By contrast, application of the 'polluter pays' principle means that less pollution is generated, either because the prices of products of industries which have to spend most on pollution control will be relatively higher (and the size of those industries therefore smaller) than if there are no pollution controls, or because regulations directly stipulate a lower level of pollution emission.

about the *efficiency* of such approaches. But, since any new measures to control pollution will involve new costs to someone, it is also necessary to consider their equity aspects. These crystallise around the two polar approaches of 'polluter pays' or 'public purse pays'. Advocates of the former argue that (social) costs incurred in using the environment should be treated no differently from costs incurred in using any other resources. In essence this viewpoint holds that society 'owns' the clean environment and therefore has a right to expect individual users of it to pay. That is, those who benefit from goods produced at a cost to the environment should have to meet that cost. The expense of pollution control is borne in the first instance by would-be polluters, but ultimately it will be passed onto the users of the products.

The 'public purse pays' viewpoint accepts that individual decision-makers are generating the wrong combination of physical commodities and clean environment. However, it sees the more appropriate cure as being for collective decision-makers to correct the result of inappropriate individual decisions. Adherents to this viewpoint justify their stand on the grounds that since society as a whole benefits from the cleaner environment, society as a whole should meet the costs incurred. In effect, a clean environment becomes a privilege to be paid for rather than a right to be expected.

The 'polluter pays' principle appears to be the sounder on grounds both of equity and efficiency, and an inter-governmental consensus appears to have been reached in its favour. As a member of the Organisation for Economic Co-Operation and Development, Australia adopted in1972 that Organisation's guiding principles governing the international economic aspects of environmental policies, including the 'polluter pays' principle.

VII

The preservation and, still more, improvement of the environment obviously requires the use of more resources for that purpose. As more resources are devoted to those ends, fewer resources than would otherwise have been available can be applied to other purposes. Using resources for pollution control conflicts with other uses of resources – with traffic control, school buildings, dry cleaning or TV sets – but this conflict is not specifically a growth problem: there is no reason for thinking that directing resources to pollution control will be *particularly* at the expense of growth-producing investment in physical equipment and human skills.

Wealthy countries will probably take out more of their growth in the form of pollution abatement than poor countries, but growing economies will also probably accommodate the required diversion of resources more readily than 'stationary' ones. It is easier to modernise plant and equipment (e.g. to incorporate pollution control mechanisms) and to engineer structural readjustments to the changing pattern of economic activity in a growth context than otherwise. More fundamentally, economic growth implies that the stock of resources (including technology), which the community has at its disposal, is continually expanding. This expansion enables people – either through their own choice or through decisions made by their governments – to exercise an option to improve their welfare in one of a number of ways. In the past this option has been exercised in favour of increasing consumption of services rather than goods, and in favour of more leisure rather than still more goods and services. Nowadays we have the opportunity that comes with growth to opt for a more pleasing environment. If that opportunity occurs in an expanding economy, opting for it need not involve an absolute reduction in presently enjoyed standards in other respects. In short, 'growth' entails a positive contribution to pollution control in a way which a 'stationary state' cannot.

VIII

The discussion so far in this Part has suggested that pollution amounts to hidden costs of production, and that when these costs are properly charged for, the output of goods and services will achieve a pattern more in keeping with the preservation of a clean environment. But how different would that pattern be? What is the extent of the change required? Will the rate of improvement in other directions be seriously retarded?

It will be clear from what has been said that the answers to these questions depend upon the priority attached to a cleaner and quieter environment. Since all human activity pollutes in some respects, the continued existence of the human species depends upon a compromise with the environment. The real issues turn upon the terms of that compromise – that is, upon the consensus reached as to the magnitude of the costs imposed by specific environmental ills, and therefore of the resources that should properly be devoted to curing them. It is clear, however, that some types of pollution can be reduced quite dramatically at relatively modest cost. The reduction in various forms of air and water pollution in London over recent years is perhaps the most widely known example of this.

The pollution control proposals being implemented in the United States today are more ambitious than in most countries, yet it is evident from estimates of the costs involved that the required redistribution of resources is not radical. The 'annualised cost' of pollution control expenditures, including measures to counter air and water pollution and to dispose of solid wastes, is estimated to rise from $10 billion in 1970 to $33 billion in 1980[34] (both totals expressed in

34 Of the *increase of $23 billion*, $9 billion relates to the estimated costs of regulating motor vehicle emissions. The estimates are given in the *Third Annual Report of the (US) Council on Environmental Quality*, (August 1972).

1971 prices). Large as these figures may appear, they represent an increase from just below one per cent to a little over two per cent of actual and prospective GNP, respectively.[35]

A diversion of an additional one per cent or so of a country's GDP to a particular use is not negligible, but a growing economy can clearly take such a diversion in its stride. Even in the period of adjustment to higher standards of environmental quality, only a small proportion of the increase in available output would need to be devoted to pollution control expenditures.

The United States' pollution control measures are expected to bring about very substantial reductions in emissions of pollutants:

> (In the US), for 1976, without new controls, iron and steel would produce over one million tons of particulates per year. Pollution controls would reduce this to 93,000 tons per year. Similarly, for kraft pulp, from 561,000 to 120,000; for grey iron foundries, from 166,000 to 29,000. Carbon monoxide emissions from the latter would be reduced from 2,220,000 tons per year to 210,000 per year. Crudely speaking, it appears that industrial pollutants can be reduced by 80 to 90 per cent through annual expenditures of the order of 5 per cent or less of the total value of the particular industrial output. For electric power generation, similar reductions can be effected at roughly 2 per cent of total power costs.[36]

There will be some industries in which large changes, and therefore large increases in costs, may be needed to counter pollution. But a few cases of spectacular cost increases would not much alter the overall proportion of resources devoted to pollution control, moderated as it would be by the numerous run-of-the-mill decisions which achieve large results for modest cost.

It is true, of course, that increasing recognition of pollution problems combined with further improvements in living standards could raise the question of even more ambitious anti-pollution objectives – and these could certainly be achieved though at increasing cost.[37]

It is also true that overall welfare may be reduced below what might have been achieved if pollution control becomes an over-riding objective regardless of the totality of considerations, or if recourse to legal restraints holds up or leads to

---

35 Overall figures for costs of pollution control program are available for five other countries for the period 1971-1975. (See the *OECD Observer*, February 1973: 9.) These costs, expressed as a percentage of GNP, for the five countries are as follows: Germany, 1.8 per cent; Italy, 0.4 per cent; Japan, 2.2 per cent; Netherlands, 1.0-1.5 per cent; and Sweden, 0.7 per cent. These figures will not be comparable as an index of effort because environmental problems will differ as will appropriate techniques; moreover, past attention or neglect will influence current requirements.

36 *IBRD, op cit*: 51.

37 It is likely, however, that technological advance will also reduce the real costs of pollution control over time, so that some improvements in standards may be possible in the future without increases in real costs.

the abandonment of important projects over issues where benefits of proceeding outweigh the costs. If pollution control standards are set so high that the costs of control clearly exceed the resulting benefits, resources will be wastefully diverted from other purposes – including perhaps other forms of environmental improvement. Moreover, it is already apparent – with the technology of pollution control only beginning to develop – that even modest expenditure can have large effects in reducing pollution.

In summary *the damage from environmental pollution in a large and growing economy with effective pollution control standards certainly need be no greater and in practice is likely to be far less than the damage in a small and slower-growing economy operating in the same area without effective pollution control measures.* The quality of the environment can be improved much more – and more quickly – by measures to counter pollution than by steps to contain economic growth. It is doubtful in any case whether action of the latter kind will be deliberately attempted; and if it were, and the improvement in living standards were slowed down as a result, the resistance to applying resources to control pollution would be so much the greater.

Part 3: Growth and its measurement

> ...with contemporary technologies and living standards, it is doubtful how far the growth of marketable output, as defined in national income statistics, is an adequate measure of the growth that is important for society... The problems of social choice, the assessment of costs and benefits of possible developments, and the selection of policy goals may therefore need to be looked at in a wider context than conventionally measured growth rates. (*OECD: The Growth of Output 1960-1980*, December 1970.)

I

Some of the confusion over the relationship between pollution and economic growth seems to stem from an over-reliance on the significance of conventional growth measures. In particular, Part I referred to the practice – more prevalent some years ago than now – of using the growth rate in 'real' GDP as an 'all purpose guide' to a country's economic performance.

The basic error here is the failure to pay heed to the *objectives* of economic activity. Just as measurements of a machine's performance are meaningless unless they bear upon the efficiency with which it performs the tasks for which it is designed, so measurements of economic performance must be related to the purpose of the economic machine. This was stated as follows in the *Supplement to the Treasury Information Bulletin: the Meaning and Measurement of Economic Growth*:

> The object of all economic activity, in the long run at least, is the satisfaction of people's demands, whether for goods and services that can be purchased in the market or for other things, tangible or intangible, that cannot.[38]

By definition things, tangible and intangible, that cannot be purchased in the market are excluded from GDP, although the output of many government services (for example, national defence), which do not have market equivalents but loom large in the economy, are represented by proxy – the cost of their purchases. Where market equivalents are available, it does not follow that the output of the relevant goods and services which are not marketed will be included – the difficulties of imputation may be too great. In the private sector, for example the services of a TV set are marketed (and therefore included) if the set is hired, but if the viewer buys a set the market equivalent of those services is excluded from GDP.[39] In the public sector the services of, for example, a government-owned school building are excluded although market equivalents exist. Again, some activities will confer benefits or impose penalties on other activities, and these effects will not necessarily be captured by GDP statistics. For example, public expenditure to relieve traffic congestion provides a future return which is included in GDP insofar as it reduces business costs, but not to the extent that it adds to the real leisure time of commuters. The latter benefits are also related to satisfying people's demands: but the ways in which they are reflected or not reflected in GDP are such that supplementary measures may also be needed.[40]

These are examples that illustrate the significance of the fact that GDP is confined, broadly speaking, to the output of goods and services that enters the market. Serious difficulties also arise in seeking to estimate changes in market output over time. Whilst this can be done with reasonable precision in terms of *current* prices – that is, the prices actually prevailing from time to time – such movements cannot indicate the 'real' growth in output because they are much influenced by changes in those prices over time. In an attempt to overcome this problem and confine the measure of growth in output as far as possible

38 *Op cit*: 5.

39 Expenditure on the *purchase* of durable goods, such as television sets is included in GDP whether the purchaser is a final consumer or a business enterprise: but only in the latter case are the services subsequently provided included in GDP. The domestic services of a housewife are an important activity which is excluded. The British economist AC Pigou once remarked that if a widower vicar paid his housekeeper a weekly wage this would represent an addition to the national income; if he married her it would be a subtraction!

40 Also, as noted earlier, the effect of pollutants on the natural environment itself is not brought into GDP. However, the use of resources to control pollution is reflected, at least in part, in GDP.

to changes in 'quantum', statisticians have developed the measure of GDP *at constant prices* by revaluing the goods and services included with a view to removing the direct effects of changes in prices.

II

Estimates of expenditure at constant prices, and the corresponding estimates of 'real' GDP as a whole which may be built up from them, are valuable – and indeed essential for some types of economic analysis. They are however very frequently misused because their inherent limitations are insufficiently recognised.

In essence, these limitations arise from the fact that relative prices of goods and services entering the computation are used as weights; and the comparisons between periods which are necessary for growth estimates involve the application of a *constant* set of weights – that is, it must be implicitly assumed, contrary to the facts, that *relative* prices or valuations remain unchanged.[41]

> In certain circumstances we may be justified in assuming that the relative values of the goods and services produced have remained constant over a period of time. If in fact the relative values have changed considerably, we may not be justified in making this assumption... In proportion as we are not so justified, the more difficult it becomes to make numerical summaries which are at all significant; and the more seriously are the changes in physical quantities resulting from changes in the 'efficiency' of the productive processes overshadowed by changes in the estimation in which the final product is held.[42]

This may appear abstract and theoretical, but an understanding of it is basic to anyone wishing to draw conclusions from constant price data.

Take, for example, the practice of quoting estimates of trends in GDP at constant prices as evidence bearing upon the effectiveness or otherwise of those policies that influence the allocation of resources between industries by affecting market prices, e.g. tariff policies. Since it is precisely through their influence on relative prices that such policies have their effects on the pattern of economic activity, measures of output that *assume* the structure of relative prices remains constant are of very qualified relevance in this context.[43]

---

41 Implicit assumptions which are contrary to the facts are not made by those who *produce* statistics at constant prices, but by those who make indiscriminating use of such statistics to measure economic growth.

42 Dr (now Sir) Roland Wilson, *Facts and Fancies of Productivity* paper read before Section G of ANZAAS at its Adelaide Meeting, August 1946: 28.

43 The higher the proportion of GDP represented by the output of industries in which productivity is growing rapidly, the more rapidly will total GDP at constant prices tend to grow: but rapid growth in productivity is not the same thing as a high *level* of productivity. There is no necessary correlation between

Another common misuse of constant price estimates arises from what they appear to show about the services sector of the economy. Services are typically less standardised than manufactured goods, and the problem of differentiating between the volume and price components of the overall change in expenditure is therefore more formidable in their case. It is generally accepted that some (net) improvements in the quality of many services are not captured by constant price estimates – that is, that apparent price increases are overstated (and output growth correspondingly understated) in this area.

Compounding the problem arising from these difficulties of measurement of the output of services is the more fundamental 'index number' problem. Even if quality improvements in services could be fully identified, it is probable that rises in their prices would be shown to be faster than rises in prices of goods. But, to the extent that this is true, the *relative* prices of services have increased. Measures such as GDP at constant prices necessarily disregard such relative changes. Those who use such measures uncritically therefore implicitly assume[44] – contrary to the fact – that the output of one unit of 'services' is no more valuable, by comparison with the output of one unit of goods, than it was at the base date.

These statistical illusions are not always appreciated. The misunderstanding shows up from time to time in suggestion that the goods-producing industries be specially encouraged and the service-producing industries discouraged[45] so as to raise the apparent rate of economic growth. The notion was referred to in *The Meaning and Measurement of Economic Growth*.

> If it were desired solely to achieve a high rate of overall productivity increase as measured statistically by figures of GNP at constant prices, efforts might be directed towards inducing the community to buy more and more of the kinds of output that appear to enhance the growth performance most – cars and other products of highly mechanised operations, for example. If, however, it were thought desirable instead to increase the proportion of national expenditure devoted to education, health and the like, or to travel or the patronage of the arts, the statistical growth in 'productivity' would be very much lower even though, in the view of many, the quality of life might thereby be much improved.[46]

The conclusion is, of course, that to seek to maximise the statistical *measure* of growth, rather than the real welfare of the community, is to miss the point.

---

the industries which are most competitive internationally and industries in which technical progress is proceeding most rapidly. Nor are industries experiencing rapid technological progress necessarily becoming more competitive: the rate of progress may be equally fast or faster in other countries.

44 See footnote 41 above.

45 The suggestion was more common in the heyday of 'growthmanship'. These days the opposite proposal is sometimes made on the grounds that goods-producing industries tend to use more mineral resources and produce more pollution per dollar of output than the services industries.

46 *Op cit*: 17.

III

In *The Meaning and Measurement of Economic Growth* it was pointed out that no one familiar with the construction of estimates of what was then called the GNP would think of attaching the significance that was being attached to them by many users.[47] The reasons for this will be apparent from the preceding section. The simple truth is that measures of trends in the market value of output, whether revalued to remove the direct effects of price changes or not, cannot be taken as comprehensive and unambiguous measures of changes in total welfare.

It is unnecessary to repeat the whole catalogue of pitfalls detailed in the earlier publication, which are illustrated by the examples cited above. It is sufficient to note that attention was drawn to problems of concept, problems of estimation and problems arising out of the necessity to tailor concepts used to the availability of data. Some of the key conclusions were:

> Like all tools of trade, estimates of GNP are meant for a particular job and they do it as well as can be expected. Difficulties arise only where they are used for jobs for which they are less well suited.[48]
>
> The particular job for which GNP figures are best suited is the description, analysis and forecasting of economic trends. `They represent a convenient "short hand" means of roughly appraising what is happening to the economy, or analysing the requirements of policy from time to time, and of portraying the inter-relationships between incomes and expenditures of the different sectors of the economy.'[49]
>
> In this context, 'constant price estimates (of GNP) indicate, over comparatively short periods free from substantial institutional change, whether economic growth appears to be taking place and whether it appears to be accelerating or slowing down. It is but a broad indicator; it certainly is not intended to be interpreted in any precise quantitative sense.'[50]

In summary, it was suggested that the attempt to identify economic growth with the growth in output at constant prices is misleading. The distinction between the two is important because certain criticisms of 'economic growth' appear to result from misinterpretation: movements in the statistic are taken as closely representing movements in economic growth.

47 *Op cit*: 13.
48 *Loc cit*.
49 *Loc cit*.
50 *Op cit*: 12.

IV

People are presumably interested in making 'right' decisions in the sense that these decisions directly or indirectly, give them what they want. A 'wrong' decision is one that leads to a different outcome from that which the decision-maker would have preferred and which could have been achieved had he decided otherwise. In the case of government decisions on behalf of the community the principles are the same – though the difficulties of making 'right' decisions are greater for many reasons: because the values that people place on many government services are not readily ascertained, because they vary greatly between individuals and because of the practical problems of assessing the full consequences of decisions even when priorities and relative valuations are known.

It will be clear from what has been said, however, that the 'rightness' of decisions cannot be judged solely by reference to their effects on GDP. People make their decisions in accordance with their own assessment of the costs and returns involved.[51] The results of particular individual decisions may or may not be registered in the national accounts; that is something which – quite rightly – is not taken into consideration by those making the decisions.

The same is true of government decisions. It was noted earlier that the process of appraisal of public sector projects and programs should not discriminate between costs and benefits that enter the GDP calculus and those that do not. The objective of general government activities is to maximise the 'output' (in terms of community welfare) for any given input of resources. The effects on national accounting aggregates are an inadequate guide in this respect because such activities are conventionally measured in the national accounts only by their cost or input, and not by their output. The rise in 'output' of the health industry cannot be adequately measured by what is spent on health services; other, and probably broad, indicators of that output have to be sought.

Because output is not an end in itself, but a means to promote the welfare of the community, it is only sensible that national policies be designed to create conditions which will enable available supplies of labour, capital and natural resources to be efficiently applied for the purposes which the community values most highly. This is not to suggest, of course that it is easy to determine what values to assign to various forms of production – and hence to the return from

51 The returns may, of course, be of many kinds and may include altruistic considerations as well as the range of other non-material values mentioned in Part I. Decisions may also be influenced by the circumstance – increasingly present in the case of the well-to-do – of not having to weigh up too carefully the pros and cons, especially on minor matters. Even those on modest incomes make many decisions, out of habit or otherwise, with little or no conscious considerations of how to get the most for their money. Nevertheless, the process involved in reaching any rational decision is essentially a benefit/cost calculus; and, although the reasoning process is expressed in many different ways, it tends to become increasingly conscious and articulated as decisions become more important.

resources in various forms. On the contrary, it can often be extremely difficult, as was shown in the discussion on environmental valuations in Part II. But it is the meeting of people's demands and preferences – individually and collectively – which constitutes the criterion. The real objective of putting available resources to their best use would not be achieved by maximising measured growth.

V

Nothing that has been said should be taken to imply that GDP and the structure of national accounts of which it forms part are not valuable tools of analysis. They are of great value in showing how the economy works and in illuminating many of the key relationships which are relevant to the formulation of policies – with respect both to the management of the economy to maintain a sound balance between available supplies and the calls upon them, and to problems of the longer term. In fact, GDP and other key aggregates provide points of reference against which may be measured not only those items of income, expenditure and product forming part of the market economy, but also the implications of using resources to provide goods and services not exchanged in the market place.

The trend in GDP at constant prices is not, however, a comprehensive measure of changes in the national wellbeing, or in the progress (if any) towards the 'good life'. Recognition of these limitations has led to two distinct strands of development directed towards their remedy.

One school advocates that additional components of human wellbeing be built into the GDP measure itself. GDP could – so it is claimed – be modified so as to take into the reckoning such negative effects as pollution, congestion and environmental degradation. Thus the measure would approach what has been called 'net economic welfare' (NEW).[52] Whilst admitting that the necessary adjustments would be relatively primitive, proponents of such a measure argue that it is better to have an inaccurate sense of what is wanted than an accurate sense of what, for some purposes, is not wanted.

As an alternative to proposals to modify the GDP concept to include 'quality of life' considerations, another school favours the development of a system of social indicators to *supplement* the conventional GDP. Their proposals do not envisage the development of a single aggregative index of human wellbeing but rather the social demands and problems which are or are likely to become major concerns of policy. It is claimed that measurement of changes in the various indicators will assist and enlighten public discussion and the decision-making processes. Considerable conceptual and methodological problems arise and it is too early to say how far this approach can successfully be developed.

---

52 The American economists, Professors William Nordhaus and James Tobin formulated this concept and it has been popularised by Professor Paul Samuelson.

VI

The conclusions of this Part so far might perhaps be summarised as follows.

The test of the success with which a country such as Australia uses its resources cannot be discerned by examining the trend in output at constant prices or any other indicator. It depends partly, but by no means wholly, on whether market prices and the implicit or explicit valuations assigned to activities outside the market reflect the preferences of its citizens. Those preferences may call for an increasing or decreasing proportion of resources to be allocated to items included in GDP. There is no basis for suggesting that arrangements which favour the provision of items which society wants but which are partly or entirely excluded from GDP are less 'material' or less 'growth-oriented' than an economic system which is designed to achieve growth only in supplies of products included in GDP.

If economic and social policies are directed to meeting the preferences of a country's citizens without using resources wastefully, the rate of growth in GDP is best regarded not as a goal or a target but rather as a result. It is the outcome of the pattern of preferences, of the efficiency of the arrangements to give effect to those preferences, and of the factors influencing the rate at which productive efficiency increases in individual productive units. A high rate of growth in the conventional statistical measure of output may be a likely result of well-directed policies: it is certainly not a necessary result. Other measures may be used to shed light on various aspects of national performance; but they cannot do so comprehensively and unambiguously, and assessments of many matters affecting national welfare must include a large subjective element.

An important factor influencing a country's rate of economic growth which has not been mentioned so far is the allocation of resources between production for current uses and for investment – that is, 'production' whether of physical equipment or human skills which adds to the economy's capacity to produce in future years. The rate of future economic growth can be increased by using fewer resources for current uses and more resources to produce items that will yield some of or all of their services in future years. But there is obviously a limit to the present sacrifices which it is sensible to make in order that one (and others) may be better-off in the future. Individuals make their own evaluations in deciding how much they will spend out of their incomes. The nation's choice is a compound not only of individual decisions but also of the decisions and policies of firms and governments.

A widely held view is that the decisions of individual consumers and enterprises will result in too little consideration of the future. This view arises in a number of contexts and it is not possible to explore all of them here. It is sufficient to say that it is not easy to find a logical chain of reasoning which leads to the conclusion that there is a general tendency for present decision-makers to neglect the interests of future generations.

The real problem, which will be considered in greater detail in the concluding chapter, is that of knowing how to take those interests into due and proper account. This can be strikingly illustrated by the wide differences in attitude between the 'growthmanship' and anti-growth schools referred to at the beginning of this paper. Both have the interests of the future at heart. Among the growthmen there is or was a view that governments should provide special encouragement to investment. This would involve some cost in present living standards, but growth would be stimulated and future living standards would therefore be higher than they would otherwise have been.

An opposite viewpoint is held by those most unequivocally in the anti-growth school. Investment in their view should not be stimulated but choked back. Far from being grateful to the present generation for sacrificing its welfare in their interest, they assert that our children and our grandchildren will curse us for condoning growth, let alone encouraging it.

One of the reasons for this latter view is the conflict that is seen between growth and the care of the environment, which was discussed in Part 2. It was suggested in that Part that the way to attack this problem was not in attempting to frustrate growth *per se* but in a proper ordering of priorities between environmental improvement and other uses of resources.

> To have growth, that is, to have more consumption tomorrow, what has to be sacrificed today is not the environment today, or even the environment tomorrow, but consumption today; for growth requires investment. How that sacrifice of consumption is to be allocated amongst various component items of consumption is a problem of the allocation of resources at any one moment of time, not a problem of the allocation of resources over time.[53]

Another argument for the view that the interests of the future require a curb on economic growth is that the physical resources are not available to sustain indefinite expansion. There is particular concern about the continued availability of non-renewable mineral resources. The next Part examines whether this concern is justified.

53 Beckerman, *op cit*: 342.

Part 4: Growth and mineral supplies

> Resources are highly dynamic functional concepts; they *are not, they become*, they evolve out of the truine interaction of nature, man, and culture. The command over energy, especially inanimate energy is the key to resource availability. And, finally, the works is not 'a bundle of hay' but a living growing complex of matter and energy, *a process rather than a thing...* the problem of resources adequacy for the ages to come will involve human wisdom more than limits set by nature. (Eric W Zimmermann, *World Resources and Industries*. (New York 1951): 814-815, 818.)

I

The economic growth of modern times has depended heavily on the use of minerals as raw materials and to provide energy. The discovery of methods of using coal rather than charcoal in forges and blast furnaces, and the subsequent application of steam power in place of water power, were critical events in the rise of industrialism in eighteenth century England.

Fears of early exhaustion are as old as the large-scale exploitation of minerals. The degree of concern has ebbed and flowed over the years, the peaks usually coinciding with periods of high prices and supply shortages that proved, with hindsight, to be temporary.

Exactly a century ago, such a temporary 'dearness and scarcity of coal' in Britain led to predictions that supplies would run out in the not-so-distant future if the exponential growth of the preceding thirty years continued, and to the appointment of a Select Committee of the House of Commons to examine the problem. In the United States fears about the long-term adequacy of non-renewable resources reached a peak in the years before World War I and again at the time of the Korean War boom, when it led to the setting up of the Paley Commission.[54] Now in the 1970s there has been a new wave of concern, not only in the United States but in many of the developed countries, that growing scarcity of non-renewable resources may pose an early threat to the continued growth of the world economy.

54 See footnote 74.

II

Many of these fears spring from comparisons of the known reserves of minerals with their present and prospective rate of use. Such comparisons appear to 'show' that many of this planet's mineral resources will be exhausted in a few decades if economic growth is maintained.[55]

It is therefore crucial to recognise that *known* reserves, or even multiples of those known reserves, are no more a guide to what ultimately usable reserves might be than they were 25, 100, 200 or 1,000 years ago. To match an extrapolated rate of consumption against the reserves which are known to exist at a particular point of time is simply to express those reserves – as defined by current technology and commercial values – in another way. A time-flow is substituted for volume. *The real question is not how known reserves compare with the prospective calls upon them, but why total known reserves are what they are.* Surprisingly, the authors of the report for the Club of Rome[56] and many others who fear that resources will be inadequate to sustain continued growth have not addressed themselves to the highly relevant question: if resources are insufficient to assure long-term adequacy, why has exploration not been stepped up so that more reserves will be found?

When the question is posed this way, the answer is obvious. There are two reasons why no one knows the extent of ultimately recoverable mineral resources. First, the search for minerals is undertaken mainly by mining companies and their efforts are directed to a specific and sensible goal: the 'proving up' of a stock of raw materials which will suffice to ensure that their decisions to spend much larger amounts on working the deposits are safely based. Secondly, the very definition of 'reserve' depends on economics and technology.

Rising demands for a mineral (as long as its price is free to move in line with that rising demand) will lead to investment in new extraction facilities and treatment plants, and to a sufficient exploration effort to satisfy the producers concerned that reserves exist to employ the facilities and feed the plants during their economic life. It will *not* lead to any interest in finding deposits that will lie idle for thirty years. That would be little more sensible than installing treatment facilities that will not be used for many years ahead.

55 The report for the Club of Rome already cited is the most conspicuous recent example; but fears on this score are very widely held.

56 For detailed commentary on the resource depletion aspects of this report, see *IBRD* and Beckerman, cited on page 109 above. For comprehensive data relating to United States and world reserves of individual minerals, discussion of the interpretation to be placed upon such data and an approach to the forecasting of supply and demand for minerals in the long-term, see *Mineral Facts and Problems,* 1970 (Washington, DC, Government Printing Office, 1970).

It follows that statements about the number of years' supply that known reserves represent give no reliable guide to the possible scale of ultimately usable reserves. At most, such statements might provide a guide to the commercial practices and motivations of mineral producers – though not as sound a guide as could be obtained from other evidence. Among the factors influencing the reserves/annual consumption ratio for a particular mineral, both globally and in particular countries, are the cost of exploration, the capital costs of mining plant and equipment, the apparent prospects for growth in demand for the mineral concerned, changes in transport costs or techniques of extraction and treatment, national security considerations and the prospects of reducing costs by discovering new reserves which are superior to existing known reserves in point of quality, accessibility or other characteristics. It is impossible to interpret statistics of known reserves without taking such factors into account. *The notion that such figures can provide evidence of impending scarcity of particular minerals is a fallacy of the crudest kind*[57] (though the abundance of known reserves of some minerals provides evidence *against* the proposition that scarcities will soon arise in those cases).

III

The conclusions of the preceding section do not depend on whether or not the proving of mineral resources is carried out entirely, or almost entirely, by business enterprises. The desirability or otherwise of governments engaging in the search for minerals need not be pursued here. It is however relevant in the present context to consider one of the reasons sometimes given for that course – that governments, which have wider responsibilities than mining companies, should seek to remove 'uncertainty' about the long term availability of minerals by engaging in comprehensive programs of exploration directed not towards discovering reserves for early use but towards compiling global inventories of available resources.

The first and obvious objection is that 'taking stock' of the world's minerals in that way would be extremely costly. That is, it would involve the use of substantial resources which might have been used for other purposes. There is a real question whether progress in raising living standards (or building up capacity to raise living standards in the future) should be retarded in the interests of seeking a greater degree of 'certainty' about the very long-term future. The answer to the question partly depends on the likelihood and consequences of a general scarcity of resources, a subject which will be taken up shortly. But there

57 Ironically, it happens that the reserves/annual consumption ratios for most key minerals have *increased* over time – that is, the exponential growth in known reserves has tended to outpace the exponential growth in consumption. If those who have taken such ratios as evidence of impending scarcity took their logic to its proper conclusion, they would have *fewer* grounds for concern now than twenty years ago.

is a much more fundamental difficulty: is the removal of uncertainty – desirable as that might be – in fact possible? The main point to have in mind in answering that question is that no one can predict, for decades into the future, the form which technical and economic progress will take.

An example may help to illustrate the point. An inventory of the world's iron ore resources in 1938 would not have included any reserves in the Pilbara region of Western Australia. Contrary to popular present-day belief, however, massive ore bodies were known to exist there. They were, in fact, mentioned in the report which led the Australian government of the day to impose its embargo on exports. The point, however, is that they were not then *economic* resources. To know that they would become so within the short space of thirty years, it would have been necessary to foresee such developments as the post-war economic growth of Japan and the slashing of real transport costs through the development of bulk materials handling equipment and the advent of giant ore carriers. Uncertainty as to the future global availability of iron ore would not have been removed by assembling data about the size and physical characteristics of ore bodies in the Pilbara or elsewhere.

Examples of this kind show that questions about the availability of raw materials to sustain continued economic growth in the long-term future cannot be answered by reference to the stock of 'reserves', and could not be even if we knew the entire stock which would be available for development in the future, given the maintenance of *present* economic and technical conditions. This is because those conditions will inevitably change quite radically as the decades pass, and in ways that defy prediction.

It is therefore not possible to ascertain the supplies of particular minerals which will ultimately be available — or, for that matter, the supplies which will be *required* in the far-distant future.[58] There are however grounds for confidence that the continued pursuit of economic growth will not leave future generations without the physical wherewithal to maintain living standards. The subject is too large to cover comprehensively within the confines of a single chapter, but there is space to explain briefly what these grounds for confidence are.

58 Although there are fears that specific minerals will be exhausted, it is hard to think of examples of exhaustion which have occurred in the past, even among the minor minerals. Moreover, it is difficult to forecast what the consequences of exhausting particular resources would be. For any particular mineral it would happen only gradually, by a process which involved a steady rise in its price. Presumably patterns of production and consumption would gradually adapt towards what they would have been had the mineral never existed in the first place. Moreover, developments in substitute materials and processes and in the pattern of demand can mean that an 'indispensable' mineral at one time might become redundant at another.

IV

As an historical fact, the long-term trend has been for the cost of mineral inputs to *decline* as a proportion of total production costs. Numerous studies of the available statistical data, spanning more than a century, have demonstrated that the tendency during this phase of unprecedented growth in the world economy and in the use of minerals has not been towards scarcity but towards abundance. In the United States the real cost per unit of minerals output was less than one-half the average 1870—1900 level by 1929; and by 1957 it was less than one-half the 1929 level.[59] Not only have there been reductions in the real cost per unit of output of most minerals, but there have also been declines in the input of minerals per unit of final output. 'Increasing costs for particular extractive products, therefore, do not signify increasing costs for extractive output as a whole, let alone for the aggregate of all goods and services.'[60]

These are points which may not have been sufficiently noted by those who take a pessimistic view about depletion of non-renewable resources. True, they relate to the past and cannot be guaranteed to continue into the future – though there is as yet no sign that they will not. But in any case the question is not of great importance for the overall scale of future growth.[61] The argument against those who fear scarcities and shortages of minerals in the future is not just that they are pessimistic about the possibilities of maintaining rapid progress in the development of new techniques and the application of presently known techniques, to the finding, extracting, processing, transporting and using of minerals. *It is rather that they are not consistent in their pessimism.* Forecasts of an indefinite exponential growth in the demand for minerals are the source of their concern; yet it is inconceivable that the development and application of new technology – which is implicitly assumed in expectations of exponentially expanding demand – could somehow pass the minerals and mineral-using industries by. It is not enough to say that sooner or later predictions that mineral supplies essential to the economy will run out must be fulfilled. Such predictions have been regularly made ever since the rise of industrialism. Past fears have proved unfounded and it is appropriate here to ask why.

---

59 HJ Barnett and C Morse, *Scarcity and Growth; The Economics of Natural Resource Availability,* (Resources for the Future, Washington, 1963): 8. This study examined the quantitative importance of various influences contributing to those results. It was shown that substitution of commodities with relatively lower or declining costs and growth in imports both contributed to the reduction in costs *but* that much the greater part of that reduction would still have occurred in the absence of either of these influences.

60 *Ibid:* 9.

61 It does of course have significant implications for the *pattern* of growth, and therefore for the future of individual industries.

V

Perhaps the basic flaw is in conceiving of the long-term availability of a particular 'resource' as an *end* in itself, rather than as an ingredient of one of the *means* of progress. The impression sometimes given that the availability of a particular mineral might give out suddenly rather than gradually is itself mistaken; and there is an associated notion that particular minerals will always be utterly indispensable for certain processes or end-uses. The latter concept may be true of the short-term but it is of the very essence of technological change that alternative methods or substitute products are invariably available in the longer-term.

Nor is it true that the need, if it were to develop, to replace increasingly scarce materials by the cheapest available alternative would necessarily impose huge and indigestible increases in costs. Fears that this may happen ignore the tendency for the elasticity of supply of resources, and the degree of substitutability between them, to increase as time goes by.

The economists' concepts of 'alternatives' and 'substitutes' may convey an impression of something less satisfactory than the original. This is not the sense in which these terms are here used. Alternative resources may be

> ...not only equal in economic quality but often superior to those replaced. Few components of the earth's crust including farm land, are so specific as to defy economic replacement, or so resistant to technological advance as to be incapable of eventually yielding extractive products at constant or declining cost. When coal, petroleum, hydro-electric power, and the atomic nucleus replace wood, peat and dung as sources of energy; when aluminium yields its secrets to technology and is made to exist, as never before, in the form of metal; when the iron in tacomite, once held there inseparably, becomes competitive with that in traditional ores – when all this happens, can we say that we have been forced to shift from resources of higher to those of lower economic quality?[62]

Implicit in fears of exhaustion of non-renewable resources is the notion that the stock of such resources can, in principle, be counted up like the stock on a shopkeeper's shelves – so many tons of iron, so many barrels of oil and so on. In fact, the level of reserves is constantly influenced, both in the short-term and the long-term, by a whole complex of ever-changing factors. There is no firm dividing line, at any point of time, between what is part of the stock and what *is* not: for reasons already indicated, statements about supplies available cannot be divorced from the current state of technology and commercial values. Scarcity does not exist as an absolute: it has to be thought of in terms of cost.

62 Barnett and Morse, *op cit*: 10.

This key point may be illustrated by a few examples. Thus, the United States Bureau of Mines has estimated that an increase of 35-40 per cent in the price of iron ore could double world reserves; a 50 per cent increase in the price of tin would raise reserves by 80 per cent; and a trebling in the price of copper would raise reserves to about 2.5 times their present level.[63] These estimates relate only to known reserves but of course, increases in prices not only lead to 'overnight' growth in the level of economically mineable ore, but also to larger *additions* to reserves. Exploration becomes more attractive, techniques of exploration and treatment which would not have been feasible at the earlier level of prices become so, recycling and reclamation of scrap and residues are encouraged, alternative materials and processes become increasingly attractive, technical methods which enable greater economy in use become more profitable, and so on.

This process of substitution and expansion in the range of alternate materials, sources and processes is going on all the time. As it continues, the possibility of large discrete leaps upward in final costs arising from growing scarcity of particular minerals is steadily receding. Numerous illustrations could be given of the increasing range of alternatives available. Aluminium has displaced or become more competitive with steel in some uses, with copper in others. As a result, bauxite has become a 'resource'.[64] Synthetic materials have displaced or become more competitive with minerals—for example, plastic piping has replaced lead in some plumbing uses.[65] Half a century ago the air was for breathing and burning; now it is also a natural resource of the chemical industry.[66] As time goes by the quality of ores becomes a less critical component in the price of many metals, while treatment and transport costs become more important.[67]

---

63 IBRD, *op cit*: 37-39. *By definition*, such estimates will necessarily show that ore bodies not now regarded as part of reserves are inferior in economic quality to those that are – in the sense that it would add to costs if these reserves, rather than as-yet undiscovered reserves, had to be used with *presently known* techniques to produce products *now known*, in the proportions required to meet *present* demands reflecting the tastes and preferences of the *existing* population in the places in which they *now* live and work. Since there will be large changes in these and other ways, estimates of what would happen if there were not are entirely hypothetical. But they do illustrate the point that scarcity is not an absolute, even for a particular commodity.

64 Bauxite is the main raw material used in aluminium production at present, though alternative aluminous materials – virtually unlimited in quantity – are also available and will probably be increasingly exploited in the long-run.

65 '...more and more of the materials input used in manufacturing plants is coming from other factories instead of from farms, mines and forests. To be sure the crude materials from which synthetics are made must still come from farms, mines, forests, or the sea, but such materials are generally worth much less than the natural materials they replace and they may be abundant rather than scarce materials.' US Bureau of the Census and US Bureau of Mines, *Raw Materials in the United States Economy 1900-1966*, (Working Paper No. 30, 1969): 11.

66 Barnett and Morse, *op cit*: 7.

67 It was stated some years ago by Mr. RT Madigan, then Managing Director of Hamersley Iron Ltd, that the low-grade iron deposits in the Pilbara region of Western Australia could amount to *100 million million tons*. On that basis the iron content of these deposits would be hundreds of times greater than the known reserves of the entire world, as estimated in the study for the Club of Rome. Similar low-grade material is exploited in North America and Europe, but there will be no need in the foreseeable future to mine low-grade ore in locations where treatment and transport costs are relatively high.

Is there any foreseeable end to this process of technological change, which is constantly 'creating' resources and opportunities for substitution?

It has been estimated, on the evidence of a large number of random samples, that the total natural occurrence of most metals in the top mile of the earth's crust is about *a million times* as great as present known reserves.[68] In purely physical terms the basic ingredients of the environment – air and water, iron and aluminium, stone and sand – are available without practical limit, and there is a constant expansion in the technical possibilities for using them to meet human needs.

The economic feasibility of many of the more radical techniques – both known and yet to be developed – is, of course, another matter; but that is because of the rapid pace of progress in extracting and using established materials in orthodox ways. If scarcities were to begin to develop, all past experience suggests that revolutionary new approaches would rapidly become practicable.

VI

It is true that the economic development of processes to use lower-grade sources of minerals and to extract raw materials from the air and the sea depends in turn upon the availability of energy supplies, and in much larger quantities than are used at present. Many see this as the key constraint. Are we not already reading of an energy crisis? What of the future, if the world economy continues to grow and the input of energy required to produce a given amount of final output becomes even greater than at present?

It is necessary to consider first the nature of the 'energy crisis':

> Much has been heard recently of an energy crisis in the developed countries, particularly the United States. This is not, of course, an ultimate crisis for the availability of sufficient resources to meet demand, but is more a crisis of *policy* on what sources of energy those countries should be reliant on, at which prices, and from where these sources should be obtained. There is still a vast potential of energy which could be tapped with changed economic circumstances or technological advance.[69]

In short, the prospect for energy supplies is no different from that for metal supplies in this respect: that there need not be *physical* shortages in total,

68 Estimate made by Commodities Research Unit, London, quoted by Beckerman, *op cit*: 338. Although statements about natural occurrences of minerals have no economic meaning, they dramatically emphasise the truth that constraints on the future availability of resources *are* economic, not physical. It is thus not valid to take known reserves and to forecast future availability on what is said to be the generous assumption that they might be capable of being doubled or even increased ten-fold. That sort of figuring misses the point.
69 IBRD, *op cit*: 9.

whatever might be the position with respect to particular fuels, or of fuels in particular countries.[70] There would be an enormous increase in available oil supplies if the world's shale oil deposits were ultimately to be developed.[71] It has been estimated that only two per cent of the world's known coal reserves will have been consumed by the year 2000.[72]

It remains to be seen how much of each of the fossil fuels are used to produce energy in the future, and by what means, in what places and on what scale. In general, energy sources are more readily substitutable for one another than raw materials; and there are also considerable possibilities for the conversion of one form of fuel into another:

> Coal can also be liquefied and refined to substitute directly for gasoline or fuel oil. It can also be gasified to substitute for natural gas. Liquefaction and gasification of coal are both approaching the margin of economic feasibility. The production of oil from oil shale is another marginal economic proposition, and it is expected that with production experience costs will be reduced further.[73]

The large-scale development of some of these processes may be accelerated by the desire of some countries to avoid excessive dependence on imported energy sources. That consideration aside, the rate of development of new processes will depend on whether (and where) they are less costly than traditional sources. If the commercial exploitation of techniques for the liquefaction and gasification of coal and the production of oil from tar sands or shale has not proceeded as

---

70 Authorities in the United States attribute current shortages of various forms of energy in that country to a large number of contributing influences. Most observers agree that concern for the environment has been of major importance – for example, there have been delays in the construction of pipelines and in the licensing of nuclear power plants, increasing difficulties in securing acceptable sizes for oil refineries, and rapid growth in petroleum usage because of the heavier fuel consumption of vehicles equipped with emission-control devices. Construction of oil refineries within the US is also believed to have been discouraged by uncertainty as to the ready availability of inputs, under the system of year-by-year or month-by-month setting of import quotas on crude supplies which was discontinued in April 1973. Demand for natural gas was stimulated, and the growth of the capacity of the industry retarded, by regulations which were designed to keep prices to users low. Without entering here into the validity or relative importance of these explanations – the issues are complex and controversial – it can be said that most observers agree that the origin of the 'energy crisis' cannot be traced primarily or largely to the depletion of mineral resources.

71 Known crude oil reserves, as given in the *Limits to Growth, op cit*: 58, are equivalent to 31 years' usage at current rates and 20 years' usage assuming that the past rate of exponential growth is maintained. *Mineral Facts and Problems* (1970), *op cit*: 190, quotes estimates by the US Geological Survey that shale oil resources in place in the land areas of the world, in shales as rich as 10 gallons to the ton or richer, may be in excess of 300 million million barrels, which is about *700 times* as great as known crude oil reserves. It is unlikely that more than a tiny fraction of these resources will ever be used, because new crude discoveries, the liquefaction of coal and the production of oil from other synthetic sources are likely to provide less costly supplies on a vast scale.

72 Quoted by Sir John Hill, chairman of the United Kingdom Atomic Energy Authority, in 'The Role of Nuclear Energy in the Total Energy Mix' *(Atom*, December 1972: 210).

73 *Economic Report of the (US) President, Annual Report of the Council of Economic Advisers*, (Washington 1971): 132.

the Paley Commission in the United States expected twenty years ago,[74] that is not because technical progress in reducing the costs of these processes has been slower than expected. *It is because progress in reducing the real costs of using conventional fuel sources in conventional ways has been faster than was then expected.*[75]

The same can be said of the development of nuclear power. Thirty years after the first controlled fission chain reaction, nuclear fission reactors are not making a large contribution to world energy supply, but they would undoubtedly have made a much larger contribution if power from conventional sources had become more expensive. In fact, the real price of conventional power has declined steeply. As nuclear technology develops, fuel costs are becoming a progressively smaller component of the cost of nuclear energy. They will soon be an insignificant component. Even if uranium had to be extracted from the sea, which is unlikely to be necessary in the foreseeable future, the additional cost would not be substantial.[76] The source of the fuel consumed in power stations will not be an important determinant of the cost of electricity used in houses in thirty years time; nor will the relative cost of operating a car depend to any significant extent on the cost of crude oil or whatever other materials may then be being processed into the fuel that cars will then be using.[77] In the decades ahead, society may face important decisions about the role of the motor vehicle, especially in the cities: but the belief that the long-term availability of fuel will be a critical consideration in those decisions can only serve to confuse the issues.

It is not possible to predict movements in the relative costs of the major energy sources several decades ahead. Nor is it possible to predict what new sources may be developed. There is the possibility of eventually producing power from controlled fusion reactions, in which case virtually limitless energy could be

---

74 The President's Materials Policy Commission (Paley Commission) submitted its five-volume analysis of the past, present and probable future of US mineral supply industries in June 1952. The Commission 'concluded that domestic crude oil production would not be able to meet domestic demand at constant costs, and anticipated supplementary supplies from oil shale and coal liquefaction by 1970. It also felt that unrestrained crude imports would be necessary to keep costs and prices from rising. What actually happened is that petroleum prices declined. Oil from shale and coal is not yet profitable, and petroleum imports are restricted under a national control program'. (*Mineral Facts and Problems*, 1970, *op cit*: 1.)

75 Statements that new means of producing energy would be 'too expensive' will usually be found on examination to depend on a comparison with costs of energy produced by 'old' means. Some of the more alarming forecasts of energy scarcity appear to rest on two assumptions that are mutually inconsistent: that supplies of traditional fuel will be inadequate; and that alternative sources cannot be developed because costs will be higher than for energy produced from traditional fuels.

76 TN Marsham and RS Pease, 'Nuclear Power – The Future' (*Atom*, February 1973: 46).

77 Even today a doubling in the cost of crude oil in Australia would add only a relatively small percentage – less than 10 per cent – to the total average cost of owning and operating a motor vehicle.

produced.[78] The sun or the tides may be harnessed. Such developments are not impossible or even highly unlikely. The question is not so much whether new developments can be effected, but when and at what cost.

If the world gradually shifts from using fossil fuels to other forms of energy in the future, it will be because those other forms become – in given locations and conditions – competitive with traditional sources in terms of cost, convenience and cleanliness. It cannot be inferred from the fact that supplies of fossil fuels are finite that the prices of such fuels must necessarily rise in the decades ahead; but it *can* be inferred that as alternative energy forms are developed, it will become increasingly necessary for fossil fuel supplies to be cheap if they are to be used at all. It is conceivable that the great bulk of the world's store of these fuels will remain in the ground (or under the sea) forever.

VII

A ton of coal once consumed is gone forever; and the same is true of a ton of iron or of other metals, with the qualification that these may be recovered in due course if resources are used for the purpose. These facts, and the common sense view that there must be a physical limit to the number of tons of coal or iron or copper in the world, are the main supports for the belief that the present generation must conserve mineral resources for its successors.

The preceding sections have however drawn attention to other important facts: that inexhaustible energy sources can be substituted for exhaustible ones, and that the eventual availability of metals is, for the future so far as it is worth talking about even in the most speculative terms, infinitely large. It follows that there is no blanket argument for physical conservation – each conservation proposal must be put to the test in terms of what is foregone to achieve its benefits.

It may, for example, be technically feasible to recycle a very large proportion of a given metal, but it would be pointless to do so if the metal can be produced more cheaply from new ore.[79] The 'waste' conserved by recycling would be offset by other 'wastes'; the ore left un-mined in the ground plus whatever other resources are involved including, directly or indirectly, other minerals and hydrocarbons.

---

78 For example, if the controlled fusion of two deuterium atoms were accomplished, it has been calculated that the energy released by the withdrawal of *one per cent of* the initial concentration of deuterium in sea water would be equivalent to *500,000 times* the world's estimated ultimate reserves of fossil fuels. (See *Resources and Man,* US National Academy of Science, Washington 1969: 230.)

79 There are, of course, other factors to be taken into account than minimising the cost of producing metal. For example, recycling may yield social benefits (e.g. cans) voluntary labour might sometimes carry out the task for nominal payment (e.g. boy scouts) but, of course, such voluntary organisations may find more attractive fund-raising activities.

It is sometimes suggested that the expectations about the future demand for a mineral which producers take into account in making their decisions about whether or not to work a deposit do not extend sufficiently far into the future, and that governments therefore have a duty to conserve mineral supplies for future generations. There will be occasions when governments accept such obligations – for example, in the interests of national security. Proposals to reserve known mineral deposits for future use require careful assessment in each case, having regard both to the possibility of safeguarding the interests of future generations and the costs of doing so. The basic problem in preventing current exploitation in order to facilitate future development is that *possible* future gains are being weighed against *certain* current losses: those in whose interests it is suggested that a certain mineral should be conserved might not turn out to want it at all, or might want it only at a fraction of its current real price.[80] Even if it could be known – and clearly it cannot be – that at a certain time in the distant future the real price of the mineral concerned would be several times the current price, there would still be no clear-cut answers to the question whether production of the mineral should be limited now in order to reduce real costs in the future. A multiple increase in the real price of one mineral or even of most minerals, would not seriously inhibit future economic growth, or change the expectation that future generations will be much better off materially than our own. Such threats as there are to these prospects do not come from the depletion of what lies in the ground.

VIII

The key conclusion of this chapter is that the effects of continuing economic growth on the availability of non-renewable resources are much more complex than is sometimes supposed. Such resources may be being 'used up', but they are also – *as an integral part of the same process* – being 'created'. It is in the twentieth century that the essential uniformity of energy and matter has been discovered, that the development of new synthetic materials has become almost commonplace, and that technological advance has become virtually continuous, each improvement creating new opportunities for further advance. The extension of knowledge about the world has not only confounded past predictions of resource scarcity but has been in directions which make such predictions less and less defensible as time goes by.

The current wave of concern about the rate of depletion of the earth's 'capital stock' of minerals sometimes appears to result in a loss in perspective. Of the legacy of capital which each generation passes on, mineral resources in

80 There is an *ad infinitum* aspect here. If the current generation arbitrarily sacrifices current ore consumption for the sake of a future generation, the future generation could logically do the same for a more future generation and so on.

the ground are only a tiny part. Far more important is the growing stock of productive and social capital in use – equipment and buildings, knowledge and technology, human skills and institutions. It is the quantity and quality of their inheritance of these things that our descendants will care about. If real minerals and energy costs were to be higher, and even much higher than at present, that would be a matter of relatively small concern to them.[81]

There is, however, in any case, no sign that real mineral and energy costs *will* be higher. Even those predicting 'Doomsday' agree that it will not arrive overnight. On their view of things, scarcities will gradually develop, driving up prices and creating increasingly difficult and eventually intolerable problems. If this is indeed the outlook for the decades ahead, however, the process should already be apparent, at least in some degree. It is not: on the contrary, the fastest rising prices in advanced economies continue to be those in the services sector. Prices in the industrial sector – the major user of energy and minerals – continue right up to the present to rise at below average rates.

There are, of course, many circumstances in which intervention by governments and supervision of private sector operations in the mining industry are essential – not only to correct disparities between private and social costs of which pollution and environmental damage are the obvious symptoms, but also to safeguard the general interest (including the interests of future generations) against wasteful and short-sighted techniques which result in ore which is or may be economic to remove now or at a future date ceasing to be so.

But conservation policy which takes the sensible form of enforcing 'best practice' is very different from that which pursues conservation on the basis of physical criteria, vaguely backed by the notion that all mineral deposits represent a 'limited' resource and are thereby 'valuable'. It is not really true that the mineral deposits our ancestors worked were 'richer' than those now exploited; some of the physical ore grades may have been higher then, but technological advance means that present-day reserves are richer in the only sense that counts: their effectiveness in achieving a given result at least real costs.

---

81 Typically an advanced economy devotes only a small proportion of its total productive effort to the winning or importation of minerals (directly or indirectly). Australia is a substantial net exporter of minerals, but even so its mineral output only represented 3.2 per cent of GDP in 1970-71. Of course the fact that a group of products are a small proportion of total output does not mean to say that they are not of critical importance: however, it is the theme of this Part of the paper that the supply of minerals as a group will not become critical. Again, the fact that an activity absorbs a small proportion of available capacity does not mean that increases in that proportion are of no importance – far from it: the total economy is the sum of activities which could be classified into small industry groups. If incomes (in the broadest sense) are to advance, there is a need to seek efficiency in *every* branch of activity. Governments will manoeuvre to the best advantage in an endeavour to obtain cheap and secure supplies of raw materials and energy for industrial and domestic use. Nevertheless, increases in the small proportion of productive effort devoted to mineral supplies would not be crippling to economic growth in the longer-term.

If we exploit this planet's mineral resources now according to current economic and technological conditions, future generations will not necessarily be any less affluent than if we made a concentrated effort to conserve mineral resources for their use. Indeed, if conservation policy took the form of slowing or stopping economic growth, they would be much less well off than they would otherwise have been. It will be in the skills and technology of future generations that their fate will lie, and they are more likely to suffer than to benefit from any well-meant but almost inevitably misdirected efforts of the present generation to anticipate the specific constellation of technical conditions and opportunities with which they will be faced.

Part 5: A question of priorities

> ... since we must rely on governments for reform and since governments reflect fairly accurately the prejudices, hopes and intellectual preconceptions of the community generally, the broad requirements of policy suggested by theory must be thrashed about and mulled over in communication and controversy between academics, scientists, politicians and the community generally until they become, as did the objective of full employment, part of the ethos of the community. (Dr HC Coombs, ABC Boyer Lectures for 1970, *The Fragile Pattern: Institutions and Man*.)

I

In Part 1 it was noted that there is increasing (though still very much minority) support for the view that economic growth must be checked or even halted altogether. The succeeding discussion has suggested that such a view can scarcely base itself on inevitabilities. There is nothing inevitable about despoliation of the environment arising out of growth of output. Nor is there anything inevitable about exhaustion of needed mineral resources arising out of continued growth.

Though there have been some widely publicised claims that an early end to growth is a veritable condition for human survival, those claims have not been backed by the solid evidence and reasoning needed to support such a drastic prescription. Once the claim of technical inevitability is rejected it becomes plain that the debate about growth is really a debate about priorities: whether they are effective in decision-making. But here the debate encounters another inevitability argument – one not of technical but of social inevitability.

The view that relatively affluent communities place far too much emphasis upon production and its increase has more substance than the notion that physical constraints will impose early limits to global economic growth. There are many strands to the argument. Some of the more important are that consumption of some products reflects status, not wants; that corporations manipulate 'wants' through advertising and other sales techniques; and that, driven on by the social compulsion of the 'rat 'race', each individual seeks to maintain or raise his *relative* position in the income structure so that the struggle to increase incomes overall is no more than a social treadmill.

Few would deny the existence of all of these phenomena, but views differ widely as to their significance, whether separately or in combination. In the final analysis a good deal obviously depends on differences in social philosophies. In this final chapter it is possible only to expose some of the issues on which judgements are likely to differ, and highlight the significance of some of the arguments for the debate about whether economic growth is worth having.

II

The ironic reflection that a major purpose of production might be to make possible socially acceptable forms of waste has cast doubt on the rationale of the process. 'Conspicuous consumption' is the term[82] adopted to describe this demand for allegedly useless goods (or aspects of goods) sought after as an outward testimony of 'pecuniary worth'. As the primitive Indian burned his pile of blankets as a token of his community standing, so, the argument goes, contemporary man encases himself in one and a half tons of metal to a similar effect.

It is one thing to acknowledge that conspicuous consumption constitutes an element in consumer behaviour. It is quite another to agree on its specific manifestations or on what to do about it. There is no more a consensus on what is 'useful' than on what is aesthetically fine. Functional engineering criteria cannot provide definitive answers. It is therefore incorrect to suppose that the concept of conspicuous consumption provides some *objective* measure of waste. It merely sets one group of values against another.[83]

Nor is the 'conspicuous consumption' thesis assisted by describing a particular valuation as involving a status symbol. Status or social acceptability in some form is important to people's participation in any society. Moreover, the suppression of one kind of pursuit of status does not necessarily mean its replacement by a kind more acceptable to the critic. Those who condemn increases in material standards of life which take the form of extra footage of car, 'useless' mechanical gadgets or modish garments are not obliged to devote any of their own expenditure to such fripperies; and they have the option, within

82 A term coined, incidentally, not in recent times but in the late nineteenth century by the American economist Thorstein Veblen.

83 Among the targets of Veblen's charges of 'conspicuous consumption' was the purchase of masterpieces of art.

limits, of seeking to persuade the purchasers of the foolishness of their actions. It is more difficult to see in such manifestations any justification for advocating a slow-down or a halt to growth.

Almost any non-subsistence purchases could be open to the charge of conspicuous consumption, but current criticism tends to concentrate on expenditure on cars and durable consumer goods. Spending on such items averages around 10 per cent of consumer spending in the advanced economies: rather more in some (including Australia) and less in others. The proportion does not appear to have increased much over time. Increased expenditure on new products tends to be offset by relatively less spending on items for which the phase of rapid growth in ownership has passed. Moreover, only extreme judgements would hold that more than a small proportion of expenditure on durable goods is of the 'conspicuous' variety. It is also at least arguable that the apparently lavish provision of these items in many households in the wealthier countries of the world should not be attributed to a misplaced ordering of priorities, but rather to a sensible response to their ready availability and low real price.[84]

The concept of conspicuous consumption has also figured in the contrast between 'private affluence' and 'public squalor'. Central to this contrast is the notion of an imbalance between the supply of those goods and services provided by the private sector and the supply of essentially complementary items by the public sector – for example, too many cars but not enough roads or parking space. Again the appropriate remedy lies in influencing priorities and the mechanisms for registering and giving effect to them, rather than in limiting the possibilities of implementing *any* set of priorities. Attitudes of sanctity towards private expenditure and parsimony towards public expenditure may properly be combatted, but there is a balance to be struck: governments may also engage in conspicuous consumption. Expansion of public spending *per se* will not rectify the supply imbalance; the real task is that of harmonising all spending, public and private, with a rational interpretation of the community's pattern of preferences (which is, of course, more easily said than done).

Personal consumer expenditures are also influenced, it is often claimed, by direct 'manipulation'. Advertising and other sales techniques frequently aim at heightening social pressures, to shame the consumer for his lack of the latest product. This is a complex issue. The point in the present context is, however, that although in the absence of persuasion techniques which contrive wants rather than inform, the pattern of consumption would doubtless be different, economic growth would not necessarily be any slower.[85] A policy of deliberately slowing or halting growth would be a costly and inefficient way of dealing with advertising: it would strike at the satisfying of wants whether contrived or not.

84 This of course reflects in turn the relatively small input of total resources – including labour and capital as well as raw materials – devoted to their production.
85 It could be in terms of *measured* GDP.

III

Another aspect of social behaviour often seen as qualifying the advantages of economic growth is the observation that a person's relative 'income' (however interpreted) as distinct from his absolute 'income' may be of importance – perhaps even predominant importance – to him. He may, for example, prefer a one per cent increase in his own command over resources, other people's remaining constant, than a five per cent increase in line with everyone else.

This notion that people are concerned in some measure with their relative incomes is another variant of the conspicuous consumption thesis, and there can be no question that there is truth in it. Our concern here, however, is with its implications for questions about whether or not economic growth is worthwhile.

Measures of income redistribution, in the interests of equity and the relief of poverty, have been introduced in most countries; these aside, what courses of social policy will be appropriate in the face of the fact that people are to some degree concerned with their position in the income structure of society rather than with their absolute incomes? It is obviously a contradiction in terms to seek to improve total relative incomes: gains for some are necessarily offset by losses to others. In fact, short of seeking to change the mores of the society, there is no practical answer available unless the total 'cake' is also growing.

It follows that, as long as people are not indifferent to their absolute incomes, policies to promote a general increase in such incomes will be seen as enhancing welfare generally. To the extent that the cult of relative income rules a community, improvements in economic welfare may be hard to come by: but it remains sensible to pursue them.

This conclusion is reinforced by two further reflections.

First, even if concern for relative rather than absolute income were more intense in an affluent community than a poor one, it would not follow that it would be more powerful and persuasive in an expanding economy than in a stationary one. On the contrary, it may well be that it is in a stagnant economy that people or groups have the stronger expectations of retaining what they hold without the subversion of change and growth. In an expanding economy relative positions may be less entrenched and less apparent, and the assumption that improvement depends on disturbing them may have a lighter hold.

Secondly, the concern of individuals with their relative income is not restricted to their position *vis-a-vis* their compatriots. They are also concerned in some measure with how they fare compared with people in other countries. Their relative position would deteriorate imposing *decreases* in welfare, if their absolute incomes remained constant while incomes in other countries increased. Even if it were the case, therefore, that people are entirely indifferent to their absolute incomes – which is very far from the truth – it would still not be sensible for one country to halt growth unless others did likewise. There is no sign of an international agreement to halt improvements in economic wellbeing.[86] Even in the developed countries it is easy for most people to think of good uses to which increased capacity can be put; elsewhere the notion of ceasing to strive for improvement would be dismissed as absurd.

IV

There is no doubt that different interpretations of social behaviour can lead to very different evaluations of the effectiveness of economic growth. Not only will there be disagreement over values – over how much emphasis to give to leisure, for example – but also the holders of a particular set of values may be accused by others of being caught up in a mindless 'rat race'. Their preference (say) for higher money income as against more leisure is the result – so it will be suggested – of the particular social context in which they pursue participation and acceptability. Those so criticised will tend to question whatever alternative is proposed. The resolution of such conflicts is a matter not for the economic but the political field.

It has been a theme of this paper that economic growth, properly interpreted, is neutral between objectives.[87] It simply expands the options. But the 'production' of the 'wrong' combination of things – for example, too many durable consumer goods and not enough government services or environmental 'goods' – can lead to the disparagement of economic growth itself by the particular groups who believe the combination is wrong.

Such disparagement has undoubtedly reinforced proposals that growth should be halted because of the alleged technical inevitabilities discussed – and rejected – in earlier Parts of this paper. Such policies are not a tenet of a widely supported political group; it is hard to envisage their operation without leading to some very unpalatable consequences such as the stifling of innovation; and they would be strongly opposed by those who see economic growth as the

86 There is the further aspect that a country taking measures to halt or drastically slow down its rate of growth could be faced with a 'brain drain' or similar consequences, and might eventually frustrate the very objectives that are held to justify action of that kind by those who advocate it.

87 That is between ultimate, long-term objectives. Policies directed towards ensuring that there is an adequate but not excessive growth in demand in the short-run, in line with the growth in capacity, must recognise the existence of 'trade-offs' between full employment, price stability, balance of payments viability and so on. But the outcome of the balancing of these aims need not involve any conflict with growth in the longer-term.

only way to improve human welfare both in its measurable and less measurable aspects. Such attitudes may, nevertheless, have their influence on decisions in a variety of fields – and in ways that may not be in the interests of anyone.

V

Time horizons are like geographical ones, so that generations in the distant future are akin to an alien people: they benefit in a general way – perhaps considerably – from the current following out of the economic calculus (as do foreigners from international trade), but their particular interests are not served. This is not surprising since those interests are not known. Were it possible to say that vital mineral deposits would be exhausted for them, or the air and water poisoned for them, these single technical absolutes would provide some guidance. But future generations are not likely to be presented with such absolutes. Whatever the present generation elects to do, there are no means of knowing what the *relative* availability of the various environmental and other resources will be in fifty or two hundred years' time; and such relativities will be worked on by an unknown technology for the purpose of meeting unknown wants. There have been many past predictions, implicit or explicit, that all of the important inventions have been made. Technology continues to grow exponentially for all that. The scientist in 1873, attempting to predict the supply of resources in 1973, would have seen as *impossible* the output of those resources which actually obtained. Yet because of the exponential nature of the growth of technology we are probably less fitted to pronounce on probabilities a hundred years hence than were our predecessors a hundred years ago.

Unborn generations cast no votes. Their political influence is by proxy, or through what there is of paternalistic foresight amongst the current generation. But if the collective frailties of present-day decision makers were to be replaced by a benign dictator 'above it all', what kinds of changes would he direct in the volume of investment and its composition? No clear-cut answer can be given, but it may be worthwhile drawing attention to some relevant points.

The projected net benefits flowing from any investment decision pass into shadow not too many years ahead. The present value of future net benefits is steadily reduced in weight through the process of discounting – that is, as preference for consumption now as against consumption at increasingly distant times is taken into account.[88] Moreover, the net benefits themselves become increasingly speculative.

Stepping up the proportion of production used for investment involves imposing a penalty on the present generation in order to make richer still those

88 See *Supplement to the Treasury Information Bulletin: Investment Analysis*, July 1966.

who through technical advance and compounding increases are likely to be richer anyway. The same is true of proposals that involve adding to the costs of investments made now for the sake of reducing the costs imposed upon, or increasing the benefits accruing to, future generations. There is no point of reference, other than the expected rate of social return criterion which guides public investment decisions generally, by which it can be shown that possible or even certain benefits for future citizens are worth the certain penalties imposed on present citizens.

The community might, of course, be ignorant and apathetic towards the welfare of future generations but it needs to be persuaded that it is so. Benefits in the remote future do not merely need to be *positive* to justify penalties on the present generation, they would need to be very large indeed in relation to current costs.

Whatever views might be held as to whether society's preferences as between present and future consumption show an excessive or deficient regard for our descendants – and there cannot be an objective answer – the 'policy' of anti-growth helps no one. It reduces the resources available to current and future generations alike.

VI

Perhaps the most important conclusion implied in what has been said in this paper is that statements 'for' or 'against' continuing economic growth abound in potential semantic tangles. Perhaps the most useful concept of 'growth' to have in mind is the process of expanding the options available to realise society's priorities.

The process of best achieving the welfare of society for the resources available will normally result in a net growth of the *per capita* output of the economic system as conventionally conceived. This growth will come from better resource allocation, improved management and skills, technological progress and net investment. It is an important *effect* because it adds to the resources of the community for meeting future social needs. But in essence the problem of providing more social (e.g. environmental) 'goods' as against more 'economic' goods is not a growth question at all. There are many problems in achieving satisfactory economic growth but the pattern of wants of the community, whether these wants are labelled economic or not, is not one of them.[89]

89 The discussion is concerned with economic growth in developed economies. In *primitive* societies the patterns of wants may be an important factor in inhibiting a people's control over their material environment.

Economic growth tends to facilitate the achievement of the community's priorities from time to time, and if that is accepted, growth cannot be the legitimate target for criticisms of those priorities.

Those who advocate checking growth or bringing it to a halt have an obligation to specify carefully what they have in mind: the danger is that the course they prescribe may reduce the options for attaining *any* commonly accepted set of priorities.

Part Two: Measuring Real Income and Wellbeing

6. Measuring Progress: The International Context

Brian Pink, Sue Taylor and Hannah Wetzler

Introduction

Progress is an idea that echoes and has echoed throughout societies across the world. The idea of progress and what it means has influenced how societies and nations understand themselves, how they change over time, and how they relate to other nations.

The idea of progress as societal improvement has a long history. Notions of national or societal progress can be traced back to early civilisations, and were discussed by the early philosophers including Aristotle and Socrates. More modern ideas around progress were further developed throughout the Reformation and the Industrial Revolution. In the nineteenth century, for example, political economist John Stuart Mill wrote about the importance of including the environment, rather than simply wealth or growth alone, in understanding national progress and he noted the importance of people developing their capabilities in order to achieve higher levels of happiness (Mill: 1848). More recently, in the twentieth century and early part of the twenty-first, as the world underwent several major economic and societal upheavals, the understanding and measurement of progress developed further, shaping how we understand it today.

This chapter paints a brief history of the development of progress measurement during the twentieth and twenty-first centuries. It examines the key events that influenced understandings of progress – such as the two World Wars, the Great Depression and the rise of key international organisations – and how to measure it. It looks at how the understanding of national progress has shifted from one of economic development towards one that includes societal wellbeing and environmental sustainability. The essay also incorporates a number of insights into the contributions made by Ian Castles (Australian Statistician from 1986-1994) in improving the statistics that inform on progress. The chapter looks at key national and international developments in the early 2000s and those following the release of the Stiglitz-Sen-Fitoussi report, and highlights the work that the Australian Bureau of Statistics has undertaken as a key player in the international statistical community. It concludes with a brief review of future international work, which will further shape how the world understands and measures progress.

Changing ideas of progress through the twentieth century

Throughout the twentieth century, economic development was a key goal for governments across the world and as a result, perhaps the most common lens through which national progress is understood. This section of the chapter charts the emergence through the century of a number of different views of progress, first through the early focus on economic growth and GDP, then an explosion of interest in charting wellbeing and human development, and finally a still emerging interest in the environment and climate change.

The rise of GDP

In 1934, Russian American economist Simon Kuznets developed Gross Domestic Product (GDP) as a tool for measuring the production or income of a country. GDP aggregates the value added of all money-based economic activities. It is based on the System of National Accounts (SNA) and allows comparisons to be made over time and between countries and regions.

GDP is the best-known measure of macro-economic activity and one of the most widely used statistics (European Commission: 2009). This is largely due to its clear methodology and clarity of concept, which is easily replicated over time and between nations. Because of this, GDP is used not only as a measure of a nation's production value and economic development more broadly, but also often as a measure of progress. To cite Ian Castles, 'No single statistic has ever claimed such attention. It became a standard against which almost all aspects of economic performance were judged' (Castles: 1973).

During WWII, the Bretton Woods conference in 1944 saw many nations come together for the purpose of taking a unified, global approach to regulating international monetary and financial order. The conference resulted in the establishment of the International Monetary Fund (IMF) and the forerunner to the current World Bank. Castles noted that after the conference, 'GDP became the main tool for measuring economic progress throughout the world' (Castles: 1973).

While GDP is a valuable and powerful statistic within itself, its use and misuse has attracted criticism. Many have argued that GDP has limitations as both a measure of economic activity, and a measure of progress more broadly. However, measuring a nation's welfare or progress using GDP was never developer Kuznets's intention for GDP; he stated 'the welfare of a nation can scarcely be inferred from a measure of national income' (Kuznets: 1934).

In Australia in 1973, Ian Castles produced the essay *'Economic Growth: Is it worth having?'* that called into question the idea of looking at national progress through the lens of economic growth alone. Castles said that economic growth should not be pursued for its own sake, but should be the result of policies directed to improving the welfare of the community without using resources wastefully. In his essay, Castles also recognised that people have different values, and therefore what some may consider progress, others would see as regress. Castles' work articulated what many others around the world were beginning to recognise, and what John Stuart Mill had noted a century earlier: that there are factors beyond economic development that are important to a nation's wellbeing.

The rise and rise of social statistics

The latter half of the twentieth century saw enormous interest in the concept of wellbeing and in issues of social concern as evidenced by: the establishment of the United Nations; enormous growth in the number and range of social statistics emerging from the Social Indicators Movement of the 1960s and 70s; and the emergence of important international initiatives such as the Human Development Index in 1990, and the Millennium Development Goals in 2000.

The establishment of the United Nations

A major international post-World War II development was the establishment of the United Nations. The United Nations supplanted the previous League of Nations, which was set up after the First World War as a forum for international cooperation. Many other nations have since joined the United Nations and it currently has 193 member states. In 1948, the United Nations General Assembly developed the Universal Declaration of Human Rights, which outlines a range of rights seen as fundamental for all people. Examples include Article 23, which addresses the right to employment in a safe and prejudice-free environment; Article 24, which addresses the right to rest and leisure; and Article 25, which addresses the right to an adequate standard of living. These universal rights have served to help frame understandings of national progress, providing aspirations for people and their quality of life.

Social Indicators movement

During the 1960s and 70s, international interest grew in how to come to grips with the scope of social statistics and how summary measures might be constructed. In 1969, the UN Declaration on Social Progress and Development attempted to document the international consensus on the meaning of progress at that time. The declaration sets out in detail the rationale, principles, objectives and means to achieving societal progress. In the declaration, the UN identified main goals for social progress and development around areas such as work life, hunger and poverty, health, education and literacy, housing and services (ABS: 2005).

At the same time, many statistical agencies began to consider how to measure societal wellbeing. In the 1960s, Raymond Bauer developed a set of Social Indicators. These were a collection of measures that aimed to assess national wellbeing by looking at the social conditions of society; '[they are] statistics, statistical series, and all other forms of evidence that enable us to assess where we stand and are going with respect to our values and goals' (Bauer: 1966). The idea of social indicators was taken up by statistical agencies around the world.

In Australia, the ABS published its first set of Social Indicators in 1976, which brought together a wide range of topics, in a single report, with the specific purpose of analysing key social issues in Australia (ABS: 1976). In 1994, in a prescient move, Ian Castles, then Australian Statistician, replaced the *Social Indicators Report* – which was struggling to keep up with the ever-expanding set of data available from the Bureau's social surveys – with *Australian Social Trends* (ABS: 1994). This publication continues to this day and has built up an impressive archive of articles across a wide range of social issues. It presents statistical analysis and commentary on a wide range of current social issues, bringing together data from many sources to tell a story about Australian life. In the preface to the first issue, noting the importance of analysing social trends, Castles wrote that 'an examination of social trends tells us not only where we are now and where we have come from, but also where we are headed' (ABS: 1994).

The Human Development Index

In 1990, the United Nations Development Program (UNDP) produced the first Human Development Index (HDI), based on the Nobel prize-winning work of Amartya Sen. The index aimed to measure progress towards human development, between countries and over time, by looking at what the UNDP considered essential dimensions of quality of human life; health, education and income. Importantly, the HDI provided an alternative to the then conventional assessments of progress.

The current index compiles composite data on national levels of life expectancy, both mean years of schooling and expected years of schooling, and gross national income per capita (at Purchasing Power Parity US$). It uses this to give an annual rank to each country based on whether people in their countries are achieving 'a long and healthy life (health), access to knowledge (education), and a decent standard of living (income)' (UNDP: 2012). More recently, the UNDP has complemented the HDI with an inequality-adjusted human development index (IHDI), which takes into account inequality between people within the nation across the three HDI dimensions.

The work of the UNDP has drawn criticism over the years. Perhaps most notably, in 1999 Ian Castles critiqued the statistical methods used by the UNDP in their reporting of data in the Human Development Report (UN Statistical Commission:

2001). He emphasised the importance of the independence, objectivity and integrity of statistical work for public policy, especially at the international level. Castles criticised the methods and accuracy of key data in the report, including the HDI, because of its composite nature and the implicit assumptions in its weighting system. He also argued that the UNDP should use real GDP per capita (PPP$), instead of GDP per capita (US$) (UN Statistical Commission: 2001). An Australian delegation (led by Mr Bill McLennan) ensured that these and other concerns were considered by the UN Statistical Commission, which ultimately led the UNDP to take steps to improve the accuracy of the Development Report.

The HDI itself has drawn criticisms for not taking into account the impacts that human development has on the environment, although there are currently plans underway to start exploring how the HDI might consider incorporating sustainability. The HDI has also been criticised for not considering other aspects of society regarded as important for human wellbeing, such as spiritual and moral needs, community and relationships.

Despite these criticisms, the UNDP Report and the HDI have demonstrated that there was a huge disparity between countries in human development, in areas such as national and per capita income, in health and life expectancy outcomes and in education. High ranking nations were seen as developed, while low ranking nations were seen as developing, and world leaders began to become more concerned with the gap between developed and developing nations.

The Millennium Development Goals

In the year 2000, the United Nations Millennium Summit marked the genesis of the Millennium Development Goals or MDGs. Building on a decade of major United Nations conferences and summits, world leaders from across the world signed up to the Millennium Declaration, which committed their nations to a global partnership to reduce extreme poverty. Out of the Declaration was born the official list of eight Millennium Development Goals, accompanied by 21 targets and 60 indicators, which served as an international tool for measuring progress towards development.

The MDGs have drawn criticism. Some of the criticisms they acknowledge and address are: that the goals are too focused on global targets, and have overlooked national circumstances and differences in initial conditions (this is particularly true of progress being made in some African countries); the broad, simple nature of the MDGs overlooks a number of other factors considered important, such as social protection and security, peace and human rights, inequality and violence against women; that the framework itself does not account for vulnerabilities to natural hazards and other external shocks; the framework provides little guidance for means to achieve the targets; and several of the goals and targets were defined imprecisely, thereby weakening accountability for the promised international support for implementing the MDG framework (UN System Task Team: 2012).

The UN System Task Team notes that 'Critics have argued that a number of these shortcomings could have been avoided if a more inclusive consultation process had taken place in formulating the MDGs.' (UN System Task Team: 2012).

In spite of these criticisms and problems, the MDGs 'simplicity, transparency and multidimensionality helped rally broad support for the goals and their achievement, and the emphasis on human development shifted policy attention well beyond the economic growth objectives that dominated previous agendas' (UN System Task Team: 2012). They have helped shaped international understandings of progress, framing progress around poverty and human development.

Environmental wellbeing

Towards the end of the twentieth century the environment emerged as an increasingly important aspect of life to people, nations and indeed globally. While the environment has been valued for millennia, either for its importance to human society or for its intrinsic value, valuing the environment and its health in a policy sense did not gain momentum until the latter half of the twentieth century.

A number of major international initiatives focused attention on the role of the environment for global progress. In 1992, the Earth Summit: the UN Conference on Environment and Development was held in Rio De Janeiro, Brazil. From this conference came Agenda 21, which set out a plan of action for developing and measuring progress in sustainable development. Since then, statistical agencies have begun to take environmental progress and sustainability into account when considering the progress of nations overall.

New views of progress for the new millennium

The new millennium saw the development of broader overarching ways to view and measure progress and wellbeing. This section of the chapter charts these new developments, highlighting some of the key initiatives underway among a plethora of activity, including the innovative Measures of Australia's Progress.

Measures of Australia's Progress

In 2002, the Australian Bureau of Statistics became the first national statistical agency to produce a broad-focused measuring tool for assessing national progress, developing what was then known as Measuring Australia's Progress (now Measures of Australia's Progress or MAP; ABS: 2002). MAP was developed to help Australians assess whether life in Australia is getting better.

MAP was a watershed. While the ABS had previously produced separate sets of indicators to measure economic and then social progress through the System of National Accounts (ABS: 2010-11) and the development of social indicators, MAP brought together for the first time a compendium of indicators on key aspects of society, the economy and the environment to help answer the question – Is life in Australia getting better?

As the first national statistical agency to produce a diverse collection of national progress indicators, MAP generated significant international interest and in many ways set the standard for other nations to think about the ways in which they can measure their own progress. In 2003, then Australian Statistician Dennis Trewin topped the society category of The Bulletin's Smart 100 awards for this work.

Since the first release of MAP, national and international interest in measuring progress has accelerated and a number of key initiatives are listed below.

OECD Global Project on Measuring the Progress of Societies

The OECD has made measuring wellbeing and progress across member countries a key priority for over a decade. Its work in measuring progress has accelerated throughout the 2000s. Building in part on the MAP initiative, the OECD, in partnership with a range of other international institutions, established a Global Project on Measuring the Progress of Societies in 2004 and has since hosted four major international dialogues and debates on measuring societal progress, which have set out a range of directions for global progress measurement. The OECD has more recently undertaken a number of major initiatives and these are discussed in the Stiglitz-Sen-Fitoussi section of the chapter below.

Treasury Wellbeing Framework

In the early 2000s, the Australian Treasury developed the Treasury Wellbeing Framework to guide its policies (The Treasury: 2011-12). The Treasury Wellbeing Framework is a qualitative framework that operates to facilitate an objective and thorough analysis of policy options for improving wellbeing. It identifies five dimensions that directly or indirectly have important implications for wellbeing, and are particularly relevant to Treasury. The dimensions do not provide a simple checklist: rather their consideration provides the broad context for the use of the best available economic and other analytical frameworks, evidence and measures. The Treasury also point out that the trade-offs between and within the dimensions need to be considered. The five dimensions of the Wellbeing Framework include the set of opportunities available to people, the distribution of those opportunities, sustainability of opportunities, overall level and allocation of risk borne by individuals and the community, and complexity of choice facing individuals and the community.

Hong Kong Quality of Life Index

The Chinese University of Hong Kong first published the Hong Kong Quality of Life Index in 2003 (The Centre for Quality of Life: 2012). The index aims to track the quality of life for the people of Hong Kong, providing policy makers and the community with a useful reference tool. This in turn aims to help make improvements in the wellbeing of the people of Hong Kong. Now an annual product, the index is a composite of statistics, which report on societal, economic and environmental wellbeing. The index uses 21 indicators from a variety of data sources, such as national statistics (e.g. unemployment rates and GDP), as well as subjective data from surveys (e.g. people's satisfaction with the government).

Monitoring Sustainable Development in Switzerland

Also in 2003, the Swiss Federal Statistical Office, together with other Swiss government departments, produced Monitoring Sustainable Development in Switzerland (also MONET, see Swiss Federal Statistical Office: 2010). The purpose of MONET is to assess whether Switzerland is 'on the road to sustainable development', by regularly reporting on the status and progress of the nation's sustainability.

MONET draws on 80 indicators (though in its simplified form it consists of 16 broad indicators), which focus on four areas:

1. Meeting needs: how well do we live;
2. Preservation of resources: what are we leaving behind for our children?
3. Decoupling (efficient use of resources): how effectively are we using our national resources?
4. Fairness: how well are resources distributed?

The indicators are presented side by side, using a traffic light approach so that people can see clearly whether progress is being made in these areas.

MONETs approach to progress through the lens of sustainability has influenced other agencies, such as Statistics New Zealand's Measuring New Zealand's Progress Using a Sustainable Development Approach. It has also helped shape thought around national progress in terms of how well a nation is promoting the current needs of its people, without compromising the needs of future generations.

The Happy Planet Index

In 2006, the new economics foundation (nef) in the UK, recognising the importance of sustainability to national progress, produced the Happy Planet Index, which took into account how well a country can achieve wellbeing sustainably (nef: 2010). The Happy Planet Index ranks nations according to how well they are doing in terms of supporting their people to live long and happy lives, while ensuring that future generations can do the same. It combines environmental impact with wellbeing to assign each country with an index, based on three measures:

- Subjective life satisfaction;
- Life expectancy at birth; and
- Ecological footprint per capita.

When it was first released, the Happy Planet Index generated huge media attention and was signalled by some as a way of comparing the true conditions of nations (nef: 2010).

Gross National Happiness Index

Another development to attract much international attention was the Gross National Happiness Index (GNHI). Developed in 2007 by the Centre for Bhutan Studies, this approach heralded a new way of thinking about progress, by focusing on the effect of growth on societal happiness and wellbeing. GNH looks at national progress in terms of advancing the happiness of its citizens, rather than the performance of the economy.

While the initial thinking around the GNHI has antecedents in the 1970s, the idea of happiness as a national goal in Bhutan can be traced back even further. A legal code from 1729 declared 'if the Government cannot create happiness *(dekid)* for its people, there is no purpose for the Government to exist' (Ura et al: 2012). In the 1970s, the idea further materialised: then King Jigme Signye Wangchuck, observing the detrimental effect of economic development on the cultural fabric of other nations, proposed measuring progress in terms wider than economic development. He declared that happiness was more important than GDP and, since then, the nation has oriented its national policy and development plans towards achieving Gross National Happiness.

In 2007, the Centre for Bhutan Studies developed this idea into a measurement of Bhutan's progress. The index uses objective and subjective responses to the Gross National Happiness Survey, which asks questions that look at whether both material and spiritual, emotional and cultural needs are being met. While this has attracted perhaps unwarranted criticism for being narrow in focus on happiness, the Centre for Bhutan Studies has responded by claiming that GNHI is an all-encompassing measure that covers a range of areas that affect the nation's wellbeing (Ura et al: 2012). The GNH index is currently linked with a set of policy and program screening tools that have a direct impact on the national policies that affect wellbeing.

Bhutan's latest index was launched at the fourth World Forum in Delhi in October 2012, and received widespread coverage including a feature article in Time magazine.

Measuring New Zealand's Progress Using a Sustainable Development Approach

In 2009, Statistics New Zealand released its report Measuring New Zealand's Progress Using a Sustainable Development Approach (Statistics New Zealand: 2009). Their approach was to look at national progress through the lens of sustainability, asking the question: 'How is New Zealand progressing towards or away from sustainable development?' The approach closely follows that of Switzerland's MONET initiative. The most recent update presents 16 indicators, which aim to answer four key questions:

1. How well do we live?
2. How well are resources distributed?
3. How efficiently are we using our resources?
4. What are we leaving behind for our children?

Canadian Index of Wellbeing

Another well-known wellbeing initiative is the Canadian Index of Wellbeing, which aims to 'measure what matters' most to Canadians (see Michalos et al: 2011). It is supported by the Canadian Index of Wellbeing Network, an independent, non-partisan group of national and international leaders, researchers, organisations and citizens. A key feature of this index is that it was developed from the ground up after a very widespread consultation with Canadians, in contrast to many other initiatives, which tend to have a top-down approach. It claims to be the only national index that measures wellbeing in Canada across a wide range of domains and draws attention to the interconnections between domains. The index is a series of composite indicators, with an index for each of its eight domains as well as an overall index. It uses an array of data taken from survey responses and national data. Data was initially released in 2009, with the complete product released in 2011.

Beyond GDP Initiative

In 2007, the European Commission, together with the European Parliament, Club of Rome, OECD and WWF, hosted the high level conference Beyond GDP. The conference focused on clarifying measures of progress, considering which indicators would be best to accurately measure progress beyond GDP. From this, they launched the Beyond GDP Initiative, which aims to improve the measures of social, economic, environmental progress, wealth and wellbeing. The initiative aims to share important information on recent developments and ongoing work in this area.

In 2009, the European Commission released the report 'GDP and beyond: Measuring progress in a changing world' (European Commission: 2009). The report contained a roadmap which outlined five actions to improve measures of progress:

1. Complementing GDP with environmental and social indicators;
2. Near real-time information for decision-making;
3. More accurate reporting on distribution and equalities;
4. Developing a European sustainable development scoreboard for measuring progress in sustainability;
5. Extending national accounts to environmental and social issues.

A watershed: The Stiglitz-Sen-Fitoussi report

Public interest in the interrelationships between economic, social and environmental aspects of life has continued to grow in communities, in governments, and internationally. The map (see Figure 1) provides an indication of the plethora of international indicator activity involved in measuring wellbeing, societal progress and sustainable development that has occurred or is currently underway.

One of the most notable developments listed on the map of initiatives is the Stiglitz-Sen-Fitoussi report which has added considerable impetus to progress measurement initiatives across the world since its release. The Commission on the Measurement of Economic Performance and Social Progress was established in 2008 by then French President Nicolas Sarkozy who was concerned that the existing measures of capturing and comparing national progress were inadequate. The Commission was led by Professor Joseph Stiglitz as its chair, with Professor Amartya Sen as chief advisor and Professor Jean-Paul Fitoussi as its coordinator, and included 19 other economists, social and political scientists, psychologists and statisticians.

The purpose of the Commission was to:

- identify the limits of GDP as an indicator of economic performance and social progress, including the problems with its measurement.
- consider what additional information might be required for the production of more relevant indicators of social progress, and
- assess the feasibility of alternative measurement tools, and to discuss how to present the statistical information in an appropriate way.

In 2009, the Commission published a report which underlined the need to understand societal progress beyond economic development. The Commissioners pointed out that while economic indicators are not sufficient measures of progress, they are not within themselves wrong, they are wrongly used. They argued that GDP is not a measure of wellbeing, and that other economic, social and environmental dimensions should be taken into account. They concluded that 'the time was right to shift emphasis from measuring economic production to measuring people's wellbeing' (Stiglitz et al: 2009).

The Stiglitz-Sen-Fitoussi report outlines thirty recommendations for improving measures of national progress. These included improving a number of traditional economic measures, measuring components of quality of life and emphasising the importance of data about improvements in sustainability. The report received huge international attention, especially from NSOs, who saw its recommendations as instruction for rethinking how to measure progress, and how they could improve their own methodologies.

The release of the report occurred at around the time of the Global Financial Crisis (GFC). The authors described the GFC as one of the worst financial, economic and social crises in history. They argued that the crisis took many economic analysts and government officials by surprise because the measurement systems used to measure and monitor the economic performance across nations failed. The main measurement systems, in the years prior to the crisis, suggested that the economy was doing far better than it was. In their opinion, this was largely due to the questionable assessments of the economic performance of the financial sector, and the limits and misuse of GDP as a measure of national economic performance. They argued that had measures which included economic sustainability (such as income indebtedness) been used, they would have revealed a more cautious view of economic performance. They argued that the excessive focus on GDP metrics – and a failure to understand the limitations of that measure – meant that alternative statistics were not given the prominence they deserve.

In a sense, many of the ideas presented by the Commission were not new. As demonstrated earlier in this chapter, many critics (such as Ian Castles) had already challenged the idea of relying solely upon economic growth to understand progress. Some countries, including Australia, were already reporting on broader measures of national progress.

Neverthertheless, the Commission brought together many new and existing ideas and suggested a number of recommendations for statistical agencies all over the world to take on board. In particular, it recommended a rethink of measurement systems and encouraged a national and global dialogue on what we care about, whether what we are striving for is achieving what we care about, and whether this is adequately reflected in our national and international metrics. Around the world, many statistical agencies and organisations responded enthusiastically to the Stiglitz-Sen-Fitoussi report. Some used its recommendations to improve their existing measures of progress, while others used it to develop new approaches to progress measurement. The key post-Stiglitz initiatives are listed below.

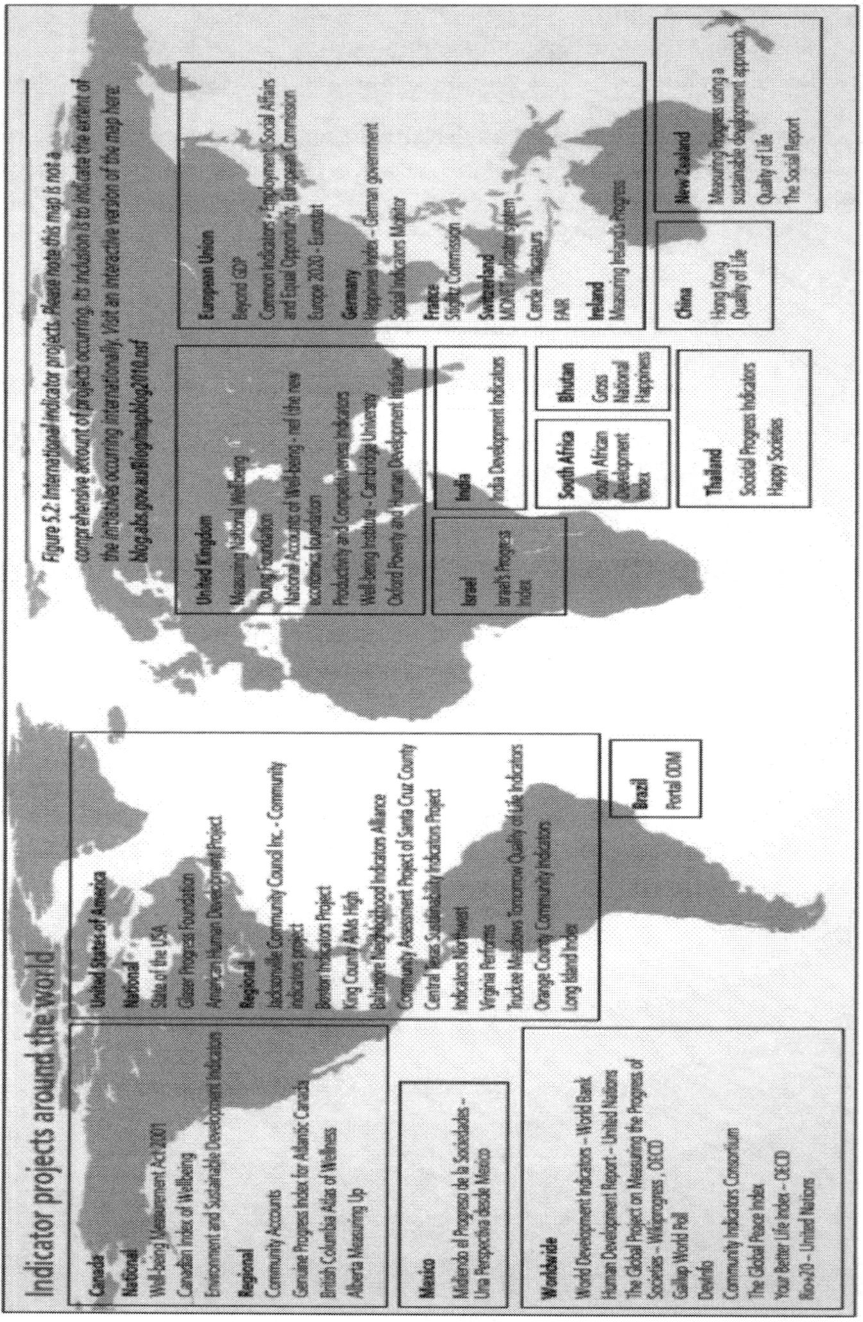

Figure 1 International map of progress initiatives

Source: ABS: 2012a.

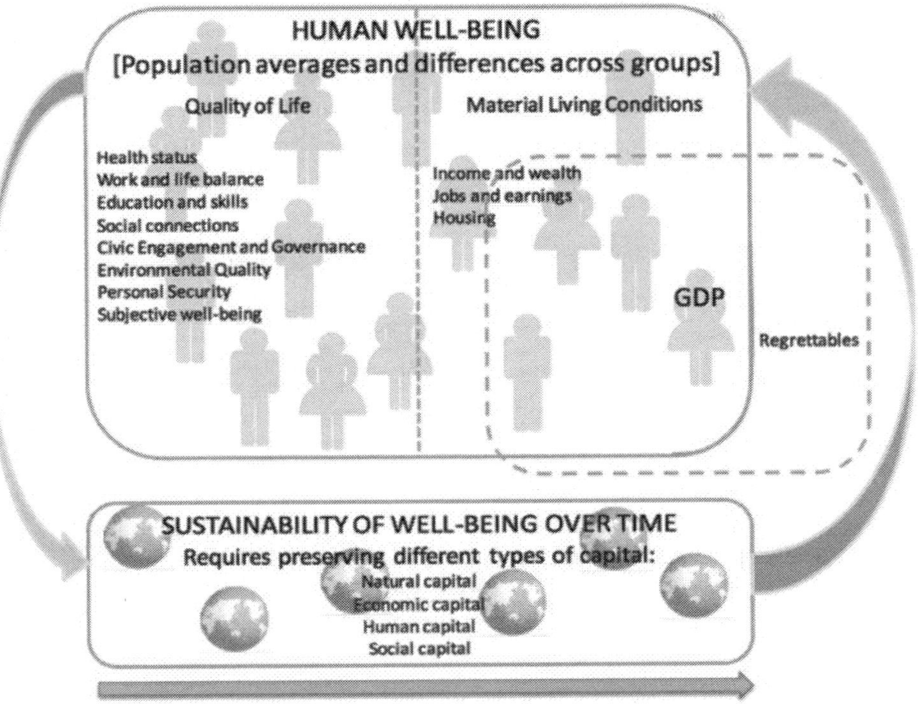

Figure 2 The OECD 'How's Life?' framework for measuring wellbeing and progress

Source: OECD: 2011b.

OECD Better Life Index

In 2010, the OECD established the online forum Wikiprogress, where people can share information and developments on measuring progress. Then in 2011, the OECD released the first Better Life Index, an online interactive tool for comparing wellbeing across nations (OECD: 2011a). This was accompanied by the How's Life report, which focused more specifically on the wellbeing of nations by looking at progress across various areas (OECD: 2011b). These initiatives are centred on individual wellbeing and track the improvement of people's lives over time. They organise indicators under two major domains: material living conditions and quality of life (see Figure 2). Complementary to these domains is a third – Sustainability of wellbeing over time – although this domain is currently outside the scope of the Better Life Index.

Measuring National Wellbeing, UK

In 2010, British Prime Minister David Cameron asked the Office of National Statistics (ONS) to measure national wellbeing as a basis for the development of new policy. As a result, the ONS has developed the Measuring National Wellbeing initiative, aimed at capturing people's wellbeing, the performance of the economy and the quality of the environment (see Office of National Statistics 2011). The ONS has undertaken a variety of approaches to determine what it is that is important to measure. In 2010-11, a national debate was held on "What matters to you?" People were able to participate in this debate through an online survey, face-to-face events and other activities.

The ONS received strong support throughout the consultation for a number of key themes important in the measurement of wellbeing. The ONS published their proposed domains and measures for measuring national wellbeing in 2012 and outlined the milestones and results to date of the ONS Measuring National Wellbeing Program. The proposed domains are: individual wellbeing, our relationships, health, what we do, where we live, personal finance, education and skills, governance, the economy, and the natural environment.

As an additional part of their Measuring National Wellbeing initiative, the ONS has been developing experimental subjective wellbeing estimates from a set of questions incorporated into their large scale Integrated Household Survey. The four questions monitor different aspects of subjective wellbeing. The survey asked respondents to rate their satisfaction in life, feelings of happiness and anxiety, and to what extent people feel the things they do are worthwhile. As subjective wellbeing is currently being considered an increasingly significant aspect of wellbeing, the ONS has been seen as a world leader in pioneering this currently experimental work.

New Zealand Treasury Living Standards framework

NZ Treasury see their role as working for the higher living standards of New Zealanders, thus improving economic performance to raise living standards. In 2011, New Zealand Treasury developed a Living Standards Framework with the intention of providing government ministers with robust, theoretically grounded and evidence-based advice that aims to improve the lives of all New Zealanders (New Zealand Treasury: 2011). They acknowledge that there are other living standards that are important in addition to material ones.

Oxfam Humankind Index

Oxfam Scotland recently undertook a national consultation to develop the Oxfam Humankind Index, first published in 2012. The Oxfam Humankind Index aims to assess Scotland's prosperity through holistic and representative measures of progress, taking into account what really matters to the people of Scotland (Oxfam Scotland: 2012). Like the ABS and the ONS, Oxfam Scotland has undertaken a consultation with the public to develop the index. Their aim is for policy makers and the community to use the index to make informed decisions based on the aspirations of the people of Scotland – whether they relate to their own wellbeing, the economy, governance or the environment.

The Australian National Development Index (ANDI)

The Australian National Development Index (ANDI) is a partnership of 40 leading community organisations, church groups, businesses, and universities which aims to create a national development index (ANDI: 2012). Still in development, the index aims to present a holistic measure of national progress and wellbeing that reflects the views of Australians.

Modelled on the Canadian Index of Wellbeing, ANDI's national progress measurement will be informed by the goals and values identified by a bottom-up approach that will be based on national consultation and research. It is expected to address progress domains, including children and young people, work and work life, environment and sustainability, and justice and fairness.

ANDI aims to work closely with the ABS and to support and complement the MAP project. For example, the results of the MAP consultation (see below) will inform the ANDI consultative work, while the ANDI consultative work will be considered as part of the ongoing evolution of MAP. The ABS has provided statistical guidance to ANDI (and included ANDI in the MAP consultations). However, the ABS is cautious to be involved with, or to produce, an index of progress. Indexes can be problematic. They are over simplistic; reducing the complexity of progress made across different domains, where progress or regress can occur, to a single number. Indexes also pose methodological issues, such as the difficulties in weighting and combining indicators from different domains (for example, how do you weight and add together progress in household income with progress in preserving threatened species, with progress in social inclusion?).

How has the ABS been developing progress measurement?

Measures of Australia's Progress dashboard

In 2010, the ABS relaunched Measures of Australia's Progress, for the first time in an entirely electronic format, and incorporating a dashboard of key social, economic and environmental headline indicators to improve accessibility and visibility and help people, at a glance, to assess whether some key aspects of life in Australia are getting better (see Figure 3). In this way, readers can review progress across the social, economic and environmental domains and understand the issues unique to each.

The dashboard approach encourages readers to consider the indicators and make their own assessment of whether Australia is, on balance, progressing and at what rate. In using a dashboard approach, the ABS has avoided the complexity and contestability of a comprehensive accounting system, which is complicated to both compile and interpret, and the potential oversimplification involved in presenting a single progress indicator.

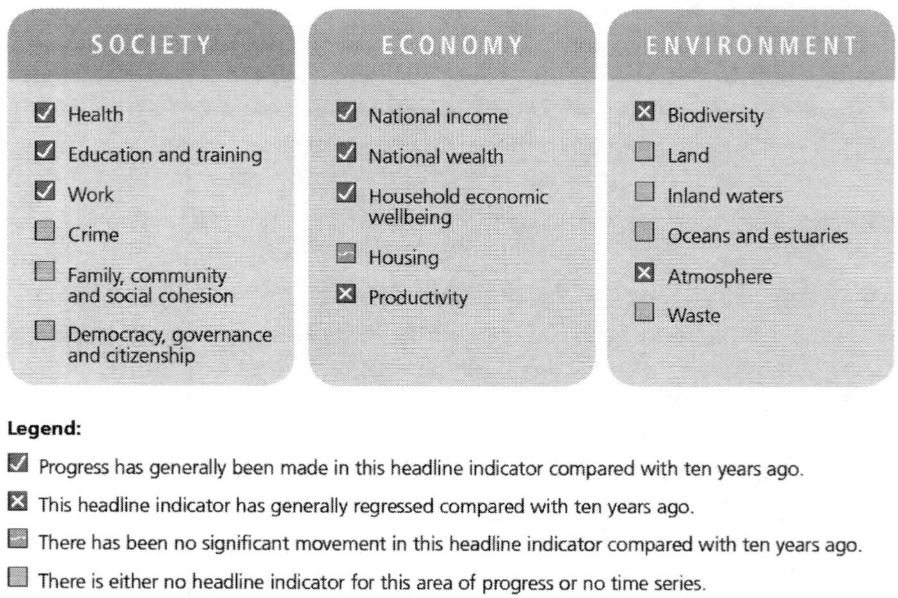

Figure 3 Measures of Australia's Progress dashboard

Source: ABS: 2012b.

MAP consultation

In addition to the changes introduced in 2010, almost a decade on from the first MAP release, and in light of recent international initiatives in progress measurement (most notably the Stiglitz-Sen-Fitoussi report), the ABS, guided by a MAP Expert Reference Panel, decided to undertake a national consultation to review MAP. ABS wanted to ensure that MAP remains relevant to today's society and continues to measure what Australian society cares about. The consultation was developed around the notion that if we are to know if we are progressing, then we need to know where we are headed. The consultation was therefore designed to ascertain from the Australian public what their aspirations were for the nation's progress. Once this had been articulated through the consultation process, the ABS would then look at the measures that might be available to inform on progress towards those goals.

The MAP consultation began in late 2010. There were several strands to the consultation, including an initial foray into the world of social media in order to engage with user groups who may otherwise be interested in the ABS and its activities, such as younger people or those who do not regularly use the ABS statistics. The ABS used various media and social media platforms, such as radio interviews, a Facebook page and, notably, a successful MAP 2.0 Blog. These provided members of the public with avenues to contribute their thoughts to the ABS on what matters most to them for the nation's progress. In order to promote the social media campaign, the ABS approached a number of prominent Australians, including Dick Smith, Michael Stutchbury, and Lauren Jackson, to contribute their aspirations about Australia's progress and these were posted on the MAP 2.0 Blog. In addition, the ABS hosted workshops across Australian capital cities, welcoming feedback from interested clients, ranging from state government stakeholders to business and community groups, and sought submissions from a range of commonwealth government agencies.

The ABS received submissions from other business and community groups and councils and examined a range of state and local government planning documents, which contained information on the goals and aspirations that guide the development of states and territories, as well as local councils. They also considered community projects, which aimed to track progress at the community level. As part of the consultation, the ABS also examined international projects being undertaken by other national statistical agencies and cross-national organisations, in order to understand how MAP fits in the broader international context.

In order to receive assistance on pulling the various consultation threads together, the ABS hosted a number of Topic Advisory Panels. These panels brought together experts from across business, community, the media, research and government sectors, and had extensive knowledge and experience in negotiating positive outcomes for the Australian public. The ABS held a number of workshops with these topic experts in order to discuss and distil the consultation feedback efficiently.

In November 2012, the ABS released the report *Measures of Australia's Progress – Aspirations for our nation: A conversation with Australians about progress* (ABS: 2012a). It details the consultation process undertaken by the ABS to discover what aspirations Australians have for national progress and provides an account of the consultation process and the feedback that the ABS received. It also sets out a framework of aspirations and themes, which were identified as important for measuring the nation's progress. A notable addition is that of a fourth domain, on governance, which received strong support through the consultation as a separate domain because of its key role as an enabler. In addition, family, community and the built environment were also identified as important to Australians.

The report marks the end of the ABS's active consultation with the Australian public, although as MAP is a constantly evolving product, members of the public are still welcome to provide feedback to the ABS. Following the release of the report, the next phase will involve working with statistical experts to find indicators that match or present data relevant to the aspirations and themes identified in the new MAP framework. The new, refreshed Measures of Australia's Progress will be released in November 2013.

ABS involvement in international initiatives to improve the measurement of wellbeing and progress

In addition to its work in improving the conceptual understanding of what progress means to Australians, ABS is currently involved in a number of international initiatives to improve particular measures of wellbeing and societal progress, namely two OECD Expert groups relating to economic statistics and the development of a household wealth framework, and an OECD Working group developing guidelines on subjective wellbeing. The ABS has also been an early adopter of the System of Environmental-Economic Accounting (SEEA). These developments are described in more detail below.

Economic statistics

Within the ABS there has for some time been a recognition that more could be done within the Australian System of National Accounts to stress the importance of the household perspective in devising measures of living standards and progress. In 2002, the ABS introduced a range of annual analytical measures of household income, consumption, saving and wealth in order to further articulate the economic experience of the household sector within the Australian economy.

Recognising the importance of measuring inequality, and noting that simple averages tend to not be reflective of the conditions of a 'typical household', the ABS has been participating in an OECD Expert Group to produce measures of disparities between groups of households which are consistent with National Accounts income and expenditure measures. The OECD analysis will be published in the first half of 2013, and following this the ABS will be publishing the results for Australia. Both of these initiatives build on the strengths of the

National Accounts, as a complete, integrated and coherent picture of the macro economy, and as describing the economic experience and living standards of Australians.

Household wealth framework

An international Expert Group, sponsored by the OECD and chaired by the ABS, is developing new international guidelines for compiling statistics on household wealth, and a comprehensive and integrated framework for statistics on household income, consumption and wealth. The Expert Group's work is expected to be published in 2013 in two OECD publications.

The first publication will provide guidance on the collection, analysis and dissemination of household wealth statistics at a detailed level. The work will address the common conceptual, definitional and practical problems that countries face in producing these statistics, and will improve the comparability of the currently available data. They will also allow statistics on household wealth to be integrated with economic wellbeing measures, such as income and consumption. Household level measures will also be comparable with broader economic measures. Harmonisation with other international standards is also an important objective of the work, e.g. the 2008 System of National Accounts, the 2011 Canberra Group Handbook on Household Income Statistics, and the recommendations of the 17th International Conference of Labour Statisticians on household income and expenditure statistics.

The Expert Group is concurrently developing an integrated framework for the joint measurement and analysis of statistics on household income, consumption and wealth. The integrated framework will bring the new wealth guidelines together with the existing standards for household income and expenditure and will underpin the production and analysis of harmonised and coherent information on the economic situation of individual households. Such a framework is needed to support the design of better-informed government policies and better targeting of programs to assist households in need. Better-informed policies hold the promise of delivering improved economic wellbeing to individuals, higher economy-wide performance, and better individual and societal outcomes across a range of dimensions of social concern.

The OECD Expert Group publications are expected to stand as a critical reference point for data compilers and users of household income, consumption and wealth data for some time. However, in due course and following 'road testing' by an increasing number of countries, consideration will need to be given to whether the outputs of the Expert Group should be refreshed, brought up to date with evolving practice, and then brought to the attention of other statistical bodies, such as the United Nations Statistical Commission, for possible endorsement as statistical standards. A similar process was followed in the case of the *2001*

Canberra Group Handbook on Household Income Statistics, which evolved into a standard, adopted with little modification, by the International Conference of Labour Statisticians (ICLS) in December 2003 (ILO, 2004).

Subjective wellbeing

In addition to the increasing interest in developing wellbeing measures, there has been growing interest throughout the world in developing measures of subjective wellbeing, that is, measures of how people feel and how they evaluate their lives. While once argued as being an immeasurable concept, in recent years it has been increasingly recognised that subjective wellbeing can and should be measured. Some argue that people's feelings and assessment of their own life are a true indication of a nation's progress.

The Stiglitz-Sen-Fitoussi report identified the importance of including measures of subjective wellbeing in any consideration of national progress. It recommended that statistical agencies should include both objective and subjective measures of wellbeing in their data on progress, including life evaluation, experiences and priorities.

The ABS has been collecting subjective measures of wellbeing since 1989, and has a collection spanning a variety of areas of interest across a number of surveys. The ABS has expanded its subjective measures, collecting data on overall life satisfaction, feelings of trust and safety, self-assessed physical and mental health, enjoyment in learning and work, self-assessed importance of culture and perceptions of the environment. The ABS continues to include and expand on ways to include subjective measures in its surveys.

Since 2010, the ABS has also been part of an OECD working group involved in formulating guidelines to enable national statistical organisations to consistently measure subjective wellbeing. The OECD recognises subjective wellbeing as having three components: life evaluation, affect (positive and negative) and having a sense of meaning and purpose in life. It is anticipated that the guidelines will be submitted to the OECD Committee on Statistics (CSTATS) for approval in 2013.

Developments in SEEA

In 2012, the System of Environmental-Economic Accounting (SEEA) was adopted as an international statistical standard by the United Nations Statistical Commission. Importantly, as an international statistical standard, the SEEA now has the same status as the System of National Accounts. The SEEA is a multipurpose, conceptual framework that describes the interactions between the economy and the environment, and the stocks, and changes in stocks, of environmental resources. Using a wide range of data, the SEEA conceptual framework provides a structure to compare and contrast information across a broad spectrum of environmental and economic issues. The development of the SEEA was driven by the desire to better understand the interactions between the economy and the environment, and to have more complete and robust information on both. This has been due to an increasing realisation that economic prosperity is dependent on the ability of the environment to supply natural resources and to absorb pollution, and that environmental policies impact on economic activity. The Stiglitz-Sen-Fitoussi report notes that:

What we measure affects what we do; and if our measurements are flawed, decisions may be distorted. Choices between promoting GDP and protecting the environment may be false choices once environmental degradation is appropriately included in our measurement of economic performance. So too, we often draw inferences about what are good policies by looking at what policies have promoted economic growth; but if our metrics of performance are flawed, so too may be the inferences that we draw. (Stiglitz et. al.: 2009)

To mark the occasion of the international adoption of the SEEA, the ABS hosted a conference 'Completing the Picture – Environmental Accounting in Practice' which aimed to assist understanding of how environmental accounts could be used and further developed in Australia. It is part of an ongoing body of work by the ABS in environmental and economic accounting, and sets out what a regular set of environmental-economic accounts might look like and how they could potentially be used.

Looking forward: The future of progress measurement

Beyond 2015

As the timeframe for the Millennium Development Goals draws to a close, the international community will direct its attention towards formulating a new set of goals. The United Nations Secretary-General Ban Ki-moon has established a High-Level Panel comprising members of civil society, the private sector and government leaders to advise him on the post-2015 agenda. He has also established a UN System Task Team to coordinate preparations for beyond 2015 and to support the work of the High-Level Panel, and requested the UN Development Group to organise country and global thematic consultations on the post-2015 agenda as input to expert and intergovernmental processes such as the High-Level Panel. Much of this work has commenced only recently, and is still in its formative stages.

Sustainable development

Twenty years on from the 1992 Earth Summit: UN Conference on Environment and Development, nations again gathered in Rio De Janeiro, Brazil to discuss progress and commitment to a plan of action for developing and measuring progress in sustainable development. The Rio+20 Conference identified a number of sustainable development themes or priorities including poverty reduction; food security and nutrition and sustainable agriculture; water and sanitation; energy; sustainable tourism; sustainable transport; sustainable cities and human settlements; health and population; promoting full and productive employment, decent work for all, and social protections; oceans; small island developing states; disaster risk reduction; forests and biodiversity; desertification, land degradation and drought; chemicals and waste; sustainable consumption and production; mining; education; gender equality and women's empowerment; and sustainable development goals. Governance processes to take the Rio+20 outcomes forward are still being established at the time of writing this essay. However, there is emerging a strong intention that the sustainable development and post-2015 agendas should converge.

OECD 4th World Forum – reflections

In October 2012, the ABS attended the 4th OECD World Forum on 'Statistics, knowledge and policy' in Delhi, India. The ABS contributed four papers, sharing results and lessons learnt from our own work on measuring national progress. The ABS showcased the recent MAP consultation, our work with the SEEA framework, the household wealth framework, and some initial thinking about measurement of aspects of governance.

OECD Chief Statistician Martine Durand summarised the key messages at the close of the World Forum. She highlighted the key achievements of the OECD community in measuring progress, including reinforcement of the global momentum in measuring progress; the growing convergence in the domains people identify as important for a good life; and the common language used to discuss progress and wellbeing. She highlighted a number of remaining challenges, such as the difficulties with measuring progress in governance, social capital and cohesion, and the built environment and mobility.

She noted growing interest in understanding progress at different levels of analysis, going beyond national aggregates alone to look at data disaggregated to consider regional progress, and progress for population groups, such as gender, across the life course, and for minority groups. She suggested that building knowledge across the international community should ultimately lead to better decision making that in turn would promote change and improvements in wellbeing through a 'virtuous cycle'.

Finally, she identified the upcoming international work for measuring progress. This includes setting an international agenda on progress goals to bring together work on wellbeing, the post 2015 agenda and the Sustainable Development Goals to create a more holistic understanding of progress.

Conclusion

Throughout the ages, nations have been interested in understanding and measuring progress. During the twentieth and early part of the twenty-first centuries, a number of major economic and societal events and the emergence of supranational institutions have been fundamental in changing the ways that countries understand and measure their own progress. More recently, notable reports such as the Stiglitz-Sen-Fitoussi Report, and the EU's Beyond GDP report, have acted as both a summary of existing ideas around understanding progress, and guidance for how statistical agencies can measure progress with more accuracy. Many national statistical organisations and other statistical bodies have responded to this guidance by creating frameworks to better measure wellbeing and progress for their nation or for comparison between nations.

Throughout this time, the ABS has been measuring progress for Australia through economic, social and environmental indicators and its flagship publication Measures of Australia's Progress. This chapter has explored some of the international initiatives, as well as developments with which the ABS is moving ahead, such as refreshing the MAP product through a large-scale consultation, and through leadership in environmental-economic accounting, economic statistics, household wealth framework development and the measurement of subjective wellbeing. As statistical agencies continue to work together on the international stage, there will be more movement towards refined understanding and better measures of progress.

References

Australian Bureau of Statistics (1976). *Social Indicators*, cat. no. 4101.0, ABS website.

Australian Bureau of Statistics (1994), *Australian Social Trends*, cat. no. 4102.0, ABS website.

Australian Bureau of Statistics (2002), *Measuring Australia's Progress*, cat. no. 1370.0.

Australian Bureau of Statistics (2005). *Informing a Nation: The Evolution of the Australian Bureau of Statistics 1905-2005*, cat. no. 1382.0, ABS website.

Australian Bureau of Statistics (2010-2011), *Australian System of National Accounts*, cat. no. 5204.0, ABS website.

Australian Bureau of Statistics (2012a). *Measures of Australia's Progress –Aspirations for our nation: A conversation with Australians about progress,* Consultation report, cat. no. 1370.0.00.002.

Australian Bureau of Statistics (2012b), *Measures of Australia's Progress*, cat. no. 1370.0.55.001, ABS website

Australian National Development Index (2012). *About ANDI,* ANDI website, viewed at 01.11.2012.

Bauer, Raymond A ed. (1966). *Social Indicators*, Cambridge, Mass., London: The MIT Press: 1.

Castles, Ian (1973). 'Economic Growth: Is it worth having?', *Treasury Economy Paper,* no. 2, Australian Government Publishing Service: Canberra.

The Centre for Quality of Life (2012). *Hong Kong Quality of Life Index,* viewed 2 March 2012.

European Commission (2009). *GDP and Beyond: Measuring progress in a changing world,* viewed 25 May 2012.

International Labour Office (2004). *Resolution concerning household income and expenditure statistics,* Seventeenth International Conference of Labour Statisticians, Geneva, 3 December 2003.

Kuznets, Simon (1934). *National income, 1929-1932,* 73rd US Congress, 2nd Session, Senate document no. 124: 7.

Michalos A, Smale B, Labonté R, Muharjarine N, Scott K, Moore K, Swystun L, Holden B, Bernardin H, Dunning B, Graham P, Guhn M, Gadermann A, Zumbo BD, Morgan A, Brooker A and Hyman I (2011). *The Canadian Index of Wellbeing: Technical Report 1.0,* Waterloo, ON: Canadian Index of Wellbeing and University of Waterloo.

Mill, John Stuart (1848). *The Principles of the Political Economy*, book 4, chapter vi.

Organisation for Economic Co-operation and Development (2011a). *Better Life Index,* viewed 26 March 2012.

new economics foundation (2010). *Measuring our progress: the power of wellbeing,* viewed 25 May 2012.

New Zealand Treasury (2011). *Working Towards Higher Living Standards for New Zealanders*, New Zealand Treasury Paper 11/02, May 2011.

Office of National Statistics (2011). *National Statistician's Reflections on the National Debate on Measuring National Well-being*, viewed 25 May 2012.

Organisation for Economic Co-operation and Development (2011b). *How's Life? Measuring Well-being*, OECD Publishing.

Oxfam Scotland (2012). *Oxfam Humankind Index: The New Measure of Scotland's Prosperity*, viewed 10 May 2012.

Statistics New Zealand (2009). *Key Findings on New Zealand's Progress Using a Sustainable Development Approach: 2008*, viewed 16 March 2012.

Stiglitz J, Sen A, Fitoussi J (2009). *Report by the Commission on the Measurement of Economic Performance and Social Progress*, Commission on the Measurement of Economic Performance and Social Progress.

Swiss Federal Statistical Office (2010). *MONET – Key Indicators*, viewed 2 March 2012.

The Treasury (2011-12). *Strategic Framework 2011-12*, Australian Government, The Treasury website.

United Nations (1969). *Declaration on Social Progress and Development*, Office of the United Nations High Commissioner for Human Rights, Proclaimed by general Assembly resolution 2542 (XXIV), 11 December 1969.

United Nations Development Program (2012). *Human Development Index*, viewed 29 February 2012.

United Nations Statistical Commission (2001). 'Report of the friends of the Chair of the Statistical Commission', *Report of the Human Development Report Office of the United Nations Development Program*, Thirty-second session, 6-9 March 2001.

United Nations System Task Team (2012). 'UN System Task Team on the Post 2015 UN Development Agenda: Realizing the future we want for all', Report to the Secretary-General, New York.

Ura K, Alkire S, Zangmo T, Wangdi K (2012). *A Short Guide to the Gross National Happiness Index*, The Centre for Bhutan Studies: Thimphu.

7. The Four Approaches to Measuring Wellbeing

John Hawkins[1]

Introduction

Discussions of the relationship between wellbeing and material progress go back a long way. One of the earliest extant comes from Aristotle:

> What is it that we say political science aims at and what is the highest of all goods achievable by action? ... It is happiness, and we identify living well and doing well with being happy...the life of money-making is one undertaken under compulsion, and wealth is evidently not the good we are seeking; for it is merely useful for the sake of something else.[2]

Economic growth in classical times was so slow as to be unobservable to those living and writing at the time.[3] Rather than writing of social progress, the Ancient Greeks mostly referred to a regression from a previous golden age.[4] Many regarded the means of achieving contentment to lie in the reduction of wants rather than an increase in output.[5] Across the world Confucian, Taoist and Buddhist theorists were similarly disinterested in expanding production.[6] The idea of economic progress only became commonly discussed with the advent of the French Enlightenment and the work of Adam Smith.[7] This was also the time when the industrial revolution had led to a marked acceleration in economic output.[8]

---

1 Thanks are due to Alex Millmow, Andrew Podger and other participants at the ASSA Crawford School Roundtable on Economic Growth and Wellbeing, and to an anonymous referee, for helpful comments. Views expressed are those of the author and not necessarily shared by organisations to which he is affiliated.

2 Aristotle (c 330BC, book 1). The Greek word eudaimonia is translated as either happiness or wellbeing.

3 Angus Maddison (2001, p 28) believes that between 0 and 1000 CE there was no average real per capita growth in GDP in either Europe or Asia.

4 This tradition goes back at least to Hesiod. Furthermore, when they did refer to increases in national wealth, the classical writers often thought it a corrupting influence; Ambirijan (1997: 33). Plato disdains avidity and cupidity, warning it leads to a gap between the citizens; Baeck (1997: 155).

5 Epicurus and Diogenes were perhaps the leading exponents of this view. It was more recently expounded by Ghandhi; Dasgupta (1993, chapter 9).

6 Hu (1988: 47, 214-5).

7 Pollard (1968). Arguably the first writer to address economic growth was Sir Josiah Child in the seventeenth century; Spiegel (1971: 151).

8 Angus Maddison (2001: 126) estimates that between 1820 and 1870 real per capita output grew by annual average of around one per cent in Western Europe. The peak growth period was over four per cent in Western Europe and over eight per cent in Japan during 1950-1973.

Other than some pioneering estimates in the seventeenth century,[9] it was centuries before discussions of national income could be informed by statistics.[10] Arguably the first official national income estimates were the work of the pioneering New South Wales statistician Timothy Coghlan, published annually starting from Coghlan (1887).[11] But Coghlan's work, far ahead of its time, was not sustained. It was not until the Keynesian revolution that interest in compiling national accounts became widespread. Much of the early development occurred in the run-up to and early stages of World War II and so the focus was on output that could be diverted to the war effort.[12] Amongst the pioneers were Simon Kuznets and the Australian economists Colin Clark and James Sutcliffe.[13]

The first official set of national accounts was prepared by the then Commonwealth Bureau of Census and Statistics and published in the 1945 budget papers as *Estimates of National Income and Public Authority Income and Expenditure*. The first macroeconomic forecasts for Australia appeared in some early drafts of the *White Paper on Full Employment* in 1945 but not in its final published version.[14] The annual, and then quarterly, national accounts attracted increasing public attention. When some questioned the desirability of economic growth, Treasury commissioned a team led by Ian Castles to address the issue.[15] After moving to the ABS, Castles initiated work on broader measures of living standards that became Measures of Australia's Progress (see below).[16]

Concerns about sustainability

But even while economists were starting to measure national income, there were some questioning the sustainability of growth. Malthus in the nineteenth century expressed concern that economic growth, in particular population growth, would tend to outstrip resources, notably farmland. He warned that the conflict was likely to be resolved by population being limited by starvation.

9 Sir William Petty (1665), a founding member of the Royal Society and friend of Samuel Pepys, estimated the national income of the United Kingdom and argued it was expanding; Deane and Cole (1969); Medema and Samuels (2003: 45-56), Rothbard (1995: 296-302); Spiegel (1971: 122-135). Ian Castles (1998) regards this as the first national income estimate. Gregory King (1688) made a more detailed attempt and there were also estimates compiled for France a little later by Boisguillebert and Vauban; Australian Bureau of Statistics (2000: 2).

10 Cairncross (1988) gives a short history.

11 See Arndt (1949), Clark and Crawford (1938: 53-55), Goodwin (1966: 473-474) and Haig (2001, 2006) for an account.

12 Daly and Cobb (1989: 70).

13 Clark (1932) on the United Kingdom and Clark and Crawford (1938) on Australia; Sutcliffe (1926). Coombs (1944) presented some 'semi-official' national income estimates for 1938-39 and projections for 1947-48.

14 Cornish (1981).

15 Treasury (1973).

16 Podger (2010).

Arguably the first rigorous analysis that looked at natural resources as a constraint on economic growth was Jevons' book *The Coal Question* published in 1865.[17] In it he presents projections indicating that coal could be exhausted by 1970, but warns that well before then the increasing price could slow economic activity. He examined the prospects for some of the renewable energy technologies of the day – windmills and waterwheels. Jevons warns of the danger of basing an economy on an exhaustible energy source; as he puts it 'encouraging a growth of industry which must prove unstable and perhaps involve all things in its fall'.[18]

Neither Malthus' nor Jevons' dire predictions came to pass in the way they feared. Both had underestimated the pace of technological innovation and the role that price signals triggered by scarcity could play in encouraging innovation. Nonetheless, as Kenneth Boulding once observed 'anyone who believes that exponential growth can go on forever in a finite world is either a madman or an economist'.[19] There are key issues of sustainability today, with climate change and peak oil probably the two most prominent aspects.

Modern attitudes to measuring wellbeing: Four approaches

While GDP and national income were never designed as a measure of wellbeing, and statisticians 'never pretended'[20] they were, they were often given this interpretation. But increasingly their unsuitability for this purpose was recognised. Arthur Pigou, the founder of modern welfare economics, argued that it is not just increases in national income that constituted improvements in national wellbeing; in particular he carefully distinguished whether the increased income was solely reflecting population growth, how it was distributed and how much it fluctuated.[21] Moses Ambramovitz concluded:

> We must be highly sceptical of the view that long term changes in the rate of growth of welfare can be gauged even roughly from changes in the rate of growth of output.[22]

A common argument runs that GDP per capita can hardly be the benchmark for achieving community satisfaction when:

---

17 William Stanley Jevons was professor of political economy at University College, London and an important contributor to the 'marginal revolution' in economics. He also built a 'logic piano', a proto-computer.

18 As a young man Jevons had worked at the Mint in Sydney for a few years. Ian Castles successfully lobbied the Powerhouse Museum to commemorate the work by Jevons in a display. See Castles (2004).

19 Cited in Brown and Singer (1996: 126). Boulding was himself an economist.

20 Trewin (1998: 110).

21 Pigou (1920: 82-92), discussed further in Spiegel (1971: 572) and Vaggi and Groenewegen (2003: 274-275).

22 Ambramowitz (1959: 21).

> In the UK the percentage reporting themselves 'very happy' declined from 52 per cent in 1957 to 36 per cent today, even though real incomes have more than doubled.[23]

There are various anomalies caused by GDP being focused on market activities. The classic example is that a man who marries his housekeeper lowers GDP.[24] Downhill skiing is included in GDP (as lift tickets are a market transaction) but cross-country skiing is not. Earthquakes can boost GDP because the destruction of buildings does not subtract from GDP but their reconstruction can add to it.

Robert Kennedy famously remarked:

> ...the gross national product does not allow for the health of our children, the quality of their education, or the joy of their play. It does not include the beauty of our poetry or the strength of our marriages; the intelligence of our public debate or the integrity of our public officials. It measures neither our wit nor our courage; neither our wisdom nor our learning; neither our compassion nor our devotion to our country; it measures everything in short, except that which makes life worthwhile.[25]

Less poetically, but at the same time, an Australian treasurer was also talking about the need for aiming at broader measures of economic wellbeing, including clean air, the physical environment, an equitable distribution of income and the needs of the disadvantaged:

> ...we must not fall too readily to exclusive worship at the altar of GNP... our prime concern should always be the social welfare of the community as a whole.[26]

A parliamentary colleague, soon also to be treasurer, argued for a focus on 'gross national wellbeing' and warned that: ...pre-occupation with economic growth is an over simplistic and misconceived approach.[27]

Bob Brown gave the following further examples:

> If I feed myself by growing vegetables in my backyard, using household waste as compost, I contribute nothing to the GNP. If I sell the vegetables and use the money to buy hamburgers, I am increasing GNP. If the

23 Jackson, (2009: 40). This 'Easterlin paradox' is widely accepted although some writers such as Stevenson and Wolfers (2008) have questioned it.

24 Pigou (1920).

25 Address at University of Kansas, 18 March 1968, Cited by Australian Bureau of Statistics (2010).

26 Bury (1969: 7-8).

27 Lynch (1973).

> crime rate rises and people start stealing my vegetables so that I have to pay someone to build an ugly barbed-wire fence around them, GNP increases still further.[28]

Indeed to its harshest critics GDP gives a 'Grossly Distorted Picture'[29] of progress towards improving wellbeing. While Treasury argued in the 1970s that GDP was a good proxy for welfare,[30] it now has its own 'wellbeing framework' in which 'consumption possibilities' are only one of five components.

These concerns have led to a desire for alternative measures that would give a better idea of whether the nation is making true progress in improving wellbeing than does GDP. There are essentially four approaches; adjusting GDP to make it more suitable, replacing it with a 'dashboard' of alternative indicators, weighting these alternative indicators to form a composite indicator, and using peoples' own reported assessments of their well-being.

Adjusted GDP

Sir John Hicks defined income as follows:

> ...we ought to define a man's income as the maximum value which he can consume during a week and still expect to be as well off at the end of the week as he was at the beginning.[31]

One approach to get closer to a measure of wellbeing is to adjust the published GDP to get closer to Hick's definition. It is worth noting that on Hicks' definition, 'sustainable income' is almost a tautology; Hicksian income is maximum sustainable consumption.[32]

Applying Hicks' approach to national income would deduct from GDP a broad measure of depreciation. Statisticians publish net national product (NDP), which is GDP less depreciation of the produced capital stock. When there is little structural change, movements in GDP and NDP tend to be quite similar. But

28 Brown and Singer, (1996: 126).

29 *The Economist*, 9 February 2006.

30 The paper, Treasury (1973: 6), while anonymous, was primarily the work of Ian Castles. It said 'obviously the pursuit of growth for its own sake misses the point: the aim must be to improve the welfare of the community. Policies directed to this latter end are likely in fact to lead to increases in the real output of the economic system per head of population and can thus fairly be described – without abuse of language – as policies for economic growth'. In Castles (1998: 353) his view was that 'I do not share the commonly held view that individual decisions are affected by the particular definition of GDP that has been adopted by the world's official statisticians...the view that decision-makers are misled is rarely supported by evidence. In my view, the GDP is a valuable and necessary, but not sufficient, measure of material progress'.

31 Hicks, (1946: 172).

32 Hamilton and Denniss (2000: 7).

over the past couple of decades the IT sector, subject to very high depreciation rates, has become a more significant share of the economy and so NDP has grown slower than GDP.

GDP includes the value of production in the economy but not all this accrues to the residents. In economies with substantial amounts of foreign ownership (or who own substantial assets in foreign countries) there can be significant differences between GDP and Gross National Product (GNP).

An increase in GNP or NDP that just arises from inflation does not represent an improvement in wellbeing. Nor is the average citizen better off if GNP or NDP rises but the population is increasing more quickly.

In terms of measuring wellbeing of residents in the country, *real net national disposable income per capita* is probably the best measure from the national accounts as currently compiled. From 2003-04 to 2011-12 it grew at an annual average rate of 2.3 per cent, considerably faster than the 1.3 per cent growth rate for GDP per capita, mostly reflecting the sharp rise in Australia's terms of trade.

Its major remaining weakness is that the depreciation deduction is limited to only produced capital, (e.g. equipment and buildings), not a broader concept of capital encompassing natural capital (e.g. forests, minerals) or ideally also environmental capital (e.g. air quality, biodiversity), human capital (e.g. education, health) and social capital (e.g. social organisations, community trust). The difficulty is that these other forms of capital are harder to measure than produced capital, which can be estimated by either surveying businesses or accumulating investment data (and applying assumed depreciation rates).

Some studies have attempted to augment GDP in other ways. For example, the coverage could be expanded beyond market activities, for example by valuing production in the home: services such as cooking, cleaning and child-minding that could potentially be done by paid workers instead. These can be valued either at the rate external workers are paid for these services or at a higher 'opportunity cost' (say, the average salary).

Conversely there are some things that are counted in GDP that arguably should not be if the purpose is to measure wellbeing. Surveys have shown that 'commuting to work is the daily activity that gives the least amount of enjoyment, with commuting home from work only marginally more enjoyable'.[33] Furthermore, commuting could be argued to be an intermediate input rather than a final act of consumption. For these reasons the costs of commuting are sometimes deducted from GDP in constructing wellbeing measures. Similar arguments are made about advertising expenditure.

33 OECD, (2011: 127).

The general result of these exercises is that at low national incomes GDP and more sophisticated measures of genuine progress move in similar ways but beyond a threshold GDP growth translates into much smaller (on some accounts no) improvements in wellbeing.[34] Some examples of these studies follow.

Nordhaus and Tobin's (1972) 'measure of economic welfare' (MEW) was an early attempt at modifying GDP to derive a better measure of true progress.[35] Activities regarded as not directly sources of utility in themselves but regrettably necessary inputs (e.g. expenditure on prisons or commuting to work) were treated as intermediate rather than final products and so excluded from GDP. They then added monetary estimates of activities (e.g. leisure, work at home) that do add to wellbeing.[36] Their MEW measure grew at an annual rate of 1.1 per cent from 1929 to 1965, compared to 1.7 per cent for NNP.[37]

Daly and Cobb's (1989) Index of Sustainable Economic Welfare also excludes 'regrettably necessary expenditures'. They construct their index for the US by first dividing household consumption by an index of distributional inequality. They then add household services (cooking, cleaning, child care), services from household durables, government provision of roads, and half of government spending on higher education and some government spending on health. They then subtract household spending on durables, most private spending on education and health, most advertising expenditure, expenditure on commuting, an estimate of the costs of urbanisation, cost of motor vehicle accidents, and the costs of water, air and noise pollution. They then make deductions for activities which undermine the sustainability of the natural resources base; the loss of farmland and wetlands, the depletion of non-renewable resources and long-term environmental damage (assumed proportional to consumption of fossil fuels and nuclear energy). They then subtract the amount of new capital required to maintain the amount of capital per worker. Finally they add the change in the US net international asset position.[38] The index grows during the 1950s and 1960s, flattens out in the 1970s and declines in the 1980s, with trends in inequality one of the main drivers.[39]

There have also been attempts to construct measures of 'Green GDP' by taking into account the consumption of natural capital, comprising resource depletion

34 Stiglitz, Sen and Fitoussi (2010: 105).

35 The authors modestly only claimed MEW was a 'primitive and experimental' attempt.

36 This can make a significant difference. Household production is equivalent to about a third of conventionally measured GDP in Finland, France and the US while including a value on leisure roughly doubles net household income; Stiglitz, Sen and Fitoussi (2010: 52-53).

37 Nordhaus and Tobin (1972: 13).

38 For a range of pragmatic and conceptual reasons they do not include some of the adjustments made by others. For example, they are sufficiently unconvinced that health and education add much to productivity in advanced economies that they do not include them in human capital calculations. They believe there are many measurement problems with leisure, so, in the absence of any significant drop in average hours worked, they leave it out. They considered excluding spending on junk food, tobacco and pornography but decided this would be too subjectively judgemental; Daly and Cobb, (1989: 402-442).

39 Daly and Cobb, (1989: 453-454).

and environmental degradation, but they have encountered resistance. President Clinton's 1993 Earth Day speech said that 'Green GDP measures would incorporate changes in the natural environment into the calculations of national income and wealth' but congressional opposition delayed the project.[40] The Chinese government attempted to introduce a 'green GDP' measure which adjusted GDP for pollution, environmental degradation and resource depletion. The initiative was short-lived, however, as the leaders of provinces dependent on heavy industry resented the reductions in their reported growth rates.[41]

The Australia Institute (AI) presented a Genuine Progress Indicator in 1997, which they updated in 2000.[42] The main features of the GPI which distinguished it from GDP were accounting for distribution, acknowledging household work, excluding defensive expenditures and accounting for depreciation of built and natural capital. The AI also deducted a proportion of spending on advertising as much of it does not contribute to wellbeing; 'many advertisements are designed to be persuasive rather than informative, creating new needs rather than fulfilling existing ones'. Unlike some similar exercises the GPI does not include the value of leisure, but does deduct the costs of overwork. The AI's GPI per capita increased over 1950-2000 but at a slower rate than did GDP (see Figure 1).

Lateral Economics developed a measure of short-term movements in Australian wellbeing in 2011, sponsored by the *Sydney Morning Herald* and *The Age*.[43] It extends the national accounts by incorporating the increase and depreciation of natural capital and human capital, through accounting for factors such as minerals discoveries, mining, education and long-term unemployment. The Herald Age Lateral Economics index (HALE) is calculated by adjusting real net national income from the national accounts. As the extent of leisure and voluntary work do not fluctuate that much over short time periods, HALE does not attempt to measure them. Congestion costs are hard to measure so no adjustment is made for them. There are adjustments for the distribution of income, based on evidence about how happiness is more sensitive to income increases at lower income levels. Mental health and obesity, and under- or over-work, detract from welfare and lead to lower values of the HALE index. Discoveries of new minerals resources are added in and depletions subtracted. Over the period 2005-2010 the HALE index grew faster than real GDP, reflecting the increase in university students and therefore increased human capital.

40 Nordhaus Panel on Integrated Environmental and Economic Accounting, (1999: 16).

41 Wenzel (2009: 40-41).

42 Hamilton and Denniss (2000).

43 *The Herald/Age-Lateral Economics Index of Australia's Wellbeing*, December 2011.

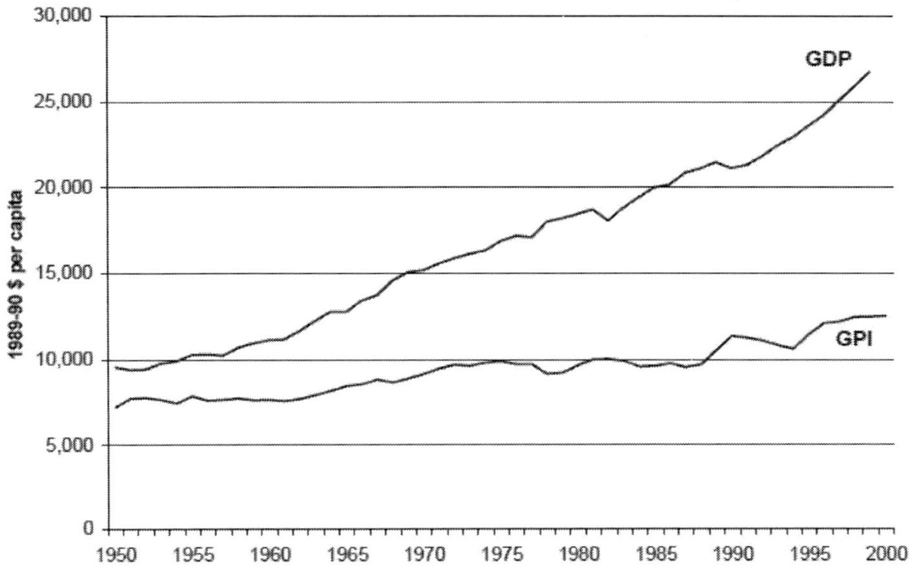

Figure 1 GDP and GPI per capita, 1950-2000

Source: ABS: 2012b.

A review of such measures for half a dozen developed economies concluded that over decades:

> All show a similar trend ... increasing with GDP (but sometimes at a lower rate) up to the 1970s, then levelling off or falling away while GDP continues to climb.[44]

Dashboard indicators

A second approach is to present a 'dashboard' or suite of indicators of various aspects of wellbeing, without attempting to condense them into a single indicator. The commonly used analogy is that when driving you are interested in the car's speed, the distance you have travelled and the amount of petrol remaining in the tank but (while the three measures are not unrelated) a single indicator that added them together would be useless.

This approach has been adopted by the ABS in *Measures of Australia's Progress*, first published in 2002.[45] This is a means of combining subjective and objective data, much of which are hard to reduce to a common denominator such as dollar values. The 2012 dashboard is show below.

44 Eckersley (1998: 20).

45 Podger (2010) says this work was initiated by Ian Castles.

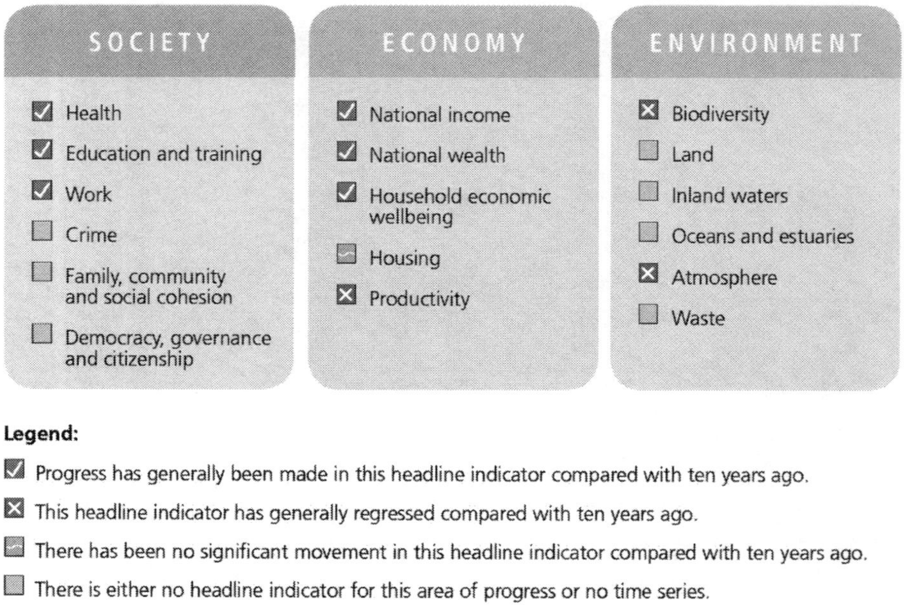

Figure 2 ABS Measures of Australia's Progress

Source: ABS: 2012b.

Composite indices

A third approach is to present composite indices, usually including GDP, but which also give weight to other aspects of wellbeing. The United Nations' Human Development Index, which combines education and life expectancy with per capita GDP, is a prominent example.[46] (Australia ranks second only to Norway on this measure.) The challenge with this class of measures is the arbitrariness of the weighting – how many extra dollars in average income is worth the same as an extra year in life expectancy?

Jones and Klenow (2010) combine data on consumption, leisure, inequality and mortality and try to weight them by their contribution to expected utility. Their measure turns out to be highly correlated with per capita GDP.

The Canadian Index of Wellbeing is another such index, giving equal weight to eight aspects: living standards, healthy populations, community vitality, democratic engagement, leisure and culture, time use, education, and the environment.

46 Ian Castles was critical of the way it was compiled; Podger (2010).

The Lagatum institute compiles an index of prosperity, based on indicators of entrepreneurship, economic performance, personal freedom, social capital, governance, health, safety and education. In 2012 Switzerland, Norway and Singapore are ranked the highest while Australia ranks tenth (doing particularly well on education, personal freedom and social capital).

Bhutan is known for aiming at, and attempting to base policy decisions on, 'Gross National Happiness' which encompasses four pillars of sustainable development, cultural values, the natural environment and good governance.[47]

The Australian National Development Index project, launched in May 2010, is aiming to create such an index with weights reflecting a consensus on the importance of various components in wellbeing.[48]

The ABS are sceptical of suggestions that the indicators in their dashboard could be weighted to form such an index:

> We prefer an approach where there is a dashboard, and where there are a range of social, economic and environmental indicators that people can look at and come to their own judgement about how they might want to weight those various measures of progress in Australia's society, and about whether they think Australian society is progressing across those key areas of interest... The difficulty is recognised by all of the people involved in these indexes – the difficulty of trying to weight those things in a way that reflects some sort of average view in Australian society of the importance of those things.[49]

As Lateral Economics comment:

> ...pure composite indices appear to have made negligible progress in dealing with the incommensurability of the various aspects of wellbeing, leading most of them to simply posit that each aspect is equally important.[50]

Ian Castles once said:

> Composite indicators are unsatisfactory because they imply there is a single answer to the question of whether life in a particular country is getting better or worse. But there can be no single answer.[51]

As another former Australian Statistician commented:

---

47 Kelly (2012).

48 Allen Consulting Group, *What Kind of Australia Do We Want?*

49 Trevor Sutton, Acting Australian Statistician, *Senate Economics Committee Estimates Draft Hansard*, 17 October 2012: 132-133.

50 *The Herald/Age-Lateral Economics Index of Australia's Wellbeing*, December 2011: x.

51 Castles (1998: 352).

> To be useful, indicators must have status: they need to be supported as valid by a wide body of Australians and preferably be underpinned by an international standard.[52]

On the other hand, the media seem to crave such a single indicator and in the absence of anything better being compiled will continue to use GDP. A composite index, or adjusted GDP:

> Is, in part, about changing the values of society…[and] the research community needs to be pushed along a bit in this area…there is considerable value in an aggregate index that attracts publicity and attention.[53]

One response is to present the dashboard in such a way that users can readily assign their own weights to produce an index. This has been done by the OCED with their Better Life Index, available at www.oecdbetterlifeindex.org.

If such websites retain the weights selected by users, then over time they can reflect the average opinion of those users, which may be a reasonable set of weights to apply to form a composite index. This is a feature of the OECD website and based on these weights Australia, Canada and Sweden have the highest wellbeing of any OECD countries.[54]

The ABS themselves have gathered some information, summarised in the cloud below, from their consultations about improving the *Measures of Australia's Progress*, on what things are more valued by the community.

---

52 Trewin (1998: 111).

53 Gregory (1998: 369). He draws an analogy; 'the Henderson poverty line illustrates how an aggregate index that is rough and ready, and certainly subjective, can play an important role in focusing and generating discussion on poverty'.

54 OECD (2011: 26).

Figure 3 ABS cloud analysis of consultation on measuring progress

Please note: This word cloud represents the range of ideas expressed during the MAP consultations. The size of the words represents how often they were raised.

Source: Australian Bureau of Statistics (2012: 5).

A relatively simple composite index that has attracted some attention is Veenhoven's 'happy life-expectancy'; a multiple of life expectancy with a survey-based measure of happiness which he shows is 'systematically higher in nations that are most affluent, free, equal, educated and harmonious'.[55]

Subjective happiness indices

A fourth approach is to ask people to assess subjectively their feelings of wellbeing or satisfaction with their life. Economists had formerly regarded such things as essentially unable to be measured properly (notwithstanding the use made of the concept of 'utility' in economic theorising). The OECD recently assessed, however, that 'an increasing body of evidence has supported the view that it is possible to gather valid measures of subjective wellbeing based on surveys'.[56] It has been noted that questions about subjective wellbeing get high response rates, consistent replies, show expected relationships with other variables and match well with biological indications of happiness or stress and assessments made by friends. They also predict behaviours such as suicide and sleep quality and outcomes such as income, marital status and mortality.[57]

55 Veenhoven (1996: 1).

56 OECD, (2011: 266).

57 OECD, (2011: 266-7); Clark, Fritjers and Shields (2008: 116-117); Kreuger et al (2009: 22-24).

Canada is the only country with a long run of official data on life satisfaction but it is now collected regularly by official agencies in New Zealand, France and Italy as well. (The collection of subjective assessments of wellbeing by national statistical agencies was recommended in the report commissioned by then president Sarkozy).[58] Gallup and Eurobarometer provide data from a broader range of countries. At an individual level, within a given country in a given year, there tends to be a strong correlation between income and satisfaction, but the correlation is much weaker across countries and across time. In particular, increases in average incomes seem to have resulted in little increase in average satisfaction. This is known as the 'Easterlin paradox'.[59] Studies that tried to explain the Easterlin paradox by including 'omitted' variables found that most other factors (e.g. life expectancy, hours worked, health, crime) that might have been expected to increase surveyed happiness did not do so, making the paradox even more puzzling.[60]

The most common explanations are that it is relative rather than absolute income that is most relevant in determining whether people are happy (at least over a certain income threshold) and that while an increase in income initially makes people happy they soon adapt their expectations and their happiness reverts to the previous level.[61]

The ABS conducted surveys of life satisfaction in 2001 and 2010,[62] but has not chosen to make it a regular component of *Measures of Australia's Progress*.

Australian Unity, in conjunction with Deakin University's Centre on Quality of Life, has been producing the Australian Unity Wellbeing Index since 2001.[63] It is based on a telephone survey of 2,000 Australians. This measures how satisfied people are with their own lives (covering health, personal relationships, safety, standard of living, achieving, community connectedness and future security) and with life in Australia in general (covering the economy, environment, social conditions, governance, business and national security). In recent surveys wellbeing generally was found to rise with income up to around $100,000 but not thereafter. As with similar studies overseas there has been no significant improvement in average life satisfaction since 2001 despite average real incomes having risen over 20 per cent since then. This is consistent with an observed

58 Stiglitz, Sen and Fitoussi (2010: 93).

59 Easterlin (1974). The data showing the paradox has been questioned by Stevenson and Wolfers (2008).

60 Clark, Fritjers and Shields (2008: 114-115).

61 Clark, Fritjers and Shields (2008); OECD (2011: 271). The adaption process is sometimes called the 'hedonic treadmill'. While a recent concept, warnings of the dangers of envy go back at least to Buddha; Dasgupta (1993: 5).

62 The latter in *General Social Survey: Summary Results*, ABS 4159.0, September 2011.

63 The latest report, referring to April 2012, can be found at http://www.australianunitycorporate.com.au/community/auwi/Pages/default.aspx.

tendency for most improvements in objective measures of wellbeing to have only temporary impacts on satisfaction which consistently returns to its average level, a phenomenon labelled 'subjective wellbeing homeostasis'.

The NAB Quarterly Australian Wellbeing Index provides another such measure. NAB also surveys consumers to produce an index of consumer anxiety.

The Melbourne Institute's HILDA survey also includes life satisfaction questions which it has been asking since 2001.[64] It differs from most indices in being 'longitudinal'; that is the same people are questioned in each survey. It also shows that average life satisfaction has remained essentially the same despite increases in average real incomes.

Conclusion

This short survey of the four main approaches has shown there is no single agreed way of measuring wellbeing. Perhaps until there is some degree of agreement, commentators will continue to use real GDP per capita despite its widely acknowledged limitations. It does at least have the virtue of being compiled on a consistent basis across time and across countries and is at least correlated with such objective characteristics of wellbeing as health, life expectancy and the environment.

While many policymakers and academics are keen for better indicators of wellbeing, and there is an increasing interest in sustainability issues and the interaction between inequality and wellbeing, there are some powerful vested interests that prefer not to have questioned whether their activities are truly benefiting overall sustainable wellbeing. This seems likely to ensure that wellbeing remains a complex and controversial concept.

References

Ambirajan S (1997). 'The concepts of happiness, ethics and economic values in ancient economic thought', in B Price (ed) *Ancient Economic Thought*, Routledge, London: 19-42.

Ambramovitz M (1959). 'The welfare interpretation of secular trends in national income and product', in *The Allocation of Economic Resources*, Stanford University Press, pp 1-22.

64 http://www.melbourneinstitute.com/downloads/hilda/Stat_Report/statreport-v7-2012.pdf.

Aristotle (c 330 BC). *Nicomachean Ethics*, translated by Ross, W, Oxford University Press, 1925.

Arndt H (1949). 'A pioneer of national income estimates', *Economic Journal*, vol 59, no 236, December: 616-625.

Australian Bureau of Statistics (2010). *Measures of Australia's Progress*, 2010.

Australian Bureau of Statistics (2012). *Measures of Australia's Progress: Aspirations for Our Nation: A Conversation with Australians About Progress.*

Baeck L (1997). 'Greek economic thought' in B Price (ed) *Ancient Economic Thought*, Routledge, London: 146-171.

Brown B and Singer P (1996). *The Greens*, Text Publishing, Melbourne.

Bury L (1969). 'Policies for growth in the seventies', address to the Economic Society of Victoria, 7 May.

Cairncross A (1988). 'The development of economic statistics as an influence on theory and policy' in D Ironmonger, J Perkins and VH Tran (eds) *National Income and Economic Progress: Essays in Honour of Colin Clark*, Macmillan Press, London: 11-20.

Castles I (1998) 'Measuring economic progress: from political arithmetic to social accounts', 8th Colin Clark memorial lecture, University of Queensland Department of Economics Discussion Paper 243, October.

Castles I (2004). ' The Curious Economist: William Stanley Jevons in Sydney', address at Powerhouse Museum, 28 October.

Clark A, Fritjers P and Shields M (2008). 'Relative income, happiness, and utility: an explanation for the Easterlin paradox and other puzzles', *Journal of Economic Literature*, vol 46, no 1: 95–144.

Clark C (1932). *The National Income 1924-1931*, Macmillan, London.

Clark C and Crawford J (1938). *The National Income of Australia*, Angus & Robertson.

Coghlan T (1887). *Wealth and Progress in New South Wales*, Government printer, Sydney.

Coombs H (1944). 'Problems of a high employment economy', Joseph Fisher Lecture in Commerce, University of Adelaide, 29 June, Hassell Press.

Cornish S (1981). 'Full employment in Australia: the genesis of a white paper', *ANU Research Paper in Economic History*, no. 1.

Daly H and Cobb J (1989). *For the Common Good*, Beacon Press.

Dasgupta A (1993). *A History of Indian Economic Thought*, Routledge, London.

Deane P and Cole W (1969). *British Economic Growth 1688-1959*, Cambridge University Press.

Easterlin R (1974). 'Does economic growth improve the human lot? Some empirical evidence?' in P David and M Reder (eds) *Nations and Households in Economic Growth*: 89-125.

Eckersley R (1998). 'Perspectives on progress: economic growth, quality of life and ecological sustainability', in R Eckersley (ed) *Measuring Progress*, CSIRO publishing: 3-34.

Goodwin C (1966). *Economic Enquiry in Australia*, Duke University Press.

Gregory R (1998). 'Summing up', in R Eckersley (ed) *Measuring Progress*, CSIRO publishing: 365-370.

Haig B (2001). 'First national accounting estimates', unpublished paper, March, Australian National University.

Haig B (2006). 'Sir Timothy Coghlan and the development of national accounts', *History of Political Economy*, Summer, vol 38, no 2: 339-375.

Hamilton C and Denniss R (2000) 'Tracking well-being in Australia: the Genuine Progress Indicator 2000', *Australia Institute Discussion Papers*, no 35, December.

Hicks J (1946). *Value and Capital*, London.

Hu J (1988). *A Concise History of Chinese Economic Thought*, Foreign Language Press, Beijing.

Jackson T (2009). *Prosperity Without Growth*, Earthscan, London.

Jevons WS (1865). *The Coal Question: an Inquiry Concerning the Progress of the Nation and the Possible Exhaustion of our Coal-mines*, Macmillan & Co, London.

Kelly A (2012). 'Gross national happiness: a tiny state's big idea that could change the world', *Guardian Weekly*, 7 December: 9.

King G (1688). *Two Tracts*, edited by George Barnett, 1936.

Kreuger A, D Kahneman, D Schkade, N Schwarz and A Stone, 'National time accounting: the currency of life', in A Kreuger (ed) *Measuring the Subjective Well-being of Nations*, University of Chicago Press.

Lynch P (1973). 'The Liberal Way', Alfred Deakin Lecture (reprinted in Buckley, B 1991 *Lynched*, Salzburg Publishing, Melbourne).

Maddison A (2001). *The World Economy: a Millennial Perspective*, OECD, Paris.

Medema S and Smauels W (2003). *The History of Economic Thought: a Reader*, Routledge, London.

Nordhaus W and Tobin J (1972). 'Is growth obsolete?', in Nordhaus W and Tobin J (ed) *Economic Research: Retrospect and Prospect, Volume 5: Economic Growth*, NBER: 1-80.

Nordhaus Panel on Integrated Environmental and Economic Accounting, 1999, *Nature's Numbers*,

OECD 2011, *How's Life? Measuring Well-being*, Paris.

Petty W (1665). *Verbum Sapienti.*

Pigou A (1920). *The Economics of Welfare*, 4th edition, 1960, Macmillan, London.

Podger A (2010). 'Adviser helped steer economic reforms' [obituary of Ian Castles], *Canberra Times*, 13 August.

Pollard S (1968). *The Idea of Progress*, CA Watts, London.

Rothbard M (1995). *Economic Thought Before Adam Smith*, Ludwig von Mises Institute.

Spiegel H (1971). *The Growth of Economic Thought*, Duke University Press.

Stevenson B and Wolfers J (2008). 'Economic growth and subjective well-being: reassessing the Easterlin paradox', *NBER working papers*, no 14282.

Stiglitz J, Sen, A and Fitoussi J-P (2010). *Mis-measuring Our Lives*, New Press.

Sutcliffe J (1926). *The National Dividend*, Melbourne University Press.

Treasury (1973). 'Economic growth: is it worth having?', *Treasury Economic Paper*, no 2, June.

Trewin D (1998). 'A framework for the presentation of indicators of national progress', in R Eckersley (ed) *Measuring Progress*, CSIRO publishing: 109-121.

Vaggi G and Groenewegen P (2003). *A Concise History of Economic Thought*, Palgrave Macmillan, London.

Veenhoven R (1996). 'Happy life-expectancy: a comprehensive measure of quality-of-life in nations', *Social Indicators Research*, vol 39: 1-58.

Wenzel T (2009). *Beyond GDP – Measuring the Wealth of Nations*, GRIN, Germany.

 Young A (1770). *Political Arithmetic.*

8. The Need for Wellbeing Measurement in Context

David Gruen and Duncan Spender[1]

This chapter aims to shed light on both the role of the Treasury wellbeing framework and Treasury's perspective on wellbeing measurement, by focusing on the broad context in which Treasury's wellbeing framework sits.

Treasury can help improve wellbeing without having in its possession a complete, agreed approach to wellbeing measurement.

- The Treasury mission requires us to serve our ministers, and the nature of democracy suggests a positive relationship between the service of ministers and improving societal wellbeing.
- The Treasury wellbeing framework reminds Treasury staff to inform their advice with an understanding that wellbeing is driven by several distinct considerations and that trade-offs will often be required. This assists ministers to make value judgements, taking into account community preferences and hence supporting wellbeing.
- The Treasury wellbeing framework requires us to undertake objective and thorough analysis using the best available tools. Rigorous application of well-worn economic tools provides us with some assurance that the policy recommendations that result are consistent with improving wellbeing.
- Provided that market and government failures are addressed, we can have some confidence that people and businesses going about their lives will tend to improve wellbeing.

Moreover, Treasury's broad wellbeing objective is accompanied by more specific – and more measurable – objectives.

So while efforts to improve and get agreement on wellbeing measures are well worthwhile, public policy agencies like the Treasury can nonetheless carry out their responsibilities in the absence of a complete, agreed approach to wellbeing measurement.

1 This chapter is a revised version of an address by the first author to the Economic Growth and Wellbeing Symposium in honour of Ian Castles AO, held by ASSA and the Crawford School at The Australian National University, 22 November 2012. We thank Harry Greenwell, James Kelly, Martin Parkinson, Andrew Podger and Angela Woo for helpful comments on an earlier draft.

This chapter briefly recaps Treasury's consideration of wellbeing and some thoughts on wellbeing measurement, before turning to how Treasury carries out its responsibilities in the absence of an agreed approach to wellbeing measurement.[2]

A longstanding focus on wellbeing

The idea that public policy should be concerned with both economic growth and broader concepts such as wellbeing is a longstanding one for both the economics profession and Treasury.

The conceptual distinction between welfare/utility and income/output was recognised by the pioneers of the discipline, including Adam Smith and John Stuart Mill. It was further explored by later economists such as Kelvin Lancaster and Gary Becker.[3]

Given this history, it should be no surprise that Treasury has for a long time incorporated both economic growth and wellbeing considerations into its analysis and advice. For example, a 1964 Treasury paper outlined the importance of measured economic activity but noted that a change in the market value of output is nonetheless not a comprehensive or unambiguous measure of the change in total welfare.[4] Many of the same points were made in the Treasury 1973 paper, 'Economic Growth: Is It Worth Having?' to which Ian Castles made major contributions.[5] A narrower approach essentially focused on growth in GDP, or in GDP per capita, would represent an overly restrictive lens through which to analyse many of the most important public policy issues.

The Treasury's conception of wellbeing has developed over time, in line with developments in economic thought. The current Treasury wellbeing framework makes clear that Treasury views wellbeing as primarily reflecting a person's *substantive* freedom, consistent with the relatively recent work of Amartya Sen.[6] People have substantive freedom if they have the capability to lead a life

2 Treasury's wellbeing framework is summarised in the attachment. For a recent detailed discussion of the Treasury wellbeing framework, its history and elements, see Kelly, James and Stephanie Gorecki 2012 'Treasury's Wellbeing Framework' *Economic Roundup*, Issue 3: 27-64. Issues with the measurement of wellbeing have been discussed in detail in Gorecki, Stephanie, David Gruen and Shane Johnson 2011 'Measuring wellbeing in theory and practice', *Treasury Working Paper No. 2011-02*, Canberra, and Gruen, David and Joanne Wilkie 2009 'New paradigms to measure progress', *Economic Roundup*, Issue 4: 1-9.

3 See, for example, the discussion of the conceptual basis for Treasury's Wellbeing Framework in Treasury 2004 'Policy advice and Treasury's wellbeing framework', *Economic Roundup*, Winter, Canberra: 2-5.

4 Treasury 1964 'The Meaning and Measurement of Economic Growth', *Supplement to the Treasury Economic Bulletin*, November, Canberra.

5 *Treasury Economic Paper No. 2*, Canberra.

6 Sen, Amartya 1999, *Development as Freedom*, Oxford University Press, Oxford.

they have reason to value. As such, substantive freedom depends not just on people's rights and liberties, but on their abilities and characteristics and the economic, social and natural environment around them.

Measuring wellbeing

Before discussing how Treasury carries out its responsibilities without there being an agreed approach to wellbeing measurement, we briefly recap some general thoughts on such measurement.

Wellbeing measurement is important. In the words of the Sen-Stiglitz-Fitoussi Commission on the Measurement of Economic Performance and Social Progress, 'what we measure affects what we do'.[7] What we measure affects judgements about the current state of affairs and what policy responses are needed. Policy choices need to be based on both reason and empirical evidence; theory and practice need to work together.

The Treasury wellbeing framework requires staff to use the best available evidence and measures. The Treasury is an intensive and extensive user of measures that, when brought together, give an indication of the wellbeing of the Australian people. Such measures also help to evaluate our performance.

But for the foreseeable future we will continue to face an array of differing approaches to wellbeing measurement, rather than having in our possession a fully agreed approach.

This is the case because a fully agreed approach to wellbeing measurement would require full agreement on the concept of wellbeing itself.

- While there is much agreement as to things that are important to wellbeing, there is no common all-encompassing conceptualisation of wellbeing. Even an individual's conception of his or her own wellbeing can be conflicted, and this conception needs to be examined and aggregated across individuals before we can arrive at an agreed concept of the wellbeing of society.
- The Treasury's wellbeing framework starts with a broad-ranging statement that wellbeing primarily reflects a person's substantive freedom to lead a life they have reason to value. This language reflects a pluralistic approach to understanding wellbeing, drawn as mentioned from the capabilities approach of Amartya Sen. The language doesn't prescribe what it is that is valued, and it doesn't say how to aggregate across individuals.

7 Stiglitz, Joseph, Amartya Sen and Jean-Paul Fitoussi 2009 'Report by the Commission on the Measurement of Economic Performance and Social Progress', *Commission on the Measurement of Economic Performance and Social Progress*: 7.

Alongside difficulties arising from conceptual differences, there are also various practical difficulties with wellbeing measurement.

- The measurement of material wellbeing involves significant difficulties with measuring quality and non-market services.
- The measurement of opportunities and capabilities involves attempting to measure what people could do, as opposed to what they actually do.[8]
- The measurement of self-reported subjective wellbeing is complicated by the various types of wellbeing that could be reported (e.g. mood happiness, life satisfaction or feelings of agency and autonomy).[9]
- And the estimation of future wellbeing involves taking a position on (at least) future preferences, discoveries, technological developments, events and population growth.

Serving ministers

Importantly, the lack of a fully agreed approach to wellbeing measurement does not pose an insurmountable problem for Treasury's use of its wellbeing framework, though it does help to focus on how the framework should be used.

Treasury's main role is to serve the people of Australia through the government of the day. That is, through its role in supporting ministers to discharge their responsibilities. Given the positive relationship between democracy and improving societal wellbeing, public servants in a democratic society should have confidence that serving their ministers, by providing advice and helping to implement policies, tends to improve wellbeing. This is true even if the measurement of wellbeing remains far from perfect.

Given the Treasury's traditional focus on economics, it is worth mentioning that this view of the positive relationship between democracy and wellbeing has strong foundations in economic theory, and is a view shared by economists who otherwise vary considerably in their world view.[10]

For instance, modern public finance theory was born more than a century ago when economists such as the Swedish economist Knut Wicksell directed

8 Measurement is a notorious problem for Sen's capabilities approach to wellbeing (Fleurbaey, Marc 2009, 'Beyond GDP: The Quest for a Measure of Social Welfare', *Journal of Economic Literature*, 47(4): 1029-1075).

9 Agency in this context refers to the capacity to act with purpose to one's advantage. This capacity is considered to be more important for subjective wellbeing as society becomes richer and basic material needs are met.

10 There is also empirical evidence of a positive relationship between democracy and subjective wellbeing measures, after controlling for economic development and initial subjective wellbeing levels (Inglehart, Ronald, Robert Foa, Christopher Peterson and Christian Welzel 2008 'Development, Freedom, and Rising Happiness: A Global Perspective (1981-2007)' *Perspectives on Psychological Science* 3(4): 264-285.

the recently developed tools of marginal theory towards an examination of government behaviour. Rather than simply assuming that government serves the public interest, Wicksell undertook an assessment of the circumstances in which government provision of public goods would be just and efficient, based on an aggregation of the interests of individuals. Importantly, his analysis explored various voting rules and highlighted the importance of universal franchise.[11]

Subsequent economists like Duncan Black and Anthony Downs explored how competition can lead rational self-interested politicians to act in the interests of the majority, while Schumpeter explored how political leadership, beyond mere representation of the median voter, can be welfare-enhancing when underpinned by periodic voting.[12] Theorists like William Niskanen and James Buchanan have explored the particular interests of public servants and politicians and the structures in which they operate, and the importance of voters being well-informed.[13] And seminal work on voting rules and group dynamics has been added by the likes of Kenneth Arrow and Mancur Olson.[14]

While these economists explored the various flaws in democratic models, they also helped build a strong economic argument linking the service of elected politicians with improvements in wellbeing.

So while public servants can sometimes be cynical about the political process, they should gain confidence from the general positive relationship between service in a democracy and wellbeing, notwithstanding difficulties in measuring that wellbeing.

---

11 Wicksell's support for universal franchise was intimately combined with support for requirements for unanimity or near unanimity in government decision-making. (See Wicksell, Knut, 1896 'A New Principle of Just Taxation' (James Buchanan trans) in Richard Musgrave and Alan Peacock (eds), 1967, *Classics in the Theory of Public Finance*, MacMillan, London.)

12 Black, Duncan 1948 'On the Rationale of Group Decision-making', Journal of Political Economy, 56(1): 23-34; Downs, Anthony 1957 *An Economic Theory of Democracy*, Harper, New York; Schumpeter, Joseph 1942 *Capitalism, Socialism and Democracy*, Fifth edition, George Allen and Unwin, London.

13 Niskanen, William 1971 *Bureaucracy and Representative Government*, Chicago, Aldine; Niskanen, William 2006 'Limiting Government: the Failure of "Starve the Beast"' *Cato Journal*, 26(3); Buchanan, James 1975 *The Limits of Liberty*, University of Chicago, Chicago. While not in the field of public finance, the economist and sociologist Max Weber provided seminal contributions on the nature of bureaucracy (see Musgrave, Richard and Peggy Musgrave 1989 *Public Finance in Theory and Practice*, Fifth edition, McGraw Hill, Singapore: 103). And in the same era as Knut Wicksell, Amilcare Puviani introduced the concept of fiscal illusion (in which there is a disconnect between awareness of government spending and awareness of (eventual) taxation) (see Lindahl, Erik 1919, 'Just Taxation – A Positive Solution' (Elizabeth Henderson trans) in Richard Musgrave and Alan Peacock (eds), 1967, *Classics in the Theory of Public Finance*, MacMillan, London: 175). The importance of voters being well informed in turn highlights the importance of freedom of political participation, speech and association and a free press.

14 Arrow, Kenneth 1963 *Social Choice and Individual Values*, Second edition, John Wiley and Sons, New York; Olson, Mancur 1965 *The Logic of Collective Action: Public Goods and the Theory of Groups*, Harvard, Cambridge, Massachusetts.

Distinguishing elements of wellbeing assists ministerial decision-making

But public servants do more than just respond to ministers; they use frameworks to advise ministers.

The Treasury's wellbeing framework reminds Treasury staff to explore, and advise ministers of the distinct impacts of policies on various considerations, such as the level and distribution of material consumption, health, and environmental amenity.

The Treasury wellbeing framework identifies five dimensions that directly or indirectly have important implications for wellbeing and are particularly relevant to Treasury. These dimensions are:

- the set of opportunities available to people, including – but not limited to – the level of goods and services that can be consumed;
- the distribution of those opportunities across the Australian people;
- the sustainability of those opportunities over time;
- the overall level and allocation of risk borne by individuals and the community; and
- the complexity of the choices facing individuals and the community.

These dimensions cover the key determinants of a person's wellbeing and the distribution of these determinants currently and across generations. They also explicitly recognise risk and complexity given the relevance of these concepts to Treasury's specific responsibilities: advising on macroeconomic policy, well-functioning markets and taxation.

In response to a particular public policy issue, Treasury may identify options that maximise the level of certain opportunities or minimise the overall level of risk or complexity. Treasury may also be able to outline how a policy affects the distribution of opportunities, risk and complexity across the population and over time (noting that the selection of a distributional measure involves normative judgements about what is being distributed, among whom, and whether the measure uses equality or adequacy as a reference point).

In doing this Treasury does not take a corporate position on whether a certain distribution is appropriate, or whether a certain weight should be given to level versus distributional considerations, or whether some types of opportunities are more important than others. Likewise, Treasury does not take a corporate position on the relative weights to apply to the five dimensions of the wellbeing framework. While Treasury advice will at times set out a preferred view based on experience and analysis, decision-making ultimately rests with ministers and elected governments, who are called to make value judgements on priorities and trade offs, taking into account community preferences and hence supporting wellbeing.

Nevertheless, the wellbeing framework helps Treasury staff assist ministers to make these value judgements.

For instance, the framework's reference to the level of goods and services for consumption is accompanied by references to various distributional concerns. This reminds staff to consider and outline impacts on both efficiency and distribution – both when the explicit purpose of a policy is to redistribute, and when it is not.

Distributional analysis may reveal that a suite of policies both assists and hinders the same group of people; such a result presumably does not serve distributional goals, whatever those goals may be.[15] It may reveal that the winners from a certain policy could compensate the losers. It may highlight community views on fairness and other reasons for considering distribution, or it may highlight differences in the distribution for one concept (such as income) but not for another (such as consumption).

So it is not the purpose of the wellbeing framework to enable staff simply to point to options that maximise wellbeing with certainty; this is impossible given the absence of an agreed approach to measuring wellbeing. Rather, the wellbeing framework helps staff set out some dimensions of wellbeing to hopefully help ministers make well-informed value judgements consistent with improving wellbeing.

Treasury draws on powerful, well-established tools to provide thorough analysis

Treasury's wellbeing framework also requires us to undertake objective and thorough analysis using the best available analytical frameworks.

Treasury faces myriad claims of market failure and needs to draw on economic frameworks to distinguish the well-based claims from the rest. Various economic frameworks are discussed in documents like the Best Practice Regulation Handbook, produced by the Office of Best Practice Regulation in consultation with agencies including Treasury. The Handbook outlines various types of

15 The combined analysis of the tax and transfer system championed by Ian Castles is an example of an approach that allows the coherence of nominally separate systems to be tested (Podger, Andrew 2011 'Ian Castles and the Henry Tax/Transfers Review', *Keynote Address – HC Coombs Policy Forum*, Australian National University, Canberra).

market failure, including monopoly and abuse of market power, asymmetric information, externalities, and non-rivalrous or non-excludable goods. It also outlines instances where government may or may not be able to improve the situation.[16]

Treasury can draw on recent economic research on systematic failures in personal decision-making, which applies to the public, but also to public officials.[17] And Treasury can also draw from literature on types of government failures, including work on fiscal illusion, the theory of second best, and barriers to policy reversal.[18]

Treasury's wellbeing framework also requires staff to gather the best available empirical evidence, in recognition that theory is always more reliable when partnered with empirics. This encompasses such techniques as modelling of distributional impacts over time and studies of fiscal impact. It also includes evidence from research in the relevant policy domains, administrative data demonstrating past experience, and cost benefit analysis, as recommended in the Best Practice Regulation Handbook.

This partnership of robust theory and available empirics can provide considerable assurance that the resulting policy recommendations are consistent with improving wellbeing, notwithstanding the absence of comprehensive wellbeing measures.

The relationship between improving personal wellbeing and societal wellbeing

A degree of assurance also comes from the nature of individuals in a market-based economy.

The Treasury's approach to wellbeing is cast from the perspective of individuals. As we have said already, Treasury considers that wellbeing primarily reflects a person's substantive freedom to lead a life they have reason to value.

This is an economic approach and is predicated on the idea that, provided that market and government failures are addressed and the government provides a

16 Australian Government 2007 *Best Practice Regulation Handbook*, Office of Best Practice Regulation, Canberra.

17 Tasic, Slavisa 2009 'The Illusion of Regulatory Competence', *Critical Review: a Journal of Politics and Society* 21(4): 423-436; Glaeser, Edward 2005 'Paternalism and Psychology' *Harvard Institute of Economic Research Discussion Paper 2097*, Harvard, Cambridge, Massachusetts.

18 Lipsey, Richard and Kelvin Lancaster 1956-57 'The General Theory of Second Best', *The Review of Economic Studies*, 24(1): 11-32; Hall, Peter 1993 'Policy Paradigms, Social Learning and the State: The Case of Economic Policymaking in Britain, *Comparative Politics*, 25(3): 275-296.

conducive environment, we should have some confidence that individuals going about their lives will tend to improve their personal wellbeing, the wellbeing of those they care for, and, in part through market transactions, societal wellbeing. (In providing a conducive environment, in general government actions will have implications for the distribution of society's resources across individuals, and for improving equality of opportunity).

This approach is consistent with Australia's democratic and market-based society, and puts the importance of wellbeing measures in context. While better wellbeing measurement will be valuable, we nonetheless have less need for such aggregate measures than do states that specialise in central planning.

Treasury has both broad and specific goals

Treasury needs to regularly assess its success or otherwise in improving wellbeing and in being an effective central policy agency with whole-of-government responsibilities, notwithstanding the difficulties in measuring such success. However, when considering Treasury's need for wellbeing measurement, it is also important to note that Treasury has been tasked with specific, more measurable, goals alongside its broad wellbeing goal.

These specific goals include the achievement of strong, sustainable economic growth, the efficient provision of Commonwealth payments to the State and Territory governments, the preparation of documents in compliance with the Charter of Budget Honesty, effective taxation and retirement income arrangements, competitive and efficient markets, a reduced regulatory burden on business, and improved housing supply and affordability.

Success against each of these goals can be measured more readily than success against the broad wellbeing goal. And, in Treasury's view, success against each of these specific goals would represent an important contribution to improving wellbeing.

A measured approach to new measures

So while efforts to improve the measurement of wellbeing are important, public policy agencies like Treasury can nonetheless carry out their responsibilities in the absence of a fully agreed, and comprehensive, approach to wellbeing measurement.

Given this, we should take a dispassionate approach when looking at efforts to improve the measurement of wellbeing. We can weigh the potential benefits of efforts to improve wellbeing measures against the costs of those efforts and the risks that resulting measures might be flawed, misused or go unused.

Conclusion

Australia is at the forefront of wellbeing measurement. The Measures of Australia's Progress project of the Australian Bureau of Statistics was ahead of its time, and continues to provide an insightful, wide-ranging and balanced dashboard of important indicators to assist public debate and understanding. This dashboard approach is the best way to grapple with perhaps the most important and challenging measurement question there can be.

It is important that we continue to counter misuse of existing measures, strive to improve individual measures, and promote consideration of a broad array of measures. There is much to gain from such efforts.

That said, it is important to note that, in the absence of a widely agreed approach to wellbeing measurement, public service and government decision-making are not blind. They continue to be guided by the democratic process, economic theory, and conscientious analysis. This is the context for Treasury's wellbeing framework, and it leaves Treasury as an eager, rather than dependent, user of wellbeing measures.

In undertaking its mission Treasury takes a broad view of wellbeing as primarily reflecting a person's substantive freedom to lead a life they have reason to value.

This view encompasses more than is directly captured by commonly used measures of economic activity. It gives prominence to respecting the informed preferences of individuals, while allowing scope for broader social actions and choices. It is open to both subjective and objective notions of wellbeing, and to concerns for outcomes and consequences as well as for rights and liberties.

Treasury brings a whole-of-economy approach to providing advice to government based on an objective and thorough analysis of options. To facilitate that analysis, we have identified five dimensions that directly or indirectly have important implications for wellbeing and are particularly relevant to Treasury. These dimensions are:

- The set of opportunities available to people. This includes not only the level of goods and services that can be consumed, but good health and environmental amenity, leisure and intangibles such as personal and social activities, community participation and political rights and freedoms.
- The distribution of those opportunities across the Australian people. In particular, that all Australians have the opportunity to lead a fulfilling life and participate meaningfully in society.
- The sustainability of those opportunities available over time. In particular, consideration of whether the productive base needed to generate opportunities

(the total stock of capital, including human, physical, social and natural assets) is maintained or enhanced for current and future generations.

- The overall level and allocation of risk borne by individuals and the community. This includes a concern for the ability, and inability, of individuals to manage the level and nature of the risks they face.
- The complexity of the choices facing individuals and the community. Our concerns include the costs of dealing with unwanted complexity, the transparency of government and the ability of individuals and the community to make choices and trade-offs that better match their preferences.

These dimensions reinforce our conviction that trade-offs matter deeply, both between and within dimensions. The dimensions do not provide a simple checklist: rather their consideration provides the broad context for the use of the best available economic and other analytical frameworks, evidence and measures.

References

Arrow, Kenneth (1963). *Social Choice and Individual Values*, Second edition, John Wiley and Sons, New York.

Australian Government (1998). *A Guide to Regulation*, Second edition, Office of Regulation Review, Canberra.

Australian Government (2007). *Best Practice Regulation Handbook*, Office of Best Practice Regulation, Canberra.

Black, Duncan (1948). 'On the Rationale of Group Decision-making', *Journal of Political Economy*, 56(1): 23-34.

Buchanan, James (1975). *The Limits of Liberty*, University of Chicago, Chicago

Downs, Anthony (1957). *An Economic Theory of Democracy*, Harper, New York

Fleurbaey, Marc (2009). 'Beyond GDP: The Quest for a Measure of Social Welfare', *Journal of Economic Literature*, 47(4): 1029 1075.

Glaeser, Edward (2005). 'Paternalism and Psychology', *Harvard Institute of Economic Research Discussion Paper 2097*, Harvard, Cambridge, Massachusetts.

Gorecki, Stephanie, David Gruen and Shane Johnson (2011). 'Measuring Wellbeing in Theory and Practice', *Treasury Working Paper No. 2011-02*, Canberra.

Gruen, David and Joanne Wilkie (2009). 'New Paradigms to Measure Progress', *Economic Roundup*, Issue 4: 1–9.

Hall, Peter (1993). 'Policy Paradigms, Social Learning and the State: The Case of Economic Policymaking in Britain', *Comparative Politics*, 25(3): 275-296.

Inglehart, Ronald, Robert Foa, Christopher Peterson and Christian Welzel (2008). 'Development, Freedom, and Rising Happiness: A Global Perspective (1981-2007)', *Perspectives on Psychological Science* 3(4): 264-285.

Inglehart, Richard and Hans-Dieter Klingemann (2000). 'Genes, culture, democracy and happiness', in Ed Diener and Eunkook (eds) *Subjective Well-being Across Cultures,* MIT Press, Cambridge, Massachusetts.

Kelly, James and Stephanie Gorecki (2012). 'Treasury's Wellbeing Framework' *Economic Roundup*, Issue 3: 27-64.

Lindahl, Erik (1919). 'Just Taxation – A Positive Solution' (Elizabeth Henderson trans), in Richard Musgrave and Alan Peacock (eds) 1967 *Classics in the Theory of Public Finance*, MacMillan, London.

Lipsey, Richard and Kelvin Lancaster (1956-57). 'The General Theory of Second Best', *The Review of Economic Studies*, 24(1): 11-32.

Niskanen, William (1971). *Bureaucracy and Representative Government*, Chicago, Aldine.

Niskanen, William (2006). 'Limiting Government: The Failure of "Starve the Beast"', *Cato Journal*, 26(3).

Olson, Mancur (1965). *The Logic of Collective Action: Public Goods and the Theory of Groups*, Harvard, Cambridge, Massachusetts.

Podger, Andrew (2011) 'Ian Castles and the Henry Tax/Transfers Review', *Keynote Address – HC Coombs Policy Forum*, Australian National University, Canberra.

Sen, Amartya (1999). *Development as Freedom*, Oxford University Press, Oxford.

Schumpeter, Joseph (1942). *Capitalism, Socialism and Democracy*, Fifth edition, George Allen and Unwin, London.

Stiglitz, Joseph, Amartya Sen and Jean-Paul Fitoussi (2009). 'Report by the Commission on the Measurement of Economic Performance and Social Progress', *Commission on the Measurement of Economic Performance and Social Progress.*

Tasic, Slavisa (2009). 'The Illusion of Regulatory Competence', *Critical Review: A Journal of Politics and Society* 21(4): 423-436.

Treasury (1964). 'The Meaning and Measurement of Economic Growth', *Supplement to the Treasury Economic Bulletin*, November, Canberra.

Treasury (1973). 'Economic Growth: Is It Worth Having?' *Treasury Economic Paper No. 2*, Canberra.

Treasury (2004), 'Policy advice and Treasury's wellbeing framework', *Economic Roundup*, Winter, Canberra.

Treasury (2011). *Treasury Strategic Framework*, Canberra.

9. The Wellbeing of the Australian People: Comments on the Treasury's Framework

Jonathan Pincus

> The methodological principle at the basis of economic science and which distinguishes it from other sciences, is the reference which it makes to a measure, namely money.[1]
>
> Productivity isn't everything, but in the long run it is almost everything.[2]

Introduction

Treasury Secretary Martin Parkinson begins the 2011-12 Annual Report thus (Treasury 2012a): 'The Treasury has a long-standing commitment to improving the wellbeing of *all* Australians by delivering quality advice to government and by providing assistance in the implementation of key policy initiatives' [emphasis added]. Then follows the now-standard Treasury statement of 'the wellbeing of the Australian people' (or TWOTAP). This statement is front and centre of Treasury's presentation of self, including in its 'Strategic Framework'. TWOTAP consists of a short general discussion of wellbeing and its importance to Treasury, followed by a list of five 'dimensions' of wellbeing, said to be of special significance to Treasury in doing its work of 'providing advice to government based on an objective and thorough analysis of options'. The framework has been discussed in a series of supporting Treasury papers and speeches.

I argue that the 'wellbeing' statement is useless or worse than useless instrumentally. For those outside Treasury, the TWOTAP list does not facilitate interrogation of the appropriateness of any specific Treasury recommendation or series of recommendations. For those inside Treasury, the existence and standing of the list should be a source of confusion and dissention.

The 'wellbeing' framework can justify Treasury's advocacy of almost any plausible policy. In particular, because TWOTAP offers a list, pure and simple, it does not and cannot give any clues about trade-offs within and between the five 'dimensions'; and this despite Treasury's claiming that the five 'reinforce

1 Ian Castles (1998: 141), quoting AC Pigou, with evident approval.

2 Paul Krugman (1994: 11).

our conviction that trade-offs matter deeply'. Moreover, TWOTAP is virtually useless for an assessment of whether in the wellbeing of the Australian people has improved, let alone whether the change has been large or small.

However, TWOTAP would have real significance, if it signals that Treasury no longer places heavy weight on improving the capacity of the economy to provide more of what Australians want and less of what they do not want. Does TWOTAP signal that Treasury is no longer the guardian of economic efficiency, broadly conceived; that Treasury is not the bulwark against the inefficient pleas of particular interests, including those represented by line departments? If not Treasury, then who?

Background

The Australian Treasury has had a deservedly high reputation. In the past, it dominated the federal policy scene through the power, subtlety and consistency of its advice. Various governments split it in two, creating the subaltern Department of Finance and Administration; added the Productivity Commission and the Australian Consumer and Competition Commission to Treasury's army of supervisors of the private sector; but also greatly expanded and strengthened Prime Minister and Cabinet (PM&C), and swelled the ranks of ministerial advisers. 'The Treasury line' may never have existed but if it did it was the pursuit of what Treasury considered best for the Australian economy. Treasury, eschewing fads and scorning sectional pleadings, could be relied upon to recommend that which Treasury believed would improve the performance of the economy, in macroeconomic and microeconomic terms. In this task, nothing was presumptively excluded from the range of matters important to Treasury.

There was a libel put around in the late 1980s and early 1990s that major government departments had been taken over by an ideology called 'economic rationalism', allegedly in the hearts of those whose secret attitudes a skilful interviewer had uncovered (see Michael Pusey 1991). However, evidence of this canker is hard to find in public documents of Treasury, including two foundational papers relevant to the discussion of national wellbeing.

'The meaning and measurement of economic growth' (Treasury 1964) canvassed technical issues in the measurement of real Gross Domestic Product (GDP). Although 'wellbeing' is not specified as a national goal, the paper took a broad view of what mattered:

> The object of all economic activity, in the long run at least, is the satisfaction of people's demands, whether for goods and services that can be purchased in the market or for other things, tangible or intangible, that cannot...Of course, while the maximum practical economic growth

> is an objective which any government is likely to accept as desirable, it would be completely unrealistic to expect a government completely to subordinate all of its policies to that aim.[3]

The paper then used defence as an example; but it is reasonable to claim that the authors also had in mind other things discussed earlier in the paper, things that people clearly value, like household production and leisure, but which are not included in GDP.

In response to the Club of Rome, in 1973 Treasury was moved to produce *Is Economic Growth Worth Having?* (Ian Castles was among those responsible.) By 'growth' was meant per capita growth, and not expansion in the sheer size of the population and economy. Yes, was the answer: 'The paper [concludes] that if what 'economic growth' is all about is carefully explained, it seems to contribute the key to achieving many of the things going to make up national wellbeing' (Foreword). Calling GDP a 'statistical shadow' of a comprehensive measure of changes in wellbeing,[4] the paper asserted that

> ...economic and social policies should not be directed towards achieving any particular statistical rate of growth [of GDP per capita] in the longer-run, but rather to the efficient use of available resources to establish and maintain those patterns of production and distribution which conform most closely to the preferences of the community...The criteria for decision-making must be related not to the achievement of a pre-ordained statistical result but to the desires of the community, as expressed by people in their capacities as consumers, workers and electors.[5]

A Treasury publication on TWOTAP, released just prior to the workshop (Gorecki and Kelly 2012: 30-31), remarked that:

> Despite these antecedents, prior to the early 2000s there had been no explicit articulation of what wellbeing meant, and in particular, how an institution such as the Treasury should be incorporating consideration of wellbeing in its policy advice.
>
> Treasury's mission statement prior to the current one focused on improving living standards, and emphasised economic policies and developments. The mission statement changed to its current form in October 1997, containing for the first time a direct reference to wellbeing as the primary objective. But with divergent internal views as to how

3 Treasury (1964: 5, 19).

4 However, maybe having 'two-bob each way', the claim was made (Treasury, 1973: 6) that policies aimed at furthering national welfare are likely to lead to increases in output of the economic system per head, that is, to conventionally defined economic growth.

5 Treasury (1973: 5).

> to interpret wellbeing, the Department initiated a process of internal discussion and debate on its meaning and application to policy analysis and advice.

These discussions and debates culminated in 'The wellbeing of the Australian people', which by 2004 had become a central element of Australian Treasury's Strategic Framework (Treasury 2004; Henry 2004); it has not changed greatly since.

Meanwhile, however, Treasury seems intent on not limiting its purview:

> We have not yet developed any single measure to summarise all that wellbeing and progress encompass, and it is fair to say that we are unlikely to. It follows, that we – policy makers, commentators and the public – ought not to rely on any single measure to provide us with an assessment of the quality of individual lives or the cohesion of society (Gruen et al 2011: 31).[6]

As will be seen, 'the cohesion of society' is not in TWOTAP.

Methodological deficiencies: A list for confusion and inconsistency

For convenience, I will first reproduce TWOTAP from the Treasury website (2012b; italics and footnote added), then discuss the content. I will argue that TWOTAP confuses categories; that it is too un-constraining to be useful; and that its efficacy seems never to have been reviewed.

> **The wellbeing of the Australian people**
>
> In undertaking its mission Treasury takes a broad view of wellbeing as primarily reflecting a person's substantive freedom to lead a life they have *reason to value*.
>
> This view encompasses more than is directly captured by commonly used measures of economic activity. It gives prominence to respecting the *informed preferences* of individuals, while allowing scope for broader social actions and choices. It is open to both subjective and objective notions of wellbeing, and to concerns for outcomes and consequences as well as for rights and liberties.

---

6 Presumably the first 'We' refers to the Treasury, which seems to compromise the disclaimer about these being "the views of the authors and not necessarily those of Treasury."

Treasury brings a whole-of-economy approach to providing advice to government based on an objective and thorough analysis of options.

To facilitate that analysis, we have identified *five dimensions* that directly or indirectly have important implications for wellbeing and are *particularly relevant to Treasury.*

These dimensions are:

- *The set of opportunities available to people.* This includes not only the level of goods and services that can be consumed, but good health and environmental amenity, leisure and intangibles such as personal and social activities, community participation and political rights and freedoms.
- *The distribution* of those opportunities across the Australian people. In particular, that all Australians have the opportunity to lead a fulfilling life and participate meaningfully in society.
- *The sustainability* of those opportunities available over time. In particular, consideration of whether the productive base needed to generate opportunities (the total stock of capital, including human, physical, social and natural assets) is maintained or enhanced for current and future generations.
- *The overall level and allocation of risk borne* by individuals and the community. This includes a concern for the ability, and inability, of individuals to manage the level and nature of the risks they face.
- *The complexity of the choices* facing individuals and the community. Our concerns include the costs of dealing with unwanted complexity, the transparency of government and the ability of individuals and the community to make choices and trade-offs that better match their preferences.

These dimensions reinforce our conviction that trade-offs matter deeply, both between and within dimensions. The dimensions *do not provide a simple checklist*: rather their consideration *provides the broad context* for the use of the best available economic and other analytical frameworks, evidence and measures.[7]

7 For comparison, the five 2004 dimensions were: '(i) the level of opportunity and freedom that people enjoy; (ii) the level of consumption possibilities; (iii) the distribution of those consumption possibilities; (iv) the level of risk that people are required to bear; and (v) the level of complexity that people are required to deal with'. The order was later changed, with distribution coming into second place; the reference to 'consumption possibilities' was replaced with 'opportunities'; 'sustainability' was one element in the original (ii).

Political but not necessarily partisan

A department is expected to assist a government in the pursuit of its legitimate objectives. In assessing policy, Treasury has long (and appropriately) taken account of several dimensions of likely impact. However, Treasury's definition of 'the wellbeing of the Australian people' is just that, Treasury's own definition: worth serious consideration, but hardly likely to receive the Rolf Schock prize in philosophy. Amartya Sen, whose capabilities framework is said to have influenced the Treasury mightily, refused to subscribe to Martha Nussbaum's list of 10 items; presumably, the same may well be the case for Treasury's five dimensions.

No philosopher has come up with a definition of 'the wellbeing' of a nation that would obtain the agreement of all those included in the nation. Even the strict Pareto criterion – make someone better off and no one worse off – would not please the envious. Envy aside, no one can devise a non-trivial policy to do what Secretary Parkinson proposed, which is to improve the wellbeing of *all* Australians. Besides, tax policy is a key matter for Treasury, and doubtless Secretary Parkinson does not believe the Mineral Resource Rent Tax improves the wellbeing of all the Australians who had invested heavily in mining stocks, either directly or through their superannuation funds.

Therefore, any Treasury definition of 'wellbeing' is doubly political: imposed on Australians by a government authority (but not a minister); and with distributional implications – some will gain, some lose from its application.

Any Treasury-initiated formulation of national wellbeing would be expected to satisfy the non-partisan test, at least notionally – neither self-serving, nor appealing to one side of politics but not the other. Maybe it does, despite the absence of the word 'productivity', one of then-Treasurer Costello's three 'Ps' (the others being population and workforce participation).

However, notional concurrence of the Government and Opposition is insufficient; the definition also has to be useful. Unfortunately, the Treasury's framework offers scant practical guidance to assist insiders or outsiders to know if, and how well, Treasury has pursued its avowed mission.

Categories

In economics, it has been usual and useful to distinguish two kinds of effects: on efficiency and on distribution – the size of the 'pie' and the shares of the 'pie'. TWOTAP has a separate 'dimension' for distribution; all the other TWOTAP 'dimensions' relate to efficiency, but in a confusing way.

The phrase, 'the set of opportunities,' would be sufficient to cover all aspects of economic efficiency, including sustainability, risk and complexity. Sustainability is the dynamic aspect of efficiency, and not a separate 'dimension'. Risk is an element in the 'set of opportunities'; it is a cost of pursuing things that people value. Accepting risk or complexity can enlarge (or reduce) the set of opportunities; similarly, working at a job that one does not especially enjoy, in order to have income that more than compensates; similarly, saving for old age involves sacrifice now for the expectation of greater benefit later. The acceptance of an appropriate level of risk (or work or saving) expands the opportunity set, and is done best when it involves making the efficient trade-offs.

That is, risk and complexity are merely two of the very many aspects of efficiency, broadly conceived: listing them separately could give the impression that they have the same significance as 'the set of opportunities available to people', whereas they are merely components of that set.

Wellbeing and trade-offs

My fundamental criticism is that, despite what is claimed by Treasury, TWOTAP as presented is incapable of providing 'a consistent basis' for Treasury advice about trade-offs. In fact, it provides no basis at all for the consideration of trade-offs. By offering a list in TWOTAP and a list only, with no clues how to deal with trade-offs, Treasury has abrogated its responsibility to provide a useful guide to its decisions and advice. Treasury signalled this dereliction of duty, back in 2004 and repeated since:

> Consistent with being primarily a descriptive tool, rather than a framework for more formal analysis, the set of dimensions are not designed to meet more formal analytic criteria, such as being comprehensive, unique or independent.

A simple checklist can guide consistent and rigorous decision-making in some instances. For example, an airplane remains on the ground unless the pilot is assured that every item on the pre-flight checklist has been ticked off: no trade-offs are permitted amongst the items. But generally, something more than a checklist is required. Businesses, for example, are urged to use the triple bottom line of people, planet, and profit, yet everyone knows that if profits are persistently absent or low, the business may be taken over or go kaput. Thus profit ranks above the other two, in a lexicographical ordering. Also, viable businesses must be willing to consider trade-offs between the items in the 3P checklist for business; and that requires placing some relative valuations or 'weights' on the various items, when designing business strategy or when forming an index of performance.

Neither ordering nor weights is found in TWOTAP. Two defects follow. Firstly, it is impossible to show that wellbeing has improved, unless there is an improvement in every single dimension. Otherwise, no summary statement about wellbeing can be made: when some items improve and some worsen, then TWOTAP offers a description, but no resolution.

Secondly, TWOTAP provides no basis upon which to choose between alternatives that both show improvements over the status quo in every dimension, but different improvements. It is not enough to say that consideration of the dimensions 'provides the broad context for the use of the best available economic and other analytical frameworks, evidence and measures,' without indicating what evidence, what measures, and how the overall judgement is made.

Moreover, the same comments apply to each of the five items in the TWOTAP list: without a rank ordering (or a set of weights), there is no way to tell if wellbeing has improved in any one of the five 'dimensions'.

When an agency is charged with dealing with a series of complex decisions, it is common (and good practice) for a set of criteria or guidelines to be enunciated. Such guidelines are most valuable when they constrain otherwise unbridled and possibly capricious discretion.[8] Good guidelines provide the principles that inform decisions and, especially, establish presumptions that clearly place the onus of proof. Take, for example, the (old) ACCC guidelines on mergers. The impact on competition was considered first, with the presumption that more competition was to be preferred over less. Thus, the onus of proof for approval of an anti-competitive merger rested with the applicants – to show that the merger was in the 'public interest', even though competition would be reduced.

TWOTAP provides no such presumptions. 'Opportunities' comes first: but there is no indication that, if a proposal does not satisfy that criterion, then it is presumptively ruled out – unless a very strong or special case is made in some other dimension. More generally: there is no indication that we should place any significance on the order in which the dimensions are listed in TWOTAP. If a trivial 'improvement' in GDP requires an arbitrary set of huge redistributions, surely Treasury would never recommend it; if a modest 'improvement' in distribution requires a significant reduction in GDP, surely Treasury would not recommend it. Surely Treasury uses filters of some kind, to sort proposals into the plausible and the implausible. No hint of that in TWOTAP – is it a case of 'We do it, but we keep it to ourselves'?

Both the OECD and ABS publish welfare indicators that are numerical or quantitative. Both agencies leave it to the user to choose whether or not to apply a rank-order or a set of weights. However, unlike the OECD and ABS, Treasury is a public policy department; and so, by offering a list of effects to consider,

8 Phillip Pettit (2003 and elsewhere) has argued for the possibility of 'group agency', of collectives that can reasonably be attributed with minds of their own, discontinuous with the mentality of the members.

and saying, in effect, 'Choose your own ordering or weights', Treasury seems to me to be abrogating its responsibility. Because TWOTAP offers no ranking or weighting system, it cannot guide Treasury consistently across time and across policy decisions.

I assume that Treasury presents the Treasurer with a recommendation with explanation, and not a summary of the completed TWOTAP list. Therefore, in order to give Treasury credit for consistency, it is necessary to assume that Treasury does have some ordering of the five dimensions (and within each), or that Treasury does have a set of weights (or range of weights) for the five dimensions (and within each) – but chooses not to reveal these to the world.

It is one thing to assert about TWOTAP that 'These dimensions reinforce our conviction that trade-offs matter deeply, both between and within dimensions'. It is quite another to make those trade-offs without any kind of ordering, or without using weights, explicitly or implicitly.

Gorecki and Kelly (2012) state that the wellbeing framework is not meant to guide day-to-day decisions. Just as well: any decision made by Treasury can be justified by TWOTAP, unless it can be shown to worsen wellbeing in all five dimensions: narrower opportunities, worse distribution, less sustainable, more risk, and more unwelcome complexity.

It must be splendid within Treasury for those with bees in bonnets: you may lose many a battle, but never mind – eventually you will win the day, under TWOTAP. I can imagine the conversation now: 'For today's policy issue, the most important question is unwanted complexity of choice – in which I happen to be expert. For yesterday's policy issue, you argued that distributional considerations were trumps; the day before, it was sustainability; and before that, it was distribution. Well, today it is complexity.'

Senior Treasury officials may reasonably plead that they exercise their informed and experienced judgement, not only in the assessment of matters that are difficult to measure (like sustainability, or unwanted complexity), but also when making an overall assessment. I have no doubt that senior Treasury officials, when making informed and impartial judgements, are not bound (and should not be bound) by the results of quantitative estimates of the effects of policy proposals. The opening quotation from Pigou via Ian Castles does not imply the contrary. A reasonable judgement about whether a specific policy would improve economic efficiency may be partly based on qualitative economic reasoning (like: a tax at a particular rate imposed on a broad base will raise revenue at lower economic cost per dollar raised than if the base were narrower); and partly based on quantitative estimates (like: our modelling indicates a sizeable increase in economic efficiency, without much churning); and partly (maybe mostly) based on insights from experience. However, it is hard for me to see how TWOTAP improves upon this necessary process, which has involved applying unannounced, unarticulated and *ad hoc* weights or ordering to the various items on and off the TWOTAP list.[9] In this regard, TWOTAP does not increase the transparency of Treasury reasoning about matters on which it gives advice – only more and timely access to Treasury and Cabinet documents would seem to offer that prospect.

Review

It is all very well to say that TWOTAP should not be used, day-to-day; but when?

Well-functioning agencies periodically review their guidelines (or have them reviewed). How have they worked in practice? Have they been followed? Consequently, how should they be changed? I found no evidence of such inquiries about TWOTAP. For what it is worth, I note that an internal 'Strategic Review of the Treasury' (Treasury 2011) suggested that the wellbeing framework was not being applied consistently throughout the department; and that SES staff thought that allocation of scarce Treasury resources between competing ends was 'one of our weakest capabilities'.[10] Moreover, the Independent Review of the Australian Government's Regulatory Impact Analysis Process (Finance 2012) noted that Treasury has a long list of items requiring Post Implementation Reviews (because no RIA was conducted), which suggests that TWOTAP may have been used extensively, instead of a RIA.

The TWOTAP dimensions themselves

What follow are comments on each of the five dimensions of TWOTAP, focusing on measurability and trade-offs.

Set of opportunities

> The set of opportunities available to people. This includes not only the level of goods and services that can be consumed, but good health

9 Treasury says that TWOTAP is not a simple checklist, which I interpret to mean that Treasury considerations are not restricted to items on the list.

10 The 'Strategic Review' was conducted internally with an external reference group. Apart from an Appendix reproducing the wellbeing framework, the only relevant discussion I could find is in the Executive Summary: 'Stakeholders generally consider that Treasury is a leader in applying rigorous economic and analytic frameworks to a variety of public and policy issues. A broad understanding of the Wellbeing Framework is an important part of Treasury culture and identity. In their responses to a survey conducted during the Review, SES considered that, although the Wellbeing Framework is valued by staff, it may not be consistently applied across the department (v)… While the effective allocation of resources between competing priorities is seen by SES staff as one of the most important capabilities for the organisation, they regard it as currently one of our weakest capabilities' (vii).

and environmental amenity, leisure and intangibles such as personal and social activities, community participation and political rights and freedoms.

Let me assume that, for this dimension, Treasury mostly relies on an index or set of indicators; otherwise, I cannot guess how Treasury goes about its assessment of whether or not the set of opportunities available to people has expanded or contracted.[11]

Conventionally, changes in the 'set of opportunities' are measured using an economic aggregate like Consumption, with the components valued at willingness-to-pay or willingness-to-supply (or cost); and with the valued bundle encompassing non-marketed as well as marketed goods and services. Every item mentioned in the second sentence quoted above, except 'political rights and freedoms',[12] can readily be accommodated within the extension of the national accounting framework offered, for example, by Nordhaus and Tobin's (1972) 'Measure of Economic Welfare': supplement the usual national aggregate for consumption, by accounting for leisure, for non-market activities, for health and longevity, and for externalities, including environmental damage. It is well known there are serious difficulties of valuation of un-marketed goods and services.[13] Nonetheless, the approach is well understood and transparent. Unfortunately, the same cannot be said about the Treasury's TWOTAP.

In its 1973 paper, Treasury made a different point, concerning policies to improve the capacity of the economy to serve the needs of the Australian people. If pollution was in excess of the 'preferences of the community', the solution lay in micro-economic reforms (e.g. making the polluter pay; or ensuring that non-renewable resources were priced properly). However, even with these in place, the trend in GDP at constant prices is not 'a comprehensive measure of changes in the national wellbeing, or in the progress (if any) towards the "good life"' (27). Two statistical remedies were briefly canvassed: supplement GDP along the lines suggested by Nordhaus and Tobin (1972); or develop a set of 'social indicators' (like the ABS's much later effort, *Measuring Australian Progress*).

In the Nordhaus-Tobin tradition, the weights given to the various items are the valuations of the individuals concerned, whether revealed in market transactions

11 In a series of Treasury papers on TWOTAP, David Gruen and others (2009, 2011) have sensible things to say about the limitations of GDP (or NNI or national consumption) as a summary measure of aggregate or average wellbeing; but so did the 1973 paper. However, my impression from reading recent Treasury papers is that some national accounts aggregate – NNI or Consumption – plays a prominent part; but details are lacking.

12 Note the absence of reference to economic rights and freedoms: politics is all?

13 Atkinson (2005) reported extensively on this issue for the British government. His main suggestion was to use (inferred) willingness to pay. But for goods and services rationed by entitlement and quantity, not price, there is no common marginal willingness to pay among consumers (as there is for those sold in ordinary markets).

or inferred from other objective evidence about subjective valuations. If there is 'market failure' – for example, if pollutants are being poured into the atmosphere without adequate charge – then the Nordhaus-Tobin approach is to include the cost of the under-priced pollution as a deduction from the aggregate of goods and services consumed. In arriving at the cost of pollution, the Nordhaus-Tobin approach is to use estimates of the values that individuals place on clearer air or on the cost of abatement. The essential aspect is that the valuations of the individuals affected are taken at face value.

In contrast, in TWOTAP, Treasury indicates that it will be 'respecting the informed preferences of individuals' and, presumably, Treasury will not be respecting what it takes to be uninformed preferences. TWOTAP refers to things that Australians have 'reason to value' – this is to distinguish them, presumably, from things that Treasury officials believe Australians value for no good reason. Clearly, behavioural economics has had its effect on Treasury. Thaler and Sunstein (2008) used the Orwellian phrase, 'libertarian paternalism', to justify subliminal manipulation of individual choices. That would be a case of 'Treasury knows better than you what is good for you, and so knows what you would choose if only you did not suffer from weakness of will or defective time preference or whatever'. Here, in contrast, TWOTAP is a case of 'Treasury knows your mind better than you do'.

However, Treasury is to be complimented for one aspect: TWOTAP makes no pretence that it is engaged in more than straight, unvarnished paternalism, with no need for a deceptive weasel word as modifier.

Treasury is the premier public service department, staffed by top-rate people, experienced in making difficult judgements on behalf of others. In this respect, the language of TWOTAP is revealing – 'informed preferences'; 'reason to value'. Who better to pass judgement on the reasons of ordinary Australians – most of whom, it must be said, lack the education and experience of senior Treasury officials – who better, than senior Treasury officials? Who better to know which preferences deserve respect, because they are informed preferences – not to be mistaken for the uniformed, presumably uninformed preferences of ordinary Australians – who better to know than senior Treasury officials?

Is there not a tone of patrician superiority in TWOTAP? Public servants may well have crafted these words, but not, it seems, as servants of ordinary Australians, whose preferences are to be judged by Treasury and, if found wanting, discounted or completely disregarded as un-informed and un-reasoned. No, these are words crafted by the masters, not the servants.

Distribution

> The distribution of those opportunities across the Australian people. In particular, that all Australians have the opportunity to lead a fulfilling life and participate meaningfully in society.

The second sentence is cant (that is, a 'pious, sanctimonious platitude') and, in particular, political cant. It goes well beyond Bob Hawke's famous promise that 'By 1990, no Australian child will be living in poverty'.

Gorecki and Kelly (2012) and other recent Treasury documents stressed the significance of Amartya Sen's 'capabilities' approach. However, it is not at all clear where this interest in Sen's work manifests itself in TWOTAP. Is this sentence it?

The first TWOTAP sentence on distribution implies that Treasury will modify its policy advice according to some estimate of the effects on the distribution of income or wealth or 'opportunities' (however these are measured).[14]

Surely redistribution is a matter for politicians, not Treasury. Politics involves the exercise of power over others, and elected politicians take from some and give to others. (The exercise of this power can be justified in a number of ways, including using the contractarian approach to politics favoured by James M Buchanan.) What roles does Treasury have here, beyond informing the politicians about the likely distributional consequences and offering advice as to what would counter them?

In a speech focusing on how to take distribution into account, David Gruen (2011: 6) chided the NZ Treasury for eschewing normative advice on distribution: this, he said, was an instance of 'reticence proclaimed a virtue...[It] does not seem possible to me to simply communicate "what the distribution is" without engaging in normative issues'.

Gruen's speech had valuable things to say about distribution, but he manages never to outline what indicators he used to measure 'improvements' in the distribution. He said that Gini coefficients and the like seem to have a smaller impact on policy than do 'measures of adequacy' – but he fails to tell us what measures of adequacy should be used. He lauds the addition of subsistence levels of consumption into the famous Atkinson-Stiglitz 1976 'separation' theorem on taxation – but fails to tell us how 'subsistence' is measured. However, I suspect that the default is that more equal is better: after telling us that Konow argued

14 For the economists, I should state that I think that the following is an empty set: policy choices that benefit all individuals. Nonetheless, I think that the concept has its normative uses (Pincus 2009).

that equality or egalitarianism is itself not an underlying principle, Gruen uses an example – involving a reduction in labour market regulation – in which movements away from earnings equality seem to be a negative.[15]

Many economists believe that efficiency and equality can clash; or, in terms of TWOTAP, that a trade-off exists between expanding the set of opportunities and making the distribution of wellbeing more ... well, more something – maybe more of what Treasury approves. Without some clear indication of what Treasury has in mind for the trade-off between these two goals, then if one goes north and the other goes south, of what use is TWOTAP?[16]

Australians have preferences about distribution of opportunities, income, wealth and power. While they may want improved wellbeing for themselves, and for their families, friends and communities, most Australians do not want to live in a country in which some people have no opportunity to enjoy a reasonable standard of wellbeing; or worse, a country in which some people have a miserable level of wellbeing. Many Australians are offended by extremes of income and wealth and power and opportunities. In a Nordhaus-Tobin-like approach to index numbers for aggregate wellbeing, the values that ordinary Australians place on these matters can be taken into account (with difficulty). Otherwise, leave distribution to the politicians.

A final remark: the Australian Constitution has a Lockean clause (51xxxi) requiring compensation on 'just terms' for property acquired by the Commonwealth 'from any State or person'. This requirement – absent or ignored in non-democratic countries – reflects a concern with the arbitrary use of power, and a respect for private property rights – that is, respect for the distributional *status quo ante*. Max Corden coined the memorable phrase, 'conservative social welfare function', to capture this latter aspect. It clashes with the assumption – seemingly pervasive at Treasury – that all incomes and assets are 'the community's', so that, if something is left in private hands, then it is only by the grace and favour of government or through government's incapacity to devise mechanisms that better achieve its goals while leaving less as private income. In his NZ speech, David Gruen (2011) remarked that 'We [Treasury] of course see rewarding effort and risk as important from an efficiency perspective, but for that reason only'. Maybe there is a typo, and the last phrase should read '...but *not* for that reason only'.[17]

---

15 '... [M]ore deregulated labour markets...reduced income inequality by improving employment outcomes [but] widened wage inequalities at the same time...[I]f work has benefits separate from income, the calculus is much more likely to be positive' (Gruen 2011). Gruen's chiding of NZ Treasury for sticking with positive description is hard to reconcile with the Australian Treasury's insistence in 2004 that TWOTAP is 'primarily a descriptive tool'.

16 Sen (1992) proposed a measure of national welfare equal to average income times one minus the Gini coefficient of inequality.

17 See Haidt (2012) for a discussion of the 'fairness/cheating foundation' in moral reasoning.

Sustainability

> The sustainability of those opportunities available over time. In particular, consideration of whether the productive base needed to generate opportunities (the total stock of capital, including human, physical, social and natural assets) is maintained or enhanced for current and future generations.

There is an old saying, with some truth-value: if you cannot measure it, you cannot manage it.

Specific attention was given to sustainability in Gorecki, Gruen and Johnson (2011):

> [F]or many stocks, particularly environmental and social capital, placing a monetary value ... is very difficult. Stiglitz et al (2009) ... recommended that a monetary index of sustainability be complemented by a limited set of physical indicators to monitor the environment – particularly in the case of irreversible or discontinuous alterations. Such an approach seems entirely sensible as we determine better ways to value the environment (27).[18]

Say that the 'productive base' is enhanced for future generations, but damaged for current. When does that enhance wellbeing, or damage it? Once again, trade-offs come into play – but once again, a checklist does not encourage consistency and transparency.[19]

Overall level of risk

> The overall level and allocation of risk borne by individuals and the community. This includes a concern for the ability, and inability, of individuals to manage the level and nature of the risks they face.

A worthy matter: but how to make it operational? And I do note the post-modernist touch – 'concern for the ability, and inability...' At least Treasury did not disavow the law of the excluded middle.

Complexity of choices

> The complexity of the choices facing individuals and the community. Our concerns include the costs of dealing with unwanted complexity,

18 On such valuations, see Wagner (1997).

19 Presumably, one reason for reticence about implementing the Stiglitz approach is that Treasury knows that even when markets for assets do exist, market prices may well be distorted by defective time preferences and the like: shadow prices everywhere, cast by the behaviourist's lamp.

> the transparency of government and the ability of individuals and the community to make choices and trade-offs that better match their preferences.

How many are there, in the behavioural economics group in Treasury, that they can not only delineate unwanted complexity in the world of choice, but also estimate the costs of dealing with it. Thaler and Sunstein should be envious.[20]

Conclusion

After the workshop, it was put to me that a main purpose of TWOTAP was internal to Treasury: to remind recent Treasury appointees of the wide range of matters that Treasury has long considered important (as the 1964 and 1973 papers attest); matters that those with great technical skills, but narrow focus, may overlook or dismiss. Certainly, in Gorecki and Kelly (2012) four of the five roles to be played by TWOTAP are internal, including, at the top of the list, 'educating staff'. Presumably, an internal document may not nudge the new recruits as effectively as a public document. But once made public, then it should be suitable for the external readership also.

The second role mentioned in the 2012 paper is 'signalling to those outside of the Treasury – individuals, organisations, other government agencies, and the Government – that our approach to public policy does not conform to simplistic stereotypes about Treasury'. If the 'simplistic stereotype' is that Treasury is seriously concerned about increasing the size of the economic pie, then TWOTAP may have satisfied that aim.

Treasury's 2012 Annual Report informs readers that the Fiscal Branch '...aims to ensure government spending arrangements are effective and that key social and economic reforms are supported. This is crucial to facilitating strong, sustainable economic growth and the improved wellbeing of Australians'.

It is a pity that Treasury does not tell us how it assesses whether policy changes would likely produce 'sustainable economic growth', let alone improve 'the wellbeing of the Australian people'; or how growth and wellbeing inter-relate.

It was reported that the experts at the symposium agreed that 'economic growth should not be constrained, so long as growth is defined not just in terms of GDP but as "expanding opportunities" (Podger 2013). For many decades, no respectable economist and certainly no senior Treasury official has advocated

20 At the workshop, it was suggested that TWOTAP should be read as referring to the complexity imposed by government (e.g. the mountains of regulation and tax code), and not to complexity of choice generally. Even after redrafting along these lines, the questions would still remain: how can Treasury delineate *unwanted* complexity, and how can Treasury measure the costs of such? Are complex BAS requirements wanted or unwanted, and by whom?

single-minded pursuit of GDP. Moreover, decades ago (as reported above) Treasury discussed how to adjust national economic aggregates for many of the items mentioned in TWOTAP, to gain a better idea of the direction and magnitude of changes in the sustainable capacity of the economy to provide what Australians value.

In earlier times, the expression commonly used in this regard was not 'expanding the set of opportunities' but 'improving economic efficiency' or 'increasing economic growth'. It was chiefly on that ground that Treasury, for example, supported a tax package involving the introduction of the GST, removal of wholesale taxes, cuts in income tax rates and compensation for some who would lose out. Economic efficiency, economic growth, improved productivity: formerly, these were given special but not overwhelming emphasis by Treasury.

In contrast, TWOTAP conspicuously avoids lexicographically ranking the items in the checklist, and eschews announcing the relative importance or weights of the various items, which normally would guide decisions about trade-offs. It is easy to find philosophical and ideological objections to ranking one dimension of wellbeing higher than another, or to using summary indices of wellbeing. But whatever reservations one may reasonably hold about these, they do not provide sufficient justification for choosing something worse.

References

Atkinson, T (2005). Final report – Measurement of Government Output and Productivity for the National Accounts, Palgrave-Macmillan.

Castles, Ian (1998). 'Measuring economic progress: from political arithmetic to social accounts' (Colin Clark Memorial Lecture), Economic Analysis and Policy 22.2: 137-146.

Department of Finance and Administration (2012). Independent Review of the Australian Government's Regulatory Impact Analysis Process (by David Borthwick and Robert Milliner) http://www.finance.gov.au/deregulation/docs/independent-review-of-ria-process.pdf

Gorecki, Stephanie, David Gruen and Shane Johnson (2011). 'Measuring wellbeing in theory and practice', Working Paper 2011-02 http://www.treasury.gov.au/PublicationsAndMedia/Publications/2011/Measuring-Wellbeing-in-Theory-and-Practice.

Gorecki, Stephanie and James Kelly (2012). 'Treasury's wellbeing framework', Economic Roundup, Issue 3, Treasury, Canberra.

Gruen, David and Joann Wilkie (2009). 'New paradigms to measure progress', Economic Roundup, Issue 4 http://archive.treasury.gov.au/documents/1689/PDF/Economic_Roundup_Issue_4_2009.pdf#page=7.

Gruen, David, James Kelly, Stephanie Gorecki and Tim Wong (2011). 'Wellbeing, living standards, and their distribution,' http://archive.treasury.gov.au/documents/2153/PDF/speech_dg_nz.pdf.

Haidt, Jonathan (2012). The Righteous Mind: Why Good People Are Divided by Politics and Religion, New York: Pantheon Books.

Henry, Ken (2004). 'Policy Advice and Treasury's wellbeing framework', Economic Roundup, Winter, Treasury, Canberra.

Krugman, Paul (1994). The Age of Diminished Expectations: US Economic Policy in the 1990s, Cambridge Mass.: MIT Press.

Nethercote, JR (2013). 'Treasury succumbs to political platitudes,' Canberra Times (Public Sector Informant), 5 February.

Nordhaus, William D and James Tobin (1972). 'Is Growth Obsolete?', in: Economic Growth, National Bureau of Economic Research, General Series No. 96, New York: Columbia University Press: 1–80.

Pettit, Phillip (2003). 'Groups with minds of their own', in FF Schmidtt, ed., Socializing Metaphysics: The Nature of Social Reality, Lanham. Md., Rowman and Littlefield.

Pincus, Jonathan (2009). 'Reflections on Microeconomic Policy Frameworks in Australia, and a Suggestion about Fairness', The Australian Economic Review 42.2: 1–10.

Pincus, Jonathan (2013). 'Treasury submits to an aim it can't measure', Canberra Times (Public Sector Informant), 2 April.

Podger, Andrew (2013). '"Political platitudes" or open-mindedness', Canberra Times (Public Sector Informant), Opinion, March 5.

Pusey, Michael (1991). Economic Rationalism in Canberra: a nation-building state changes its mind, Cambridge, England and Melbourne: Cambridge University Press.

Thaler, Richard H and Cass R Sunstein (2008). Nudge: improving decisions about health, wealth, and happiness, New Haven: Yale University Press.

Treasury (1964). 'The meaning and measurement of economic growth', Supplement to the Treasury Economic Bulletin, http://archive.treasury.gov.au/documents/1689/PDF/Treasury_1964_The_meaning_and_measurement_of_economic_growth.pdf.

Treasury (1973). 'Economic growth: is it worth having?', Treasury Economic Paper No. 2, Canberra, http://archive.treasury.gov.au/documents/1689/PDF/Treasury_1973_Economic_Growth_is_it_worth_having.pdf.

Treasury (2004). Policy advice and Treasury's wellbeing framework, Economic Roundup, Winter, http://archive.treasury.gov.au/documents/876/HTML/docshell.asp?URL=Policy_advice_Treasury_wellbeing_framework.htm.

Treasury (2011). 'Strategic review of the Treasury', http://www.treasury.gov.au/~/media/Treasury/About%20Treasury/Our%20Department/Strategic%20review/Downloads/A9RC613.ashx.

Treasury (2012a). Annual Report 2011-12. http://www.treasury.gov.au/PublicationsAndMedia/Publications/2012/Treasury-Annual-Report-2011-12.Treasury (2012b). Australian Treasury Strategic Framework 2011-12. http://treasury.gov.au/~/media/Treasury/About%20Treasury/Our%20Department/Strategic%20framework/Downloads/Treasury%20Strategic%20Framework_20110802.ashx.

Wagner, Richard E (1997). 'Parasitical Political Pricing, Economic Calculation, and the Size of Government', Journal of Public Finance and Public Choice 15: 135-146 (accessed at http://mason.gmu.edu/~rwagner/PolPrice.pdf).

10. Subjective Wellbeing and the Mismeasure of Progress

Richard Eckersley

Introduction

The past two decades have seen a remarkable surge in interest in measuring the progress of societies. The debate has focused on adequacy of economic indicators, notably per capita income or GDP (gross domestic product). Measures of subjective wellbeing (SWB) are attracting particular attention, with several national statistical agencies, including the Australian Bureau of Statistics (ABS), examining their value for inclusion in sets of indicators of national progress.

The statistical models of progress have a high degree of internal consistency: all or most of the dominant indicators are correlated. Some economists say GDP is associated with so many other measures of progress (including SWB) that we might as well continue to use GDP. Some SWB researchers, on the other hand, say SWB is associated with so many other, objective measures of progress, we should use SWB. Most researchers, however, opt for a mix of subjective and objective indicators.

So what is the problem? My argument is that conventional indicators of progress, including GDP and SWB, are measuring Westernisation or modernisation, rather than optimal social progress or development. While the concepts may overlap, they are not the same thing. At best, the qualities being measured may be desirable, even necessary, but are not sufficient. At worst, the benefits of modernisation are being counted, but not its costs, including those associated with excessive materialism and individualism (to say nothing of its environmental impacts, with which I am not concerned here).

In other words, indicators focus on those qualities that modernisation emphasises and celebrates, such as material wealth, education, democratic governance, the rule of law, human rights and individual freedom. Valuable though these qualities are, they do not represent the sum total of what makes a better life.

The goal of progress should be to improve people's quality of life, not just to raise their standard of living. Quality of life is the degree to which people enjoy – or societies provide – the conditions of life (social, economic, cultural, environmental) that are conducive to total wellbeing (physical, mental, social and spiritual). Quality of life is both subjective and objective, as much a matter of how we feel about our lives as about the material conditions in which we live. Subjective wellbeing has been defined in many ways, but is usually measured on a scale of self-reported happiness or life satisfaction.

I set out in more detail the case against orthodox models and measures of progress in several recent papers (Eckersley: 2006a, 2009, 2012, in press). The orthodox view places Western liberal democracies at its leading edge; other evidence suggests they may be, in some respects at least, societies in decline. Reconciling these views is no simple matter.

In this chapter I want to take two aspects of SWB that are raised by a new paper by Ed Diener and his colleagues, which is one of the most persuasive and compelling accounts in favour of SWB measures (Diener, Inglehart, Tay: in press). The first is the gap – or contradiction – between personal life satisfaction and social discontent; the second concerns the role of personal freedom in SWB.

All these matters would have been of keen interest to Ian Castles. They reflect both the continuities in the debate about progress and its developments and advances since his time. In his response to the papers presented at the 1997 conference, 'Measuring national progress: Is life in Australia getting better, or worse?', Ian said that he had listened to the presentations with a sense of déjà vu (Castles: 1998). I suspect he would say the same about these symposium papers. Ian concluded by saying that while GDP was sometimes misused, the view that decision-makers were misled is rarely supported by evidence. 'In my view, GDP is a valuable and necessary, but not sufficient, measure of material progress.'

Ian even drew on SWB measures to support his case at an ASSA workshop later that same year (Castles: 1997). In his presentation, a critique of the Human Development Index and the Genuine Progress Indicator, he stated that the objective indicator of wellbeing which correlated best with the subjective measure of wellbeing was GDP per head:

> It would be unwise to draw strong inferences from these findings, but it is interesting that an indicator which was never intended to be a measure even of *economic* welfare should appear to be better correlated with the subjective wellbeing measure than several indicators which embrace non-economic aspects of wellbeing, and also of a composite indicator which was designed to embrace economic and non-economic aspects.

Ian and I were often on opposite sides of the debate about progress, although I had great respect for his statistical knowledge and rigour; our differences were more philosophical. I do think, for example, that governments have been misled

– or mistaken – in persisting with a model of material progress, focused on growth in GDP, in the face of growing evidence of its declining benefits and rising costs, including to wellbeing (Eckersley: 2005, 2006a, b).

Personal satisfaction and social disquiet

The new paper by Diener and colleagues carefully reviews the reliability, validity and sensitivity of life satisfaction measures. They argue that several types of data indicate that the measures validly reflect the quality of people's lives. These lines of evidence include: differences between nations in life satisfaction, which are associated with differences in objective conditions; differences between groups who live in different circumstances; patterns of change in life satisfaction before, during, and after significant life events; and prediction by life satisfaction scores of future behaviours such as suicide.

Despite this, they remain cautious about using SWB indicators to inform national policy decisions. The measures are useful in research on individual wellbeing, but there are questions about applying them to policy that need more analysis and research, they say.

> Life satisfaction can provide an added window on what is going well or badly in a society, as experienced by the citizens themselves. There are specific instances where life satisfaction measures can help illuminate current policy debates, but being able to tie the scores to factors that bear on policy is essential. Given their low cost and ease of administration it is desirable that societies adopt measures of life satisfaction to supplement current economic and social indicators. At the same time it must be recognised that life satisfaction measures have clear limits, and provide only one type of information to policy makers. Thus, additional types of objective and subjective indicators are needed.

The authors report research findings that help to explain something that I have pointed out repeatedly in my writing: asking people about life in general or the lives of others gives a very different result from asking them about their own lives (Eckersley: 2000a,b, 2005, 2009, 2012, in press).

In the study in question, political questions sometimes came before, and sometimes after, the life evaluation question. People's life evaluation scores were lower when they followed the political questions (a draft stated that the scores were 'substantially lower' and that this item-order effect was 'relatively large'). Inserting a buffer or transition question – 'Now, thinking about your personal life, are you satisfied with your personal life today?' – between the political questions and life evaluation largely eliminated this item-order effect. The authors suggest the effect might have been due to the way questions were interpreted rather than to the priming of certain information. 'The political questions at the beginning of the interview may have induced respondents to think the survey was about people's lives embedded in the context of societal and political affairs.'

The findings are significant because they reveal the extent to which the standard use of SWB measures discounts the social environment. Surely when we use SWB as a social indicator, a measure of progress, we want to put people's individual lives into a wider context. In contrast, for example, a question I have used in several surveys explicitly includes this social context (as well as broadening the focus beyond the individual): 'Thinking now about the overall quality of life in Australia, taking into account social, economic and environmental conditions and trends, would you say that life in Australia is getting better, worse or staying about the same?' (Eckersley: 2000a, b, 2005). This question is arguably better suited to assessing subjectively national progress. It also produces markedly different results: most people say they are happy and satisfied with their lives; however, when it comes to trends in quality of life, pessimists outnumber optimists. Yet this approach is neglected compared to the growing interest in SWB measures.

The difference in perspectives is highlighted in the headline of a story in *The Atlantic* in 2012: 'Americans are losing confidence in the nation but still believe in themselves' (Penn: 2012). The article states:

> In a wave of pessimism that has been pervasive throughout the last decade (perhaps the longest running in American history), Americans believe their country is heading in the wrong direction, that our values are weathering, that their generation is worse off than their parents' generation, and that their children will be still worse off. Americans believe that political corruption, too much focus on material things, and the influence of money in politics are weakening our values and standing in the world. They believe elected officials reflect and represent mainly the values of the wealthy and think the economic system is unfair to middle- and working-class Americans. And they believe that Wall Street is more like a cancer than an engine for economic growth.

In 2011, *Time* magazine reported a poll showing that the United States is going through 'one of its longest sustained periods of unhappiness and pessimism ever', adding that it is 'hard to overstate what a fundamental change this represents' (Penn: 2011). Two-thirds of Americans believed the past decade was one of decline, not progress, for the US (68 per cent) and that the greatest threat to the long-term stability of the US came from within, not from outside, the country (66 per cent). A half said the past decade was one of the worst in the past 100 years (47 per cent) and that American children today would be worse off than people were when they grew up (52 per cent).

Australia ranks at or near the top of many international comparisons of quality of life and development. Unlike the United States and Europe, it escaped the global financial crisis relatively unscathed: there was no recession, unemployment didn't rise, and national debt is manageable. A refrain in public debate is that Australians have nothing to whine about. Yet, the public mood in Australia is sour; dissatisfaction with government is high. In a 2009 survey, only 24 per cent of people said quality of life in Australia was getting better (ANU Poll: 2009). In another 2009 survey, Australians generally saw themselves today as being richer, but unhappier (or no happier), than they were in the previous few decades (Auspoll: 2009). While 77 per cent said Australians' material standard of living was higher than 20 years ago, 58 per cent felt emotional wellbeing was lower.

The findings stand in stark contrast to people's high levels of self-reported personal happiness and life satisfaction. Why do we persist in telling only half the story?

The mixed blessings of freedom

The second issue raised in the Diener paper has to do with equating progress with modernisation.

The authors say that the theory of evolutionary modernisation states that people's values and life strategies change as they move from subsistence-level scarcity to high levels of economic and physical security. At low levels of development, sheer survival tends to be the dominant goal and happiness is closely linked with whether one has enough of life's basic necessities. As people attain higher levels of economic and physical security they attach greater importance to having free choice in how to live their lives. They present data on international comparisons showing this: as we move from low-income nations to high, financial satisfaction becomes less important to overall life satisfaction, and free choice becomes more important.

A lot of research shows that personal freedom is a major determinant of progress and human development in cross-country comparisons. In another study, Inglehart and his colleagues linked happiness to the extent to which a society allows free choice; free choice was, in turn, associated with economic development, democratisation, and social liberalisation (Inglehart, Foa, Peterson, Welzel: 2008). Yet studies of the role of freedom in health, both empirical and theoretical, tell a different story (Eckersley: 2002, 2006b, 2009).

Freedom can be disturbing as well as exciting: while it creates new opportunities for personal experience and growth, it also carries risks of social dislocation and isolation, and a cultural attenuation that makes identity and belonging problematic. This is particularly clear in the sociological work on the centrality of individualisation to late-modern or postmodern life, which is marked by perceived insecurity, uncertainty and risk, and a lack of clear frames of reference.

A new study in Finland – which, with other Scandinavian countries, does well in international comparisons of progress and development – casts fascinating light on this question (Lindfors, Solantas, Rimpela: 2012). It assessed changes in fears for the future of Finnish youth, based on adolescent health and lifestyle surveys carried out in 1983, 1997, and 2007. A total of 17,750 students aged 12-18 were asked an open question: 'When you think about your life and the future in general, what three things do you fear the most?'

Surprisingly, fear of war and terrorism fell over the period, as did fear of environmental disasters. Fear about work and education did not change much, again surprising given the changes in these areas. However, other, more personal fears rose: failure and making wrong choices (from seven per cent to 16 per cent), future family and partnership (seven per cent to 14 per cent), loneliness (five per cent to 20 per cent), accidents (six per cent to 12 per cent), health (16 per cent to 41 per cent), and death (17 per cent to 39 per cent).

The authors conclude that perceptions of risks have become more individualised, thus supporting late-modernist theory. The results highlight the fact that adolescents' images of the future act as a mirror of the times, reflecting the values and ethos of society and its social and cultural norms and their changes over time. 'Cultural and societal changes, including emphasis on individual choice and increased uncertainty, seem to create perceptions of uneasiness and insecurity in young people's transitions to adulthood,' the authors write.

The existential dimension of the analysis can be taken further. In psychology, terror management theory argues that fear of our mortality is a powerful motivation for humans, and we construct personal and cultural means to manage it, to allow us to accept the inevitability of death: worldviews, values, beliefs, rituals. So the Finnish findings, showing increased fear of death, might be further evidence of how Western culture is failing us.

The Diener paper – and the broader SWB literature – does not address this paradox of freedom, although I have noted it in earlier papers. One possibility, which links both the issues I have discussed, is that there is a bias in SWB measurement in favour of individualistic societies, in which people place less emphasis on the social context and more on personal aspects of life.

Conclusion

For all their advantages, I believe SWB measures are still missing critical dimensions of human wellbeing: the more intangible, cultural and moral aspects of life that reflect and reveal the depths of the human psyche and the complexities of human affairs. These are the factors that have a major influence on belonging, identity and meaning in life, and so provide the foundation for a sense of intrinsic worth and existential certainty and confidence that are crucial elements of wellbeing.

Replacing or supplementing money with happiness or life satisfaction as a measure won't solve the problem. Although research has revealed the importance of things other than money to wellbeing, there remains a substantial gap in the new progress measures, even those incorporating SWB. Orthodox approaches underestimate the degree to which 'progress' as we measure it is contributing to an existential deficit that is affecting the health and wellbeing of all of us, rich and poor alike. This 'psychosocial dynamics' perspective is largely absent from the political, and even scientific, debate about progress.

However, I admit to being puzzled by these issues. I am impressed by the consistency of SWB findings, the many aspects of life they do seem to reflect. At the same time, SWB researchers seem reluctant to respond to my criticisms, and to venture outside the narrow world of SWB and its correlates to take other, more diverse data into account. This stance can produce what I have called a 'false consensus' that can take hold within scientific disciplines and research fields: an agreement about what is right and important that the wider evidence does not justify.

My work involves transdisciplinary synthesis (Eckersley: 2005, 2010). It ranges well outside social indicators to include, for example, an analysis of the patterns and trends in young people's physical and mental health (Eckersley: 2011). I seek coherence in the overall conceptual picture rather than precision in the empirical detail. The approaches are complementary: they can draw on, inform and balance each other. Yet the value of synthesis is widely overlooked.

My perspective puts me at odds with most empirical approaches, including that of statisticians. I've taken this up with both the Australian Bureau of Statistics and the Australian Institute of Health and Welfare, arguing, for example, that while life expectancy (the most widely used health indicator) may be rigorous, it does not capture the growing importance to health of non-fatal, chronic, physical and mental illness. In avoiding 'sins of commission' (drawing on less rigorous data), statisticians and researchers risk committing 'sins of omission' (not using all the available data). The result can be a failure to get as full and true a picture of life today as they otherwise might.

I suspect my approach would also put me at odds with Ian Castles, who was a formidable advocate for statistical precision and rigour. However, we should not be surprised that what makes a good life – in all its richness, diversity, complexity and subjectivity – defies ready, or precise, quantitative evaluation, including through the use of GDP or SWB. We may be making progress in measuring progress, but we have further to go than many researchers and statisticians appreciate.

References

ANU Poll (2009). October 2009 frequencies. Canberra: The Australian National University.

Auspoll (2009). Community attitudes to children and young people. Canberra: Australian Research Alliance for Children and Youth.

Castles I (1997). Measuring wealth and welfare: why HDI & GPI fail. Symposium: wealth, work, wellbeing. Academy of Social Sciences in Australia, 10 November.

Castles I (1998). Short responses. In R Eckersley (ed) Measuring progress: Is life getting better? Collingwood, VIC: CSIRO Publishing: 351-353.

Diener E, Inglehart R, Tay L (in press). Theory and validity of life satisfaction scales. Social Indicators Research. Doi: 10.1007/s11205.012.0076.y.

Eckersley R, Dear K (2002). Cultural correlates of youth suicide. Social Science and Medicine 55 (11): 1891-1904.

Eckersley R (in press). A psychosocial dynamics model of progress and development. Encyclopedia of Quality of Life and Well-being Research. SpringerReference.com

Eckersley R (2000a). The mixed blessings of material progress: Diminishing returns in the pursuit of happiness. Journal of Happiness Studies 1 (3): 267-292.

Eckersley R (2000b). The state and fate of nations: Implications of subjective measures of personal and social quality of life, Social Indicators Research 52: 3-27.

Eckersley R (2005). Well and Good: Morality, meaning and happiness, 2nd edition. Melbourne: Text.

Eckersley R (2006a). Progress, sustainability and human wellbeing: Is a new worldview emerging? International Journal of Innovation and Sustainable Development 1940: 306-317.

Eckersley R (2006b). Is modern Western culture a health hazard? International Journal of Epidemiology 35: 252-258.

Eckersley R (2009). Population measures of subjective well-being: How useful are they? Social Indicators Research 94 (1): 1-12.

Eckersley R (2010). The hazards of synthesis. Australasian Science, July-August, p 40.

Eckersley, R (2011). A new narrative of young people's health and wellbeing. Journal of Youth Studies 14 (5): 627-638.

Eckersley R (2012). Whatever happened to Western civilization? The cultural crisis, 20 years later. The Futurist 46 (6), Nov-Dec: 16-22.

Inglehart R, Foa R, Peterson C, Welzel C (2008). Development, freedom, and rising happiness: A global perspective (1981-2007). Perspectives on Psychological Science 3 (4): 264-285.

Lindfors P, Solantaus T, Rimpela A (2012). Fears for the future among Finnish adolescents in 1983-2007: From global concerns to ill health and loneliness. Journal of Adolescence. Doi: 10.1016/j.adolescence.2012.02.003.

Penn M (2012). Americans are losing confidence in the nation but still believe in themselves. The Atlantic, 27 June.

Penn MJ (2011). The pessimism index. Time, 30 June: 28-29.

Note: All Eckersley publications are available at: http://www.richardeckersley.com.au.

11. Measuring Wealth and Welfare: Why HDI and GPI Fail[1]

Ian Castles

Earlier this year [1997], the World Bank released *World Development Indicators,* a comprehensive database of statistics relating to the wealth and welfare of the world's peoples.The new annual publication provided some 600 indicators for nearly 150 countries. In his Foreword to the hard-copy version, the Bank's President, James Wolfensohn, expressed the hope that the new publication

> will become the principal mechanism by which the world measures progress in reducing poverty and in enriching the lives of people everywhere.[2]

At the masthead of Chapter 1, the World Bank reproduced the celebrated injunction of Sir William Petty, inventor of the concept of national income, to members of the Royal Society of London – *No word might be used but what marks either number, weight or measure.* The authors of the new compendium were quick to point out that Petty's concerns went beyond the national income to such factors as 'the Common Safety' and 'each Man's particular Happiness'.

The Bank's invocation of the name and work of Sir William Petty was particularly apt. The underlying principle of his great work *Political Arithmetick*, written in 1676, was that the condition of England and its people could be represented in numbers. Moreover, Petty argued that these numbers – 'development indicators' in modern terminology – could be applied to 'policy, by the name of *Political Arithmetic*', and that government had a responsibility to ensure the accuracy of the information upon which policy was founded:

> Now the Observations or Positions expressed by *Weight and Measure,* upon which I bottom the ensuing Discourses, are either true, or not apparently false, and which if they are not already true, certain, and evident, yet may be made so by the Sovereign Power... ...I hope all ingenious and candid persons will rectifie the Errors, Defects and Imperfections, which probably may be found in any of (my) Positions... Nor would it misbecome Authority it self, to clear the Truth of those Matters which private Endeavours cannot reach to.[3]

---

1 First presented in 1997 at the Academy of the Social Sciences annual symposium.

2 World Bank (1997). *World Development Indicators*, pv.

3 Petty, Sir William (1676). Political Arithmetick in Hull, CH (ed) *The Economic Writings of Sir William Petty,* Cambridge, *1899*, vol. 1: 244-5. The reference to 'policy by the name of *Political Arithmetic*' is quoted in Strauss, E (1954). *Sir William Petty: Portrait of a Genius*: 184.

Generalising from Petty's example, the World Bank authors claimed that 'Since the seventeenth century, economists have viewed development as a means of improving standards of living and the quality of life in very broad terms'. But they did not believe that the 'quality of life' itself could be represented in numbers: the aim of *World Development Indicators* was to enumerate various *indicators* of 'life's quality'. Judgements about the relative importance of individual indicators needed to recognise that

> ...values differ greatly from individual to individual, reflecting different aspirations, conceptions, abilities and tastes – and from society to society, reflecting culture and tradition.[4]

But the World Bank economists did observe that one of the 600 indicators – GNP per capita – had a particular significance. They cited the results of a study undertaken jointly by Partha Dasgupta, professor of economics at Cambridge, and Martin Weale, director of Britain's National Institute of Economic and Social Research, which had established 'a strong correlation between the rankings of 48 developing countries for GNP per capita (adjusted for purchasing power parity) and their rankings for five other indicators (life expectancy, infant mortality, adult literacy, political rights and civil rights).[5]

This cross-country study of the relationship between 'quality of life' indicators was used by Professor Dasgupta in his monograph, *An Inquiry into Well-Being and Destitution*, from which the World Bank authors quoted an important finding:

> ...recent suggestions that national income is a vastly misleading index are not borne out by this exercise. We can do better than merely rely on national income, but we wouldn't have been wildly off the mark as regards an ordinal comparison of countries had we relied exclusively on national income per head.[6]

The nature of this relationship between national income and other measures of wellbeing and quality of life was a subject of intense interest to our late friend and colleague Fred Gruen, who is sadly missed from the Academy's Symposium this year and who would certainly have been an active participant if he were with us. In a 1996 paper entitled `The Quality of Life, the National Interest and the Role of Economics',[7] Fred drew extensively on the study by Weale and Dasgupta, and followed the same methodology to produce 'an assessment of the quality of life in Australia using available comparative surveys'.

---

4 World Bank (1997), *op cit*: 3.

5 Dasgupta, Partha and Weale, Martin (1992). 'On Measuring the Quality of Life' in *World Development* 20: 119-31.

6 Dasgupta, Partha (1993). *An Inquiry into Well-Being and Destitution*, Oxford.

7 Gruen, Fred (1996). 'The Quality of Life, the National Interest and the Role of Economics'. Contribution to a series of seminars entitled 'Dialogues on Australia's Future' in honour of Professor Ronald Henderson.

Professor Gruen noted that the Weale and Dasgupta finding of a strong relationship between average real incomes and various aspects of the quality of life in developing countries was confirmed by the evidence used in Ronald Inglehart's monograph *Culture Shift in Advanced Industrial Societies,* which had identified strong and statistically significant positive relationships between GDP per head and 'mean life satisfaction' in the richer countries.[8]

Professor Gruen took issue with 'arguments advanced in the 1995 Boyer Lectures (and elsewhere) that Australia has neglected such social values as trust, reciprocity and mutuality in a narrow drive for competition and wealth creation' and he concluded that

> Cross-national evidence suggests strongly that, in countries with high average real incomes, people tend to believe that 'most people can be trusted'. Practically all studies available so far suggest a positive relationship between real incomes and the various aspects of the quality of life which can be measured. This suggests that the decline in trust in many of Australia's institutions over the years is as likely to have been produced by our poor economic performance – rather than being the result of concentrating too much on wealth creation ... and not enough on 'the quality of life'.[9]

It is only in recent years that the availability of internationally comparable real income and quality of life indicators for a large number of countries has enabled relationships between these measures to be tested. The accumulating evidence of strong correlations between these variables is significant, because economists have traditionally been reluctant to draw conclusions about economic welfare, let alone welfare more generally, from macro-economic aggregates.

As long ago as *1912,* in his seminal work *Wealth and Welfare,* AC Pigou, professor of political economy at Cambridge, held that the 'national dividend' is only part of 'economic welfare'; that 'economic welfare is ... a part of a part of (total) welfare'; and that 'anything in the nature of rigid inference from effects on economic welfare to effects on total welfare is out of the question'.[10]

In *1946,* Australia's Dr (later Sir) Roland Wilson took a similar view:

> 'Well-being' is somewhat wider than 'economic welfare', and 'economic welfare' comprehends more than the market-valued wealth which is the refuge of some economists but the only stock-in-trade of the economic statistician. Even if our productivity measures were all inclusive, and

8 Inglehart, Ronald (1990). *Culture Shift in Advanced Industrial Society,* Princeton University Press.

9 Gruen, Fred (1996). *Op cit,* Executive Summary: 2.

10 Pigou, AC (1912). *Wealth and Welfare,* London: 3-11.

> completely accurate within their limits, it is clear that they would not necessarily serve as complete indexes of well-being, even defined in a quasi-economic sense.[11]

And in 1976 Richard Stone, who had been the chief architect of Britain's official national accounts 35 years earlier, pointed out that:

> ... the figures ... [of GNP] measure the unduplicated output of goods and services per head of the population ... [But] welfare depends on much besides the availability of produced goods and services: according to the tastes prevailing in different cultures, a good climate, space, tranquility, a sense of security, a sense of freedom, and many other things which do not enter into the national accounts will be prized as well as an abundance of goods and services. However, estimates of output are useful in themselves and are an essential element in any attempt to measure ... welfare.[12]

The evidence from cross-country studies of strong correlations between real GDP per head and other measures of wellbeing might have been expected to provide a strong fillip to the development and maintenance of internationally comparable estimates of GDP and its components. In fact, however, the trend has been all the other way.

In an address to the congress of the International Statistical Institute at Beijing in 1995, Jean-Claude Milleron, Under-Secretary General of the United Nations and former head of INSEE, France's national statistical office, expressed the view that, in this area, 'we cannot continue to be as weak as we are today'. Mr Milleron nominated the need for 'improved international comparisons of major macroeconomic aggregates' as one of two 'particularly urgent' priorities which called for 'major investigations, both conceptually and empirically' in order to strengthen the global statistical system.[13]

But it was not to be. The Statistics Division of the United Nations can no longer afford to support the International Comparison Project (ICP), which was developed at the University of Pennsylvania in the late 1960s as the major source of internationally comparable price and output data. The importance of this project for researchers into wealth and wellbeing may be judged from the fact that the number of citations of its benchmark monographs and the associated

11 Wilson, Roland (1947). *Facts and Fancies of Productivity* (Paper read, as a Presidential Address, before Section G of the Australian and New Zealand Association for the Advancement of Science, August 1946), Melbourne: 18.

12 Stone, JRN and G (1976). *National Income and Expenditure,* (8th ed), London: 151.

13 Milleron, J-C (1995). 'Global Aspects of a Statistical System in the World Today', *Bulletin of the International Satistical Institute: Proceedings, 50th Session*: 1759-75.

Penn World Tables which had been listed in the Social Science Citation Index by early 1995 had exceeded 1000, and the number of different (first) authors represented in the list exceeds 600.[14]

The interest of researchers continues. At the International Statistical Institute meeting in Istanbul last August, an invited papers session on the topic 'International multilateral measurement of purchasing power parities and real income' included a paper by Professor Prasada Rao of the University of New England, one of the newly elected Fellows of the Academy of the Social Sciences [in Australia] who is present at this Symposium; and Professor Alan Heston of the University of Pennsylvania, a leader in ICP research, will participate in a seminar on `The Asian Economies in the Twentieth Century' at Griffith University later this month.

But the ICP itself is under review and, unless new sources of funds can be found, it will be wound up. Earlier this year, I undertook a review for the OECD of its 'purchasing power parity' program, upon which the ICP relies for its estimates of internationally comparable price and output data for richer countries such as the United States, Japan and Australia. My report, which was discussed at a meeting of national accounts experts in Paris last week, argued that the staffing input of 2.5 staff years which the OECD currently devotes to this program falls far short of the minimum staffing allocation required for the compilation of reliable statistics in this area. The future of this program is also in serious question.

The Human Development Indicator (HDI)

Whilst the Statistics Division of the United Nations no longer has the funds to support the international comparisons of macro-economic aggregates which Jean-Claude Milleron rightly sees as a vital element in the global statistical system, another arm of the world body – The United Nations Development Program (UNDP) – is able to devote substantial resources to publishing and promoting its own interpretation of the significance of indicators of wellbeing which have been compiled elsewhere.

The UNDP has devised a Human Development Index (HDI), which is calculated annually and published in its *Human Development Report*. The purpose of the HDI is to compare the relative level of 'human development' of the peoples of the world. Specifically, the HDI

14 Information provided by Professor Robert Summers, from a citation list prepared in mid-1995 for a proposal submitted to the US National Science Foundation.

> ...measures the average achievements in a country in three basic dimensions of human development - longevity, knowledge and a decent standard of living. A composite index, the HDI thus contains three variables: life expectancy, educational attainment (adult literacy and combined primary, secondary and tertiary enrolment) and real GDP per capita (in PPP $).[15]

The HDI has gained enormous attention, not least because the UNDP presents the results in a way that is calculated to gain maximum attention in the world's media.

By way of contrast, the format of the tables in the World Bank's *World Development Indicators* is not calculated to win media attention: countries are listed in alphabetical order so that, for most of the 600 indicators, the list begins with Albania and ends with Zaire. If James Wolfensohn is to achieve his hope that the Bank's publication becomes 'the principal mechanism by which the world measures progress...in enriching the lives of people everywhere', the Bank may need to change this form of presentation.

The format in which the Human Development Office of the UNDP presents the annual HDI results is more 'media-friendly': the countries of the world are listed in the order of their assessed performance in the achievement of 'human development'. In 1997, Canada headed the list for the fourth year running, with a score of 960 points out of a possible 1000; whereas Sierra Leone, at the bottom (country number 175), gained only 176 points.

In presenting the annual HDI results, the Human Development Office takes every opportunity to pursue its own agenda. Despite the accumulating evidence of strong correlations between real GDP and other 'quality of life' indicators, the presentation of the HDI results is geared to the promotion of the contrary view.

One technique which is adopted is to include in each year's HDI table a column showing the 'Real GDP per capita rank minus HDI rank'. These differences are highlighted in the text of the *Human Development Reports*. In the 1997 *Report* for example, countries whose HDI rank greatly exceeded their GDP rank were praised for 'effectively translat[ing] the benefits of economic growth into improvements in the lives of the people'; and the countries whose GDP rank greatly exceeded their HDI rank were held by the UNDP authors to have 'considerable scope for distributing the benefits of economic growth more equitably'.[16]

15 United Nations Development Program (1997). *Human Development Report:* 14.

16 *Ibid:* 46.

The authors of the *Human Development Report* are less than candid in arguing for the usefulness and validity of the HDI. In the 1997 *Report*, for example, the Index was presented as an initiative which has found increasing favour among those concerned with the measurement of human wellbeing:

> Although greeted with controversy when first launched in 1990, the HDI has found an increasing following as a simple measure of human development. The HDI provides an alternative to GNP, for assessing a country's standing in basic human development or its progress in human development over time.[17]

Somewhat disingenuously, there was no mention of the judgement on the HDI made by Partha Dasgupta in *An Inquiry into Well-Being and Destitution:*

> ...the index is not much good: it has too many unappealing properties ... HDI is also excessively partial.[18]

Professor Dasgupta also expressed the view that the HDI did not have much normative significance, and that when its authors had attempted to give an account of what the normative significance of the index was, they had ended up 'merely describing HDI'. It is important to recognise that these critical assessments of the HDI were concerned solely with the *technical* properties of the index: Dasgupta's verdict that the index was 'not much good' would still have been made even if all of the underlying data entering into the composite measures were of the highest quality. But in practice the HDI is far worse than it is in theory, because the quality of many of the data sources used in compiling the measure is quite poor.

The consequences of the use of data on the reliability of the HDI can readily be demonstrated by a comparison of the relative performance of Australia and New Zealand in the 'human development' stakes, as assessed by the UNDP. In the 1997 competition, New Zealand was ranked ninth on the HDI ladder and Australia was ranked 14th. This overall result was solely attributable to the education component of the HDI, because Australia's ranking was above New Zealand's on both of the other component indexes which went into the overall HDI. Australia ranked equal seventh on the life expectancy index, whereas New Zealand ranked only equal 21st; and Australia was ranked 18th on the real GDP per capita index, whereas New Zealand was 24th.

Australia's poor showing in the education component of the HDI, *vis-a-vis* New Zealand's, was in turn, solely attributable to this country's supposedly much lower 'combined first-, second- and third-level gross enrolment ratio'. According

17 *Ibid*: 19.

18 Dasgupta, Partha (1993). *Op cit*: 77-8.

to the *Human Development Report* which in turn attributed the data to UNESCO, Australia ranked equal 28th (with Poland and Fiji) on this measure, whereas New Zealand ranked fourth in the world in its overall education enrolment ratio. Among the countries which the UNDP ranked above Australia on the education enrolment criterion of human development were Belarus, Libya, Turkmenistan, Peru, South Africa and Namibia.

Fortunately, we have far better data on education enrolment ratios in Australia, New Zealand and other OECD countries than those published by the UNDP. They are compiled by the OECD's Centre for Educational Research and Innovation, and are regularly published in the OECD's *Education at a Glance*. The most recent issue of this publication[19] provided estimates of net enrolment rates in all levels of education for each single year of age between the ages of 15 and 24. These figures show that Australia's education enrolment ratios were higher, not lower, than New Zealand's.

In short, Australia's *true* HDI rank is well above New Zealand's on all three of the component indexes and, *a fortiori,* on the composite index. The UNDP'S finding to the contrary is solely a reflection of a statistical aberration in UNESCO data. Yet the UNDP results receive wide coverage in the Australian media, and our politicians and commentators debate the causes of this country's slide down the ladder of human development, including by comparison with New Zealand, as if it were a fact.

Naively, most Australians assume that comparisons which are made in a publication of an arm of the United Nations are reliable and authoritative. How can they be expected to know that Partha Dasgupta, Frank Ramsay Professor of Economics at Cambridge University, considers that the HDI measure is 'not much good'? Or that the comparisons are vitiated by better statistics produced by another international institution?

It must be presumed that, in many other countries, the political and public debate is influenced by naive assessments, made in New York by the Human Development Office of the UNDP, about whether the countries concerned have or have not been successful in translating the benefits of economic growth into improvements in the lives of their people.

Deficiencies in data quality, of the kind which have been illustrated by the Australia/New Zealand example, should be sufficient in themselves to discourage such sweeping and patronising judgements – and one does not have to be knowledgeable about the relevant data to be sure that many of these judgements are unsound.

19 OECD (1996). *Education at a Glance:* OECD Indicators, (4th ed, issued 9 December 1996): 122.

There was, for example, a table in the 1997 *Human Development Report* which showed seven pairs of countries which had, according to the heading, 'similar HDI, different income, 1994'.[20] The authors failed to reveal the fact that the 'different income' levels were calculated by converting GNP in national currencies to US dollars on the notoriously unsatisfactory basis of prevailing exchange rates. Yet they must have known that the only valid way to measure relative income levels is by correcting for differences in purchasing power, because this is the basis used for the GDP measure which the creators of the HDI used for its 'standard of living' component.

The first of the seven comparisons in the table is between New Zealand and Sweden. New Zealand's slightly higher HDI than Sweden's is set against the 'fact' that Sweden's GNP per capita was 91 per cent higher than New Zealand's in 1994. According to a table showing GDP per capita in purchasing power parity terms for the same year in the same report,[21] the excess of Sweden's real product per head over New Zealand's was only 13 per cent, not 91 per cent. As average life expectancy in Sweden was higher than in New Zealand, the latter country's higher HDI was entirely attributable to its higher education enrolment ratios in the UNESCO data. Data from the OECD'S Centre for Educational Research and Innovation again show that the figures which were used in the compilation of the HDI are wrong.

The next of the comparisons in the UNDP table shows Barbados as having a higher HDI than Singapore, notwithstanding that Singapore's GNP per capita was well over three times higher than that of Barbados in exchange rate terms and nearly twice as high in purchasing power parity terms. As Singapore's average life expectancy was also higher than its comparator, the supposedly lower level of human development in Singapore is entirely attributable to the education component of the index – and, in particular, to an adult literacy rate of only 91 per cent compared with 97 per cent in Barbados. It is relevant to note that Professor Dasgupta found 'that the adult literacy rate is a rogue index' which was poorly correlated with other 'quality of life' measures,[22] and it should be obvious in any case that observed differences in adult literacy ratios which exceed 90 per cent would reveal little about contemporary levels of human development.

Similar comments can be made about each of the other comparisons in the UNDP table. The similarity of the HDIs for South Africa and Sri Lanka would be remarkable if GNP per head was indeed nearly five times as great in the former country as in the latter, as the figures in the table wrongly indicate. But

---

20 UNDP (1997). *Op cit*: 46.

21 *Ibid*: 146.

22 Dasgupta, Partha (1993). *Op cit*: 116.

it is scarcely worthy of mention if the real margin of difference is only 31 per cent, as the purchasing power parity comparison would have shown it to be. Equally, it would indeed be a matter for remark that Gambia had the same HDI as Mozambique if the former country's GNP per head was really nearly four times as great as the latter. But since the purchasing power parity estimates show both countries as having about the same level of product per head this comparison is again a case of 'Similar HDI, *similar* income', rather than the reverse phenomenon which the table purports to list.

The UNDP lends itself quite unashamedly to the use of the HDI as a tool for political advocacy. When last year's *Human Development Report* was launched in Ottawa, the UNDP's news release stated that 'For the third year in a row, the report ... placed Canada at the top of its Human Development Index' and went on to point out that:

> The report singles out Canada as a leader in translating economic wealth into the well-being of its citizens, a point which the Hon. Pierre Pettigrew, Minister for International Cooperation, underlined in his comments at the launch. 'In the present context of fiscal restraint,' he said, `it requires a tremendous amount of political will, consensus and co-operation, at all levels, to continue channelling economic growth into human development through investments in education, health and other public goods, and to ensure that the benefits of growth are equitably shared – both here at home and in developing countries.'[23]

The news release for the 1996 launch also stated that the United States ranked second in the HDI, and Japan third. As these two countries also rank among the world's leaders in GDP per head, the results do not sit well with the claim that the HDI provides an alternative to GNP for assessing a country's standing in basic human development. It could be argued, moreover, that an alternative measure to the GDP per head *should* put the United States and Japan well down the 'league table', because these two countries are frequently believed, including by many of their own citizens, to have failed to translate their economic wealth into a high, and well-distributed, 'quality of life'.

'Quality of life' is a subjective concept. The available indicators of subjective wellbeing are drawn together in the 'World Database of Happiness', which is maintained by the Department of Social Sciences at Erasmus University, Rotterdam in the form of 'a register of scientific research on subjective appreciation of life'. This database provides a comparison of the 'average appreciation of life' in 48 countries in the early 1990s.[24] The seven countries in

23 UNDP (1997). Press Release 'Human Development Report 1996: Moving from "Inequitable to Inhuman"'.

24 Cited in Wearing, Alexander J and Headey, Bruce (1997). 'Measures and Correlates of Subjective Well Being'. Paper given at the conference 'Measuring National Progress: Is life in Australia getting better, or worse?' Canberra, 3-5 July 1997.

which the average appreciation of life was highest, according to this measure, were the three Benelux countries, three of the Scandinavian countries (Sweden, Denmark and Iceland) and Ireland. Next, with an equal ranking, were Australia and Switzerland.

As we have seen, the three medal winners in the 1996 HDI Olympics were Canada (gold), the United States (silver) and Japan (bronze). The 'average appreciation of life' in all of these countries was below that in the nine countries which have just been named. Canada, ranked first in 'human development', was 20th out of 48 in 'average appreciation of life'; the United States, ranked second in 'human development', was tenth in 'average appreciation of life'; and Japan, ranked third in 'human development' in 1996 (and first in the early 1990s) was 25th out of 48 in 'appreciation of life'.

It is also of interest to note that New Zealand, which was ranked five places *above* Australia in the HDI list, was seven places *below* Australia in the 'appreciation of life' list.

An obvious question which arises from the fact that the HDI is not highly correlated with the subjective measure of 'appreciation of life', is whether there is a higher correlation between 'appreciation of life' and GDP per head, or between 'appreciation of life' and some other objective indicators. For the purposes of this paper, I have attempted to test these relationships for the countries which are included both in the World Bank list of nearly 150 countries (most of which are developing countries) and the 'World Database of Happiness' list of 48 countries (most of which are developed countries). For the 43 countries which figure in both lists, crude measures of correlation were calculated as the average *difference* between the average 'appreciation of life' rank and the rank on each of the comparator objective indicators, ignoring sign.

According to this test, the objective indicator of wellbeing which correlates best with the subjective measure of wellbeing is GDP per head (an average difference of 7.8 places). This is followed by HDI (an average difference of 8.2 places), life expectancy (an average difference of 8.9 places) and infant mortality (an average difference of 9.6 places). It would be unwise to draw strong inferences from these findings, but it is interesting that an indicator which was never intended to be a measure even of *economic* welfare should appear to be better correlated with the subjective wellbeing measure than several indicators which embrace non-economic aspects of wellbeing, and also of a composite indicator which was designed to embrace economic and non-economic aspects.

The Genuine Progress Indicator (GPI)

The Genuine Progress Indicator (GPI) for the United States was developed in San Francisco by Redefining Progress, an organisation 'whose purpose is to stimulate broad debate over the nature of economic progress and the best means of attaining it'. It was presented in an article in the October 1995 issue of the *Atlantic Monthly,* entitled 'If the GDP is Up, Why is America Down?'[25] and a more detailed methodological paper.[26]

The same name has been adopted for indicators with a similar purpose which have subsequently been produced for other countries, including Australia. The Australian indicator, which has been developed by Dr Clive Hamilton, was published recently as a discussion paper by the Australia Institute.[27]

The present paper is concerned with the GPI for the United States. As Dr Hamilton has followed different procedures in developing a GPI for Australia, the discussion which follows does not necessarily apply to his more sophisticated indicator. It is clear that some of the most serious deficiencies in the American GPI have been avoided in the Australian model.

The creators of the United States GPI were extremely critical of the measures of output produced by the world's official statisticians. They held that growth in GDP, as measured by our 'antiquated' national accounting system, is 'an artifact of history', 'a relic of another era' and 'a barricade of abstraction that separates us from economic reality'; and they accused the statisticians of 'rigging the books':

> Honest national accounting would inject a large dose of accountability to the political process. It would stop politicians and interest groups from hiding bad policy behind what amounts to a rigged set of books.[28]

The *Atlantic Monthly* article also included some strong criticism of the economics profession:

> ... no field has grown more tightly shut than economics, whose basic orthodoxies have persisted for at least a hundred years ... the generation that developed the GDP, and for which the GDP distilled an entire world view, is now mainly retired. The students and disciples of that generation are well into their middle years, rumbling along on mental capital from long ago.

---

25 Cobb, Clifford *et al* (1995). 'If the GDP is Up,Why is America Down?', the *Atlantic Monthly,* Boston, October.

26 Cobb, Clifford *et al* (1995). *The Genuine Progress Indicator: Summary of Data and Methodology,* San Francisco.

27 Hamilton, Clive (1997). *The Genuine Progress Indicator: A new index of changes in well-being in Australia,* Australia Institute, Discussion paper, no. 14, October 1997.

28 Cobb, Clifford *et al.* (1995). *Op cit*: 45.

The uncritical acceptance of the validity of these comments is a telling indicator of the esteem in which the economists and statisticians are held. In an article in *The Australian Financial Review* in June 1996, Lindsay Tanner, the Federal Shadow Minister for Transport, asserted as a 'basic point' that 'our political and economic analysis is shackled to a system of measurement from the world of Chubby Checker and the FJ Holden'.[29] And following a presentation by Ted Halstead, the founder and president of Reinventing Progress, at a conference in Canberra last July,[30] the *Canberra Times* asserted in an editorial that Mr Halstead had 'persuasively debunked the notion that GDP is a *useful* measure of a nation's real economic wealth or well-being', and that this measure 'says *nothing* about the quality of life enjoyed by citizens' (emphases added).[31]

It is a moot point whether the GPI is useful in measuring wellbeing, or says something about the quality of life. Its creators have a rare faith in numbers. For example, they hold that television viewing contributes to family breakdown, turning children 'into ardent, GDP-enhancing consumers'. As 'Even those unwed teenage mothers are bringing new little consumers into the world', a negative adjustment was made to the GPI to allow for the genuine regress which was assumed to result from television watching by children. The adjustment was calculated as follows:

> ... we estimated the time involved in these families as hours per day per household) times (365 days per year) times (number of households in the US) times (the proportion of households with children) times ($0.30).[32]

Another negative adjustment was made for 'divorce', which was calculated by multiplying the number of divorces in the United States by $5000 and the number of children affected by $7500, as 'a rough estimate of lifetime damage including such things as counselling, health costs and difficulties at school, work and in personal relationships'.

These are precisely the kinds of adjustments which the economist Arthur Okun, in a 1971 paper, strongly urged national accountants to 'resist at all costs':

> It is hard to understand how anyone could seriously believe that GNP could be converted into a meaningful indicator of total social welfare. Obviously, any number of things could make the nation better off without raising its real GNP as measured today: we might start the list with peace, equality of opportunity, the elimination of injustice and violence, greater brotherhood among Americans of different racial and

29 Tanner, Lindsay (1996). 'Time for an indicator of real progress' in *Australian Financial Review*, 4 June 1996.

30 Halstead, Ted (1997). The Science and Politics of New Measures of Progress: A United States Perspective', presented at Conference on 'Measuring National Progress', Canberra, 3 July.

31 *The Canberra Times, (*1997). 'Food for thought on the economy', 7 July.

32 *Ibid:* 21.

> ethnic backgrounds, better understanding between parents and children and between husbands and wives, and we could go on endlessly. To suggest that GNP could become *the* indicator of social welfare is to imply that an appropriate price tag could be put on changes in all of these social factors from one year to the next. This is ... asking the national income statistician to play the role of a philosopher-king, quantifying and evaluating all changes in the human scene (emphasis in original).[33]

A detailed commentary on the criticisms of the GDP by the creators of the GPI, and a detailed evaluation of the GPI itself, would require a lengthy paper in itself. All that will be attempted here is a comparison of how the two concepts handle one key issue: the measurement of the interaction of the government and non-government sectors. This was, of course, the central aspect of the working of a mixed economy which the system of national accounts was devised to illuminate.

The conventional national accounts include in GDP the expenditure of government. The reason for this was explained in JR Hicks' seminal paper entitled 'The Valuation of the Social Income':

> ... if we accept the actual choices of the individual consumer as reflecting his preferences (clearly we must do so for these purposes), then I do not see that we have any choice but to accept the actual choices of the government, even if they are expressed through a Nero or a Robespierre, as representing the actual wants of society.[34]

By contrast, 'the GPI does *not* include most government expenditures'. The creators of the GPI explain that

> The main reason is that [government expenditures] are largely defensive in nature; they protect against erosions in the quality of life, rather than enhancing that quality of life. (This is literally the case regarding the largest government service outlay, defence.)[35]

The counter argument to this view of the San Francisco think-tank in 1995 was mounted by Nassau Senior, first professor of political economy at Oxford University, in his lectures at Oxford in 1828:

> Those writers who have maintained that whatever is raised by taxation is deducted from the revenue of the country, seem to have been led to this conclusion by observing that the object of government is to occasion not positive but negative effects, not to produce good, but to

33 Okun, Arthur M (1971). 'Social Welfare Has No Price Tag' in United States, Department of Commerce, *Survey of Current Business*, 50th Anniversary Issue, July 1971: 129-30.

34 Hicks, JR (1940). 'The Valuation of the Social Income' in *Economica*, May 1940.

35 Cobb, Clifford, *et al* (1995). *Op cit*: 16.

> prevent evil...But it must be recollected that the mere prevention of evil is one of the principal objects even of individual expenditure. We do not build houses because it is pleasant to breathe the confined atmosphere of a room, but because roofs and walls are the only means by which the inclemency of the seasons can be avoided. We do not buy drugs for our pleasure, but to avert or remove disease. Yet no one ever thought what he spends on medicines and on house rent a deduction from his income. ...
>
> And it may be asked, in what respect does each man's contribution towards the means by which the community is to be protected against internal and external violence and fraud differ from his contribution to a Friendly Society ... ? It is true that, if the protection could be less expensively obtained, the fund for the maintenance of labour would be increased. But this is merely an exemplification of [the principle] that the extent of the fund for the maintenance of labour depends mainly on the productiveness of labour. If fewer fleets, and armies and magistrates could preserve the peace, ... the labouring classes would, *ceteris paribus,* be better off, just as they would be better off if fewer husbandmen or artisans could produce ... the same quantity of corn; that is, if labour were more productive in supplying food.[36]

Commenting on the argument that 'regrettable necessaries' should be excluded from GDP, Edward Denison was to make a similar point in 1971:

> It yields the false result that we are equally well off whether, in the same circumstances, we ride or must walk to work, freeze or are comfortable, do or do not obtain medical care when we are sick, or provide or do not provide for national security. Needs and provision to meet them must be separately evaluated.[37]

Not all of the propositions mounted by Senior in 1828 and Denison in 1971 are beyond argument. Some of them have, indeed, continued to be argued within the profession whose basic orthodoxies are supposed by the creators of the GPI to have persisted for at least 100 years. In this case, the orthodoxy has persisted for closer to 200 years, but that does not mean it is immutable.

In the meantime, those who support the exclusion of the expenditure of government from the measure of progress should know the implications of this exclusion.

---

36 Senior, MW (1858). *Political Economy,* London: 183.

37 Denison, Edward (1971). In *Survey of Current Business,* January 1971: 15. Cited in Okun, Arthur M (1971), *op cit*: 132.

One implication, of course, is that 'genuine progress' according to the GPI will occur whenever the provision of services by government is replaced by private provision. For example, if the entire system of publicly provided schools in the United States were to be privatised, and parents were obliged to pay for their children to be educated in the same way as they are now obliged to pay for them to be fed, the GPI would record a huge leap in 'genuine progress' because of the resulting rise in private consumption. The GDP would not be significantly affected, because in this case the increase in expenditure on private consumption would be substantially offset by a corresponding decrease in government consumption expenditure.

Some technical consequences of the GPI treatment of government expenditure should be noted. At present, most children in the United States attend schools operated by government authorities. This means that expenditure on the salaries of most of the nation's school-teachers is entered into the GPI calculation at zero. The number of hours worked by some of these teachers is *greater* than the number that they are presumed to wish to work, in which case the GPI requires a deduction from the zero figure. Other teachers work *fewer* hours than they would prefer, and in this case the GPI again registers a negative figure, even though there is no positive figure from which to make the deduction. Again, most teachers at public schools incur expenditures in travelling to work, and the time that they spend on commuting is not available for them to spend on other activities: under the GPI methodology these commuting costs are also deducted from incomes which have not been counted in the first place.

Yet the creators of the GPI maintain that it is the GDP which is 'a barricade of abstraction that separates us from economic reality'.

Another consequence of the GPI treatment of government activity needs to be noted. The GPI rises if a government introduces or raises substantially the charges for entry into museums or national parks, because the GPI assumes that only private spending can achieve 'genuine progress': government spending on (say) national parks is, in the view of the GPI's creators, only preventing regress. Yet it should be obvious that output is the same, whether the government's expenditure on national parks is financed by charges on users or by taxation.

Again it is difficult to contest the proposition that it is the GDP which records the 'economic reality', and that it is the GPI which fails to provide 'an honest set of books'.

One final point needs to be made. The proponents of the HDI and the GPI have criticised the concepts of the economists and the national accounts statisticians in strong terms, but they have shown little inclination to submit their alternative concepts to critical scholarly scrutiny, or to acknowledge and respond to the substantial criticisms which have been made. In this field, the economists and national accountants have maintained a tradition of open inquiry since Sir William Petty invited 'all ingenious and candid persons' to rectify the 'errors, defects and imperfections' in the argument of his *Political Arithmetick* in 1676.

The conferences of the International Association for Research in Income and Wealth (IARIW) and the Association's Journal *Review of Income and Wealth* provide fora in which the issues discussed in this paper are regularly and freely debated. A paper in the September 1996 issue of the *Review* by Markos Mamalakis of the University of Wisconsin deserves special mention. Its subject is indicated adequately by its title: 'Misuse and Use of National Accounts as a Welfare Indicator: Selected Analytical and Measurement Issues'. Mamalakis' abstract indicates that his

> ...evaluation of deductions and additions to the System of National Accounts (SNA) made by [a number of scholars] in their research on extended product and income accounts and improved indicators of welfare reveals numerous unresolved analytical and measurement issues; and *reaffirms the usefulness of the SNA as a fundamental, initial, welfare indicator* (emphasis added).[38]

For a statistician who was formerly responsible for Australia's national accounts, and who believed himself to be producing 'an honest set of books', this is a reassuring conclusion.

38 Mamalakis, Markos J (1996). 'Misuse and Use of National Accounts as a Welfare Indicator: Selected Analytical and Measurement Issues', *Review of Income and Wealth*, September 1996: 293.

12. Measuring Economic Progress: From Political Arithmetick to Social Accounts[1]

Ian Castles

I am delighted to give the Eighth Colin Clark Memorial Lecture. The Department of Economics, the Economic Society of Australia in Queensland and the Queensland Treasury are to be congratulated upon their initiative and their continuing support, and I give special thanks to the department for honouring me with the invitation to present the 1998 lecture, and for its welcome to me in recent days.

Previous speakers in the series have contributed much to the development of our knowledge of the work of one of the most influential scholars of the century, and our understanding of its significance. But there is much more still to be learned. As Jim Perkins and Alan Powell observed in their 'affectionate memoir' in 1990, 'it would take a small army of biographers, historians of economic thought and bibliographers to evaluate properly the man, economist, scholar and polemicist whose works span more than half a century'.[2]

The particular perspective on Clark's life work which I have chosen to explore in today's lecture is that of its connection with the art and science of 'political arithmetick': the term coined by William Petty in the late seventeenth century to denote the systematic assembly of numerical information for public policy purposes.

Colin Clark himself acknowledged his indebtedness to, and affinity with, the political arithmeticians in his preface to the first edition of *Conditions of Economic Progress*:

> ...economics was started on the right lines by Gregory King and Sir William Petty at the time of that astonishing flowering of the English scientific spirit in the later 17th century. ... We need to return to the spirit of those two brilliant pioneers from whom even now we have much to learn.[3]

1 First given as the Eighth Colin Clark memorial lecture of The University of Queensland in October 1998.

2 Perkins, JON and Powell, Alan A (1990). 'Colin Clark, 1905-1989: An Affectionate Memoir', *The Economic Record* December: 329-341.

3 Clark, Colin (1940). *Conditions of Economic Progress*, London, Macmillan.

We can only speculate on the origins of Clark's interest in these political arithmeticians. It may not be merely coincidental that he began his post-secondary career at Brasenose College, Oxford – the College at which Petty had been vice-principal nearly three centuries earlier. Clark was to note with relish that in his (Clark's) day, Brasenose 'had a great reputation for athletic prowess, philistinism and drinking'.[4]

It is also possible that Clark's interest in these 'brilliant pioneers' was fired by his brief association with AM (later Sir Alexander) Carr-Saunders, who as Professor of Social Science at Liverpool supervised Clark's work on the Social Survey of Merseyside in 1929. Clark was later to acknowledge that he had 'learnt a great deal from [Carr-Saunders'] highly original work on sociology and on demography',[5] and he may well have learned at this time of the seminal contributions of Petty and King to the development of demography as the central core of what was then 'political arithmetick' and what might now be termed 'social science'.

Petty was a polymath. He became professor of anatomy at Oxford at the age of 28, and in the following year 'went to Ireland as physician-general to the army, which was no sinecure in a country ravaged by the plague and other lethal epidemic diseases'. He was a 'persistent inventor', pursuing his design for a twin-hulled ship through four prototypes. One of the founders of the Royal Society, 'he read a number of communications to the Society on topics varying from dyeing practices in the clothing trade to the testing of mineral waters and (achieved) a formidable and serious literary output on economic, demographic, naval, medical and scientific subjects'. As political arithmetician, Petty's achievement is summarised by Phyllis Deane, in the *International Encyclopedia of the Social Sciences* in the following terms:

> Petty's claim to fame as an economist lies not so much in his originality or his theoretical ability as in his analytical skill. His insistence on measurement and his clear schematic view of the economy make him the first econometrician, and he was constantly evolving and using concepts and analytical methods that were in advance of his time. His evaluation of the gain from foreign trade in 'Another Essay in Political Arithmetick Concerning the Growth of the City of London' ... is based on a statement of the benefits of the division of labor and specialization and was written a century before Adam Smith's famous account. ... He was the author of the first known national income estimates ... some of the calculations in his *Treatise of Taxes and Contributions* and elsewhere are essentially exercises in what is now called 'cost-benefit analysis'. He was the first writer, so far as we know, to grasp the concept of the velocity of money...[6]

4 Clark, Colin (1977). 'The "Golden" Age of the Great Economists', *Encounter*, 48: 84.

5 *Ibid*: 85.

6 Deane, Phyllis (1969). 'Petty, William' In *International Encyclopedia of the Social Sciences*, vol 12: 66-68.

Gregory King is less well known. At the time that Colin Clark described him as a 'brilliant pioneer', and for at least another quarter-century, he did not rate an entry in the *Encyclopedia Brittanica*.

Like the higher-profile Petty, King was a polymath. He 'was a well-informed topographer and surveyor', and was the designer of the district of Soho in London, 'whose streets and squares were all projected by him, and most of the first articles for building thereof'. He supported himself for many years as a mapmaker and engraver, including by the preparation of maps of London and Westminster at a scale of 100 feet to the inch. He is also recorded as being 'a skilled and well-known genealogist', 'a successful practising accountant' and a teacher of bookkeeping. He learned to play the violin, and 'was convivial to the point of organising an annual meeting of persons bearing the surname "King"'.[7] But his lasting fame is as a political arithmetician, and Phyllis Dean's assessment is again worth quoting:

> King was a scholar rather than a politician. Perhaps this was why he never published his estimates, being content to make them freely available as a basis for economic policy making or analysis ... He was primarily interested in finding the exact truth about the dimensions of the national economy, so far as the available data would let him. It is evident from the notes and communications which have survived that he was completely honest about the limitations of his material and amazingly methodical in his use of it. And the more modern scholars have probed his methods and uncovered new sources of his notes, the more they have tended to admire his results. His famous 'Scheme of the Income and Expenses of the Several Families of England', given in his *Natural and Political Observations and Conclusions Upon the State and Condition of England (1696)*, and his international comparisons of national income and expenditure for England, France, and Holland in his *Of the Naval Trade of England A° 1688 and the National Profit Then Arising Thereby (1697)* were based essentially on guesswork, but as explicit statements of the views of a particularly well informed observer they are profoundly revealing. They ... became benchmark data of immense value to students of long-term growth.
>
> All King's estimates were made with an accountant's meticulous concern for internal consistency, and in this respect his national income estimates were in advance of any calculations made in this field until the mid-twentieth century. It is possible to extract from [his] national income and balance of payments estimates ... a complete, articulated set

7 Glass, DV (1965). 'Two Papers on Gregory King' in Glass, DV and Eversley, DEC *Population in History: Essays in Historical Demography*, London, Edward Arnold (Publishers).

> of double-entry social accounts as well as an abundance of detail on the content of national income, output, and expenditure in 1688 and 1695. He also made estimates of the national capital, its content and its rate of increase through the seventeenth century. His population estimates were based on careful analyses of actual enumerations for particular places, corrected for technical errors and adjusted to a national basis, on assumptions that modern demographers (basing their judgements on the results of nineteenth-century census enumerations) have found to be both consistent and plausible. His schedule of the relation between changes in the price of wheat and deviations from the normal wheat harvest ... represents a piece of demand analysis of a kind that we find in no other source until the early twentieth century.[8]

In 1966, a full quarter of a century after Colin Clark's invocation of Gregory King's name in the preface to his own great pioneering work, the English historical demographer Peter Laslett wrote of King in the following terms:

> However much the contemporary student of historical social structure sees himself as an explorer of unknown territory, he feels that King has been there before him, in the 1690s ... (I)t has only now begun to be realised what a remarkable feat it was for him to have drawn up the one and only attempt at a complete social description ever made anywhere in pre-industrial Europe, and to have done so 150 years before the Registrar-General began to collect the mass of complicated evidence which we now think is necessary for the purpose.[9]

It is not surprising that Colin Clark was attracted to the *subject matter* of the works of Petty and King: in essence, they were seeking to answer the same demographic, sociological and economic questions which Clark had been addressing for more than a decade, and was to continue to address for more than 50 years.

But Clark's plea to his contemporaries, in the preface to his great work, did not relate to the subject matter studied by the political arithmeticians: his reference was to the *'scientific spirit in the later 17th century'* (emphasis added), and it was from this 'spirit' of Petty and King that he believed 'even now we have much to learn'.

Clark saw himself as possessing this 'scientific spirit' – as being, in fact a 'scientist'. Explaining to Chris Higgins why he had never stood for Parliament in Australia, after standing three times as a Labour candidate in Britain, Clark said

8 Deane, Phyllis (1969). 'King, Gregory' in *International Encyclopedia of the Social Sciences*, vol 8: 385-86.

9 Laslett, Peter (1973). 'Introduction' to the *Earliest Classics*, Gregg.

> ...it had become clear to me I had not got the right personality for politics. It's a different world, really. I am, or tried to be, a scientist, whereas politicians have to deal with action. It is a fundamental distinction.[10]

And Colin Clark drew another fundamental distinction between 'economic scientists' and 'economic theorists'. Here is the argument, as developed in the 1940 preface which has already been cited:

> The hard *scientific* discipline has yet to be learned, that all theories must constantly be tested and retested against observed facts, and those which prove wrong ruthlessly rejected. Theory has a valuable, indeed an essential, part to play in the development of economic *science*. But it must be theory which respects facts, not tries to supersede them. ...there is room for two or three economic theorists in each generation, not more ... The rest of us should be economic *scientists*, content steadily to lay stone upon stone in building the structure of ordered knowledge.[11]

One of the fascinating pieces of information uncovered by George Kenwood and Alan Lougheed in their 'official history' of *Economics at the University of Queensland* is that a Department of History and Economic *Science* was projected as part of the Faculty of Arts at this University in 1911.[12] There was in fact, nothing unusual about this terminology in the first half of the century.

In his great work *Wealth and Welfare*, published in 1912 and soon prescribed at the University of Queensland, AC Pigou said that:

> The methodological principle at the basis of economic *science*, and which distinguishes it from the other social *sciences*, is the reference which it makes to a measure, mainly money.[13]

The probable reason for the contraction of 'economic science' to 'economics' is also given in *Wealth and Welfare* Pigou explained that the

> purpose of economic investigation ... is not primarily scientific, if by science we intend the single-eyed search for knowledge for its own sake. It is rather practical and utilitarian, concerned chiefly to lay bare such parts of knowledge as may serve, directly or indirectly, to help forward the betterment of social life. Hence, the failure of economic welfare to act as a barometer of total welfare is of slight importance. For what we wish to learn is, not how large welfare is, or has been, but how its magnitude would be affected by the introduction of causes, which it is in the power of statements or private persons to call into being.[14]

---

10 Higgins, Christopher I (1989). 'An Interview: Colin Clark', *The Economic Record*, December: 297.

11 Clark, Colin (1940). *Op cit*: xy.

12 Kenwood, AG and Lougheed, AL (1997). *Economics at the University of Queensland 1912-1997*: 1.

13 Pigou, AC (1912). *Wealth and Welfare*: 8.

14 *Ibid*: 4.

In March 1930, at the age of 24, Colin Clark was suddenly placed in a position of potential influence over 'statesmen' with the power to introduce 'causes' which would enhance the welfare of the people of Great Britain. To his complete surprise, Clark was appointed to the staff of the newly formed Economic Advisory Council. For Clark, it was a deeply disillusioning experience. As he was to recall nearly 40 years later, the Council was 'a weird and wonderful organisation indeed'. It was chaired by the Prime Minister, Ramsay MacDonald, and included the Chancellor of the Exchequer, Philip Snowden, and three other Ministers. Among the 15 other members were three economists (GDH Cole, JM Keynes and Sir Josiah Stamp); a physicist and a geneticist who 'knew nothing whatever about economics' but contributed 'lengthy memoranda to the Council's proceedings'; some prominent bankers and businessmen 'who talked far too much, mostly about their own troubles'; Ernest Begin, leader of the Transport and General Workers' Union; and the economic historian RH Tawney.[15]

Before long, Clark was to recall, 'we were engaged in interminable committees about the need for "training more biologists", and for international measures of locust control'. Meanwhile – and this information comes not from Clark but from the history of the Council published in 1977 – the Treasury refused to buy an adding machine for Colin Clark.[16]

Meanwhile, the economic situation was rapidly worsening and it was becoming increasingly apparent that 'the Economic Advisory Council, as then constituted, was not the appropriate body to advise on what was, after all, an economic problem'. And so a committee of [five] economists, chaired by Keynes, was appointed to review 'the whole problem of the Great Depression'.

Importantly for our story, Colin Clark was 'permitted to attend most ... of the meetings' of this Committee and 'to circulate ... some calculations I had made, comparing the industrial production index with the employment figures for manufacturing industries ... indicating that product per man-year had been showing a moderate rate of improvement during the 1920s; thus, amongst other things, justifying some rise in real wages'.[17]

As Clark told Chris Higgins in 1988, his idea would now be seen as an elementary one, but 'in those days it was novel...'.[18] Keynes was impressed, and encouraged Clark to develop the work. Keynes also recommended him for the lectureship in statistics at Cambridge which Clark took up in 1931 and retained until he came to Australia in 1937.

Even more importantly, Keynes gave strong support to the publication of Clark's first book *The National Income 1924-1931*. Recommending the manuscript to

15 Clark, Colin (1977). *Op cit*: 85.

16 Howson, Susan and Winch, Donald (1977). T*he Economic Advisory Council 1930-1939*: 25.

17 Clark, Colin (1977). *Op cit*: 87-88.

18 Higgins Christoher I (1989). *Op cit*: 298.

Daniel Macmillan, Keynes said 'that Clark's work, on this and allied subjects, is quite outstanding and that he is likely to become the recognised authority, in the course of time. ...Clark is, I think, a bit of a genius – almost the only economic statistician I have ever met who seems to me quite first class.'[19]

Keynes was equally enthusiastic after reading the finished book. In a letter to Clark on 2 January, 1933, he wrote:

> I have just finished reading your book carefully ... I think that it is *excellent*. An enormous step forward. ...You have quite convinced me that *gross* output, gross investment, gross savings, etc. is the natural way to work and not with the net, and I have been re-writing my definitions and equations on those lines. I am sure it is an improvement.

Keynes proceeded to explore what he described as 'an interesting possibility' relating to the size of the multiplier and the normal growth rate, which had been suggested to him by the tables in the last chapter of Clark's book. And Clark responded with further calculations and the observation 'this really is rather fascinating. It certainly beats Physics'.

We can guess that Clark and Keynes had at some time talked about Clark's scientific background: his degree at Oxford had been in chemistry, and the subject of his thesis had been the radio-chemistry of uranium and thorium.

Some years later, Keynes was to pen his famous lines about Stanley Jevons as

> ...the first theoretical economist to survey his material with the prying eyes and fertile, controlled imagination of the natural scientist. ... It is remarkable, looking back, how few followers and imitators he had in the black arts of inductive economics in the fifty years after 1862. But today [that is, 1936] he can certainly claim an unnumbered progeny, though the scientific flair which can safely read the shifting sands of economic statistics is no commoner than it was.[20]

Clark liked Keynes' phrase about the 'prying eyes and fertile, controlled imagination of the natural scientist', and knew that it applied to some degree also to himself. But it is doubtful whether he realised the closeness of the parallels between himself and Jevons.

First, they had both begun their post-secondary education with the study of chemistry.

19 Keynes, JM (1971-89). *The Collected Writings of John Maynard Keynes*, (30 vols.) All of the cited quotations in correspondence with or about Colin Clark are from *The Collected Writings*.

20 Keynes, JM (1951). 'William Stanley Jevons' in *Essays in Biography*. 2nd ed: 268.

Secondly, they had both, at the age of 23, been engaged in social surveys of cities – Jevons in Sydney in his remarkable solo effort which survives in manuscript in the Public Library of New South Wales – but regrettably remains unpublished, Clark as a member of the staff of the New Social Survey of London which attempted to reproduce Charles Booth's survey in the 1890s – a survey which Professor Graeme Davison of Monash has shown may well have been modelled in important respects on Jevons' study.[21]

Thirdly, Jevons and Booth were both born in Liverpool, where Clark was to work with Carr-Saunders on another social survey.

Fourthly, both Jevons and Clark turned heavily towards quantification – towards political arithmetic – and both produced, at the age of 26, path-breaking studies, which earned Keynes' admiration. Both of them were writing alone without support. We have already seen what Keynes said about Clark's pioneering study on the national income: here is what he had to say about Jevons' study, *A Fall in the Price of Gold Ascertained and its Social Effects Considered*.

> For unceasing fertility and originality of mind applied with a sure touch and unfailing control of the material, to a mass of statistics, involving immense labours for an unaided individual ploughing his way through with no precedents and labour-saving devices to relieve his task, this pamphlet stands unrivalled in the history of our subject.[22]

There are still other parallels. Both Jevons and Clark worked as public servants in Australia, both of them acknowledged freely that their official duties were not heavy, and both of them used the resulting free time to pursue innovative scientific work with enormous energy and skill.

Finally, and importantly for our theme, both were deeply interested in the work of their predecessors, including the political arithmeticians of the seventeenth century. In his T*heory of Political Economy,* praised by Keynes as 'the first modern book on economics', Jevons reported that, although the celebrated law of demand

> is 'commonly attributed' to King, he was unable to find it in the full reproduction of King's *Observations* contained in *George Chalmer's Estimate of the Comparative Strength of Great Britain (1802)*. The fact that Davenant elsewhere made full acknowledgement to King also led Jevons to suggest that the law is 'perhaps' due to Davenant.[23]

21 Davison, Graeme (1996) 'The unsociable sociologist – WS Jevons and his Survey of Sydney, 1858'. Conference on `Natural Sciences and Social Sciences', Humanities Research Centre, Australian National University, 9 September.

22 Keynes, JM (1951). *Op cit*: 271.

23 Creedy, J (1986). 'On the King–Davenant "Law" of Demand', *Scottish Journal of Political Economy*: 194-95.

Jevons went on to observe that he knew

> nothing more strange and discreditable to statists and economists than that in so important a point as the relations of price and supply of the main article of food, we owe our most accurate estimates to writers who lived from one to two centuries ago.[24]

Let us now return to 1933, when Clark wrote with excitement to Keynes that the work on which they were jointly engaged 'certainly beats physics'. Soon after this, Clark contributed an important essay to a collection of studies of the economic problem which was planned and edited by GDH Cole. The following extracts convey the flavour of Clark's thinking at this time:

> [In his last] two budgets Mr Neville Chamberlain has resignedly faced, as if it were something to do with the weather, conditions of declining income and production...
>
> What neither of our British Chancellors – iron or wooden – seemed to have realised is the effect which government policy can have on the size of the national income, as well as the effect which a decline in the national income, fatalistically accepted, must perforce have upon government policy...
>
> ...If somebody would invent a new system of mathematics whereby every country should import less and export more, he would be doing the world a great service; but under our present rules of arithmetic it is impossible. The balances of trade of all the countries in the world, some being positive and some being negative, must of necessity add up to zero...
>
> ...The biggest scope for public investment lies in the restoration of the activity of municipal housing and the rapid proceeding with slum clearance schemes, road programs, rural water supply and sewage, small holdings and afforestation, and a great deal of new school building and replacement...
>
> Everyone of them represents work which would permanently enrich the country, and the fact that we prefer to leave labour and resources idle rather than to undertake such work, because as we say there is not enough money in the country, merely proves that we are all mad.
>
> A really big program of public works would lead to a big consequential demand for productive materials such as cement, steel and bricks. The

24 Creedy, J (1986) *op cit*: 193.

> effect of increasing the purchasing power of the workers would also be to improve the demand for a great many other commodities of staple consumption...
>
> ...(T)he main planks in a program of monetary recovery ... must be a big policy of public investment, some plan of recovery for private investment, and the expansion of the purchasing power of those who need it most, by social services and by a forward wage policy which keeps pace with technical progress.[25]

Keynes' appreciation of Colin Clark's capacities was again evident in an exchange of letters between them in 1938.[26] Clark wrote to Keynes from New Zealand on 1 February, saying that his 'address till August will be University of Western Australia' and concluding:

> I am reaching the conclusion I want to stay in Australia. People have minds which are not closed to new truths, as the minds of so many Englishmen are: And with all the mistakes Australia has made in the past, I still think she may show the world, in economics, politics, education and technology, in the next twenty years.

In his reply, Keynes said that he was 'rather dismayed' with this paragraph, 'though not taken entirely by surprise'. He urged Clark to return to Cambridge first, noting the necessity of laying 'the foundations for a proper department of *statistical realistic economics*' at that University and strongly implying that Clark should be its head.

The rest, as they say is history. Clark rejected the offer of a professorship in Adelaide but accepted an offer from the Queensland government. He was a public servant in this State for 14 years, before returning to academia for the remainder of a long and productive career for which he should have received the Nobel Prize in Economics – as Heinz Arndt said in the obituary for the Academy of the Social Sciences in Australia.[27] And the department of 'statistical realistic economics' was in due course established at Cambridge as the Department of Applied Economics under Richard Stone, who had been Clark's student. Stone played the leading role in the development of the internationally agreed System of National Accounts and for this and other contributions to 'statistical realistic economics' he *did* receive the Nobel Prize. But Colin Clark's legacy to us of 'statistical realistic economics' is no less rich and varied, and his injunction to economists to embrace 'the scientific tradition of the seventeenth century pioneers' is as apt today as it was in 1940.

---

25 Clark, Colin (1933). 'Investment, Savings and Public Finance' in Cole, GDH (ed.) *What Everybody Wants to know about Money: A planned outline of monetary problems*. London. Gollancz.

26 Keynes, JM (1971-1989). *Op cit*.

27 Arndt, HW (1989). 'Colin Clark' in *Academy of the Social Sciences in Australia Annual Report 1988-89*: 50-52.

13. The Mismeasure of Nations: A Review Essay on the Human Development Report 1998[1]

Ian Castles

The annual *Human Development Report,* published for the United Nations Development Program (UNDP) by the Oxford University Press, is promoted by the UNDP as 'the only comprehensive guide to global human development available on the market' (UNDP 1998c). Since the series was launched in 1990, these reports have been extraordinarily influential. According to Amartya Sen, speaking at a memorial meeting for the originator of the series, Mahbub ul Haq, on 15 October 1998, the *Human Development Report* 'had a profound effect on the way policy makers, public servants and the news media as well as economists and other social scientists view social and economic advancement'. Professor Sen went on to describe the *Report* as 'one of the major sources of information and understanding of the social and economic world' (Sen 1998).

The release of each *Human Development Report* has become a significant global event. The 1998 report was launched on 9 September at The Hague City Hall and 'in more than 100 capitals worldwide'. In support of the report's theme of 'Consumption for human development', visitors to the launch and the associated events 'were able to purchase ecologically and socially sound products at a consumer's market; sit in on small workshops and discussion groups on consumption issues; and visit displays on development and the environment by dozens of non-government organizations' (UNDP 1998d).

In all, *Human Development Report 1998* was published in ten languages: English, French, German, Italian, Portuguese, Spanish, Catalan, Arabic, Japanese and Russian. The associated *Human Development 1998 Database* on diskettes facilitates the compilation of tailored reports on the 'demographic, social, economic and environmental issues of human development'. Prospective users are advised to 'simply select one or more of 353 social indicators, select from 174 countries and/or 28 regional aggregates and run with the report'.

With unconscious irony, the 1998 *Report* refers to the difficulties for local and national producers that arise from 'the opening of consumer markets with a constant flow of new products':

---

1 *Review of United Nations Development Program, Human Development Report 1998.* New York: Oxford University Press; This paper was first published in *Population and Development Review* 24 (4) (December 1998): Reprinted with the permission of the Population Council. Except where otherwise indicated, all figures and tables in this chapter are Castles' own.

> Market research identifies 'global elites' and 'global middle classes' who follow the same consumption styles, showing preferences for 'global brands'. There are the 'global teens' ... inhabiting a 'global space', a single pop-culture world, soaking up the same videos and music and providing a huge market for designer running shoes, t-shirts and jeans. (UNDP 1998a: 6)

This review will argue that the *Human Development Report* is itself the quintessential 'global brand' of the 1990s, and that its dominant position in the global market for information on the social and economic world owes little to its intrinsic qualities and much to the packaging and promotional efforts of its multinational sponsor.

Statistical misunderstandings and errors

For every reader of the *Human Development Report,* there are thousands who read newspaper items purporting to summarise its contents. As few journalists can be expected to read and comprehend a 240-page report, most of the articles are taken from news releases produced in the UNDP's Public Affairs Department.

The role of these news releases is well illustrated by the 'media advisory' for an invitation-only advance briefing on the *Human Development Report 1998,* which was hosted by the UNDP Administrator at a New York restaurant just one week before the global launch at The Hague. The release was headed 'Despite record-high global consumption, ranks of poor, hungry and homeless are growing in rich nations as well as poor'; and it claimed that 'homelessness and illiteracy in industrialized countries continue to rise, according to the *1998 Human Development Report ...*' (UNDP 1998b).

Perhaps no one noticed, but the *Report* did not say this. All of its claims about poverty and illiteracy in the industrial countries related to the situation at a point in time, not to trends over time. Reference was made to rising levels of malnutrition in Eastern Europe and the Commonwealth of Independent States, but few readers would have thought of these countries as 'rich nations'. The key observation about hunger was unexceptionable if platitudinous: it 'is not as pervasive' in the industrial countries as in the developing countries (UNDP 1998a: 27).

By way of contrast, the key observation about homelessness in the industrial countries was obviously wrong. In the 1997 volume it had been argued that 'the most extreme housing deprivation is to have no home, and worldwide, an estimated 100 million are homeless' (UNDP 1997a:29). In the 1998 *Report,* however, it was said that 'around 100 million are thought to be homeless' in the developing countries alone and that 'more than 100 million are homeless' in the industrial countries (UNDP 1998a: 2, 25, 27). Taken together with population data, these figures imply that the homeless represent only two per cent of the population of the developing countries, but eight per cent of the population of the industrial countries. Clearly one or both of these percentages must be wrong.

There are well-known methodological problems in measuring homelessness, and most studies agree that the number of 'homeless people' at a particular time is not a satisfactory indicator. Alternative approaches have yielded more carefully stated conclusions: for example, 'In New York nearly a quarter of a million people, more than 3 per cent of the city's population, have stayed in a shelter at some point in the past five years' (UNDP 1997a: 29). But the claim in *Human Development Report 1998* is that more than 100 million people in the industrial countries *are* homeless ('a shockingly high number amid the affluence'), not that this number of people have experienced homelessness (UNDP 1998a: 27).

In the same list of bullet points, under the heading 'Measuring human poverty in industrial countries', the 1998 *Report* asserts that 'Unemployment among youth (age 15-24) has reached staggering heights, with 32 per cent of young women and 22 per cent of young men in France unemployed, 39 and 30 per cent in Italy and 49 and 36 per cent in Spain' (UNDPa: 27). All of these figures are wrong, the correct percentages being far lower than those cited. For 1995 – the reference year in the table from which the figures are drawn – nine per cent of young women and seven per cent of young men in France were unemployed. In Italy the figures were 14 per cent and 12 per cent, and in Spain 18 per cent and 16 per cent.

The errors relating to youth unemployment in this year's *Report* can be attributed to inadequate documentation in the 'Human Development Indicators' section of the *Report* itself. In 1998, for the sixth successive year, this section included statistics of the 'youth unemployment rate' in industrial countries (UNDP 1998a: 192); but, as in earlier *Reports* the compilers failed to mention that the rates relate unemployment to the labor force in the relevant age/sex group, not to the population in that group. As a result, it is likely that many readers of the *Reports*, and many of the users of the *Human Development 1998 Database*, will have made the same mistake as this year's authors. The ILO, the OECD and many national statistical offices are striving to remove common misunderstandings about the scale and nature of youth unemployment in the industrial countries that the UNDP is helping to create.

Additional sources of confusion have been introduced in the 1998 *Report* with the unveiling of 'the new human poverty index (HPI-2)'. According to the authors, this index 'shows conclusively that under-consumption and human deprivation are not just the lot of poor people in the developing world' (UNDP 1998a: 2).

One element of HPI-2 is a measure identified as 'People not expected to survive to age 60 (% of total population) 1995' (UNDP 1998a: 28, 186). This indicator does not represent the percentage of those living in 1995 who could not expect to live until the age of 60, but the percentage of a hypothetical population *born in 1995* who would not survive to age 60 if that population were subject at each age to the mortality rates of 1995.

Again the authors of the *Report* appear to have misinterpreted their selected indicator. They say that 'Nearly 200 million people [in the industrial countries] are not expected to survive to age 60' (UNDP 1998a: 27), this being the product of the population of the industrial countries (about 1200 million) and the proportion of persons not surviving from age zero to age 60 at 1995 mortality rates (16 per cent). The proportion of persons not surviving from their present age will, of course, be much lower. And the number of people in the industrial countries who are not expected to survive from their present age to age 60 is about 100 million, not 200 million.

In any case, the key point is that mortality rates are decreasing at all ages. During the twentieth century, expected survival rates from birth to age 60 in such countries as Britain and France have increased from about 45 per cent to about 90 per cent (Keyfitz and Flieger 1968: 324, 525; UNDP 1998a: 28, 186). In these countries, the chance of survival from age zero to age 60 is now greater than was the chance of survival from age zero to age one in 1900. Of course, there are still 'millions' who will not survive to age 60, but it is somewhat perverse to present this as a manifestation of 'human deprivation'.

The Human Development Index: Crude measure or policy guide?

The First Human Development Report (1990) introduced a new measure of human development. Indicators of life expectancy, educational attainment, and income were combined into a composite 'human development index' (HDI). In his speech at the memorial meeting for Mahbub ul Haq in October, Amartya Sen recalled his initial doubts about trying 'to catch in one simple number a complex reality about human development and deprivation'. But Sen explained that he came to accept Haq's view that the HDI was valuable 'as an instrument of public communication'. This 'deliberately constructed crude measure' was a means of 'getting the ear of the world through the high publicity associated with [its] transparent simplicity ...' (Sen 1998).

But the proponents of HDI saw other benefits in the 'transparent simplicity' of the index. It was argued in the first *Report* that 'Too many indicators could produce a perplexing picture – perhaps distracting policy makers from the main overall trends'; and that 'Having too many indicators in the index would blur its focus and make it difficult to interpret and use' (UNDP 1990: 11, 13). The world was encouraged to believe that this simple device not only enabled 'people and their governments to evaluate progress over time' but also permitted the determination of 'priorities for policy intervention' (UNDP 1994: 91).

Successive reports promoted the UNDP's special new product. In the second *Report* (1991), it was claimed that the HDI was 'a reliable measure of socio-economic progress' (UNDP 1991:15). Readers were referred to a technical note in which the 'robustness' of the HDI had been established by statistical tests:

> Another way to check the index is to try a different weighting. Suppose we take the product of the three measures and then take the cube root – that is, the geometric rather than the arithmetic mean. This is the same as the equally weighted sum of the logarithms of all three variables. Taking the log of life expectancy, the log of literacy and the log of income ... – and arranging them – gives a new index that also has an extremely high rank correlation with the original HDI ... (UNDP 1991: 88).

The conclusion was that 'the HDI, simple as it is, stands up as a robust device for making intercountry comparisons' (UNDP 1991: 89). In the 1995 *Report,* readers were assured that 'the HDI has been found to be a robust measure: even when different weights are tried, the country HDI values do not change significantly' (UNDP 1995: 122). Many development economists were less impressed. Allen Kelley argued in this journal that the HDI 'offers only limited insights beyond those obtained by small modifications to simple measures of economic output' (Kelley 1991: 315). And in *An Inquiry into Well-being and Destitution,* Partha Dasgupta judged the index to be 'not much good; it has too many unappealing properties [and] ... is also excessively partial' (Dasgupta 1993: 107).

There are grounds for believing that the vigorous promotion of the merits of the HDI has encouraged a simplistic approach to public policy and administration in many developing countries. In the 1995 *Report,* it was said that 'Its rankings [had] opened healthy competition among countries to improve their human development status' – that is, their HDI score (UNDP 1995: 119). and the 1998 *Report* records that president Fidel Ramos of the Philippines had 'asked the National Statistical Coordination Board to include the human development index regularly in the system of statistics used to track variations across provinces', and had 'directed the Department of Interior and Local Government to closely monitor provincial and municipal human development indices – and to institute rewards for good performance' (UNDP 1998a: 18).

As a 'deliberately constructed crude measure' that was devised as a means of 'getting the ear of the world', the HDI may not be a satisfactory indicator of the performance of provincial administrators. For reasons that will be explained below, it may also be an unsatisfactory tool for monitoring progress and determining priorities for policy intervention.

The HDI in practice: Country examples

Madagascar, Mauritius and Tanzania

From the outset, the creators of the HDI reflected the complex concept of 'human development' as a single number. A country's human development performance was related to its potential by means of a crude comparison of its relative ranking in 'league tables' of HDI rank and GNP per capita. In the HDI table in each *Human Development Report,* countries were categorised according to whether their 'HDI rank' was above or below their 'GNP rank'.

In this year's *Report* [1998], two island-countries in the Indian Ocean are featured in the discussion of these relative rankings. Madagascar, which is almost as large as Texas, is one of four low-income countries that are said to 'rank higher on the HDI than on GDP per capita (PPP$ [purchasing power parity dollars]), suggesting that they have converted economic prosperity into human capabilities very effectively' – an achievement described as 'noteworthy.' Mauritius, 1000 kilometres to the east of Madagascar and smaller than Rhode Island, is one of four 'more affluent' countries whose 'ranking on the HDI is lower than that on GDP per capita (PPP$), suggesting that they have failed to translate economic prosperity into correspondingly better lives for their people'. This is described as 'particularly disturbing' (UNDP 1998a: 20).

The following table, which is drawn entirely from statistics in the *Human Development Report 1998*, provides an alternative perspective on the development record of these two countries:

	Madagascar	Mauritius
Land area ('000 ha)	58,154	203
Total real GDP ($PPPbn)	10	15
Real GDP per capita ($PPP)	673	13,294
Life expectancy at birth (years)	58	71
Under five mortality rate (per 1,000 live births)	164	23
Population without access to safe water (%)	66	2
Population without access to health services (%)	62	0
Population without access to sanitation (%)	59	0
Children not reaching grade five (%)	72	1
Adult illiteracy rate (%)	54	17

In 1955, Sir Arthur Lewis identified Mauritius as a country that faced problems in achieving development because its population was 'much too large in relation to agriculture, and at the same time much too small to support a wide range of industrial development' (Lewis 1955: 324). Almost 40 years later, another eminent development economist, Partha Dasgupta, pointed out that Mauritius had been placed first in a 'ranking of living standards data of 48 of the world's poorest countries' and commented that 'Her presence at the top of our ranking was a revelation to me' (Dasgupta 1993: 113). Lewis would not have believed it possible that Mauritius would achieve a level of real GDP per head 20 times that of Madagascar.

While Mauritius has succeeded beyond all expectation, Madagascar has continued to disappoint. The country is regarded by the World Bank as having 'enormous potential for growth', with 'abundant and varied natural resources'. But as a result of its failure to turn these resources to advantage, it is now

> ...among the poorest countries in the world. Poverty has increased and deepened substantially over the past two and a half decades, with real per capita income decreasing 40 percent between 1971 and 1991. The poverty assessment estimates that 70 per cent of the population are poor and 59 per cent are extremely poor (World Bank 1997: 88-90).

It is little short of tragic that the 'team of eminent economists and distinguished development professionals' who prepare the *Human Development Report* have told the world that poverty stricken Madagascar has turned its 'economic prosperity into human capabilities very effectively'; and that affluent Mauritius has 'failed to translate economic prosperity into correspondingly better lives for [its] people'.

Regrettably, these examples from this year's *Report* are part of a consistent pattern of misleading commentary on the relative performance of different countries. In the 1995 *Report* it was claimed that 'A look at the highest positive and negative differences between HDI and real GDP per capita ranks shows clearly that such countries as Costa Rica and Madagascar used their economic growth to enhance the lives of their people' (UNDP 1995: 22). The fact was that Madagascar had had no economic growth to 'use': between 1965 and 1996, its GNP per capita had *decreased* at an average rate of two per cent per annum (World Bank 1998: 24). But the authors of the *Reports* had become so enmeshed in the scrutiny of 'positive and negative differences' that they had lost sight of realities that in the absence of the HDI would have been painfully obvious.

The 1996 *Report* quoted with approval a statement by Julius Nyerere, who had been President of Tanzania for over 30 years: 'Every proposal must be judged by the criterion of whether it serves the purpose of development – and the purpose of development is the people' (UNDP 1996: 46). Notwithstanding their leader's rhetoric, the people of Tanzania are among the very few in the world who are even poorer than those of Madagascar, and their life expectancy at birth is seven years shorter. Yet Tanzania is also in the list of four low-income countries who are complimented in this year's *Report* for their noteworthy achievements in converting their 'economic prosperity into human capabilities very effectively'.

Oman

In the early *Reports,* oil-rich Oman was seen as the worst performer in the 'negative difference' stakes. With an HDI rank 56 places below its GNP rank, the first *Report* (1990) listed it first among a group of countries 'that ...have yet to translate their income into corresponding levels of human development' (UNDP 1990: 16). In the second *Report* (1991), Oman was included in a group of 'countries whose HDI rank is 20 or more places lower than their per capita income rank, showing that they have considerable potential to improve their human development levels – by spending their incomes better and planning their investment priorities more wisely' (UNDP 1991: 15). And in the third *Report* (1992), Oman was again singled out for its alleged failure to translate its high income into a commensurate HDI:

> ...Oman has a per capita income two and a half times that of Costa Rica, but its literacy rate is one-third of Costa Rica's, its average life expectancy is nine years less and its child mortality rate is two and a quarter times higher. All this can be reduced to the information that Oman has an HDI of 0.589, while Costa Rica's HDI is 0.842 - 43% higher. (UNDP 1992: 20)

The issues of principle that are raised by figuring of this kind will not be pursued here, except to note that they are not disposed of by tests of 'robustness', such as comparisons of results with the cube root of the product of three component measures. But there is also a practical question that has received little attention in the debate over the HDI: the quality of the underlying data.

When the index first appeared in 1990, the estimated expectation of life at birth in Oman in the reference year (1987) was given as 57 years – less than in China, India, Pakistan, Brazil, Thailand, Philippines, Turkey or Iran. It is now estimated that life expectancy in Oman in 1985-90 was in fact 68 years – greater than in all of these countries (United Nations 1998). The charge that Oman had failed to translate its income level into corresponding levels of human development was made on the assumption that the country's average life expectancy was in the lowest quartile of the world's population: we now know that it was in the highest quartile. The original calculations of Oman's 'deprivation' with respect to life expectancy in 1987, on a scale of zero to one, was 0.60; on the estimates now available, Oman's 'deprivation,' for the same year and calculated on the same basis, would have been 0.24.

The first HDI calculations assumed that the adult literacy rate in Oman in 1985, on the basis of an estimate made by UNDP itself, was 30 per cent. UNESCO has now published an estimate that Oman's adult literacy rate in 1993 was 60 per cent (UNESCO 1998a). This implies that the rate in 1985 was far higher than the 30 per cent which the UNDP estimated in the 1990 and 1991 *Reports*; and that the country's level of adult literacy in the 1990s has been substantially higher than the figure of 35 per cent that was published in every *Human Development Report* from 1992 to 1997 (and that went into the calculation that Costa Rica's HDI was 43 per cent greater than Oman's).

The estimates of 'mean years of schooling' were even more astray, and here the errors are inexplicable. The HDI calculations in the 1992 *Report* put the 'mean years of schooling' in Oman at only 0.9 years, compared with 5.7 years in Costa Rica. These figures were clearly inconsistent with UNESCO data, which showed that Oman had established a system of universal primary education. In fact, the UNESCO *Statistical Yearbook 1992* (UNESCO 1993) gave the gross enrolment rates at primary level in 1990 as: Oman, 103 per cent (up from 60 per cent in 1980) and Costa Rica, 102 per cent (down from 105 per cent in 1980). At the secondary level the rates were: Oman, 54 per cent (up from 14 per cent in 1980) and Costa Rica, 42 per cent (down from 48 per cent in 1980).

At the time of the 1992 *Human Development Report*, Oman's per capita income was two and a half times that of Costa Rica. By 1996, Oman's margin of advantage over Costa Rica had been reduced to one-third (World Bank 1998). It was becoming difficult to suggest that Oman had failed 'to translate [its] income into corresponding levels of human development,' as had been alleged in the 1990 *Report*. This was not because Oman had suddenly begun 'spending [its] income better and planning [its] investment priorities more wisely', as the authors of the 1991 *Report* had urged (1991: 15). It was because circumstances beyond its control had diminished the country's income (thereby reducing the 'negative difference' between its HDI and GNP rankings).

The crude technique of cataloguing these positive and negative differences implicitly assumes that a country's progress in enhancing life expectancy and literacy levels can be sensitive to such temporary phenomena as rises and falls in the price of oil. It should always have been obvious that this assumption was invalid, and specifically in the case of Oman the 1997 *Report* effectively acknowledged that the judgements made in earlier reports had been unsound:

> Beginning in 1970, Oman undertook a comprehensive program of human development, achieving some of the most rapid advances ever recorded. Life expectancy has increased by 30 years ... Improvements in education have been even more impressive ... Most health problems associated with poverty and lack of schooling have been controlled or

> eradicated ... Advances in health and education have been accompanied by rapid advances in other areas of human development ... Oil revenues ... made possible such rapid progress and such a high standard of living. But without the commitment to human development, Oman might have been wealthy but unhealthy. Oman has been a global pace-setter in human development. (UNDP 1997a: 28).

Only five years earlier, the originator of the *Human Development Report*, Mahbub ul Haq, had singled out Oman as the prime example of a country that was 'wealthy but unhealthy':

> ...beyond the confusing maze of GNP numbers, beyond the curling smoke of industrial chimneys, beyond the endless fascination with budget deficits and balance of payments crises – it is people who matter. Costa Rica has a per capita income only one-third that of Oman but its literacy rate is three times higher, its life expectancy ten years longer, and its people enjoy a wide range of economic, social and political freedoms. (Haq 1992: 1)

Costa Rica

As this extract exemplifies, Costa Rica has always been seen by the HDI team as the prime example of a country that has become healthy without needing to be wealthy. The 1990 *Report* listed it first in a table headed 'Top 15 countries in democratic human development' and asserted that 'Costa Rica shows that assigning a high priority to social sector expenditures, coupled with well-structured across-the-board policies, can dramatically improve the human condition despite only moderate growth and a poor distribution of income' (UNDP 1990: 16, 51). The 1991 *Report* proclaimed that 'Costa Rica remains an outstanding example of human development in Latin America – and the world' (UNDP 1991: 59). And, as already noted, the 1992 *Report* put Costa Rica's HDI at 43 per cent higher than Oman's.

In the 1994 *Report*, Costa Rica was one of seven listed countries whose 'HDI rank is far ahead of their income rank, showing that they have made more judicious use of their income to improve the capabilities of their people' (UNDP 1994: 5). The similar comment on Costa Rica and Madagascar in the 1995 *Report* has already been cited. Both the 1996 and 1997 *Reports* singled out Costa Rica and Viet Nam as countries that had 'effectively translated the benefits of economic growth into improvements in the lives of their people'; and the 1996 *Report* also identified Costa Rica, together with Canada, China and Sri Lanka, as 'countries that convert income into capabilities more effectively than others, countries that constitute the "human development frontier" of efficiency' (UNDP 1996: 31, 67; 1997a: 46).

This year's *Report* gives special praise to Costa Rica as 'a global leader in environmental sustainability'. In a box in the chapter 'Agenda for Action', the country's 'coherent package' of environmental protection policies is outlined. These policies appear to rely heavily on public relations activities:

> The hundred cleanest companies in Costa Rica are named annually, and a green seal of quality is given to gas stations with the best records in preventing air and water pollution and in treating waste water. A red stamp is for those with the worst records. The government and civil society also apply moral suasion by using ad campaigns to convince people that a healthy environment is good in itself, contributes to human wellbeing and is good for tourism. (UNDP 1998a: 99)

Summaries of Costa Rica's own human development reports (UNDP 1997b), which are the outcome of a project sponsored by a consortium of national and international institutions (including UNDP, the European Union, and the Council of State Universities), take a quite different view of Costa Rica's environmental record. The first report, published in 1995, was critical of the fact that 'the country's economic growth [had] relied heavily on depredation of the country's natural endowment'; that 'agroecological limitations of natural resources have not been taken into account'; and that 'even worse, the nation's developmental goals have been reached, in good part, at the expense of those resources'. With the country's primary forest coverage reduced from 56 per cent of its area in 1960 to 22 per cent in 1990, the report warned that 'If this pace continues, Costa Rica will exhaust its primary forests within eight years...'

Comments in other sections of this report, and in a second report published in 1996, did not support the glowing views of Costa Rica's human development performance espoused in successive *Human Development Reports*. The country reports pointed out that 'one in five children between 5 and 11 works and 78% of the youth [labor force] have only an incomplete primary education'; that 62 per cent of all heads of households did not finish primary school; that 'nearly 25% of adolescents between 12 and 17 years old work with almost no job skills'; that 'children and adolescents watch TV an average of 6.7 hours per day, while receiving less than 5 hours of school'; and that 'In spite of governmental public relations campaigns, the majority of the people thought that the current administration's performance was 'bad' or 'very bad' (UNDP 1997b).

Remarkably, the *Human Development Reports* for the UNDP have not drawn upon these comments in Costa Rica's own human development reports. In this year's *Report* for example, no mention is made of the finding that Costa Rican children spend far *more* time watching television than in school, although this was highly relevant to a section of the *Report* headed 'Information imbalances', which referred to findings that children in Japan and the United States spent *almost as much* time watching television as in school (UNDP 1998a: 64). As 'one of the major sources of information and understanding of the social and economic world' (to use Amartya Sen's phrase), one might expect the *Human Development Report* to provide the same details about information imbalances in the 'outstanding example of human development in Latin America' as it does for countries such as Japan and the United States.

Korea

This year's *Report* includes a chart headed 'Similar HDI, different income', which shows graphically that the HDIs of Costa Rica and the Republic of Korea are virtually the same, while Korea's real GDP per capita is almost twice as great. According to the explanatory text, the chart shows that 'The link between economic prosperity and human development is ... neither automatic nor obvious' (UNDP 1998a: 20). As in earlier *Reports*, the authors have reified the abstract concepts 'economic prosperity' and 'human development' as GDP and HDI numbers and have thereby *assumed* that the link between HDI and human development (unlike the link between GDP and human development) is automatic and obvious. In fact, the view that Korea and Costa Rica are at a similar level of human development would not be entertained, but for the fact that the near-identity of their HDIs gives it a superficial plausibility.

Between 1965 and 1996, Korea's average rate of growth of GNP per capita was 7.3 per cent per annum, the fastest rate of growth that has ever been achieved by a major economy over a 30 year period. As Costa Rica's per capita GNP growth rate over the same period was a very modest 1.2 per cent per annum (World Bank 1998), it appears that Korea's level of real per capita income increased between the mid-1960s and the mid 1990s from less than one-third to almost double that of Costa Rica.

Because the HDI calculations 'reflect the diminishing returns to transforming income into human capabilities' (UNDP 1990: 12), Korea's much higher per capita income raises its HDI by only 0.009 relative to that of Costa Rica. There are several reasons why a near-doubling in income would have a much larger impact on enlarging people's choices than this small difference in the HDI implies. Perhaps the most important is that the concomitant decrease in the amount of time that people need to spend in order to earn any given level of income provides them with the opportunity to choose more leisure, an aspect of human welfare that is not taken into account in the HDI. According to estimates prepared by Andrew Harvey for the United Nations (United Nations 1995), Koreans – both women and men – devote less time to work and household chores, and have more 'free time', than their counterparts in more than 20 other countries for which statistics are available (including all of the main industrial countries).

The rate of development in the educational attainment of Korea's adult population has been without precedent for a major country. Between 1960 and 1990, the average total years at schools and higher institutions of the population aged 15 and older increased from 4.25 years to 9.94 years. As a proportion of the average for the OECD countries, average years at school of the population aged 15 and older rose from 60 per cent to 110 per cent. The proportion of Korea's population aged 15 and older who had been at secondary school or higher rose from 20 per cent in 1960 (compared with 38 percent for the OECD total) to 76 percent in 1990 (compared with 63 per cent for the OECD) (Barro and Lee 1993). As noted above, the proportion in Costa Rica was far lower (UNDP 1997b). The much higher level of educational attainment in Korea than in Costa Rica is disregarded in the HDI, except to the extent that it is reflected in a fractionally higher level of adult literacy.

According to UNESCO estimates (1998b), average length of schooling in Korea had reached 14.5 years in 1995, which was higher than in Sweden (14.3 years) and Switzerland (14.0 years). Average length of schooling in Costa Rica was 10.3 years in 1995, which was lower than in all OECD countries except Turkey and also lower than in many other countries of Central and South America – including Peru (12.4 years), Chile (11.8 years), Cuba (11.3 years), Dominican Republic (11.2 years), Brazil (11.1 years), Jamaica (11.0 years) Trinidad and Tobago (10.8 years), Venezuela (10.5 years), and Colombia (10.5 years). The far higher level of average time in school in Korea *vis-a-vis* Costa Rica is not fully reflected in the 'gross enrolment ratios' component of their respective HDIs.

The only element of the HDI in which Costa Rica ranks higher than Korea is 'life expectancy at birth' which is five years greater in Costa Rica. This has a huge impact on the relationship between the HDIs of the two countries (0.027). But the infant mortality rate, which is disregarded in the HDI because it 'is almost perfectly correlated with life expectancy' (UNDP 1995: 121), is far lower in Korea (six infant deaths per thousand births, compared with 13 per thousand in Costa Rica).

Conclusion

The review of the HDI by Allen Kelley, published in this journal[2] in 1991 and cited earlier, was entitled "The Human Development Index: 'Handle with care'" (Kelley 1991). Eight more *Human Development Reports* and eight more HDI 'league tables' have demonstrated the need for even greater care in handling the index – and more circumspection by the UNDP in promoting the usefulness of its product.

2 *Population Development Review.*

References

Barro, Robert J and Jong-Wha Lee (1993). 'International comparisons of eductional attainment', *Journal of Monetary Economics* 32, no. 3: 363-394.

Dasgupta, Partha (1993). *An Inquiry into Well-being and Destitution*. Oxford: Clarendon Press.

Haq, Mahbub ul (1992). *Human Development in a Changing World*. UNDP Occasional Paper 1. New York.

Kelley, Allen C (1991). 'The Human Development Index: 'Handle with care,'" *Population and Development Review* 17, no. 2:315-324.

Keyfitz, Nathan and Wilhelm Fleiger (1968). *World Population*. Chicago and London: University of Chicago Press.

Lewis, W Arthur (1955). *The Theory of Economic Growth*. London. George Allen and Unwin.

OECD (1997). *Education at a Glance: OECD Indicators*. Paris.

_______(1998). *Quarterly Labour Force Statistics* Number 2. Paris.

Sen, Amartya (1998). 'Mahbub ul Haq: the courage and creativity of his ideas', speech at the Memorial Meeting for Mahbub ul Haq, 15 October. UNDP website.

UNDP (1990). *Human Development Report*. New York: Oxford University Press.

_______(1991). *Human Development Report*. New York: Oxford University Press.

_______(1992). *Human Development Report:* New York: Oxford University Press

_______(1993). *Human Development Report*: New York: Oxford University Press

_______(1994). *Human Development Report*: New York: Oxford University Press

_______(1995). *Human Development Report*: New York: Oxford University Press

_______(1996). *Human Development Report:* New York: Oxford University Press

_______(1997a). *Human Development Report*: New York: Oxford University Press

_______(1997b). 'Indicators and democratic governance: Measuring sustainable human development in Costa Rica'. UNDP website.

_______(1998a). *Human Development Report*. New York: Oxford University Press

______(1998b). Media Advisory. 'Invitation-only press luncheon on 2 September to preview UNDP's 1998 *Human Development Report'*, UNDP website.

______(1998c). 'About the *Human Development Reports'*, UNDP website.

______(1998d). '*Human Development Report*: News and Events', UNDP website.

UNESCO (1993). Statistical Yearbook 1992. Paris.

______(1998a). *Statistical Yearbook 1997*. Paris.

______(1998b). *World Education Report 1998*. Oxford: UNESCO Publishing.

United Nations (1995). *Statistics and Indicators on the World's Women*. New York.

______(1997). *The Sex and Age Distribution of the World Populations:* The 1996 Revision. New York.

______(1998). *World Population Prospects:* The 1996 Revision. New York.

World Bank (1997). *Poverty Reduction and The World Bank: Progress in Fiscal 1996and 1997*. Washington DC.

______(1998). *World Development Indicators* 1998. Washington, DC.

14. Measuring Economic Progress[1]

Ian Castles[2]

1. The Evolution of the International League Table

Economists have been inquiring into the nature and causes of the wealth of nations for centuries,[3] but the regular and systematic construction of official quantitative measures of relative economic progress is a phenomenon of recent decades. A key role in this transformation was played by Colin Clark, who held that '[c]omparisons of economic welfare between one community and another, one economic group and another, and between one time and another, are the very framework of economic science' (Clark 1951: 16).

Clark's Joseph Fisher Lecture in Commerce at the University of Adelaide in 1938 was a milestone, because it was in this lecture that the idea of using the national accounts framework to express the average incomes of countries at a common price level was first developed and applied. Drawing upon material from what was his forthcoming book, *Conditions of Economic Progress*,[4] Clark attempted to quantify 'the absolute levels of economic progress so far achieved in different countries'. He explained that this was a difficult statistical task consisting 'in essence...of measuring the real national income of the countries concerned, which amounts to the same thing as the actual equivalent of goods and services produced...*measured at an international price level*' (Clark 1938: 9, emphasis added).

In the course of the lecture, Clark presented estimates of the average income per occupied person at work in various countries in 1936 or 1937, measured in international units of purchasing power (IUs). One IU equalled the average amount of goods and services purchasable with one American dollar, over

1 This paper was presented at a Reserve Bank of Australia conference in 1995 and published as a chapter in the Bank's 1995 book, *Productivity and Growth*. Except where otherwise indicated, all figures and tables in this chapter are Castles' own.

2 This paper could not have been produced without the invaluable assistance, and numerous helpful suggestions, of John Romalis. I am also indebted to many others at the Reserve Bank of Australia and particularly thank all staff of the Bank's library for superlative support. The views expressed here are, of course, my own.

3 In fact, the full title of the most famous economics text, published in 1776, was *An Inquiry Into the Nature and Causes of the Wealth of Nations*, by Adam Smith.

4 The first edition of *Conditions of Economic Progress* was published in 1940, and was dedicated to 'W Forgan Smith, LL.D, Premier of Queensland, A Far-Seeing Patron of Economic Science'.

the period 1925-1934. According to these calculations, the highest average real income per occupied person at that time was in New Zealand (2,040 IUs), followed in order by the United States (1,948 IUs), Great Britain (1,402 IUs) and Australia (1,363 IUs).[5]

The significance of Clark's pioneering work in comparing average income levels in different countries at international price levels has now been recognised.[6] In the 1990s however, inter-country comparisons of real product and incomes are no longer the province of individual scholars. The United Nations International Comparison Program (ICP), which began in 1967, has developed into a world-wide statistical enterprise which aims at obtaining internationally comparable data on total and per capita gross national product (GNP), by taking account of the purchasing power differences of the currencies in which national estimates were originally compiled.[7] In 1985, the ICP conducted a benchmark exercise, the results of which were published in 1994 (UN 1994).[8] For this phase of the ICP (Phase V), comparisons were initially made within six regions or country groups: Africa, the Caribbean, Asia and the Western Pacific, the EEC, a broader European grouping comprising the European Comparison Program (ECP), and the OECD. Since each study employed the same technique, regional results could be linked to form a global comparison if a country was represented in more than one of the regions, or through bilateral comparisons between two countries belonging to different regions. The global framework of this exercise is illustrated in Figure 1.[9]

In the *World Bank Atlas 1995*, ICP results were extended to non-participating countries, and extrapolated to 1993 for participating countries, in order to present, for around 130 countries, a new measure of GNP per capita converted at purchasing power parity (PPP). This PPP-based measure was designed to offer '...an alternative view of a country's income level relative to others *by using international prices to value domestic production*' (World Bank 1995: 2, emphasis added).[10] According to the World Bank's rankings (the current official 'league

5 See Clark (1938: 9) for further details.

6 See Arndt (1979: 121-124) and references cited therein.

7 See United Nations and Commission of the European Communities (1994), hereafter referred to as UN (1994).

8 Organisations participating in various aspects of the benchmarking exercise included the World Bank, the University of Pennsylvania, the Statistical Division of the United Nations Secretariat (UNSTAT), the Statistical Office of the European Communities (EUROSTAT), the Organisation for Economic Co-operation and Development (OECD), the Economic Commission for Europe (ECE), the Economic and Social Commission for Asia and the Pacific (ESCAP) and the Austrian Central Statistical Office.

9 For a detailed exposition see UN (1994: 9-19).

10 However, readers are asked to note that '...because of differing statistical systems and methods of collection among economies, the indicators are *not always strictly comparable* in coverage and definition' (World Bank 1995: 2, emphasis added). It was not made clear, however, that the range of error involved in the PPP estimates is far greater, and the conceptual issues raised are far more formidable, than in the case of other country indicators published by the Bank (such as the demographic characteristics of countries, their exports and imports, or the industrial origin of their GNPs). Nor was it mentioned that the responsibility for

table'), the relative average income levels of the 25 richest countries in 1993 were as shown in Table 1: the bracketed figures show the rankings in the late 1930s, according to the estimates given by Clark in his Joseph Fisher Lecture.

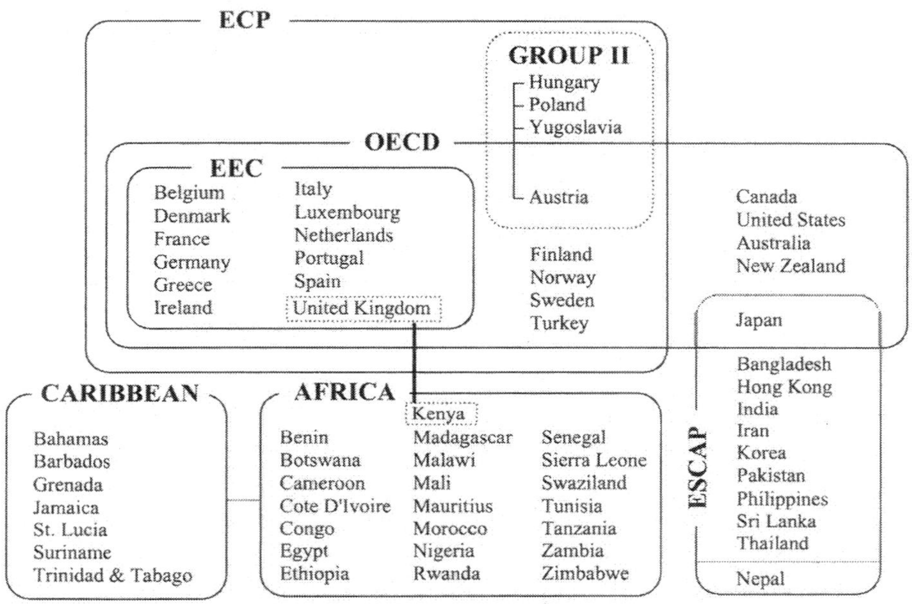

Figure 1 Global Framework of the 1985 ICP

Source: UN (1994).

As was to be expected, the aspect of the new comparisons that attracted most attention in the Australian media was the indicated relationship between Australia's income level and those of the most successful economies to its north. Under the heading 'Aust slides below HK and Singapore', the *Australian Financial Review* noted that 'Australia...lags well behind Singapore and Hong Kong in the World Bank's alternative new purchasing power parity measure of material living standards, which adjusts individual country's per capita [GNP] for their price levels'.[11] This was a correct interpretation of the reported estimates but, as we shall see, it is questionable whether the reported estimates for the relevant countries reflect the reality.

Another aspect of the reported comparisons deserves emphasis. The current official league table shows most of the rich countries as having quite similar levels of average income. Australia, with an indicated average per capita income

PPP estimates does not rest with national statistical authorities (with the single exception of the Austrian Central Statistical Office), but with the international organisations and other coordinating bodies listed in footnote 8 above.

11 *Australian Financial Review*, 3 January 1995: 5.

in 1993 of int$18,490, was one of ten countries with average incomes of between int$17,500 and int$19,500. And Australia stood in the middle of 20 countries whose average incomes were within a range of +/- 20 per cent of the Australian average. Only the United States and four small and atypical countries were above this range. This concentration of the average income levels of the richer countries in a relatively narrow range suggests that the oft-used league table analogy is inapposite, and the associated concentration of attention on precise rankings is misplaced.

A league table of teams in a sporting competition records unambiguously the precise outcome of a series of contests, according to pre-determined rules. If the purpose of the rankings is to separate the teams which reach the finals from those that failed to do so, it is irrelevant that the margin between the lowest ranked of the former and the highest ranked of the latter may be a fraction of a percentage point on a countback.

For a number of reasons, the rankings in Table 1 have no such significance. First, they have been determined following the application of PPPs rather than actual exchange rate parities, so they do not report the output of a competition (even in the sense of 'competition for markets'). Second, the numbers summarise the outcome of a myriad of transactions and are, therefore, inevitably subject to large errors of measurement. Third, even if the terms of every transaction were known and were included in the calculations, there would be no 'correct' way of aggregating those transactions in order to establish, without ambiguity, the average real income of one country compared with another. Finally, and most importantly, there is no agreement, and there is no prospect of agreement, about the concept of 'income' of which it is always better to have more rather than less.

Depending on the context, our interest might be in the measure of output that is aggregated in the system of national accounts or in alternative measures. For example, our interest might be in measures of output that take account of items not identified in the national accounts; such as unpaid and voluntary work, changes in stocks of natural resources, or in measures which seek to comprehend less tangible aspects of wellbeing or the quality of life. Our interest might be in a measure of income per some unit; such as per hour worked, per capita, per employed person, or some augmented measure of labour,[12] or per unit of some composite of factor inputs. Alternatively, our interest might be in the income of individuals in particular circumstances; for example, the median wage and salary earner, the retired or the unemployed, or the income of particular types of households (such as single income or single parent households).

12 Such as one that allows for differences in education, skills and/or experience.

Table 1 GNP per capita at purchasing power parities in 1993 international dollars

Rank	Country	Int$
1	Luxembourg	29,510
2	**United States (2)**	**24,750**
3	Switzerland(b)	23,620
4	United Arab Emirates(b)	23,390
5	Qatar(b)	22,910
6	Hong Kong	21,670
7	Japan	21,090
8	Germany(a)	20,980
9	Singapore(b)	20,470
10	Canada	20,410
11	France	19,440
12	Norway	19,130
13	Denmark	18,940
14	Austria	18,800
= 15	**Australia (4)**	**18,490**
= 15	Belgium	18,490
17	Italy	18,070
18	Netherlands, the	18,050
19	**United Kingdom (3)**	**17,750**
20	Sweden	17,560
21	Iceland	17,160
22	Bahamas, the(b)	16,820
23	Cyprus(b)	15,470
24	**New Zealand (1)**	**15,390**
25	Finland	15,230
34	Korea(c)	9,810
35	Argentina	8,630
37	Malaysia	8,630
45	Thailand	6,390
75	Indonesia	3,140
80	Philippines	2,660

Source: See Appendix.

Notes:

(a) Former Federal Republic of Germany.

(b) Obtained from regression estimates.

(c) Republic of Korea

Figures in parentheses are the rankings of relative average income levels from Clark (1938).

Int$ are international prices denominated in 1993 US dollars.

In short, the measurement of income levels at PPPs raises formidable conceptual and practical difficulties which are not properly recognised in bland explanations that 'international prices' have been used to value domestic production, or that the estimates are 'not always directly comparable'. Even if all of these difficulties could be overcome, there would be marked shifts in the rankings of the high-income countries of the 1990s depending on which concept of income or output was seen as most relevant for the purpose at hand.

The dangers of the league table approach to the assessment of economic performance were encapsulated by Stein (1990: A16):

> ...a moment's reflection will show that [our] standard of living, or... personal welfare,...does not depend on our being ahead of anyone else... Our real problem...is not to get richer than someone else or to get richer faster than someone else but to be as good as we can be, and better than we have been, in the areas of our serious deficiencies, such as homelessness, poverty, ignorance and crime.

Stein (1990) was actually speaking of the American experience. However, in the Australian context, similar concerns about league tables have been expressed. The Vernon Committee (1965), in its assessment of Australia's post-war development and prospects for future growth, was reluctant to compare economies and claimed that Australia's performance could not be judged by '... its place in any simple ranking of so called advanced countries...' (para 2.21). More recently, Gruen (1986) has been critical of such rankings, arguing that Australia's slide down the 'totem pole' of per capita income has given rise to somewhat exaggerated concerns about the nation's economic performance. He has maintained that non-economic factors probably 'loom large' in any adequate explanation of why some countries achieve faster growth than others.

It is not the purpose of this paper to deny that summary measures of average per capita incomes, arranged in the form of league tables, may be a useful analytical tool. It will be argued, however, that there is a need for greater circumspection in the use of such comparisons, and for a more informed understanding of their limitations. In particular, it needs to be recognised that aggregates of values cannot meaningfully be compared 'at international prices' if there are large differences in the price *and* quantity relativities applicable to many of the components.

The paper is organised as follows. Section 2 presents estimates of relative real GNP per capita over this century. Sections 3 to 5 deal with a range of conceptual and practical difficulties associated with the identification of these relativities. Alternative approaches are then considered in Sections 6 to 8. They are shown to yield rankings of economic performance that differ significantly from those in conventional tables. Section 9 then reflects upon the way in which measures of Australia's relative economic performance reflect social choices. Section 10 places these choices in an historical context, and some impressions of earlier relativities are offered. Finally, conclusions are drawn.

2. Indicative estimates of 'real' GNP *per capita*: 1900–1993

The 'official' World Bank (1995) estimates of relative contemporary income levels in Australia and in 16 other countries are exhibited in a long-term context in Figure 2. The 1993 official estimate of Australia's real GNP per capita is backcast to 1900, using IMF estimates of annual growth rates in recent years and those reported by Maddison (1989) for earlier years to construct the time series. (For detailed data description see the Appendix.) Comparable time series for six groups of other countries have been constructed and plotted against the estimates for Australia.

The vertical scale in each panel of Figure 2 is logarithmic, so that equal vertical distances represent equal *proportional* differences in estimated levels of GNP per capita at purchasing power parities (in international prices denominated in 1993 US dollars). According to these estimates, the bunching of the average real incomes of a large number of countries at about the same level is a relatively recent phenomenon: before World War I, the indicated average real income levels in the United States and Australia were around twice those of most countries of continental Europe, which in turn were about twice those of the highest income countries in Asia (the Philippines and Japan).

Figure 2 presents the picture of Australia's relative position over time which has come to be generally accepted. On the one hand, the per capita growth rates of most countries in Europe, and of several countries in East Asia, have been much faster than that for Australia. In fact, the estimates suggest that many of these countries have now achieved an indicated average income level that is at least comparable to, and in several cases is higher than, Australia's. On the other hand, however, the country's per capita growth rate has been substantial in an absolute sense (for example, at a rate sufficient to provide each generation with a standard of living notably superior to its predecessor).

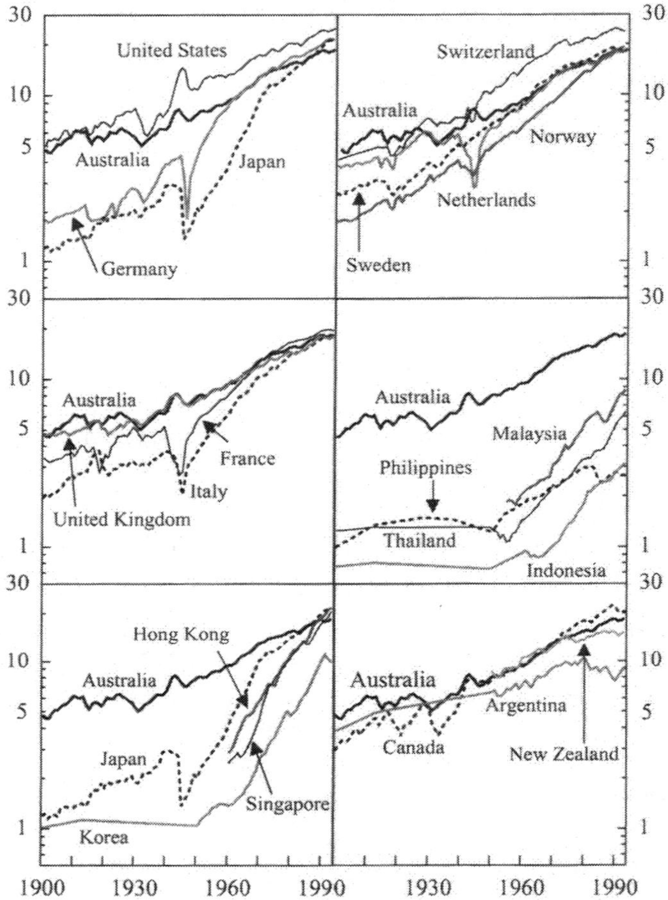

Figure 2 Real GNP per capita in selected economies (see Appendix for data drawn upon)

Source: Author's calculation (see Appendix for data drawn upon).

Much concern has been expressed in Australia in recent times about the decline in the country's relative position on the real income scale.[13] This loss of relativity has arisen because the *growth rate* of Australia's real GDP has been lower than that of most other high-income countries; it does not depend on the reliability or otherwise of the results of PPP studies. Most of the countries whose average real incomes were formerly much lower than Australia's have now 'caught up'.[14]

13 This debate has been well articulated by Gruen (1986), and more recently by Dowrick and Nguyen (1989) and Dowrick and Quiggin (1993).

14 For a detailed discussion of the phenomenon of catch-up and convergence see Dowrick and Nguyen (1989) and Dowrick in Reserve Bank (1995). *Productivity and Growth.*

However, for the reasons advanced by Stein (1990), and because of fundamental questions about whether meaningful relativities can be established in the first place, this should not of itself be cause for concern.

A final general point is that the focus of attention on the countries at the top of the league table introduces selectivity: the countries on this list are those that have always been near the top, or have had the fastest growth in average real incomes, in the modern era. We are, therefore, comparing ourselves with the countries that have been most successful. Whilst Australia is not among the leaders of this elite, we are clearly ahead of most of the pack.

But what precisely do measures of real income levels indicate about relative economic performance? There are many conceptual and practical difficulties associated with benchmarking these measures to form international comparisons. Backcasting data to form an historical profile of relativities poses even further challenges. The strategy adopted in this paper is to demonstrate the limitations of real income levels as indicators of relative economic performance, and then to provide alternative evidence of relativities, both for the benchmark period and for specific episodes.

3. Methodological problems of the ICP approach

Although indicative estimates of real GNP per capita are expressed in 'international prices denominated in 1993 US dollars' the observations charted in these figures should not be seen as estimates of value, but as *index numbers of relative economic quantities*.[15] The essence of ICP comparisons lies in the *relativities* of average magnitudes between countries and over time, and the expression of those relativities in terms of international prices denominated in US dollars is purely a matter of convenience. The results could be expressed in any other currency: for example, those for the 20 countries participating in the ECP 1985 (see Figure 1) were initially reported in terms of international prices denominated in Austrian schilling.

The real GNP per capita estimates published by the World Bank for 1993 were derived from estimates initially relating to other years in a variety of ways. Those for the countries of the European Union were extrapolated from benchmark EUROSTAT estimates for 1990; those for other OECD countries were also extrapolated from 1990, from an extension of the EUROSTAT study by the OECD;[16] those for other countries participating in the ICP were extrapolated

15 For a discussion on the concept of economic quantity, see Wilson (1946), especially 6-8.

16 This study relied to a substantial extent on product specifications developed for the purpose of making PPP and real product comparisons between European countries.

from the 1985 reference year of that program; and those for countries not participating in the ICP (including Singapore) were estimated from the results for participating countries by regression analysis.[17]

In brief, the best-performing regression models utilise capital city price surveys conducted as part of a program designed to equalise the real incomes of public servants and business executives assigned to countries around the world. While the price indices designed for this group do not properly reflect the prices or relative quantities of goods consumed by nationals of these countries, a structural relationship was found between the measures of purchasing power derived from these price surveys and those derived from the prices ordinarily used in the ICP. This relationship was then used to form PPP comparisons with non-ICP countries.

The accuracy of these regression estimates, in terms of a 95 per cent confidence interval, is guessed to range from +/- 60 per cent for low-income countries, to +/- 15 per cent for countries with per capita incomes up to seven tenths of that of the United States (Summers and Heston 1991: 341-342). Given the similarity of the PPP-adjusted per capita estimates reported in Table 1, these wide confidence intervals suggest that the reported rankings are of particularly low significance for countries (such as Singapore) that did not participate in the ICP. In addition to this basic qualification about the interpretation of league table rankings, there are several specific difficulties which affect the reliability of ICP comparisons.

Summers and Heston (1991) present the outcome of the ICP in its most extensive form and outline the methodological approach of the ICP benchmark studies in the following terms:

> Basically, an ICP benchmark study is a pricing exercise. Prices of hundreds of identically specified goods and services prevailing in each participating country are collected and processed. The price comparisons that emerge are estimates of price parities for each country's currency at a number of aggregation levels, including an overall purchasing power parity...The price parities and PPPs are used to convert the countries' national currency expenditures to a common currency unit, thus making real quantity comparisons across countries possible.
>
> The ICP divides up...GDP into about 150 detailed categories (approximately 110 consumption, 35 investment and 5 government). All of a country's individual final output items are assigned to one or another of the categories. The ICP central office works with national

17 A description and assessment of the methods used to extend PPP comparisons to non-ICP countries is provided by Kravis and Lipsey (1990: 21-26,43-48).

> data of two sorts from each participating country: national prices for between 400 and 700 particular items; and national expenditures for each of the 150 detailed categories.
>
> For the prices to provide a meaningful basis for determining relative quantities, *it is of the utmost importance that they refer to the same items*, that is, of the same quantity and quality, *from country to country*. ...To this end, specification manuals giving closely detailed technical descriptions of over 1,500 commodities, services and labour inputs have been developed that cover the universe of all items priced in any country (Summers and Heston 1991: 329, emphasis added).[18]

The emphasised statement may appear to be the obvious expression of an essential requirement of a program that seeks to provide reliable estimates of real quantities. In fact, it conceals a fundamental problem. The practical situation is that the items which are identical in quantity and quality *between* countries are often *not* the items which are most typical or representative of the relevant area of expenditure *within* every country. In the countries in which the items priced are less typical of the purchases made, it would usually be the case that the more typical items provided the buyer with better value for money than the items priced in the ICP. Indeed, it is the 'value for money' consideration that has, in many cases, made a particular product 'typical' of spending. The resulting economies of scale may well make that product progressively cheaper than the more internationally comparable alternatives. The point is best illustrated by some examples.

The list of passenger cars in EUROSTAT's 1985 PPP study, for which the OECD sought prices from its non-EEC members, included 10 diesel engine and 81 petrol-engine vehicles. Of the latter, only five had an engine capacity exceeding two litres. But no cars representative of the bulk of the Australian market (locally produced models with an engine capacity of three litres of more) were included in the OECD comparison. In the outcome, therefore, nominal expenditure on passenger vehicles in Australia was revalued for PPP purposes using a price parity relating to vehicles that were not typical of the Australian market.

For refrigerators, the OECD 1985 list taken over from EUROSTAT's comparison included five single-door models which had an average capacity of 170 litres; and 11 two-door models with an average capacity of 290 litres. At this time the Australian consumer magazine *Choice* reported that 50 per cent of the Australian refrigerator market was held by two-door cyclic-defrost models, and tested 13 such models (nine of which were of Australian or New Zealand manufacture) which had an average capacity exceeding 350 litres.[19] The refrigerator in the typical Australian kitchen was grossly under-represented in the PPP comparison.

18 See also Kravis, Heston and Summers (1978) for a discussion of these measurement issues.

19 *Choice*, October 1984: 34-39.

The statistical experts at the OECD have recognised this problem and, in cooperation with the statistical agencies of non-EEC member countries, have sought to take some account of it (mainly by being less rigorous about ensuring precise identity of specifications than the Summers and Heston paper suggests is necessary). There are, however, limits to the scale of the *ad hoc* improvements which can be effected in this way when the resources available for the purpose, both at the OECD and in the national statistical offices, are minuscule. There can be little doubt that the PPP estimates for Australia (and also for Canada, New Zealand and the United States) are substantially affected by the fact that the list of items for which prices are sought was initially prepared for the purpose of supporting comparisons between European countries. A program which had recognised the need to take account of North American and Australasian conditions from the outset would probably have identified significantly higher levels of real product, relative to those of European countries, than does the ICP.

4. Conceptual problems in inter-country comparisons

Having regard to these enormous practical and conceptual difficulties, it is perhaps surprising that the ICP results have been accepted by most scholars as reliable and accurate measures of relative levels of real income, and even of living standards or economic welfare, between countries and over time. In contrast, Colin Clark's estimates of the average income in different countries in the late 1930s were greeted with considerable scepticism, largely because of the conceptual constraint known to statisticians as 'the index number problem'. The significance of the index number problem in relation to comparisons of real income was well articulated in 1939 by E (later Sir) Ronald Walker, Professor of Economics at the University of Tasmania. In an essay published soon after Clark's Joseph Fisher Lecture, Walker suggested that, for scientific purposes, the term 'standard of living' should be abandoned; and he considered that a concept such as the average real income:

> ...can be calculated, and has meaning, only if we accept certain conventions, which rest on assumptions regarding similarity of culture. But...the comparisons in which we would be most concerned are comparisons between countries...in which these conventions cannot be accepted. Our conclusions, therefore, are somewhat negative. Not only are most international comparisons of living standards misguided in intention, but those to which approval can be accorded are practically impossible; except between nations which resemble each other so closely as to rob the comparisons of much of their interest. The most useful work in this field, from the scientific viewpoint, will be found

> not in the reduction of highly doubtful differences in living standards to spuriously precise indexes, but in the comparative study of the actual content of typical family budgets of different classes in the relevant countries.[20]

In raising these doubts about the possibility of making quantitative comparisons of real income levels between countries with widely differing cultures, Walker was repeating concerns that had been voiced for decades by statisticians and economists. Perhaps their most famous expression was by Keynes (1909) in an essay entitled 'The Method of Index Numbers with Special Reference to the Measurement of General Exchange Value', for which he won the Adam Smith prize for that year.

Keynes criticised official British estimates of relative levels of real wages in different districts of the United Kingdom. He reproduced from the official report a statistical table which purported to show that real wages in London were three per cent higher than in Ireland, and then rearranged the same information in a way which appeared to show that real wages in London were two per cent *lower* than in Ireland (see Great Britain (1908)). He claimed that both results were arbitrary:

> The arbitrary element enters in when we decide what standard quantity of food corresponds to a given standard quantity of house-room. ...If the standard is fixed for all districts with reference to what is actually the standard in London, we get one result; and if we fix it with reference to what is actually the standard in the Midlands or in Ireland, we get a different result. Which of these standards we choose is, from all points of view, wholly arbitrary (Keynes 1910: 180).

In his more detailed exposition, Keynes distinguished between two kinds of difficulty which arose in the use of index numbers to measure economic quantities:

> In the first kind, the quantities in question are perfectly definite and capable of measurement, but the information at our disposal is incomplete. Our task consists in making as accurate a measurement as we can by using what statistics we have. In the second kind the quantity itself is not, in the strictest sense, capable of numerical measurement at all. We must adopt some conventional, but practically useful, measure and our task mainly consists in elucidating the quantitative aspect of the concept in question...

20 See Walker (1939: 61,64). Following a distinguished diplomatic career, Sir Ronald Walker was to be appointed Australia's first Ambassador to the OECD in 1971. In 1930, when he had been a PhD student at Cambridge, Walker 'had been invited...to become a member of the famous Political Economy Club...which met every Monday evening during term in Keynes's rooms in King's College... . When Walker was in Cambridge... Colin Clark regularly attended meetings' (Cornish 1991: 60).

> We have in 'the cost of living' a conception which is *prima facie* measurable. We should say that the comparison of the cost of living in two different places requires no more than the collection of the necessary statistics. Reflection shows, however, that this is not the case. The difficulty in comparing the cost of living of two sets of people who live under very different conditions is not a statistical one. It depends upon the intrinsic difficulty of saying what scale of living under one set of circumstances corresponds to a given scale of living under a different set. The two things may be numerically incommensurable (Keynes 1909: 53, 62-63).

The difficulty to which Keynes was alluding must be distinguished from a different issue with which it is commonly confused: that of the difficulty (or impossibility) of making inter-personal comparisons of utility. As Keynes was to argue in his final exploration of the problems of comparisons of purchasing power, more than 20 years later:

> ...we do *not* mean by purchasing power the command of money over quantities of utility. If two men both spend their incomes on bread and both pay the same price for it, the purchasing power of money is not greater to the one than to the other merely because the former is hungrier or poorer than the latter. The purchasing power of money is not different to two individuals with equal incomes because one has greater powers of enjoyment than the other. A redistribution of money incomes which has the effect of increasing the aggregate of utility does not in itself affect the purchasing power of money (Keynes 1930: 96).

Thus the particular problem which limited the possibility of comparing average purchasing power was that:

> ...the composite commodities representative of the actual expenditure of money-incomes are not stable in that constitution as between different places, times or groups. They are unstable for three reasons — either (1) beacause the need which the object of expenditure is intended to satisfy... varies, or (2) because the efficiency of the objects of expenditure to attain its purpose varies, or (3) because there is a change in what distribution of income between different objects is the most economical means of attaining the purpose. The first of those reasons we may classify as a change in tastes, the second as a change in environment, and the third as a change in relative prices. For these reasons every change in the distribution of real incomes or in habits and education, every change in climate and national customs, and every change in relative prices and in the character and qualities of the goods offering for purpose, will affect in some degree the character of average expenditure (Keynes 1930: 95-96).

Keynes went on to examine a number of possible methods of arriving at approximations of the relative purchasing power of incomes, distinguishing between the direct method of comparing incomes of similar persons and various indirect methods of comparing prices of equivalent composite commodities. But there were limits to all of these methods, which Keynes explained in typically piquant illustrations:

> We are not in a position to weigh the satisfactions for similar persons of Pharaoh's slaves against Fifth Avenue's motor cars, or dear fuel and cheap ice to Laplanders against cheap fuel and dear ice to Hottentots... We cannot hope to find a ratio of equivalent substitution for gladiators against cinemas, or for the conveniences of being able to buy motor cars against the conveniences of being able to buy slaves (Keynes 1930: 104-109).

It is arguable that the differences between the objects of consumption which were available to the many in 1930, and to the few in classical times, were not greater than those which are available to the many in 1995, compared with those available to the few in 1930. The problems of comparing purchasing power 'as between different places, times or groups' in the late 20th century are even greater than those that troubled Keynes, but a world which constantly demands the quantification of the unquantifiable appears to be unable to come to terms with the notion that 'two things may be numerically incommensurable'.

Keynes' doubts about PPP comparisons between groups with widely differing expenditure patterns were not the cautions of an insecure statistician, fearful of sacrificing detail by striking an average, but the strongly stated verdict of one of the greatest economists after decades of serious reflection. It is remarkable that they have been so quickly set aside, in the uncritical acceptance in recent times of league table comparisons of economies between which there are massive differences in 'the character of average expenditure'.

5. The 'index number problem' in practice

An example of this uncritical acceptance has already been given: the reporting of the *World Bank Atlas*, PPP-adjusted estimates of real per capita incomes in Australia compared with Hong Kong and Singapore. Such comparisons ignore the serious logical problems identified in the preceding section. In order to demonstrate this, the relationship between the ICP 1985 price and quantity relativities for the main components of final national consumption of Australia and Hong Kong will be examined in some detail.[21]

---

21 It is not possible to compare these relativities for components of the final national consumption expenditure of Singapore, the other country whose rise in the *World Bank Atlas* rankings was prominently

These relationships are plotted in Figure 3 for each of 20 broad commodity groups. Each of the observations is itself an aggregation of the price and quantity relativities of each commodity within the group and, as such, has its own index number problems. Of the 20 broad commodity groups, there are only four for which the relative per capita quantity consumed in Hong Kong lies between two-thirds and one and a half times that in Australia. And of the 16 commodity groups for which the quantity relative lies outside this wide range, there are six for which the bilateral price relative *also* lies outside that broad range.

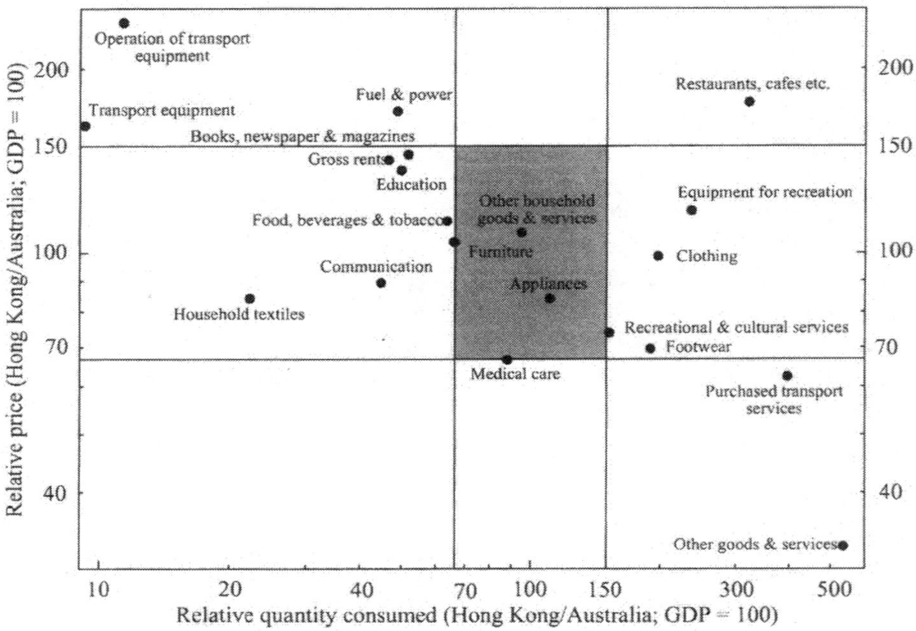

Figure 3 Relative prices and relative quantities consumed in Australia and Hong Kong in 1985.

Source: See Appendix.

Suppose that the relative *prices* of all commodities in the two countries had been the same, so that, for example, the average price of a given quantity of medical care bore the same relationship to the average price of a given quantity of clothing in each. In that case, each of the observations in Figure 3 would lie along a horizontal line at 100, and the relative GDPs of the two countries could be calculated without ambiguity (assuming there were no measurement problems) by valuing the various different commodities, produced in differing proportions between the two countries, at that constant relative-price relationship.

reported in the Australian media. Singapore has not participated in the ICP, but other information, discussed in Section 8 below, suggests that the index number problem which is illustrated here in respect of the Hong Kong/Australia comparison, would apply with equal or greater force in the case of a Singapore/Australia comparison.

Alternatively, suppose that the relative *quantities* of all commodities consumed in the two economies were the same. In that case, each observation would lie along a vertical line at 100, and an unambiguous computation of the relative price levels of the two countries could be achieved by weighting all of the various price relativities of each individual commodity between the countries by the amount of each commodity consumed.

In fact, however, the ICP results plotted in Figure 3 show that the price *and* quantity relativities of commodity groups differ greatly between Australia and Hong Kong.

In short, the conditions identified by Keynes under which an *approximate* comparison of real quantities could be made are not fulfilled. It is important to recognise that the problem of comparing the PPP and real product relationships between two countries as different as are Australia and Hong Kong would still be there, even if we had perfect knowledge of the quantity and price of every transaction in both countries in the reference period. As Keynes pointed out, the problem with which we are confronted is not a statistical one, but one that arises from 'the intrinsic difficulty of saying what scale of living under one set of circumstances corresponds to a given scale of living under a different set'.

When the World Bank authors made the seemingly simple statement that the PPP-adjusted real income estimates take into consideration the purchasing power differences of the currencies in which the national estimates were originally compiled, they are implicitly asserting that (to use Keynes' words), 'the comparison of the cost of living in two different places requires no more than the collection of the necessary statistics'. But PPP-adjusted measures cannot provide satisfactory measures of the relative real product or the relative price levels in Australia and Hong Kong, because the problem of aggregation is intrinsic. It cannot be overcome (but is, unfortunately, obscured) by multilateral comparisons in which expenditures are revalued in 'international prices' rather than in the prices of one or both of the countries which are the subject of comparison.

As it happens, the ICP revaluation of 1985 nominal expenditures in terms of international prices showed similar levels of per capita final national consumption in Australia (int$7,946) and Hong Kong (int$7,710). On average, per capita expenditure on the purchase and operation of transport equipment in Australia was over ten times greater than in Hong Kong, and per capita expenditure on the purchase of transport services (fares) was over three times greater in Hong Kong than in Australia. As Figure 3 shows, there were also large differences in the opposite direction in the price relativities for these groups.

A necessary implication of the existence of such large differences in price and quantity relativities is that the aggregation of the expenditures at international prices is an artificial exercise. The transactions did not take place at international prices and, if international prices *had* prevailed in each of the markets, the quantities of the various commodities consumed would have been entirely different. In the outcome the relative real income for each country depends to an important extent upon the degree to which the price and quantity relativities for that country differs from the corresponding average relativities for the entire group of participating countries.

The extent to which ICP comparisons can be affected by the aggregation of expenditures at hypothetical rather than actual prices may be judged by a specific example from the 1985 benchmark study. According to the estimates published by the OECD (OECD 1987), the *nominal value* per head of final expenditure on gross rent in Portugal, *at national prices* converted to US dollars at the prevailing exchange rate, was US$85 (OECD Table 16). The so-called *real value* per head of the same component *at average EEC prices* was estimated at US$677 (OECD Table 6). The *real value* per head when measured *at average OECD prices* was US$855 (derived from OECD Tables 7 and 8). And the so-called *real value* per head of final expenditure *at international prices* was US$1,100 (UN 1994, Table 3).

Thus the expenditure on gross rent in Portugal in 1985 was estimated to be 13 times greater when measured at international prices than when measured at the actual values recorded by Portugal's national accountants. Other components of final expenditure in Portugal (the purchase of transport equipment, for example) were estimated to be a *smaller* total in international prices than at the prices which were actually paid.

In Table 2, the so-called real value of expenditure on gross rents in Portugal (US$1,100) is placed in a different context. The table shows the estimated '*per capita* real value of final expenditure' of 'gross rents' in OECD countries in 1985. All of the information is reproduced from a table in the official report on Phase V of the ICP (UN 1994, Table 3), with the ranking presented in the form of a league table.

It is obvious from casual inspection that the comparisons in Table 2 do not indicate the relative standards of housing in the OECD countries in 1985. No study of housing conditions at that time could have concluded that Spaniards were better housed on average than Americans; or that Japanese were better housed on average than Australians; or that Portuguese were better housed on average than New Zealanders. Such comparisons are immediately recognisable as wrong by anyone familiar with the housing conditions prevailing in these countries, or with the available statistical information bearing directly on the subject. Yet the real expenditures on gross rent are a significant component of the ICP estimates of real GDP which have attracted such widespread and uncritical attention.

Table 2 Per capita real value of final expenditure on gross rents at international prices in 1985 US dollars

Rank	Country	Int$
1	Spain	1,851
2	Japan	1,789
3	Denmark	1,787
4	United States	1,710
5	Sweden	1,681
6	United Kingdom	1,657
7	Italy	1,582
8	Australia	1,579
9	Canada	1,511
10	France	1,326
11	Finland	1,254
12	Luxembourg	1,233
13	Belgium	1,183
14	Austria	1,138
15	Netherlands, the	1,129
16	Germany	1,124
17	Portugal	1,100
18	New Zealand	1,067
19	Norway	890
20	Ireland	727
21	Greece	539
22	Turkey	161

Source: See Appendix.

6. An alternative approach

The fact that measures of relative real product or relative price levels cannot be satisfactorily measured tends to support the view expressed by Walker that the only international comparisons of living standards to which approval can be given are 'practically impossible'. Walker did, however, suggest an alternative approach which he believed could provide more useful results: 'the comparative study of the actual content of typical family budgets of different classes in the relevant countries' (Walker 1939: 64).

Figure 4 provides an illustration of the approach that Walker advocated. The comparison is again between Australia and Hong Kong, with three pie charts for each country showing the patterns of household expenditure (other than on housing) of low, middle and high-income groups in the late 1980s.[22] For the low-income group – representing the 50 per cent of households with the lowest incomes – the relevant charts show that the 'all other' category absorbed 65 per cent of the non-housing expenditure of Australian households, compared with only 38 per cent for the corresponding households in Hong Kong. The *ratio* of the largely discretionary 'all other' component to expenditure on food rises in Hong Kong from 74 per cent at the lower income level to about 130 per cent for the high-income group; in Australia, the corresponding ratio rises from 260 per cent at lower incomes to over 360 per cent at the high income level.[23]

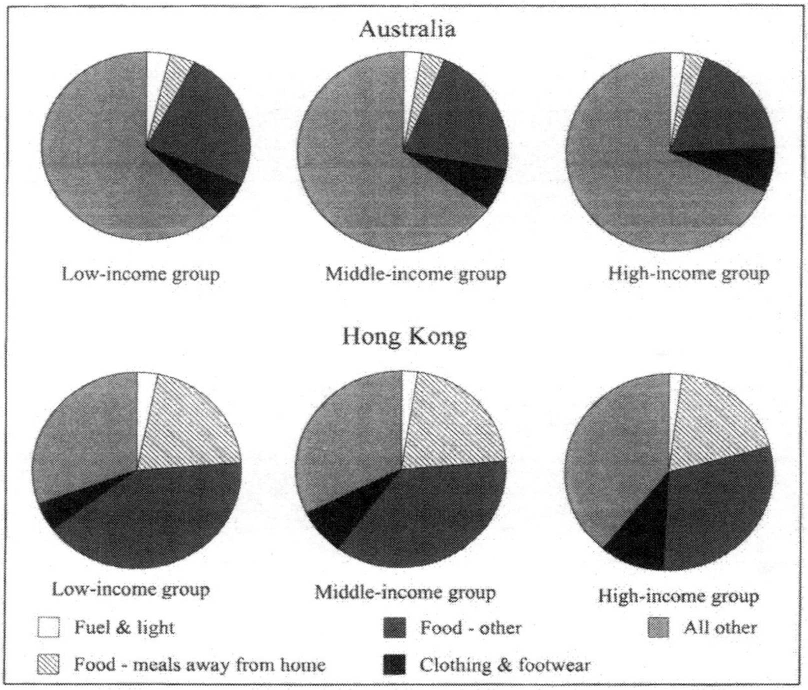

Figure 4 Expenditure shares excluding housing in Australia and Hong Kong.

Source: See Appendix.

There is thus a striking contrast between the picture shown by a bilateral comparison of the patterns of household spending of different income groups in the two countries, and that shown by a comparison of their real income levels

22 For details of sources see the Appendix.

23 As would be expected, the ratio of 'all other' expenditure to expenditure on food also rises over time for any given income group. In the case of Hong Kong, this ratio increased from 66.6 per cent in 1979/80 (Hong Kong Census and Statistics Department (1981, Appendix 7)) to 74 per cent in 1989/90.

at so-called international prices. In the one case, the differences are extremely large; in the other, they are negligible. The contrast does not mean that the ICP comparison is 'wrong', in that the result could be corrected by the substitution of additional or more precise estimates of particular expenditures or prices. It is rather that the ICP type of comparison is *impossible* for the reasons carefully stated by Keynes.

The central point is really quite a simple one. The 'real' value of a money income can only be measured in terms of the goods and services which could be purchased in the markets where that income is actually spent, and cannot be affected by the structure of prices in other markets.

Although the comparative analysis of household expenditure at different income levels does not, of itself, indicate 'real' levels of income or the PPPs of different currencies, it may provide useful guidance on these matters. For example, the analysis exhibited in Figure 4 shows that the proportion of household expenditure devoted to 'fuel and light' was somewhat higher in Hong Kong than in Australia in all three of the income groups which are identified. Other sources reveal that the per capita residential use of electric power (which represents a high proportion of this expenditure component in both countries) is well over twice as great in Australia as in Hong Kong (OECD/IEA 1994a, 1994b). Taken together, these indicators reveal that the unit cost of power for domestic use is, relative to average incomes, much lower in Australia; and that the per capita quantity of power consumed was far higher in Australia.

7. 'Comparison-resistant' items

Of course, analyses of household expenditures cannot indicate relative real levels of spending in those areas of final demand for which the real level of consumption of individual households is not closely related to their expenditures. Important examples are the imputed rent of owner-occupied dwellings and publicly provided or subsidised education and health services.[24] These are, however, precisely the areas in which the ICP approach to inter-country comparisons of real income also encounters its most serious difficulties.

The difficulties in estimating real levels of expenditure on gross rents have already been discussed. In this case, it can be argued that the process of revaluation of the nominal expenditures recorded in the national accounts at international prices is circular and unnecessary. As the individual national estimates for imputed rents have been built up from information about the

24 These are not minor issues. In Australia in 1990, imputed rent was estimated to be 12.8 per cent of household disposable income, while government expenditure on health and education was 11.5 per cent.

physical stock of dwellings derived from censuses and housing surveys, the most reliable way of estimating relative real expenditures would be to utilise that information, and to use the national estimates of nominal values only for weighting purposes. In fact, the ICP attempts to make estimates of rentals for 'finely specified housing units', such as a country's rent for an apartment in a 20-year old multi-storeyed building, of 120 square metres, with central heating and one bathroom (Summers and Heston 1991: 330).

Summers and Heston recognise that an implication of this approach is that location effects on rentals are ignored, but that it is unclear how, even in principle, such an important effect should be treated. The scale of the potential errors that may result from the ICP treatment is illustrated in Figure 5, which compares the per capita 'real' expenditure on gross rents in selected OECD countries in 1990, as estimated in the OECD benchmark PPP study (OECD 1992). It is obvious that the relativities shown in the figure, like those shown for the 1985 benchmark in Table 2, are seriously awry, presumably because the rental deflators used to revalue nominal expenditures differ from the (mainly imputed) rental values which were used by the national accountants to estimate nominal expenditures in the first place.

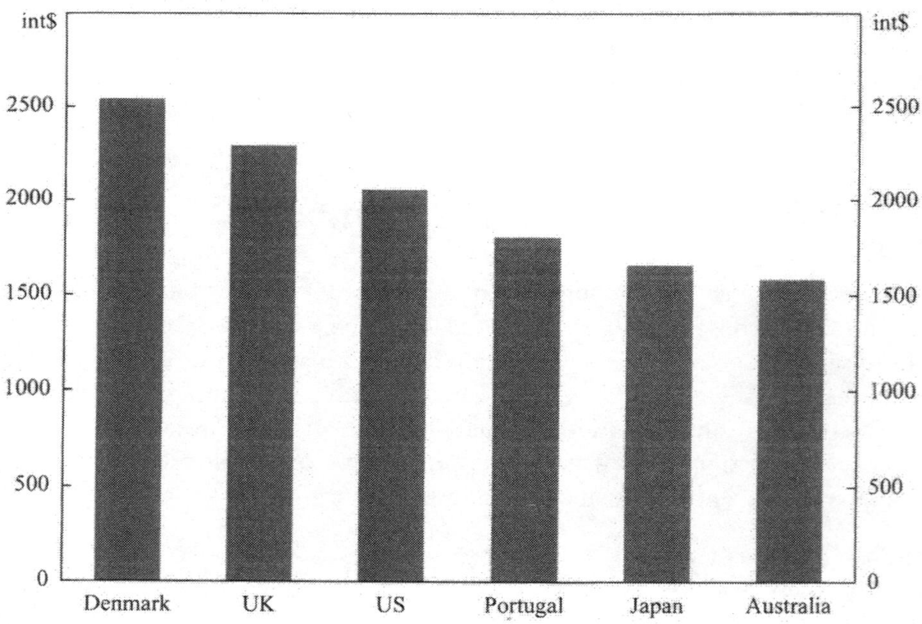

Figure 5 Gross rent in selected OECD countries

Source: See Appendix.

For example, in a bilateral PPP comparison between Australia and the United Kingdom for 1958, it was estimated that real expenditure on housing was 21 per cent higher in Australia than in the United Kingdom, whether measured in British or Australian relative prices (Haig 1968: 45). The implication of the OECD estimates that per capita expenditure on dwellings, on a PPP-adjusted basis, was 30 per cent *lower* in Australia in 1990 is implausible, particularly in the light of the commonly held view that investment in housing in Australia has made a disproportionately heavy call on domestic savings in recent decades.

According to the OECD estimates, per capita 'real' expenditure on dwelling rents was also higher in Japan than in Australia in 1990. This finding is at odds with general opinion in both countries, and with a mass of statistical evidence. In 1939 Colin Clark recorded, on the basis of 'the results of a recent survey', that the average floor area of houses in Queensland at that time was 1,275 square feet (118.5 square metres);[25] and the average floor area of new dwellings completed in Australia increased from 160 square metres in 1983 to 185 square metres in 1993.[26] By comparison, the average floor area of houses in Japan in 1988 was 89 square metres.[27] These figures suggest that the PPP-adjusted estimates of real expenditures on gross rents in Australia would have been far higher had they correctly captured the physical characteristics of the housing services to which the ICP comparisons must necessarily be restricted.[28]

The ICP principals also acknowledge the '...particularly thorny problem of somehow valuing services that are not priced in the market...' in areas such as general government, medical care and education (Summers and Heston 1991: 330). The solution that has been adopted, as in the national accounts, is to derive price parities for these categories on the basis of input comparisons. As in the dwellings case, however, this approach could be implemented more reliably by the direct use of available data on real inputs (e.g. numbers and utilisation of hospital beds, numbers of health professionals and para-professionals), rather than by attempting to deflate relevant components of expenditure by average bed-day costs or the average income of nurses.

An indication of the possible effect of the ICP procedure of revaluing nominal expenditures with measures of input prices, even in 'comparison-resistant' areas such as health care, is provided in Figure 6. These figures compare World Health Organisation (WHO) data on the numbers of physicians and nurses in relation to population in selected countries in the late 1980s with the 1985 ICP estimates of 'real' per capita final national consumption expenditure on health care in

25 From the Colin Clark papers, Fryer Library, University of Queensland.

26 As reported in the Australian Bureau of Statistics' *Australian Social Trends 1994* (ABS Cat. No. 4102.0: 156).

27 *Japan Statistical Year Book 1993-94*: 596. For a comparison of the size and equipment of housing between Sydney and Japanese cities, see Castles (1992: 92-121) also publised as chapter 21 in this book.

28 However, it is not relevant to an evaluation of the reliability of the ICP data that physical characteristics may be an inadequate measure of the quantum of housing services consumed.

the same countries. The latter estimates imply that per capita expenditures on health care, when measured in international prices, are over two and a half times greater in Japan than in Canada, and nearly twice as great in France as in Australia or New Zealand. Even in the absence of other information, these wide margins of difference would have appeared implausible; and the WHO data on the numbers of health professionals suggest that any differences may, in fact, be in the opposite direction to that indicated by the ICP estimates.

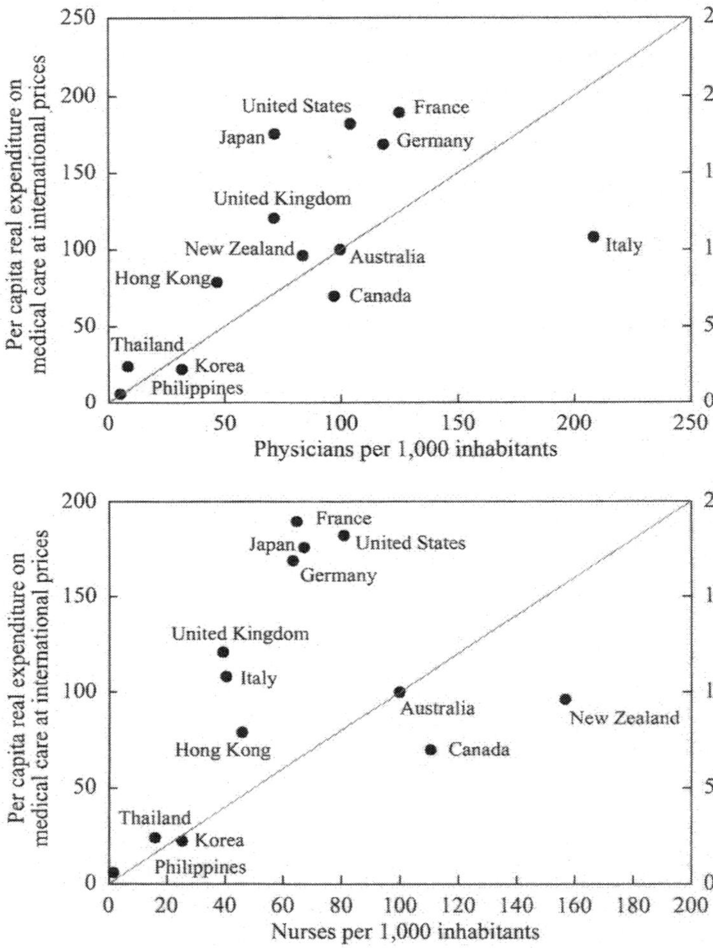

Figure 6 Real expenditure on medical care in 1985 v. numbers of physicians and nurses (Australia = 100)

Source: See Appendix.

8. The evidence from non-official surveys

In the two preceding sections, it has been shown that the estimate of Australia's relative real per capita product emerging from official PPP studies appears to be improbably low when compared with indications from other sources of information – from household expenditure patterns in relation to comparisons with Hong Kong, and from various quantity measures in relation to comparisons with a number of countries for components of expenditure which have been identified as 'comparison resistant'.

In this section, the ICP results are tested against those of three non-official studies – the celebrated 'Big Mac' index published annually by *The Economist* since 1986; the surveys of prices and wages around the globe that have been published by the Union Bank of Switzerland (UBS) at approximately three-year intervals since 1970; and a recent study of relative living standards using the revealed-preference principle, by Dowrick and Quiggin (1993).[29]

The Economist has explained that the Big Mac index was devised 'as a light-hearted guide to whether currencies are at a "correct" level.'[30] But its promotion as a measure of value has not been entirely in jest. The worldwide survey of the price of a standard hamburger at McDonald's is, in a sense, at the opposite extreme to the ICP. Instead of pricing hundreds of commodities, services and labour inputs which 'cover the universe of all items priced in any country' and then weighting the resulting price relativities with the aid of detailed dissections of expenditure, the price of a single commodity is taken as representative of all final prices (though many significant intermediate prices have entered into that final price, including those of several foodstuffs, packaging, various categories of labour services, fuel and power, commercial rents and so on).

Although presented as a price parity, the Big Mac index can be used to denominate real product. In fact, it is instructive to think of a league table based on alternative units of measurement. In Table 3, each country's average per capita income is expressed as an index in relation to Australia's: first on a conventional PPP basis; and second in terms of Big Macs.[31]

In nearly all cases, Australia's 1993 GDP was relatively higher (and in some cases very substantially higher) when expressed in Big Macs rather than in international dollars according to the World Bank's PPP measure. Hong Kong was, however, a significant exception: its per capita GDP was, when expressed in Big Macs, far higher than that of any other country shown in Table 3.

29 They used a revealed preference approach whereby observed consumption was assumed to be the preferred element in a given budget set.

30 *The Economist*, 15 April 1995: 78.

31 Using the April 1993 prices reported in *The Economist*, 17 April 1993: 83.

Also shown in Table 3 are the results of a similar computation from the most recent Union Bank of Switzerland survey (UBS1994). The 1993 nominal per capita GDP of each country has been divided by the nominal total cost, in the June quarter of 1994, of the basket of 111 goods and services, weighted by European consumer habits, which are included in the UBS survey. The resulting per capita GDPs, expressed in UBS basket units, have then been calculated as indices (Australia = 100). A similar procedure has been followed to calculate component indices for other groups of items in the UBS survey. These are charted in Figure 7.

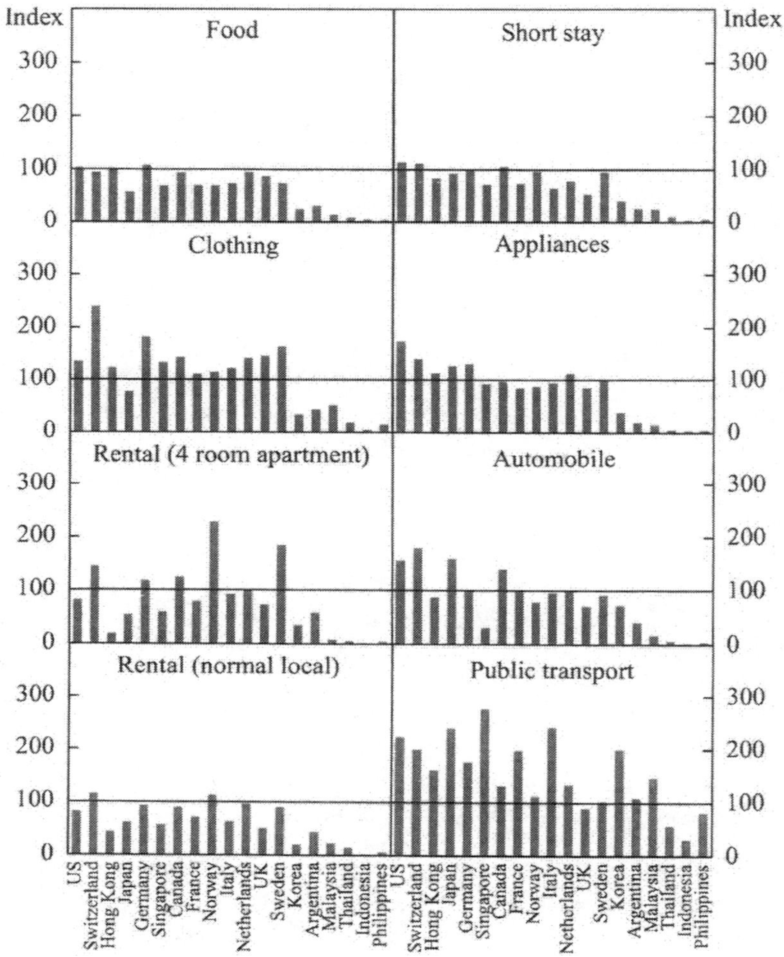

Figure 7 GDP per capita expressed as an index of selected baskets of goods and services (Australia = 100)

Source: See Appendix.

By comparison with the ICP, on which the official league table of real incomes is based, the 1994 UBS study was of modest dimensions, but it was not minuscule. More than 20,000 data items were collected by the UBS's correspondent banks and by its foreign branches and representative offices in 53 cities. In most cities the information was collected by two units working independently of one another. The entire body of data was then analysed by the Economic Research Department at the Bank's Head office in Zurich, thus ensuring a degree of central coordination which could not be matched by the ICP (which has responsibilities for various aspects of coordination located in New York, Washington, Paris, Philadelphia, Luxembourg, Geneva, Vienna and Bangkok). The results of this substantial survey, as reported in Table 3 and Figure 7, support two significant generalisations.

First, they confirm the indications from other evidence that Australia's relative real per capita income is understated in the official PPP estimates. Compared with *most* of the countries shown in the figure, the indicated level of per capita GDP is higher (and in several cases substantially higher) when measured in UBS basket units than when measured in international dollars at the PPPs revealed by the ICP. The significance of this conclusion is strengthened by the fact that the UBS basket is based specifically on European consumer habits, and would therefore be expected to be cheaper in European cities than a basket which took greater account of American, Asian or Australasian expenditure patterns for the purpose of comparisons with cities on those continents.[32]

Second, the purchasing power of per capita incomes in the various countries differs markedly between individual expenditure groups. These results, therefore, serve to reinforce the reservations that have been made in previous sections about the possibility of measuring, on a single scale, the average real incomes of communities living under very different conditions.

Given that communities do live under different conditions, one approach is to account for the revealed preference implicit in the choices. The results of the study using the revealed-preference principle are best reported in the words of one of the authors:

> ...we demonstrate that once proper account is taken of purchasing power, and also of leisure, the average standard of living in Australia is probably higher than in Japan. We base this assessment on detailed OECD data supplied by the Australian Bureau of Statistics...which gives a breakdown of 1990 GDP by prices and quantities for forty categories of goods and services.
>
> Our judgment that Australians are, on average, better off is based on the revealed preference principle. A resident of Australia who is earning average Australian hourly wages *could* have afforded to buy the Japanese

32 New Zealand was not represented in the UBS survey.

> bundle of goods and services if she had worked Japanese hours. The fact that she *actually* chose the Australian bundle is taken as evidence of a higher standard of living, particularly since the average resident of Japan could not have afforded the Australian bundle of goods, services and leisure. ...On this basis we make the judgment that Australia's average living standards rank somewhere in between tenth and twelfth in the OECD,... ahead of Japan (Dowrick 1993: 3).[33]

In other words, differences in the relative structure of prices between countries can nullify conclusions based on measures of GDP 'at international prices'.

Table 3 Alternative league tables

World Bank 1993			Big Macs 1993			UBS 1994		
Rank	**Country**	**Index**	**Rank**	**Country**	**Index**	**Rank**	**Country**	**Index**
1	United States	133.9	1	Hong Kong	161.0	1	Switzerland	131.2
2	Switzerland	127.7	2	United States	112.2	2	FRG	121.2
3	Hong Kong	117.2	3	Singapore	108.8	3	US	116.9
4	Japan	114.1	**4**	**Australia**	100.0	4	Canada	111.2
5	FRG	113.5	5	Japan	99.8	5	Austria	108.9
6	Singapore	110.7	6	FRG	99.4	6	Denmark	107.6
7	Canada	110.4	7	Canada	93.6	7	Belgium	106.5
8	France	105.1	8	Switzerland	90.7	8	Netherlands	104.7
9	Denmark	102.4	9	Austria	81.5	9	**Australia**	100.0
10	Austria	101.7	10	Netherlands	72.0	10	Sweden	93.5
= 11	**Australia**	100.0	11	Belgium	69.5	11	Japan	91.4
= 11	Belgium	100.0	11	Belgium	69.5	11	Japan	91.4
13	Italy	97.7	13	Denmark	68.3	13	Italy	89.2
14	Netherlands	97.6	14	Sweden	67.6	14	UK	82.8
15	UK	96.0	15	Italy	63.4	15	Singapore	78.0
16	Sweden	95.0	16	UK	63.1	16	Hong Kong	75.5
17	Korea	53.1	17	Malaysia	26.9	17	Argentina	35.8
18	Argentina	49.4	18	Korea	26.2	18	Korea	34.7
19	Malaysia	46.7	19	Argentina	22.0	19	Malaysia	19.0
20	Thailand	34.6	20	Thailand	10.4	20	Thailand	10.3
21	Indonesia	17.0	21	Indonesia	4.5	21	Indonesia	4.2

Note: Rankings refer to this subset of countries only.

Source: See Appendix.

33 As Dowrick (1993) acknowledges, an alternative explanation of observed differences in consumption and leisure is simply that Australians and Japanese might have fundamentally different tastes. However, he finds that variations in OECD consumption patterns are explicable as responses to the different price structures in each country.

9. Australia as a 'different' society

The impression of Australia as a 'different' society is found not only in studies of the revealed preferences of Australians, but in the impressions of visitors and temporary residents over the years. As one external commentator observed in 1985:

> Australia is not a carbon copy of other modern democracies, even of those with whom it has close and continuing relations and is commonly compared. ...Australia is different today; it was different in the 19th century. It was prosperous, very prosperous, when many nations now wealthy were not so at all. Australia retains some residual memory of its earlier great affluence – an affluence based on speculation, built on hazard and greed. While international statistical comparisons suggest that the very rich are now to be found elsewhere in the world, Australians are concerned...with what some see as a growing cupidity and materialism at home. A more fundamental concern, certainly, is whether Australia will continue to do well in the fiercely competitive economic world of the future, whether so easygoing a society will be able to accommodate itself to the demands of a new kind of industrial order...(Graubard 1985: v, viii).

There is evidence that, from the earliest days of the nation's great era of relative affluence, the Australian 'bundle of goods, services and leisure' was weighted more towards leisure than the bundles of other countries. In January 1857, Stanley Jevons, later to become one of the great economists, attended 'a very grand cricket match between Sydney and Melbourne...; it was in the Domain which from its natural beauty and splendid position and the immense number of orderly people in it presented one of the most beautiful spectacles I ever saw'. Writing to his brother in England, the 21-year-old Jevons went on to describe the huge attendances at the match, calculating that 'nearly one quarter of the population was at the match at one time and the business of the town was quite interrupted'. And then he concluded:

> I take this to be a sign, not of laziness, but that the people are so well today as to be able to spare more holidays and really to enjoy themselves more than the people of other countries (Jevons 1856).[34]

A similar conclusion was expressed more than a century later by the OECD (1972) in its first annual review of the Australian economy:

> No one can doubt that there are differences in social attitudes among countries...in the relative value placed on work and leisure, on money-making, on duty and discipline – *which cannot help but affect the rate of*

34 Jevons' observation is confirmed by the historian G Blainey: 'Sydney and Melbourne led the world in having Saturday afternoons off for working men and that meant they were free to attend sporting events' (*The Weekend Australian*, 17-18 June 1995: 26).

> *economic growth*. Australians, though no more consistent in their demands on life than other people, have for long leaned towards the view...that economic growth is not everything (OECD 1972: 28, emphasis added).

Jevons and the OECD reviewers clearly approved of the priority which Australians accorded to leisure and to the pursuit of 'non-economic' goals. But there has been another strand in the Australian national culture with which economists have been less comfortable, the manifestations of which may provide the key to the relatively slow apparent growth in real incomes during the 20th century which is exhibited in Figure 2. It was identified by WK (later Sir Keith) Hancock in his remarkable book *Australia*, published in 1930:

> The Australians have always disliked scientific economics and (still more) scientific economists. They are fond of ideals and impatient of technique. Their sentiments quickly find phrases and their phrases find prompt expression in policies. What the economists call 'law' they call anarchy. The law which they understand is the positive law of the State... the democratic State which seeks social justice by the path of individual rights. The mechanism of international prices, which signals the world's need from one country to another and invites the nations to produce more of this commodity and less of that, belongs to an entirely different order. It knows no rights, but only necessities. The Australians have never felt disposed to submit to these necessities. They have insisted that their Governments must struggle to soften them or elude them or master them... (Hancock 1930: 86).

The characteristic Australian distrust of market signals and dislike of what Hancock called 'scientific economics' (now known as 'economic rationalism') had its most lasting and influential expression in the celebrated Harvester Judgment in 1907 – just a few months before Keynes' public questioning of the validity of the official estimates of relative real wages in London, the Midlands and Ireland.

HV McKay, the dominant figure in the Australian agricultural implements industry had applied to Mr Justice Higgins, the new President of the Commonwealth Arbitration Court, for a declaration that the wages he paid were 'fair and reasonable', and that therefore his machines should be exempt from the excise duty on harvesters. Higgins rejected the application, on the grounds that the wages paid at the Sunshine harvester plant did not, in his opinion, provide for an unskilled labourer 'the normal needs of an average employee, regarded as a human being living in a civilised community'. Higgins was later to explain the reasoning which led him to this decision in the following terms:

> Many household budgets were stated in evidence, principally by house-keeping women of the labouring class; and, after selecting such of the budgets as were suitable for working out an average, I found that in Melbourne, the average necessary expenditure in 1907 on rent, food

> and fuel, in a labourer's household of about five persons was one pound twelve shillings and five pence, but that as these figures did not cover light, clothes, boots, furniture, utensils, rates, life insurance, savings, accident or benefit societies, loss of employment, union pay, books and newspapers, tram or train fares, sewing machine, mangle, school requisites, amusements and holidays, liquor, tobacco, sickness or death, religion or charity, I could not certify that any wages less than 42 shillings per week for an unskilled labourer would be fair and reasonable (Higgins 1915: 15).

As it happens, the information which provided the British Board of Trade with the capacity to calculate relative real wages in different districts of the United Kingdom can also be used, in conjunction with contemporary Australian data on prices in Melbourne, to estimate the relative level of the wage which Higgins believed was necessary to meet the minimum needs of an unskilled labourer and his family.

In Figure 8, the purchasing power over British and Australian food baskets of the wage rate specified in the Harvester Judgment of 10.5 pence per hour (42 shillings for a standard 48 hour working week) is compared with the purchasing power of the hourly wage of an engineering labourer at that time in London, Leicester in the English Midlands and Dublin. As the figure shows, the Harvester rate was, in real terms, *twice* the London rate and *three times* the prevailing rate in Dublin.

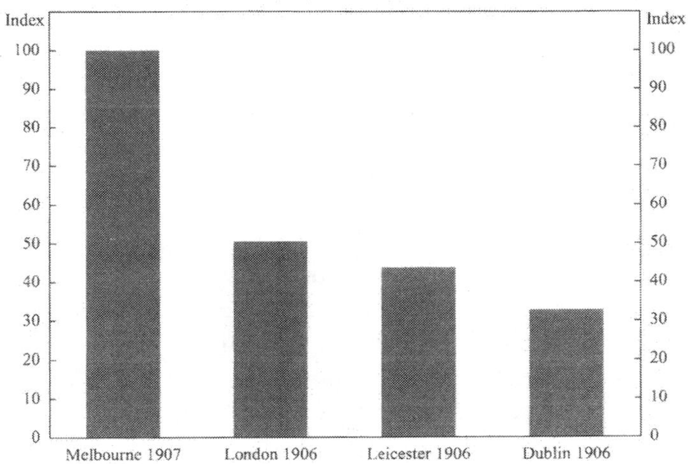

Figure 8 Purchasing power of unskilled labour (Melbourne, Harvester Judgment = 100)

Source: See Appendix.

The scale of the 'average necessary expenditure...on rent, food and fuel' for a family of five in Melbourne in 1907 was a matter of opinion, and the level which was judged by Higgins to be necessary was austere by the standards of the 1990s. But it was certainly not austere by the British standards at that time, and it was far above the standards which prevailed in the leading cities on the continent of Europe.

The real quantities of housing, food and fuel which could have been bought in Melbourne in 1907 with a weekly sum of 'one pound twelve shillings and five pence' were considerably greater than the quantities in the basket used by the British officials to judge the relative costs of living in different cities in the United Kingdom in 1908; and it would in any case have been impossible at that time for unskilled labourers in Britain (or anywhere in Europe) to earn a wage sufficient for the assessed needs of a family of five.

In Higgins' view – and it was a view which had the support of most Australian politicians at the time – an industry which could not afford to pay the level of wages that the Arbitration Court judged to be 'fair and reasonable' should not receive protection. The practical consequence of this view was that many Australian industries had to be supported by high and increasing levels of protection in order to survive and to pay the wage rates decreed by the Arbitration Court.

10. The league table before the wars

According to the estimates charted in Figure 2, Australia's level of real GNP per capita was only slightly higher than that of the United Kingdom in the years preceding World War I. Acknowledging that there are significant differences between the concepts being measured, this does not appear to be consistent with the large differences in real wage rates which were discussed in the preceding section and illustrated in Figure 8.[35]

The probable reason for the apparent inconsistency is that the relativities shown in Figure 2 are not correct. In previous sections of this paper, it was shown that average real incomes in Australia in the 1990s are probably substantially higher, relative to those in many other countries including the United Kingdom, than the conventional estimates on a PPP basis show. If this is the case, the relativities in the estimates which would be backcast to 1900 are equally astray.

35 Williamson (1991) puts the real wage rate for manufacturing workers in Australia 15 per cent above the UK real wage rate and 40-60 per cent above real wage rates in other European countries, but well below those of the United States and Canada. Williamson's comparative real wage data are based on national data for nominal wages and retail prices but then converted into comparable figures using PPPs for four benchmark years. They are thus subject to the problems discussed earlier.

And differences in the end-point relativities are only one of the possible sources of error in the long-period estimates. There would be serious hazards in the backward projection of national estimates of real product over long periods, even if the underlying information was of high quality and the changes in economic structure were modest.[36]

It follows that estimates of relative average real income levels in past periods can only be relied upon if they are built up from contemporary data, and that the use of year-by-year estimates of GDP at constant prices should be restricted to the identification of the profile of short-run changes. Over long periods, economic growth rates should be seen as summary measures of the apparent rate of movement which has been observed between successive 'snapshots', not as the means by which the scale of change between two distant years can be determined.

There is, however, an important advantage of the 'snapshot' approach to the measurement of relative real average incomes between countries and over time. The approach does not require that estimates be made of every individual expenditure component and every individual price parity – a procedure which, as we have seen, is difficult enough to achieve contemporaneously. Instead, it can rely on the approach which Ronald Walker suggested would prove to be more useful in any case: 'the comparative study of the actual content of typical family budgets of different classes in the relevant countries' (Butlin 1962: 10).[37]

Some preliminary estimates based on this approach were made for five countries in the pre-World War I period, using official family budget studies, and are exhibited in Figures 9 and 10. The results bring out very marked differences between the patterns of expenditure in, on the one hand, the United Kingdom and France and, on the other, the United States, Australia and New Zealand. The estimates also provide pertinent information on the relative positions and average levels between countries. These clearly suggest that the differences in real average incomes between the countries of the Old World and the 'NIEs'

36 For the period before the commencement of the official estimates, the Australian estimates of real product are derived from Butlin (1962). In that monograph Butlin states that 'any attempt to deflate series of gross domestic product and gross capital formation over long periods must be regarded with the greatest suspicion; our attempt is no exception' (31). Despite Butlin's emphatic disclaimer, Australian and international scholars have relied upon his estimates to assess the level of average Australian incomes, relative to those in other countries, in the relevant period.

37 In June 1995, the Australian Bureau of Statistics published *A Provisional Framework for Household Income, Consumption, Saving and Wealth* (ABS Cat.No.6549.0) which defined a conceptual map relating data in these fields, so as to lay the foundation for the further development of statistics concerning the economic wellbeing of households. It is in this area that the more cohesive development of consistent and relevant definitions and concepts, nationally and internationally, is most necessary in order to support the information needs of policy makers.

of those days were much larger than the presently accepted estimates, which have been derived as an outcome of the backward projection of modern PPP calculations.

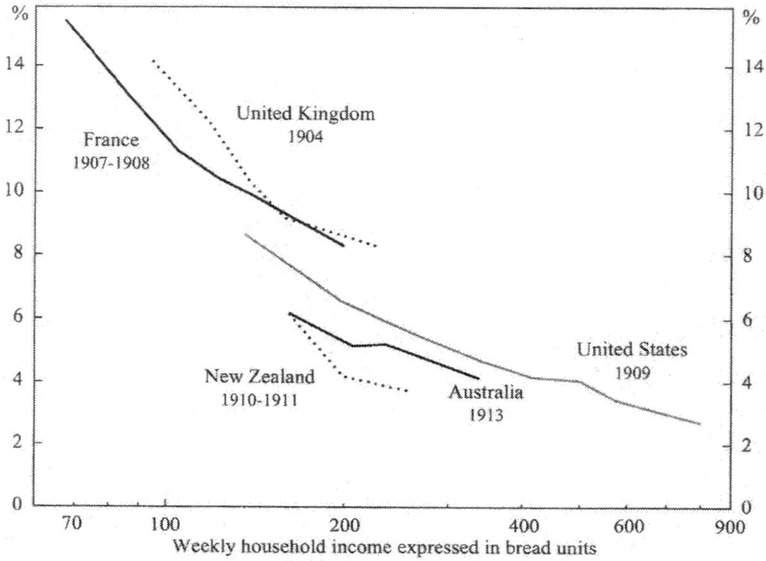

Figure 9 Expenditure on bread and flour as a percentage of income (1904-1913)

Source: See Appendix.

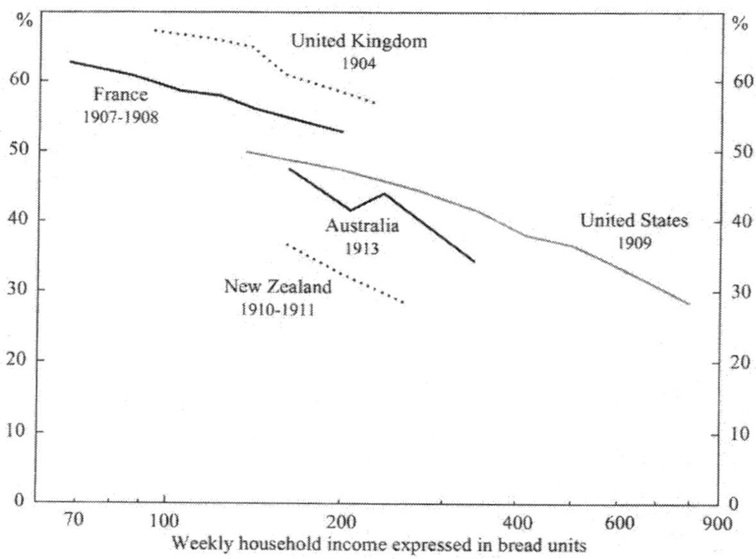

Figure 10 Expenditure on food as a percentage of income (1904-1913)

Source: See Appendix.

11. Conclusion

Our review of the available evidence about relative living standards and real incomes in the Australia of the 1990s reveals a need for great caution. Nonetheless, economists and national-accounting statisticians of the late 20th century have been comfortable with expressing diverse observations as averages, and then adjusting and manipulating those averages according to hypothetical assumptions – such as that prices are constant or that prices are the same as somewhere else or everywhere else. Although these simplifications are necessary if inter-country and inter-temporal comparisons of real incomes are to be made at all, it should not be forgotten that they not only involve summarisation (i.e. the loss of some part of the truth), but also the making of assumptions which do not hold in (and may often differ markedly from the facts of) the real world.

This need for caution combined with the results of the review makes it reasonable to conclude that the concerns that have their origin in Australia's position in the conventional league table are misplaced. The statistics are subject to measurement errors which are potentially large enough to invalidate the conclusions commonly drawn from them. Even if the measurement problems could be resolved there are important conceptual issues which would remain. The representation of the outcome of macroeconomic performance by a single measure involves an excessive degree of summarisation and loss of detail. Consequently, the policy issues surrounding Australia's comparative position and performance must be addressed within a multi-dimensional framework that acknowledges the serious and possibly fatal weaknesses of conventional statistical measures in capturing the scale and the subtlety of economic change. In particular, it must recognise the features which distinguish Australia from other modern societies.

Our review also shows that league tables for the early part of this century (often produced by backcasting current figures) are equally misleading. Australia, at that time, was a country with a small population and labour force relative to its abundant natural resources. Moreover, a distinctive feature of Australia was the setting of comparatively high real wages. Indeed, this was the mechanism by which the high real incomes generated in the resource-based industries were transferred to provide the owners and workers in many other industries with higher incomes than the PPP-adjusted value of what they had produced.

We have emphasised the statistical and conceptual problems in measuring the comparative position of Australia, but we would not seek to deny that there has been some considerable 'sliding down the international league scale' during this century. Yet again, however, the concerns expressed in reactions to the World Bank's league table seem, at least in part, to be misplaced. To start with the part where there are genuine reasons for concern, there is little doubt that attempts to protect economic factors from foreign competition and the cost of change has been a principal constraint on economic growth. To quote Gruen, growth was sacrificed because '...our social organisation tended to produce that outcome' (Gruen 1986: 193). However, two other factors have also been at work and do not give cause for concern because they are the direct outcomes of Australia's unique position early this century and of the responses of Australian institutions to that position. First, to the extent that Australians place different values on work and leisure than other countries and give a relatively high priority to those aspects of life which are not included in the conventional national accounts, *measured* growth rates will be relatively low. Second, Australia provided its contribution to the international process of convergence of per capita income by choosing to distribute the resource wealth through relatively high real wages and encouraging a wider dispersion of resources through fast population and labour force growth. In fact, this, more than any other factor, may explain the relatively slow growth in average per capita real incomes in Australia through this century.

Appendix: Data sources for figures and tables

Figure 2 Real GNP per capita in selected economies (1900-1993)

Estimates of 1993 real GNP per capita are PPP estimates sourced from the *World Bank Atlas 1995*: 18-19). For recent years these estimates are backcast for Australia, Canada, France, Germany Italy, Japan, Netherlands, Norway, Sweden, Switzerland, UK and US using growth rates in GDP per capita calculated using estimates of population and constant price GDP reported in IMF (1995). The estimates were then backcast from 1989 using movements in GDP reported in Tables A6, A7 and A8 of Maddison (1991) and movements in population reported in Tables B2, B3 and B4 of Maddison (1991). For the remaining countries, comparable series were produced using the sources reported in the list below.

Figure 3 Relative prices and relative quantities consumed in Australia and Hong Kong in 1985

Relative quantities consumed were derived from Table 1 of UN (1994), setting relative GDP in each country to 100. Relative prices were derived from Tables 10 and 1 of the same publication, by dividing the nominal expenditures in Table 10 by the quantities reported in Table 1, setting the relative price of GDP to 100.

Figure 4 Expenditure shares excluding housing in Australia and Hong Kong

Australia: ABS Household Expenditure Survey 1988-89 (ABS Catalogue Nos 6530.0 and 6535.0). Hong Kong: Hong Kong Year Book 1989-90, Expenditure Weights.

Figure 5 Gross rent in selected OECD countries

Gross rent and water charges item of OECD (1992, Table 1.3).

Figure 6 Real expenditure on medical care in 1985 v. numbers of physicians and nurses (Australia = 100)

Data on per capita real expenditure on medical care at international prices were obtained from UN (1994,Table 3). Data on physicians and nurses per 1,000 inhabitants were obtained from the World Health Organisation.

Figure 7 GDP per capita expressed as an index of selected baskets of goods and services

Nominal GDP estimates in national currencies for second quarter 1994 were obtained from IMF (1995). Latest IMF (1995) nominal GDP estimates were for Singapore, Argentina, Indonesia and Malaysia were for 1993; and 1992 for Luxembourg and Thailand. Estimates for 1992 and 1993 were converted to 1994 prices using consumer price indices published in IMF (1995). These estimates were divided by population estimates for each country, obtained by extrapolating 1993 mid-year population estimates by the average population growth rate for the period 1988 to 1993, with population statistics sourced from IMF (1995). For Hong Kong, 1993 GNP per capita in US$ was obtained from World Bank (1995), converted to local currency, and converted into 1994 prices using consumer price index data sourced from *Hong Kong Monthly Digest* of *Statistics,* March 1995 (Census and Statistics Department, Hong Kong).

Prices of commodity baskets were obtained from Union Bank of Switzerland (1994). Nominal GDP per capita was then divided by the cost of each of these baskets, with the resultant index set to 100 for Australia. The clothing index is a weighted average of the separate indices for women's clothing (60 per cent weight) and men's clothing (40 per cent weight). Automobile cost includes taxes and the cost of a 15,000-kilometre service. The short stay basket is made up of an overnight stay for two in a hotel, two evening meals with a bottle of red house wine, a taxi ride within the city centre, a rental car for half a day, cinema tickets for two, two 'Big Macs' and two public transport tickets.

Figure 8 Purchasing power of unskilled labour (Melbourne, Harvester Judgment = 100)

Australia: Commonwealth Bureau of Census and Statistics, Labour and Industrial Branch Report No. 2: 47.

UK: Report of an Enquiry by the Board of Trade into Working-class Rents, Housing and Retail Prices, Together with the Standard Rates of Wages Prevailing in Certain Occupations in the Principal Towns of the United Kingdom, Great Britain Parliament, Accounts and Papers (1908).

Derived as a geometric mean of indices of purchasing power over Australian and UK consumption baskets, with Melbourne set to 100.

Figure 9 Expenditure on bread and flour as a percentage of income (1904-1913) and Figure 10 Expenditure on food as a percentage of income (1904-1913)

Australia: Commonwealth Bureau of Census and Statistics, Labour and Industrial Branch Report No. 4: 13, 19, 26.

France: *Report of an Enquiry by the Board of Trade into Working Class Rents, Housing and Retail Prices, Together with the Rates of Wages in Certain Occupations in the Principal Industrial Towns of France*, Cd.4512(1909).

New Zealand: New Zealand Government Department of Labour, *Inquiry into the Cost of Living in New Zealand, 1910-11* (1912): 10, 13, 22. Flour consumption was estimated to be 30 per cent of bread consumption.

United Kingdom: *Report of an Enquiry by the Board of Trade into Working-class Rents, Housing and Retail Prices, Together with the Standard Rates of Wages Prevailing in Certain Occupations in the Principal Towns of the United Kingdom*, Great Britain Parliament, Accounts and Papers (1908).

United States: *Report of an Enquiry by the Board of Trade into Working-class Rents, Housing and Retail Prices, Together with the Standard Rates of Wages Prevailing in Certain Occupations in the Principal Towns of the United States of America 1909* (1911).

Table 1 GNP per capita at purchasing power parities in 1993 international dollars

World Bank (1995).

Table 2 Per capita real value of final expenditure on gross rents at international prices in 1985 US dollars

UN (1994).

Table 3 Alternative league tables

The World Bank 1993 ranking is sourced from World Bank (1995).

Country	Dates	Data Sources
Argentina	1900-50	Data for 1890, 1913, 1950 are available from Maddison (1993); exponential interpolation is used to produce an annual series
	1950-90	Penn world Table (Mark 5.6a)
	1990-93	IMF (1995)
Korea	1900-53	Interpolated series using data for 1890, 1913, 1950, 1973 from Maddison (1993)
	1953-90	Penn World Table (Mark 5.6a)
	1990-93	IMF (1995)
Thailand	1900-50	Interpolated series using data for 1890, 1913, 1950 from Maddison (1993)
	1950-91	Penn World Table (Mark 5.6a)
	1991-93	Asian Development Bank, Asian Development Outlook
Indonesia 1900-60	1900-60	Interpolated series using data for 1890, 1913, 1950, 1973 from Maddison (1993)
	1960-92	Penn World Table (Mark 5.6a)
	1993-93	IMF (1995)
Hong Kong	1960-92	Penn world Table (Mark 5.6a)
	1992-93	Asian Development Bank, Asian Development Outlook
Malaysia	1955-92	Penn World Table (Mark 5.6a)
	1992-93	IMF (1995)
Philippines	1900-50	Interpolated series using data for 1900,1913, 1929, 1938, 1950 from Maddison (1989)
	1950-92	Penn World Table (Mark 5.6a)
	1992-93	IMF (1995)
Singapore	1960-92	Penn world Table (Mark 5.6a)
	1992-93	IMF (1995)
New Zealand	1951-92	Penn world Table (Mark 5.6a)
	1992-93	IMF (1995)

For the Big Macs 1993 ranking, nominal GDP per capita in 1993 was calculated employing the same methods and sources used for Figure 7. These estimates were then divided by the local currency price of a Big Mac in 1993, sourced from *The Economist*, 17 April 1993: 83. 1994 Big Mac prices were used for Singapore and

Austria from *The Economist*, 9 April 1994: 92. 1995 Big Mac prices were used for Indonesia and Thailand from *The Economist,* 15 April 1995: 78. An index was then constructed with Australia set to 100.

The UBS 1994 ranking was calculated in the same manner and using the same sources that were employed in constructing the indices plotted in Figure 7. The relative cost of the UBS basket of 108 goods and services (excluding rents) in the different countries was adjusted to reflect rents by multiplying the cost of that basket by the UBS index of prices including rent and dividing by the UBS index of prices excluding rents.

References

Arndt, HW (1979). 'Colin Clark', *International Encyclopedia of the Social Sciences,* Vol. 8, Macmillan and Free Press, New York: 121-124.

Butlin, N (1962). *Australian Domestic Product Investment and Foreign Borrowing* 1861 to 1938-39 Cambridge University Press, Cambridge.

Castles, I (1992). *'Living Standards in Sydney and Japanese Cities: A Comparison'* in K Sheridan (ed.) *The Australian Economy in the Japanese Mirror*, University of Queensland Press, St Lucia: 91-121.

Clark, C (1951). *Conditions of Economic Progress,* 2nd Ed., Macmillan and Co Ltd, London.

Clark C (1938). *'Australian Economic Progress Against a World Background',* The Joseph Fisher Lecture in Commerce, given on 9 August 1938, Adelaide, Hassel Press, Adelaide. Cornish, S (1991). 'Edward Ronald Walker', *Economic Record,* 67(196): 59-68.

Dowrick, S (1993). 'Australia's Long Run Macroeconomic Performance: Living Standards, Productivity, Investment and Employment', paper presented to the University of Melbourne Conference on 'Economic Rationalism?: Economic Policies for the 90s', 15-16 February.

Dowrick, S and D Nguyen (1989). 'OECD Comparative Economic Growth 1950-85: Catch -up and Convergence', *American Economic Review,* 79 (5): 1010-1030.

Dowrick, S and J Quiggan (1993). 'Australia, Japan and the OECD: GDP Rankings and Revealed Preference', *Australian Economic Review* 1st Quarter: 21-34.

Graubard, S (1985). 'Preface', *Daedalus,* 144(1): v-xii.

Great Britain Parliament, Accounts and Papers (1908). 'Report of an Enquiry by the Board of Trade into Working-class Rents, Housing and Retail Prices, Together with the Standard Rates of Wages Prevailing in Certain Occupations in the Principal Towns of the United Kingdom'.

Gruen, F (1986). 'How Bad is Australia's Economic Performance and Why?', *Economic Record*, 62(177): 180-193.

Haig, B (1968). Real Product, Income and Relative Prices in Australia and the United Kingdom, Australian National University Press, Canberra.

Hancock, W (1930). *Australia*, Ernest Benn Limited, London.

Higgins, H (1915). 'A New Province for Law and Order, Industrial Peace Through Minimum Wage and Arbitration', *Harvard Law Review*, XXIX: 13-39.

Hong Kong Census and Statistics Department (1981). 'Report of the Household Expenditure Survey, 1979-80 and the New CPI System'.

IMF (1995). International Financial Statistics, May International Monetary Fund, Washington, DC.

Jevons, WS (1856), in R Black and R Konekamp (eds), *Papers and Correspondence of WS Jevons*, Vol. 2, London, Macmillan for the Royal Economic Society, 1972.

Keynes, JM (1909). 'The Method of Index Numbers with Special Reference to the Measurement of General Exchange Value', in *The Collected Writings of John Maynard Kaynes*, Vol XI, Economic Articles and Correspondence: Academic, The Macmillan Press Ltd, London, 1983: 49-156

Keynes, JM (1910). 'Board of Trade Index Number of Real Wages', in *The Collected Writings of John Maynard Keynes*, Vol. XI, Economic Articles and Correspondence: Academic, The Macmillan Press Ltd London, 1983: 180-182.

Keynes, JM (1930). *A Treatise on Money*, Macmillan and Co, London.

Kravis, I and R Lipsey (1990). 'The International Comparison Program: Current Status and Problems', NBER Working Paper No. 3304.

Kravis, IR Summers and A Heston (1978). International Comparisons Program: Current Status and Problems', NBER Working Paper No. 3304.

Kravis, IR Summers and A Heston (1978). *International Comparisons and Real Output and Purchasing Power*, Johns Hopkins, Baltimore.

Maddison, A (1982). *Phases of Capitalist Development*, Oxford University Press, Oxford.

Maddison, A (1989). 'The World Economy in the 20th Century', Development Centre Studies, OECD, Paris.

Maddison, A (1991). *Dynamic Forces in Capitalist Development, A Long-Run Comparative View,* Oxford University Press, Oxford.

Maddison, A (1993). 'Explaining the Economic Performance of Nations 1820-1989', Australian National University Working Papers in Economic History No. 174.

OECD (1972). *OECD Economic Surveys, Australia,* No. 1, December 1972, OECD, Paris.

OECD (1987). *Purchasing Power Parities and Real Expenditures, 1985,* OECD Department of Economics and Statistics, Paris.

OECD (1992). *Purchasing Power Parities and Real Expenditures, EKS Results,* Vol. 1, 1990, OECD Statistics Directorate, Paris.

OECD (1993). *Purchasing Power Parities and Real Expenditures, GK Results,* Vol. 2, 1990, OECD Statistics Directorate, Paris.

OECD/IEA (1994a). *Energy Statistics of OECD Countries, 1991-1992,* OECD, Paris.

OECD/IEA (1994b). *Energy Statistics and Balances of Non-OECD Countries, 1991-1992,* OECD Paris.

Reserve Bank (1995). *Productivity and Growth.* Reserve Bank of Australia.

Stein, H (1990). 'Who's Number One? Who Cares?', *Wall Street Journal,* 1 March 1990.

Summers, R and A Heston (1991). 'The Penn World Tables (Mark 5): An Expanded Set of International Comparisons, 1950-1988', *Quarterly Journal of Economics,* 106(2): 327-368.

Union Bank of Switzerland (1985), *Prices and Earnings Around the Globe, 1985 Edition,* Union Bank of Switzerland, Zurich.

Union Bank of Switzerland (1994). *Prices and Earnings Around the Globe, 1994 Edition,* Union Bank of Switzerland, Zurich.

United Nations and Commission of the European Communities (1994). *World Comparisons of Real Gross Domestic Product and Purchasing Power, 1985, Phase V of the International Comparison Program,* United Nations, New York.

University of Pennsylvania (1995). *Penn World Table (Mark 5.6a),* The Center for International Comparisons, University of Pennsylvania, 15 January.

Vernon Committee (1965). Report of the Committee of Economic Enquiry, Commonwealth of Australia, Canberra.

Walker, E (1939). 'International Comparisons of Standards of Living', in F Eggleston *et al.* (eds), *Australian Standards of Living*, Melbourne University Press: 45-64.

Williamson, JG (1991). *The Evolution of Global Labor Markets in the First and Second World Since 1830: Background Evidence and Hypotheses*, Harvard Institute of Economic Research Discussion Paper No. 1571, October.

Wilson, R (1946). 'Facts and Fancies of Productivity', Presidential Address to Section G, Australian and New Zealand Association for the Advancement of Science: 6-8.

World Bank (1995), *The World Bank Atlas*, Washington, DC.

15. Reporting on Human Development: Lies, Damned Lies and Statistics[1]

Ian Castles

Popular opinion is mistaken in attributing the *bon mot* about 'lies, damned lies and statistics' to the American humorist Mark Twain, and Twain himself was probably mistaken in attributing the jest to the British statesman Benjamin Disraeli. In fact, the lasting slur upon statistics and statisticians was first brought to public notice in 1892, by one of the leading statisticians of the day.

As a senior public servant, Robert Giffen, head of the statistical department in the British Board of Trade, would have thought it improper to use the word 'damned' in a public address. But he introduced his paper on 'International Statistical Comparisons', presented to the first meeting of the Australasian Association for the Advancement of Science (AAAS) in Hobart, with the following sentences:

> An old jest runs to the effect that there are three degrees of comparison among liars. There are liars, there are outrageous liars and there are scientific experts. This has lately been adapted to throw dirt upon statistics. There are lies, there are outrageous lies, and there are statistics. Statisticians can afford to laugh at ... jests at their expense... The statistics ... are not lies in themselves: it is only in the handling of them that the lying takes place.[2]

Measuring human development: The Australian contribution

In the late twentieth century the word 'damned' has become harmless, but 'lying' has become too strong a word for what most people see as a peccadillo: the misuse of statistics without any deliberate intent to deceive. So the title of today's Symposium offers us a softer alternative: there are facts, there are statistical estimates and there are fancies.

1 Originally published in Academy of the Social Sciences in Australia *Annual Symposium 1999*. Except where otherwise indicated, all figures and tables in this chapter are Castles' own.

2 Giffen, Robert (1892). 'International Statistical Comparisons' in Australasian Association for the Advancement of Science, *Report of the Fourth Meeting*, Hobart: 463.

This title also pays tribute to the late Dr (later Sir) Roland Wilson, who as Commonwealth Statistician of Australia presented the celebrated paper 'Facts and Fancies of Productivity' to a meeting of ANZAAS, the successor body to the AAAS, in Adelaide in 1946. And the theme of today's meeting provides us with the opportunity to remember the extraordinary contribution that Australian scholars have made during the past century to the measurement of economic progress and to the knowledge of the conditions required for its achievement.

As many in today's audience know, the world's first official estimates of national income were produced by Timothy Coghlan, Government Statistician of New South Wales, in the 1890s; and the first comprehensive comparisons of the relative real incomes of different countries were produced by Colin Clark, a former Fellow of this Academy, in the late 1930s.

Roland Wilson's contribution has not been adequately recognised. His paper on the measurement of productivity was a masterly survey of the 'pitfalls in the way of those who seek to chart the course of material progress in mere figures'. Emphasising that 'well-being' was wider than 'economic welfare', and the latter concept 'comprehends more than the market-valued wealth which is the refuge of some economists but the only stock-in-trade of the economic statistician', Wilson went on to explore the reasons for 'the gradual divergence of wellbeing from productivity':

> Another example ... is the growing tendency for work to become play, and thus to fall outside the statistician's measurement of productivity. With greater leisure more 'non-economic' work is done at home, such as household repairs, gardening and simple manufacture. Moreover, it is probably true that larger numbers of people spend longer hours in unpaid activity for charitable and social betterment purposes ...[3]

Another major Australian contributor to the recognition of the richness and variety of 'human development' was Wilson's predecessor Charles Wickens. In his paper 'Human Capital', presented to the ANZAAS conference in Wellington in 1923, Wickens recalled Oliver Goldsmith's reference to the 'hastening ills' which befall lands 'where wealth accumulates and men decay'. He questioned 'whether, as a matter of fact, the net result of such a process would not be a diminution of wealth in the proper sense', and asserted that there could 'be no worse policy in any community than that under which the health of the citizens is sacrificed to the increase of material goods'. According to Wickens' estimates, the value of Australia's 'human capital' was about 'three times the whole of the material capital, both private and public'.[4]

3 Wilson, Roland (1947). *Facts and Fancies of Productivity*, Melbourne: 19.

4 Wickens, Charles H (1924). 'Human Capital' in *Report of the AAAS* (Wellington): 536-554.

The dangers of international statistical comparisons: Robert Giffen, 1892

In his address to the AAAS in 1892, Robert Giffen argued that 'knowledge of the condition and growth of communities in the mass' was 'unattainable except by statistics'. But he wished to bring to attention 'the principal dangers in the handling of statistics to which the inexpert, and some of us perhaps who think we are expert, are exposed, through the too ready comparison with each other of figures which apparently are applied to facts of a like kind, but which really cover dissimilar facts'. With the 'extensive development of statistical abstracts, hand-books, year-books, manuals, dictionaries, statistical atlases and such like works of reference', there was a special need to be alert to these dangers in the field of international statistical comparisons:

> Accustomed to see quantities, which are really dissimilar in kind, placed together under the same heading, which is done primarily for the mere purpose of reference, we come to neglect the dissimilarity in our speech, and, by and by, in thought... The numbers of ... production, imports and exports, and money wages in different communities are compared as if they in all cases meant the same things, and without any preliminary discussion of what the figures really do mean. All this is essentially mischievous, and is contrary to the most elementary lessons in the study of statistics. It is the part of the student to re-act against the temptation to which he is exposed to use works which are only good for reference in this haphazard fashion.[5]

Giffen supported his argument with a wealth of examples. He showed that comparisons of school populations in different countries often failed to take into account the differences in length of the school year; comparisons of crime rates ignored differences in the efficiency of police services; comparisons of wage levels glossed over differences in the occupational mix of the labour force and in the 'purchasing power of money in different places'; and comparisons of aggregate wealth needed to be 'accompanied by statistics of relative income ... and the like information'. All such comparisons were therefore vulnerable to the 'short cuts of the amateur partisan':

> All the leading branches of statistics without exception ... give numerous illustrations of the dangers of taking ... figures ... from dictionaries or works of reference at haphazard for international comparison... [T] he figures as such may be right enough ... but [their] exact meaning ... may require a great deal of elucidation... There are ... many errors

5 Giffen, Robert (1892). *Op cit*: 464.

> [in circulation] respecting the conditions of most communities, partly derived from and partly nursed by, the rash use of statistics with a more or less conscious bias towards a desired conclusion.[6]

At the end of the twentieth century, our statistical measures of wellbeing and of human development are far more advanced than they were a century ago, but it is a moot point whether there has been a corresponding advance in society's understanding of itself. To an extent that Giffen would have regarded as unimaginable a century ago, packaged information has displaced scholarship as the source of knowledge about the world in which we live.

Monitoring human development: The eclipse of the social sciences

It was easy for Robert Giffen to include himself among those 'who think we are expert'. He was the leading official statistician in the world's leading trading nation, at the zenith of British power and influence. Within weeks of his return from Australia, he was elected a Fellow of the Royal Society of London.

In the same year, one of Britain's leading academic statisticians, Karl Pearson, published *The Grammar of Science*, a classic work which made large claims for statisticians (including social statisticians) as scientists:

> The field of science is unlimited... *The unity of all science consists alone in its method, not in its material*... The facts may belong to the past history of mankind, to the social statistics of our great cities, to the atmosphere of the most distant stars, to the digestive organs of a worm, or to the life of a scarcely visible bacillus. It is not the facts themselves which form science, but the method in which they are dealt with.[7]

In the 1990s, social statisticians can no longer 'afford to laugh at ... jests at their expense'. Robert Giffen turned out to be the last social scientist to be elected to the academy which in earlier years had welcomed: William Petty, author of the first estimates of national income; John Graunt, the first demographer; Robert Malthus, the pivotal figure in the history of population studies; and Stanley Jevons, the 'first economist effectively to introduce index-numbers of prices into Monetary Science'.[8]

---

6 *Ibid*: 486.

7 Castles, Ian (1998). 'The Methods of the Social Scientist', in Australian Research Council *Challenges for the Social Sciences and Australia*: 2. 295-6 (emphasis in original).

8 Keynes, JM (1930). *A Treatise on Money*: 1. 80.

The UNESCO/ICSU world conference on science: Budapest, June 1999

The closing of ranks against social scientists by one of the world's oldest and most prestigious academies symbolises a strange paradox of the twentieth century. At its end we are told, rightly, that we live in an 'information society', and that the fostering of a 'knowledge economy' offers the only way forward for countries such as Australia whose present prosperity is supposed to have been built upon a wealth of natural rather than human resources. Yet there is less recognition than there was in Giffen's day that 'knowledge of the condition and growth of communities in the mass' is 'unattainable except by statistics'.

The place of the social sciences in UNESCO provides a case in point. Julian Huxley, the Organisation's foundation Director-General (and a Fellow of the Royal Society), declared in 1947 that 'Science in UNESCO's program ... must be taken to include all aspects of the pursuit and application of the organised knowledge of phenomena'.[9]

Social scientists might therefore have expected that UNESCO would lead the way in recognising the value of their disciplines: it is certainly not obvious that 'the social statistics of our great cities' are less worthy of scholarly attention than 'the digestive organs of a worm'.

But in the 1990s UNESCO gives scant recognition to the place of the social sciences in 'the pursuit and application of the organised knowledge of phenomena'. Earlier this year, its Director-General, Federico Mayor, gave the following explanation of UNESCO's decision to join with the International Council of Science (ICSU) to convene the World Conference on Science (WCS):

> Science reigns triumphant. Never has it been so powerful and influential. It has conquered diseases which have decimated whole populations. It has abolished exhausting physical labour and wearisome repetitive tasks. It has vanquished distance and pushed back the frontiers of knowledge of the infinitely large and the infinitely small, in both the inanimate and the living world...
>
> [But] ... humanity has the right to ask science to give priority into processes of global disruption and ways of coping with them. What's more, all citizens have the right to ask science to further our understanding of the mechanisms of inequality and exclusion which are gradually undermining peace and democracy... One major purpose of this meeting [the WCS] will be to see that the benefits of science

9 Huxley, Julian (1947). *UNESCO: Its Purpose and its Philosophy*: 34.

> go primarily to all those who have hitherto been unreached. Their conditions can only improve if they have access to the mighty power of science.[10]

There was no suggestion that there might be a place for political scientists, historians and economists in promoting 'our understanding of the mechanisms of inequality and exclusion', nor recognition that the establishment of the conditions of economic progress and human development might be a more complex matter than giving all citizens 'access to the mighty power of science'.

One of the preparatory documents for the WCS ('aimed at facilitating the understanding of the draft Agenda') assured prospective participants that 'Scientific research is increasing our knowledge and ability to understand complex systems and processes in an ever-wider range of scale in space and time'. But the UNESCO/ICSU Secretariat that prepared the document had a limited understanding of the complex systems and processes of human societies, as the following extract reveals:

> Growing inequalities on all fronts ... today beset the world. The patterns of disparities are now more complex and contrasted. As one of many instances that illustrate the situation on a global scale, we recall that 20 per cent of humankind shares 86 per cent of the total private consumption. Within and between countries the benefits of education, culture, health services and other factors of human and social well being are ever more unequally distributed.[11]

At its final session, the Conference approved a Declaration proclaiming that global problems such as poverty, environmental degradation and inadequate public health were associated '*in particular* ... with population growth', and urging 'Governments and scientists of the world [to] address ... the *increasing* inequalities in health across different countries'.[12] No empirical evidence was provided for these highly debatable propositions.

The UNDP's *Human Development Report*

There was, however, one statistical 'fancy' in the WCS documentation, reported as if it was a fact: '20% of humankind shares 86% of the total private consumption'. This statement was obviously based on the UNDP's *Human Development Report 1998*, which claimed that:

10 Mayor, Federico (1999). 'Science to what purpose?' *The UNESCO Courier*, May: 9.

11 World Conference on Science (1999a). *Introductory Note to the Science Agenda – Framework for Action*: 1.

12 World Conference on Science (1999b). *Declaration on Science and the Use of Scientific Knowledge*. (emphasis added).

> Globally, the 20% of the world's people in the highest-income countries account for 86% of total private consumption expenditures – the poorest 20% a miniscule 1.3%.[13]

In other words, private consumption per capita in the rich countries was *66 times* greater than in the poorest countries. A chart on the opposite page of the report, headed 'Consumption is distributed inequitably', showed the 86 per cent allegedly shared by the 'richest 20%' in green, the 12-13 per cent shared by the 'middle 60%' in white and the 1.3 per cent of the 'poorest 20%' in black.[14]

The final chapter of last year's *Report*, headed 'Agenda for Action', asked rhetorically 'What would happen if the trends in consumption of the past 25 years were to continue for another 50? Where would that leave the world in the mid-21st century?' The answer, in part, was as follows:

> The consumption of the fifth of the people in the world's poorest countries would still be well under $2000 – not even 3% of the rich country average at that time and under 10% of rich country levels today.[15]

The 'not even 3%' figure tells us that in 50 years time, if the trends of the past 25 years continue, consumption of the fifth of the world in the rich countries would still be over *30 times* greater than that of the fifth of the world in the poorest countries.

Yet on the back of its front cover, the 1998 *Human Development Report* tells its more vigilant readers that one of the stacks of blocks featured on the cover represents the ratio of the consumption levels of 'the 20% of people who live in the richest countries' to that of those of 'the 20% of people in the poorest countries'. This ratio is given as *'16 times as much'*.[16]

The difference between the ratio of 16:1 shown in the explanation of the 'stack of blocks' and the ratio of 66:1 given in the main text of last year's *Human Development Report* presumably arises because the former figure allows, and the latter figure does not allow, for differences in price levels between countries. The discrepancy is not a trivial one: yet the officials of the peak science bodies that prepared the documentation for the WCS, who reported as fact that the world is beset by 'growing inequalities on all fronts', were apparently unaware of its existence.

---

13 UNDP (1998). *Human Development Report 1998*: 2.

14 *Ibid*: 3.

15 *Ibid*: 86.

16 *Ibid* (emphasis added).

The UNDP's *Human Development Report 1999*, which was released ten days after the WCS concluded its deliberations, repeated the claims about global inequalities which had attracted headlines in earlier years. Under the heading 'Stark disparities between rich and poor in global opportunity', a chart showed the 'Richest 20%' had 86% of 'world GDP', the 'Middle 60%' had 13 per cent and the 'Poorest 20%' had one per cent of 'world GDP'.[17] As GDP was defined in the 'Definitions of statistical terms' as 'The total *output* of goods and services for final use *produced* by an economy ...',[18] the *Report* gave the clear impression that the statistics quoted related to *real* output. In fact these percentages, like the similar figures relating to consumption expenditure in the 1998 *Report*, relate to the *nominal* value of production in national currencies, converted to a common currency (US dollars) on the basis of prevailing exchange rates.

These comparisons are spurious, as is apparent from the fact that in 1996 the UNCTAD secretariat, using data provided by the HDR Office itself, estimated that the proportion of the world's GDP produced by the richest quintile of the global population – ranking countries by their GDP per capita (PPP$) – was 64.4 per cent in 1960 and 63.7 per cent in 1991.[19]

The final chapter of the *Human Development Report 1999* recalled the report of the Pearson Commission in 1969:

> Nearly 30 years ago the Pearson Commission report began with the recognition that 'the widening gap between the developed and the developing countries has become the central problem of our times.' Today, global inequalities in income and *living standards* have reached *grotesque* proportions. The gap in per capita income (GNP) between the countries with the richest fifth of the world's people and those with the poorest fifth widened from *30 to 1 in 1960*, to *60 to 1 in 1990*, to *74 to 1 in 1995*.[20]

The emphasised words in this extract invite the conclusion that, over a 35-year period, per capita real expenditure on goods and services by the richest fifth of the world's people has more than *doubled* by comparison with that of the poorest fifth. Yet the figures from last year's report which have already been quoted imply that, if the trends of the past 25 years continue for the next 50 years, the corresponding ratio will be *halved* over the period. And the ratio of 74 to 1 between the top and bottom quintiles in the latest report does not sit easily with the ratio of 16 to 1 for 'overall consumption' cited on the back of the cover of last year's report.

---

17 UNDP (1999). *Human Development Report 1999*: 2.

18 *Ibid*: 254 (emphasis added).

19 UNCTAD (1996). *The Least Developed Countries: 1996 Report*: V.

20 UNDP (1999). *Op cit*: 104-05 (emphasis added).

These massive contradictions arise from the mixed use, without explanation, of nominal (constant prices and constant exchange rates), nominal (current prices and current exchange rates) and real (international prices) data on output, income and expenditure in the statistics in the *Human Development Report*.

The contradictions are equally apparent in the confused presentation of data on energy use. For example, a table in the latest report[21] presents, for each of over 120 countries, the 'Commercial energy use: GDP output per kilogram (US$) 1996'. It is explained in a footnote that the ratios represent the 'Estimated real GDP (at 1987 prices) divided by kilograms of oil equivalent of commercial energy use'. No indication is given, either in the table or elsewhere, that '*real* GDP (at 1987 prices)' in 1996 means '*nominal* GDP in national currencies in 1996, revalued at the average prices in the specified country in 1987 and converted into $US at the exchange rate which prevailed in 1987'. As the 'Definitions of statistical terms' in the report define 'GDP' as 'The total *output* of goods and services for final use produced by an economy',[22] most readers would infer that the ratios are comparisons of energy use in relation to output – that is, of energy efficiency.

In fact, the Human Development Report Office itself is (or was) under the same impression. In the 1994 report it was claimed that the energy use was very inefficient in many developing countries:

> There is tremendous scope for reducing energy input per unit of output. For example, the energy consumed for every $100 of GDP is 13 kilograms of oil equivalent in Japan, 18 in Germany, *35 in the United States*, 50 in Canada and 254 in Romania. Energy use is *even more inefficient* in developing countries: as high as *187 kilograms* of oil equivalent for every $100 of GDP *in China*...[23]

The claim that more than five times as much energy is used per unit of GDP in China as in the United States is clearly erroneous. It may be compared with estimates by Angus Maddison. In *The Chinese Economy in the Twentieth Century*, under the heading 'The analytical relevance of PPP conversion', Maddison states that

> My own estimates... suggest that *China consumes... less* [energy per unit of output] *than... the United States*...[24]

As in previous years, the claims in *Human Development Report 1999* that global inequalities were rising and had reached 'bizarre proportions' received massive

21 *Ibid*: 201-204.

22 *Ibid*: 254 (emphasis added).

23 UNDP (1994). *Human Development Report 1994*: 18 (emphasis added).

24 Maddison, Angus (1998). *Chinese Economic Performance in the Long Run*. Paris: OECD: 154 (emphasis added).

and uncritical coverage in the world's media. As well as publishing extended reports from their own correspondents at the Canberra launch, several Australian newspapers reproduced equally uncritical reviews from overseas. A London correspondent's report claiming that 'the gap between rich and poor widens inexorably' was reported in Melbourne under the heading 'The vacuum at the heart of the new world disorder' and in Canberra under the heading 'Putting morality into the globalisation equation'. Other headlines included 'Massive wealth divide exposed', 'Poverty gap grows wider', 'Globalisation brings further world injustice', 'Let's abandon the race to the bottom' and (from a Chicago correspondent) 'Rich getting richer as poor nations struggle on fringes of the global village'.[25]

Succeeding sections of this paper will question the validity of the statistical evidence that underpins these claims of ever-widening inequality. This is not to doubt the existence of a *wide* gap in average living standards between rich and poor countries, nor to question that this gap widened in the early phases of modern economic growth. Most economic historians have recognised such a phenomenon, and have seen it as an ineluctable consequence of the fact that modern economic growth had to begin somewhere.

But it is fanciful to suppose that inter-country inequalities were still widening in the final decade of the millennium. The persistence of the myth in the face of massive statistical evidence to the contrary says much about the state of the social sciences in today's world.

Colin Clark and the discovery of 'the gap'

I have already referred to Colin Clark's pioneering comparisons of the relative real incomes of different countries, which were published in *The Conditions of Economic Progress* (1940). As Heinz Arndt has pointed out, this book, 'by supplying the first substantial evidence of the gulf in living standards between rich and poor countries, helped awaken Western opinion to the problems of underdevelopment'.[26] Writing in the late 1930s, Clark found the world to be

> ... a wretchedly poor place. ... Oft-repeated phrases about poverty in the midst of plenty, and the problems of production having already been solved if only we understood the problems of distribution, turn out to be the most untruthful of modern cliches.[27]

25 *The Age* (Melbourne) and *The Canberra Times*, 11 July 1999.

26 Arndt, HW (1990). 'Colin Clark as a Development Economist' in *World Development*, 18, 7: 1046.

27 Clark, Colin (1940). *The Conditions of Economic Progress*: 2-4.

Angus Maddison, then aged 14, read the Australian economist's book in the public library near his home at Darlington, Durham. He was 'fascinated at the way [it] quantified what was going on in so many countries' and, in a memoir published in 1994, acknowledged its 'lasting effect' on his subsequent research agenda'.[28] In the Kuznets Lectures at Yale University in 1998, Maddison paid tribute to Colin Clark's *magnum opus*:

> At the time that [*The Conditions of Economic Progress*] appeared it was quite sensational in its breadth of perspective, and it demonstrated clearly the usefulness of a quantitative approach in clarifying the dimensions of economic performance and potential and the wide divergence between countries.[29]

With hindsight, it is easy to equate the gap that Clark identified with the 'north/south gap' which the Pearson Commission identified 30 years later as 'the central problem of our times'. But this is a simplistic view. Colin Clark's statistical snapshot did indeed show that there was a wide gulf between average incomes in the countries and those of poor countries in the inter-war years, but his painstaking assembly and analysis of the empirical evidence enabled him to explain this gulf within the context of a comprehensive theory of economic development.

Clark's recognition that 'the gap' was not immutable has been confirmed by the striking changes in relativities that have occurred in the six decades since the publication of his book. For example, the estimates which were of such interest to the young Angus Maddison showed average incomes in Brazil as higher than those in Italy; average incomes in Chile as higher than those in Japan; and average incomes in Argentina as higher than in all of these countries, and higher than in France, Germany, the Netherlands, Belgium and the Scandinavian countries.

In 1969, at the half-way point between the publication of *The Conditions of Economic Progress* and the present, the Pearson Commission still counted South Africa in 'the north', and Spain, Greece and Portugal in 'the south'. And, even now, the Population Division of the United Nations counts the Ukraine among the 'more developed regions' of the globe, and the Republic of Korea (with more than six times the average income of the Ukraine) among the 'less developed regions'.[30]

---

28 Maddison, Angus (1994). 'Confessions of a Chiffrephile' in *BNL Quarterly Review*, June: 435.

29 Maddison, Angus (1998). 'Pioneers of Empirical Macromeasurement, 1665-1995' (The Twelfth Kuznets Lectures): 9.

30 World Bank (1969). *Partners in Development*: 358-359.

Such a distinction could only be justified on historical or geographical criteria: Europe was, and for the most part still is, 'more developed' than Asia. But the consistent application of these criteria would require that Japan be included in the 'less developed regions'.

As well as significant changes between countries, the past two generations have seen dramatic changes in conditions within countries. Angus Maddison has told of his memories of the sickly and tubercular children of the unemployed in the north of England in the early 1930s, and of seeing 'nowhere so depressing [as Gateshead] ... until visiting Calcutta thirty years later'.[31] The poor of Britain are now less poor, but it would be a simplistic distortion of history to portray this change as 'the rich getting richer'.

The conditions of economic progress: Colin Clark's views

In *The Conditions of Economic Progress*, Colin Clark set out 'to give as much information as possible on the subject which after all concerns us most – namely to find the conditions under which we can hope for the greatest degree of economic progress in the future'.

Colin Clark's search for the conditions which could provide the *greatest* degree of economic progress in the future is easily open to the interpretation that he believed that societies should pursue the maximum possible growth in the output of material goods and services per head of population. Nothing could be further from the truth. Clark's view of the significance of 'economic growth' and of the role of the economist was well summarised in the following passage:

> The desire for greater leisure will of course conflict with the desire to increase output of goods and services; and security for particular individuals and groups is often incompatible with maintaining a full rate of economic progress. On these two issues, and on other conflicts between purposes which may arise, it is not the business of the economist to make a decision. It is the business of the community as a whole in its collective or political capacity. It is the duty of the economist to inform the community, carefully and objectively, of the gains and losses which will follow each decision... If to all of these questions economics is to give a scientific and quantitative answer, its foundations must be firmly

31 Maddison, Angus (1994). *Op cit*: 435.

> built upon the ascertained facts of the production and distribution of goods and services. Only by the disciplined study of the facts of the present and the past can we make judgements upon the future.[32]

The following list of qualifications to the notion that economic progress can be measured as the output of goods and services per head of population are taken from the opening pages of the first edition of *The Conditions of Economic Progress*:

> When ... we say that the average American enjoys greater economic welfare than the German, the German than the Italian, the Italian than the Indian, or present-day Europeans than their ancestors a century ago, we are perfectly well aware that the relative merits of these civilisations are not necessarily described by this economic ordering. A community making great economic progress may lack, and an economically unprogressive community may possess in full measure, the other values of life, such as a sense of contentment and of hope for the future...
>
> Leisure is an element in economic welfare, and more precisely we can define economic progress as the attaining of an increasing output of ... goods and services [which are customarily exchanged for money] for a minimum expenditure of effort, and of other scarce resources, both natural and artificial...
>
> A productive system leading to great inequalities of income between one person and another, or to great instability of income, even if it produces a higher output of goods and services, should be regarded as creating less economic welfare than a system from which these features are absent...
>
> For certain countries ... the quoted figures of national income require to be reduced for the effects of wasting of natural assets in minerals and timber. This applies more strongly in the case of agriculture. No calculations have ever been made in any country as to the extent of exhaustion of natural fertility of soils and pastures... Though it is unfortunately as yet impossible to give even the most approximate numerical valuation of this destruction of natural resources in different parts of the world, the reader must carry in mind throughout very serious qualifications when examining all agricultural and pastoral statistics.[33]

---

32 Clark, Colin (1940). *Op cit*: 18.

33 *Ibid*: 1-26.

Clark went on to criticise the 'rather ignorant sophistication' of economists who 'say that it is impossible to compare the level of income between two communities or between two individuals, or even between the same individual at different times', and defended the view that 'economic welfare can be compared between times and places':

> Purposive scientific generalisation differs from the meaningless accumulation of facts only in that the former uses the method of *comparison*. Comparisons of economic welfare between one community and another, one economic group and another, and between one time and another, are the very foundation of economic science. Anything which can be done to promote the scope and improve the technique of such comparisons is of fundamental importance.[34]

Despite Colin Clark's efforts to 'give as much information as possible' about 'the ascertained facts of the production and use of goods and services' and his explicit recognition that the world was 'a wretchedly poor place', his findings were not well understood except by some economists and statisticians. In an influential book published a quarter of a century later, with a foreword by Julian Huxley, a chapter entitled 'The cornucopian economists' explicitly nominated Colin Clark (as evidenced by his major book) among 'some economists and agronomists'

> ... who hold that the way to eliminate poverty in the world is to ignore population problems and concentrate solely on a more aggressive use of the earth and its materials, and that, given such use, there could be enough of everything to go around, no matter what numbers of people had to be supplied. It is necessary to discuss these men because, although their cornucopian theories do not seem to me to correspond to any observable facts of life in the vast, overpopulated, underdeveloped areas of the world, they are nevertheless sometimes eagerly hailed as economic optimists.[35]

Human development and economic growth

To the best of my knowledge, all recognised economists accept the substantial validity of Colin Clark's reasons for rejecting the notion that the maximisation of the marketable output of goods and services should be the chief end of human activity. Most economists in today's audience would therefore agree

34 *Ibid*: 26-27.

35 Appleman, Philip (1965). *The Silent Explosion*: 21, 141.

with the proposition, which has been argued in successive issues of the *Human Development Report* since the series began in 1990, that there is 'a tension between wealth maximization and human development'.

They would, however, be surprised to find that the reports regularly portray economists (and, indeed, other social scientists and 'policy-makers') as being 'obsessed' with the former objective to the exclusion of the latter. Consider, for example, the following extract from the 1994 *Report*:

> Only during the 20th century did the social sciences become increasingly concerned with economics – and economics with wealth rather than with people, with the economy rather than with the society, with the maximization of income rather than with the expansion of opportunities for people. Although the obsession with materialism may be recent, the preoccupation of economists and policy-makers with augmenting 'national treasure', in surplus trade balances, dates back at least to the mercantilists, who preferred to concentrate on material success rather than with the development of human lives.
>
> The dominant contemporary tradition of focusing exclusively on such variables as per capita gross national product or national wealth is a continuation – certainly an intensification – of the old opulence-oriented approach. And it is this low road of regarding humanity as an instrument of production – rather than the high road of acknowledging the universality of life claims – that fits well with the reputation of economics as a 'dismal science'.[36]

In fact, of course, economics was dubbed the '*dismal science*' not because its practitioners believed that humanity was merely an instrument of production, but for precisely the opposite reason. As I have pointed out elsewhere, the phrase had its origin in an 1849 article by the English historian Thomas Carlyle, who was prompted by reports of a strike by plantation workers in the West Indies to launch an attack on 'the dismal science' (emphasis in original) 'which ... reduces the duty of human governors to that of letting men alone'. Arguing that 'supply and demand' could not be 'the all-sufficient substitute for command and obedience among two-legged animals of the unfeathered class', Carlyle urged that 'pigs with pumpkins' be made to work 'with beneficent whip'.[37]

---

36 UNDP (1994). *Op cit*.

37 Carlyle, Thomas (1849). 'Occasional Discourse on the Negro Question', *Fraser's Magazine*, December [expanded version published separately as *Occasional Discourse on the Nigger Question*, 1853 and with the *Latter-Day Pamphlets*, 1858].

Carlyle's unpleasant diatribe would not be worth recalling, but for the spirited response it evoked from the economist John Stuart Mill, who portrayed Carlyle as 'revolving in an eternal circle around the idea of work':

> In opposition to the 'gospel of work', I would assert the gospel of leisure, and maintain that human beings *cannot* rise to the finer attributes of their nature compatibly with a life filled with labour... To reduce very greatly the quantity of work required to carry on existence is as needful as to distribute it more equally; and the progress of science, and the increasing ascendancy of justice and good sense, tend to this result.[38]

As I have shown, many twentieth-century economists have said much the same thing. The view that contemporary economists are obsessed with augmenting 'national treasure' reveals a fundamental misconception about the nature and purpose of economic studies.

Inter-country and gender inequalities in health

I have referred to the UNESCO/ICSU paper submitted to the WCS last June, which asserted that 'between countries, the benefits of ... health ... are ever more unequally distributed', and that 'the patterns of disparities [in general] are now more complex and contrasted'. I have also noted the *Declaration* subsequently endorsed by the conference that referred, *inter alia*, to 'increasing inequalities in health across different countries'.

If there is evidence to support these assertions, it might be expected that it would be found in the international comparisons of health status published annually in the WHO's excellent *World Health Report*.[39] I have not been able to find such evidence in the tables in the latest report showing changes over time. The tables certainly support the statement that there are large inequalities in health, but not the generalisation that those differences are increasing. Almost without exception, they point to the contrary view.

The most universal and widely used measure of changes in health status over time and between countries is, of course, the average expectation of life at birth. Table 1 shows, for the 33 countries which had a population of over 30 million in 1997, the UN Population Division's estimates of the average expectation of life in 1952 and in 1997 (strictly speaking, for 1950-55 and 1995-2000).[40]

---

38 Mill, John Stuart (1850). 'The Negro Question', *Fraser's Magazine*, February (emphasis in original).

39 World Health Organization (1999). *World Health Report*.

40 United Nations 1998. *World Population Prospects 1950-2050: The 1998 Revision*.

Table 1 Specified countries: Life expectancy at birth 1952-1997 (ranked by increase in life expectancy in years, 1952-1997)

	Population Millions	Life expectancy Years		Increase 1952-97	
				Years	% (a)
	1997	1952	1997	1952-97	1952-97
China	1244	40.8	69.8	29.0	64.4
Indonesia	203	37.5	65.1	27.6	61.3
Vietnam	76	40.4	67.4	27.0	60.0
Turkey	63	43.6	69.0	25.4	56.4
Pakistan	144	38.9	64.0	25.1	55.8
Korea, Republic of	46	47.5	72.4	24.9	55.3
India	966	38.7	62.6	23.9	53.1
Egypt	65	42.4	66.3	23.9	53.1
Myanmar	44	36.9	60.1	23.2	51.6
Iran	65	46.1	69.2	23.1	51.3
Thailand	60	47.0	68.8	21.8	48.4
Mexico	94	50.6	72.2	21.6	48.0
Bangladesh	123	36.8	58.1	21.3	47.3
Philippines	71	47.5	68.3	20.8	46.2
Colombia	40	50.6	70.4	19.8	44.0
Japan	126	63.9	80.0	16.1	35.8
Brazil	164	51.0	66.8	15.8	35.1
Spain	40	63.9	78.0	14.1	31.3
Nigeria	104	38.5	50.1	13.6	30.2
Italy	57	66.0	78.2	12.2	27.1
Congo, Democratic Republic of	48	39.1	50.8	11.7	26.0
France	58	66.5	78.1	11.6	25.8
Poland	39	61.3	72.5	11.2	24.9
Tanzania, United Republic of	31	37.0	47.9	10.9	24.2
Argentina	36	62.5	72.9	10.4	23.1
Ethiopia	58	32.9	43.3	10.4	23.1
Canada	30	69.1	79.0	9.9	22.0
Germany	82	67.5	77.2	9.7	21.6
South Africa	39	45.0	54.7	9.7	21.6
United Kingdom	58	69.2	77.2	8.0	17.8
United States	272	69.0	76.7	7.7	17.1
Ukraine	51	66.9	68.8	1.9	4.2
Russian Federation	148	67.3	66.6	-0.7	-1.6
Total: 'The World (b) of which:	4745	46.3	67.3	21.0	46.7
'The South' (b)	3784	41.1	65.3	24.2	53.9
'The North' (b)	961	67.0	75.4	8.4	18.6
'The North/South gap' (b)		**25.9**	**10.1**	**-16.2**	**-35.3**

(a) Increase in life expectancy as percentage of period over which increase was achieved (45 years).

(b) Population represents the total of the specified countries. The data represents the average of the specified countries in each region, weighted by their population in 1997. Thus the estimates for 'The World', 'The South' and 'The North' are, in effect, fixed-weighted indices relating to the specified countries in each of these regions.

Source: United Nations 1998. *World Population Prospects 1950-2050: The 1998 Revision.*

The countries are ranked according to the absolute increase in life expectancy during the period. The data shown for 'The World', 'The South' and 'The North' represents the averages of the countries specified in the table (whose combined population amounts to more than 80 per cent of the global total), weighted by the populations of the countries in 1997.

The key points are that the weighted average life expectancy in the specified countries of 'The South' increased during the 45-year period by 24 years, compared with a weighted average increase of only eight years in 'The North'. As a result, the 'North/South gap' decreased from 26 years to 10 years, or by over 60 per cent.

The figures in the final column of the table are of particular interest. These show the increase in average life expectancy in each of the countries, expressed as a percentage of the period (45 years) over which the increase was achieved. In 10 countries, with a combined population amounting to more than half of the world total, this proportion exceeded 50 per cent for the entire 45-year period.

The declines in mortality that are reflected in these increases can only be described as extraordinary. In his paper 'World resources and world population', presented to the United Nations Scientific Conference on the Conservation and Utilization of Resources in 1949, Colin Clark noted as a phenomenon that

> ... in a mere 12 years, from 1923 to 1935, the Japanese expectation of life rose from 42.6 years to 48.3 years.[41]

Clark's example represented an increase in average life expectancy equivalent to 47.5 per cent of the period of 'a mere 12 years' over which it was achieved. It would have been unimaginable in 1949 that such a rate of increase could be maintained on average for half a century, in countries with a majority of the world's population.

Table 2 looks at the United Nations' estimates of life expectancy from a gender perspective. In this table, the 33 countries are ranked according to the excess of the average life expectancy of females over that of males.

41 Clark, Colin (1949). 'World Resources and World Population' in *UNSCCUR Proceedings*, 1: 15-27.

Table 2 Specified countries: Life expectancy by gender 1952-1997 (ranked by excess of life expectancy of females over males in 1997)

	Population Millions	Male Total years		Female Excess over male years	
	1997	1952	1997	1952	1997
Russian Federation	148	62.5	60.6	8.0	12.2
Ukraine	51	63.3	63.8	6.3	9.9
Poland	39	58.6	68.2	5.6	8.7
Brazil	164	49.3	63.1	3.3	7.9
France	58	63.7	74.2	5.8	7.8
Korea, Republic of	46	46.0	68.8	3.0	7.2
Argentina	36	60.4	69.7	4.7	7.1
Colombia	40	49.0	67.3	3.3	7.0
Spain	40	61.6	74.5	4.7	7.0
United States	272	66.2	73.4	5.8	6.7
South Africa	39	44.0	51.5	2.0	6.6
Germany	82	65.3	73.9	4.3	6.3
Thailand	60	45.0	65.8	4.1	6.2
Italy	57	64.3	75.0	3.5	6.2
Japan	126	62.1	76.8	3.8	6.1
Mexico	94	48.9	69.5	3.6	6.0
Canada	30	66.8	76.1	4.8	5.7
United Kingdom	58	66.7	74.5	4.9	5.3
Turkey	63	42.0	66.5	3.2	5.2
Viet Nam	76	39.1	64.9	2.7	4.7
China	1244	39.3	67.9	3.0	4.1
Indonesia	203	36.9	63.3	1.2	3.7
Philippines	71	46.0	66.5	3.1	3.7
Myanmar	44	35.6	58.5	2.6	3.3
Egypt	65	41.2	64.7	2.4	3.2
Congo, Dem Rep of	48	37.5	49.2	3.1	3.1
Nigeria	104	35.0	48.7	3.0	2.8
Tanzania, U Rep of	31	35.6	46.8	1.0	2.3
Pakistan	144	40.2	62.9	-2.6	2.2
Ethiopia	58	31.4	42.4	3.0	1.9
Iran	65	46.1	68.5	0.0	1.5
India	966	39.4	62.3	-1.4	0.6
Bangladesh	123	38.3	58.1	-3.4	0.1
Total: 'The World (a) of which:	4745	45.2	65.3	2.2	4.1
'The South' (a)	3784	40.4	63.8	1.3	3.2
'The North' (a)	961	64.2	71.5	5.5	7.7
'The North/South gap' (a)		**23.8**	**7.7**	**4.2**	**4.5**

(a) See footnote (b) to Table 1.

Source: United Nations 1998. *World Population Prospects 1950-2050: The 1998 Revision.*

A point of particular interest which emerges from Table 2 is that in 1997 the average life expectancy of males in 'The North' was *7.7 years greater* than that of males in 'The South', but *7.7 years less* than that of females in 'The North'. Since the early 1950s, the 'North/South gap' had narrowed by 16 years and the 'gender gap' had widened by two years.

Inter-country and gender inequalities in education

In exploring the claim by the UNESCO/ICSU Secretariat for the WCS that the benefits of health 'are ever more unequally distributed' between countries, we are faced with an immediate dilemma. The countries of 'The North' had already achieved universal primary education and universal adult literacy before estimates of primary school enrolment rates and of literacy among adults were available for many countries of 'The South'. There will therefore be a contraction, by definition, in the 'North/South gap' revealed in these human development indicators.

We need also to note that, if the statement by the UNESCO/ICSU Secretariat is true, the empirical supporting evidence should be available from UNESCO itself. The organisation is, upon its own testimony, 'the leading source of statistical information on education systems around the world', and 'the only universal organization entitled, by virtue of its Constitution, to ask Member States to provide it, on a systematic basis, with statistical data in all its fields of competence'.[42]

To the best of my knowledge, none of the available empirical evidence lends support to the generalisation that there is ever-increasing inequality in the provision of the benefits of education – though it is true, as Gavin Jones points out, that the record in some regions has been disappointing.[43] Some relevant information is presented in Table 3, which compares the combined gross enrolment ratios (GERs) for first-, second- and third-levels of education for 1970 and 1997, in respect of all of the countries with a population of over 30 million in 1997 for which UNESCO publishes comparable data for 1970 and 1997.

42 UNESCO (1997). *Draft Program and Budget 1998-1999*: 109.

43 See Gavin Jones' paper in Academy of the Social Sciences in Australia *Annual Symposium 1999*.

Table 3 Specified countries: Combined gross enrolment ratios 1970-1997 (ranked by percentage increase in combined gross enrolment ratios)

	Population millions	Combined GER		Increase 1952-97	
		%	%	points	% (a)
	1997	1970	1997	1970-97	1970-97
Ethiopia	58	7	24	17	343
Nigeria	104	20	54	34	270
Pakistan	144	19	43	24	226
Tanzania, U Rep of	31	17	33	16	194
South Africa	39	50	93	43	186
Egypt	65	39	72	33	185
Brazil	164	49	80	31	163
Indonesia	203	40	64	24	160
China	1244	44	69	25	157
Colombia	40	47	71	24	151
Korea, Republic of	46	61	90	29	148
India	966	38	55	17	145
Spain	40	66	92	26	139
Myanmar	44	40	55	15	138
France	58	70	92	22	131
Italy	57	63	82	19	130
Thailand	60	46	59	13	128
Argentina	36	62	79	17	127
Mexico	94	55	70	15	127
Japan	126	67	85	18	127
United States	272	75	94	19	125
Canada	30	79	99	20	125
Bangladesh	123	28	35	7	125
Philippines	71	66	82	16	124
Turkey	63	50	61	11	122
Congo, Dem Rep of	48	43	39	-4	91
Total: 'The World' (b) of which:	4226	45	66	21	147
'The South' (b)	3643	41	62	21	153
'The North' (b)	583	71	91	20	128
'The North/South gap' (b)		**30**	**29**	**-1**	**-25**

(a) Combined gross enrolment ratio (GER) for 1997 expressed as index (GER for 1970 = 100).

(b) See footnote (b) to Table 1.

Source: UNESCO (1999). Statistical Yearbook 1999.

In this table, the countries are ranked according to the percentage increase in their combined GER over the 27-year period. The GERs for the specified countries in 'The South', weighted by their respective populations, increased by 53 per cent over this period, whereas the GERs for the specified countries in 'The North' increased by 28 per cent. Even if the comparison is made in terms of the rise in the number of percentage points, the increase in 'The South' was fractionally greater than in 'The North'. Among individual countries, the largest increases in terms of percentage points were in South Africa (43 percentage points), Nigeria (34 points), Egypt (33 points) and Brazil (31 points).

Table 4 presents the GERs for females for each of the countries over the 27-year period. The increase in the GERs for females in the specified countries of 'The South' exceeded 70 per cent over this period, compared with an increase of 33 per cent in the specified countries of 'The North'. The system of ranking of the countries in this table has been prompted by observations made by our Cunningham Lecturer, Professor Jack Caldwell, in his address at the National Club earlier this year:

> ... the degree of convergence in the education of the sexes in much of the world is remarkable. In great swathes of Asia and Latin America the extent of secondary schooling for girls is much above what it was in the West in the 1950s. Schooling ... implies subsequent full-time employment. In every country in the world where the majority of girls have at least three years' secondary education, the majority of women work and fertility is at replacement level or below.[44]

In the light of these comments, the ranking of countries in Table 4 is according to GERs in 'The South' in 1997 and in 'The North' in 1970. This form of presentation brings out the fact that, in 1997, the combined GERs for females in South Africa, the Philippines, the Republic of Korea, Argentina and Brazil were higher than the corresponding ratio for any of the specified countries in 'The North' in 1970.

44 Caldwell, JC (1999). 'Population...Explosion or Implosion?' Address at theNational Press Club, Canberra, 17 March 1999.

Table 4 Specified countries: Combined gross enrolment ratios – females 1970-1997 (ranked by gross enrolment ratios in 'The South' in 1997 and in 'The North' in 1970)

'The South'	'The North'	Population millions	Combined GERs: Female	
			%	%
		1997	1970	1997
South Africa		39	53	94
Philippines		71	66	85
Korea, Republic of		46	57	84
Argentina		36	63	82
Brazil		164	48	77
	Canada	30	76	102
	United States	272	73	97
Colombia		40	47	71
	France	58	70	94
Mexico		94	51	69
China		1244	39	67
Egypt		65	29	66
	Japan	126	64	83
	Spain	40	62	94
Indonesia		203	35	61
Thailand		60	43	59
	Italy	57	59	83
Myanmar		44	36	54
Turkey		63	39	54
Nigeria		104	15	48
India		966	27	47
Tanzania		31	13	32
Bangladesh		123	17	31
Congo, D Rep of		48	9	31
Pakistan		144	30	28
Ethiopia		58	4	18
Total: 'The World' (a) of which:		4226	39	62
'The South' (a)		3643	34	58
'The North' (a)		583	69	92
'The North/South gap (a)			**35**	**34**

(a) See footnote (b) to Table 1.

Source: UNESCO (1999). *Statistical Yearbook 1999.*

Inter-country inequalities in real income

Inter-country inequalities in real income, or GDP per capita, have received more attention in the 1990s than inequalities in other 'factors of human and social well-being'. An important reason for this has been the introduction and growing influence of the UNDP's *Human Development Report*, which was launched in 1990. According to Amartya Sen, speaking at a memorial meeting for the originator of the series, Mahbub ul Haq, on 15 October 1998, this *Report* has 'had a profound effect on the way policy makers, public servants and the news media as well as economists and other social scientists view social and economic advancement'.[45]

Ironically, the *Report* appears to have had the opposite effect to that intended by its founders. Their purpose was to focus attention on a more comprehensive concept of human development than GDP per head, and the human development index (HDI) was devised as a measure of such a concept. In practice, however, the main interest of the media has not been in the HDI, but in the sections of the *Report* and the accompanying publicity which purport to show that there has been a rapid and unprecedented widening in global income disparities.

Unlike the estimates of global income distribution made by Colin Clark in 1940 and those presented to us by Angus Maddison this morning, the estimates used in the text of the *Human Development Report*, and emphasised in the promotional material for the *Report* are *not* 'firmly built upon the ascertained facts of the production and distribution of goods and services'. In failing to take into account the large and varying differences in price levels between countries, they fail to provide the scientific and quantitative 'comparisons of economic welfare between one community and another, one economic group and another, and between one time and another' which Clark held to be 'the very foundation of economic science'.

Table 5 provides 'scientific and quantitative' comparisons of GDP per head in 1960, 1990 and 1997, for all of the countries with a 1997 population of over 30 million in respect of which such data can be calculated in 1997 PPP$ from tables in the *Human Development Report 1999* (for 1990 and 1997) and *Human Development Report 1998* (for 1960). It also shows, for each country, annual growth rates over the long-term (1960-97) and in the 1990s (1990-97). Countries are ranked by their growth rates in the 1990-97-period.

45 Sen, Amartya (1998). 'Mahbub ul Haq: The courage and creativity of his ideas', speech at the Memorial Meeting for Mahbub ul Haq, 15 October. UNDP website.

Table 5 Specified countries: Gross domestic product per capita 1960, 1990, 1997 (ranked by percentage per annum increase in GDP per capita 1990-1997)

	Population millions	GDP per capita				
		1997 PPP $int. (a)			% per annum	
	1997	1960	1990	1997	1960-97	1990-97
China	1244	416	1582	3130	5.5	9.7
Korea, Republic of	46	1131	8963	13590	6.7	5.9
Indonesia	203	845	2387	3490	3.8	5.4
Thailand	60	1073	4619	6690	4.9	5.3
India (b)	966	711	1290	1670	2.4	3.9
Argentina	36	6919	8069	10300	1.1	3.5
Bangladesh	123	703	862	1050	1.1	2.8
Colombia (b)	40	3246	5908	6810	2.1	2.0
Pakistan	144	505	1362	1580	3.1	1.9
Egypt	65	712	2704	3050	3.9	1.7
Turkey	63	2465	5879	6350	2.5	1.6
Spain	40	4697	14314	15930	3.3	1.5
United States	272	14419	26466	29010	1.9	1.3
Japan	126	4516	22001	24070	4.5	1.3
United Kingdom	58	9993	18970	20730	2.0	1.3
Brazil	164	2531	5991	6480	2.5	1.1
Mexico (b)	94	3902	7792	8370	2.1	1.0
Italy	57	6911	19046	20290	2.9	0.9
France	58	8571	20761	22030	2.6	0.8
Philippines	71	2257	3342	3520	1.2	0.7
Canada	30	9678	21623	22480	2.2	0.6
Nigeria	104	961	908	920	-0.1	0.2
South Africa	39	5712	7797	7380	0.7	-0.8
Congo, D Rep of	48	2613	1724	880	-3.0	-10.0
'The World' (c) of which:	4151	2425	5485	6561	2.7	2.6
'The South' (c)	3510	1032	2332	3237	3.1	4.8
'The North' (c)	641	10056	22749	24761	2.5	1.2
'The North/South gap' (c)		**9.7:1**	**9.8:1**	**7.6:1**	**0.6**	**3.6**
Weighted by population:						
'The World' (c) of which:	4151				3.3	4.5
'The South' (c)	3510				3.4	5.2
'The North' (c)	641				2.7	1.2
'The North/South gap' (c)					**0.7**	**4.0**

(a) 1997 data is as given in UNDP, *Human Development Report 1999*, Table 1: 134-37. The data for 1990 has been calculated using the growth in GDP per capita (1987 US$) from 1990 to 1997, as given in UNDP, *ibid* Table 6: 151-54. The data for 1960 has been calculated by the same method, but using GDP *per capita* (1987 US$) for 1960 as given in UNDP, *Human Development Report 1998*, Table 5: 140-43.

(b) GDP per capita (1987 US$) data for 1996 in UNDP (1999) *op cit* has been updated to 1997 using the growth rates in GDP per capita in IMF *World Economic Outlook*: May 1999.

(c) See footnote (b) to Table 1.

Source: Author's own calculations.

The levels and growth rates of GDP per head are also shown for 'The World' (i.e. the weighted average of the specified countries, whose combined population exceeds 70 per cent of the global total), 'The South' and 'The North'. The weighted average growth rates for these regional aggregates are shown on two bases:

- using GDP weights (i.e. weights that take account of the level of GDP per head in each country as well as the country's population); and
- using population weights (i.e. weights that take account of the population of each country, but not of its GDP per head).

On the latter basis of comparison the growth rates for the regional aggregates do not depend on the absolute levels of GDP per head in different countries, and are therefore independent of whether the 'purchasing power parity' or the 'exchange rate' method has been used to establish those relative levels.

In commenting on Table 1, I described the increases in life expectancy in the developing world since the early 1950s as 'extraordinary', and supported this judgement by citing Japan's experience in the inter-war period, as reported in 1949 by Colin Clark. The increases since 1960 in GDP per head in the developing world shown in Table 5, which are broadly consistent with those given by Angus Maddison in Table 3 of his paper to this Symposium, can be seen to be equally extraordinary by placing them in the perspective of judgements made in December 1948 by another great development economist, Dr (now Sir) Hans Singer:

> As a result of the preoccupation of economists with national data and national problems... there has been a general tendency to assume that there has been a rise in per capita incomes the world over during the last two generations and also that there has been some progress towards a more equal distribution of income. This optimism cannot be seriously sustained if we think in terms of world income... While it is true that in some of the *individual* countries incomes and even per capita incomes have been rising, though at very uneven rates, the average or median world income is almost certainly smaller now than it was in 1913.
>
> The reason for this is that in the determination of average international incomes the underdeveloped countries, with their expanding populations, acquire a constantly increasing weight. The situation is perhaps best described as follows: a shrinking proportion of the world population has been rapidly raising its standard of living, while the living standard of an increasing majority of the world population has been rising much more slowly or has remained stationary. The improvement

> within the first group and the very slow improvement in the second group are, however, swamped by the shift in relative numbers from the first group to the second...
>
> In terms of world income, the situation has probably deteriorated during the last three generations in respect to all three Pigovian criteria: average size, equality of distribution, and stability over time. If we define the 'average' world income as that of the median world citizen, the spectacular improvement which has occurred at one extreme and which has fascinated economists and other observers becomes irrelevant. Such considerations perhaps lean over backward in the direction of gloom, but they may be a useful corrective of the prevailing view of the situation.[46]

This must be regarded as a well-informed assessment at the time that it was made. With the benefit of the estimates of modern economic growth that Angus Maddison and others have developed in recent decades, it seems clear that Singer's judgement did indeed 'lean over backward in the direction of gloom'. But Maddison's estimates suggest that the average rate of growth in income per head in the developing countries between 1870 and 1950 (Singer's 'last three generations') was well below one per cent annually.

The average growth rate of three per cent per annum achieved over the entire period from 1960 to 1997 is therefore without precedent. Moreover, the fact that the rate was even higher on a population-weighted basis shows that the benefits of this growth were widely spread: in our own time, the situation has almost certainly improved with respect to the Pigovian criterion of equality of distribution.

In 'The North', the growth rate of per capita incomes contracted sharply in the 1990s, but in 'The South' there was a marked acceleration. The trend was interrupted in 1997 by the 'Asian crisis', but it is already clear that the check was only a temporary one. The last decade of the millennium was almost certainly the first decade in history in which the average real incomes of most countries in which most of the world's poor lived increased at an average rate of three per cent or more. The objective evidence provides no support for the prevailing belief that inter-country inequalities in real income have been widening during the past decade.

46 Singer, HW (1949). 'Economic progress in under-developed countries' in *Social Research*: March, 1-2.

16. International Comparisons of GDP: Issues of Theory and Practice[1]

Ian Castles and David Henderson

Introduction

This article combines a general theme, which though not new remains a subject of lively debate, with specific instances, illustrations and proposals for change. Our chief concern is with how international comparisons of real GDP and GDP per head are best made. We set out the case for using purchasing power parity (PPP) converters for this purpose, rather than exchange rates, and give reasons for rejecting various arguments that are still widely made to the contrary.[2] In doing so, we give instances of the differing current practices of international agencies, argue the case for greater uniformity and consistency, and make suggestions for improvement.

In developing the general theme, we start with a number of preliminary points, some of them familiar and elementary but pertinent nonetheless, relating to the measurement of output, and of changes in output over time, in individual countries. We then turn to consider the international comparative dimension, where much though not all of the argument proceeds on parallel lines. Under both headings, a basic and invaluable source is Chapter 16 of the 1993 System of National Accounts (SNA), and we have also drawn on an illuminating recently published paper by William Nordhaus.[3] Following these general expository sections, we turn to specific and topical cases. First, we list and comment on some mistaken but still-continuing ways of presenting and interpreting international comparative data, by a range of individuals and official agencies. Second, we review briefly the extent to which the consistent use of PPP converters has

1 First publised in *World Economics*, volume 6:1, Jan - Mar, 2005: 55 - 66.

2 The choice is often presented as being between PPP converters and 'market exchange rates' (MERs); but since it is debatable how far past and present exchange rates can be viewed as 'market-determined' we use here a more neutral term. Later in the text, when quoting or referring to other authors who speak of MERs, we place the term in inverted commas.

3 *System of National Accounts 1993*, prepared and published by five international agencies – the European Commission, the IMF, the OECD, the United Nations and the World Bank – and approved by the statistical authorities of their member governments. William Nordhaus, 'Alternative Measures of Output in Global Environmental Models: Purchasing Power Parity or Market Exchange Rates?'; revised version of a paper prepared for an Experts Meeting of the Intergovernmental Panel on Climate Change (IPCC) in January 2005. It is available at ppp_02085.doc. Another valuable reference is Irving B Kravis, 'Comparative Studies of National Incomes and Prices'. *Journal of Economic Literature*, Vol. XXII, March 1984.

been incorporated into the work of the leading international agencies that are responsible for issuing international comparative data. Third, we summarise the actions that governments still need to take in order to ensure more accurate and more consistent treatment and presentation of these data. In a short annex we reproduce an earlier note by one of us which outlines a specific proposal for improvement on a broad front.

Among the international organisations whose current practice is open to question, one that we note in particular, because of its topical aspects, is the Intergovernmental Panel on Climate Change (IPCC). We have presented elsewhere a critique of the Panel's handling of economic issues; and within this critique, one element concerns the way in which inter-country comparisons of real GDP, and hence GDP per head, have been made in IPCC documents. Mistaken procedures have been adopted, and the IPCC has shown itself resistant to changes in these and unclear as to what is at stake. Such mistakes are to be found in particular, though not only, in the *Special Report on Emissions Scenarios* (SRES), which was published in 2000 as one of the documents that entered into the Panel's Third Assessment Report. The SRES provided, as its main single product, a range of projections of greenhouse gas emissions covering the period from 1990 to 2100.[4]

The Panel is now well into the preparation of its Fourth Assessment Report (AR4), which may well come to 3,000 pages and is due for completion in 2007. It has dismissed both our critique and our suggestions for wider participation in its economic work;[5] and as part of this reaffirmation of the status quo, it has determined that 'the SRES scenarios provide a credible and sound set of projections, appropriate for use in the AR4'. Hence this particular instance of the case for reform on the international scene is especially topical: IPCC member governments have to act promptly if the decision to retain the SRES as the point of departure for AR4 is to be reconsidered – and, more broadly, if the economic aspects of this coming report to governments are to be handled in a more informed and professionally representative way than is now the case. Because of this immediate relevance, the work and procedures of the IPCC and one of its twin parent agencies, the United Nations Environment Program (UNEP), are featured in the two final sections of the paper.[6]

---

4 While the main single target of our critique has been the SRES, our concerns extend to the IPCC process and milieu *as a whole*, including the Panel's parent agencies and its sponsoring departments in member governments. The concerns are summarised in an article by one of us (Henderson) in the quarterly *Newsletter* of the Royal Economic Society for January 2005. This piece has now been reprinted in *Energy and Environment*, Vol 16 No 2 (2005).

5 A formal IPCC press release of December 2003, now posted on the Panel's website, says that 'In recent months some disinformation has been spread questioning the scenarios used by the IPCC', and refers to us as 'so called "two independent commentators"'.

6 The IPCC was established in 1988 as the joint creation of the UNEP and the World Meteorological Organisation.

Prices and quantities: Measuring and interpreting changes within an economy

Nominal and real changes in output and expenditure

For any country or individual economy for a specific period of time (normally a year), its GDP is defined in terms of the value of the output of goods and services produced within the economy over that period. For any given year, past or present, the outputs that enter into GDP are measured and valued at the prices prevailing in that year: the starting point is an estimate of the value of output at current prices, or nominal GDP.

To define and measure changes in aggregate output, or real GDP,[7] such initial current-price estimates have to be corrected for year-to-year changes in the average price level of the goods and services concerned: for GDP, as for other economic time series, 'Changes in the values of flows of goods and services can be directly factored into two components reflecting changes in the prices of the goods and services concerned and changes in their volumes' (SNA 1993: 379). Only by eliminating price effects, and valuing each year's GDP accordingly, is it possible to derive a consistent measure of changes in output.

Such a measure is indispensable for establishing a true record of the past, for analysing and interpreting economic events and relationships, and for assessing current macroeconomic policy choices. As the SNA notes (para.16.1) one objective is

> to assemble a set of interdependent measures which make it possible to carry out systematic and detailed analyses of inflation and economic growth and fluctuations.

For all the above purposes, a necessary first step is to separate out price and quantity elements.

Both nominal and real GDP can be expressed either as an output total, where the component parts comprise value added in different industries or sectors of or the economy, or as an expenditure total, made up of final expenditures plus exports less spending on imports. Although the items that make up the two aggregates are thus different, the totals are constrained to be the same: both emerge from the same matrix of transactions in goods and services for the period in question. Changes over time in real GDP are defined as equal whether particular estimates relate to output or to expenditure.

7 The SNA suggests (para.16.72) that the term 'volume GDP' is preferable to 'real GDP'. We use 'real' here because of its greater familiarity.

In separating price changes from quantity changes, both practical and analytical problems necessarily arise, and in neither case are there unique and agreed solutions.

Problems of estimation

The chief practical problems relate to the collection and interpretation of data. The process of separating the price and quantity components of economic time series is not costless. Resources have to be devoted to the collection, processing, interpretation and publication of data relating to prices and quantities over the relevant period or periods. Again, improvements in the quality of these data do not come free of charge. There is an inescapable trade-off between, on the one hand, wider and more detailed coverage and more firmly based results, and, on the other, keeping costs within reasonable limits. Inevitably, there is room for disagreement about how the balance should be struck. But no one doubts that the derivation of estimates of real GDP is necessary, or that improvements in the reliability of such estimates are to be welcomed as such.

No matter how detailed and meticulous the inquiries may be that yield estimates of changes in real GDP, there will remain room for doubt and for differences of view. Three factors in particular are involved here. One is changes in the quality of goods and services that may not be fully reflected in their prices. A second is the appearance of new products and the disappearance of older ones, so that the lists of goods and services entering into output over the period under review may not be identical. Both these factors loom larger if the GDP estimates in question relate to changes over a substantial period. A third problem arises from the presence of (to quote para.16.4 of the SNA) 'non-market goods and services whose valuation is difficult at current as well as constant prices'. However, the existence of these significant and unavoidable problems does not put in question the need for reliable estimates of changes in real GDP, nor does it make long-run intertemporal comparisons inadmissible.

Questions of interpretation

As to analytical aspects, there is admittedly no single and unique formula for measuring changes in a country's real GDP, since different sets of price weights can be used to value the respective outputs. If for example a comparison is being made between two years, outputs can be valued at the prices of the earlier year, thus yielding a Laspeyres quantity index (expressed as $\Sigma p_1 q_2 / \Sigma p_1 q_1$); at those of the later year, yielding a Paasche index ($\Sigma p_2 q_2 / \Sigma p_2 q_1$); or at an average of the two, as in the Fisher index. If the series is to extend over several years, the range of choice is wider, the possibilities of chaining come into play and the choice of reference year may become an issue. Once again, however, these inherent features of the exercise do not put in question its purpose or its rationale. For one thing, there is now broad agreement on index number choices and procedures, as reflected in the recommendations set out in para. 16.73 of SNA 1993. More fundamentally, the fact that index number problems are inescapable, and that different ways of treating them can be defended, does not affect the need to derive estimates of real GDP as an essential measure of the course of economic change.

The choice of index number formula can be linked to a second and possibly more contentious analytical issue. This concerns the significance to be attached to estimates of real GDP over time: just what is it that is being measured, or should ideally be measured?

Although these are deep waters, we believe that a contrast can be drawn between two approaches or modes of interpretation. In the evolution of economists' thinking on the subject, issues of the definition and measurement of real GDP have often been considered in relation to its status as a measure or indicator of an economy's performance: thus in a classic and influential article published in 1940, John Hicks referred to, and joined himself with, 'a long line of economists who have sought in the Social Income an index of economic welfare, of the wealth of nations'.[8] This orientation, or way of thinking, characterises what the SNA refers to (paras 16.21-30) as 'the economic theoretic approach to index numbers', in which 'the observed quantities may be assumed to be functions of the prices, as specified in some utility or production function'. Thus measures of real GDP are (or can be) interpreted as reflecting underlying shifts in individual utilities of consumers (where expenditure is under consideration) or in the economy's production possibility frontier (where the focus is on output); and a lot of work has been done to define precisely, first, the conditions under which this relationship would hold good, and second, the price deflators that it would then be appropriate to use.

In our view, an alternative (or complementary) approach is possible, in which the movement in real GDP is viewed and interpreted, at least initially, in more neutral terms. It can be defined, in the first instance at any rate, as no more than the estimated volume component of a series that is originally given in value terms, i.e., in current prices. As such, its status is descriptive only: in itself, it does not pretend to convey information about changes in welfare or production possibilities, any more than an index of the volume of exports or of industrial production does. The relationship of real GDP – or, more strictly, real GDP per head – to economic welfare represents a second and separate stage of inquiry, in which various other influences have to be taken into account,

8 JR Hicks, 'Valuation of Social Income', originally published in 1940 in *Economica,* reprinted as Chapter 3 of *Wealth and Welfare: Collected Essays on Economic Theory*. Volume 1, Oxford, Blackwell, 1981.

starting with changes in the terms of trade over the period in question. To be sure, this positivist approach leaves open the choice of price deflator. However, adopting it does not prejudice the choice, nor does it affect the broad agreement on index numbers referred to above. Moreover, and as will be seen below, such a neutral interpretation of real GDP estimates may be seen as more appropriate in the context of many international comparisons.

The irrelevance of exchange rate changes

In estimating current-price GDP series, as also in correcting these for price changes so as to derive a series for changes in real GDP, only the prices at which the outputs for each year were actually transacted are relevant. Just as the real or volume component of current-price GDP is the output produced, or the real final expenditure incurred, within the country or economy concerned, so the price component is derived from the prices at which the goods and services in question were bought and sold within it. Hence in constructing measures of price and output changes, *exchange rate changes do not enter in:* to 'correct' a real GDP series for such changes is wrong.

A recent instance of such an error, which itself follows in the footsteps of others, is to be found in Jagdish Bhagwati's book *In Defence of Globalization* (New York, Oxford University Press, 2004). In Chapter 13 of the book Bhagwati refers to 'the perils of gung-ho international financial capitalism'. He states there (199), by way of illustrating those perils, that in the financial crises which affected five East Asian economies in the 1990s:

> Per capita incomes tumbled to almost one-third of their 1996 level in Indonesia, with the other crisis-stricken Asian countries showing declines ranging from a quarter to nearly half of the 1996 levels.

From the source that Bhagwati quotes, which itself gives another source, it becomes apparent that these figures refer to changes in GDP per head as between calendar years. However, actual GDP per head for Indonesia, according to standard published data, fell by only about one-twelfth, as opposed to two-thirds, between 1996 and its lowest subsequent point in 1998. Again, the corresponding largest falls for four other 'crisis-stricken' countries over the period 1996-99 ranged, not from 'a quarter to nearly half of the 1996 levels', but from 7½ per cent in the case of South Korea to just under 14 per cent for Thailand.[9] The alarmist numbers that Bhagwati quotes, and which he believes to carry implications for the external policies that developing countries should

9 The figures that we quote here, and others that appear below, are taken from Angus Maddison, *The World Economy: Historical Statistics* (Paris OECD Development Centre, 2004).

follow, appear to reflect some process of revaluing GDP totals so as to reflect the big falls in exchange rates that occurred during the crises. This is not how changes in real GDP are defined and measured.[10]

The argument here can be extended from the record of the past to projections of the future. Just as with past changes, the prospective growth of real GDP in an economy is defined and measured with reference to output and expenditure at constant domestic prices. It is wrong either to adjust the results of such a projection by building in assumptions about possible future changes in the exchange rate, or to rest the projection itself on such assumptions. When assessing or modelling the possible future growth of output, the exchange rate does not directly enter in.

Prices and quantities: Cross-country comparisons

Nominal and real differences in output and expenditure

Where comparisons between two countries are in question, whether for a given year or over a series of years, there is a close analogy with the procedures that are called for, and the problems that arise, when making estimates of changes over time in real GDP for a particular economy.

As in the inter-temporal case, the point of departure for a cross-border comparison is the respective estimates of GDP in value terms; that is, at current prices. These current price estimates are given in the respective currencies of the two countries. The GDP of the one economy can thus be translated into that of the other, often though not always straightforwardly, by conversion at the average exchange rate for the period in question. But just as the current price estimates for a single country for two different years take no account of price *changes* as between the two, so an exchange-rate-based conversion of the money GDP of two countries in a particular year takes no account of price *differences* between them. *It therefore does not yield a measure of comparative output.* Only by eliminating price effects, and thus valuing each country's GDP at a common set of prices, it is possible to derive a valid measure of differences in real GDPs. For cross-border comparisons as for inter-temporal estimates of real GDP, price

10 To be sure, in such episodes changes in GDP per head are not the whole story. Because of the very large turn-round in their current account balances, the crisis-affected countries, as Martin Wolf has noted, had to 'reduce spending in relation to national incomes by an amount equal to 15.5 per cent of their combined GDP' – a huge adjustment in so short a time. Further, real incomes were reduced by adverse changes in the terms of trade – which, however, are not correctly measured by the fall in nominal exchange rates.

and quantity components have to be separated out, so that the respective GDPs are expressed in a common set of prices. This is achieved by the use of PPP (purchasing power parity) ratios or converters.

The SNA gives clear guidance on this matter. In its opening chapter, it specifies (para.1.38) that:

> When the objective is to compare the volumes of goods or services produced or consumed per head, data in national currencies must be converted into a common currency by means of purchasing power parities and not exchange rates ... Exchange rate converted data must not ... be interpreted as measures of the relative volumes of goods and services concerned.

Just as with inter-temporal comparisons, attention may be focused on differences in either real output or real expenditure; and here again, the two totals are defined as being equal. It is true that most cross-country PPP comparisons have so far been made with reference to final expenditures rather than output totals, but this is largely for reasons of data availability.

Again as with inter-temporal comparisons, and largely for the same reasons, both practical and analytical problems arise in making the separation between prices and quantities.

Problems of estimation

The practical problems are the same in kind, though they are often worse in degree. Here again, resources have to be devoted to the collection, processing, interpretation and publication of data relating to the prices of comparable goods and services in the two countries; and in doing so, it is necessary to make judgements as to what is genuinely comparable. Again, improvements in the quality of such estimates are not costless, and there is the same trade-off between achieving wider and more detailed coverage and keeping costs within acceptable bounds. Again, similar problems may arise because differences in quality are not reflected in price differences, because the respective product lists are not identical, and from the presence of non-marketed goods and services. All these problems can be more serious in cross-country comparisons than when changes in a single economy are in question: the SNA notes (para.16.81) that 'there is little doubt that it is more difficult to compile reliable international than inter-temporal price indices'. But as with intertemporal comparisons, the existence of the problems does not undermine the case for making comparative estimates which relate to real GDP, rather than using actual exchange rates on no better grounds than that they are readily available, and despite the fact that they do not yield measures of comparative output.

Questions of interpretation

The analytical issues that arise are likewise similar. As in the inter-temporal case, the results that emerge will depend on the choice of price weights: index number problems arise in the same way and for the same reasons. Thus for a particular year the respective outputs of goods and services (or real expenditures) can be valued at the prices of Country A ($\Sigma A_p B_q / \Sigma A_p A_q$) or of Country B ($\Sigma B_p B_q / \Sigma B_p A_q$): the choice is precisely analogous to that between a Laspeyres and a Paasche index for a comparison in a single country as between two years. In this case also, there may be good arguments for using an average such as the Fisher index. Again as with intertemporal comparisons, the fact that these index number problems have to be faced does not undermine the case for the deflating the value series in national currencies by a suitable price index, so as to derive a measure of differences in real GDP.

In the international context also, the question arises as to how such differences are to be interpreted; and here again, the same argument as for inter-temporal comparisons can be made for adopting a neutral or 'positive' interpretation. Indeed, the argument is stronger, since cross-country differences, where the economies in question may have widely different properties, are more liable to put in question the assumptions that enter into the construction of 'economic-theoretic' measures of comparative GDP. Thus PPP-based estimates of cross-country differences in real GDP are best viewed, at any rate initially, as no more than that. They are measures of comparative outputs, neither more nor less. *As such, they do not measure comparative living standards, productivity or welfare,* though they can be used, along with other evidence and on clearly specified assumptions, to throw light on all of these.

The irrelevance of exchange rate changes

Since exchange rate changes, past or prospective, do not enter into measures of changes in the real GDP of a single economy, they are not relevant when comparing differences in real GDP growth across countries. Recent comparative data relating to the US and the Euro Area can serve to illustrate the point. From recent OECD published data, it appears that between 2001 and 2004 the aggregate GDP of the Euro Area rose by an estimated 3.3 per cent, as compared with 9.6 per cent for the US. Over the same period the euro rose in relation to the US dollar by some 38 per cent; and this occurred despite the fact that there was little difference in the respective increases in the two domestic price levels.[11] Hence a series for Euro Area GDP at constant prices, if converted from

11 These figures are taken from OECD Economic Outlook, No. 76, December 2004. The estimated rise in the consumer price index for the Euro Area between 2001 and 2004 is 6.5 per cent, which compares with 6.6 per cent for the US. The corresponding figures for the GDP deflator are 6.5 per cent for the Euro Area and 5.6 per cent for the US.

euros to US dollars at the rates that prevailed, would show a rise of over 40 per cent for the period. Conversely, the corresponding series for the US, if converted from dollars to euros, would show a fall of over 20 per cent. But neither of these two figures has any economic meaning, nor do they offer alternative estimates for changes in real GDP. These latter estimates are what they are: they are derived, without reference to exchange rate changes, by correcting each of the respective value series for GDP for changes in domestic prices. In this particular comparison, they would not be affected if the movement of exchange rates over the period had been in the opposite direction. Since exchange rate variations have no bearing on how the growth of output is defined and measured, they have no bearing on comparative growth rates. In this context also, they do not enter in.

The above example also serves to illustrate a related point. It is well recognised that making cross-country conversions of GDP at actual exchange rates, rather than using PPP converters, causes the gap between rich and poor countries to appear as much greater, chiefly because the prices of non-traded goods are typically lower in poor countries. This overstatement of the gap in real GDP and GDP per head is often viewed, with good reason, as an argument in favour of using PPP-based estimates when comparisons between these two groups of countries are in question. But the argument against bringing in exchange rates is a general one, which applies to other comparisons also. As is shown by the above example of the Euro Area and the US – and many other past instances could be cited[12] – market exchange rates may have a momentum of their own, which is unrelated to changes in the outputs or price levels of the countries concerned. In such cases, actual exchange rates give seriously misleading results if used to make comparisons of output as between countries even with similar levels of real GDP per head. It is not only as between rich and poor countries that the *Purchasing Power Parity theory* (or hypothesis), according to which exchange rates reflect and move in line with comparative national price levels, has not been borne out by actual events.

The argument here can be extended to the measurement of combined GDP totals, with the above figures again taken as an illustration. A measure of the change in the combined GDP of the Euro Area and the US, as between 2001 and 2004, has to be a weighted average of the 3.3 per cent increase for the one and the 9.6 per cent for the other, and the weights should reflect the relative size of the two economies. Since the US economy grew faster over the period, its relative weight for 2004 should be higher than for 2001. If however the respective GDPs

12 For example, Irving Kravis, in the article mentioned above, noted (2) that 'exchange rate conversions indicate that Japan's per capita GNP was 47 per cent higher than that of the United Kingdom in 1978 and 5 percent lower than the UK level in 1980 ... The Japanese constant price series for GNP shows an increase of about 8 per cent on a per capita basis while the UK constant price series shows an approximate decrease of one per cent'.

are converted at actual exchange rates, the reverse change occurs: because of the appreciation of the euro: the Euro Area GDP appears as having increased in relation to that of the US. Such a result does not make economic sense. In measuring the growth of output for two or more countries grouped together, or for the world as a whole, the appropriate weights are the comparative real sizes of the economies concerned in some agreed base period, and these can be derived only from a PPP-based comparison. The correct procedure, as summarised by Nordhaus in the abstract of the article cited above, is to combine 'cross-sectional PPP measures for relative incomes and outputs' with 'national accounts price and quantity indexes for time-series extrapolations' (and also, we may add, for estimates of past growth).[13]

Exchange rate-related confusions: Projecting the closure of an imagined gap

In some model-based projections, such as those that enter into the SRES, it has been the practice to start with base-year cross-country (or cross-region) GDP data valued at actual exchange rates. These are treated, wrongly, as yielding measures of real GDP per head; and as a result, the initial gap in GDP per head between rich and poor countries is greatly overstated: thus in the SRES the ratio of GDP per head in 1990 in the OECD group to that of the Asian developing countries is put at close to 40 to 1, as compared with a figure of around 9 to 1 that emerges from Maddison's estimates. Building in this overstated gap increases the apparent scope for future convergence in GDP per head: convergence is defined in nominal rather than real terms, though such a notion has little if any economic meaning. If such 'nominal convergence' is built into a model, it gives rise to projections of output and GDP per head for developing regions which are higher than they would have been if the base year figures had been correctly derived, from PPP-based comparisons, and the gap had accordingly been smaller. In such inflated projections for the growth of GDP in poor countries, therefore, there are two elements, one genuine and the other imaginary. The first reflects higher growth in real GDP per head, correctly defined, while the second represents no more than the assumed closure of an imaginary initial gap.

In some models, a further element, which should likewise have no place, enters into 'nominal convergence'. The assumption is made, and reflected in projections, that in the case of initially poor countries the gap between 'MERs' and PPP converters, which arises from relative poverty, will be gradually closed over time. By tracing out the projected path of such a change, it is possible to express

13 Where cross-border comparisons extend to more than two countries, the analogy with intertemporal comparisons no longer holds good, and a question arises as to how best to 'multilateralise' comparisons. The issues which then arise are reviewed in all three of the sources cited in footnote 2 above.

the GDP of the groupings of poor countries either in the original 'MER' units or in terms of exchange rates that are projected to converge on what are taken to be PPP values. The bizarre result of such a procedure is that, to quote a recent article by Richard Tol, 'Developing countries grow slower with a purchasing power exchange rate than with a market exchange rate'.[14] But as already noted, the projected growth of output for any country or group of countries has to be derived from national price and quantity measures, suitably weighted by relative outputs where more than one country is involved. Assumptions relating to the possible future course of exchange rates are not relevant to the choice of a unit of account for valuing projected GDP, whether for a single economy or for a group of countries. Exchange rates, whether past or projected, do not enter into the measurement of changes in real GDP. Where output is in question, there is no such thing as 'MER growth rate' or a 'PPP growth rate'. These are no more than figments of modellers' imaginations. They acquire meaning only in relation to a process of assumed 'nominal convergence' which itself has no economic meaning.

A puzzle

If the above arguments hold good, a question at once arises. If exchange-rate-based cross-country comparisons of GDP are analogous to current-price inter-temporal comparisons of GDP for a single economy, in that neither yields a valid measure of comparative real GDP, how is it that the need to correct for price changes is universally accepted in the latter case but widely rejected in the former? Answering this question throws light both on the rationale of PPP-based measures and on some reasons currently given for not accepting them for what they are.

PPP and 'MER': Some still-prevalent mistakes

Misconstruing PPPs

The meaning and rationale of PPP measures remain subject to various ill-founded notions. One such notion is that they do not arise from, or reflect, actual transactions. For example, Professor Lord Desai, in an intervention last year in the House of Lords (21 April 2004), expressed the view that

> nobody pays their bills in purchasing power parity: they pay it in real money, which is based on market exchange rates.

---

14 Richard Tol, 'Exchange Rates and Climate Change: an Application of *FUND*'. Within the SRES, a so-called PPP-based set of projections is given as a variant of the MESSAGE scenario group.

The fact is that PPP converters, as is clear from the index number formulae quoted above, are built up from detailed price comparisons that are based on actual purchases made in the respective domestic currencies in each of the countries concerned. For any pair of countries, and for all market transactions covered, 'real money' is involved.

A related argument is that while exchange rates are really existing entities, the values of which are known, PPP converters are no more than artificial constructs. Thus a group of authors associated with the SRES have argued, in responding to the critique of the Report that we had made, that

> ...the main appeal of market exchange rates is that they can actually be *observed* in the market transactions. In contrast, PPP need to be estimated by statistical offices and international organizations.[15]

But as just noted, PPP converters are derived from information relating to actual observed market transactions. It is true that they have to be estimated, and that different weighting procedures will yield different results: but the same is equally true of the price indices that are used to deflate current price series in order to derive estimates of real GDP for a single country. Even where 'MERs' can be readily observed, they do not yield a measure of differences in output.

On similar lines, some commentators view PPP converters as inferior *ersatz* exchange rates. In contrast to actual observed exchange rates, PPP estimates are portrayed as a costly and questionable rival product, built up from the obscure labours of statisticians round the world whose time could have been better spent. But PPP converters are not, and do not pretend to be, exchange rates: they are price index numbers that result from systematic inter-country price comparisons. Their purpose and rationale is to enable cross-country comparisons of output to be made, while at the same time yielding cross-country price comparisons which are of interest in their own right. The fact that they may be subject to uncomfortably wide error margins – as a result of data limitations, problems of comparability, and the relatively modest resources that often go into their compilation – is not a reason for giving up the task of producing and improving them, still less is it an argument for using exchange-rate-based conversions. As Jacob Ryten has correctly observed, 'The only viable alternative to the use of inadequate PPP-based estimates is better PPP-based estimates'.[16]

---

15 The quotation is taken from p.191 of 'IPCC SRES Revisited: A Response', by a group of 15 authors, published in *Energy and Environment*, Vol. 14, Nos 2 and 3, 2003.

16 Jacob Ryten, 'MERs, PPPs and IPCC: illusion and reality'. *Energy and Environment*, Vol. 15. No. 3, 2004.

Misdefining the rationale of PPP-based comparisons

A widely held mistaken belief is that PPP converters are appropriate for making international comparisons of GDP aggregates only when those comparisons relate to 'living standards': when comparing outputs and shares in world GDP, and in computing total world GDP, a 'MER'-based measure of some kind should be used. For example, Richard Cooper has argued, in a letter to *The Economist* (18 June 2004), that:

> ... how best to measure global output depends on the purpose of the measurement. Some variant of PPP is surely needed to compare standards of living across countries but for that we do not need global output. If we are interested in the vigour of global demand, national demand (and output) must be added by using market exchange rates, not PPP rates.

A similar distinction enters into the long established and still continuing practice of the World Bank, as expressed in its *World Bank Atlas*. The Director of the Bank's Development Data Group, in writing to one of us recently, expressed the view that 'we all agree that comparisons of welfare between countries are better stated using purchasing power parities'. When it comes to output, however, the latest edition of the *World Bank Atlas*, which is subtitled *Measuring Development*, states (6) that:

> While more than 80 percent of the world's people live in developing countries, their economies in 2003 produced goods and services worth \$7.1 trillion, about one-fifth of the world's total output ... To make comparisons between countries, local currencies must be converted to a common value ... Valuations based on exchange rates better measure the tradable value of a country's output and a country's relative importance in the global economy.

As against such ways of thinking, the following points are relevant.

- Global output is the sum total of the outputs of the countries that comprise the world economy. These can be compared one with another only by correcting for differences in the prices of the goods and services that enter into output - that is through the use of PPP converters.
- It makes no sense to argue, as the World Bank does, that 'exchange rates better measure the tradable value of a country's output', since there is no basis for estimating the comparative tradable value of non-tradable goods.
- In a world where exchange rates are often volatile, and often do not track changes in national price levels, there is no satisfactory basis for choosing a particular rate, or constellation of such rates, as valid or representative for cross-country comparisons of output. In this connection, it is worth noting

that even trade volumes, for country groupings as well as for individual economies, are computed without reference to the exchange rates that prevailed: export and import values are deflated by their own price or unit value indices.

- It is unclear what economy-wide national accounts aggregate, to be distinguished from real GDP and potentially divergent from it, is supposed to be the appropriate measure, with PPP converters as a basis, for making comparisons of 'living standards'. As noted above, cross-country PPP-based comparative figures for GDP do not measure, and do not claim to measure, differences in living standards.
- In the letter quoted above, Cooper refers to the problems of making accurate cross-country price comparisons, 'reflecting both the difficulty of finding truly comparable goods and services in different countries, then deciding how to weight them'. But the problems are no different in kind from those that arise in making long-run comparisons for individual economies.

A variant of the 'living standards' line of thinking finds expression, among other places, in the article by Richard Tol already quoted. The notion here is that the function of PPPs is to measure and compare inter-country differences in the cost of buying 'a standard basket of goods'. This too is a misapprehension. PPP converters are not defined with reference to a specific 'basket': their purpose (to repeat) is to enable estimates to be made of cross-country differences in real GDP, and following from this, of movements in the real GDP of country groupings and the world as a whole. Each economy has its own 'basket', which comprises its own aggregate output of goods and services.

In one more misdefining comparative output in this latest edition of its *Atlas,* the World Bank gives further currency, in the excerpt quoted above, to a widely repeated but seriously misleading statement. The statement is to the effect that the developing countries, with 80 per cent of the world's population, produce (or, on some interpretations, 'receive') only 20 per cent of total world GDP, while the rest produce (or, on some interpretations, 'take' or control) the remaining 80 per cent. This comparison is a favourite one with the President of the Bank, James Wolfensohn; and indeed it occurs in the most recently published issue of *World Economics*, in an article written by two World Bank staff members.[17] A more soundly based estimate, derived from PPP-based comparative data, is that the current share of developing countries in world GDP is well over 40 per cent.[18]

---

17 Kirk Hamilton and Ian Johnson, 'Responsible Growth to 2050', *World Economics*, Vol 5, no 4, October-December 2004. Three outrageous variations on the '80/20' theme, one of them from Wolfensohn, are quoted in David Henderson, *The Role of Business in the Modern World: Progress, Pressures and Prospects for the Market Economy,* London, Institute of Economic Affairs, 2004 (83-4) and Washington, DC, Competitive Enterprise Institute, 2004 (91-2).

18 Angus Maddison's estimates for 2001 would suggest a share of 42.5 per cent, while rapid growth in China and India since that year may well have pushed this figure up a bit. IMF projections for 2005 suggest a figure of close to 43 per cent.

Treating the issue as trivial or unimportant

In some quarters, the choice between exchange-rate-based and PPP-based conversions is wrongly seen as of little or no consequence. Thus in the IPCC press release of December 2003, referred to in footnote 4 above, the statement is made that 'the economy does not change by using a different metrics (PPP or MEX), in the same way that the temperature does not change if you switch from degrees Celsius to Fahrenheit'. A different variation on this theme of inconsequence was provided last April by Lord Desai, in his remarks in the House of Lords already quoted. He advanced then the view that, '... whether one takes one measure of GDP or another is very much a matter of taste'.

In weighing such dismissive assertions, the case of China today is instructive (though many other instances could be given). Last year one of us (Henderson) made the following comment, to no visible effect, on a speech by the present Leader of Her Majesty's Opposition:

> Michael Howard is quoted in today's *Times* (29 April) as saying that China's GDP is now close to that of Britain, and that the UK is the fourth largest economy in the world. Howard should know, and certainly his advisers should, that these are highly questionable statements. In my opinion, they are seriously misleading... Taking Angus Maddison's most recent estimates, which are for 2001, the GDP of China in that year appears as 3.8 times that of the UK. China is now easily the second largest economy in the world, while the UK comes seventh.

Over the period 2001-04 the gap has widened, since Chinese GDP appears to have grown by well over one quarter, as compared with an increase in the UK of some 7.5 per cent. Hence the ratio of Chinese to British GDP might now be put at around four and a half to one – and indeed, a figure of approximately 4.4 for 2005 is indicated by recent IMF data.

Whether the GDP of China today is roughly equal to that of the UK or well over four times as large is neither a mere matter of taste nor a trivial issue of choosing between two equivalent 'metrics'. The same is true of broader contrasting estimates of the gap in GDP per head between rich and poor countries. Thus in the recent report of the 'World Commission on the Social Dimension of Globalization', commissioned by the International Labour Office (ILO), the relative gap for the period 2000-02 between the twenty richest and the twenty poorest countries in the world is put at 120 to 1, whereas a PPP-based estimate would suggest a figure of around 40 to 1.[19]

---

19 *A Fair Globalization: Creating Opportunities for All,* Geneva, International Labour Office, 2004: 37. The figure of 40 to 1 is based on Maddison's estimates. The World Commission report was reviewed by one of us (Henderson) in *World Economics,* Vol 5 No 3, October-December 2004. Among the members of the Commission were two prominent academic economists, Professors Deepak Nayyar and Joseph Stiglitz.

Misleading figures for GDP can go together with correspondingly misleading figures for GDP-related ratios. A recent instance is contained in a study published last year by the International Energy Agency (IEA), entitled 'Analysis of the Impact of High Oil Prices on the Global Economy'. In reviewing the impact across countries, the study provides comparable measures of oil intensity, defined as 'primary oil consumed per unit of GDP'. In deriving this figure for different countries and country groups, the GDP of the countries covered is expressed in a common unit of measurement through conversion of national currencies into US dollars at actual exchange rates. As a result of this procedure, it is wrongly made to appear that (to quote a leading instance from the IEA text) India 'uses more than two and half times as much oil as developed countries per unit of GDP'. This again is not an instance merely of 'Celsius versus Fahrenheit'. It is not a trivial matter, nor a matter of indifference in judging the impact of higher oil prices on the Indian economy, whether that economy uses well over twice as much oil per unit of GDP as developed countries, as asserted by the IEA, or (as PPP-based estimates would suggest) much the same amount.

In all cross-country economy-wide comparisons, as also in relating such series as energy use or CO_2 emissions to GDP, it is real GDP – in other words, output – that is relevant. Only conversion of nominal GDPs through PPP converters yields a measure of cross-country differences in output: and the substitution of PPPs for 'MERs' in defining and measuring such differences can have a significant or even dramatic effect on how the world appears and how events and relationships are interpreted.

Disregarding evidence

In weighing the twin rival criticisms of PPP converters just outlined – that using them makes no difference to anything that matters, and that they have their uses but these do not extend to measuring differences in real GDP – facts and figures can shed some light. Again, the case of China today provides a good example. On an exchange-rate-based comparison, the share of China in world GDP in 2003 was close to 4 per cent, while for a PPP-based computation the figure can be put at around one-eighth. In considering which of these two widely divergent estimates may be nearer to the mark, the following illustrative data are of interest:

- *Agriculture:* According to the FAO database (FAOSTAT), in 2004 China's estimated share of the global output of selected agricultural commodities was: cereals, 19 per cent; fibre crops, 25 per cent; fruit, 15 per cent; vegetables, 50 per cent; roots and tubers, 26 per cent; meat, 28 per cent; eggs, 45 per cent; wool, 15 per cent; and milk 4 per cent.

- *Industrial commodities*: According to the Industrial Commodities Yearbook 2000, produced by the Statistics Division of the United Nations Department of Economic and Social Affairs, in 2000 China's share of the global output of major industrial commodities was: iron ore, 18 per cent; wheat flour, 31 per cent; cotton yarn, 40 per cent; cotton woven fabrics, 48 per cent; woollen woven fabrics, 29 per cent; sulphuric acid, 25 per cent; cement, 37 per cent; crude steel ingots, 17 per cent; refrigerators for household use, 18 per cent; washing machines for household use, 25 per cent; colour television receivers, 39 per cent; telephones, 49 per cent; and watches, 26 per cent.
- *Communications*: From information in the *Human Development Report 2004*, published by the United Nations Development Program (UNDP), it can be calculated that in 2002 China accounted for 20 per cent of the world total of telephone mainlines, 18 per cent of the world's cellular telephone subscribers and 10 per cent of the world internet subscribers.
- *Energy:* According to *Energy Balances of Non-OECD Countries 2001-2002*, published by the IEA, China in 2002 produced 12 per cent of the world's energy and accounted for 12 per cent of the world's total primary energy supply. China was responsible for 10 per cent of the total generation of electricity, and also for 10 per cent of the final consumption of electricity for all uses.

In the light of such evidence, it is absurd to argue that the choice between exchange rate-based and PPP-based estimates of the comparative size of the Chinese economy is arbitrary, unimportant, or no more than a matter of personal taste. Further, it is not credible to maintain, which as just noted the World Bank has recently done, that 'the tradable value of China's output', and its relative importance in the global economy, are better indicated by the country's share of global GNI measured at actual exchange rates (4 per cent) than by the corresponding share measured at purchasing power parities (12 per cent).

PPP and 'MER': The thinking and practice of international agencies

Official responsibility for the production and diffusion of international comparative economic data rests primarily with international agencies, though those agencies are subject to direction and supervision by their member governments. Over the past 15 years or so, there has been what Angus Maddison has termed a 'creeping acceptance' among the agencies of the case for basing comparisons of real GDP on PPP estimates, rather than relying on exchange rates, and for modifying published official statistics accordingly. However, as the following brief notes on agency practice suggest, the creeping process still has a long way to go.

IMF

A major step was taken in 1993 by the International Monetary Fund (IMF), when PPP-based weights were adopted as the basis for computing changes in world GDP in the Fund's *World Economic Outlook* (WEO). Since then the Fund's analyses of the world economy have relied entirely on PPP-based measures for inter-country comparisons of income and output and estimates of changes in world GDP. At the same time, however, the Fund's *International Financial Statistics* database, which presents 'MER' conversions, is a widely used source of GDP estimates from 1948 onwards; and by maintaining these series for all countries, the IMF is helping to perpetuate the inappropriate use of data that are based on such conversions.

OECD

Chronologically, the first displacement of exchange-rate-based estimates by a PPP-based alternative may well have been in the OECD, where the decision was made in 1990 to use estimates of GDP (PPP) to determine the country weights in the OECD-wide consumer price index. A similar reweighting was later introduced for the totals presented in the Organisation's *Economic Outlook*. However, in the Organisation's annual *National Accounts of OECD Countries: Main Aggregates* exchange-rate-based GDP comparisons are published in parallel with their PPP-based counterparts; and the main tabular presentation of comparative levels of GDP in *Monthly Economic Indicators* is done (a) in current prices and exchange rates and (b) in the prices and exchange rates of 2000.[20] Again, in its new publication, OECD Factbook: *Economic Environmental and Social Statistics*, the Organisation has incorporated uncritically exchange-rate-based data provided by the IEA.

IEA

Although one of the IEA's lapses has been noted already, a further word is in order here. The Agency's current practice is inconsistent. Its flagship publication is the biennial *World Energy Outlook*, which presents itself, on the back cover of its 2002 edition, as 'the authoritative source for projections of

20 In an OECD publication entitled OECD *Environment Outlook 2001*, it was stated (66) that the OECD countries accounted for 80 per cent of world GDP, which of course was an exchange-rate-based (and misleading) figure. However, this report appears to have had no successors.

global trends in energy supply and demand, trade and investment and carbon dioxide emissions'. Since the 1998 volume, all of the projections of output in successive editions of the *Outlook* have been PPP-based, and none has been expressed in terms of 'MERs'. The 2002 edition includes the statement (40, note 4) that:

> All GDP data in this report are expressed in 1995 dollars using purchasing power parities (PPPs) rather than market exchange rates...*This is important in analysing the main drivers of energy demand or comparing energy intensities among countries* (italics added).

Notwithstanding this firm (and correct) statement of doctrine on how to measure energy intensities, the Agency published last year (as noted above) comparative figures for oil intensities which, by contrast, incorporate exchange-rate-based conversions and hence give seriously misleading results. Again, its *Energy Balances of OECD Countries 2000-01:2003* edition presented an analysis of the relative importance of the OECD countries collectively in the world economy, and of their relative energy intensity as a group, which relied entirely on 'MER'-based estimates of GDP.[21] And the discussion in the text of the 2004 edition of the companion document (*Energy Balances of Non-OECD Countries*) assumes without explanation that 'world GDP' is the aggregate of country GDPs using exchange rates. On p. 1.50 it is stated that:

> In 2002, the world GDP experienced a 1.9% growth explaining in part a 2.2% growth in Total Primary Energy Supply. From 1971 to 2002 as an annual average, the growth of GDP and in TPES were respectively, 2.9% and 2.2%.

The GDP increases quoted here are incorrect. As one of the tables in the publication shows, estimated PPP-based world GDP increased between 2001 and 2002 by 2.9 per cent, not 1.9 per cent – so that it was higher, not lower, than the growth in TPES. Further, it can be seen from the same table that the annual average growth of world GDP from 1971 to 2002, correctly measured, was not 2.9 per cent but 3.3 per cent.

World Bank

Conspicuous inconsistencies of treatment are likewise to be seen in the past and current practice of the World Bank. In the 1997 edition of its annual publication, *World Development Indicators* (WDI), the bank gave estimates for a range of countries relating energy use to GDP in which the GDP figures

21 It included the statement, which belongs with the class of groundless '80/20' assertions already referred to, that 'In 2001, about 19per cent of the world population lived in the OECD, but more than 80 per cent of the world GDP was created in its 30 member countries'.

had been converted into US dollars using actual exchange rates: and it then said, misleadingly, that 'Per dollar of GDP, developing countries produce four times the carbon dioxide that high income economies do' (p.113). These same errors entered into the next two editions of WDI, but were corrected in the 2000 edition. However, the President of the Bank continued to use exchange rate conversions of GDP in his public speeches and in his personally signed 'Foreword' to each issue of the WDI and the *World Bank Atlas*; and in WDR 2003, published on the eve of the Johannesburg World Summit on Sustainable Development, the Bank repeated the statements that it had made in the late 1990s about the allegedly high relative consumption of energy in relation to GDP in non-OECD countries, which were said to use '3.8 times as much energy per dollar of GDP [as OECD countries]'.

When it comes to comparative figures for GDP, the bank publishes, for example in its annual *World Development Report,* country estimates and group and world totals on both a 'MER' and a PPP basis: the two are shown together in the same table, as though they had equal claims to validity. At the same time, and as noted above, in its flagship publication, the *World Bank Atlas*, the Bank continues to give prominence and a special status to flawed exchange-rate-based comparative figures, for reasons which do not hold water.

This is not an impressive record, especially for an organisation that lays special claim to economic expertise. It is high time for the Bank to improve further its handling and presentation of international comparative data, so as to ensure acceptable standards of accuracy and consistency.

UNDP

A recent case of change for the better is that of the United Nations Development Program (UNDP), in the context of its annual *Human Development Report* (HDR). Although from the outset in 1990 the Report made use of PPP-based comparative figures, in the issues for 1992 and subsequent years the authors used exchange-rate-based estimates of GDP to make exaggerated and well publicised claims about the extent of global inequality in incomes and to argue that inequality was continuing to widen (although PPP-based estimates showed the opposite).

Following the release of the widely quoted 1999 *Human Development Report,* one of us (Castles) made extensive statistical criticisms of the treatment there of trends in global poverty and inequality. At the request of the 2000 meeting of the UN Statistical Commission, those criticisms were examined by a group of expert statisticians constituted as the Friends of the Chair of the Commission. The report of this group upheld the main criticisms. In particular, it took the view that HDR 1999 had made a 'material error' (i.e. one which left the reader with 'a fundamentally distorted view of the phenomenon being described') in using national accounting aggregates converted into $US at current exchange rates to compare output and living standards between countries. The HDR Office of the UNDP accepted the criticism, and has improved its statistical presentation and reporting in subsequent issues of the Report.

SRES, IPCC and UNEP

Among the recent reports which have given approving currency to the 'material errors' contained in the 1999 HDR are the SRES, two major IPCC reports that formed part of the Panel's Third Assessment Report of 2001, and a leading publication of the United Nations Environment Program (UNEP) which is one of the IPCC's two parent agencies (the other is the World Meteorological Organisation).

As noted already, the SRES starts from an assumption that 'MER'-based estimates and projections of GDP can be taken as a measure of relative levels of economic activity. Consistently with this point of departure, the Report presents estimates of energy intensity which are misleading in the same way as those just referred to from the IEA and (in some earlier years) the World Bank. For example, two charts in the Report (pp.97 and 125) show alleged historical trends in comparative energy intensities, but both use 'MER'-based GDP as the denominator. The SRES contains 17 double-columned pages of references, yet the SNA is not listed there: it is possible that none of the 53 authors, 4 review editors and 89 expert reviewers who took part in the preparation of the Report were aware of the System and what is said in it.

It is not only in the SRES that similarly inappropriate exchange-rate-based comparisons are to be found in recent IPCC documents. The Panel operates through three Working Groups, each of which produced its own full-scale report as part of the Third Assessment Report. WGI is concerned with scientific aspects of climate change, WGII with the prospective impacts of such change and ways of adapting to it, and WGIII with mitigation of the impacts. In the WGIII Report, the old-style HDR is taken as the source for comparisons of GDP per head between rich and poor countries which are exchange-rate-based. The report quotes an early HDR as saying that 'in 1998 the richest fifth of the world population received 82.7% of the global income, which is nearly 60 times the share of the income received by the poorest fifth (1.4%)'; and the text goes on to quote the 1999 HDR as showing that since 1988 this relative gap had widened.[22] In the WGII Report also, these same UNDP comparisons are referred to, while misleading statements are made about the nature and purpose of PPP-based comparisons.

---

22 *Climate Change 2001: Mitigation*. A Report of Working Group III of the Intergovernmental Panel on Climate Change. Cambridge, Cambridge University Press, 2001: 97.

As just noted, the UNDP which was a prime source for these IPCC reports has now admitted its error, and has affirmed that international comparisons of real GDP should be PPP-based. This change of front on the part of the UNDP may have come too late to influence the drafting of the SRES and the two IPCC Working Group reports. One might however have expected that by 2003 news of the change would have reached the IPCC milieu, to be taken into account in a high-level conference organised by the Panel early that year in preparation for AR4. To the contrary: in the published proceedings of this conference one of the three current Vice-Chairs of the Panel, Professor Mohan Munasinghe, quoted yet again the same kinds of misleading international comparisons, long since disowned by the agency that had produced them, which had been referred to in the report of WGIII.

News of the UNDP's change of front was likewise not picked up by the UNEP, which made similarly misleading statements about 'the gap', also based on the 1999 issue of the HDR, in a major report which appeared in 2002.[23] In this flagship document it is also stated, contrary to the facts, that 'per capita incomes have risen *only marginally* in most regions [since 1972], *with the exception of* Europe and North America' (italics added).[24] The UNEP press release for the report says that over 1,000 people contributed to its preparation. It seems likely that, even aside from their shaky economic history, none of these persons was aware either of the admission made by the UNDP or of the existence of the 1993 SNA.

Paths to improvement

To ensure more accurate and more consistent treatment of international comparative data requires action by the member governments of responsible international agencies; but a wider understanding and agreement among economists and economic statisticians generally would be valuable in itself and would help to create and stiffen official resolve.

The main change required, a straightforward one, is agreement on the basic point that exchange-rate-based international comparisons of nominal GDP do not yield differences in output: to measure such differences, prices have to be directly compared, and PPP converters estimated accordingly. From this it follows (1) that comparative figures such as are to be found in the publications

23 UNEP, *Global Environment Outlook 3: Past, present and future perspectives*, London, Earthscan, 2002: 36.

24 On Maddison's estimates, average per capita incomes in Asia (excluding Japan), with 57 per cent of the world's population in 2001, almost trebled between 1972 and 2001. For China the increase was more than fourfold, while for the rest of developing Asia it was 129 per cent. The corresponding increase in per capita incomes in Europe and North America, with less than 12 per cent of the world's population in 2001, was 78 per cent.

of several international agencies, and are taken as the point of departure of the SRES, are misleading; (2) that to offer exchange-rate-based international series as an acceptable representation of historical events, and a data base that can be safely used by modellers, is a questionable practice; (3) that to make use of exchange-rate-based comparative GDP data in computing such ratios as energy intensities and emissions intensities is inadmissible; and (4) that in computing estimated changes in real GDP for country groupings or for the world as a whole, PPP-based weights should be used. Acceptance of these principles would open the way to major improvements in agency practice.

Official acceptance largely depends on actions, preferably taken in concert, within two areas of responsibility and expertise in member governments: first, national statistical offices; and second, the central economic departments of state – that is, treasuries, ministries of finance or economics, and, where they exist, agencies such as the US Council of Economic Advisers. In both areas, the basis for action has to be greater awareness of the issues, and of the scope for improving present international statistical systems and practice. A possible first step could be the setting up of a special commission of inquiry, along the lines of the UN Statistical Commission's 'Friends of the Chair' referred to above, but with wider sponsorship and terms of reference.

A special case

Among the various international mechanisms affected, the IPCC and its two supporting agencies constitute a special case. Here prompt action is called for, in the context of AR4, while resistance to change is strong and determined. We believe that a necessary first step is that national statistical offices and central economic departments of state should now become involved in the IPCC process; but the Panel, in responding to our critique, has rejected any suggestion of change. The opening paragraph of the official press release referred to above says of the IPCC that

> It mobilises the best experts from all over the world, who work diligently on bringing out the various reports ... The Third Assessment Review of the IPCC was released in 2001 through the collective efforts of around 2000 experts from a diverse range of countries and disciplines. All of IPCC's reports go through a careful two stage review process by governments and experts and acceptance by the member governments composing the Panel.

In relation to economic aspects, however, there is good reason to question the claims to authority and representative status that the IPCC makes on its behalf. We do not question the numbers of those involved, their diligence, or the existence and observance of formal review processes. But we think that when it comes to the treatment of leading economic issues, the IPCC milieu is neither fully competent nor adequately representative. We also hold that building in peer review is no safeguard against dubious assumptions, arguments and conclusions if the peers are all drawn from the same restricted professional milieu.[25]

Fortunately a straightforward route to wider official involvement in the IPCC process exists for the taking. For the economic departments and agencies in OECD member countries, an instrument is to hand for their prompt collective engagement: it is the OECD itself. They should act now to ensure that IPCC-related economic issues are placed on the agenda of the OECD's Economic Policy Committee, where they could be reviewed by the Organisation's Economics Department, in conjunction with its Statistics Directorate and Environment Directorate.

Beyond officialdom

It is not only in official circles that greater awareness, together with closer acquaintance with generally agreed principles of national income accounting, could help to clear a path to improvement. As the preceding text has shown, there remain surprisingly wide differences of opinion among economists on how these issues should be viewed and handled: we have cited here the cases of several leading members of the profession whose current opinions, though not necessarily identical or consistent with one another, are at variance with what is laid down in SNA93. We hope that the arguments we have advanced here will help to increase awareness, to widen professional debate, and to extend the area of agreement.

ANNEX I

Improving the International Statistical System: Building on Angus Maddison's Work

The text that follows formed the basis for a presentation by one of us (Henderson) at a conference held in Canberra in 1999 by the Academy of the Social Sciences in Australia. The case that it makes is still pertinent today.

In my remarks this morning, I paid tribute to Angus Maddison's work as a source of data, analysis and ideas on the long-continuing story of economic growth and change across the world. Much could be said about his contribution, but here I want to stress three aspects of it in particular:

25 It is not only in relation to economic aspects that such queries have been raised about the IPCC process and its results by critics writing about other subject areas.

- First is its *range* in both space and time. In principle, though subject of course to availability of data, every country in the world is covered. In every case, statistical series are laid out, and quantitative evidence presented, as far back in history as the often limited sources will permit.
- Second is *comparability*: estimates of GDP, as of some connected series too, are expressed in common units of measurement, so that comparisons can be made across countries and between different periods of time. Related to this is a third key aspect, which is that of
- *Continuity*: for most countries of the world, from whatever date the available evidence makes this possible, continuous annual series are presented.
- For the harassed user of figures, these three features combine to yield a store of published data which within its limits – for to be sure, not all the relevant aspects of economic change are covered – is uniquely rich, accessible and convenient to use. No other source in the world compares with it. In particular, the statistical output of the various international agencies, incorporating though it does, directly and indirectly, the work of thousands of professionals, has not to my mind yielded a comparably useful product of the same kind.

I believe that what Maddison has done offers ideas and lessons for improving the present international statistical system. In my view, one element in a program of improvement should take the form of a conscious attempt to build on Maddison's achievement and his vision of what is needed. His example should be followed, and his work continued, refined and extended, by the international agencies and the governments that support them.

Let me illustrate and clarify this notion with a concrete example to show the kinds of improvements I have in mind. Here I draw on my own experience – my own sad experience, let me add, since it relates to one of the failures of my years as Head of what was then the Economics and Statistics Department of the OECD.

Among its many statistical publications, the OECD produces an annual volume entitled *OECD Historical Statistics*.[26] Its coverage is restricted, quite properly, to the OECD member countries. Within this limit, care is taken to try to ensure that the figures are internationally comparable; and as compared with Maddison, the volume covers a much wider range of headings and series. So far, so good; but there are two serious limitations.

- The series go back only as far as 1960, the time of the earliest beginnings of the Organisation.
- Even for the years that have passed since then, the value of the publication as an historical source is fatally undermined by two features. First, it gives

26 No longer true. Alas, since this presentation was made, the OECD has actually discontinued the publication.

data only for selected years, not continuous annual series; and second, many of the figures are presented in the form of year-to-year percentage changes, although these are useful only for short-term analysis.

During my time at the OECD I tried to remedy this situation. I decided that, rather than remodelling *OECD Historical Statistics*, we would replace it with a new, more ambitious and better-designed product. This would so far as possible take all the series back to 1900; and in every case, again subject only to availability of data, continuous annual figures would be shown: the idea was to establish a comprehensive '20th century data base' for the OECD countries. Two eminent scholars, Charles Feinstein and Angus Maddison, agreed to direct the project as consultants. With their help we drew up a project proposal. All that remained was to raise the quite modest sum of money required to get the new publication launched; but in this our best efforts, which I dare say were less skilful than they could have been, proved unavailing. None of the sources that we approached, public or private, was interested in supporting such a venture.

Despite its failure to take off, I think my idea at OECD was a good one. I would like to see a project of this kind designed and put into effect today, preferably covering the world as a whole and not just the OECD area (though an OECD venture would be an excellent start). I think that agencies and governments should now work towards establishing and maintaining a comprehensive and accessible database for the world, and for individual countries and groupings of countries within it.

I have put this suggestion in the context of long-run historical series, but it applies equally to recent developments and newly emerging statistics. My concern is not only for quantitative economic historians and historically minded economists, but also for commentators on the events of today and tomorrow. I would like to see current and newly published data made available within a similar comprehensive and accessible framework, which at present they are not.

As to roles and procedures, there are various possible lines of action, and I will not consider them today. The main thing now is to get the idea itself more fully worked out and put into circulation.

Part Three: Measuring Inequality

17. What Can We Learn from International Evidence on Trends in Income Distribution?

Henry Ergas[1]

Introduction

In an essay comparing living standards in Australia and Japan, Ian Castles described the challenge for policymakers as being that of using 'the skills and strengths of their peoples to improve opportunities for the enhancement of their well-being in its broadest sense' (Castles, 1990: 16). There was, he noted, 'little point in trying to encapsulate the differences [in wellbeing] in any single measure' (*ibid*: 15), but that hardly meant one should not attempt to measure carefully what could be measured. It was in that spirit that Castles undertook several international comparisons of living standards and income distribution, including between Australia, Japan, Sweden and the United States (Castles, 1984, 1990).

Read today, those comparisons stand out for the care Castles took to rest his assessment on a sound analytical base. Indeed, there are respects in which those comparisons remain unmatched, notably in adjusting PPP exchange rates to reflect differences in consumption baskets by income group. Thus, Castles was particularly attentive to the fact that relative prices were lower in Australia than in comparator countries for the goods and services which feature particularly prominently in the consumption baskets of lower income households. Although the biases in PPP exchange rates are well known (Almås, 2012), they are rarely taken into account and even more rarely as scrupulously as they were by Castles.

Castles' attention to those adjustments is both a testament to the quality of his work and suggestive of the motivations underpinning his comparisons of income distribution. Although his presentation is anything but polemical, it is difficult to resist the impression that his studies responded, at least in part, to claims that the distribution of incomes in Australia was unequal by international standards. Castles showed that that view was unduly simplistic, and that while the distribution of incomes in Australia was perhaps less equal than in Sweden

1 Many thanks but no blame due to Jonathan Pincus, Peter Whiteford, Alex Robson, Peter Crone, David Henderson and Andrew Podger.

(though more equal than in the United States and Japan), living standards for low-income Australians were still very high both in comparative and absolute terms.

Since then, concerns about distribution have, if anything, become more pronounced – indeed, the previous Treasurer claimed that the distribution of income and wealth is the commanding issue facing Australians (Swan, 2012). That claim will be surprising to those who recall John Kenneth Galbraith's *The Affluent Society*. 'Few things are more evident in modern social history', Galbraith wrote in what was certainly no paean to free markets, 'than the decline of interest in inequality as an economic issue' (Galbraith, 1958: 82). The reason for that decline, said Galbraith, was simple: the triumph of economic growth, which ensured prosperity (at least in its 'private affluence' variety) through rising incomes for all, rather than by shuffling incomes around.

By the time Castles wrote, however, that phase was over, and even economic growth itself was contested as a value, provoking Castles into a brilliant defence of economic growth (Castles, 1973). In such a mood of (poorly informed) pessimism, the focus on issues of distribution was perhaps understandable. But once growth returned, that focus did not disappear. On the contrary, writing at the end of a remarkable phase of global economic expansion, which had lifted hundreds of millions of people out of misery, Angel Gurria, the Secretary General of the OECD, called 'fears of rising income inequalities and poverty' issues that 'require correcting the asymmetries in the costs and benefits of globalization' (OECD, 2008: 3). Returning to the theme in 2011, in a preface to an OECD report on trends in income distribution, the Secretary-General expressed those views yet more strongly. 'Popular discontent' about income distribution, he wrote, 'is spreading rapidly'; and rightly so, for the OECD report 'dispels the assumption that the benefits of economic growth will automatically trickle down to the disadvantaged' (OECD, 2011: 18-19). That the 400-page OECD report never discussed the relation between economic growth and income distribution did not prevent the Secretary-General from concluding that 'without a strategy for inclusive growth', including tax and other measures to 'counter rising inequality', 'inequality will continue to rise' (OECD, 2011: 19).

That those views have wide resonance is difficult to doubt. And it is indeed true that the distribution of income in most OECD countries has become somewhat more unequal, though any such conclusion involves a number of issues of measurement and interpretation discussed below. But before turning to those issues it is worth noting quite how small the changes have been relative to the concerns they have provoked.

The rise in the Gini coefficient for the distribution of market incomes in Australia is a case in point. From 1985 to the present, the Gini coefficient for market income increased by some 0.06 points. Using the methodology set out in Blackburn

(1989), that rise corresponds to shifting around six per cent of average market income from those below the median market income to those above it. Of course, expressed as a share of below median incomes, that proportion would be higher, say 12 per cent. However, merely over the much shorter period from 1995 to the present, real market incomes for the bottom decile more than doubled (calculated from OECD, 2011: 23).

As a result, if it is indeed correct that – as Kuznets (1955) famously surmised – periods of growth based on rapid structural change involve an initial widening in the distribution of market incomes, the slight rise in inequality seems a small price to pay. Additionally, it is readily seen that if policies aimed at reversing the rise in inequality reduce economic growth, their costs, even to those they are aimed at assisting, could readily exceed the benefits.

The case for caution in tinkering with market-driven changes is all the stronger in Australia, where it is not clear that there is a problem policy needs to solve. On the contrary, developments in the Australian income distribution seem something of a success story. It is helpful to set out some features of that story as background (noting that they are discussed more fully by Peter Whiteford and Robert Bray, in this volume) before turning to the substance of this paper.

Simplifying to a headline level the basic trends over the period from the mid-1980s to the onset of the Global Financial Crisis (drawn from OECD, 2008 and OECD, 2011, and highlighting, in italics, the different income concepts) are these:

- As in other OECD countries, the largest single factor changing the *distribution of market income* was changes in the distribution of labour earnings;
- However, the OECD data suggest that in contrast to what happened elsewhere, we experienced a compression in the *distribution of real wages*, as the relative wages of lower paid workers increased;
- But the impact of this on the *distribution of earnings from employment* was partly offset by changes in average hours worked, which diminished at the bottom end of the wage distribution while increasing at the top. While these shifts also happened elsewhere, a difference in Australia was that hours increased for that group whose relative wages fell (that is, above the median of the wage distribution), while falling for those for whom they increased (that is, below the median of the wage distribution). Had the responses gone the other way – in other words, had labour supply been elastic – the changes in hours would have reinforced, rather than offset, the change in the wage distribution, as happened in the United States;
- At the same time, as unemployment diminished and participation increased, the *distribution of market income in the working age population* became somewhat more even, relative to the distribution of income from employment, as also tended to happen (albeit to differing extents) elsewhere;

- Nonetheless, taking account of taxes and income transfers, there was some increase in the Gini coefficient for the *distribution of disposable income* between households, probably in the order of 0.03 points.

That this story has many positive features is clear. For instance, increased participation was related to strong demand for labour, greater flexibility in employment contracts and the associated increased availability of part-time work, reduced effective marginal tax rates for some income earners and restrictions on access to, and the generosity of, some income transfers. At the same time, the change in the pattern of hours (whereby hours increased significantly for high income earners, while diminishing for low income earners) could reflect socially desirable responses to lower marginal tax rates at the top and to the greater availability of part-time work at the bottom and in the middle of the earnings distribution.[2] To that extent, these factors would move the economy in the direction of a more efficient use of resources.

Yet it is also clear that there are questions. For instance, the compression of the real wage distribution might reflect a greater net *supply* shift than elsewhere towards better skilled workers, or it could reflect a lesser net *demand* shift towards better skilled jobs. In other words, there must at least be the possibility that there was less technological change than elsewhere and/or that it was less skill-biased.

Equally, while the change in hours could reflect the socially desirable responses set out above, the pattern of that shift does seem somewhat unexpected, as one would have expected labour supply to be relatively elastic below the median income level and relatively inelastic at the higher end of the income distribution. While the observed shifts were slight, it remains the case that had that pattern of elasticities held, as in the United States, the changes in hours would have accentuated rather than offset the impact of changes in wage relativities on the distribution of earnings. Yet hours diminished at the bottom, where relative wages were rising, and increased at the top. Moreover, at the top, the participation rate of married women in couples with at least one income earner seems to have increased less than elsewhere, though the earnings of those who did work increased in line with elsewhere. Given those trends, it may be that the tax and transfer systems continue to discourage labour supply both at the lower and at the upper end of the income distribution.[3]

Addressing these questions would go far beyond my scope. But they do highlight the complexities involved in disentangling changes in the distribution

---

2 The recession of the early 1990s may have been a stronger factor in increasing part-time employment in that period, but part-time job growth subsequently remained strong even as the unemployment rate fell to or even below the Non-Accelerating Inflation Rate of Unemployment.

3 It is of course possible for labour supply curves to be backwards bending, but, absent policy distortions, it would be surprising for them to be in the backward sloping segment at both the top and the bottom of the wage distribution.

of incomes – much as Castles said about economic growth, those changes are not an instrument governments can sensibly seek to control directly: they '"come out" of the complex of decisions made by governments, institutions and individuals ... (and are) to be neither pursued nor shunned' (Castles, 1973:1). It is in the light of, and by reference to, those complexities that in this chapter I seek to make four points: first, not all apparent increases in income inequality are a bad thing; second, not all apparent reductions in income inequality are a good thing; third, even those aspects of the trends that might be problematic may not be as worrying as commonly made out; and fourth and last, some of the proposed policy approaches central to what the OECD Secretary-General has termed 'inclusive growth' merit a healthy degree of skepticism.

Not all increases in inequality are bad for you

Were incomes merely endowments, there would be little justification for distributing them unequally, rather than on the basis of needs.[4] In reality, however, incomes are sensitive to investments in effort and in foregoing current consumption for the sake of future abilities. Moreover, market prices for the capabilities created by those investments play an important allocative role, guiding the investments themselves and ensuring acquired skills (and innate abilities) are put to their most highly valued uses. Since redistributive policies distort those signals, 'we cannot', as Arthur Okun used to say, 'have our cake of market efficiency and share it equitably'.

All that is not likely to be contentious, at least among those who have given these matters any thought. Indeed, even the late GA (Jerry) Cohen, an eminent political philosopher and unrepentant Marxist, only a few years ago concluded, after a life time of efforts to show the opposite, that attempts to bypass the informational and incentive functions of market prices were utopian (Cohen, 2009). But none of that means changes in income distribution should necessarily be viewed benignly; and it is understandable that an apparent widening in disparities would at least give rise to questions and possibly concerns. However, in answering those questions, it is crucial to look behind the simpler indicators.

There is, in particular, a risk that relying on aggregate measures of income distribution will hide important shifts occurring within the aggregate – shifts that are more to be applauded than condemned. Three examples make the point.

First, there is considerable evidence that the earnings gap between men and women has narrowed. Thus, examining data for the United States, Welch

4 Giving kidney transplants to those who need them, but not to those who don't, is unequal (in Rae's sense of 'lot regarding inequality', which gives the same shoes to all, despite differences in foot size – Rae, 1981) but not inequitable, at least in Aristotle's sense of proportionate equality.

(1999) finds that over the period from 1967 to 1997 representation in the upper quarter of the market income distribution increased five-fold for white women and ten-fold for black women (admittedly, in the latter case, from a very low base). Equally, examining data for the UK, Goldthorpe and McKnight (2006) find that while age/earnings profiles for women in higher-level occupations in 1975 resembled those of women in lower-level occupations, by 1999 they were aligned on the higher and significantly steeper profiles for men.

These moves towards gender equality in pay have given rise to increased dispersion in the overall income distribution not only directly but also through assortative mating, i.e. the tendency for more highly educated men to marry more highly educated women – with the OECD (2011: 207) estimating that after the change in the dispersion of male earnings, assortative mating was the second largest contributor to the increase in the inter-decile ratio of Australian household incomes (that is, the ratio of market earnings in the top to the bottom decile).

There has, to that extent, been a decrease in *between*-group inequality matched by a corresponding rise in *within*-group and *aggregate* inequality. Put simply, as women earned a market return that better reflected their skills, the effect was to increase the variance of women's incomes (as between low and high skill women) and of incomes overall. But is difficult to see how that could be a bad thing – on the contrary, it is the largely predictable result of decreasing inequality between segments of society (as anticipated in Rae, 1981).

Secondly, *cross-sectional* measures of income distribution (that is, the distribution across the relevant population at one point in time) may obscure changes that work through income variation *over time* (i.e. longitudinally) and that potentially increase dispersion in a cross-sectional sense while not doing so (and indeed raising all or most incomes) over lifetimes.

Consider, for example, declines in the depreciation rate of individuals' earnings abilities, i.e. the postponement, perhaps as a result of the greater share of human capital in individual's bundle of capabilities or of improved overall health, of the age at which the returns to experience decline. Such a postponement, if it leaves mean incomes unchanged (and so is mean-preserving in income for a given stock of experience and education) increases the slope of age/earnings profiles in the Mincerian equation relating wages to education and experience; it therefore increases inequality in the cross-sectional income distribution (Welch, 1999). However, over time, all currently less experienced workers will become more experienced, and so for a pure mean-preserving change, lifetime inequality is unchanged. And if the fall in the depreciation rate increases incomes and more generally wellbeing, as is likely, this change too is to be welcomed rather than condemned.

Third and last, a similar problem with cross-sectional distributions arises from changes in risk-aversion.

As Friedman and Savage noted in their classic paper on choice under uncertainty, 'occupations differ greatly in the variability of the incomes they offer, (and) individuals, in choosing among occupations, are making choices analogous to those they make when they decide whether to buy insurance or to gamble' (Friedman and Savage, 1948: 279). This is important because as incomes rise, individuals should become more willing to bear risk.[5] As societies grow richer, one would therefore expect a greater share of economic activity to involve relatively risky choices, which in turn gives rise to a higher dispersion of realised income in each period (Halaby, 2003).

Over time, however, repeated risky bets will yield a lifetime distribution of returns that is more equal, while consumption smoothing will ensure the distribution of consumption is less unequal than the cross-sectional distribution of income. Moreover, the greater willingness to bear risk – be it through the choice of self-employment, of riskier forms of dependent employment and/or of increased investment in relatively risky financial assets – will increase incomes overall (as the cost of risk bearing falls), making this change also one to be welcomed.

It is difficult to know how large an impact changes in risk aversion have had on overall changes in income distribution. While the dispersion of incomes from self-employment has increased, accounting decompositions suggest these have made a relatively small contribution to increased dispersion in earnings (OECD, 2011: 238). As for the impact of returns on financial assets, these too made a small, but in this case rising, contribution to measured inequality, though less so in Australia than elsewhere (OECD, 2011: 239). Shifts towards riskier forms of employment have not, however, been considered in the literature, though there is evidence that the use of forms of remuneration more dependent on performance, and hence involving greater risk, has made a significant contribution to increased earnings dispersion, at least in the United States (Lemieux, Bentley MacLeod and Parent, 2007).

None of this, however, is to deny that the main source of changes in the earnings dispersion in the advanced economies concerns increases in the returns to skill, and especially to the higher levels of skill (relative both to low-level skills and to mid-level, routine, skills). This reflects a combination of skill-biased technological change (Goldin and Katz, 2008) and of factors that increase the international tradeability of routine information processing tasks (Acemoglu and

5 If individuals have roughly constant relative risk aversion, absolute risk aversion decreases significantly with income. For instance, with log utility, in which utility = LN(c), absolute risk aversion is (1/c), so individuals with one-tenth as much 'c' have ten times as high a level of absolute risk aversion.

Autor, 2010). In the immediate, such a change has winners and losers, though on net, the benefits are likely to be substantial. Without changes in relative earnings, however, the signals to adjust to that change would be weakened, and in particular, the incentives for long-term skill acquisition would be reduced.

As a result, while this change can create immediate issues for those whose relative market earnings have declined (and obviously so if their earnings decline in absolute terms), the key long run issue is with whether adaptation can occur to an increased skill premium – an issue considered in the discussion of policy proposals below.

Not all reductions in inequality are good for you

Just as not all increases in conventional measures of income dispersion are bad, so not all reductions in dispersion are good.

A striking case, with some relevance to current Australian policy debates, is that of wage compression associated with collective bargaining and employment protection laws.[6] As a general matter, international comparisons show that stronger unions and higher levels of collective bargaining are associated with a narrower wage and earnings spread, as are more stringent employment protection laws (Blau and Kahn, 1996). Those narrower wage spreads reduce labour force participation rates, especially among the unskilled (Blau and Kahn, 1996). Moreover, while employment protection laws reduce the rate at which protected workers transition to unemployment, they increase the duration of those spells of unemployment, with the second effect being greater than the first (Blanchard and Portugal, 1998).

As a result, employment protection laws lead to a higher equilibrium rate of unemployment. So as to counter that effect, since the 1990s many governments have granted exemptions to the laws for workers on temporary or contingent contracts, allowing those contracts to act as a pressure valve in the labour market (Rueda, 2008). The overall impact is twofold: a compression of wage differentials, reducing measured dispersion in the earnings distribution (Atkinson and Brandolini, 2006); and a sharp split in the labour market between 'insiders' and 'outsiders', with the former in highly protected jobs while the latter bear the vast brunt of cyclical and structural changes.

6 Employment protection laws impose restrictions on the ability of employers to dismiss employees or alter their conditions of employment. They affect earnings by changing the distribution of bargaining power between employers and the protected employees and make it easier for unions to secure agreements that provide rents to the employees with the greatest weight in union decision-making.

In France, for instance, one of the few OECD countries where the wage dispersion has fallen over time, temporary employment contracts account for some nine per cent of all jobs but generate 80 per cent of employment turnover in French establishments (DiPrete, Goux, Maurin and Quesnel-Vallee, 2006). Workers on temporary contracts face a risk of unemployment that is up to ten times greater than that of permanent employees, both because the hazard rate is so high and because their unemployment durations are long (Maurin, 2010). Moreover, that higher risk is not offset by higher expected earnings when in employment. The resulting differential in risk exposure therefore amounts to a reduction in the 'full wage', relative to the nominal rate of pay; but that reduction is not reflected in the income distribution data, which consequently understates the dispersion in effective income.

The economic costs of these distortions obviously go far beyond the understatement of income inequality. High turnover in temporary jobs – whose duration is usually limited by statute – discourages employers from investing in employee skills, thereby preventing employees from accumulating experience that would increase their lifetime earnings, which reduces the rate of growth of productivity (Dolado and Stucchi, 2008). At the same time, the difference in effective (risk-adjusted) earnings between insiders and outsiders increases competition for the protected jobs, leading to costly forms of rent dissipation, including over-investment in credentialing (Maurin, 2010). Additionally and somewhat paradoxically, international comparisons of public opinion surveys show that stronger laws against dismissal increase insiders' fear of being made redundant, doubtless because the consequences of losing one's job are so severe in terms of the likely duration of unemployment and the associated permanent income loss (Clark and Postel-Vinay, 2008). The result is a stronger correlation between earnings and perceived income insecurity than in countries with more flexible labour markets, setting the basis for politically powerful coalitions that push for high public employment and generous welfare benefits (Rehm, Hacker and Schlesinger, 2012), with fiscal consequences all too apparent in Europe's current difficulties.

The fact that the measured dispersion of labour income has increased less in countries with stringent employment protection laws is therefore hardly an indication of success. But all this is missed in simple comparisons of cross-sectional income distributions, which regularly imply that narrower means better.

Some changes could be bad for you

None of that, however, implies the appropriate attitude to changes in income distribution is one of indifference. Rather, cogent concerns have been expressed about the risks of hardship for those at the bottom, the dangers of privilege accruing to those at the top, and the longer-term implications of a widening income distribution for mobility and equality of opportunity. But while these issues cannot be dismissed lightly, they do need to be kept in perspective. I consider each of them in turn.

Poverty

At least in Australia, the persistence of poverty is reasonably close to the OECD average (OECD, 2008: 157-8, 171), with the HILDA data suggesting relatively low three-year persistence. Moreover, even for those at the bottom of the distribution, rising incomes reduce the risk of relative deprivation: if poverty is defined as an income lower than half the median income of a decade earlier (rather than with respect to the median income of today), the proportion in poverty is reduced by over 50 per cent and is reasonably low by international standards (OECD, 2008: 130). Additionally, the poverty gap – defined as the proportion of the poor living with disposable incomes far below the poverty line – is low, absolutely and by international standards (OECD, 2008: 128), again suggesting a risk of hardship that is low and likely to be tightly localised in groups with multiple sources of disadvantage, such as Indigenous Australians.

All this confirms the more general, but crucial, point that the distribution of consumption is far more equal than that of income: for instance, a recent study by the ABS using national accounts data finds that while the inter-quintile ratio[7] for wages and salaries is in the order of 6.5, the inter-quintile ratio for actual individual consumption is only 1.6 (Smedes, 2012), reflecting consumption smoothing and the redistributive impact of taxes and transfers. Even assuming some error in these ABS estimates, other ABS sources (notably the Household Expenditure Survey, which may have the opposite bias) suggest a consumption gap of around three to one, which is still a very significant reduction relative to the difference in wages and salaries.

That hardly means there are no concerns: the plight of localised groups, especially Indigenous Australians, calls for a more effective policy response. Additionally, a point stressed in Castles (1984 and 1990) seems relevant. Castles noted that prices for income-inelastic goods, relative to those for income-elastic goods, were low in Australia, compared to the other countries for which he had

7 The ratio of the relevant share to the top quintile to that share for the bottom quintile.

data (the United States, Sweden and Japan). That increased the relative living standards of low-income households, as did the abundant availability of low-priced or un-priced resources (such as camping grounds and playing fields).[8]

In recent years, however, charges for utilities, public transport and government-provided facilities have risen sharply, with especially steep increases in water and electricity prices (RBA, 2012:61). While those increases have been to a degree offset by income transfers, taper provisions in the compensation tend to increase effective marginal tax rates, accentuating the disincentives for full-time work and increasing the risk of 'poverty traps'.

Top incomes

Seen in international perspective, the income share of the top one per cent of income earners tends to move relatively closely with aggregate concentration (Leigh, 2007). In Australia, the increase in that share has been modest: the income share of the top five per cent of income earners rose from 16 per cent in 1973 to around 20 per cent in 2009/10 – still far below the 40 per cent level it reached in 1922.

In relative terms, the trend since the 1980s is very similar to the trend in other rich English-speaking countries, with the share for the richest one per cent of taxpayers roughly doubling from five per cent to 10 per cent between 1980 and 2007. It is worth noting, however, that the share of the top one per cent was in comparative terms very low in 1979-80, so that the doubling of the income share put Australia post-2000 in the same range as France and Japan, but significantly lower than Canada or the United Kingdom, and about half the share of the richest one per cent in the USA.[9]

Nonetheless, as the former Treasurer's recent essay shows (Swan, 2012), few issues have raised as much ire, bearing out both Tocqueville's observation that democracy can fan 'a debased taste for equality' (Tocqueville, 1969: 57) and Hancock's conclusion that Australians – a people that 'loves oratory, and does not love statistics' – are inclined to be 'merciful to the average' and suspicious of the best, indulging the 'destructive vandalism of the weak' (Hancock, 1931: 143, 146, 304). Yet there is no shortage of factors that would lead one to expect the top income share to have increased in recent decades. These include:

- The rapidly growing absolute size of firms and their internationalisation, which has increased the size of managerial hierarchies and intensified international competition for talent, with the largest benefits accruing to

8 For instance, Castles estimated that on a per capita basis, Sydney residents had access to four times as many public open space sites as residents in Kyoto and eight times as many as residents in Tokyo. As for public playing fields and tennis courts, these were ten to twenty times greater (Castles, 1990:15-16).

9 I am grateful to Peter Whiteford for the data presented in this paragraph.

English-speaking executives (reflecting the role of English as the lingua franca of global business);

- More intense product market competition and improvements in corporate governance, which have also increased the returns on management skill and intensified competition in managerial labour markets;
- Better techniques for monitoring and measuring executive performance, which have increased the role of performance-related pay and allowed the highest performing managers to capture a greater part of the potential gains from trade;[10] and
- Reductions in top marginal tax rates, which may have increased labour effort by the top decile.[11]

Indeed, the vast literature on the rise in top earnings finds that any one of these contributes significantly to the trend, and that many suffice, or come close to sufficing, to explain the entire observed change (see for instance Veall, 2012). As a result, a higher share of top earners in the overall income distribution is in itself no indication of inefficiency.

Additionally, as with poverty, persistence at the top of the Australian income distribution seems to be relatively low, with an annual exit rate from the highest one per cent of income earners that, at nearly 40 per cent, is significantly above that in Canada (where it is around 30 per cent) and the United States (around 27 per cent) (OECD, 2011: 353).[12] Also high is the effective average tax rate on Australian top income earners, which is three percentage points higher than that in Canada, five percentage points higher than that in Sweden and 10 percentage points higher than that in the United States (OECD, 2011: 363).[13]

That said, it is true that the assistance provided to the financial system during the Global Financial Crisis may create significant issues of moral hazard going forward, including in terms of executive pay; but those issues seem best addressed directly, rather than being a question of the long-run trend in the income distribution as such.

As a result, it is difficult to put much weight on the concerns that have been expressed about top incomes, at least from an economic perspective. However,

---

10 These techniques reduce agency problems in the shareholder-manager relationship and hence reduce the waste those problems create in terms of foregone productivity improvements (the 'agency loss'). This increases the gain to hiring good managers and hence should give rise to higher earnings.

11 The OECD provides data for the top quintile, which shows a slight increase in hours worked – see OECD, 2011:188.

12 Paul Samuelson used to quote Schumpeter to the effect that the top floor in capitalism's best hotels was invariably full, but always with different people. Turnover rates of 30 per cent or more are certainly reminiscent of Schumpeter's *bon mot*.

13 As Peter Whiteford has pointed out to me, these estimates refer to labour income taxes and do not include social security contributions. However, social security contributions are usually slightly regressive, so excluding them is unlikely to change the international comparison. Moreover, for Australia, they do not include the superannuation guarantee.

those concerns have been paralleled by claims that a rising share of top incomes could compromise the functioning of democratic institutions. The explicit or implied parallel is with the United States where, it is argued, political donations distort the democratic process.

These claims are difficult to evaluate. There is no doubt politics has become more capital intensive (Aldrich, 1995); the question is whether that has allowed the very wealthy, as their share of aggregate income rises, to exercise greater influence. At least as matters now stand, the evidence is inconclusive. Morris Fiorina, a leading contemporary scholar of American politics, does not list income shares as a factor affecting the current difficulties of the American political system (Fiorina, 2009), although there are scholars who have come to the opposite conclusion (Gilens, 2012). As for the recent highly critical study by leading scholars Thomas Mann and Norman Ornstein, while they are deeply concerned by the role of money in US politics, they regard it as essentially a second order issue and term reform proposals 'quixotic', though that may reflect pessimism as to the prospects for change (Mann and Ornstein, 2012:127-130). Meanwhile, research into Congressional voting patterns finds that very broad interest groups – such as those representing retirees, public sector employees and environmentalists – are as effective as narrower interest groups, and in some cases more so, in shaping agendas and outcomes (Grossmann, 2012; and Trumbull, 2012).

Given mixed findings for the United States, the contention that the far more limited increase in the share of top earners in the Australian income distribution threatens democracy seems exaggerated. This is all the more the case given the characteristics of the Australian political system, including the relatively centralised nature of the political parties and the fact that unions – not wealthy individuals – are the largest and most stable source of external resource transfers (with almost all of the transfers unions make going to a single party).

None of that is to deny that wealthy individuals have recently played an important role in Australian politics, with the influence of property developers on the New South Wales Labor government being well documented (Cavalier, 2102) and giving rise to seemingly serious issues of corruption (Freestone and Williams, 2012:204-5). That said, the roots of the problem lie less in income distribution than in government policies (particularly with respect to land use and planning restrictions) that create rents politicians can allocate on a discretionary basis – indeed, the distortions to income distribution (in terms of the high returns to certain forms of property development) have tended to arise *from*, rather than *cause*, the government policies, although they may then ensure those policies are perpetuated. As a result, those issues seem best addressed by reforming policy so as to remove the rents at issue, together with increased transparency, tighter controls on political donations (including by unions) and strengthened measures against corruption, rather than by tinkering with the overall distribution of income.[14]

Social mobility

This leads to the third and final source of concern which is with longer-run social mobility. Ultimately, social mobility goes to equality of opportunity, which is not only a core element in the legitimacy of market systems but also central to efficiency: if talent is widely distributed across income groups, precluding the talented children of poorer people from contending for the more senior positions in society, while reserving some of those positions for the less talented offspring of richer people, is an inefficient allocation of resources. The question is therefore whether increased inequality in the distribution of incomes reduces social mobility, and hence results in such an inefficiency.

As typically defined, equality of opportunity involves an equal chance to participate in the race, rather than an equal chance to win it – as the chances of winning should be sensitive to ability, which is at least partly inheritable.[15] Those chances are also sensitive to attributes such as diligence and ambition, that even staunch egalitarians (for instance Dardarnoni, Fields, Roemer and Puerta, 2006) recognise ought to affect outcomes, despite their correlation with family background. That recognition notwithstanding, economists and sociologists typically assess the degree to which there is equality of opportunity by examining outcomes rather than prospects, and in particular, by measuring the correlation between parental income (or education) and the income (or education) of children.[16]

This creates an obvious difficulty, in that it is hardly clear how high or low this coefficient needs to be to correspond to 'equal opportunity' – a difficulty made all the greater by the somewhat counterintuitive fact that the intergenerational correlation in outcomes will be higher the larger the variance of talent in the population, the more important talent is in determining outcomes and the more efficient is education in complementing talent (Grawe and Mulligan, 2002; Jencks and Tach, 2006). That said, the best estimate for the United States is that genetic factors associated with the inheritance of talent account for one third to

14 This is all the more the case as many of the instances of corruption involved developers who operated on a relatively small, local scale and were far from being part of the 'top .01%'.

15 John Rawls, for example, defines 'fair equality of opportunity' as meaning that 'those with similar abilities and skills ... and (who) have the same willingness to use them, should have the same prospects of success regardless of their initial place in the social system' (Rawls, 1971:73).

16 In some cases, the focus is not on the intergenerational correlation but on the coefficient in a regression equation relating parental attributes to those of children. The links between these parameters, and the issues involved in their interpretation, are analysed in Jencks and Tach, 2006.

one half of the observed intergenerational correlation (Jencks and Tach, 2006), with other factors (such as attitude and values) possibly accounting for another third (as suggested by Dardarnoni, Fields, Roemer and Puerta, 2006).

Assuming inheritability is no lower in Australia than in the United States, and given that the absolute size of the intergenerational persistence coefficient is significantly lower in Australia than in the United States (Blanden, 2009; Björklund and Salvanes, 2011), there is little reason to believe Australia does not provide 'equal opportunity', at least for non-indigenous Australians. The strong demand for permanent residence in Australia by migrants whose aspirations largely involve upward mobility by their children seems to confirm the view that Australia still provides great scope for social advancement.[17]

The question nonetheless is whether an *increase* in income inequality is likely to compromise equality of opportunity going forward. The answer is that there is not strong evidence to believe it would. To begin with, the relationship, even on a cross-sectional basis, between income distribution and social mobility is far from clear-cut: France has a significantly lower Gini coefficient than Canada or Australia, but significantly higher intergenerational persistence, i.e. lower mobility (Smeeding, Erikson and Jäntti, 2011). Moreover, even within countries, significant increases in measured income inequality do not appear to have reduced social mobility, possibly reflecting the fact that greater inequality increases the incentive to invest in achieving upward mobility, even if it increases its difficulty (Blanden, 2009; Erikson and Goldthorpe, 2010; and Lee and Solon, 2008). And of course, an increase in the earnings dispersion may itself reflect an increase in mobility, if it arises from an increase in the importance of talent as a determinant of the earnings distribution (Jencks and Tach, 2006; and Grawe and Mulligan, 2002).

Ultimately, the differences in social mobility between advanced market economies are surprisingly small – as Blanden (2009) points out, even the large gap in measured intergenerational persistence between Sweden and the United States is not statistically significant. That is perhaps unsurprising: there is an openness, common to those economies, that creates scope for talent and movement. Changes in the income distribution, especially on the rather limited scale of recent years, seem unlikely to materially alter that picture, at least at an aggregate level.[18]

17 Indeed, in my view, there is great, under-utilised, scope to use migrant demand for entry and permanent residence as between possible host countries as an indicator of relative quality of life and of social mobility.

18 They may nonetheless worsen poverty traps for particular groups in the population, which are perhaps best dealt with through targeted responses (though the efficacy of those responses has, at least so far, not been especially high).

Fashionable policy responses may do more harm than good

In short, while the changes that have occurred in the distribution of income raise legitimate questions, there is little reason to think they have been grossly problematic. Moreover, many aspects of those changes reflect factors that increase both efficiency and equity. That notwithstanding, they have given rise to myriad policy proposals, and especially to suggestions that spending should be increased on education, that taxes should be raised on high incomes and that some form of bequest tax should be introduced. I now turn to consider, somewhat sceptically, each of these proposals.

Increased spending on education

The observed increase in the returns to skill is suggestive of an increase in the private and (potentially) social returns on education, leading to proposals for greater public spending on education as a way of assisting individuals to adjust and of promoting social mobility.

Underlying these proposals is the presumption that individuals and families are credit constrained (and hence cannot realise their desired level of investment in skills) and/or that there are social returns to education that exceed the private returns (and hence result in under-investment). Moreover, assuming initial levels of public spending are reasonable, the arguments for an increase must involve some increase in these underlying factors – i.e. a greater likelihood of credit constraints or of externalities preventing existing efforts from attaining efficient outcomes.

There is no evidence of an increase in the externalities associated with education – indeed, greater private returns to skills suggest individuals are capturing at least a reasonable share of the increased social value of education and experience. Indeed, if performance measurement in the workplace has improved, it may be that individuals are capturing an increased share of that social value.

As for credit constraints, the theory seems to be that a widening in the income distribution increases the risk that low-income households will be unable to finance the investment they would wish to make in skill development, restricting adjustments to changes in labour demand by current workers and reducing social mobility between generations. In practice, however, a general increase in spending on education would be a poorly targeted way of dealing with adjustment by the existing generation of workers; the question must therefore be whether it would facilitate otherwise unachievable but desirable social mobility between generations and do so in a manner that involved benefits that exceeded the spending's opportunity costs.

That spending increases would meet these criteria is at best unproven.

To begin with, relatively little is known about the degree to which credit constraints restrict social mobility,[19] and even less about whether those constraints have become more binding. It would be surprising if they had, given that incomes have increased significantly at all points in the income distribution and that relatively generous financial assistance is already provided to education.

Additionally, there is little evidence to suggest that the extent to which educational systems entrench or offset family background effects bears any simple relationship to public spending on education, at least at the levels of expenditure typical of advanced economies. Rather, the characteristics of educational systems (for instance, in terms of decentralisation and choice) seem a more important determinant (Schuetz, Ursprung and Woessmann, 2008; Björklund and Salvanes, 2011; and Hanuschek and Woessman, 2011). Without structural reform of those systems, it is unclear why greater spending would lead to better outcomes – and with structural reform, it may not be needed or efficient (in the sense of yielding benefits that exceed costs).

Last and related, the possibility must be acknowledged that increased public spending, rather than benefiting social mobility, would largely be captured by the providers of education, or would simply strengthen the advantage of those who could fund education for themselves, while crowding out potentially more efficient private efforts (Peltzman, 1973; Checchi, Ichino and Rustichini, 1999; and Jencks and Tach, 2006).[20]

As a result, the best that can be said for this proposal is that the case in its support has not been made.

Increased taxes on the rich

Proposals to increase effective tax rates on very high incomes have almost invariably accompanied expressions of concern about the rise in top incomes and have even been taken up by the OECD (see OECD, 2008 and 2011). However, as noted above, effective average tax rates on high incomes are already high in Australia by international standards, and the question must be what impact increases in those tax rates would have.

---

19 The extent to which credit constraints bind social mobility depends on the joint distribution of educational potential and financial resources (Becker and Tomes, 1979; Grawe and Mulligan, 2002); in countries which are already relatively meritocratic, the partial inheritability of ability implies this is most likely to be an issue in middle-income families, a supposition borne out by evidence for Canada (see Corak and Heisz, 1999) and hence is unlikely to be much affected by a widening of the income distribution at its tails.

20 The fact that families with far lower income levels have made and continue to make large investments in education in the rapidly growing Asian economies, and that those investments seem relatively effective both in terms of educational outcomes and of social mobility, is certainly consistent with this possibility. See James and Benjamin, 1988 and Lynn, 1988 on Japan, Amsden 1989 on Korea and Lemos, 2012 on China.

This can be seen by considering the revenue-maximising tax rate – i.e. the rate that raises the greatest revenue from top-income earners, regardless of its efficiency consequences. That rate can be calculated using some simple parameters of the income distribution and of the elasticity of taxable income (which is usually defined in terms of the response of income to the share of income a taxpayer retains, and hence is a positive number: for estimates, see Gruber and Saez, 2002).[21] Thus, using Canadian parameters for the top income distribution (Veall, 2012: 33) the revenue from a marginal increase, starting from an initial marginal rate of 50 per cent,[22] is negative for values of the elasticity of taxable income above 0.6, which is within the range of reasonable estimates.

It is therefore not apparent that an increase in the tax rate would raise any revenue – rather, it could place the tax on the wrong side of the Laffer curve. At the same time, half or more of the response would be a real fall in social output, reducing welfare. This could, in other words, be an exercise in cutting off one's nose to spite one's face, which is hardly a sensible basis for public policy.

Bequest taxes

A final proposal, again commonly associated with concerns about top incomes, is to introduce taxes on bequests or other forms of inheritance. As with all other taxes, these have obvious incentive problems, aggravated by the fact that *inter vivos* gifts must be policed to prevent evasion. But there is a more fundamental incoherence in these taxes, at least as a way of enhancing social mobility.

In effect, if dynastically aware families[23] face a choice between investing in the education and general integration into working life of their children on the one hand, or investing in financial assets on the other (as in Becker and Tomes, 1979), a tax on bequests simply leads to an inefficient shift in the composition of investment to the former. This has the perverse result of increasing educational inequality (Grawe and Mulligan, 2002). It is difficult to believe this is the outcome its proponents have in mind. While the extent of any such effect is an empirical question, it does emphasise the need for a more sophisticated approach to such taxes than their advocates usually display.

---

21 The formula for the maximum revenue raising tax rate is $1/(1 + ea)$, where e is the elasticity of taxable income and a is the Pareto coefficient.

22 This is not an unreasonable starting point, given an average effective rate of about 40 per cent (OECD, 2011: Table 9.7), a consumption tax of 10 per cent and a payroll tax of say three per cent. Veall sets out the Canadian and international estimates, defining the marginal increase in terms of the tax that raises an additional dollar, assuming no behavioural response.

23 That is, families that internalise the welfare of future generations.

Conclusions

Public attitudes to income distribution, and public policies in respect of income distribution, are relatively closely related to beliefs about the inherent justice or otherwise of social outcomes (Bénabou and Tirole, 2006; Brooks and Manza, 2006; and Jasso, 1999). They also reflect the public's beliefs about the inherent legitimacy, costs and effectiveness of redistribution (McCall, 2012). The focus on executive pay arising from the GFC, combined with long-run shifts in income distribution, are likely to have affected those aspects of public opinion, at least potentially creating pressures for further government intervention.

Yet there is little reason to believe that there is a serious problem in Australia with income distribution. While the distribution of market incomes has widened slightly, that seems related to factors that are likely to increase efficiency and in some cases (such as the closing of gender gaps in pay) equity. Moreover, despite that widening, market incomes at all levels of the income distribution have increased strongly. In contrast, at least some countries that have adopted policies that narrow the distribution of market incomes – such as employment protections laws and measures aimed at promoting collective bargaining or centralising wage setting – have not only suffered in terms of economic growth but also in terms of equity. And many of the policies advocated by local supporters of redistribution could well have the same effect. Paying close attention to the lessons of international experience, as Castles so clearly did, should be crucial in assessing the risks those policies involve.

References

Acemoglu, D and Autor, D (2010). 'Skills, Tasks and Technologies: Implications for Employment and Earnings', *National Bureau of Economic Research Working Paper Series*, Working Paper 16082.

Aldrich, John H (1995). *Why Parties? The Origin and Transformation of Political Parties*, University of Chicago Press, Chicago.

Almås, I (2012). 'International Income Inequality: Measuring PPP Bias by Estimating Engel Curves for Food', *American Economic Review*, 102(1): 1093–1117.

Atkinson, AB and Brandolini, A (2006). 'The Panel-of-Countries Approach to Explaining Income Inequality: An Interdisciplinary Research Agenda', in Morgan, SL, Grusky, DB and Fields GS (eds), *Mobility and Inequality*, Stanford University Press, Stanford CA.

Becker, GS and Tomes, N (1979). 'An Equilibrium Theory of the Distribution of Income and Intergenerational Mobility', *Journal of Political Economy*, 87(6): 1153-1190.

Bénabou, R and Tirole, J (2006). 'Belief in a Just World and Redistributive Politics', *The Quarterly Journal of Economics,* 121(2): 699-746.

Berry, MJ (1977). 'Inequality' in Davies et al *Australian Society: a sociological introduction,* Longman Cheshire, Melbourne: 18–54,

Björklund, A and Salvanes, KG (2011). 'Education and Family Background: Mechanisms and Policies', in Hanushek, EA, Machin, S and Woessman, L (eds) *Handbook of the Economics of Education*, Volume 3, Elsevier, Amsterdam.

Blackburn, M (1989). 'Interpreting the Magnitude of Changes in Measures of Income Inequality', *Journal of Econometrics,* 42: 21-25

Blanden, J (2009). *'How Much Can We Learn From International Comparisons of Intergenerational Mobility?'*, Centre for the Economics of Education, CEE DP 111, London School of Economics.

Blanchard, O and Portugal, P (1998). 'What hides behind an unemployment rate: comparing Portuguese and US Unemployment', *National Bureau of Economic Research Working Paper Series*, Working Paper 6636.

Blau, FD and Kahn, LM, (1996). 'International Differences in Male Wage Inequality: Institutions versus Market Forces', *Journal of Political Economy,* 104 (4): 791-837.

Brooks, C and Manza, J (2006), 'Why Do Welfare States Persist?', *Journal of Politics,* 68 (4): 816–827.

Castles, I and others (1973). *'Economic Growth: Is it Worth Having?'*, Treasury Economic Paper No. 2, Australian Government Publishing Service, Canberra.

Castles, I (1984). 'Money income distribution and redistribution in Australia, Sweden and the United States', Paper presented to the *57th ANZAAS Congress 24th August 1987,* James Cook University of North Queensland, Australian Bureau of Statistics.

Castles, I (1990). *'Living Standards in Sydney and Japanese cities: A Comparison',* manuscript subsquently published (1994) in *'The Australian economy in the Japanese mirror',* Sheridan, K (ed), University of Queensland Press, St Lucia, Queensland.

Castles, I (1997a). 'Measuring Economic Progress: From Political Arithmetick to Social Accounts', *Economic Analysis and Policy,* 28(2): 137-146.

Castles, I (1997b). 'Measuring Wealth and Welfare: why HDI and GPI fail', Paper presented to the Academy of Social Sciences in Australia *Symposium: Wealth, Work, Well-Being…* , 10th November 1997.

Cavalier, R (2012). 'The Labor Party' *in* Clune, D and R Smith *Labor in Office in NSW 1995-2011*, Allen & Unwin, Sydney: 3-14.

Cohen, GA (2009). *Why Not Socialism?*, Princeton University Press, Princeton, N.J.

Checchi, D, Ichino A and Rustichini, A (1999). 'More equal but less mobile? Education financing and intergenerational mobility in Italy and in the US', *Journal of Public Economics*, 74: 351–393.

Clark, A and Postel-Vinay, F (2008). 'Job security and job protection', *Oxford Economic Papers*, 61: 207–239.

Corak M and Heisz, A (1999). 'The Intergenerational Earnings and Income Mobility of Canadian Men: Evidence from Longitudinal Income Tax Data', *Journal of Human Resources*, 34(3): 504-533.

Dardarnoni, V, Fields, GS, Roemer, J and Puerta, MLS (2006). 'How Demanding should Equality of Opportunity Be, and How Much Have We Achieved?' 'in Morgan, SL, Grusky, DB, and Fields GS (eds), *Mobility and Inequality*, Stanford University Press, Stanford CA.

Davies, AF, Encel, S and Berry, MJ (eds) (1977). *'Australian society: a sociological introduction'*, Longman Cheshire, Melbourne.

de Tocqueville, A (1969). *Democracy in America,* Lawrence, G. (tr), Mayer, JP (ed), Doubleday, Garden City NY.

DiPrete, TA, Goux, D, Maurin, E, and Quesnel-Vallee, A (2006). 'Work and pay in flexible and regulated labor markets: A generalized perspective on institutional evolution and inequality trends in Europe and the US', *Research in Social Stratification and Mobility*, 24: 311–332.

Dolado, JJ and Stucchi, R (2008). 'Do temporary contracts affect TFP? Evidence from Spanish Manufacturing firms', *IZA Discussion papers* No. 3832.

Erikson, R and Goldthorpe, JH (2010). 'Has social mobility in Britain decreased? Reconciling divergent findings on income and class mobility', *The British Journal of Sociology,* 61(2): 211-230.

Fiorina, MP with Abrams, SJ (2009). *Disconnect: the Breakdown of Representation in American Politics*, University of Oklahoma Press: Norman.

Freestone, R and P Williams (2012). 'Urban Planning' *in* Clune, D. and R. Smith *Labor in Office in NSW 1995-2011*, Allen & Unwin, Sydney: 193-206.

Friedman, M and Savage, LJ (1948). 'The Utility Analysis of Choices Involving Risk', *Journal of Political Economy,* 56(4): 279-304.

Galbraith, JK (1958). *The Affluent Society*, The Houghton Mifflin Company, Cambridge, MA.

Gilens, S (2012). *Affluence and Influence: Economic Inequality and Political Power in America*, Princeton University Press: Princeton, N.J.

Goldin, C and Katz, LF (2008). *The Race between Education and Technology*, Harvard University Press, Cambridge MA.

Goldthorpe, J and McKnight, A (2006). 'The Economic Basis of Social Class' 'in Morgan, SL, Grusky, DB, and Fields GS (eds), *Mobility and Inequality*, Stanford University Press, Stanford CA.

Grossmann, M (2012). *The Not-So-Special Interests: Interest Groups, Public Representation, and American Governance,* Stanford University Press, Stanford CA.

Grawe, N and Mulligan, C (2002). 'Economic Interpretations of Intergenerational Correlations', *The Journal of Economic Perspectives*, 16 (3): 45-58.

Gruber, J and Saez, E (2002). 'The elasticity of taxable income: evidence and implications', *Journal of Public Economics,* 84: 1–32.

Halaby, CN (2003). 'Where Job Values Come from: Family and Schooling Background, Cognitive Ability, and Gender', *American Sociological Review*, 68 (2): 251-278.

Hancock, WK (1930). *Australia*, Ernest Benn, London.

Hanuschek, EA and Woessman, L (2011). 'The Economics of International Differences in Educational Achievement', in Hanushek, EA, Machin, S and Woessman, L (eds) *Handbook of the Economics of Education*, Volume 3, North Holland, Amsterdam.

James, E and Benjamin, G (1988) *Public Policy and Private Education in Japan,* Macmillan Press.

Jasso, G (1999). 'How Much Injustice is There in the World? Two New Justice Indexes', *American Sociological Review*, 64(1): 133-168.

Jencks, C and Tach, L (2006). 'Would Equal Opportunity Mean More Mobility?' in Morgan, SL, Grusky, DB, and Fields GS (eds), *Mobility and Inequality*, Stanford University Press, Stanford CA.

Kuznets, S (1955). 'Economic Growth and Income Inequality', *The American Economic Review*, 45(1): 1-28.

Lee, C-I and Solon, G (2008). 'Trends in Intergenerational Income Mobility', *The Review of Economics and Statistics*, 91(4): 766–772.

Leigh, A (2007). 'How Closely Do Top Income Shares Track Other Measures Of Inequality?', *The Economic Journal*, 117: 619–F633.

Lemieux, T, Bentley MacLeod, W and Parent, D (2007) 'Performance Pay and Wage Inequality', *National Bureau of Economic Research Working Paper Series*, Working Paper 13128.

Lemos, G (2012). *The End of the Chinese Dream: Why Chinese people fear the future,* Yale University Press, New Haven and London.

Lynn, R (1988). *Educational Achievement in Japan,* ME Sharpe, Inc, Armonk, NY.

Mann, TP and Ornstein, NJ (2012). *It's Even Worse Than It Looks: How The American Constitutional System Collided With The New Politics Of Extremism,* Basic Books, Perseus Books Group, New York.

Maurin, É (2010). *La Peur Du Déclassement: Une Sociologie Des Récessions,* La Republique des Idees, Seuil, Paris.

Morgan, SL, Grusky, DB, and Fields GS (eds), (2006). *Mobility and Inequality,* Stanford University Press, Stanford CA.

OECD (2008). *Growing Unequal? Income Distribution and Poverty in OECD Countries,* OECD, Paris.

OECD (2011). *Divided We Stand: Why Inequality Keeps Rising,* OECD, Paris.

Peltzman, S (1973). 'The Effect of Government Subsidies-in-Kind on Private Expenditures: The Case of Higher Education, *The Journal of Political Economy,* 81(1): 1-27.

Rae, D (1981). *Equalities,* Harvard University Press, Cambridge MA.

Rawls, J (1971). *A Theory of Justice,* Harvard University Press, Cambridge, MA.

Rehm, P (2011). 'Risk Inequality and the Polarized American Electorate', *British Journal of Political Science,* 41(2): 363–387.

Rehm, P, Hacker JS and Schlesinger, M (2012). 'Insecure Alliances: Risk, Inequality, and Support for the Welfare State ', *American Political Science Review,* 106(2).

Reserve Bank of Australia (2012). *Statement on Monetary Policy,* Reserve Bank of Australia, Sydney.

Rueda, D (2008). *Social Democracy Inside Out: Partisanship and Labor Market Policy in Advanced Industrialized Democracies,* Oxford University Press, Oxford.

Schuetz, G, Ursprung, HW and Woessmann L (2008). 'Education policy and equality of opportunity', *Kyklos,* 61(2): 279-308.

Smedes, M (2012). 'Measuring Household Disparities in a National Accounts Framework', *Presentation to the Economic Society of Australia: Seminar Series,* 14 November, National Accounts Branch, Australian Bureau of Statistics.

Smeeding, TM, Erikson, R and Jäntti, M (2011). 'Introduction' in Smeeding, TM, Erikson, R and Jäntti, M (2011). *Persistence, Privilege, and Parenting:The Comparative Study of Intergenerational Mobility,* Russell Sage Foundation, New York, NY.

Swan, W (2012). 'The 0.01 Per Cent: The Rising Influence of Vested Interests in Australia', *The Monthly*, 76.

Trumbull, G (2012). *Strength in Numbers: The Political Power of Weak Interests,* Harvard University Press, Cambridge MA.

Veall, MR, (2012). 'Top Income Shares in Canada: Recent Trends and Policy Implications', Presidential Address to the *Canadian Economics Association.*

Welch, F (1999). 'In Defense of Inequality', *The American Economic Review*, 89 (2): 1-17.

18. Changes in Inequality in Australia and the Redistributional Impacts of Taxes and Government Benefits

J Rob Bray

Introduction

This paper is concerned with trends in income inequality in Australia over recent decades and the impact of government taxes and benefits. It comprises three main sections. The first considers some of the broad changes which may have contributed to changes in the distribution of income; the second tracks shifts in the distribution of income; and the third considers the contribution of specific components of income, in particular government taxes and benefits, to the level and change in income inequality.

In presenting this as a quantitative analysis the paper utilises three main sources of data – the ABS Survey of Income and Housing (SIH), the ABS Household Expenditure Survey (HES) and the Household Income and Labour Dynamics Australia (HILDA) survey.[1] There are several reasons for this. The first is as a simple test of the robustness of the findings, ensuring that these are not simply the artefact of any particular dataset. The second is that each of these data series can contribute some unique elements to the analysis. The HES provides the longest reliable time span and permits the analysis of extended measures of income; the SIH, while less long running than the HES, has been conducted more regularly over the period for which it is available; and HILDA, while having the shortest time span, is available annually and also enables the longitudinal analysis of trends.

For the most part the paper is concerned with the disposable incomes, that is the total cash income, including government cash transfers, less income tax, that households have available to them to enable their consumption of goods and services, and to save, or repay debts associated with earlier or later consumption.

1 This paper uses unit record data from the Household, Income and Labour Dynamics in Australia (HILDA) Survey. The HILDA Project was initiated and is funded by the Department of Families, Housing, Community Services and Indigenous Affairs (FaHCSIA) and is managed by the Melbourne Institute of Applied Economic and Social Research (Melbourne Institute). The findings and views reported in this paper, however, are those of the author and should not be attributed to either FaHCSIA or the Melbourne Institute.

The data has been equivalised[2] to take account of variations in the size and composition of the household.[3] In the third section a wider measure of income is considered, taking into account the value of some non-cash benefits, indirect taxes and the value of owner-occupied housing.

Is income an adequate basis for considering inequality?

While income is perhaps the most frequent focus for the study of inequality, at least in western countries, it is far from being the only variable that can, or indeed should be, considered. Although usually seen as a measure of the capacity of individuals to support their consumption, the relationship between income and consumption, while present, is often far from complete, especially in survey data.

Table 1 shows the correlations between equivalised disposable income and a range of other measures of household income, consumption, wealth[4] and wellbeing. While all of the correlations between the different measures of income, consumption and wealth are positive and robust, and those between these and the measures of adverse outcomes, such as financial stress and hardship, are robust and negative, the coefficient values are quite low given the extent to which the concepts are frequently considered to be synonymous.

A consequence of these results is, as noted above, that considerable caution needs to be exercised in the interpretation of data on income inequality. While low levels of measured income may be associated with low levels of consumption and low wealth, for many this is not the case. It can also be suggested that a change in the distribution of any one of these may not necessarily be reflected in the others.

---

2 In this paper the 'revised OECD' scale is used. This uses a weight of 1 for the first adult in the household, 0.5 for subsequent adults and 0.3 for children under the age of 15 years. It should be noted that while equivalence scales play an important role in making such adjustments, they are essentially crude instruments, and the use of different scales may generate different results.

3 The use of the household as the measure of aggregation essentially requires an assumption that resources are pooled within households. While there is some evidence that pooling is far from complete, including differences by gender, there are limited alternatives which can be used in this type of analysis. While traditionally 'income units' have been used in some Australian analysis, this requires an equally or potentially more demanding assumption, that resources are not shared between income units. (Income units represent 'economic units' within families and households, typically separating out the incomes of parents and any dependent children from those of other residents, including older children who are not undertaking full-time study.)

4 While the use of equivalisation has gained wide acceptance in the analysis of income, there is less agreement on how wealth should be analysed. For this reason wealth is shown on an equivalised, per capita and total household basis.

Table 1 HES, correlation between income, consumption and wealth, 2009-10

	Equivalised disposable income	Equivalised final income	Equivalised goods & services expenditure	Equivalised expenditure (a)	Equivalised wealth	Wealth per capita	Household wealth	Hardship (b)	Hardship & cashflow (c)	Financial Stress (d)
Equivalised disposable income	1.000									
Equivalised final income	0.959	1.000								
Equivalised goods and services expenditure	0.502	0.390	1.000							
Equivalised expenditure (a)	0.627	0.564	0.700	1.000						
Equivalised wealth	0.366	0.395	0.221	0.376	1.000					
Wealth per capita	0.324	0.352	0.206	0.343	0.995	1.000				
Household wealth	0.433	0.464	0.247	0.428	0.983	0.961	1.000			
Hardship (b)	-0.120	-0.106	-0.107	-0.095	-0.047	-0.044	-0.055	1.000		
Hardship & cashflow (c)	-0.153	-0.148	-0.120	-0.123	-0.075	-0.072	-0.085	0.801	1.000	
Financial stress (d)	-0.323	-0.278	-0.351	-0.284	-0.113	-0.102	-0.136	0.513	0.623	1.000

(a) Goods and services expenditure, income tax, mortgage principal repayments, superannuation and life insurance.

(b) Number of 'hardship items'. Because of a shortage of money a person has: 1. sought assistance from a welfare/community organisation; 2. was unable to heat their house; 3. had gone without meals; or 4. had to sell or pawn something.

(c) Sum of (b) and number of 'cashflow items'. Because of a shortage of money a person has: 1. been unable to pay an electricity, gas or telephone bill on time; 2. been unable to pay their car registration or insurance on time; 3. sought financial help from family or friends.

(d) Sum of (c) and 'missing out'. Because a person cannot afford to they have not had: 1. a night out once a fortnight; 2. a special meal once a week; 3. family or friends over for a meal once a month; 3. an annual holiday of a week or more away from home; 4. they have purchased second-hand rather than new clothing; 5. been unable to spend time on leisure or hobby activities.

Person weighted, all results significant at $p < 0.001$.

Source: Derived from ABS HES 2009-10 CURF.

Finally a strong assumption underpinning most inequality analysis is that income is equally valued by all within society and hence it is an appropriate focal point for the analysis. This is an assumption which neither allows for heterogeneity of preferences across the population, including individual trade-offs between work and leisure, nor potentially, as income is usually treated as being linear, to any diminishing returns on the value of money.

The measurement of income

Central to the analysis of the distribution of income is the quality of the data collected and made available for analysis. This has two elements of particular import, the quality of the data, and its conceptual basis.

Over recent decades ABS have made considerable efforts to improve their measurement of income, both conceptually, and in collection and processing. Taking this into account, more recent estimates of income may be considered superior to those in earlier surveys. This though has come at the price of comparability over time.[5] For this reason in some of the analysis of income inequality based on the SIH and the HES multiple measures of income have been constructed to build more compatible time series, or at least provide periods of overlap.

A major conceptual question arising with existing income statistics is the general exclusion of capital gains or the draw down in capital assets. Although seen as a robust strategy under some conceptualisations of income it also has weaknesses. It is inconsistently applied to superannuation where a drawdown of capital as a pension or annuity is treated as income. Similarly while efforts are made to include salary sacrificed superannuation contributions as income, compulsory contributions are not identified. Related to the approach to capital gains is the treatment of apparent losses from investments, including residential property investment and small business operations. In the 2009-2010 SIH, for example, some 8.3 per cent of adults (aged 15 years and over) report having weekly income from residential property. Of these just 30.8 per cent report making a profit, 49.0 per cent report a loss and 20.2 per cent that they break even. Similarly 30.7 per cent of people running their own business report that it makes a loss or just breaks even. Across the adult population as a whole some 5.1 per cent report making a loss on either property, own business or investments. In many cases these recurrent losses are offset by future capital gains.

5 Very frequently it is not possible to retrospectively adjust for these. This is for two reasons. The first is the data available in the CURFs, while containing considerable detail especially in some latter surveys, cannot always be disaggregated sufficiently or may simply not have been collected on an appropriate basis. The second is that even modelling of components based on later information may not be possible where the incidence of a practice, for example salary sacrifice, has varied across time and across population subgroups. In this case the situation is further clouded by the fact that there is variation across individual respondents as to whether these amounts had been included in their originally reported levels of income.

With increasing diversity in working patterns a frequently neglected component of income analysis is the costs people incur in earning this income and possibly shifts in the value of home production associated with changes in external employment. Where analysis, such as this, is being conducted over a period of changing patterns of workforce participation, to the extent these are not taken into account, this may well distort some of the findings. Unfortunately few tools exist within the current set of income measures to address these.

What might have affected income inequality in Australia?

The pattern of income distribution in a society can be affected by many factors. Some of these arise from the operation of labour markets, some from government interventions and others because of the decisions of individuals. These latter can be based on many preferences including the degree to which they wish to trade off income for leisure.

For this paper a number of these are considered below:

- The rates of payment across different occupations, industries and skill levels and the resultant patterns of earnings dispersion;
- Levels of workforce participation, including the impact of involuntary joblessness, and choices about workforce participation, especially within families, and across a person's lifecycle;
- Linked in part to the above, the proportion of economically inactive households, including those drawing down assets;
- Levels of dependence on income support and the rate at which this is paid, both relative to earnings and the relative rates between payments;
- The impact of other government transfers, including support for families; and
- The impact of taxation, in particular its progressivity.

The nature of some of these emphasise the need for caution in the social interpretation of changes in the pattern of income distribution, and in particular concepts such as inequality. For example, an increased level of inequality may arise from an increase in the proportion of partners in couples who participate in the workforce, or from an increase in the number of retirees as a result of demographic change and the degree to which people have built up savings through the superannuation system.

Earnings

Over recent decades there has been increasing dispersion of earnings in Australia. Figure 1 shows the trends in the real earnings[6] of full-time non-managerial workers in the period since 1975.[7] In 2010 this group of workers represented some 89.3 per cent of all full-time employees – with the balance being managerial employees.[8] Over the whole period the ratio of earnings at the ninetieth percentile relative to the tenth percentile has increased from 2.02 to 2.79, and relative to median earnings from 1.50 to 1.78.

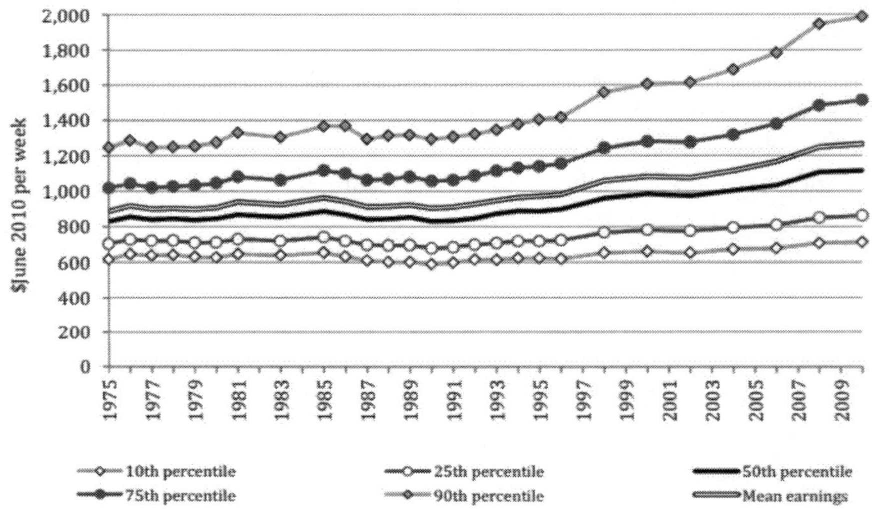

Figure 1 Employee Earnings and Hours Survey, real earnings of full-time non-managerial adult workers at selected percentiles, 1975-2010

Note: Since May 2006 ABS has ensured that earnings include amounts which are 'salary sacrificed'. This series has smoothed the impact of the introduction of this approach.

Source: ABS EEH Cat No 6306.0 various editions.

6 Income adjusted for changes in prices as measured by the CPI. An issue outside the scope of this paper is the relevance of the expenditure weighted CPI as a measure of price change for population subgroups and other related questions about the methodology of the CPI.

7 This data is from the ABS Employee and Earnings and Hours collection (ABS Cat No 6306.0). This is an employer-based survey with the data being largely taken directly from payroll systems. It can therefore be considered to be less affected by reporting error than that derived from household surveys – such as the similar series which can be extracted from the Survey of Employee Earnings, Benefits and Trade Union Membership (EEBTUM) (ABS Cat No 6310.0).

8 While the omission of this latter group may tend to underestimate the level of higher incomes, the definition of managerial includes supervisory roles with many non-managerial workers being paid at relatively modest levels. Around a third of all managerial employees are paid less than the median earnings of non-managerial employees although 56 per cent are paid above the seventy-fifth percentile. In addition including only full-time employees may mean that these rates of growth are not wholly reflective of the considerable numbers of persons who are employed part-time. However attempting to develop a series of hourly rates to take this into account is limited by data availability and the accuracy of reported hours of work.

A second feature of this chart is the extent to which rates of earnings growth have varied over time. Most marked is the limited growth in earnings between the mid 1970s and mid 1990s and strong growth in the period since then, although this latter appears, potentially as a consequence of the Global Financial Crisis (GFC), to have flattened out in the period between 2008 and 2010.

As shown in Table 2, while the real median earnings of these full-time adult non-managerial employees grew at an annualised rate of 0.4 per cent between 1975 and 1996,[9] the rate of growth rose to 1.6 per cent between 1996 and 2010. For workers at the twenty-fifth percentile of earnings the annualised growth rate of 1.3 per cent between 1996 and 2010 compares with a rate of 0.1 per cent in the preceding period.[10]

Table 2 EEH, Real earnings of full-time non-managerial adult workers at selected percentiles, 1975-1996 and 1996-2010

	1975	1996	Change	Annualised change	1996	2010	Change	Annualised change
	$2010		%	%	$2010		%	%
10th percentile	616	619	0.4	0.0	619	711	14.9	1.0
25th percentile	702	722	2.8	0.1	722	862	19.4	1.3
50th percentile	829	898	8.4	0.4	898	1115	24.1	1.6
75th percentile	1018	1155	13.5	0.6	1155	1513	31.0	1.9
90th percentile	1246	1416	13.7	0.6	1416	1986	40.2	2.4
Mean earnings	887	981	10.7	0.5	981	1266	29.0	1.8
Federal minimum wage	485	502	3.4	0.2	502	544	8.3	0.6
				Ratio				
p90/p10	2.02	2.29			2.29	2.79		
p90/p50	1.50	1.58			1.58	1.78		
p25/p50	0.85	0.80			0.80	0.77		
p10/p50	0.74	0.69			0.69	0.64		

Source: ABS EEH Cat No 6306.0 various editions.

Many factors underlie these trends, and while these are not explored here they are very relevant to interpreting changes in the distribution of income. For

9 This rate of income growth may however understate the effective remuneration of people over this period. The period also saw a reduction in working hours for many employees from 40 hours per week to 38 and the introduction of superannuation – in particular between 1991 and 2003 when the level of employer contributions increased from three per cent of wages to nine per cent.

10 The growth of earnings recorded over this period in Australia highlights some differences between the Australian and US experience. While real median earnings of full-time non-managerial employees in Australia grew by 34.5 per cent between 1975 and 2010 (31.6 per cent for males and 46.7 per cent for females), in the US the median earnings of male full-time, year-round workers grew by just 2.0 per cent, although that of women grew by 33.4 per cent. (US Census Bureau 2012, Table P-38)

example, between 2001 and 2011 the proportion of the population aged 15 to 64 years with a bachelor degree or higher qualification increased from 17.0 per cent to 23.7 per cent, and the proportion with any non-school qualification increased from 47.2 per cent to 56.5 per cent. (ABS Cat No 62270DO001_201105, 2011, Table 8.) With such a shift in this aspect of human capital, it is to be anticipated that there would be changes in the distribution of earnings reflecting returns to this investment.

Workforce participation

Most household income is derived from the participation of household members in the workforce. Hence it would be expected that the distribution of income would be affected if the pattern of participation changes. This section considers two aspects of this participation – employment patterns within households and the impact of retirement and demographic change.

One of the many elements of change in the pattern of employment in Australia in recent decades has been increasing workforce participation by women, and, within couple families, an increase in dual earner couples. Between June 1994 and June 2011, as illustrated in Figure 2, the proportion of couples with a reference person aged 15 to 64 years which had both members engaged in the workforce, rose from 54.4 per cent to 64.4 per cent. Conversely the proportion with a single earner only fell from 32.4 per cent to 26.6 per cent, and with neither member employed from 13.2 per cent to 7.0 per cent. Although many of the second earners in these households only work part-time, and many, especially those with younger children, incur considerable costs in participating in employment, overall this type of shift is likely to increase income polarisation between households, reflecting the different earning capacity of households with zero, one and two employed persons. Amongst couples with children the shift away from the traditional single breadwinner model has been particularly marked. Between 1981 and 2010 the proportion of such families with a single full-time employed person has fallen from 51.4 per cent to 29.5 per cent, while the proportion with two income earners has grown from 40.9 per cent to 60.7 per cent.

Across the income distribution it is a combination of both the rate of pay and the period worked which impacts on household incomes. Table 3 shows the average rate of pay of all employed persons in the household, the average aggregate hours worked by these people and the proportion of households which have such an employed person, by income quintile.

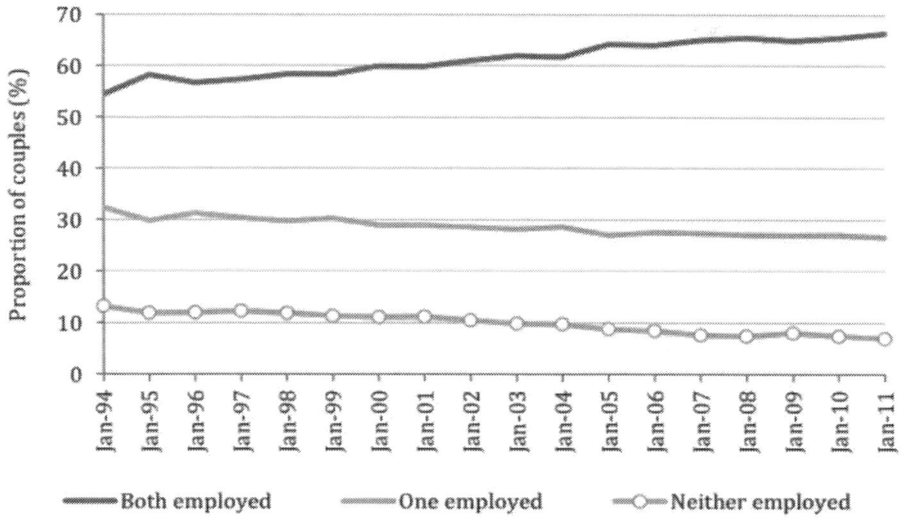

Figure 2 Labour Force Survey, couple households with reference person aged 15-64 years, employment status of couple, 1994-2011

Source: Labour Force Australia, Cat No 6291.0.55.001 Tables ST FA4_aug04 and ST FA4.

Table 3 HES hours worked and rate of pay equivalised household disposable income decile, 2009-10

Equivalised disposable income quintile	Average hourly wage of all employed persons ($ph)	Hours worked by employed persons (Hours)	Proportion with at least one employed person (%)
1	14.4	37.9	13.7
2	15.9	38.8	24.1
3	19.0	42.3	54.9
4	21.1	49.1	77.3
5	23.2	57.3	89.0
6	25.0	63.0	90.8
7	28.3	70.2	92.7
8	30.4	76.3	95.9
9	35.4	75.9	97.3
10	57.1	77.4	95.0

Notes: Includes wage and salary and own business income. Population restricted to those households reporting an average hourly earnings rate of $5 per hour or more. This leads to some underestimation of the proportion of households with an employed person.

Source: ABS HES CURF 2009-10.

Relative to the first decile, a household in the fifth decile is 6.5 times more likely to have a person in employment, and if they do, the household receives an average rate of pay, across all employed persons, 62 per cent higher and these people work some 51 per cent more hours. Compared to this household in the fifth decile, a household in the top decile is only 6.7 per cent more likely to have at least one person in employment, and on average works 35 per cent more hours in aggregate, but receives an hourly rate almost 150 per cent higher.

Consideration also needs to be given to the effect of demographic change on workforce participation, in particular the increasing numbers of older, largely retired, households. Between 1976 and 2010 the proportion of households with a reference person aged over 65 years is estimated to have increased by some 24 per cent, rising from some 14.2 per cent of households to 17.6 per cent (see Figure 3).

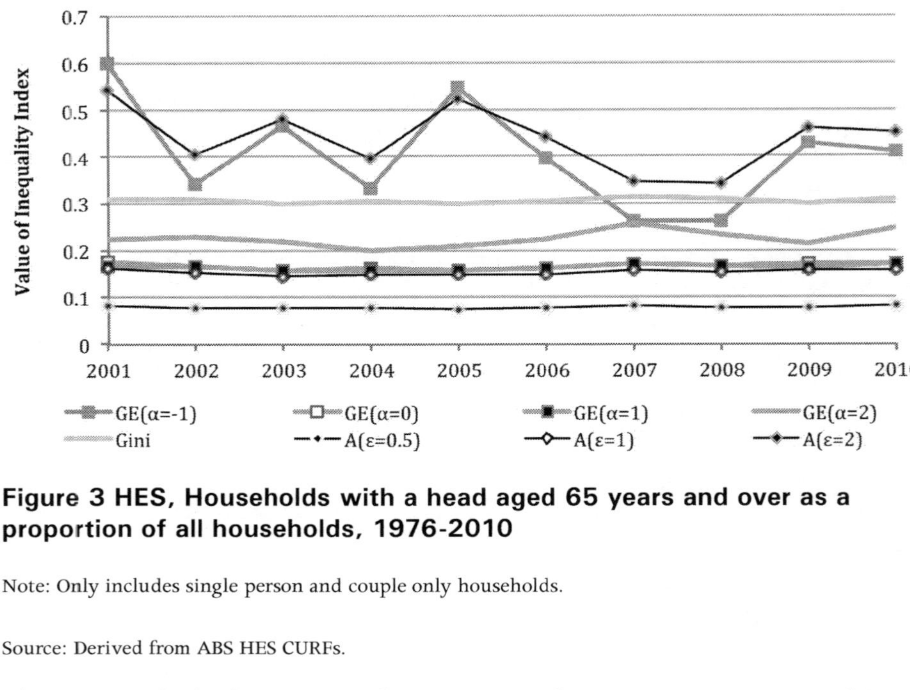

Figure 3 HES, Households with a head aged 65 years and over as a proportion of all households, 1976-2010

Note: Only includes single person and couple only households.

Source: Derived from ABS HES CURFs.

This is a trend which is projected to continue. The 2010 Intergenerational Report (Treasury 2010) suggests that the proportion of the population aged over 65 years will increase from 13.5 per cent in 2010 to 16.4 per cent in 2020 and 22.7 per cent by 2050. More specifically they indicate: 'As the number of aged people increases, their lower rates of participation are projected to pull down the total labour force participation rate from 65.1 per cent in 2009-10 to 60.6 per cent by

2049-50.' (*ibid*: 12) Along with this, it also forecasts a decline in the number of hours worked – in large part because of the higher proportion of the workforce comprised of older workers and women.

Because of their lower levels of income[11] the growth in the proportion of these households is likely to result in an increase in apparent income inequality. This may be partially offset by the extent to which increasing levels of superannuation savings will see higher incomes amongst many of the households in retirement. Though this may of course increase inequality within this subgroup of households headed by an older person.

As previously noted this increase in the use of superannuation as a source of income may also exacerbate the problems of income measurement.

Income support and other transfers

Income support and other government transfers play an important role in providing or supplementing the incomes of many Australian households. The extent of these payments can be seen in analysis by the Melbourne Institute on the HILDA survey that reports that in

> 2008, 36 per cent of persons were living in a household in receipt of income support at the time of interview, and 39 per cent lived in households that had received income support payments at some stage in the preceding financial year.

They note though that 'rates of receipt are somewhat lower among workforce-age persons, at 30 per cent for the current week and 34 per cent for the preceding financial year' (Wilkins et al 2011: 41).

11 While a major fall in income with age may have welfare implications - and hence the fact that the elderly tend to have lower incomes can be seen as an issue of concern as it signals a fall in their capacity to consume – and cannot simply be set aside as a consequential effect of demographic change, the case for this is open to some debate. While theory suggests that people will smooth consumption over their lifetime, empirical evidence suggests that consumption tends to decline with age. Furthermore a falling level of current income is often associated with drawing down on savings. This, as discussed earlier, is not consistently recognised in many concepts of income as a measure of economic resources.

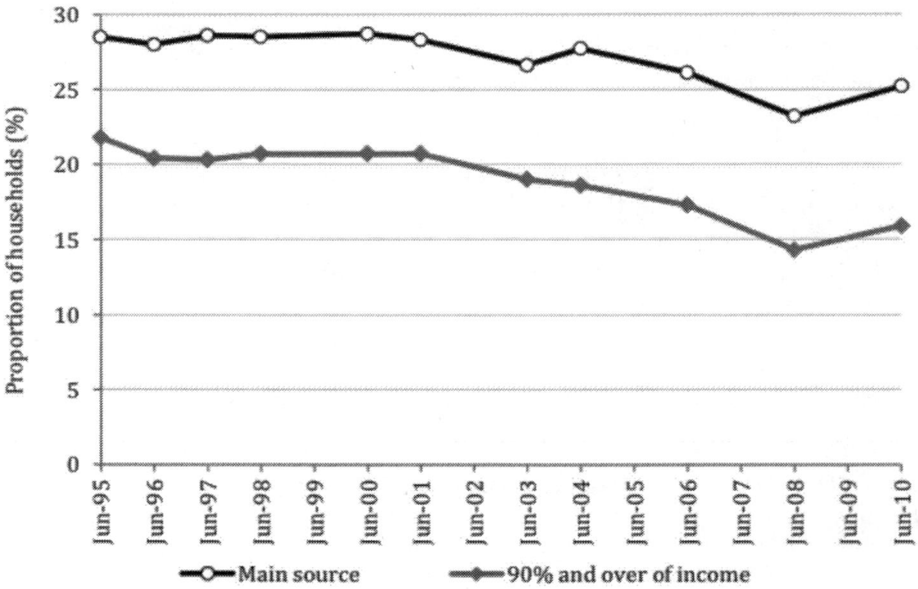

Figure 4 SIH, Proportion of households dependent upon government transfers, 1995-2010

Source: ABS (2011) Cat No 65230DO001, Table 3.

The proportion in receipt of this assistance has however not been stable over time. Figure 4, using data from the SIH and a broad definition of transfers which include both income support and family payments, shows the proportion of households which have transfers as their main source of income, and those for which transfers account for 90 per cent or more of their income. While these shares were largely stable for most of the 1990s, since then they have shown a considerable decline. The proportion for households for whom transfers were their main source of income peaked at 28.7 per cent in 2000 before dropping to 23.7 per cent in 2008. The proportion who reported that more than 90 per cent of their income came from transfers fell from a peak of 21.8 in 1995 to 14.3 per cent in 2008. In both cases these proportions then increased a little in 2010 reflecting the impact of the GFC.

All other things being equal, in a system such as Australia's where income support is tightly targeted, it can be anticipated that a decline in the extent of reliance on transfers, which arises because people are no longer eligible to receive an income-tested payment, will result in a reduction in the level of inequality.

A second impact of the transfer system on income distribution is the rate at which payments are made, both relative to earnings and within the payments system.

As shown in Figure 5, a substantial difference has emerged in the rate at which different income support payments are made. This is a result of different approaches to indexation[12] as well as one-off changes introduced in the 2009-10 budget, which, in particular, impacted on the rate of payment of the pension for single pensioners.[13]

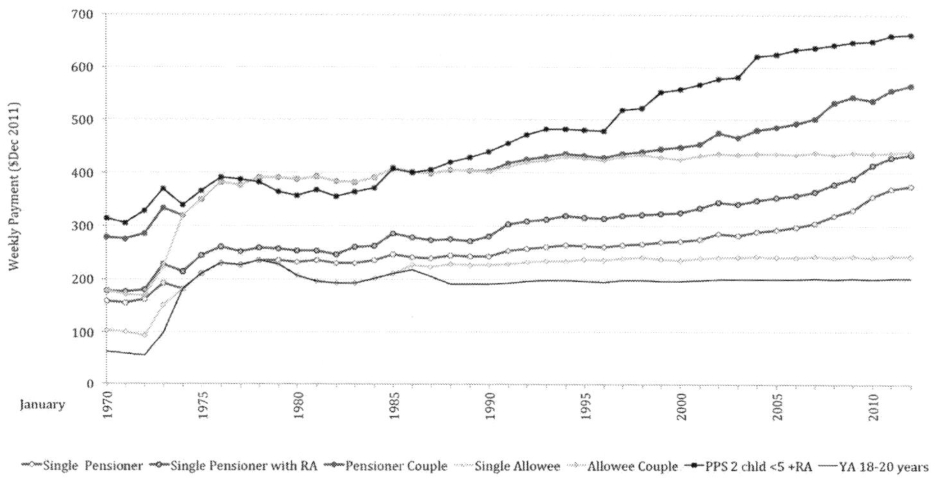

Figure 5 Real weekly rates of payment, selected income support payments, 1970-2012

Source: FaHCSIA 2012, Section 5.2 and other administrative collections.

These differential rates of payment, especially when compared with the situation in the late 1970s when all payments were made at a common rate and even much of the 1990s when the differences between the payment rates were relatively small, are likely to be reflected in increasing income inequality.

A further impact of transfer payments concerns the provision of support for families. The level of support provided to families with children has also grown over time, as well as being extended to many households in the workforce. This not only impacts directly on the income distribution, but also the relative outcomes for those with and without children.

---

12 Since the 1980s, while allowance type payments such as Newstart and Youth Allowance have been adjusted for price changes only, pensions are adjusted to maintain a relativity with earnings as well as providing protection against changes in prices.

13 The pension rate shown in the table includes the value of bonuses paid to Older Australians/Seniors in 2001, 2006, 2007 and 2008, but excludes the 2008 Economic Security Bonus Payment, as this formed part of a much wider payment.

Income tax

The second major intervention by government which impacts on the distribution of disposable income is income tax.

Traditionally most income tax systems have been progressive with higher tax rates being levied against those with higher incomes. This approach reflects both an assessment of the relative capacity of individuals to pay tax, and explicit redistributive goals. Since 1999-2000 as illustrated in Figure 6, there have been substantial changes in the rates at which income tax is levied at particular income levels. Particularly marked are the changes in 2000-01 and again in 2006-07. While a simple chart such as this does not illustrate the full range of changes including changes to taxation offsets, shifts between the use of tax and the transfer system to deliver assistance, or trade-offs between direct and indirect tax (in particular the introduction of the GST in July 2000), it nevertheless shows how thresholds have moved and the effective marginal tax rates have reduced over wide bands of income.

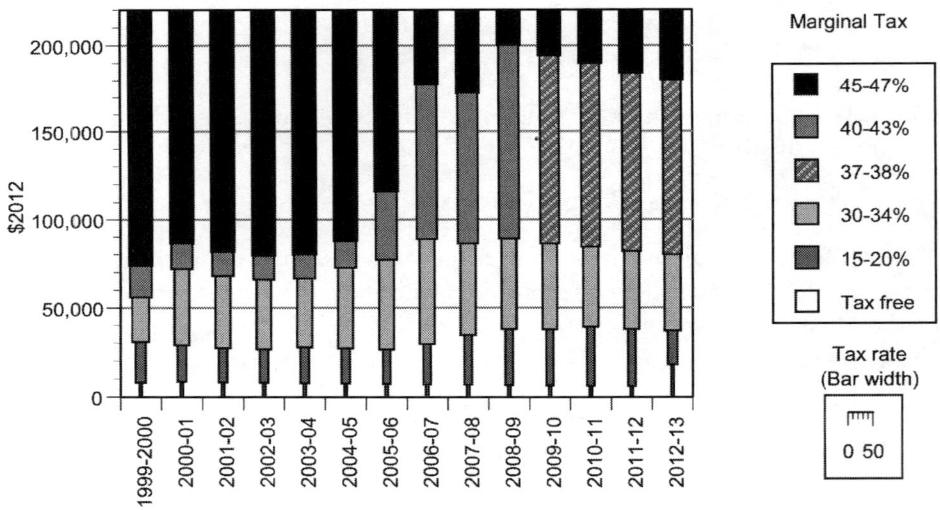

Figure 6 Income tax scales, 1999-2000 to 2012-2013

Note: Bar width indicates relative tax rate.

Source: ATO (2012a, b).

The cumulative impact of the changes between 2000-01 (that is, just after the specific changes introduced along with the GST) and 2009-10, along with changes in the distribution of income amongst taxpayers,[14] are shown in Table 4.

14 The population of taxpayers varies as a proportion of the total population depending not just on the income of individuals – that is, low income individuals are excluded from the data - but also by changes in the real value of the minimum tax threshold. Where the threshold is held flat in nominal terms – as it has over a

As this shows, the actual pattern in changes in the average rates of taxation at different points of the distribution is complex. For the bottom vingtile the average rate of taxation fell by 1.18 percentage points, the amount of reduction then increased up to the seventh income vingtile where it peaked at 3.94 percentage points – a reduction in the average tax rate paid from 15.4 per cent to 11.4 per cent. The rate of reduction then declined reaching a low in the sixteenth vingtile at 0.93 percentage points. After this the rate of decline again commenced to increase until it reached a reduction in the average rate of income tax paid of 2.25 percentage points for the five per cent of taxpayers with the highest incomes.

Also noticeable in the table are changes in the income share received at various points in the distribution. In particular, the share of total income received by the top five per cent of taxpayers increased from 19.8 per cent in 2000-01 to 20.5 per cent in 2009-10. Despite the fall in their average tax rate over the period the share of taxation they paid increased from 31.3 per cent to 33.5 per cent.

Table 4 Income tax, average rates of taxation and shares of income and tax by total income vingtile, 2000-01 and 2009-10

Vingtile of taxpayer	Total income		Income Tax Payable		Share of income		Share of tax		Average tax rate	
	2000-2001	2009-10	2000-2001	2009-10	2000-2001	2009-10	2000-2001	2009-10	2000-2001	2009-10
	$m				%					
1	3,489.0	7,976.9	118.0	175.9	1.0	1.4	0.2	0.1	3.4	2.2
2	4,902.0	10,028.3	273.0	399.7	1.5	1.7	0.4	0.3	5.6	4.0
3	6,101.0	11,681.7	481.0	690.4	1.8	2.0	0.6	0.6	7.9	5.9
4	7,274.0	13,286.9	700.0	900.8	2.2	2.3	0.9	0.7	9.6	6.8
5	8,368.0	14,724.9	875.0	1,082.3	2.5	2.6	1.1	0.9	10.5	7.4
6	9,359.0	16,052.3	1,071.0	1,348.1	2.8	2.8	1.4	1.1	11.4	8.4
7	10,305.0	17,314.9	1,399.0	1,674.2	3.1	3.0	1.8	1.4	13.6	9.7
8	11,249.0	18,549.4	1,728.0	2,118.1	3.3	3.2	2.2	1.8	15.4	11.4
9	12,178.0	19,932.1	2,032.0	2,598.6	3.6	3.5	2.6	2.2	16.7	13.0
10	13,142.0	21,417.9	2,338.0	3,106.3	3.9	3.7	3.0	2.6	17.8	14.5
11	14,159.0	23,038.1	2,654.0	3,663.4	4.2	4.0	3.4	3.0	18.7	15.9
12	15,248.0	24,833.5	2,989.0	4,271.9	4.5	4.3	3.8	3.6	19.6	17.2
13	16,446.0	26,811.6	3,353.0	4,952.4	4.9	4.7	4.3	4.1	20.4	18.5
14	17,760.0	29,025.2	3,753.0	5,713.1	5.3	5.1	4.8	4.7	21.1	19.7
15	19,296.0	31,638.9	4,210.0	6,553.8	5.7	5.5	5.4	5.4	21.8	20.7
16	21,080.0	34,699.4	4,743.0	7,483.5	6.3	6.0	6.1	6.2	22.5	21.6

substantial period - more low-income earners may become liable to pay tax even if their income has remained flat over time. This in itself will result in an apparent concentration of earnings at the top of the population. Over short time frames this effect is likely to be negligible.

Vingtile of taxpayer	Total income		Income Tax Payable		Share of income		Share of tax		Average tax rate	
	2000-2001	2009-10	2000-2001	2009-10	2000-2001	2009-10	2000-2001	2009-10	2000-2001	2009-10
17	22,947.0	38,298.3	5,421.0	8,581.6	6.8	6.7	7.0	7.1	23.6	22.4
18	25,801.0	43,351.0	6,574.0	10,465.9	7.7	7.6	8.4	8.7	25.5	24.1
19	30,974.0	53,515.3	8,822.0	14,230.7	9.2	9.3	11.3	11.8	28.5	26.6
20	66,655.0	117,523.6	24,365.0	40,315.6	19.8	20.5	31.3	33.5	36.6	34.3
Total	**336,733.0**	**573,700.1**	**77,899.0**	**120,326.4**	**100.0**	**100.0**	**100.0**	**100.0**	**23.1**	**21.0**

Source: Australian Taxation Office (2012 c) Table 9; Australian Taxation Office (2003) Table 9.

The complex pattern of these changes also makes it difficult to simply interpret the overall impact. On balance, at least at this level of aggregation the overall impact on rates is to increase relative progressivity. However, changes in progressivity across taxpayers, associated with lower average tax rates and potentially increasing earnings dispersion, does not necessarily mean that the tax system has been more redistributive across the population as a whole.

Trends in inequality

As seen above there are many reasons to expect that the pattern of income distribution has changed over recent decades. While some of these may be considered to be enhancing equality, on balance they appear to be more inclined towards an increase in inequality. This section examines the major data series introduced earlier to identify the degree to which there have been changes in the distribution of income in Australia, in particular over the past decade, but more generally since the 1970s. The focus as discussed previously is on equivalised disposable income inequality and the Gini is used as the main measure. This section considers in turn the results gained from analysis of the three major data collections identified above, the SIH, HES and HILDA. While the analysis of the SIH and HES mainly use current income, in some selected tables, and in the analysis of HILDA, annual data is used.

Measures of inequality

For the most part this paper uses the Gini coefficient as the main measure of inequality. The case for this approach is however not clear-cut.

On one hand the measure is:

- The most commonly used measure and as such is familiar to most users;

- Has a relatively simple statistical basis and links to the Lorenz curve (as it is essentially the area between the line of uniform distribution and the Lorenz curve of the income distribution, expressed as a proportion of the area under the line);
- Able to handle zero and negative values of income;
- Relatively easy to decompose, in particular with regard to income source.

On the other hand, it lacks the deliberate construction of the Atkinson and Generalised Entropy measures which demand a choice of parameter to reflect the value attached to specific forms of inequality. Also, in common with other single value measures, because of the myriad ways in which inequality can arise at different points of the distribution, it is not necessarily, by itself, fully informative of changes in inequality.[15] As with other single measures there is also no normative basis for interpreting any particular level of the measure. That is, while it is generally recognised that extremes of inequality, or for that matter equality, may be associated with adverse outcomes, there is no particular basis for considering what an 'appropriate' level might be. Because of this there is a frequent tendency to assess all shifts towards a higher level of inequality as being negative, and any drops as being a positive.

SIH

For the purposes of this analysis, data since 1990 has been used. Over the period to 2009-10 twelve surveys have been undertaken. These however have used a number of different income definitions. While the ABS has published consolidated series of key statistics including the Gini coefficient for the current income measure for the period since 1994-95, they caution

> Estimates presented for 2007-08 and 2009-10 are not directly comparable with estimates for previous cycles due to the improvements made to measuring income introduced in the 2007-08 cycle. Estimates for 2003-04 and 2005-06 have been recompiled to reflect the new treatments of income, however not all new components introduced in 2007-08 are available for earlier cycles (ABS 2011, Cat No 6523.0: 11).

15 A distribution can be unequal in many different ways. For example, it may be unequal because those at the bottom of the distribution have very little, while the balance of the population has higher but relatively evenly distributed incomes. Alternatively it can arise because most of the population has relatively similar incomes and a small subgroup has very substantially higher incomes. Although the subtleties of these distributions can be presented in graphic forms – such as Lorenz curves which plot the cumulative distribution of ranked income across the population, they cannot be seen in a single value measure.

As seen in Figure 7, which includes estimates derived from the CURFs using a series of different definitions, this is clearly the case and indeed the ABS series seeks to link the series rather than provide a more substantive common definition.

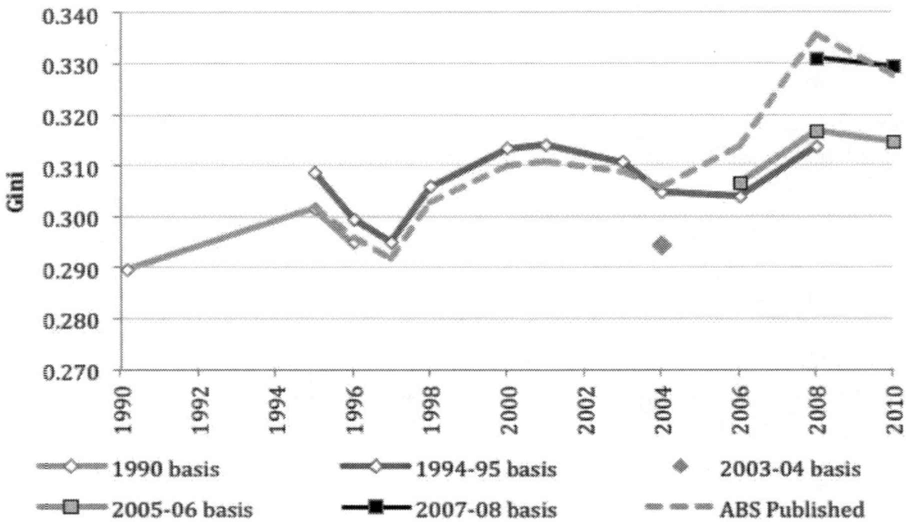

Figure 7 SIH, Current equivalised disposable income, estimated Gini, using different income definitions, 1990-2010

Note: Data plotted at the end of each financial year in which the survey was conducted.

Source: Derived from ABS SIH CURFs and ABS 2011, Cat No 6523.0.

Given the apparent close overlaps between the definitions using the 1990, 1994-95 and 2005-06 bases over the period when data is available or can be derived under multiple income definitions, it is reasonable to consider a composite of these to be more indicative of trends over time. This would suggest that inequality of current equivalised disposable income, as measured by the Gini, rose from around 0.290 in 1990 to a peak of around 0.314 in 2000-01 before declining to a low of 0.304 in 2005-06. After this point it increased again to reach a level of 0.317 and 0.315 in 2007-08 and 2009-10 respectively.

The pattern shown in the annual data from the SIH (Figure 8) is somewhat different – suggesting a slow but consistent rise between 1998-99 to 2002-03, from a Gini of 0.296 to 0.310, before accelerating rapidly to reach a Gini of 0.345 in 2006-07 with a slight decline to 0.305 in 2008-09.[16]

16 An unusual feature of the distribution of this annual income relative to the distribution of current income is the identification of higher inequality in the distribution of annual income. Intuitively it could be

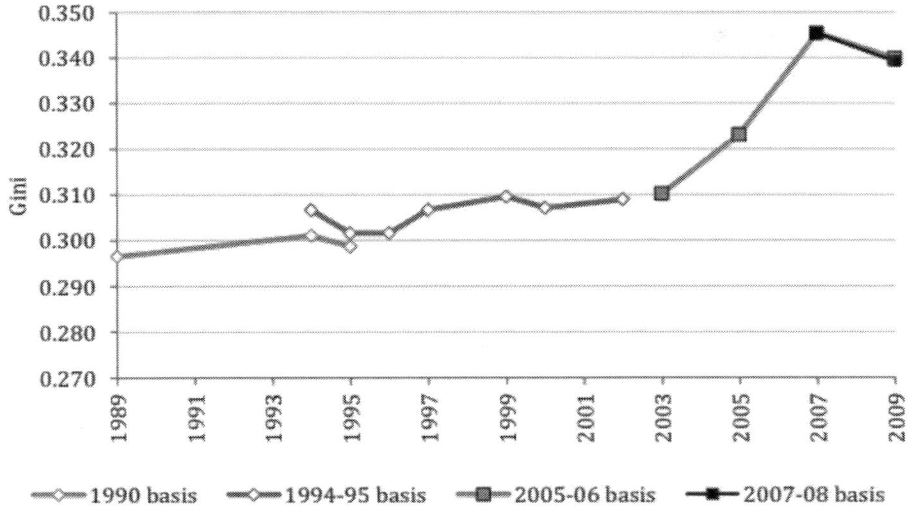

Figure 8, SIH, Annual equivalised disposable income, estimated Gini, using different income definitions, 1989-1990 to 2008-09

Note: Data plotted at the end of each of the financial years for which it was collected.

Source: Derived from ABS SIH CURFs.

The underlying trends in real current equivalised income, as measured in terms of the average income per decile are shown in Figure 9. This repeats the earlier pattern of limited if any income growth until the mid 1990s then steady increases for most groups to the early 2000s followed by rapid growth until 2007-08, after which they tended to be steady or decline.

The chart also shows the marked differences in income growth over the period. While the income of the top decile increased by 73.6 per cent over the whole period, that of the lowest decile increased by just under half this, 32.4 per cent. Although there was some dispersion at almost all points of the income distribution, most apparent has been the way in which the income growth of the top ten per cent of the population has far exceeded that of all other groups. The pattern of growth of this one decile is also very similar to the pattern of change in the Gini coefficient across the period.

expected that over a longer period of time there would be greater income smoothing and hence a lower level of inequality. As seen in later data from HILDA where income is smoothed over a number of years, the level of measured inequality drops.

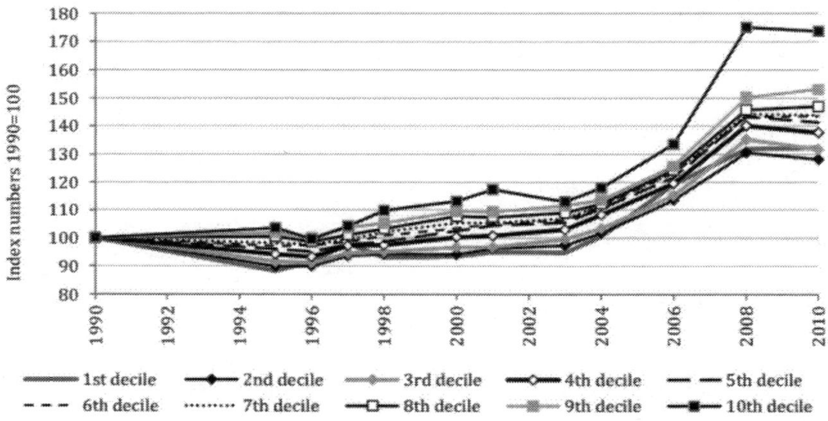

Figure 9 SIH, Mean real equivalised disposable current income by income decile, index numbers, 1990 to 2009-10

Source: Derived from ABS SIH CURFs.

HES

As with the SIH, deriving a long time series from the HES is not straightforward. In addition to changes in definitions of income and whether or not tax data was collected or imputed, a particular problem is caused by the relative treatment of negative incomes. As discussed earlier, the data from the HES has been subject to some edits to seek to derive a more consistent series.

Figure 10 shows the results of a number of different treatments of those households with zero or negative incomes, either in aggregate or for some income components. These include: setting all negative incomes to zero, setting the contribution of own business and investment to zero where the combined total is negative; bottom coding all records below the fifth percentile to the fifth percentile value, and simply excluding records with negative and zero values. In all cases these treatments have been applied to the series which has been adjusted to maximise comparability over time.

As illustrated, the approaches can make a considerable difference in the value of the point estimates of the Gini coefficient. This is particularly marked in the 1993-94 HES, with the smallest differences showing in 2009-10.

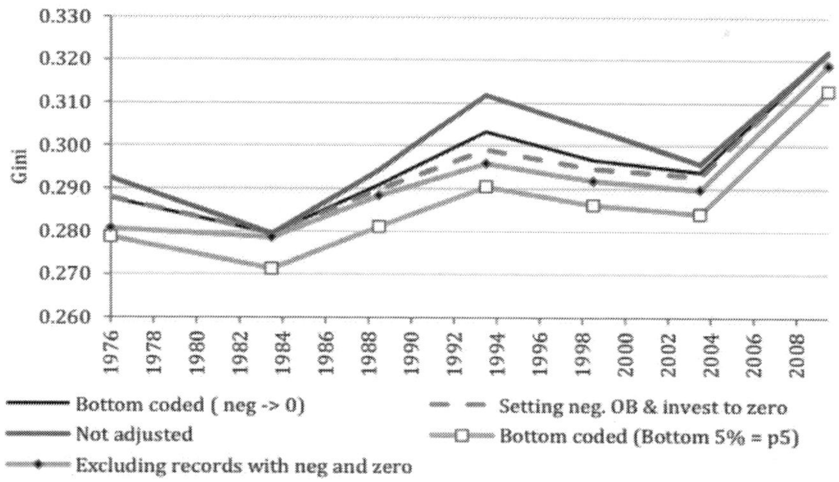

Figure 10 HES, Current equivalised disposable income, estimated Gini, using different income treatments, 1976-2010

Note: OB = Own Business.

Source: Derived from ABS HES CURFs.

Notwithstanding these differences, all of the series show a similar pattern, although differing in the magnitude of the change. This pattern comprises: a fall in inequality as measured by the Gini between 1976 and 1984; before rising to a peak in 1993-94; declining until 2003-04; and then increasing sharply to 2008-09. The overall shift in the Gini ranged from an estimated increase of 0.030, from 0.293 and 0.322 in the 'non-adjusted' series, to 0.038 in the series which excluded negative and zero incomes – an increase from 0.281 to 0.319.

The HES also allows one to consider changes in consumption inequality. Because the definition of consumption in 1976 included the principal component of home loan repayments for owner occupied housing, direct comparisons on current definitions cannot be made consistently across the period. Figure 11 plots the trend in the Gini coefficient using three different treatments of housing costs.

When compared with the income-based estimates, these data suggest a similar decline in inequality between 1976 and 1984, much slower growth until 2003-04, without the pronounced peak in 1994, and then a strong increase to 2009-10, although this last movement was less than half the growth in the income measures. The increase in the Gini coefficient over this period was much less than that recorded for income – ranging from 0.007 where all housing costs are excluded to 0.014 where all housing capital repayments are included in the measure of consumption. These are quite modest changes.

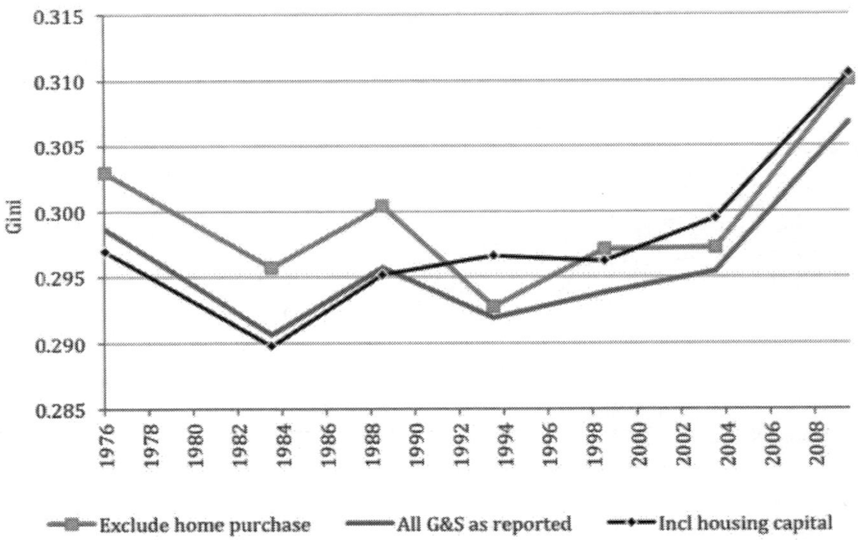

Figure 11 HES, Equivalised consumption, Gini, using different treatments of home purchase costs, 1976-2010

Source: Derived from ABS HES CURFs.

The pattern of income growth underlying these HES results is shown in Figure 12. As with the data from the SIH, this points to a concentration of income growth in the second half of the period (and indeed negative results for all but the second vingtile between 1976 and 1994), and much stronger growth for those households with the highest five per cent of incomes.[17,18]

17 It is noted that, as these surveys are cross-sectional, these rates of growth are based on comparing those households at a particular point in the income distribution in the first period with the set of potentially different households at that point in the second period. No information is available on whether or not these households are common across surveys. This latter style of analysis requires the use of longitudinal data.

18 Notwithstanding the specific impact of the growth in these higher incomes on income distribution, analysis suggests that even if households in the top vingtile of income are excluded, the trends in inequality presented earlier persist.

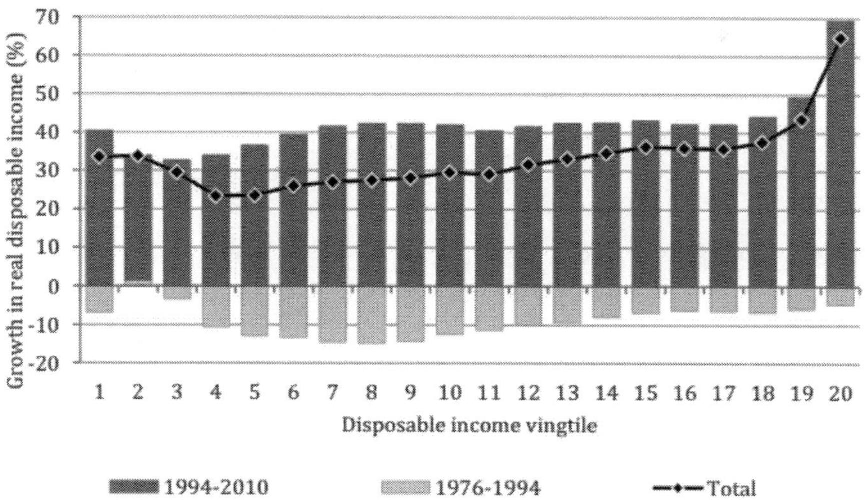

Figure 12 HES, Growth in equivalised real household disposable income, 1976-2010

Source: Derived from ABS HES CURFs, 1976, 1993-94 and 2009-10.

The distribution of equivalised disposable income, in the form of Lorenz curves is plotted in Figure 13 for 1976, 1999 and 2000.

Visually this provides an impression that between each of these three time periods inequality increased, as shown by the consecutive Lorenz curves moving to the right and further away from the line of equality (the diagonal line). More detailed analysis, using percentile points of the distribution, suggests that this is not the case between 1976 and 1999 as the two lines cross. Indeed up to the seventeenth percentile the 1976 line is dominated by the 1999 line, with this again occurring from the ninety-seventh percentile onwards. This reflects the phenomena seen in the earlier chart of income growth of smaller falls in income for these groups, and indeed the slight gain for the second vingtile, relative to the middle.

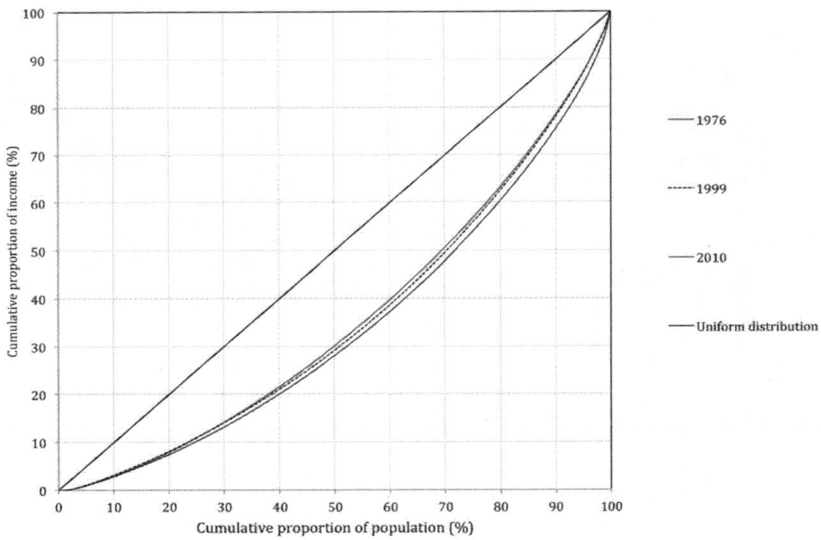

Figure 13 HES, Equivalised disposable income, Lorenz curves, 1976, 1999 and 2010

Source: Derived from ABS HES CURFs, 1976, 1998-99 and 2009-10.

In the case of the comparison between 1999 and 2010, with the exception of the first two percentile points, the 1999 distribution dominates. Given the extent to which these very low incomes are more likely to be strongly affected by how various income losses are treated, there are strong grounds to suggest that dominance has been established and hence income in 2010 was unequivocally less equally distributed.

This finding though is only a partial insight into the possible changes in welfare over this period. As was seen above, the period since 1999 was also marked by strong income growth. The effect of this can be seen in the Generalised Lorenz Curves, Figure 14.

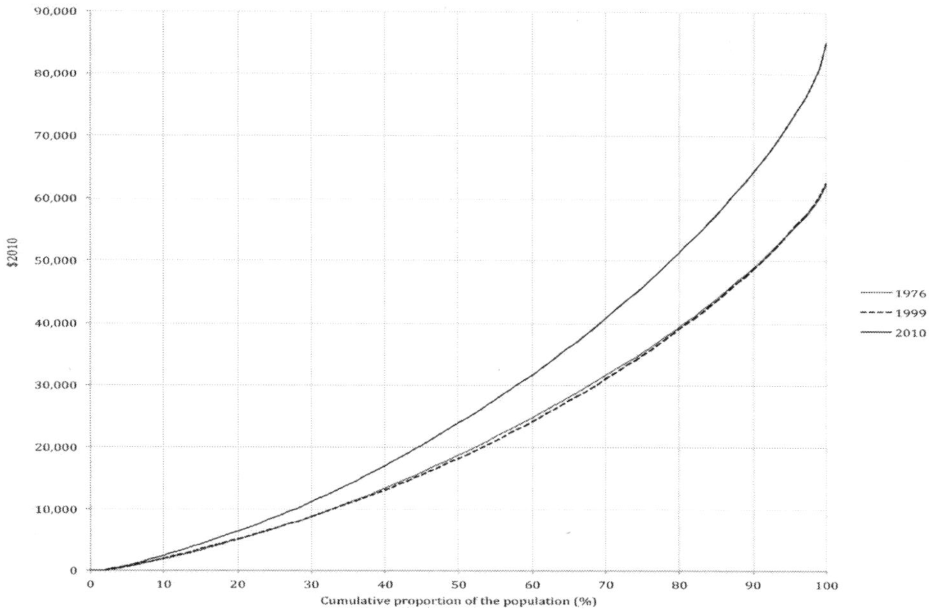

Figure 14 Equivalised disposable income, generalised Lorenz curves, 1976, 1999 and 2010

Source: Derived from ABS HES CURFs 1976, 1998-99 and 2009-10.

In this it is clear that the 2010 distribution clearly dominates those of the previous years, that is, there were gains in income by the population across the income distribution.

HILDA

The HILDA dataset varies from the ABS series in a number of ways. The most prominent of these is its longitudinal basis, a characteristic which will be considered later in this section. A further feature is that unlike the other datasets discussed here, the HILDA dataset is subject to revision over time. In particular as additional information is obtained from subsequent waves of the survey, it is possible to improve on the imputation of missing values in earlier waves. A consequence, from the perspective of analysis, is that estimation of particular population parameters can vary depending upon the specific release of HILDA used. This, as is illustrated in Figure 15, is the case with estimates of the inequality of the income distribution.

While there is considerable fluctuation in the Gini coefficient between the series and over time, there appear to be no strong or consistent time trends. The main HILDA Wave 10.0 file result indicates that in 2010 the Gini at 0.314 was virtually the same as the 0.315 in 2001. Using the series with zero and negative disposable incomes excluded, the value of the Gini coefficient at both the beginning and end was 0.308.

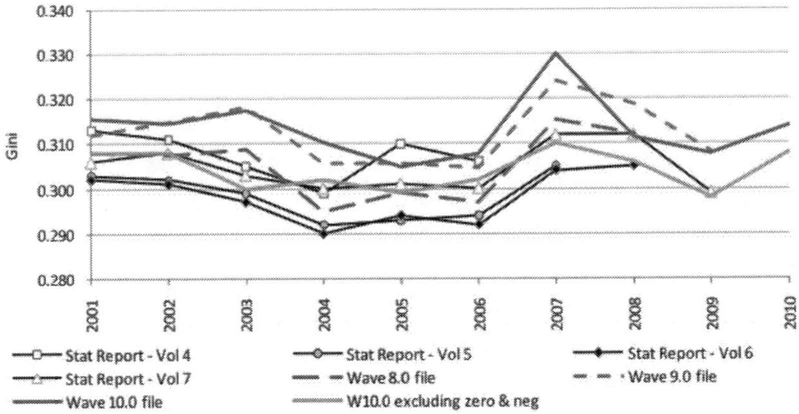

Figure 15 HILDA, Equivalised disposable income, Gini, various sources

Source: Derived from HILDA, Wave 8.0, 9.0 and 10,0 c files, Wilkins *et al* 2009, 2010 and 2011.

The Gini is though not the only instrument for measuring inequality and changes in inequality over time. Figure 16 and Figure 17 present estimates derived from a number of different methodologies, firstly income ratios at different points in the income distribution, and secondly the Atkinson and General Entropy/Theil measures. For these charts records with negative and zero incomes have been excluded as a number of these measures cannot deal with these values and are sensitive to the value which is substituted.[19]

Looking at the income ratios, changes are on the whole slight, although some particular patterns show through. In the case of the p75:p25 ratio, that is the income of a person at the seventy-fifth percentile of the income distribution relative to a person at the twenty-fifth percentile, the ratio fell from being above 2.1 in each of the first five waves of the survey to below in the second five waves. Overall it fell from 2.13 to 2.08 – a 2.4 per cent change. There were also falls in the p75:p50 ratio (-2.2 per cent), the p90:p50 ratio (-2.0 per cent) and the p90:p10 ratio (-1.6 per cent). These figures are surprising in that this data does not appear to reflect the much stronger income growth at the top of the income distribution seen in the other series over the 2000s. This is potentially

19 The sensitivity of measures to the use of substitute values for observations with negative or zero values is discussed in Appendix 3 to the User Guide to the 2009-10 HES and SIH (ABS Cat NO 6503.0 2012).

a consequence of the growth being most concentrated in the very top of the income distribution and hence not impacting as much on the actual cut-off point for the top vingtile.

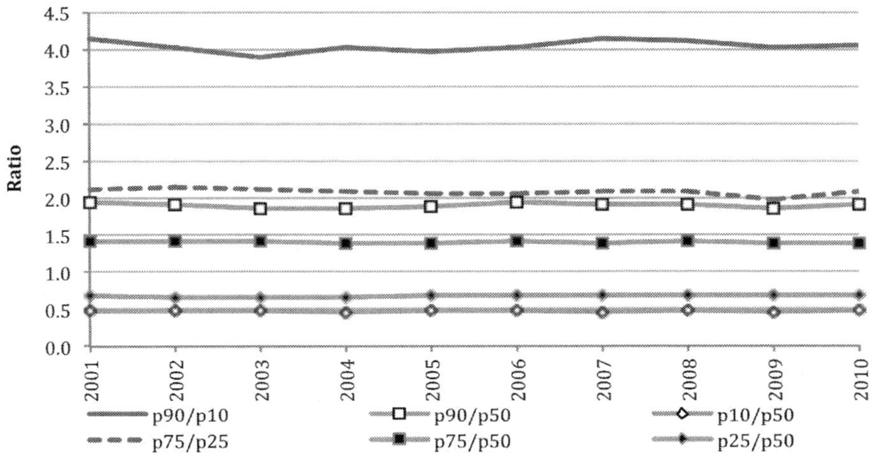

Figure 16 HILDA, Equivalised disposable income, excluding negative and zero observations, selected income ratios, 2001-2010

Note: Excludes records with a negative or zero disposable income.

Source: Derived from HILDA Wave 10.0.

The Atkinson and Generalised Entropy measures shown in Figure 17 differ in one important aspect from the Gini in that they require the user to choose a particular parameter which reflects the specific characteristics of inequality they are particularly interested in.

- In the case of the Atkinson measure the ε value reflects a level of inequality aversion. A higher ε – typically a value of 2 – makes the measure particularly sensitive to changes in inequality at the bottom of the income distribution.
- The choice of the α parameter in the Generalised Entropy measure plays a similar role with more negative values, making the index more sensitive to income shares between those on lower incomes and more positive values, increasing its sensitivity to differences in income shares amongst those with high incomes.

The data suggests an erratic, but overall downward trend in inequality amongst those on lower incomes, especially up until 2008 (Atkinson $\varepsilon = 2$ and Generalised Entropy $\alpha = -1$) but less change at other points – although the Generalised Entropy measure with $\alpha = 2$ lifts somewhat in the latter part of the period, suggesting that there have been some inequality increasing changes in the income share amongst those with higher incomes.

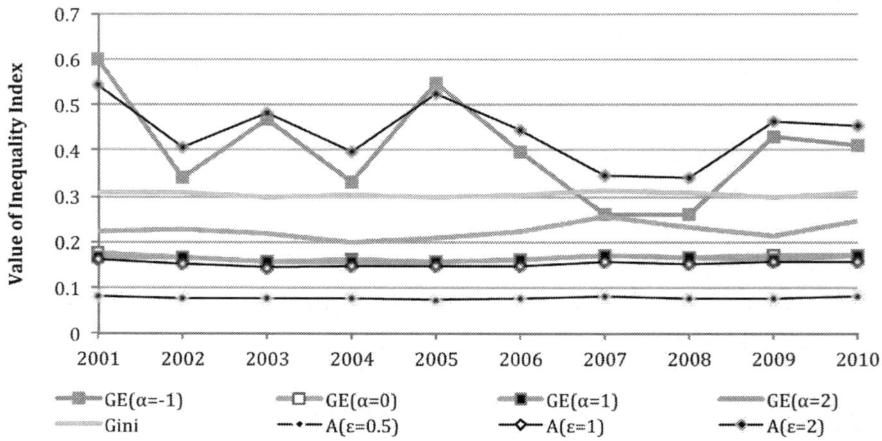

Figure 17 HILDA, Equivalised disposable income, excluding negative and zero observations, selected inequality measures, 2001-2010

Note: Excludes records with a negative or zero disposable income.

Source: Derived from HILDA Wave 10.0.

Figure 18 presents two further assessments of inequality trends from the HILDA survey. For these a balanced panel has been used – that is looking at the experience of those for whom data are available for all waves of the HILDA survey. In this analysis the population has been divided into three cohorts – those who were under 25 years in Wave 1, those aged 25-49 years at that time and those aged 50 years and over. This was done as it would be anticipated that these groups may have different experiences over time – the first in terms of leaving parental homes and establishing their own households and participating in the workforce, the third in regard to withdrawal from the work force, with the second representing a group which was likely to have continuously high levels of participation.

Two series are plotted for each of these groups. The first is, for each year, the Gini coefficient for current equivalised disposable income in that year. The second is the Gini coefficient of people's average income over the whole ten-year period.[20] This latter, for all cohorts, sits well below the annual data. This suggests that income is more evenly distributed when a longer time period is considered, or put another way, that cross-sectional analysis of income distribution picks up some transient elements of income, or errors in the reporting of this. Using the

20 As in all of the analyses involving equivalised measures, the analysis is undertaken on the basis of population weighting, effectively allocating to each person within a household the equivalised income of the household in which they live at that point in time. In this analysis it is the average of these which has been used, even where it involves people who may have lived in a number of different households over the period.

average of income over the ten-year period produces estimates of the Gini which are 0.050 below the annual figures. For example, over the ten-year period the annual figures for the Gini for the total balanced panel range between 0.301 and 0.327, with an average of 0.311, the Gini for income aggregated over the period is 0.259. This clearly indicates that income inequality when viewed over a longer time scale is not as severe as shorter term snapshots indicate.[21]

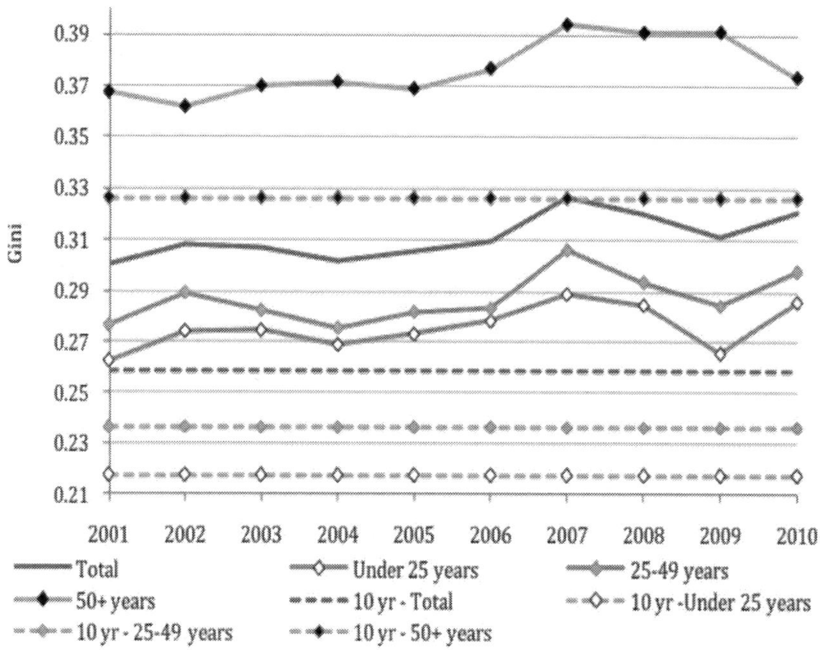

Figure 18 HILDA, Equivalised disposable income, balanced panel, population cohorts based on age in Wave 1, within group Gini, 2001-2010

Source: Derived from HILDA Wave 10.0.

Returning to the annual estimate a second feature of this chart is that, in contrast to the cross-sectionally weighted analysis, there is some suggestion of increasing inequality over the period. This is particularly marked in the 25-49 year-old entry age cohort where the Gini has increased from 0.276 to 0.284. However, for all series, the level of inequality in the second half of the decade is higher than in the first.

21 For this analysis, income in each year has simply been adjusted for changes in the CPI to produce time consistent real values. An alternative approach would be to also include a time discount value to reflect the tendency of individuals to prefer current over future consumption.

An overall perspective

Figure 19 plots the Ginis for a selection of the major income series together. Although individual series show considerable volatility and there are periods of marked inconsistency between series, it is not unreasonable to conclude, with the exception of the cross sectional series derived from HILDA, that there has been a general upwards shift in the Gini coefficient, in particular since 1990. The magnitude of this is around 0.025. Recent OECD analysis reports that between 2000 and the late 2000s there were increases in inequality of a similar magnitude in Denmark (0.022), Germany (0.031), Switzerland (0.024) and the US (0.021); conversely there were marked falls in Greece (-0.038), Spain (-0.025), and Great Britain (-0.018) (OECD 2011).

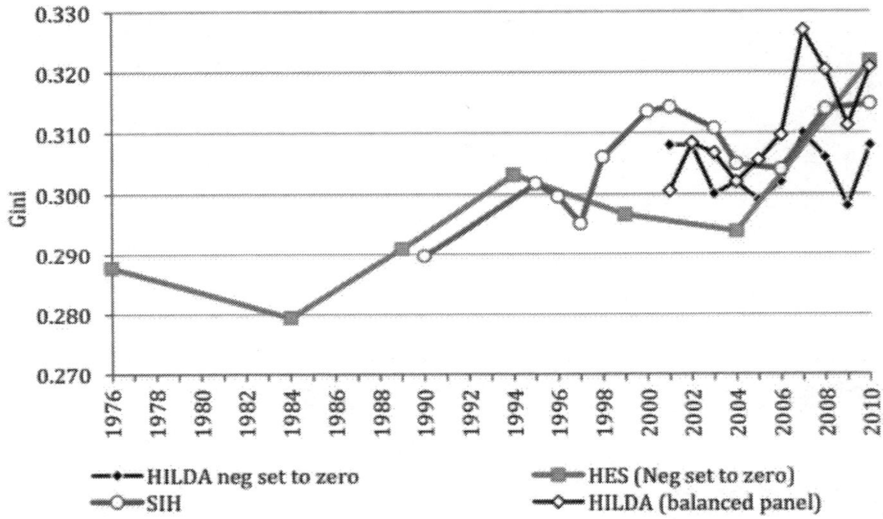

Figure 19 HES, SIH and HILDA, equivalised disposable income, Gini

Notes: HES, series derived from HES CURFs to maximise backwards compatibility, negative household incomes set to zero.SIH: series derived from SIH CURFs, 1990 & 1994-95 using 1990 basis, 1996-2008 using 1994-95 basis, 2010 using 2005-06 basis. HILDA derived from wave 10.0, a) using cross-sectional weights negative incomes set to zero; b) balanced panel using longitudinal weights.

Source: Derived from HES, SIH and HILDA Wave 10.0.

Perhaps more significant to wellbeing, these shifts in income distribution in Australia, in particular since 2000, have been accompanied by very strong real income growth. This has resulted in households, across the income distribution, having increased resources for consumption and other purposes.

What impacts on the income distribution?

This section addresses the question: what are the factors which contribute to the patterns of income distribution seen in the previous section and changes in these over time? In particular it considers the roles of the tax and transfer systems.

The approach used for this is factor decomposition of the Gini coefficient using the 'natural decomposition' approach proposed by Shorrocks (1982). This takes the final distribution of income, typically disposable income, and seeks to identify the relative contributions of each of the components of income to this distribution. In essence it performs this by considering the covariance between the distribution of this particular income component, and the distribution of the population as ranked by the aggregate concept of income.

This however is not the only approach which is available, and a range of different approaches have been developed across the literature. These include:

- Lerman and Yitzhaki (1985) propose the use of a relative marginal effect – or elasticity of inequality to a source income – as a focus for decomposing the effect of different sources. This does not consider the decomposition of the existing income components per se but rather considers the impact of a marginal uniform proportional shift in any one source of income on inequality;
- A 'sequential accounting decomposition' of inequality. This involves the derivation of a sequential set of income estimates, adding an additional source each time, then calculating the inequality measure for these and ascribing the change in inequality to the additional source of income. This approach is commonly seen in OECD publications.
- Shapley decomposition (Chantreuil and Trannoy 2013; Shorrocks 2013) this uses a game theory approach repeating games by eliminating components (replaced by the mean or zero) and then uses the average value derived from all possible sequences to estimate the relative contribution.
- Lastly there are a number of regression-based approaches to decomposition as well as various non-parametric approaches.

As hinted at by the existence of this range of methods, even across the most recent literature, there is limited consensus on the most appropriate methodology. This is far from trivial as the results of any decomposition can be very sensitive to the approach given and individual approaches may provide markedly different estimates of the relative contribution of components. In addition there are reasonable grounds for having strong reservations around most of the methods. Some aspects of this are discussed further in Appendix A.

Although there are arguments for using a number of the approaches, the natural decomposition has been adopted in this paper for a number of reasons. In the first instance, in parts of the analysis up to ten sources of income are considered. The sensitivity of the sequential approach to the order in which components are included makes it poorly suited to this approach. Secondly there is a strong intuitive attraction to the focus in the natural decomposition methodology on the relationship of the income element being considered and the final income distribution, rather than considering distributions of the population which, as in the sequential approach, are re-ranked in each iteration as additional elements are included. In addition the approach provides a direct linkage to the calculations of the marginal effect – with this latter providing a useful tool for the consideration of policy options, rather than just being a descriptive approach.

Finally, in considering this type of decomposition of inequality by source, it needs to be emphasised that only direct effects are being described, and that causation is much more complex. Hence, while these measures, for example, seek to describe the actual quantitative effect of tax paid to the final distribution of income, this is quite a different question to the actual impact of taxation on the distribution of income which includes a diversity of behavioural and other responses (Creedy and Hérault 2012).

Disposable income

In 2010 the Gini coefficient of equivalised disposable household income, as derived from the HES, was 0.329. This can be decomposed, as shown in Figure 20, into the following contributions: wage and salaries 0.382, income from a person's own business 0.030, from salary sacrificed amounts of earnings from these two sources 0.017, investment income 0.046, superannuation 0.012, other income 0.002. Offsetting these, income support payments made a negative contribution of -0.041, family payment -0.012, and income tax -0.108. Private transfers made a very small positive contribution of 0.001.

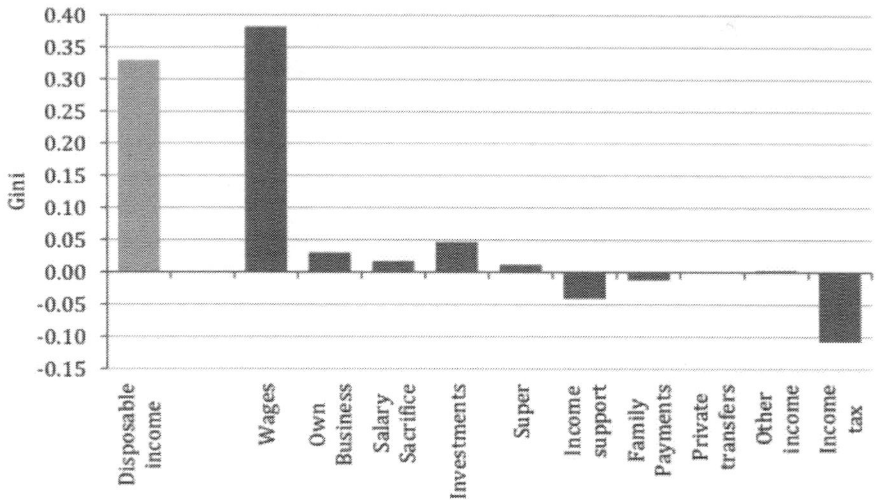

Figure 20 HES, Equivalised disposable income, Gini decomposition by source, 2010

Source: Derived from ABS HES 2009-10 CURF.

That is, the final Gini of 0.329 reflects the impact of the negative -0.161 effect of the tax transfer system on the 0.490 Gini of private income, with the bulk of this effect resulting from the progressive nature of the income tax system.

As discussed in Appendix A, alternative approaches to the decomposition provide different estimates of the relative role of the tax and transfer system in contributing to the lessening of inequality. In particular the sequential accounting approach suggests a stronger role for transfers. In approaching this from a policy perspective there is also merit in considering the Lerman and Yitzhaki relative marginal effect. This is derived directly from the natural decomposition, being the proportional share of the contribution to the inequality of the income source less its share of income. Taking this further transformation, the contribution of income tax of -0.108 represents -32.8 per cent of the overall Gini. Subtracting the income tax share of disposable income (-18.6 per cent) from this, generates an elasticity of -14.2 per cent. The same transformation on the combined effect of transfers is -28.2 per cent. This indicates that a uniform proportional change in transfers will have a stronger effect on the distribution of income than a similar change in taxation.

Role of second earners

This form of decomposition can be undertaken in many different ways to look at the effect of different income sources. Given earlier discussion of the changing composition of employment in couple households, Figure 21 splits the effect of earned income (wages and salaries and own business including salary sacrifice) between first and second and other earners (with the first earner being defined as the person in the household with the highest earned income).

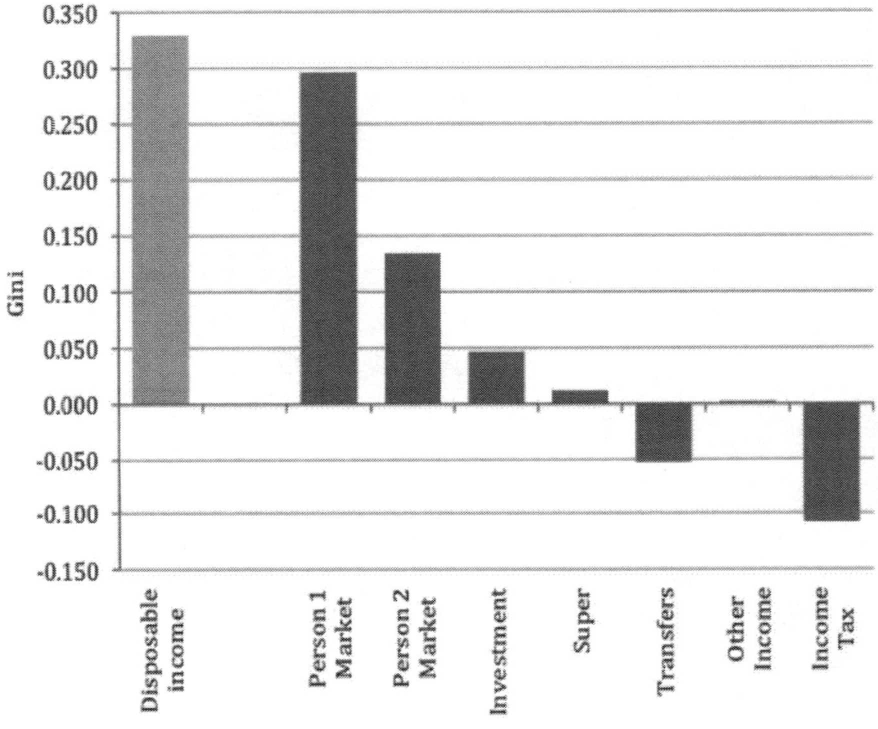

Figure 21 HES, Equivalised disposable income, Gini decomposition by source – impact of first and second earner income, 2010

Source: Derived from ABS HES 2009-10 CURF.

In this case we see that the distribution of income to the first earner contributes 0.296 to the disposable income Gini, while that of the second and other earners adds a further 0.134. Given that first earners contribute on average 2.7 times the income of second and subsequent earners, their relative contribution to the Gini of 2.2 times, suggests that the incomes of second and subsequent earners add disproportionately to inequality across households.[22]

22 The extent of this may be overstated as a consequence of the use of concepts of income and of equivalence scales which do not take account of the costs of employment. That is, under the approach used here it is assumed that two households with the same disposable income and the same household structure are in equivalent situations regardless of whether one or two people (or indeed no person) is in employment.

The role of second and further income earners in shaping the income distribution is further considered in Figure 22. This plots, for vingtile groups, the value of income derived from the above sources. While employment income for the first person plays a significant role from the fifth vingtile upwards,[23] second earner income only makes a substantial contribution from the ninth vingtile, where it represents around 23 per cent of the earned income of the household. This proportion then increases to reach 36 per cent of the earned income of households in the sixteenth vingtile before declining to 24 per cent of the earned income of households in the top vingtile.[24]

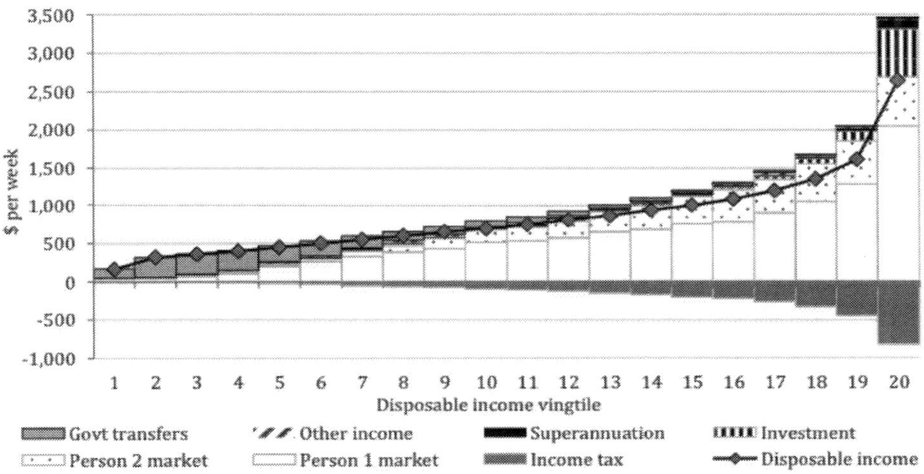

Figure 22 HES, Components of equivalised disposable income, by income vingtile, 2009-10

Source: Derived from ABS HES 2009-10 CURF.

Also apparent in the chart is the extent to which superannuation and investment income flows to higher income households. Almost 80 per cent of all investment income is received by the 20 per cent of households with the highest disposable incomes, with just over 58 per cent flowing to the five per cent of households that comprise the top vingtile. While the distribution of superannuation is not quite so marked, nevertheless some 44 per cent flows to those in the top 20 per cent of the income distribution, and a quarter to those households in the top five per cent.[25]

23 In technical terms, as the data are population weighted each vingtile represents five per cent of the population living in households with these characteristics. For convenience in discussion this is presented in terms of the vingtiles representing five per cent of the households.

24 While there is some evidence of second earners across all of the vingtiles, the net contribution of these in the lower vingtiles is small. In the first vingtile, because the first and second earner have been defined on the basis of relative earnings, while the average earnings of the first person (as an average across all of the households) is $40 per week, this is offset by an average negative income of -$8 for second earners.

25 This result is likely to represent the history of superannuation rather than as a prospective finding for the future impact of superannuation. It is probable that this distribution reflects the fact that until the

Broader concepts of income

Government intervention in the relative wellbeing of households is not limited to direct cash transfers and income tax. It also includes government benefits in kind – such as health, education and other welfare services, and the impact of indirect taxes including the GST. In addition those households in owner occupied housing gain a flow of services from this. These additional elements generate a broader concept of total income.

The value of these services is estimated by ABS and available in the HES CURF (see ABS 2012).[26]

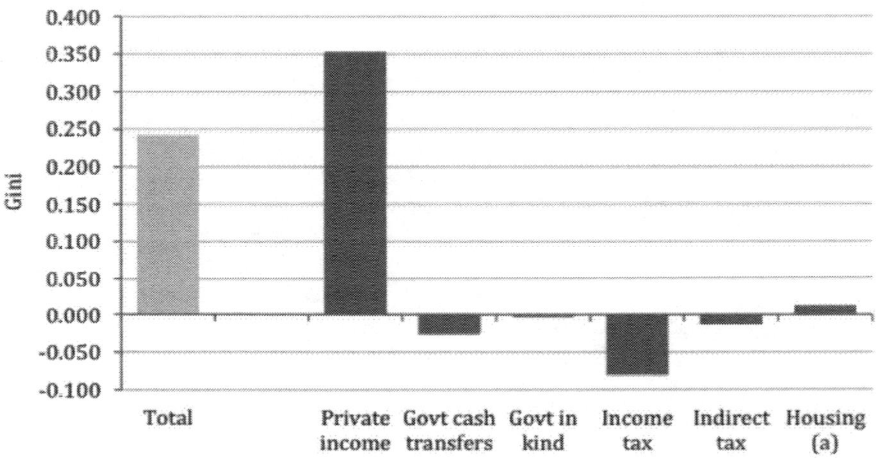

Figure 23 HES, Total income, Gini decomposition, 2009-10

(a) Imputed value of home ownership and private housing subsidies.

Source: Derived from ABS HES 2009-10 CURF.

When this broader notion of income is used, the Gini coefficient falls to 0.242 – substantially below the 0.329 when income is defined in terms of disposable

introduction of the superannuation guarantee, the main groups with superannuation were relatively well-paid employees in the public sector and selected management positions in some areas of the private sector.

26 Full details of the approach used by the ABS are provided in the cited publication. Government assistance in kind, described by ABS as 'social transfers in kind' are defined by the Bureau to 'consist of goods and services provided free or at subsidised prices by the government. In this study, allocation of social transfers in kind was restricted to those arising from the provision of education, health, housing, social security and welfare services, and electricity concessions and rebates'. The methodology for allocating these to households vary – but in large part they are either allocated on an average basis to those who are known to receive services – such as children at school, or allocated on an 'insurance basis' across populations based on known levels of relative use – such as health care which is allocated on the basis of age, gender and state.

income.[27] This then can be decomposed into the impact of private income 0.353, and the value of imputed rent for owner occupied dwellings and privately subsidised rental accommodation 0.012, being offset by government cash transfers -0.026, government assistance in kind -0.003, income tax -0.080 and indirect taxes -0.013.

In considering these results it should be noted that the contribution to the overall Gini of total income from sources such as private income, cash transfers and direct taxation varies from those seen above, with regard to the distribution of disposable income. The key reason for this is that the use of different income measures, as discussed previously, results in a different ranking of households when this is performed using different concepts of income. For example, a household which lives in an owner-occupied house with a number of children attending education may see themselves now ranked in the income distribution above a household with a similar level of income but where the children are not studying and where the household is renting.

Impact of taxes and transfers over time

As has been seen previously, income taxes and transfers both play a role in countering the degree to which market income is distributed unequally across households. This section is concerned with how this may have changed over time. While having this specific focus, the analysis will also consider other components of income.

HES

Analysis of the HES data for this purpose has been limited to the period since 1984. The main reason is that the taxation data in the earlier 1976 survey is tax 'as reported' rather than imputed and, on the basis of later surveys and analysis of the apparent changes in the role of income tax, this suggests there is evidence that levels of taxation may be under-reported.

---

27 In this analysis this broader definition of income has again been equivalised by the use of the revised OECD scales. It is less clear, even to the extent these scales may be appropriate for the use of identifying relative needs for disposable income, whether they are entirely appropriate to the use of these broader concepts. For example, given that expenditure on education is allocated to children attending school, the use of a divisor which is more heavily weighted to the number of adults in the household does not seem appropriate. Again there are few simple solutions to this.

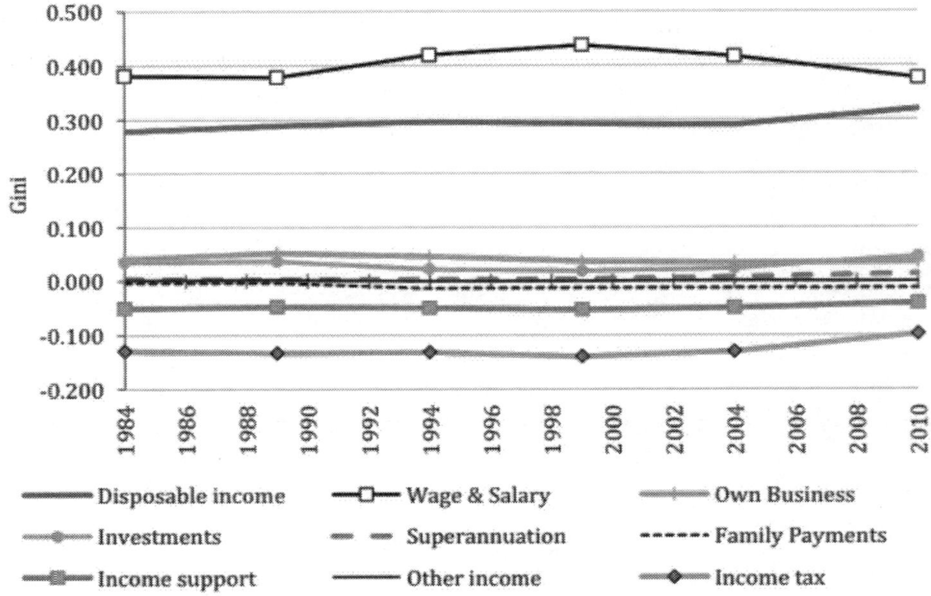

Figure 24 HES, Equivalised disposable income, decomposition of Gini 1984-2010

Source: Derived from ABS HES CURFs 1984 to 2009-10.

Considering in turn the components of income shown in Figure 24 (excepting other income which has only a minor effect on the pattern of income distribution):

- The contribution of wage and salary income to inequality, in addition to being the major contributor, increased from 0.381 in 1984 to a peak of 0.437 in 1999 before declining to 0.377 in 2010, a little below the level it was at the beginning of the period.
- The contribution of own business income to overall inequality was in a range of 0.041 to 0.052 for the first three periods, that is 1984 to 1994. It then shifted downward to be in the range of 0.034 to 0.037 for the second three periods from 1999 to 2010.
- Investment income displayed some fluctuation in its contribution to overall inequality over the period making a contribution of 0.034 and 0.037 in 1994 and 1998, before declining to 0.022 in 1994 and 0.018 in 1999, before rising to 0.024 in 2004 and 0.046 in 2010.
- Superannuation made a slight positive contribution to the overall pattern of inequality of 0.003 to 0.004 up to 1999 before increasing to 0.007 in 2004 and 0.014 in 2010.

- The impact of family payments was small in 1984 and 1988 at -0.003 in each period, before increasing substantially to -0.013 in 1994 and remaining at or very close to that level over the rest of the period.
- Income support made a relatively consistent offsetting contribution to inequality of around -0.048 to -0.053 over the whole period, except for 2010 where it dropped to -0.041
- Income tax also had a negative impact on the level of inequality over the period. This was in the range of -0.130 to -0.134 for the first three periods, rising to -0.140 in 1999 before declining back to its earlier levels in 2004, before falling very sharply to -0.098 in 2010.

The summary impact of these changes is illustrated in Figure 25. The chart shows, for the period between 1984 and 1999, and then between 1999 and 2010, the change in contribution of each of the components to the Gini coefficient of the distribution of disposable income.

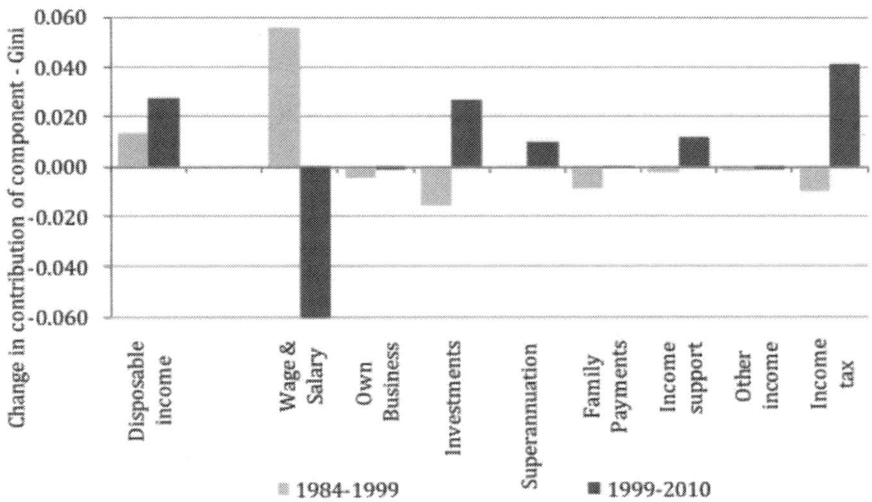

Figure 25 HES, Change in contribution of components of income to overall inequality 1984 to 1999 and 1999-2010

Source: Derived from ABS HES CURFs 1984-2009-10.

Over the first period the main effect was an increasing contribution towards inequality from wage and salary income offset by declines in the contribution of most other elements. Over the past decade the situation has been quite different: the role of wage and salary income as a contributor to inequality has declined while that of capital income from investments and superannuation has increased, and the offsetting role of income support has fallen. Most marked however has been the very large decrease in the offsetting role of taxation (resulting in a positive contribution to the change in inequality). A similar but lesser change is seen in the role of income support payments.

HILDA

Although HILDA showed a very slight decline in inequality over the past decade – a contrast with the results from the HES and SIH, as shown in Figure 26 – the pattern of change in the relative contributions of the components is very similar to that identified in the HES. The contribution to inequality of earned income (from wages, salaries and own business) fell strongly over the period, income from capital (investments and superannuation) increased its impact on income inequality, while income support payments played a less marked role in offsetting inequality. While the decline in the role of income tax in offsetting inequality was not quite as marked as seen in the HES, it remains very strong.

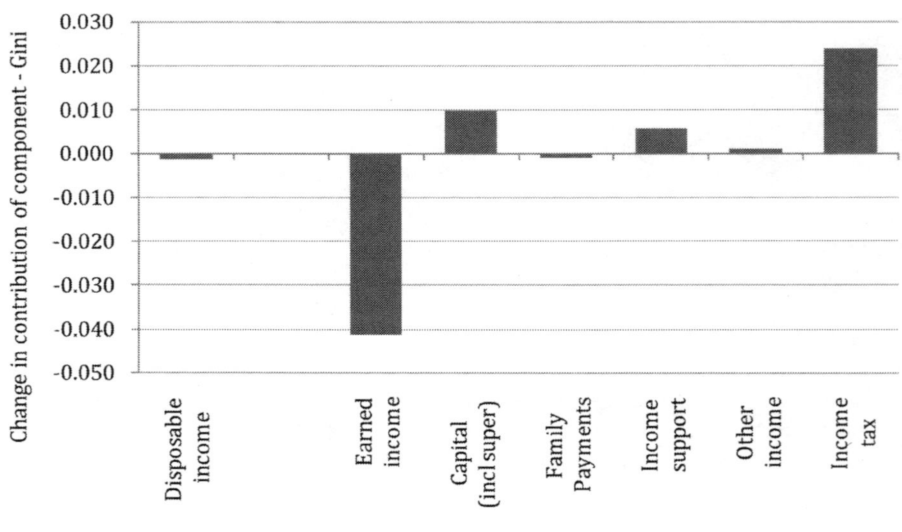

Figure 26 HILDA, Change in contribution of components of income to overall inequality 2001-2010

Source: Derived from HILDA Wave 10.0.

A more detailed analysis of the contributions of these components to inequality over the period is shown in Figure 27. As with the HES data this suggests that most of the decline in the offsetting role of income tax is in the post-2006 period. Although peaking at -0.142 in 2002, the impact of taxation in 2006 remained strong at -0.137 in 2006 before declining to -0.116 in 2010.

The role of income support varied a little more over the period, although again showing a reduction in its offsetting role. In the early 2000s it was around or above -0.04 before falling to a low of -0.028 in 2009, and rising to -0.034 in 2010.

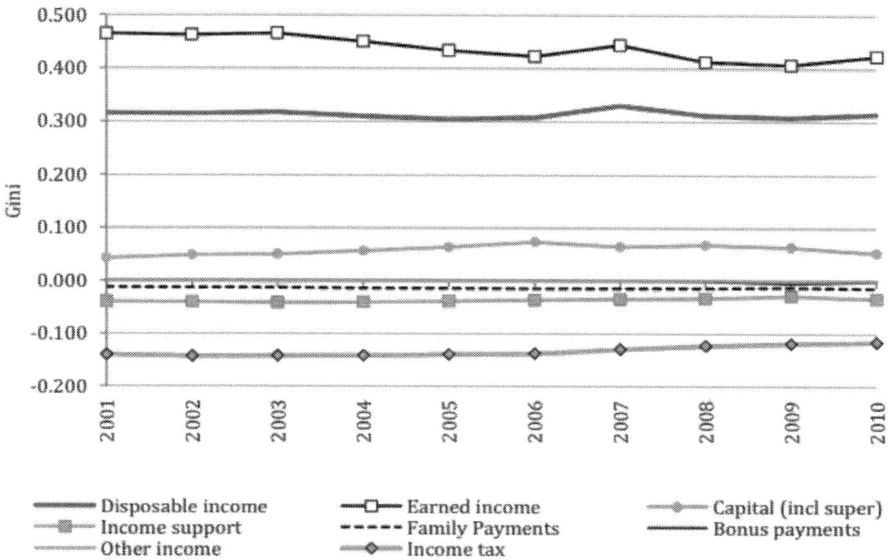

Figure 27 HILDA, Equivalised disposable income, decomposition of Gini 2000-2010

Source: Derived from HILDA Wave 10.0.

SIH

Figure 28 and Figure 29 show the contribution of income tax to overall inequality as recorded in the SIH, firstly with regard to current income and secondly with regard to annual income. While there are some differences in the period up to 1995, since then both series suggest that there was an increase in the offsetting role income tax played up until around 2000, after which this role diminished. While the two series do not wholly coincide on timing, certainly the pick up was more marked in the latter half of the decade.

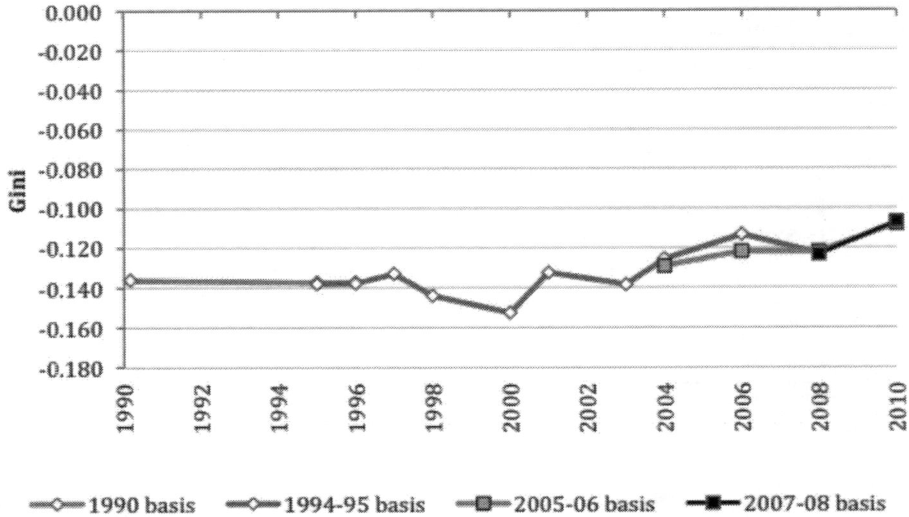

Figure 28 SIH, Current equivalised disposable income, contribution of income tax to Gini, using different income definitions, 1990-2010

Source: Derived from ABS SIH CURFs 1990-2010.

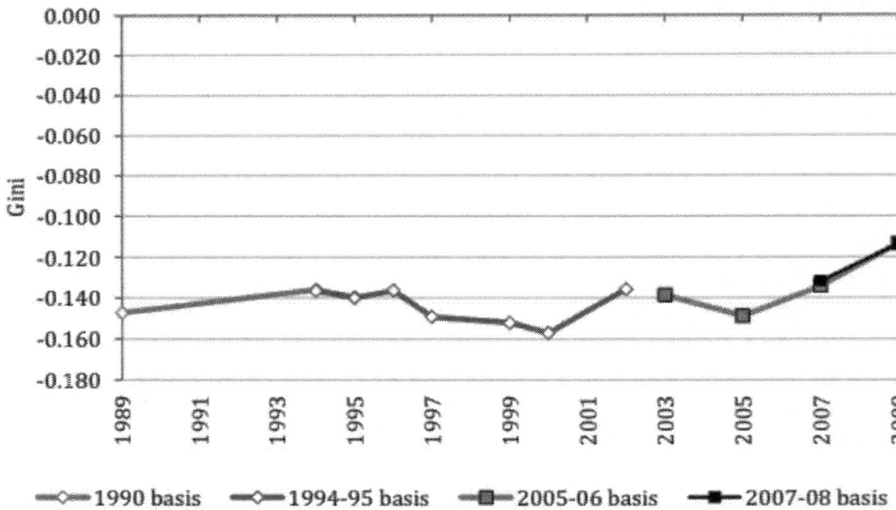

Figure 29 SIH, Annual equivalised disposable income, contribution of income tax to Gini, using different income definitions, 1990-2010

Source: Derived from ABS SIH CURFs 1990-2010.

The annual data suggests that the decline from 2000 has been around 0.044 with most of this (-0.036) occurring between 2005 (-0.149) and 2009 (-0.114).

The current data series suggests a decline of 0.025 to 0.045 to the 2010 level of -0.107, depending upon whether 2001 (-0.153) or 2000 (-0.132) is used as the base year.

These estimates compare with 0.042 from the HES for the period between 1999 and 2010, and 0.024 from HILDA between 2001 and 2010. In looking at the pattern of the data, and in particular the movement in 2000, one issue which needs to be considered in explaining these trends is the impact of the changes in direct taxation associated with the introduction of the GST, as well as the ongoing changes to the taxation system that have been documented earlier.

Conclusions and reflections

Analysis of the distribution of income in Australia suggests that over recent years there has been an increase in income inequality and that the traditional tools of income distribution, progressive income tax and transfer payments have been playing a lesser role in counterbalancing the impact of the distribution of other sources of income. Indeed the decomposition of the sources of inequality would suggest that the decline in the function played by these has been the main factor contributing to the increase in inequality.

Specifically, while the results vary from source to source and the methodology used, the analysis indicates:

- Income inequality in Australia, as measured by the Gini, has risen by some 0.02 to 0.03 since the mid 1990s with much of this increase occurring since the mid 2000s. In the case of the SIH, using current data, this is an increase from 0.295 to 0.314.
- In the past decade the extent to which income tax reduces inequality has fallen. The change identified represents a decrease in its offsetting impact on the Gini of some 0.02 to 0.04
- A similar reduced impact is seen in the role of transfer payments. In this case the reduction in the offset to the Gini is around 0.005 to 0.01.
- Taken together these factors would appear to be responsible for the overall decline, although it is noted that many other components have moved in different directions at the same time. However all three surveys considered in the analysis indicate that changes in the distribution of wage and salary income over the past decade has been towards equalising the income distribution.

This finding though needs to be taken with some caution.

- On technical grounds the measurement of income is fraught with both practical and conceptual limitations, and while income may be better measured in many household surveys than it has in the past, this has brought with it problems in building consistent datasets to allow for the analysis of income over time. In addition as a measure of household resources, current income measures do not account well for some dimensions such as capital gains, and few surveys identify well the range of non-cash benefits which play an important role in wellbeing. It is also well established that for many households income does not reflect either their level of consumption, or of wellbeing. An additional set of technical problems arises in measuring income inequality. In particular the use of single value measures of inequality does not capture the different ways in which inequality can occur. These technical problems of inequality measurement are even more complex when attempting to identify the contribution of different income components to final income inequality.
- While inequality would appear to have increased more strongly since the early to mid 2000s, this has also been accompanied by a strong increase in household incomes which, while favouring higher income households, has been well distributed across the income distribution including those households with the lowest incomes.
- It is difficult, in the context of income inequality, to make normative judgements about some of the factors which may have contributed to this. For example the increasing proportion of dual income households is likely to have increased the level of inequality relative to those with one income. Similarly population ageing had resulted in an increase in the number of retired incomes, many of which are drawing upon superannuation and other savings, as well as potentially facing lower income needs.
- More specifically the lesser role of the government transfers in redressing income inequality needs to be seen in the light of a decline in the proportion of the population which is in receipt of these payments and the lesser reliance by households on these payments as their major source of income. In the case of the role of taxation, again the lesser role of income tax in income distribution must be considered in the context of changes to taxation policy which have seen an overall reduction in the average tax rate from 23.1 per cent to 21.0 per cent with particularly strong reductions in the average rate of tax paid by those in the lower half of the distribution of taxpayers.

These cautions do not however mean that the question of income distribution should simply be ignored, but rather argues a need for us to improve our techniques and data, and not treat any results in isolation from a wide range of other economic and social objectives and priorities.

Further, in forming any judgements about income inequality and its trends, the question must be asked as to why one is concerned? It can be suggested that in itself income inequality, within certain bounds, is of relatively little import, but rather its study serves more as a guide to two other questions. The first is whether it is a symptom of some more fundamental problem within society; the second is whether it brings with it consequences which may be adverse to society.

Related to this is a final question: even if trends in income distribution provide a means for exploring these questions, is its use as an indirect approach appropriate, or should attention be given more directly to other forms of inequality? These might include opportunities for education, access to health care, ability to engage in leisure and other activities which a person may value, freedom from discrimination or ability to exert power. While it can be argued that income plays an important role in achieving some of these opportunities, for others this may not necessarily be the case.

References

Araar A (2006). *On the decomposition of the Gini Coefficient: an Exact Approach, with an illustration using Cameroonian data*, Centre interuniversitaire sur le risque, les politiques économiques et l'emploi, Working Paper 06-02.

Araar A and Duclos J-Y (2013). User Manual DASP version 2.3, DASP: Distributive Analysis Stata Package, Université Laval, PEP, CIRPÉE and World Bank .

Australian Bureau of Statistics (1986). *1984 Household Expenditure Survey, Australia, Summary of Results*, Cat No 6530.0, ABS, Canberra.

Australian Bureau of Statistics (1987). *1984 Household Expenditure Survey, Australia, Effects of Government Benefits and Taxes on Household Income*, Cat No 6537.0, ABS, Canberra.

Australian Bureau of Statistics (2010). *Standards for Income Variables, 2010*, Cat No 1287.0, ABS Canberra http://www.abs.gov.au/AUSSTATS/abs@.nsf/Lookup/00AD7C0C516A9508CA2576E400144852?opendocument, ABS, Canberra.

Australian Bureau of Statistics (2011). *Education and Work Australia, May 2011*, Cat No 62270DO001_201105, ABS, Canberra.

Australian Bureau of Statistics (2011). Household Income and Income Distribution, Australia, 2009-10, SIH 2009-10 Detailed Tables Cat No 65230DO001, Table 3, ABS, Canberra.

Australian Bureau of Statistics (2012). Household *Expenditure Survey and Survey of Income and Housing, User Guide, Australia, 2009-10,* Cat No 6503.0, ABS, Canberra.

Australian Bureau of Statistics (2012). *Employee Earnings, Benefits and Trade Union Membership*, Cat No 6310.0, ABS, Canberra.

Australian Bureau of Statistics (2012). *Labour Force, Australia, Detailed - Electronic Delivery, Oct 2012*, Cat No 6291.0.55.001, ABS, Canberra.

Australian Bureau of Statistics (2012). *Government Benefits, Taxes and Household Income, Australia, 2009-10*, Cat No 6537.0, ABS, Canberra.

Australian Bureau of Statistics (Various years). *Employee Earnings and Hours,* Australia, Cat No 6306.0, ABS, Canberra.

Australian Taxation Office (2003). *Taxation Statistics 2000–2001*, Australian Taxation Office, Canberra.

Australian Taxation Office (2012a). *Individual income tax rates for prior years,* http://www.ato.gov.au/content/73969.htm last accessed 10 November 2012.

Australian Taxation Office (2012b). *Individual income tax rates* http://www.ato.gov.au/individuals/content.aspx?doc=/content/12333.htm last accessed 10 November 2012.

Australian Taxation Office (2012c). *Taxation statistics 2009–10,* Australian Taxation Office, Canberra.

Brewer M and Wren-Lewis L (2011). *Why did Britain's households get richer? Decomposing UK household income growth between 1968 and 2008-09,* IFS Briefing Note 125, Institute of Fiscal Studies.

Chantreuil F and Trannoy A (2013). "Inequality decomposition values: the trade-off between marginality and efficiency", *Journal of Economic Inequality,* 11: 83-98.

Commonwealth Department of Housing, Community Services and Indigenous Affairs (FaHCSIA) (2012). *Guide to Social Security Law Version 1.191,* http://guidesacts.fahcsia.gov.au/guides_acts/ssg/ssg-rn.html

Cowell FA and Fiori CV (2010). *Inequality Decompositions,* Amsterdam , AIAS, GINI Discussion Paper 4.

Creedy J and Hérault N (2012). *Decomposing Inequality and Social Welfare Changes: The Use of Alternative Welfare Metrics,* Working Papers in Public Finance 06/2012 Victoria University of Wellington.

Fuest C., Niehues J., Peichl A. (2010). "The Redistributive Effects of Tax Benefit Systems in the Enlarged EU", *Public Finance Review,* 38 (4): 473-500.

Garcia-Peñalosa C and Orgiazzi E (2013). *Factor Components of Inequality: A Cross-Country Study,* Aix Marseille School of Economics Working Paper 2013 –Number 18.

Heshmati A (2004). *A Review of Decomposition of Income Inequality,* Discussion Paper No 1221, IZA, Bonn.

Immervoll H and Richardson L (2011). *Redistribution Policy and Inequality Reduction in OECD Countries: What Has Changed in Two Decades?* Discussion Paper No. 6030, IZA Bonn.

Immervoll H, Levy H, Lietz C, Mantovani D, O'Donoghue C, and Sutherland H (2005). *Household Incomes and Redistribution in the European Union: Quantifying the Equalising Properties of Taxes and Benefits,* EUROMOD Working Paper No. EM9/05.

Jędrzejczak A (2008). "Decomposition of the Gini Index by Sources of Income", *International Advances in Economic Research,* 14:441-447.

Jenkins SP and Van Kerm P (2009). "The Measurement of Economic Inequality," in *The Oxford Handbook of Economic Inequality* Salverda W, Nolan B and Smeeding TM (eds), Oxford University Press.

Kimhi A (2009). *On the Interpretation (and Misinterpretation) of Inequality Decompositions by Income Source,* Discussion Paper No 9.09, The Center for Agricultural Economic Research, The Hebrew University of Jerusalem.

Lambert PJ (2013). "Mini-symposium on the Shapley value: The 1997 paper by Frédéric Chantreuil and Alain Trannoy, and the 1999 paper by Anthony F. Shorrocks", *Journal of Economic Inequality,* 11: 79-82.

Lerman RI and Yitzhaki S (1985). "Income Inequality Effects by Income Source: A New Approach and Applications to the United States", *The Review of Economics and Statistics,* Vol 67 No 1: 151-156.

OECD (2011). *Divided we stand, Why inequality keeps rising,* OECD, Paris.

OECD (2011). *Factbook 2011: Economic, Environmental and Social Statistics,* OECD, Paris.

Okamoto M (2011). "Source decomposition of changes in income inequality: the integral-based approach and its approximation by the chained Shapley-value approach", *Journal of Economic Inequality,* 9: 145-181.

Sastre M and Trannoy A 2002). "Shapley Inequality Decomposition by Factor Components: Some Methodological Issues", *Journal of Economics*, Supplement 9: 51-89.

Sen, AK (1995). *Inequality Reexamined*, Harvard University Press.

Shorrocks AF (2013). "Decomposition procedures for distributional analysis: a unified framework based on the Shapley value", *Journal of Economic Inequality*, 11: 99-126.

Suoniemi I (2000). *Decomposing the Gini and the variation coefficients by income sources and income recipients*, Labour Institute for Economic Research, Helsinki.

Treasury (2010). *Intergenerational Report 2010 Australia to 2050: future challenges*, Treasury, Canberra.

U.S. Census Bureau (2012). *Median weekly earnings of part-time wage and salary workers by selected characteristics Table P-38*, Current Population Survey, Annual Social and Economic Supplements. http://www.bls.gov/cps/cpsaat38.pdf

Wang C and Caminada K (2011). *Disentangling income inequality and the redistributive effect of social transfers and taxes in 36 LIS countries*, Munich Personal RePec Archive Paper no 32861.

Wilkins, R, Warren, D and Hahn, M (2009). *Families, Incomes and Jobs, Volume 4: A Statistical Report on Waves 1 to 6 of the Household, Income and Labour Dynamics in Australia Survey*, Melbourne Institute of Applied Economic and Social Research, The University of Melbourne.

Wilkins, R, Warren, D, Hahn, M and Houng, B (2010). *Families, Incomes and Jobs, Volume 5: A Statistical Report on Waves 1 to7 of the Household, Income and Labour Dynamics in Australia Survey*, Melbourne Institute of Applied Economic and Social Research, The University of Melbourne.

Wilkins, R, Warren, D, Hahn, M and Houng, B (2011). *Families, Incomes and Jobs, Volume 6: A Statistical Report on Waves 1 to 8 of the Household, Income and Labour Dynamics in Australia Survey*, Melbourne Institute of Applied Economic and Social Research, The University of Melbourne.

Appendix A: Alternative approaches to decomposition of inequality by source

This paper has primarily used the Shorrocks approach to the decomposition of income inequality by source. As has been discussed, this is not the only approach. This attachment compares the results of this methodology with others which have been used in contemporary analysis.

This comparison is illustrated in Table 5. The analysis has been undertaken on current income in the 2009-10 HES survey, and for the purposes of analysis a three-source model has been adopted. This breaks income into private income, government transfers and income tax. In all cases the inequality measure which is being decomposed is the Gini coefficient. The methodologies shown are:

- Shorrocks' factor decomposition as used in the text;
- Lerman and Yitzhaki's (1985) extension of this to identify the relative marginal effect of each of the components. As indicated in the paper, this is not strictly decomposition of the existing income components but rather informs on the potential relative impact of changes in any one of these income sources on the Gini. (As an elasticity it implies, using the value of -0.282 the marginal effect of transfers as shown in the table, that a uniform 10 per cent increase in transfers will result in a 0.009 – or 2.8 per cent reduction in the Gini.);
- Two Shapley decompositions, as this method requires the elimination of particular components of income in its derivation it is necessary to replace the component with a constant. Two methods are usually proposed, the first is the simple elimination of the component – that is setting it to zero, the second is setting it to its mean value;
- Three examples of the sequential accounting approach to decomposition. As noted this commences with one element of income, estimates the Gini for this, and then adds other elements of income, and recalculates the Gini for these components together. It then identifies the differences between these two Ginis as the contribution made by the additional income component. This sequence is then repeated for additional elements of income. The three models shown use a difference sequencing of private income (P), income tax (I) and transfers (T). The three sequences shown are Private/Transfers/Income tax; Private/Income Tax/Transfers; and Transfers/Private/Income tax.

The natural decomposition and marginal effect have been calculated using a user-written Stata routine, the Shapley decomposition has been undertaken using the dsginis command which is part of the DASP add-on package to Stata and the sequential accounting approach has used the Stata ineqdec0 command written by Stephen Jenkins. In all cases data has been equivalised using the modified OECD equivalence scale as discussed previously. The first panel of the table shows the decomposition of the Gini (or in the case of the marginal effect the elasticity) and the second, the relative contribution each source of income makes to the income distribution.

Table 5 HES 2009-10, Alternative approaches to decomposing factor components of inequality

	Natural		Shapley		Sequential accounting		
	Decomposition	Marginal effect	Zero	Mean	PTI	PIT	TPI
			Gini				
Private	0.490	0.424	1.400	0.318	0.471	0.471	-0.297
Transfers	-0.053	-0.282	-0.229	0.009	-0.101	-0.116	0.667
Income Tax	-0.108	-0.142	-0.842	0.002	-0.041	-0.026	-0.041
	0.329		0.329	0.329	0.329	0.329	0.329
			Relative contribution				
Private	1.487		4.252	0.966	1.431	1.431	-0.900
Transfers	-0.160		-0.695	0.026	-0.306	-0.351	2.026
Income Tax	-0.328		-2.557	0.007	-0.125	-0.080	-0.125

Source: Derived from ABS HES CURF 2009–10.

As shown there is little consistency in the estimates of the relative contribution to inequality across the methodologies.

In the first instance two of the approaches – the Shapley with mean replacement and the sequential accounting approach which commences with transfer payments – generate results which appear implausible. When eliminated elements of personal income are replaced by the mean value, all components of income are identified as increasing inequality using the Shapley approach. This result has been previously identified by Araar (2006), who notes that the mean replacement approach is most appropriate where the interaction effect between the components is null. This is clearly not the case where income tax is dependent upon the level of private income, and where income support flows primarily to households with inadequate levels of income to support themselves. It is also discussed in Shorrocks (2013: 118), who notes that this zero replacement approach provides a more intuitive analysis of the impact of a uniform poll tax or subsidy.[28] In the case of the sequential accounting approach the result highlights the sensitivity of this method to the sequence in which income elements are considered.

---

28 Interestingly the behaviour of the natural decomposition approach to this very impact is the major criticism of the natural decomposition approach in Feust, Niehues and Peichl (2010).

The second aspect of these approaches is the relative roles of the tax and transfer systems. Whereas the natural decomposition and the Shapley with a zero replacement suggest that the impact of the income tax system on reducing income inequality is double to almost four times that of the transfer system, the sequential accounting approaches suggest the inverse. Depending upon the order in which the decomposition is undertaken, it estimates the role of the tax system to be only 40 per cent to a little over 20 per cent as great as the transfer system. This difference also highlights the sensitivity of the sequential approach to ordering. While it might be possible to argue plausible sequencing to some elements, these often simply represent established accounting identities rather than logical sequences. Further the issues become much more difficult to resolve when multiple sources of income are considered.

While the estimated marginal effect of the transfer system is estimated to be about double that of the income tax system, it is to be recalled that this is an elasticity to a change in the component, and that the actual magnitude of a proportional change in the taxation system is larger than that of a similar change in the transfer system.

The discrepancy between the natural decomposition and sequential approach to decomposition in regard to the role of taxes and transfers is not unique to the Australian income distribution but is rather more deeply embedded in the methodology. Wang and Caminada (2011), in a study of 36 countries included in the Luxembourg Income Study, report that across all of these countries on average transfers account for 85 per cent of the overall redistribution and taxes just 15 per cent – with the only exception being Guatemala (*ibid*: 14). Fuest, Niehues and Peichl (2010) consider the two methods in a study of redistribution in the EU and in discussion suggest that the difference between the approaches is a function of the normative foundations and that both approaches should be considered.

Finally, as has been suggested previously, caution needs to be taken in the interpretation of these source decompositions as being causal elements. This further step requires much more than a decomposition, including taking into account the behavioural responses of people to the particular components and the effect this may on both the component itself, and on other possible sources of income.

Appendix B: Notes on data sources

HES

The Household Expenditure Survey is the longest standing household survey conducted by the ABS for which regular Confidentialised Unit Record Files are available. The survey was initially developed with the purpose of weighting the Consumer Price Index, although it has increasingly been used for more diverse purposes with latter iterations containing data on wealth and financial hardship. In addition, since 1984 the ABS has also generated estimates of the impact of non-cash government benefits and indirect taxes. The HES was conducted in 1974-75, 1975-76, 1984, 1988-89, 1993-94, 1998-99 2003-04 and 2009-10, and data from all but the first of these have been used in this analysis.[29]

A number of these characteristics make the HES, while smaller in sample size than some other household surveys, an attractive basis for income distribution analysis.

The files have been subject to some editing to attempt to build a more consistent time series.

Over time there have been many changes to the concept of income used in the surveys. Central to these is the inclusion in most recent data of income from overtime and bonuses, better recording of amounts salary sacrificed and the use of current estimates of income from investments and own business, rather than basing these on data from the previous financial year.

In all surveys used in this analysis, other than the 1975-76 survey, income tax data has been imputed. In 1984 while ABS published aggregate data (ABS Cat No 6537.0 1987) showing the imputed values, these have not been included on the CURF. As the difference between the reported average level of tax of $80.07 (ABS Cat No 6530.0 1986) and the imputed tax $91.60 is quite substantial, an imputation exercise has been undertaken with this being benchmarked to the ABS published series. It is not possible to undertake such an accurate imputation on the earlier file.

While the 2003-04 and 2009-10 data files contain some information on income components in a form which maintains some backward compatibility, data on the imputed value of income tax on these is not provided (or in the case of

29 The 1974-75 HES has been excluded from analysis as it was restricted to state capital cities and Canberra, and ABS has not released a CURF.

2009-10 is the same as for the current definition); adjustments have been made for this. Other processing has been undertaken to obtain estimates of full-time employment amongst the self-employed in the first two surveys.

SIH

The Survey of Income and Housing is today the main ABS survey on household incomes. It is conducted more frequently than the HES and utilises a larger sample of households. In 2009-10 the ABS conducted the HES in association with the SIH and income data are harmonised across the two surveys. As with the HES there have been frequent improvements over time in the quality of data from the SIH, both with regard to definitions and in the collection process.

While CURFs are available from the 1982 and 1986 Income Distribution Surveys (as the SIH was then called), analysis in this paper is limited to the 1990 IDS onwards. This decision is largely based on the absence of imputed estimates of income tax in these earlier surveys.

Specifically this paper used data from the 1990, 1994-1995, 1995-96, 1996-97, 1997-98, 1999-2000, 2000-01, 2002-03, 2003-04, 2005-06, 2007-08 and 2009-10 surveys. With the exception of the 1990 survey which was conducted between October to December 1990, the SIH data has been collected over a period of a year with a small sample being taken each month. In this paper no attempt to derive a single consistent series over time has been made, however where possible, overlapping series have been estimated. These have used the ABS variables which contain income data classified on previous survey bases. In these cases no attempt has been made to adjust the ABS estimate of income tax.

HILDA

The HILDA Survey is a longitudinal panel survey which commenced in 2001. The survey which has annual waves of data collection was initiated, and is funded, by the Australian government through the Department of Families, Housing, Community Services and Indigenous Affairs (FaHCSIA) (now the Department of Social Services). It is managed by the Melbourne Institute of Applied Economic and Social Research at the University of Melbourne.

No edits have been undertaken to the data as it is presented here. As noted, the results of inequality analysis based on HILDA may vary from those published in other research. This can arise because of the extent to which HILDA is subject to edits, both to data and to weights, between releases. The analysis here used the Wave 10.0 in-confidence release. The income data in this file has not been subject to top-coding.

19. What Difference Does Government Make? Measuring Redistribution in a Comparative Perspective

Peter Whiteford

Introduction

Government policies in all countries affect the distribution of household income. In high-income countries, they do so through a range of programs but most directly through the cash transfers paid to households and the direct taxes and social security contributions collected from them. In addition, other social spending programs and other forms of taxes impact on households. Different welfare states may pursue a variety of social objectives, with the balance and priority given to each of them varying across both countries and between programs. A critical issue that all governments confront – particularly when considering policy reforms – is whether the redistributive and other policy objectives of society could be more effectively or efficiently achieved through a different mix or design of policies.

The appropriate level and structure of public spending and taxation is currently high on the policy agenda in Australia. The recent Grattan Institute report *Budget pressures on Australian Governments* (Daley, 2013) argued that Australian federal and state governments potentially face a combined annual deficit of around four per cent of GDP by 2023, of which around 2.5 per cent of GDP would be at the Commonwealth government level. In a subsequent address at the Per Capita think tank speech in late April the Prime Minister foreshadowed a reduction in projected tax revenues by the end of this financial year of around $12 billion, leading to the need for 'urgent and grave Budget decisions'. In a speech to the Institute of Public Affairs in early May, the Shadow Treasurer, Joe Hockey said that 'attacking spending' and 'looking for structural saves' was increasingly urgent, and he referred to a speech given at the Institute of Economic Affairs in London in 2012 where he argued that 'all developed countries are now facing the end of the era of universal entitlement. Addressing the ongoing fiscal crises will involve the winding back of universal access to payments and entitlements from the state'.

It is interesting to note in this context that a recent OECD working paper (Rawdanowicz, Wurzel and Christensen, 2013) on 'The Equity Implications of

Fiscal Consolidation' found that a cut in transfer spending of three per cent of GDP would increase income inequality in Australia to a larger extent than any other OECD country. As discussed below, the reason is that Australia has the most target-efficient transfer system in the OECD, so that a cut back of this magnitude would very adversely impact low-income groups.

This suggests that in deciding which policy directions to follow to bridge the budget gap, it is necessary to have a clear understanding of the distribution of welfare state spending, as well as how spending is financed. Australia is well placed in relation to information on the distributional impacts of government spending and taxing, notably because of the work of Ian Castles and others at the Australian Bureau of Statistics (ABS).

In March 1987, the ABS released *The Effects of Government Benefits and Taxes on Household Income* (ABS Catalogue No. 6537.0), which presented the results of a study of the effects of government benefits and taxes on the distribution of income of households in 1984, based primarily on data collected in the 1984 Household Expenditure Survey, supplemented by relevant data from other sources. Subsequently in May 1987 the then Social Welfare Research Centre at the University of New South Wales held a workshop on the study at which Ian Castles presented a paper on 'The Effects of Government Benefits and Taxes on Household Incomes: Estimates for Australia and Other Countries' (Saunders, 1987). As noted by Saunders (1987) this paper provided a stimulating and welcome addition to the literature on the effects of government benefits and taxes on the distribution of income in modern economies. The paper also illustrated the important lessons to be learnt from comparisons between countries with different social policy environments.

The Australian Bureau of Statistics subsequently published further studies using data from the Household Expenditure Surveys for 1988-89, 1993-94, 1998-99, 2003-05 and 2009-10 (Catalogue No. 6537.0).

Ian Castles and the ABS also contributed to improvements in international statistics in this area. An International Expert Group on Household Income Statistics, known as the 'Canberra Group', was established in 1996 at the initiative of the ABS in response to a growing awareness of the need to address the common conceptual, definitional and practical problems that national statistical offices face in the area of household income distribution statistics.

The primary objective of the Canberra Group was to enhance national household income statistics by developing relevant standards on conceptual and practical issues. To improve international comparability, the group developed and recommended international guidelines and standards. The Final Report of the Canberra Group was published in 2001.

The *Canberra Group Handbook on Household Income Statistics, Second Edition* was published in 2011 by the United Nations Economic Commission for Europe. The updated volume provides a consolidated reference for those involved in producing, disseminating or analysing income distribution statistics. It reflects current international standards, recommendations and best practice in household income measurement. It also contains updated and expanded information about country practices in the field of statistics and provides guidance on best practices for quality assurance and dissemination of these statistics.

The second edition of the *Handbook* was prepared by a small international task force of experts from national statistical offices and international agencies, under the endorsement of the Bureau of the Conference of European Statisticians. The ABS played a leading role in the update, filling both the chair and editor roles for the task force.

The work of the Canberra Group is also reflected in changes that the ABS has made over the years to its series of income surveys. The ABS has conducted household income surveys since the late 1960s, although it is only surveys since 1982 that are comprehensive and available for public analysis. There have been major changes in methodology over the years, giving rise to a diversity of estimates of inequality. While changes have been made on a regular basis, recent changes are most significant. In 2007-08 the ABS revised its standards for household income statistics following the adoption of new international standards, which followed in turn from the work of the Canberra Group.[1] In summary, these changes mean that the income measure is more comprehensive and thus better captures the extent of income inequality in Australia. However, the observed increases in income levels and in income inequality in recent years are likely to be exaggerated, although this means that inequality was higher in previous years than previously measured.

This chapter reviews the evidence on the redistributive impact of the Australian welfare state and how it has changed over time. It also discusses the comparative performance of the Australian welfare state and seeks to identify the implications of different analytical approaches for Australia's performance relative to those in other OECD countries.

Section 2 commences the main analysis by looking at how the design of Australia's welfare state differs from those in other OECD countries and summarises the

1 Implementation of the broader income measure in 2007-08 resulted in an $85 increase in mean weekly gross household income, compared to the previous definition, a difference of roughly five per cent. The inclusions affected 3.4m households in total (43 per cent). Most of the impact was on employment income, which increased by $89 per week on average. The inclusion of non-cash employment benefits and bonuses had the most impact ($43 and $32 per week respectively). In 2007-08, the Gini coefficient on the new basis was 0.331, which is higher than that compiled on the former basis (0.317). This reflects that most of the changes have been at the higher end of the income distribution i.e. the fourth and highest quintiles.

conventional view in the social policy literature on the effectiveness of the Australian welfare state. In brief, this conventional view is that Australia is not very effective in reducing inequality despite high levels of progressivity in spending and taxes, primarily because of the low levels of spending and taxation. The most recent evidence from OECD income distribution studies supports this view, but in section 3 I argue that there are significant conceptual and practical limitations to this approach. Section 4 looks at the implications of broadening the concept of resources for Australia's comparative performance. I conclude with a discussion of a number of further issues that could be considered in international comparisons of the effectiveness of welfare state arrangements and in comparisons of welfare state outcomes.

The Australian welfare state and its impacts

The Australian social security system differs markedly from those in other OECD countries. In Australia payments are flat-rate and financed from general taxation revenue, and there are no separate social security contributions; benefits are also income-tested or asset-tested, so payments reduce as other resources increase. Importantly, payments are not time-limited and continue for as long as people remain entitled.

In 2012, social expenditure in Australia was estimated to be 18.7 per cent of GDP (including pensions, unemployment payments, family payments, healthcare and community services) compared to an OECD average of 21.7 per cent, a level lower than the United States and Japan, and the tenth lowest in the OECD (OECD, 2013).

With taxes at about 27 per cent of GDP in 2008 compared to an OECD average of close to 35 per cent, Australia is the sixth lowest-taxing country in the OECD. Because of the absence of social security contributions, income tax takes a higher share of total tax revenue than in many other OECD countries, averaging 55-60 per cent of total revenue since 1980, compared to an OECD average of around one-third.

It is also important to note that the interactions between the tax and benefit systems can have significant implications for perceptions of levels of spending and also for redistribution. Adema and Ladaique (2005) show that accounting for private social benefits and the impact of the tax system on social expenditure has a significant equalising effect on estimated levels of social effort across OECD countries. For example, direct taxes (including social security contributions) paid on cash transfers are five per cent of GDP in Sweden and Denmark, but are less than 0.5 per cent of GDP in Australia. Indirect taxes on goods and services bought by benefit recipients are over two per cent of GDP in Nordic countries, but less than half that level in Australia. Non-pension tax expenditures (either tax credits similar to cash benefits or tax concessions aimed at stimulating the provision of private social benefits, but not including support for pensions) are of limited value in Nordic countries, but are close to two per cent or more of GDP in the USA (but only 0.4 per cent of GDP in Australia). Australia, however, has the highest level of pension tax expenditures in the OECD (Whiteford, 2010).

Australia also has a higher than average level of private social spending (Adema and Whiteford, 2010), with most spending on short-term sickness being provided by employers, and since 1992 mandatory private pensions have grown to cover more than 90 per cent of employees. The value of superannuation funds has grown from around 20 per cent of GDP in the early 1980s to more than 100 per cent by 2012, with annual payouts (mainly lump sums) exceeding public spending on age and related pensions.

Liberal, residual or radical?

Australia is often regarded as the epitome of the 'liberal' or residual welfare state; Esping-Andersen (1990) found Australia to have the lowest score on his de-commodification index, while Korpi and Palme (1998) found Australia was the only example of a targeted (rather than basic security) welfare state. These characterisations are disputed, however, by Gruen (1989) and by Castles and Mitchell (1990, 1993) who argue that Australia is one of a distinctive 'radical' group of nations, focusing its redistributive effort through the design of instruments rather than high expenditure levels.

When considering the redistributive impact of alternative transfer systems it is important to note that their design features differ in significant respects. Two of the most important features relate to the way benefits are *funded* – that is, the different ways in which programs are financed – and *structured* – that is, the relationship between benefits received and the past or current income of beneficiaries. Using these criteria, the social welfare systems of OECD countries are often characterised as either 'Bismarckian' or 'Beveridgean' (Werding 2003). In the first, social programs are based on social insurance principles, with earnings-related benefits, entitlement based on contribution records and funding through employer and employee social security contributions. In the second, policies are generally characterised by universal provision, with entitlement based on residence and in some cases need, and with benefits that are flat-rate and financed through general taxation. As previous discussion has suggested and later discussion will show, Australia can be considered a 'hyper-Beveridgean' welfare system.

A related way of classifying and evaluating alternative welfare state arrangements is on the basis of the forms of redistribution emphasised in different institutional arrangements. Rather than focusing on the early architects of the welfare state this classification looks to the architecture itself. Barr (1992, 1999, 2001) points out that the main objective of transfer systems in most OECD countries is to provide *insurance* in the face of adverse risks (unemployment, disability, sickness) and to *redistribute across the life-cycle*, either to periods when individuals have greater needs (e.g. when there are children in the household) or would otherwise have lower incomes (such as in retirement). Barr (2001) describes this as the 'piggybank objective'.

The second main objective of the welfare state can be described as 'taking from the rich to give to the poor' (what Barr calls the 'Robin Hood' motive). Targeting of benefits is usually justified as a means of achieving the Robin Hood objective. Bismarckian-type welfare states can be characterised as giving priority to the piggy-bank objective, while Beveridgean-type welfare states give priority to the Robin Hood objective.

I would argue that the characterisation of Australia as a 'radical' welfare state is apt. Australia is the strongest example of a country using the 'Robin Hood' approach to the welfare state (Barr, 2001), relying more heavily on income-testing and directing a higher share of benefits to lower-income groups than any other OECD country. The poorest 20 per cent of the population receives nearly 42 per cent of transfer spending; the richest 20 per cent receives only around three per cent. As a result, as shown in Figure 1, in 2005 the poorest fifth received twelve times as much in cash benefits as the richest fifth, the highest ratio in the OECD and about 50 per cent more than the next most targeted country, New Zealand (Whiteford, 2010).

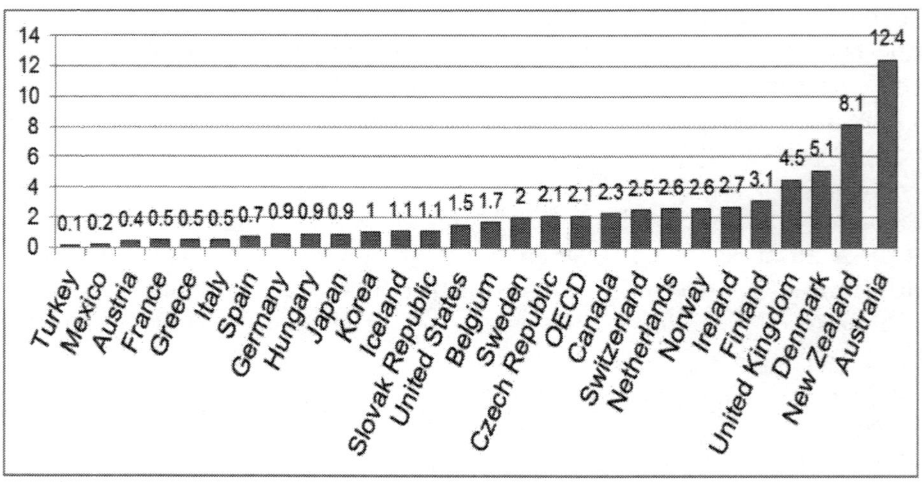

Figure 1 Progressivity of transfers, 2005. Ratio of cash benefits received by poorest 20 per cent of households to richest 20 per cent

Source: Whiteford, 2010.

It is also worth noting, however, that the targeting of benefits in Australia is reinforced by the relatively high concentration of household joblessness (Whiteford, 2009); in this sense part of the reason why benefits are spread more widely across the income distribution in other countries is that people receiving social security payments are more likely to live in households with others not receiving payments; to some extent this implies that in these countries, inequality is 'hidden' within the household.

Because of its design features, Australia also has the most 'target efficient' system of social security benefits of any OECD country (OECD, 2008; Whiteford, 2010). Australia also has one of the most progressive systems of direct taxes of any OECD country (OECD, 2008), but the progressivity of taxes in Australia is not a consequence of particularly high taxes on the rich, but reflects the fact that lower-income groups in Australia pay much lower taxes than similar income groups in other countries (with the exception of the United States and Ireland). This is a result of the low level of direct taxes on social security recipients; effectively, any individual fully reliant on a social security payment will pay no income taxes.

The extent to which the Australian welfare state redistributes to the poor is determined by the interactions between the tax and social security systems, both in terms of the size of taxes collected and benefits paid and the distribution of taxes and benefits. Figure 2 shows 'net redistribution' to the poorest 20 per cent of the population around 2005 (Whiteford, 2010). This is calculated by estimating the level of spending on social security benefits as a percentage of household disposable income and then taking account of how much of this goes to the poorest fifth. The same procedure is used to calculate how much tax is paid by people in that group, which is then subtracted from the benefits received to give 'net redistribution to the poor'.

Even though Australia spends below the OECD average on social security benefits, the distribution of benefits is so progressive, and the level of taxes paid by the poor is so low, that Australia redistributes more to the poorest 20 per cent of the population than any other OECD country except Denmark (which spends about 80 per cent more than Australia).

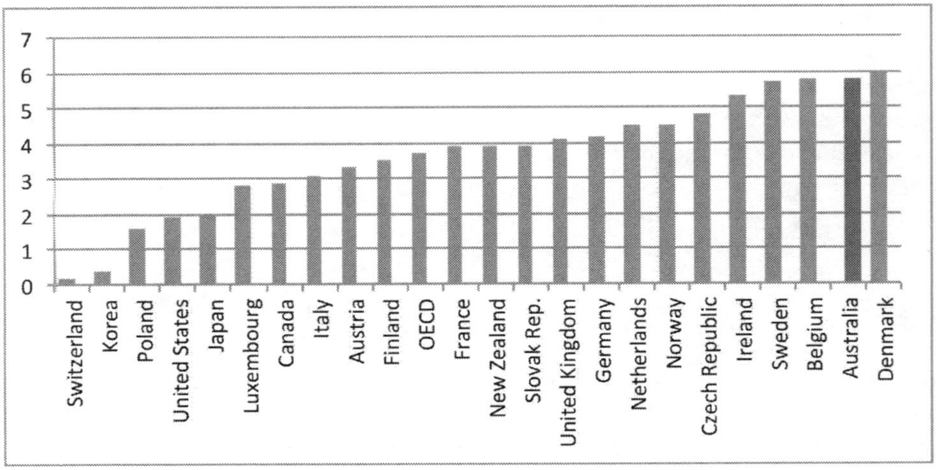

Figure 2 Net redistribution to the poor, 2005. Cash benefits after direct taxes received by poorest 20 per cent of households as a percentage of household disposable income

Source: Whiteford, 2010.

The differing designs of social programs influence the distribution of household incomes in different ways. In assessing these impacts it is important to distinguish between *progressivity* and *redistribution*. *Progressivity* refers to the profile of benefits when compared to market or disposable incomes; how large a share of benefits is received by different income groups? For example, do the poor receive more than the rich from the transfer system? *Redistribution* in contrast refers to the outcomes of different tax and benefit systems; how much does the benefit system actually *change* the distribution of household income?

The figures given above show that Australia has the most targeted and the most progressive transfer system among all rich countries, but this does not mean that it has the most redistributive system. This is because the level of redistribution is a product both of the progressivity of spending and the volume of spending – Australia has high progressivity but low spending. Put simply, a high spending but less progressive system may redistribute more than a low-spending but more progressive system. In this context, it is also important to look at the whole distribution and not just the poorest 20 per cent, as has been done in Figure 2. So what does the evidence show?

Figure 3 shows the most recent OECD (2013) figures on the level of household income inequality around 2010. Australia has the eleventh highest level of inequality among OECD countries, ranking between Canada and Japan. This represents a further change in Australia's ranking in recent years: OECD (2008) found that around 2005, Australia ranked fifteenth highest in the OECD, and just below the OECD average, while OECD (2011) found that in 2008 Australia had the eighth highest level of inequality in the OECD. The change in Australia's ranking between 2005 and 2008 reflects the changes made to ABS income surveys discussed previously, while the change between 2008 and 2010 reflects the accession of Chile to the OECD and the inclusion of Spain and Portugal in the 2010 figures but not the 2008 figures, plus a small fall in inequality in Australia in this period, which caused Australia to fall below Japan in rankings.

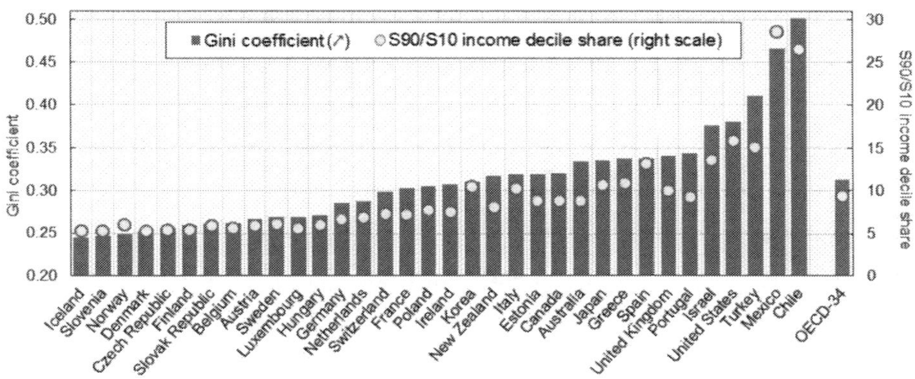

Figure 3 Level of inequality, OECD countries, around 2010

Source: OECD, 2013.

Figure 4 shows estimates calculated from the OECD (2013) database of the redistributive impact of cash transfers and direct taxes on income inequality as measured by changes in the Gini coefficient. Figure 4 shows that inequality reduction in Australia is currently the seventh lowest in the OECD, with the Gini coefficient for disposable income after taxes and transfers being less than 0.15 Gini points, with inequality reduction being greatest in Ireland at just over 0.25 Gini points. Overall this suggests that while Australia has the most progressive and target-efficient transfer system in the OECD, it is not particularly effective at reducing inequality.

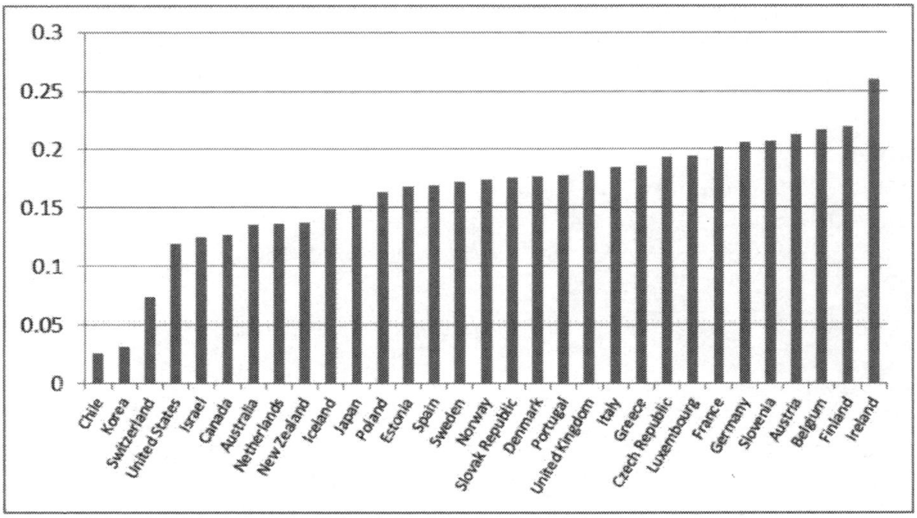

Figure 4 Reduction in inequality through transfers and taxes, OECD countries, 2010. Percentage point difference in Gini coefficient

Source: Calculated from OECD, 2013.

Why is this so? The main argument offered by some analysts is that referred to above, and discussed in more detail in Whiteford (1997) and Whiteford (2010): the Australian welfare state is less effective at reducing inequality than higher-spending welfare states because we simply fail to spend enough on social security transfers or raise enough in taxes to significantly reduce underlying inequality. Paradoxically, this is precisely because we have less middle class welfare than other countries (Barr, 1990; Korpi and Palme, 1998). This is because the degree of redistribution achieved by a benefits system depends on the 'quantum' of benefits as well as the progressivity of the formula for allocating benefits (Barr, 1992). A means-tested program with a highly redistributive formula may achieve limited redistribution if spending is low. That is, while the Australian system is more efficient than others, it is not as effective at reducing poverty (Mitchell, Harding and Gruen, 1994) or inequality. In contrast, a high cost, earnings-related system may achieve greater redistribution by providing more generous basic benefits (Korpi and Palme, 1998; Saunders, 1994). Other countries reduce inequality to a greater extent than Australia, because their tax and social security systems take a larger share of national income.

These arguments are of considerable significance to debates about the future of the Australian welfare state. They imply that if we wish to reduce inequality, then we should actually increase the level of taxes and welfare spending. Moreover, it suggests that we can achieve greater redistribution between rich and poor even if we have a less progressive tax system (for example, by increasing the GST) and a less targeted social security system (more universal or even earnings-related benefits).

In earlier work (Whiteford and Kennedy, 1995; Whiteford, 1997, 2010) I have argued that there are a number of significant problems with such an analysis. Overall, the weight of these arguments is that the apparent failure of the Australian approach to redistribution to substantially reduce inequality is at least partly an artefact of the methods used to measure inequality and income redistribution. The discussion that follows argues that international comparisons have a number of biases that may lead to a mis-estimation of the redistributive impact of the welfare state, because the methodological framework used to reach these conclusions is usually incomplete.

Measuring income inequality: The standard approach and its problems

An accounting framework for household income

By definition, any numerical assessment of income inequality must deal with a range of technical questions (Gruen, 1989; Whiteford, 1997), including the concept of living standards, the measure of material resources, the treatment of wealth, the time period over which income is measured, the unit assumed to share income, and the treatment of families or households with differing needs. All income distribution studies must make precise decisions about each issue. For many issues there is no one 'correct' answer so the choice of a particular approach is arbitrary in the sense that there can be good reasons for making different choices. But results can differ significantly if different decisions are made about any issue

Underlying all comparisons of welfare state outcomes is a framework for analysing the process of income distribution and redistribution (Esping-Andersen 1990). The results presented above employ what Ringen (1987) has called 'the standard approach' to analysing income distribution data. As set out in Table 1, essentially this is an accounting framework for relating different income components and for deriving aggregates such as gross income and cash disposable income. When using microdata, this framework is applied to each household's income to produce the income measures identified. These household or income unit accounts are aggregated and analysed to produce measures of distribution and redistribution for the population as a whole. The redistribution achieved by taxes or transfers is calculated by comparing income shares, Gini coefficients, or poverty indexes at different stages in the process outlined.

Table 1 The Income Accounting Framework

Wages and salaries +
Self-employment income +
Property income =
1. Factor income +
Occupational and private pensions =
2. Market income +
Social security cash benefits (universal, income-related, contributory) +
Private transfers +
Other cash income =
3. Gross income -
Income tax (and employee social security contributions) =
4. Cash disposable income x
Equivalence scales =
5. Equivalent cash disposable income

Source: Whiteford, 2010.

While this framework has been used by virtually all international studies – including the results given in Figure 4 – there are obvious limitations to the approach. These problems are discussed below, and include: the counterfactual against which to measure redistribution; the comprehensiveness of the income framework, particularly the omission of important components of the welfare state from standard analysis; and the relationship between public and private welfare. In many ways these problems are interlinked, although the discussion below separates them.

These problems affect analysis of the degree of underlying inequality; they affect the measurement of the effectiveness and efficiency of the welfare state itself; and they affect the measurement of the final outcomes of redistributive policy. Consequently, they also impact on any policy inferences drawn from international comparisons. It is extremely important to note that the work of the Canberra Group is designed to address a number of these conceptual and methodological issues and as a result of their work the ABS, the OECD and Eurostat have augmented their analyses of income distribution. These broader measures go a long way to reducing the problems to be discussed, although there are a number of important challenges remaining.

The counterfactual

Any assessment of the distributional impact of the welfare state involves a comparison of the observed distribution with a counterfactual – the hypothetical distribution existing in the absence of the policies evaluated (Pedersen, 1994). Table 1 relies on a counterfactual in which the welfare state has had no behavioural effects on the 'underlying' income distribution. The framework is linear, implying that the distribution of market incomes precedes the operation of the tax-transfer systems, and there have been no interactions between them, apart from the direct effect of government programs in reducing inequality. Crucially, it is also assumed that the wide variations in the scope of different welfare states have had the same (zero) behavioural impact in each country.

As argued by Layard (1977) and Reynolds and Smolensky (1977), however, to the extent that the welfare state displaces private savings or other activities, the standard approach exaggerates market or private income inequality and then exaggerates the amount of redistribution achieved by the welfare state. At the simplest level this can be seen as a result of adverse behavioural incentives associated with welfare state programs, for example, incentives to lone parenthood said to be associated with welfare benefits for lone parents (Murray, 1984) or lengthening durations of unemployment potentially caused by extended entitlements to unemployment insurance. In particular, however, in countries with generous public pensions, the standard approach implies that middle class individuals are plunged into market income poverty on retirement simply because it is the government, rather than the market, that provides their pensions: generous earnings-related public pensions are then measured as being very effective at reducing inequality, in part because they restore middle-income retirees to their pre-retirement ranking. Effects of this sort are not so much behavioural as mechanical.

How should we rank?

As noted above, in the standard approach the degree of redistribution achieved by cash transfers is measured as the difference between the Gini coefficient (or other inequality measure) for market incomes and the Gini coefficient for gross incomes, and the redistributive effect of taxes is measured as the difference between the Gini coefficient for gross incomes and that for disposable incomes. The question therefore is how much of this redistribution is due to the re-ranking associated with welfare state programs.

Table 2 shows the effects of using different income concepts for ranking households on the distribution of benefits and taxes. For example, if households are ranked by their private incomes then the cash benefits received by the poorest 20 per cent of Australians are 29 times as great as those received by the richest quintile, while the income taxes paid by the richest 20 per cent are 756 times those paid by the poorest 20 per cent. In this context, it is worth noting that cash benefits are income-tested on the basis of private income, so as a measure of the degree of targeting in the benefit system this is arguably the most appropriate income concept to rank by.

However, if households are ranked by their gross income (i.e. private income plus cash transfers) then the progressivity of both direct and indirect spending is measured as being much lower, as is the progressivity of income taxes, while the distribution of indirect taxes actually becomes somewhat more pro-poor. This re-ranking occurs because some people with measured low private incomes do not receive social security benefits. As noted by the ABS (2012), 'Some households report extremely low and even negative income in the survey, which places them well below the safety net of income support provided by government pensions and allowances. Households may under-report their incomes in the survey at all income levels, including low-income households. However, households can correctly report low levels of income if they incur losses in their unincorporated business or have negative returns from their other investments'. Some of these apparently low-income households do not claim social security benefits. So re-ranking occurs because these people stay in the bottom quintile, while some people receive enough in social security to move them up the income distribution. It is also worth noting that while some social security payments are not taxable, it could be argued that gross income is the most appropriate income concept to assess the progressivity of taxes on income, since income taxes are paid out of gross income.

Ranking by disposable income increases the measured progressivity of cash benefits and transfers in kind but reduces the apparent progressivity of direct and indirect taxes. The earlier results in Figure 4 are based on ranking by disposable income, and these results suggest that progressivity in the distribution of transfers has increased since the first OECD results for 2003, since the Q1/Q5 ratio has increased from around 12 to 1 to nearly 15 to 1 since then. However, the progressivity of income taxes has declined since 2003 when the richest quintile paid nearly 69 times as much in tax as the poorest quintile, with the most recent figure being close to 49 times as much.

Ranking by final income causes significant changes with all measures of the progressivity of taxes and transfers being lower. This reduced progressivity reflects large scale re-ranking of households, with older people benefiting from large transfers in kind through the health care system, while higher income households with children benefit from education spending.

Table 2 Effects of different income rankings on distribution of benefits and taxes, Australia, 2009-10

Private income	Social assistance benefits in cash	Taxes on income	Social transfers in kind	Taxes on production
		Private income		
Lowest quintile	$435	$1	$455	$105
Highest quintile	$15	$756	$234	$273
Ratio*	29.00	756.00	1.94	2.60
		Gross income		
Lowest quintile	$281	$2	$319	$89
Highest quintile	$45	$809	$363	$309
Ratio*	6.24	404.50	0.88	3.47
		Disposable income		
Lowest quintile	$323	$15	$442	$114
Highest quintile	$22	$731	$239	$275
Ratio*	14.68	48.73	1.85	2.41
		Final income		
Lowest quintile	$224	$38	$293	$142
Highest quintile	$43	$745	$305	$263
Ratio*	5.21	19.61	0.96	1.85

Note: The figures for the lowest and highest quintiles are the dollar values in 2009-10 of the average benefits received and taxes paid by the income quintile. The ratios for social assistance benefits and social transfers received are the ratio of the lowest quintile to the highest quintile; the ratios for taxes on incomes and taxes on production are the ratio of the highest quintile to the lowest quintile.

Source: Calculated from ABS, Government Benefits, Taxes and Household Income, Australia, 2009-10, Catalogue No. 6537.0.

Overall it is apparent that the income measure used for ranking households has a significant impact on the assessment of the progressivity of the different transfer and tax instruments, and that more comprehensive income measures show lower progressivity than do less comprehensive income measures.

Having said this, it is also important to note that more comprehensive income measures show much lower income inequality than less comprehensive measures, although there are differences according to the ranking measure. Table 3 shows the Q5 to Q 1 ratio for different income concepts and different rankings. When households are ranked by their private incomes, equivalised private income is very unequally distributed with the highest income quintile having incomes more than 21 times as great as the lowest income quintile; the receipt of social security benefits reduces this disparity to about 6 to 1 and the deduction of income taxes reduces this further to under 5 to 1. In-kind transfers reduce this further to just under 3 to 1, while indirect taxes increase this marginally. When households are ranked by their final income, however, the Q5/Q1 ratio for private income is less than 8 to 1 showing that most of the reduced progressivity is due to the re-ranking of people in terms of their private income. Put another way, disparities in final income vary by much less when different income rankings are used than do disparities in private income.

Table 3 Income disparities under different income rankings, Australia, 2009-10. Q5/Q1

	Private income	Gross income	Disposable income	Disposable income plus transfer in kind	Final income
Equivalised private income	21.47	6.03	4.81	2.97	3.01
Equivalised disposable income	13.71	6.21	5.10	3.11	3.21
Equivalised final income	7.96	5.44	4.62	3.51	3.80

Source: Calculated from ABS, Government Benefits, Taxes and Household Income, Australia, 2009-10, Catalogue No. 6537.0.

Is there a 'right' income measure by which to rank households? The answer is probably no. In this context, it is worth noting that the equivalence scales used to adjust for household size are those related to cash incomes, but receipt of transfers in-kind raises complex issues relating to the needs of households. For example, generally households receiving large benefits from health care spending are experiencing illness or disability and their needs for health care are not captured by conventional equivalence scales.

Do the issues raised by re-ranking have implications for an assessment of the effectiveness of the Australian tax-transfer system? The answer appears to be yes – the income measure used for ranking can have major implications for the measurement of redistribution across countries.

Figure 5 shows two measures of the 'effectiveness' of the tax and benefit systems in reducing income inequality in OECD countries: the percentage reduction in income inequality when moving from market income to disposable income (in the top panel), and the absolute point difference between these two measures (in the bottom panel) (OECD, 2008).

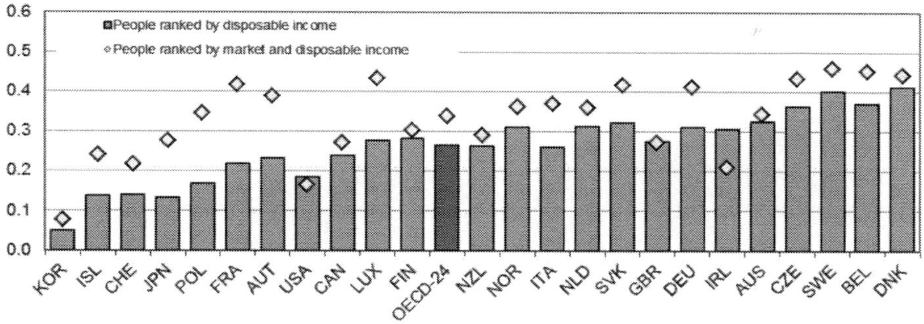

Figure 5a Differences in inequality before and after taxes and transfers in OECD countries. Difference in concentration coefficients, mid-2000s. Percentage reduction

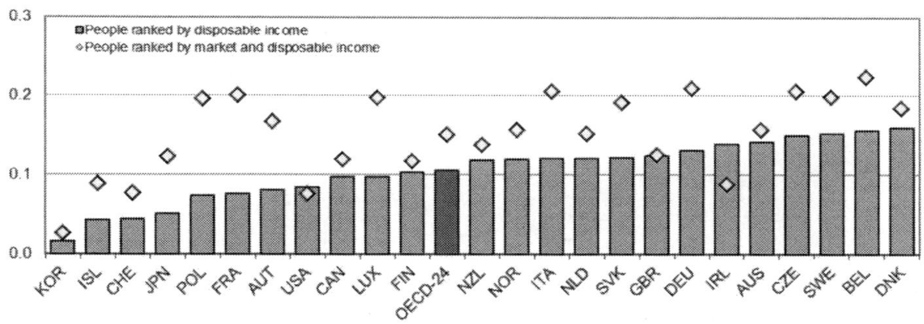

Figure 5b Differences in inequality before and after taxes and transfers in OECD countries, Difference in concentration coefficients, mid-2000s. Point reduction.

Note: Countries are ranked, from left to right, in increasing order of the percentage point reduction in the concentration coefficient achieved by household taxes and public cash transfers, based on people ranked by their household disposable income. Bars are computed based on grouped data for average market and disposable income, by deciles of people ranked by their household disposable income. Diamonds are computed based on individual data, with people ranked by market income (for the Gini coefficient of market income) and ranked by disposable income (for the Gini coefficient of disposable income).

Source: OECD income distribution questionnaire.

These measures are calculated in two ways. In the first approach (shown as diamonds), inequality in the distribution of market income is computed by ranking people by their level of market income. On this measure, on average, across the twenty-four countries covered, the tax and transfer systems lower income inequality by around one-third (i.e. around 0.15 Gini points), with declines ranging from around 45 per cent in Denmark, Sweden and Belgium to less than eight per cent in Korea.

In the second approach (shown as bars) the Gini coefficient for market income is based on people ranked by their disposable income, that is, individuals are ranked by where they end up 'after' redistribution, rather than where they were placed 'before' redistribution. On this second measure, the reduction of inequality achieved by taxes and transfers is a little more than one-fourth (i.e. 0.11 points), with declines ranging from around 40 per cent in Sweden and Denmark to five per cent in Korea.

The difference between the two measures of redistribution is a result of the re-ranking of some households as a consequence of welfare state programs (Ankrom 1993). A comparison between the two measures suggests that, in some OECD countries, a very significant part of the redistribution measured by the standard approach reflects such a re-ranking of people. In particular, the countries where the re-ranking effect is most significant are those where public pensions account for more than 90 per cent of the total disposable income of the retirement-age population (i.e. Austria, Belgium, France, Italy, Luxembourg and Sweden). In contrast, re-ranking is lower in Korea, the United States, Canada, Finland, the United Kingdom, Ireland and Australia, where public pensions are 50 per cent or less of the disposable income of the retired.

The effect on Australia's relative performance is very large, primarily because there is little difference between the Australian results on the two rankings. Using the percentage point reduction in the Gini coefficient Australia moves from being the fifteenth most effective country in the OECD in reducing inequality to the fifth most effective. Australia also ranks fifth in terms of the proportional reduction, although it can be argued that since this measure is sensitive to the degree of inequality in market incomes, it is the point reduction that gives a more accurate picture of the extent of redistribution.

It is important to note, however, that this does not change Australia's ranking in terms of inequality of disposable incomes; all it suggests is that other OECD countries are not so effective in reducing inequality through the welfare state as the standard approach implies. This suggests that redistribution is exaggerated because the 'original' level of private income inequality is not as high as estimated. The level of disposable income inequality is unaffected by this adjustment. It should also be remembered that this conclusion applies to the period around 2005 (specifically 2003 in the case of Australia), and there is evidence that the redistributive impact of taxes and transfers declined somewhat between 2003 and 2008, but increased between 2008 and 2010, partly due to the fiscal stimulus in 2008 and 2009 and the pension increase in 2009.

Broadening the measure of resources

A second major set of issues relates to the fact that the standard framework is incomplete. Most income surveys include information only on cash transfers and direct taxes, which form different fractions of overall government activity in different countries. Most standard comparative studies ignore the impact of broad-based consumption taxes and government non-cash benefits such as health, education and public housing. Consumption taxes tend to be regressive by income, and are much higher in large welfare states than in small welfare states. Non-cash benefits tend to be less progressive than targeted or universal cash transfers, but vary in significance by less than cash benefits.

The effects of government services and indirect taxes

The Australian evidence

The discussion of the standard approach has focused on the impact of cash transfers and direct taxes, but governments also redistribute resources to households through the provision or financing of public services, and they also finance spending through indirect taxes. A comprehensive accounting of the impact of government therefore needs to take these into account. As noted earlier, the ABS has published estimates of the redistributive impact of non-cash benefits and indirect taxes for 1984, 1988-89, 1993-94, 1998-99, 2003-04 and most recently for 2009-10, with the first estimates being prepared while Ian Castles was Australian Statistician. As with income distribution statistics, major changes have been made to the methodologies for imputing the value of non-cash benefits and indirect taxes, with the result that the series is not fully comparable over time.[2]

Figure 6 shows ABS estimates of income disparities by income concepts for successive studies from 1984 to 2009-10. It is particularly important to note that households are ranked by gross income quintiles, and income measures are not equivalised. In 1984 the highest gross income quintile received 6.1 times the disposable income of the poorest quintile, but after adding non-cash benefits and deducting indirect taxes, this disparity was reduced to 4.5 to 1. Over the period shown, income disparities widened for disposable income, but initially narrowed in respect of final income, before rising again in the 1990s. As noted,

2 Up until 1998-99, the ABS did not adjust by equivalence scales and households were ranked by gross income. In 2009-10 major improvements were made: a more comprehensive measure of private income, including net imputed rent for owner-occupied dwellings and the net benefit that can be attributed to households living in subsidised private rentals; improvements to the allocation of transfers in-kind for health benefits, housing benefits and child care assistance; inclusion of electricity concessions provided by state/territory governments for the first time; and, improvements to the methodology for estimating taxes on ownership of dwellings.

the latest two studies involve a changed definition of private income since they include imputed income from owner-occupied housing and private rental subsidies. This broadening of the income concept has a substantial impact on disposable income inequality, with the Q5/Q1 ratio for disposable income being lower in 2003-04 and 2009-10 than shown using the different income measure for 1998-99.

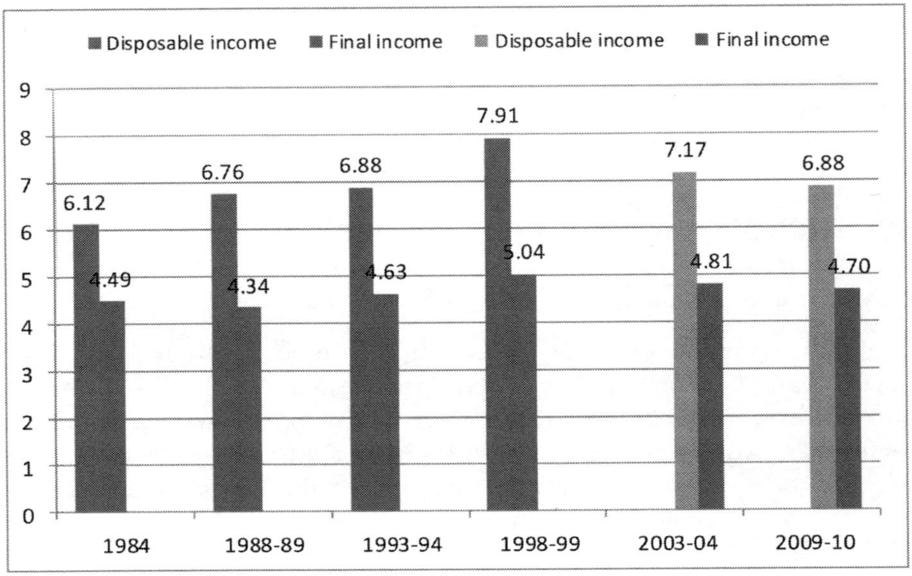

Figure 6 Income disparities by income concept, Australia, 1984 to 2009-10. Ratio of Q5 to Q1

Source: Calculated from ABS, Government Benefits, Taxes and Household Income, various years.

These figures are of interest in showing trends over the longer term, but conceptually results for equivalised income concepts are preferred.

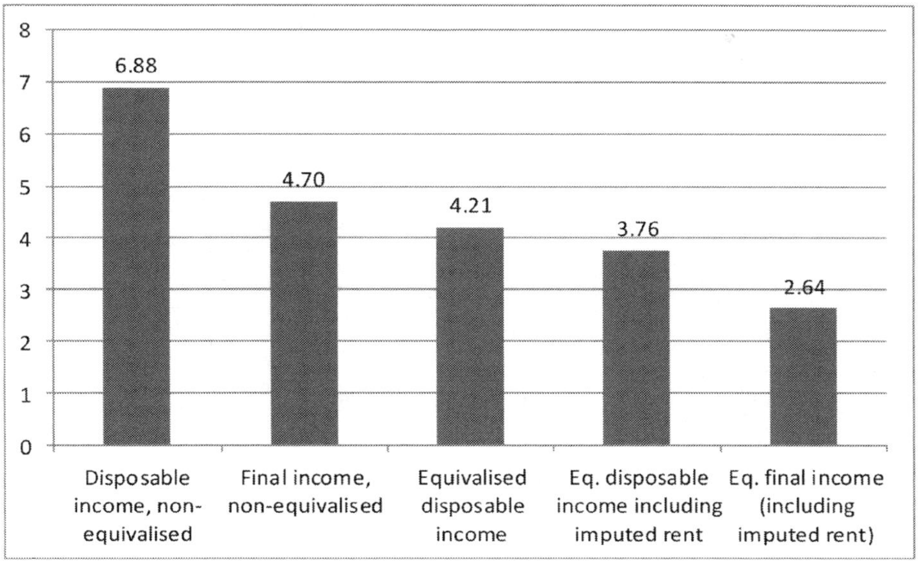

Figure 7 Income disparities by income concept, Australia, 2009-10. Ratio of Q5 to Q1

Source: Calculated from ABS, Government Benefits, Taxes and Household Income, 2009-10.

Figure 7 shows equivalised household income distributions for different income concepts in 2009-10. Including the impact of imputed rent and taking account of non-cash benefits and indirect taxes significantly reduces estimated inequality. Adding imputed rent to disposable income reduces disparities by close to 11 per cent and adding non-cash benefits and indirect taxes reduces this measure of inequality by a further 30 per cent.

A recent Productivity Commission Staff Working Paper (Greenville, Pobke and Rogers, 2013) calculates that the Gini coefficient for equivalised final income (excluding imputed income from owner-occupied housing and other housing subsidies) increased from 0.248 in 1988-89 to 0.270 in 2009-10. They also calculate that the Gini for equivalised disposable income in the same data (the 2009-10 Household Expenditure Survey) was 0.344 and the Gini for equivalised disposable income plus non-cash benefits but excluding indirect taxes was 0.257, suggesting that spending on non-cash benefits reduces inequality by 0.087 Gini points or about 25 per cent, but indirect taxes raise inequality by 0.013 Gini points or about five per cent.

The international evidence

International studies of the impact of government cash and non-cash benefits and direct and indirect taxes have been undertaken for some considerable time.

The UK Central Statistical Office has published such estimates since the 1960s with figures available online for results from 1977 onwards. Their approach influenced the ABS in undertaking their first study based on the 1984 Household Expenditure Survey. Ian Castles himself undertook an early comparative study in his 1987 paper referred to earlier, in which he compared results for Australia in 1984, New Zealand in 1981-82, and Sweden, the United Kingdom and the United States in 1984 (although a differing approach in the USA meant that some comparisons were limited, and results for Sweden and the United States do not take account of non-cash benefits and indirect taxes).

Table 4 shows some of these results, presenting Gini coefficients for private, gross, disposable income, disposable income and indirect benefits and for final income. The results are also adjusted for household size, although this adjustment is relatively crude, as the Castles study did not have microdata for the other countries. Table 4 shows that disposable income inequality was lowest in Sweden and highest in the United States, with Australian income inequality being second highest, although the gap between Australia and the USA was considerable. However, non-cash benefits appear to have had a stronger equalising effect in Australia than in the United Kingdom or New Zealand, and indirect taxes had a very small impact in all three countries. The overall result was on the basis of final income – Australia was slightly less unequal than New Zealand or the United Kingdom, but the differences were very small. Overall, the impact of this broadening of the income concept appears to have been a small degree of re-ranking of countries in the middle of this limited international distribution.[3]

Other relatively early comparative studies of the effects of non-cash benefits on income distribution include Smeeding, Saunders *et al* (1992) and Whiteford and Kennedy (1995). Smeeding, Saunders *et al* (1992) compare the impact of including the value of health and education benefits in income for Australia, Canada, Germany, the Netherlands, Sweden, the United Kingdom and the United States, plus imputed income from owner-occupied housing in these countries, apart from Australia and the UK. Adding these non-cash benefits had a relatively minor impact on income disparities in West Germany and Sweden, with larger impacts in the United States and Canada and the most significant effect in the Netherlands, which ranked third lowest in terms of disposable income inequality but lowest in terms of final income inequality, primarily due to the effects of imputed housing income. Smeeding, Saunders *et al* (1992)

3 It is worth noting that if the Q5 to Q1 ratio is used rather than the Gini coefficient, then the United Kingdom was slightly less unequal than Australia, which suggests that some care should be taken with conclusions based on this ratio, given the greater validity of the Gini coefficient as a measure of overall inequality.

found that the impact on relative poverty rates was much greater, particularly in Australia and the United Kingdom, where poverty rates fell by two-thirds and half, respectively.

Table 4 Approximate Gini coefficients for alternative income measures in five countries, early to mid-1980s

	Private income	Gross income	Disposable income	Disposable income and indirect benefits	Final income
Ranked by private income					
Australia	0.469	0.363	0.314	0.263	0.263
New Zealand	0.433	0.336	0.290	0.267	0.266
Sweden	0.521	0.294	0.258	-	-
United Kingdom	0.491	0.354	0.311	0.269	0.264
Ranked by gross income					
Australia	0.462	0.370	0.325	0.278	0.279
United Kingdom	0.486	0.363	0.324	0.288	0.286
United States	0.459	0.406	0.369	-	-

Source: Castles, 1987, Table H: 14.

Whiteford and Kennedy (1995) replicated this methodology, but were able to add imputed housing benefits for Australia and the United Kingdom, but not for the Netherlands and Sweden. Their results were broadly similar to Smeeding, Saunders *et al* (1992), although it can be noted that the reduction in inequality achieved was greatest in Australia. Once again, the effects on relative poverty rates were much greater than the effects on income inequality.

Since that time there have been many studies that take account of the impact of non-cash benefits, as well as studies that take account of the effects of indirect taxes. However, in quite a number of these studies the two instruments of redistribution are assessed separately. For example, in the study *Growing Unequal*, the OECD (2008) analysed the distributional effects of non-cash benefits in OECD countries around 2000, assessing the impact of health, education, social housing and other community services on income disparities.

Figure 8 shows the reduction in income disparities estimated by the OECD (2008), with the reduction in the Q5 to Q1 ratio varying between 0.5 in Luxembourg (i.e. from 3.8 to 3.2) and 2.6 in the USA (from 7.1 to 4.6).

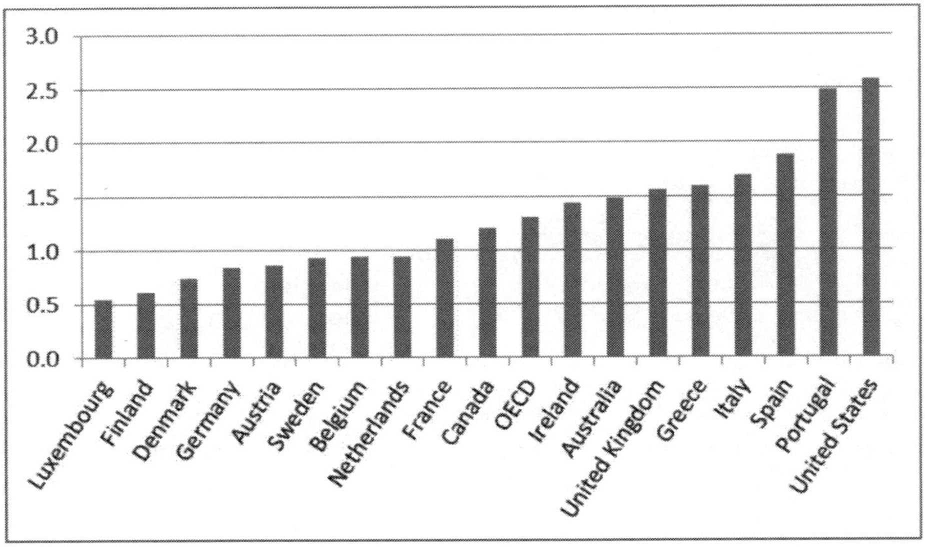

Figure 8a Reduction in inter-quintile share ratio after inclusion of non-cash benefits, selected OECD countries, around 2000. Reduction in ration of Q5 to Q1

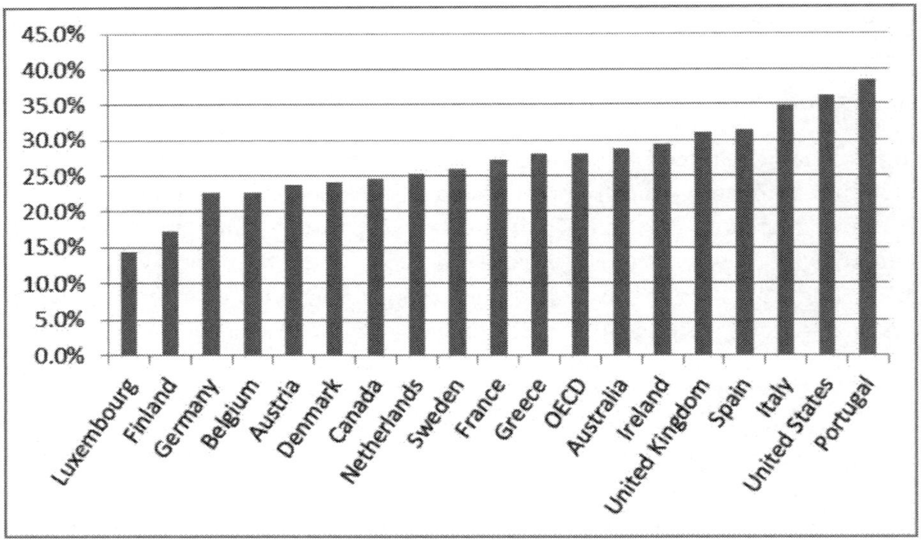

Figure 8b Reduction in inter-quintile share ratio after inclusion of non-cash benefits, selected OECD countries, around 2000. Percentage reduction in ratio of Q5 to Q1

Source: Calculated from OECD, 2008: 234.

The reduction estimated for Australia was slightly above average from 5.0 to 3.5, or by nearly 29 per cent. Generally speaking it was found that public spending on health had the largest impact in reducing income disparities, with the effect being about 50 per cent higher on average, but being nearly twice as important in Australia than the impact of education spending. While the inclusion of non-cash benefits had no effect on Australia's international ranking (staying the fifth most unequal of these countries) a number of countries did change their ranking, but mainly to a limited degree; Finland, however, fell four places from second least unequal to sixth least unequal.

The subsequent OECD report, *Divided We Stand: Why Inequality Keeps Rising* (2011, Part III, Chapter 8) undertook a similar analysis on a wider range of countries for the period around 2007. In Australia the reduction in the interquintile share ratio was estimated to be from 5.35 to 3.81 or 29 per cent, a percentage reduction identical to the earlier results and around the average of the 27 countries included. However, OECD (2011) also calculated the effects on the reduction in the Gini coefficient, which in the case of Australia was 17 per cent, below the OECD average of 20 per cent, and equal fourth lowest among these countries. This resulted in a relatively large change in Australia's international ranking, so that it fell from seventeenth to twenty-first in the OECD ranking on the basis of the Gini coefficient.

The main factor behind this is that spending on non-cash benefits in Australia was the lowest among these countries as a percentage of disposable income – around 19 per cent of disposable income compared to an OECD average of 29 per cent and a high of 41 per cent of disposable income in Sweden.

However, as with spending on cash transfers, spending on non-cash benefits in Australia appears to be very target efficient. The reduction in the Gini coefficient in percentage points per unit of non-cash spending was the fourth highest in the OECD, while the reduction in relative income poverty per unit of spending was the highest in the OECD. Overall, income poverty in Australia was reduced from 15 per cent to 7.9 per cent, the equal fifth largest poverty reduction effort. Overall, this suggests that Australia's welfare state design is more effective in reducing poverty than it is in reducing inequality.

OECD (2011) also found that spending on education benefits in Australia was the lowest in the OECD as a percentage of household disposable income and spending on health care was the equal lowest, and spending on early childhood education and care was the second lowest. The OECD did not have figures on spending on public housing in Australia, and while public housing is tightly targeted to the poor, the low level of benefits (about one quarter of one per cent of average household disposable income and 3.3 per cent for the lowest quintile) is unlikely to change the results at all. However, the OECD also did not have figures for Australia for spending on long-term elderly care services, and these are much more significant.

The impact of indirect taxes

Neither OECD (2008) nor OECD (2011) includes the impact of indirect taxes in their measure of incomes. In 2010 taxes on goods and services in Australia amounted to 7.3 per cent of GDP, the fourth lowest level in the OECD, exceeding only Japan, Switzerland and the USA. The OECD average was 11.0 per cent of GDP and the highest level was in Hungary where taxes on goods and services were around 16 per cent of GDP.

The case for taking account of the impact of these taxes has been put by Warren (2008):

> ... while personal income and social security taxes on employees are a significant proportion of GDP, they are just part of the total tax burden. For many countries high consumption taxes are accompanied by low personal income taxes and *vice versa*. ... These differences imply that any inter-country comparison of the impact of government taxes on individuals which omits consumption taxes will yield biased results because of both the different level and mix of these taxes. ... The case for including consumption taxes along with personal income tax and employee social security contributions taxes in any inter-temporal or cross-country comparisons of the impact of government tax policies is therefore clear. Even if the contribution and composition of consumption taxes remained similar and unchanged over time and between countries, studies focusing only on personal income tax and employee social security contributions will provide a partial assessment because the incidence of these two groups of taxes is significantly different (2008: 10).

While country studies of the distributional impact of all government taxes have a long history starting from the 1960s (Warren, 2008), international comparisons have been more limited; Warren (2008) identifies three cross-national studies – Garfinkel, Rainwater and Smeeding (2006), Harding, Warren and Lloyd (2007) and O'Donoghue, Baldini and Mantovani (2004).

O'Donoghue, Baldini and Mantovani (2004) provide the widest potential base for comparison of consumption taxes in Australia with EU countries. Comparing their results with the most recent ABS study of the *Impact of Government Benefits and Taxes* shows that the level of indirect taxes on consumption at 10.1 per cent of equivalised household disposable income is lower in Australia than in any of the 12 EU countries they studied, although Luxembourg at 10.3 per cent and the Netherlands at 11.5 per cent are not much higher than Australia. But in half of these EU countries, consumption taxes exceed 15 per cent of equivalised disposable income and in France and Ireland the level of consumption taxes is twice as high as in Australia, at 19.6 per cent and 20.5 per cent, respectively.

The impact of VAT in these 12 European countries is much greater than the impact of GST in Australia. Precise comparisons are not possible due to the different ways in which results are reported[4] but in Australia the GST raises 6.6 per cent of equivalised disposable income from the bottom quintile and 3.5 per cent from the richest quintile. In Europe VAT paid by the second decile ranges from a low of 11.9 per cent of disposable income in Luxembourg to more than 23 per cent in Sweden and France; correspondingly the amount collected from the second richest decile ranges between eight and 15 per cent of disposable income. These results suggest that while the regressivity of these consumption taxes is lower than in many European countries, there are EU examples where the distribution is not dissimilar to Australia. For example the ratio of GST collected from the bottom quintile to GST collected from the richest quintile as a percentage of equivalised disposable income in Australia is 1.88 to 1, whereas the corresponding ratios for the poorest decile to the richest decile ranges from 1.4 to 1 in Belgium to 5.6 to 1 in Sweden, with other countries showing ratios of between 2 and 4 to 1.

O'Donoghue, Baldini and Mantovani (2004) also look separately at the impact of excise duties, which are generally more regressive than VAT. However, excise duties play a much smaller role in countries with high VAT rates, but are more significant in Ireland and the UK. For example, excise duties are equivalent to 6.5 per cent of equivalised disposable income in the United Kingdom and 9.8 per cent in Ireland but range between two and five per cent in other countries in the study, which is comparable to Australian taxes on alcohol, tobacco and motor vehicle fuels of 2.7 per cent of disposable income.

In his own study, Warren (2008) analyses the broad impact of non-cash benefits and indirect taxes in 24 OECD countries around 2000. He finds that in-kind public services generally reduce the Gini index of income inequality, but including consumption taxes partly offsets the positive redistributive effects of in-kind public services. This offset is on average only some nine per cent of the impact of including in-kind services, but as much as 22 per cent for Turkey and 18 per cent for Mexico, Netherlands and Greece and only two per cent in the United States, and three per cent in Australia, Japan and Sweden. Overall, Australia's inequality ranking 'improves', falling from the tenth highest on the basis of cash disposable income to the twelfth highest on cash income plus indirect benefits to the thirteenth highest on final income.

It is worth noting, however, that Warren's estimates of the impact of consumption taxes is based on the distribution of consumption taxes in Australia, adjusted to other countries by the relative ratios of other countries' consumption taxes to GDP relative to Australia in 2002. This is because a truly comprehensive study of

4 Specifically, Australian results are reported for quintiles and EU results for deciles.

the impact of consumption taxes would require a multi-country team working over many years. It thus abstracts away from differences in consumption patterns across income groups in each country and from differences in the base and rate of different consumption tax regimes. Given that the Australian GST taxes food at a zero rate, for example, while most EU countries tax food at between five and ten per cent, and Denmark at 25 per cent, it is likely that Warren's estimates for EU countries understate their regressive impact.

Employer social security contributions

A related but even more significant gap in the standard framework is the complete absence of employer social security contributions in standard income distribution analyses. Given that these taxes are paying for a large part of social security spending in some countries, but do not exist in Australia or New Zealand, and are very low in Denmark and relatively low in the remaining English-speaking countries, their absence from welfare state comparisons is particularly problematic (Whiteford, 1995).[5] For example, using LIS data for the 1980s Whiteford and Kennedy (1994) calculated that the average transfers received by Australian households were just over half the average taxes paid. In France, in contrast, transfers were around 2.75 times the taxes measured as being paid by households – French households were apparently getting nearly two-thirds of their social security system 'for free'! It is employer social security contributions that fill this gap in France, but because they are paid by employers to government they do not pass through households and do not appear in household income surveys.

Employer social security contributions can be considered deferred earnings similar to employer-provided superannuation. For example, the United Nations Provisional Guidelines for Income Statistics (1977) advocated the inclusion of employers' contributions to social security schemes as part of wage and salary income in income surveys. The Canberra Group made a similar recommendation, noting that employer contributions should be counted both as part of market income and as part of taxes. Since 2007 Eurostat has collected information on employer social security contributions as part of the Survey of Income and Living Conditions (EU-SILC). However, while these data are now collected they are not included in the main income aggregates either as part of gross income or taxes paid (Atkinson and Marlier, 2010). Warren (2008) also does not analyse the distributional impact of employer social security contributions, but this is because his remit was to evaluate the impact of consumption taxes.

---

5 O'Donoghue *et al* (2004) estimate that employer social security contributions range between three to four per cent of equivalised disposable income in Denmark and Ireland and 6.8 per cent in the United Kingdom to more than 20 per cent in Sweden, France and Belgium.

The progressivity of employer social security contributions varies across countries; many countries have contribution floors which provide a degree of progressivity, while many also have contribution ceilings which reduce progressivity.[6] The effect of including employer social security contributions in private income and taxes would be to increase inequality in private incomes, since this approach treats them effectively as part of the wage package, and those who are unemployed, on welfare or retired would not receive this form of income. Moreover, including employer contributions as part of taxes would mean they would have no effect on inequality in disposable incomes, but the degree of redistribution achieved by the welfare state would increase in those countries with these taxes. This would therefore move in the opposite direction to the effect of re-ranking.

It could be argued that the Superannuation Guarantee plays an analogous role in Australia. There are strong arguments for considering employer superannuation contributions, both those under the SG and additional contributions, as being part of the wage package, implying that they should be included in private income. The common practice of advertising salaries as inclusive of superannuation and the origin of compulsory superannuation as a trade-off in national wage cases under the Accord strengthen the case for this view. Moreover those benefiting from higher-than-mandated employer contributions would undoubtedly regard their overall living standards as being reduced if employers reduced superannuation contributions. Superannuation contributions are not paid to government, however, while employer social security contributions are, and superannuation is therefore not part of government welfare state redistribution as conventionally defined, even though it is mandatory.

Assessing the combined effect of non-cash benefits and indirect taxes

As discussed earlier, ideally to identify the distributional impact of different welfare state arrangements it would be best to make the analysis as comprehensive as possible. Unfortunately, there are no multi-nation comparative studies that allow a more precise measure of the impact of non-cash benefits combined with the impact of indirect taxes. However, it is possible to compare results based on a very similar methodology used by the Office of National Statistics in the United Kingdom and also used by the ABS in Australia.

6 On the other hand, if those below contribution floors are not entitled to benefits, the overall progressivity of the tax-transfer system might be reduced.

Table 5 shows estimates of the components of final income for different income quintiles in Australia and the United Kingdom in 2009-10 with income components adjusted to Australian dollars using purchasing power parities.

Table 5 Components of final income for income quintiles, Australia and United Kingdom, 2009-10

	Bottom	2nd	3rd	4th	Top	All households
Australia						
Private income	13817	38219	69346	105166	189425	84102
Cash benefits	16841	16007	8707	3598	1147	9229
Benefits in kind	23046	23046	19135	15642	12461	18614
Direct taxes	-782	-3493	-8395	-15798	-38114	-13556
Indirect taxes	-5944	-7195	-9072	-11054	-14339	-9542
Final income	46978	66635	79670	97606	150580	88847
United Kingdom						
Private income	10882	24367	51836	85174	174889	69429
Cash benefits	15453	18590	13783	8866	4472	12232
Benefits in kind	16962	16282	15914	13835	11502	14899
Direct taxes	-2683	-4939	-10889	-18866	-43781	-16232
Indirect taxes	-6657	-7782	-10011	-12092	-16706	-10649
Final income	33958	46517	60633	76917	130376	69681

Source: Calculated from Office for National Statistics, *The Effects of Taxes and Benefits on Household Income, 2009/10* and Australian Bureau of Statistics, *Government Benefits, Taxes and Household Income, 2009-10*. UK values are adjusted by purchasing power parities to Australian dollars with one pound equal to $2.25.

Private incomes are higher for all income groups in Australia, while on average cash benefits are higher in the United Kingdom except for the lowest income quintile. Benefits in-kind are higher in Australia for all income groups, while direct and indirect taxes are lower in Australia for all income groups, and as a result final incomes are higher in Australia for all income groups. In addition, as could be expected, while the overall average private and final incomes for all households are similar (more so in the UK than in Australia), the effect of redistribution is to increase the incomes of low-income groups and reduce the incomes of high-income groups. For example, the final income of the poorest income quintile in Australia is 3.4 times their private incomes, while for the richest quintile their final incomes are 79.5 per cent of their private incomes; the corresponding figures for the United Kingdom are 3.1 and 74.5 per cent.

To assess the effects of these different income components on inequality, Table 6 shows an estimate of the distribution of benefits and taxes in each country, the weight of benefits and taxes, and the impact of benefits and taxes on income disparities.

As a starting point, it is worth noting that the two studies suggest that overall income disparities are narrower in Australia than in the United Kingdom, as the Q5 to Q1 ratio for final income is 3.21 in Australia and 3.84 in the United Kingdom. However, the Australian data include imputed income from owner-occupied housing which will have an inequality reducing effect not included in the calculations for the United Kingdom.

Table 6 Impacts of taxes and benefits on income distribution, Australia and United Kingdom, 2009-10

	Distribution	Weight	Impact
Cash benefits			
Australia	14.7	10.4	-7.5
United Kingdom	3.4	17.6	-9.3
Direct taxes			
Australia	48.7	15.3	-1.1
United Kingdom	16.3	23.3	-1.1
Non-cash benefits			
Australia	1.85	21.0	-2.0
United Kingdom	1.47	21.4	-3.1
Indirect taxes			
Australia	2.41	10.7	+0.9
United Kingdom	2.51	15.3	+1.3

Notes: *Distribution* is the ratio of the benefits received by the poorest quintile to those received by the richest quintile and the ratio of the taxes paid by the richest quintile to those paid by the poorest quintile, respectively. *Weight* is the level of benefits and taxes as a percentage of final income. *Impact* is the difference between the Q5 to Q1 ratio as a result of adding each income component. Households are ranked by equivalised disposable income using the modified OECD equivalence scale. In Australia, non-cash benefits are added before indirect taxes are deducted, while in the United Kingdom indirect taxes are deducted first.

Source: Calculated from Office for National Statistics, The Effects of Taxes and Benefits on Household Income, 2009/10 and Australian Bureau of Statistics, Government Benefits, Taxes and Household Income, 2009-10.

The progressivity of cash benefits is greater in Australia than in the United Kingdom, with the poorest quintile of households receiving nearly 15 times as much as the richest quintile, compared to a ratio of 3.4 to 1 in the United Kingdom. However, the overall weight of benefits in the United Kingdom at

17.5 per cent of final income is greater than in Australia at 10.4 per cent of final income, and this greater weight means that the UK benefit system actually reduces income disparities by more than the Australian benefit system.

Similarly, even though the direct tax system is more progressive in Australia than in the United Kingdom, the greater volume of taxes in the UK means that the two systems reduce disparities to a very similar degree. Comparisons of the impact of non-cash benefits are complicated by the fact that the approach used varies between countries, with the ABS adding non-cash benefits to disposable income before deducting indirect taxes, while the ONS in the UK deducts indirect taxes before adding non-cash benefits. This difference in ordering does not affect either the progressivity of these benefits or taxes and their weight but will have an effect on their measured impact, since the starting point differs between countries. However, these figures suggest that non-cash benefits reduce inequality to a somewhat greater extent in the UK than Australia, but that indirect taxes have a stronger effect in the UK in widening disparities. It is also worth noting that in both countries indirect taxes appear to increase disparities by about as much as direct taxes reduce disparities, but as noted above taxes are necessary to pay for the spending which appears most effective in reducing inequality.

Taking account of wealth and imputed income from owner-occupied housing

It has long been recognised that a significant feature of economic wellbeing in Australia is its relatively high level of home ownership (Castles, 1997), which has led to a relatively high level of personal wealth. Indeed, according to the 2012 Credit Suisse Global Wealth Report, Australian wealth per adult in 2012, at USD 355,000, was the second highest in the world – after Switzerland and ahead of Norway. Its median wealth of USD 194,000 is the highest in the world. The composition of wealth is heavily skewed towards real assets, which form 64 per cent of the total. The level of real assets per adult in Australia is now the second highest in the world after Norway, in part reflecting high house prices. Compared to the rest of the world, very few Australians have a net worth that is less than US$10,000. This reflects factors such as relatively low credit card and student loan debt. The proportion of those with wealth above USD 100,000 is the highest of any country – eight times the world average. With 1,571,000 people in the top one per cent of global wealth holders, Australia accounts for 3.4 per cent of this group, despite having just 0.4 per cent of the world's adult population.

The fact that median Australian wealth is the highest in the world contributes to the fact that by international standards Australia also appears to have one of the least skewed distributions of net worth in the developed world. Figure 9 shows a simple measure of 'skewedness' – the ratio of mean net worth to median net worth.

Apart from Italy, Australia has the lowest ratio of mean to median net worth in these countries; it is notable that the Scandinavian countries and Switzerland have the most skewed wealth distributions. A recent study by the European Central Bank (2013) found that Germany and Austria have distributions of net worth that fall between the levels shown for France and Norway, while Cyprus, Spain and Greece have distributions that are similar to Italy. While a number of Southern European countries appear to have less unequal wealth distributions than Australia, the much greater level of net worth in Australia could be expected to have a stronger equalising effect.

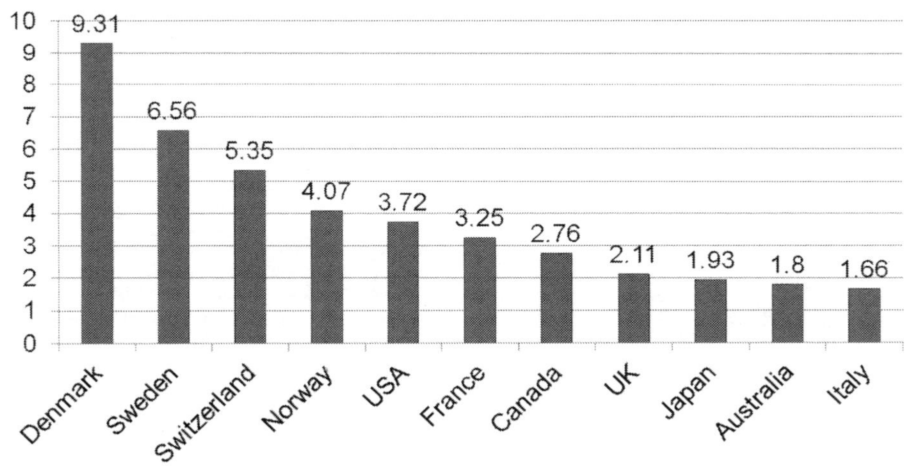

Figure 9 Australia's wealth distribution is one of the least skewed in the OECD. Ratio of mean to median net worth, 2011

Source: Calculated from Credit Suisse, 2012.

The ABS has undertaken surveys of net worth in Australia since 2003-04, and it is their figures that are used in the Credit Suisse (2012) report. The level of inequality in net worth is strongly influenced by the measure by which net worth is ranked. When households are ranked by net worth, wealth is much more unequally distributed than disposable income, and net worth has become much more unequally distributed than income – the Q5 to Q1 ratio increasing from around 42 to 1 in 2003-04 to 62 to 1 in 2009-10.

A very different picture appears, however, when households are ranked by their disposable income – that is when the joint distribution of net worth and income is considered. Overall, when households are ranked by disposable income the

Q5 to Q1 ratio for net worth is around 3.2 to 1; that is net worth is less unequally distributed than disposable income. The main reason for this is that owner-occupied housing accounts for about half of all net worth, and the Q5 to Q1 ratio for housing is only around 2 to 1. Other non-financial assets (e.g. vehicles and dwelling contents) are even less unequally distributed. Total liabilities tend to fall most heavily on the richest quintile. This pattern reflects the life-cycle accumulation of assets, so that older people tend to own their homes outright, while younger and higher-income groups are still acquiring assets and thus have more substantial debts.

While the distribution of net worth ranked by disposable income is less unequal than the distribution of disposable income, there is evidence of growing inequality in its impact since 2003-04. Figure 10 shows that disparities in net worth have widened somewhat, even though disparities in owner-occupied dwelling wealth narrowed slightly. Two factors seem important – an increase in disparities of financial assets held by different income groups and reduced disparities in liabilities, which therefore reduce the net worth of higher-income groups less than in the past.

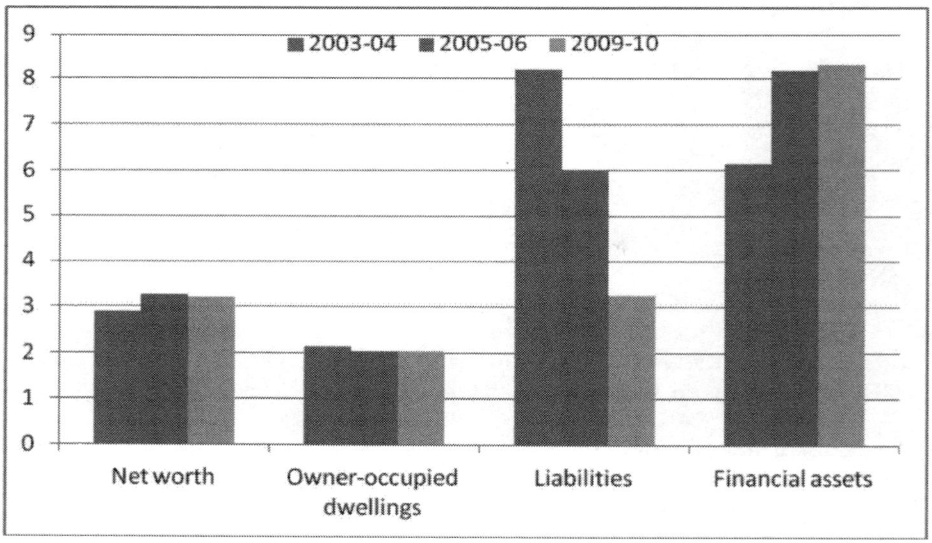

Figure 10 Trends in distribution of household net worth, Australia, 2003-04 to 2009-10. Q5/Q1

Source: Calculated from ABS, Household Wealth and Wealth Distribution, Australia, various years.

Following the recommendation of the Canberra Group, Eurostat has collected information necessary to calculate the benefits of imputed rent since 2007. Imputed rent has been added for all households that do not report that they pay full rent, either because they are owner-occupiers or because they live in accommodation rented at a lower price than the market price, or because the accommodation is provided rent-free. However, Eurostat note that the inclusion of imputed rent in the standard EU-SILC income concept would have a significant impact on all income-based indicators and would create a serious break in the time series as imputed rent could not be included in the indicators prior to 2007 due to the unavailability of the required data.

Chapter 7 of Atkinson and Marlier (2010) presents estimates of the distributional impact of moving from measures of disposable income to incomes augmented with imputed rents for 25 European countries in 2007. In the Netherlands and Norway, adding imputed rent actually increases the Gini coefficient, while in France it has no effect; in the remaining countries, the distributional impact ranges from negligible to a reduction in the Gini coefficient of up to 0.036 Gini points, with the impact being largest in the United Kingdom, followed by Estonia and Spain. Imputed rent also raises average incomes in most countries, again with the exception of the Netherlands and Norway, with the increase in average incomes being highest in Hungary at around 23 per cent.

The ABS has also included estimates of imputed rent in a number of its income surveys, with the most recent estimates being for 2009-10. In 2009-10, imputed rent is estimated to raise average household incomes from $848 per week to $905 per week, an increase of 6.7 per cent overall. For owners without a mortgage the increase in average income was around 20 per cent, while for those renting from state or territory housing authorities the increase was 17 per cent.

In 2009-10, the addition of imputed rent to equivalised household disposable income in Australia was estimated to reduce the Gini coefficient from 0.328 to 0.309, a reduction of 0.019 Gini points. This reduction in inequality was exceeded in nine of the 25 countries of Europe in the Atkinson and Marlier report (2010), while the increase in mean income was lower than in all but seven European countries. The apparently surprising result that imputed rent has a relatively minor impact on mean income in Australia reflects the fact that imputed rents in both the ABS and Eurostat studies not only includes imputed rent from owner-occupied housing, but also includes the value of public housing subsidies, which are much more significant in a large number of European countries. For example, in 2009-10 only 3.9 per cent of Australian households were public renters, with a further five per cent paying reduced rents or living rent-free. In contrast nearly 18 per cent of the UK population lived in households not paying market rents and nearly one quarter in Hungary, with nine other European countries having higher shares of reduced rent tenants than Australia. It is likely to be this factor that explains Australia's relatively low ranking in the contribution to average incomes despite its very high level of housing wealth. However, it is also important to bear in mind that this stronger equalising effect of public housing in many European countries was already included in estimates of the impact of government non-cash benefits on income distribution, so that the further addition of imputed income from owner-occupied housing would be likely to have a stronger effect in Australia than is suggested by these figures.

Conclusions

Broadening the measure of resources has important implications for assessments of the impact of the welfare state on income levels and on inequality, as well as having implications for understanding the effectiveness of Australia's welfare state compared to those in other developed countries.

To sum up, measures of the effectiveness of welfare state redistribution are biased due to the counterfactual underlying any such evaluation – that the welfare state has not affected the distribution of private income and that the differences in welfare state design across countries have had the same zero effect on private incomes. Given that the counterfactual is by definition unobservable, the most that can be said is that when households are ranked by their 'endpoint' rather than by their starting point, the degree of redistribution achieved by the welfare state in many countries is significantly less than is conventionally measured. This is not the case to the same extent in Australia (or other English-speaking countries), which implies that the degree of redistribution achieved in Australia is higher than conventionally estimated. Having said this, this specific effect does not alter the level of inequality in disposable incomes: Australia is more effective than conventionally measured, but no less unequal in outcomes.

On the other hand, taking account of non-cash benefits raises living standards across the income distribution and reduces inequality. The reduction in the inter-quintile ratio in Australia appears to be close to the OECD average, but the reduction in the Gini coefficient is less than the OECD average; the result is that when measured by the Gini coefficient Australia's inequality ranking worsens somewhat. This may be due to an incomplete accounting, as neither public housing nor nursing home care are included in the data for Australia used in the OECD comparative studies. Inclusion of public housing, however, is unlikely to have a large impact in Australia, due to the low share of households in this tenure.

Taking account of indirect taxes on consumption is likely to improve Australia's relative ranking in terms of inequality, both because the weight of indirect taxes is lower and because the structure of indirect taxes appears likely to be less regressive than in many European countries. The size of this effect is unclear, however, as cross national studies of the impact of indirect taxes are not common.

Adding imputed income from owner-occupied housing also raises household incomes and reduces inequality in living standards, and seems likely to improve Australia's international ranking. Again, the available evidence on this is not definitive because existing studies simultaneously take account of both the benefits of imputed income from owner-occupied housing and the benefits of government-subsidised public housing. As noted above, because public housing is less prevalent in Australia it is plausible that owner-occupied housing provides a larger share of the redistributive effect here. In addition, existing comparative studies of the impact of non-cash benefits also include the impact of public housing, so it would be important to avoid double counting its impact on the level of inequality across countries

Finally, the effects of employer social security contributions and employer provided private fringe benefits need to be considered. If they are added to private income and then not counted in disposable income, then the effect would be to increase the extent of redistribution but not alter the extent of disposable income inequality. However, in the case of employer contributions to private pensions it can be argued that they should be counted in a comprehensive measure of resources, since they are an addition to net worth. Similarly, the earnings of superannuation and private pension funds also increase net worth, although earnings can be negative as well as positive.

An important point that comes out in this review is that the Australian welfare state is likely to be relatively more effective in reducing income poverty than it is in reducing income inequality as measured by the Gini coefficient. This is not surprising given that the design of the Australian welfare state emphasises targeting and therefore poverty alleviation. Given that cash transfers in Australia are more targeted to the lower half of the income distribution than in any other OECD country, it is unsurprising that the Gini coefficient – which is well known to be sensitive to changes in income in the middle of the distribution – should be reduced less in Australia. Whether this is problematic or not depends on values about the objectives of the welfare state.

Overall, broadening the definition of income to take account of the factors discussed here shows higher living standards and lower inequality and relative poverty in most countries, and it also narrows the difference between measured outcomes in different countries. However, despite the work of the Canberra Group and national and international statistical agencies in significantly improving the comprehensiveness of household income surveys, questions remain about the methodology of comparative analysis of welfare state outcomes.

References

Adema, W and Ladaique, M (2005). *Net social expenditure*, Labour market and social policy occasional paper, OECD, Paris.

——and Whiteford, P (2010). 'Public and private social welfare', in *Oxford handbook of comparative social policy*, ch. 8, Oxford University Press.

Atkinson, A and E Marlier (eds), (2010). Income and Living Conditions in Europe, Eurostat, Brussels. http://epp.eurostat.ec.europa.eu/cache/ITY_OFFPUB/KS-31-10-555/EN/KS-31-10-555-EN.PDF

Australian Bureau of Statistics, (various years), *The Effects of Government Benefits and Taxes on Household Income*, ABS Catalogue No. 6537.0, Canberra.

——(various years), Household Wealth and Wealth Distribution, Australia, Catalogue No. 6554.0, Canberra.

Barr, N (1992). 'Economic theory and the welfare state: a survey and reinterpretation', *Journal of Economic Literature*, vol. 30, June.

——(1999). 'Fundamentals of social security analysis', *Australian Social Policy*, 1999/1: 7-29.

——(2001). *The welfare state as piggy bank: information, risk, uncertainty, and the role of the state*, Oxford University Press, Oxford.

The Canberra Group (2001). *Expert Group on Household Income Statistics: Final Report and Recommendations*. Ottawa.

—— (2011) *Canberra Group Handbook on Household Income Statistics, Second Edition*, United Nations Economic Commission for Europe, Geneva.

Castles, F (1997). 'The Institutional Design of the Australian Welfare State'. *International Social Security Review*, 50 (2): 25-41.

Castles, I (1987). 'The effects of government benefits and taxes on household incomes: Estimates for Australia and other countries'.

Credit Suisse (2012). Global Wealth Report, Credit Suisse, Zurich.

Daley, J (2013). *Budget pressures on AustralianGovernments*, Grattan Institute, Melbourne.

Esping-Andersen, G (1990). *The three worlds of welfare capitalism*, Polity Press, Cambridge.

Garfinkel, I, L Rainwater, and TM Smeeding (2006). 'A Re-examination of Welfare State and Inequality in Rich Nations: How In-Kind Transfers and Indirect Taxes Change the Story'. *Journal of Policy Analysis and Management* 25(4): 855–919.

Greenville, J, Pobke, C and Rogers, N (2013). *Trends in the Distribution of Income in Australia*, Productivity Commission Staff Working Paper, Canberra.

Gruen, FH (1989). *Australia's Welfare State – Rearguard or Avant Garde?* Discussion Paper No. 212, Centre for Economic Policy Research, Australian National University.

Harding, A, Warren, N, and Lloyd R (2007). 'Beyond conventional measures of income: including indirect benefits and taxes', in *The Distributional Effects of Government Spending and Taxation* (ABA festschrift for Tony Atkinson) edited by Micklewright J and Jenkins. T., (OUP:Oxford), pp84-102

Korpi, W and Palme, J (1998). 'The paradox of redistribution and the strategy of equality: welfare state institutions, inequality and poverty in the Western countries', *American Sociological Review*, vol. 63, no. 5.

Layard, R (1977). 'On measuring the redistribution of lifetime income', in MS Feldstein and RP Inman (eds), *The economics of public services*, Macmillan, London.

Mitchell, D, Harding, A and Gruen, F (1994). 'Targeting Welfare', *Economic Record*, 70, 10: 315-340.

O'Donoghue, C Baldini, M and Mantovani, D (2004). 'Modelling the redistributive impact of indirecttaxes in Europe: an application of EUROMOD', EUROMOD Working Papers EM7/01, EUROMOD at the Institute for Social and Economic Research.

Office for National Statistics, (2011). *The Effects of Taxes and Benefits on Household Income, 2009/10*, Newport.

Organisation for Economic Co-operation and Development (OECD) (2008). *Growing unequal: income distribution and poverty in OECD countries*, OECD, Paris.

Organisation for Economic Co-operation and Development (OECD) (2011). *Divided we stand: Why inequality keeps rising*, OECD, Paris.

Pederson, AW (1994). *The welfare state: still no answer to the big questions?* LIS working paper, CEPS/INSTEAD, Luxembourg.

Rawdanowicz, L, E Wurzel and A Christensen (2013). 'The Equity Implications of Fiscal Consolidation', *OECD Economics Department Working Papers*, No. 1013, OECD Publishing. doi: 10.1787/5k4dlvx2wjq0-en

Reynolds, M and Smolensky, E (1977). *Public expenditures, taxes and the redistribution of income: the USA, 1950, 1961, 1970*, Academic Press, New York.

Ringen, S (1987). *The possibility of politics*, Clarendon Press, Oxford.

Saunders, P (ed) (1987). *Redistribution and the welfare state: estimating the effects of government benefits and taxes on household income, proceedings of a workshop held at the University of New South Wales, 13 May 1987*, reports and proceedings, no. 67, Social Welfare Research Centre, University of New South Wales.

Saunders, P (1994). *Welfare and Inequality*, Cambridge University Press, Melbourne.

Smeeding, T, Saunders, P, Coder, J, Jenkins, S, Fritzell, J Hagenaars, A, Hauser, R, and Wolfson, M (1992). *Noncash Income, Living Standards and Inequality: Evidence from the Luxembourg Income Study*, LIS Working Paper, CEPS/ INSTEAD, Luxembourg.

United Nations (1977). *Provisional Guidelines on Statistics of the Distribution of Income, Consumption and Accumulation of Households*, New York.

Warren, N (2008). *A review of studies on the distributional impact of consumption taxes in OECD countries*, OECD social, employment and migration working paper, OECD, Paris.

Werding, M (2003). 'After another decade of reform: do pension systems in Europe converge?', *CESifo DICE Report*, vol. 1/2003.

Whiteford, P (1995). 'The Use of Replacement Rates in International Comparisons of Benefit Systems', *International Social Security Review*, 48, 2/95, 3-30.

—— (1997). 'Targeting welfare: a comment', *Economic Record*, vol. 73, no. 220, March: 45-50.

——(1998). 'Is Australia particularly unequal?', in P Smyth and B Cass (eds), *Contesting the Australian way: states, markets and civil society*, Cambridge University Press, Melbourne.

—— (2010). 'The Australian tax-transfer system: architecture and outcomes,' *Economic Record*, 86 (275), 528-544.

Whiteford, P and Kennedy, S (1995). *Incomes and Living Standards of Older People: A Comparative Analysis,* UK Department of Social Security, Research Report No. 34, HMSO, London.

20. Money Income Distribution and Redistribution in Australia, Sweden and the United States 1984[1]

Ian Castles

This paper compares the distribution of household money incomes in Australia, Sweden and the United States, and examines the association between the private incomes and cash benefits received and the direct taxes paid by various household groups within each of the three countries.

Over the years, many attempts have been made to compare the distribution of the money incomes of families in Australia with the corresponding distribution in other countries. In a review of the literature published in 1978 in the Surveys of Australian Economics series for the Academy of Social Sciences in Australia, Richardson commented:

> The hazards of international comparisons of income distribution are severe. Briefly these hinge on the non-comparability of definitions of family and income; the possibility of substantial sampling error; and the inability of any existing measure of private income to reflect the value of government-provided goods and services. It is plain that even the most careful analysis should be taken as suggestive rather than conclusive. Despite the difficulties and the very tentative nature of the conclusions, a number of studies attempt this comparison of family incomes.[2]

After summarising these studies, she concluded:

> Despite the overwhelming consistency of the evidence suggesting Australia has a very equal distribution of income, reservations remain.[3]

During the subsequent decade, much new information on the distribution of incomes in Australia has become available. The Australian Bureau of Statistics (ABS) undertook surveys of income in 1978-79 and 1981-82, and a Household Expenditure Survey in 1984.[4]

---

1 Presented to the 1987 ANZAAS Congress in Townsville on 24 August 1987. Published by the Australian Bureau of Statistics as a monograph. Except where otherwise indicated, all figures and tables in this chapter are Castles' own.

2 Richardson, S, 'Income Redistribution, Poverty and Redistributive Policies' in Gruen, FH (ed.) *Surveys of Australian Economics*. Volume 2: 26.

3 *Ibid*: 27.

4 Another income survey was conducted in 1985-86, but results are not yet available.

The output from these surveys has eased some of the difficulties of comparisons between Australia and other countries in this area. The problem of non-comparability of definitions of 'family' between countries has been diminished by the release of Australian data on various bases - income units, families and households; there is some evidence that the degree of non-comparability of estimates on a current income basis with those on an annual income basis may have been overstated;[5] and steps have been taken towards adjusting private income measures to reflect the value of government-provided goods and services.[6]

Despite these advances, it remains the case that international comparisons of the distribution of household incomes are subject to problems of non-comparability of a kind that have long since been addressed – and largely overcome – in other statistical areas by the adoption of international conventions (e.g. the United Nations System of National Accounts, International Monetary Fund conventions for balance of payments statistics, International Labour Office conventions for statistics of employment, etc).

The present paper presents a comprehensive comparison of the distribution and redistribution of money incomes in Australia and Sweden on an income unit basis (that is, for units consisting of a couple or single person and their children if any), and some more limited comparisons between Australia and the United States on a household basis (that is, for units consisting of a group of people living together). For both studies, the method adopted was to match the published results from the 1984 surveys of money income in the overseas countries with corresponding data from the ABS Household Expenditure Survey 1984. The objective is to show how household survey data can be used to compare the structure of income distribution and redistribution between countries.

The detailed bilateral comparisons are contained in attachments to the paper. Although the Australia/Sweden and Australia/United States comparisons are on quite different bases, the data strongly suggest that the distribution of household incomes in Australia is less equal than in Sweden and more equal than in the United States. They also suggest that, although the purchasing power of money incomes in Australia is lower on average than in the United States and higher

5 As Table A in Attachment A shows, the distribution of household incomes on a current income basis from the 1984 Household Expenditure Survey was very similar to the corresponding distribution on an annual income basis from the 1981-82 Income and Housing Survey.

6 Estimates of the value of government-provided goods and services for Australia are given in Australian Bureau of Statistics *Household Expenditure Survey Australia 1984: The Effects of Government Benefits and Taxes on Household Income* (ABS Cat. No. 5237, April 1987). Estimates for Australia, New Zealand and the United Kingdom are compared in Castles, I, 'The Effects of Government Benefits and Taxes on Household Income: Estimates for Australia and Other Countries' in Saunders, P (ed.) 'Redistribution and the Welfare State: Estimating the Income Effects of Government Benefits and Taxes on Household Income'. *Social Welfare Research Centre Reports and Proceedings, No. 67*, August 1987.

on average than in Sweden, the real value of the money incomes of *low-income* households in Australia is higher than in the United States and lower than in Sweden.

As this example shows, estimates of relative average real income levels for entire populations are of limited value in assessing the real incomes of specific groups within countries. Other illustrations of the limitations of global comparisons of real income levels will emerge from the discussion of the main findings of the Australia/United States studies in this paper.

Money incomes of income units in Australia and Sweden 1984

Statistics Sweden has conducted an 'Income Distribution Survey' annually since 1973. The income units used in the survey are described as family units, and are defined as follows:

> Family units consist of cohabitants (married or unmarried) with or without children less than 18 years old, or single persons with or without children less than 18 years old.[7]

The ABS Household Expenditure Survey 1984 (HES) was, as the name implies, a survey of households (spending units) rather than of income units. For purposes of this section of the paper, the income data collected for individual members of households has been aggregated to produce data for 'income units', which are identical to 'family units' as defined in the Swedish income distribution surveys.[8]

The detailed tables in Attachment A present comparable information for income units (IUs) from the Australian HES and from the Swedish Income Distribution Survey 1984. The tables make use of concepts and classifications of income, income units, income unit quantiles, consumption units and real values. These are defined and explained in the next section.

---

7 Statistics Sweden, Statistical Series Be 21 SM 8601, *Income Distribution Survey in 1984: Income Development of Families in 1975-1984*: 16. The main results of the 1984 Income Distribution Survey are published in this publication and in Statistical Series Be 21 SM 8603, *Income Distribution Survey in 1984: Income Distribution of Families in 1984*.

8 'Income unit' as defined here is similar to, but not identical with, the definition used by the ABS in its income and expenditure surveys. For the latter definition see, for example, ABS *Household Expenditure Survey 1984: the Effects of Government Benefits and Taxes on Household Income*: 80.

Concepts and classifications

Two concepts of *income* are used in the comparisons: 'private income' and 'disposable income'. 'Private income' includes all money receipts, other than government pensions and benefits, which are received regularly by any member of the income unit. 'Disposable income' represents private income plus direct benefits received less direct taxes paid.[9] In some of the tables the net difference between private income and disposable income ('net cash transfers') is disaggregated into 'direct benefits received' and 'direct taxes paid'.

The comparisons are made for *income units* in three age groups: 18-19 years; 20-64 years; and 65 years or more. Most of the tables relate to the '20-64 years' age group. In this age group, income units are classified into four broad categories:

1. married couple without children;
2. married couple with children;
3. single parents;
4. single persons;

and further subdivided according to the employment status of adult members and (for income units with children) the number of children. The '65 years or more' age group is subdivided into married couples and single persons.

The various populations of income units are divided into *quantiles*, so that the structure of incomes within those populations can be expressed by means of average values of private or disposable income within each quantile. The main quantiles used are 'deciles' – i.e. 10 per cent groupings of the estimated population when income units are ranked in ascending order according to each income unit's total private or disposable income. Many of the tables also show comparable average values for the 5 per cent and 2.5 per cent of the relevant income unit population with the highest incomes, and for the 5 per cent of the relevant population with the lowest incomes. The tables of distributions also show a 'co-efficient of concentration', which is an approximation of the Gini co-efficient calculated from the average incomes for each decile.

In order to provide a rough adjustment of the 'income per income unit' data to take account of the differing needs of income units of varying size and

9 'Direct benefits' represent the total of regular cash payments received directly from government, without any requirements to provide goods or services in return for the payment, by all members of the income unit. 'Direct taxes' represent, for Australian income units, the total personal income tax and health insurance levy of all members of the income unit; and, for Swedish income units, all 'negative transfers' as defined in Swedish Income Distribution Survey publications (over 98 per cent of negative transfers in 1984 were direct taxes paid to central and local governments). The direct tax for Australian income units was modelled in the same way as in ABS *Household Expenditure Survey 1984: The Effects of Government Benefits and Taxes on Household Income*: see discussion on pages 2, 79 and 83 of that publication.

composition, income data in some of the tables are presented in terms of averages per *consumption unit* (CU). An income unit consisting of a married couple only is taken as 1 CU, with a single person income unit regarded as equivalent to 0.6 CU and children 0.25 CU.[10] This yields the following 'equivalence ratios':

	Consumption unit
Single person only	0.60
Single parent, one child	0.85
Married couple only	1.00
Single parent, two children	1.10
Married couple, one child	1.25
Married couple, two children	1.50
Married couple, three children	1.75

The *real values* for Australian income units are money values in Australian currency, but with the average weekly values from HES data converted to average annual rates. The values for Swedish income units are converted from Swedish kroner to Australian dollars using OECD estimates of the Purchasing Power Parity (PPP) of the two currencies in relation to private final consumption expenditure. The relative average money incomes of the various income unit categories are therefore expressed in estimated 'real values', and specifically in terms of their relative capacity to purchase goods and services entering into the private final consumption expenditure of households.[11] The same PPP ratio (Skr7.2 = $A1) is used for all income unit types and at all income levels. The presentation of all of the money income comparisons in terms of a uniform purchasing power measure does not, of course, affect the relativity between income magnitudes *within* each of the countries.

10 In Swedish Income Distribution Survey publications, a slightly different consumption unit is used: a single person is taken as 0.95 consumption units, a couple as 1.65 consumption units and children as 0.40 consumption units. Converted to 'couple units', the relevant ratios are: couples = 1.00 consumption units, single persons 0.576 consumption units and children 0.242 consumption units. The different equivalence ratios used in the published Swedish income distribution tables do not affect the comparisons in Attachment A.

11 Purchasing power parity (PPP) estimates for Australia, Sweden and a number of other countries have been compiled by the OECD from information supplied by national statistical offices (including Australia), and are to be published in *National Accounts: Volume 1 – Supplement* (forthcoming). Summary estimates have been published in ABS, *Gross Domestic Product at Purchasing Power Parity in OECD Countries 1985* issued August 1987. The purchasing power parity of private final consumption expenditure in terms of national currency units per US dollars in 1985 was Skr8.88 for Sweden and $1.24 for Australia, implying that the Skr/$A relationship in terms of average OECD prices was 7.16: 1 in that year. Allowing for the (fractionally) higher increase in the implicit price deflator for private final consumption expenditure in Australia in 1985, the implied ratio for 1984 is Skr7.2=$A1. It should be noted that no allowance is made for the fact that, to the extent that the provision of services by government without charge or at less than full cost (e.g. on health and education functions) differs between the two countries, the 'real value' of income available for expenditure on other goods and services cannot be accurately represented by private final consumption expenditure adjusted by the PPP ratio.

Main results

The comparisons in the 28 Australia/Sweden tables in Attachment A cannot be summarised in a few paragraphs. This section provides some illustrations of the way in which the tables can be used to compare the structures of income distribution and redistribution in the two countries.

The aged population

The most striking difference in the demographic structure of the two countries is the much larger aged population in Sweden. This is brought out in the first column of Table A1. For each 100 income units in the under 65 age group, there were 34 income units in the 65 years and over age group in Sweden and only 19 income units in this group in Australia.

It follows from this much higher proportion of aged income units in Sweden that the aggregate of net cash transfers to the aged population would need to have been almost twice as great in relation to the income of the non-aged population in order to achieve the same relative level of income support per aged income unit in Sweden as in Australia. In fact, Table A1 shows that net cash transfers to the aged in Sweden were far greater than this.

Expressed as a proportion of the total private income of non-aged income units, net cash transfers to the 65 years and over aged group amounted to 14.2 per cent in Sweden compared with only 4.5 per cent in Australia (Table A1). Measured against the money income of the working population, net payments for the income support of the aged were thus more than three times greater in Sweden than in Australia.

Although the level of net cash transfers per aged income unit was much higher in Sweden than in Australia, the average money disposable income of aged people in the two countries was virtually the same in terms of the purchasing power parity (PPP) estimates used in this study (Table A27), and the average in each income decile was also quite similar (Table A28). These outcomes reflect two factors: the higher average levels of private income per aged income unit in Australia; and the effects of income tests in reducing or eliminating the entitlement to benefits of aged people with significant private incomes in Australia, but not in Sweden.

Non-employed working age population

In the case of the working age population, the most marked difference between the two countries was in the proportion of income units in which there was no employed adult. Such units are usually dependent on government benefits for all or most of their income.[12]

12 Not all income units in which there was no employed adult were mainly dependent on government benefits: in Australia there would, for example, have been significant numbers of early retirees with superannuation benefits or other private incomes.

Whereas the proportion of aged to working age income units was much higher in Sweden than in Australia, the proportion of 'dependent' income units in the working age group was much higher in Australia than in Sweden. For each 100 income units in the 20-64 age group in which at least one adult was employed, the number of units in which no adult was employed was 27 in Australia and only 12 in Sweden (Table A4). Moreover, nearly 80 per cent of the much smaller population of 'dependent' units in the working age group in Sweden consisted of single persons, whereas most of the 'dependent' units in Australia were couples with or without children and single parents (Table A4).

The proportion of couples without children in the 20-64 age group with neither partner employed was, at 19 per cent, much higher in Australia than in Sweden – five per cent (Table A4). The difference was mainly attributable to a lower average retiring age in Australia: over five-sixths of the non-employed couples without children in the 20-64 age group in Australia were in the 55-64 age group. In Sweden, the universal old-age pension and the earnings-related pension are available to all aged persons who are otherwise eligible, whether they retire or not.[13]

Among income units with children, the proportion in which the sole parent or both parents were not employed was 16 per cent in Australia but less than four per cent in Sweden. The proportion of single parents who were not employed was 64 per cent in Australia compared with only 16 per cent in Sweden, and the proportion of couples with children in which neither partner was in employment was eight per cent in Australia and about one per cent in Sweden.

Comparison of private and disposable income distributions

The detailed tables provide numerous comparisons of the distributions of the private and disposable incomes of various population groups. This section illustrates one way in which the data can be used. The share of the total income of selected populations of income units with children which is received by the *50 per cent with the lowest incomes* is compared for the two countries and, for each country, for private and disposable incomes.

In the case of *all couples with children*, the income shares for private and disposable incomes were:

13 US Department of Health and Human Services, Social Security Administration, *Social Security Programs Throughout the World 1985*: 242.

Share of income of 50 per cent of married couple with children income units with lowest:	Australia %	Sweden %
Private incomes	24.1	33.4
Disposable incomes	**33.2**	**39.5**
Difference	**9.1**	**6.1**

Source: Table A17 in Attachment A.

The table shows that, in Australia, the share of the 'lower half' in disposable incomes was nine percentage points higher than their share of private incomes – but it was still fractionally below the share of the 'lower half' in *private* incomes in Sweden.

The larger increase in the income share between the two income concepts in Australia (nine percentage points) than in Sweden (six percentage points) is entirely attributable to the benefits paid to the substantial numbers of income units in Australia with neither partner employed. For income units with *one partner employed* the income shares were fairly similar in both countries:

Share of income of 50 per cent of married couple with children, one employed income units with lowest:	Australia %	Sweden %
Private incomes	32.4	32.9
Disposable incomes	**36.7**	**38.7**
Difference	**4.5**	**5.8**

Source: Table A18 in Attachment A.

For 'married couple with children' income units with *both partners employed* – which outnumbered one-worker couples in a ratio of more than five to one in Sweden but which were about the same in number as one-worker couples in Australia (Table A4) – the corresponding figures were as follows:

Share of income of 50 per cent of married couple with children, two employed income units with lowest:	Australia %	Sweden %
Private incomes	31.4	36.0
Disposable incomes	**34.8**	**40.6**
Difference	**3.4**	**4.6**

Source: Table A19 in Attachment A.

The tables show that the impact of cash transfer systems in redistributing income between income units cannot be evaluated in isolation from factors such as the employment status of the members of those units. The point emerges even more clearly from similar data relating to single parent income units. For *all single parents*, the income shares for private and disposable incomes were:

Share of income of 50 per cent of single parent income units with lowest:	Australia %	Sweden %
Private incomes	2.0	23.8
Disposable incomes	**32.1**	**39.3**
Difference	**30.1**	**15.5**

Source: Table A23 in Attachment A.

Restricting the comparison to income units in which the single parent is employed – 36 per cent of the total in Australia and 85 per cent in Sweden – the income shares of the 'lower half' were as follows:

Share of income of 50 per cent of employed single parent income units with lowest:	Australia %	Sweden %
Private incomes	23.8	31.1
Disposable incomes	**34.7**	**40.3**
Difference	**10.9**	**9.2**

Source: Table A24 in Attachment A.

Taxes and benefits

Most income units in Sweden paid more in direct taxes, but received more in direct benefits, than corresponding units in Australia. In both countries, however, the net cash transfers (direct taxes paid minus direct benefits received) were equivalent to about 15 per cent of the private income of all income units in the 20-64 years age group (Table A6) and about 20 per cent of the private income of units in the 20-64 age group in which there was at least one employed adult (Table A12).

The similarity in the proportion of net transfers to private income in the aggregate did not extend to particular categories of income units. For example, one-worker couples with children in Sweden received more in direct benefits than they paid in direct taxes, whereas in Australia the direct taxes paid by this group exceeded benefits received by an amount equivalent to about 17 per cent of private income. By contrast, the net cash transfers paid by two-worker couples with children were equivalent to about 21 per cent of private income in both countries (Table A5).

Money incomes of households in Australia and the United States 1984

The income survey used for the United States comparison was the March 1985 Current Population Survey (CPS) conducted by the Bureau of the Census. The Census Bureau has combined data from the Annual Housing Survey, the Income Survey Development Program and the Internal Revenue Service, as well as the CPS results to derive estimates of after-tax income which are designed *inter alia* to 'measure...differences in purchasing power between subgroups of the population.'[14]

The detailed tables in Attachment B present comparable information for households from the Australian HES and from the study of after-tax incomes for 1984 by the US Bureau of the Census. The tables make use of concepts and classifications of income, households, household income deciles, consumption units and real values. These differ in many respects from those used in the Australia/Sweden comparison. They are defined and explained in the next section.

Concepts and classifications

Two concepts of *income* are used in the Australia/United States comparisons: 'before tax income' and 'after tax income'. 'Before tax income' is identical to the 'gross income' concept used in HES and other ABS income survey publications – i.e. it includes government cash pensions and benefits as well as all other money receipts received regularly by any member of the household. 'After tax income' is similar to the HES concept of 'disposable income', except that the deductions from gross income include property taxes (US) and general rates (Australia) paid on owner-occupied dwellings. The United States estimates of taxes are based on a simulation which allocated to households direct taxes equivalent to 98.5 per cent of the relevant taxes according to independent estimates.[15]

14 All of the estimates used in the tables in Attachment B are derived from US Bureau of the Census *After-Tax Money Income Estimates of Households: 1984* (*Special Studies, Series P-23, No. 147*), except for the estimates for consumption units used to calculate average incomes per consumption unit in the lower half of Table B2. The latter estimates use information about numbers of children in households of different types from other Census Bureau publications relating to the March 1985 CPS.

15 The taxes allocated in the simulation procedure compare with independent estimates of tax liabilities or collections as follows:

	Simulation $bn	Independent estimate $bn
Federal income tax	293.9	302.1
State income taxes	66.6	61.9
Payroll tax on households	115.7	117.3
Property taxes	40.8	43.4
	517.0	524.7

The Australian estimates were also based on a simulation, which resulted in 97 per cent of the revenue collected by government being allocated to households.

The comparisons are made for five *household* types:

1. Married couples with no children under 18;
2. Married couples with children under 18;
3. Female householder, no husband present, with children under 18;
4. Single person households;
5. All other;

and are also made for households in six age groups of the person nominated as 'head', and for households in owned and rented dwellings.

The populations of households (but not of individual types of households) are ranked in ascending order of their before-tax incomes and divided into *deciles*.[16] The distributions of before tax and after tax income in gross income deciles are also compared in the form of 'co-efficients of concentration' for both countries.

The population of households of different types is again expressed in terms of the number of *consumption units*, using the same equivalence ratios as were used in the Swedish comparison.

Estimated *real values* of the average before-tax and after-tax money incomes are also calculated for 'all households', and for 23 household categories (five household types, six ages of household head, two forms of housing occupancy and 10 before-tax income deciles.)

The real values are calculated by converting United States dollars to Australian dollars using OECD estimates of the purchasing power parity of the two currencies in relation to private final consumption expenditure. The same PPP ratio (A$1 = 84 US cents, or $US1 = A$1.19) is used for all household categories. The presentation of the money income estimates in this form does not affect the relativity between average incomes for particular household categories *within* each of the two countries.

Main results

The Australia/United States comparisons in Attachment B are much less comprehensive than the Australia/Sweden comparisons in Attachment A. The

16 Deciles are not identified in the US Census Bureau publication; the decile averages in the Attachment B tables have been calculated by interpretation from tables in the source document. They correspond closely with the quintile averages in a table in the introductory text of the source document.

tables provide some comparable estimates for Australia and the United States relating to all households, classified by type (i.e. household composition), age of head, nature of housing occupancy and gross income decile. A summary table (Table 8) shows direct taxes paid as a percentage of gross income for each of the housing types identified.

Of the five household types distinguished in the estimates in Attachment B, *married couples with children* had the highest incomes in both countries. When the estimates are expressed on a 'per consumption unit' rather than a 'per household' basis, however, *couples without children* had much higher incomes in both countries. The average after-tax real income per consumption unit of married couple households without children was 34 per cent higher than for couples with children in the United States, and 25 per cent higher in Australia (Table B2).

Household type

The proportion of *single parent* households is much higher in the United States than in Australia. For every 100 married couple households with children, the number of female single parent households was 22 in the United States compared with nine in Australia (Table B1). The average income of female single parent households is much lower than the average income of all households in both countries. On a 'per consumption unit' basis, the average after-tax income of such households was 51 per cent of the average for all households in the United States and 68 per cent of the average for all households in Australia (Table B2).

Age of household head

There is a marked difference between Australia and the United States in the relative incomes of the young and the old (Table B4).

Expressed on a 'per person' basis, the average income of Australian *households with heads under 25 years of age* was *higher* than for any other age group, both before tax and after tax. In the United States, by contrast, the average income per person of households with heads under 25 years was *lower* than for any other age group, both before tax and after tax.

On the same 'per person' basis, the average income of Australian *households with heads over 65 years of age* was *second-lowest* of the six age groups distinguished in the study; and the average income of United States households in this age group was *second-highest* of the six age groups.

Nature of housing occupancy

In both countries, the average income of renter households was lower than the average income of owner-occupiers. The per capita after-tax income of households renting the dwellings they occupied was six per cent lower than that of owner-occupiers in Australia, and 26 per cent lower in the United States (Table B5).

Household gross income deciles

When all households were ranked in ascending order of their gross incomes, the share of the 10 per cent of households with the highest gross incomes in total income was about 2.5 percentage points greater in the United States than in Australia. This was true both in 'before tax' and 'after tax' terms (Table B6).

The co-efficient of concentration for *after-tax* incomes of all households in the United States was the same as the corresponding co-efficient for the *before-tax* incomes of all households in Australia.

In Australia the average income after tax per person in the highest household gross income decile exceeded that in the lowest decile in the ratio of 3.4 to 1. The corresponding ratio in the United States was over 10 to 1 (Table B6).

Direct taxes as percentage of income

Federal income tax took a much greater proportion of gross incomes in Australia than in the United States (20 per cent compared with 12 per cent). There were, however, two significant types of direct taxes in the United States which had no counterpart in Australia: state indirect taxes (three per cent of gross income) and payroll taxes levied on employees and the self-employed (five per cent of gross income). With the addition of these taxes, the overall proportion of gross incomes taken in direct taxes was virtually the same in both countries (Table B7).

The proportion of gross incomes paid in all direct taxes was significantly higher in the United States at lower income levels, but much the same in the higher income deciles:

	Australia %	United States %	Difference %
Direct taxes as percentage of gross income in:			
Lowest 10%	3.4	7.1	+3.7
Second decile	3.6	7.1	+3.5
Third decile	5.3	10.4	+5.1
Fourth decile	12.7	13.4	+0.7
Fifth decile	16.1	15.7	-0.4
Sixth decile	18.7	18.2	-0.5
Seventh decile	21.0	19.7	-1.3
Eighth decile	22.4	21.7	-0.7
Ninth decile	23.9	23.7	-0.2
Highest 10%	29.1	28.7	-0.4
Overall average	21.1	21.5	+0.4

Source: Table B8 in Attachment B.

The similarity between the two countries in the proportion of gross income taken in direct taxes in the six highest gross income deciles was also reflected in similar percentages of gross income paid in direct taxes for most household types, for most age groups of household head and for households renting or owning the dwelling they occupied (Table B8).

Because average real household incomes are significantly higher in the United States than in Australia, the similarity in the ratios of direct taxes to gross incomes at given levels of income *defined in relation to the structure of incomes within each country* is not inconsistent with Australian tax/income ratios which were higher at given levels of income *defined in relation to their purchasing power*. The following table shows that, on the latter basis, direct tax rates were two to four percentage points higher in Australia over a wide range of household incomes:

	Australia %	United States %	Difference %
Direct taxes as percentage of gross income, at real gross income of:			
$A15,000	13.2	11.2	-2.0
$A20,000	17.3	14.0	-3.3
$A25,000	20.1	16.2	-3.9
$A30,000	21.8	18.3	-3.5
$A35,000	23.0	19.4	-3.6
$A40,000	24.1	20.6	-3.5

Source: Derived by interpolation from Tables B6 and B7 in Attachment B.

Concluding comments

This paper has shown that there are very substantial differences between Australia, Sweden and the United States in the distribution of household money incomes. Estimates of the relative per capita real income levels for entire populations may not reveal much about the real household incomes of particular groups within a country. There are major differences between countries in the degree of concentration or dispersion of household incomes, both in the aggregate and for groups of households which are relatively homogeneous in terms of family composition and the employment status of household members. Differing structures of cash transfers have an important impact on the distribution of disposable incomes, but differences in the degree of dispersion of private incomes appear to have an even larger influence. Whilst analysis of the distribution of income of all households can go some distance towards identifying the key features of the structure of household incomes, there is no substitute for detailed comparisons at the level of disaggregation undertaken in the Australia/Sweden study reported in this paper.

Attachment A

Australia and Sweden 1984: List of tables

A: Distribution of total household income among households: period income from 1981-82 Income and Housing Survey and current income from 1984 Household Expenditure Survey

All income units

A1: Number, average real private and disposable income, and total real private and disposable income, by age groups

A2: Persons and employed persons per 100 income units, by private income quantiles

A3: Average real income by income quantiles:

(a) Private income, units ranked by private income

(b) Disposable income, units ranked by private income

(c) disposable income, units ranked by disposable income

Income units in 20-64 age group

A4: Number, by income unit type and employment status

A5: Average real private and disposable income, by income unit type and employment status

A6: Average real private income, cash transfers and disposable income, by income unit type

A7: Average real disposable income, by disposable income quantile

With no employed adult

A8: Average real income by income quantiles:

(a) Private income, units ranked by private income unit

(b) Disposable income, units ranked by disposable income unit

With at least one employed adult

A9: Persons, employed persons and consumption units per 100 income units, by private income quantiles:

(a) Married couples without children

(b) Married couples with children

(c) Single parents

(d) Single persons

(e) All income units

A10 Average real private income, by private income quantiles:

(a) Married couples without children

(b) Married couples with children

(c) Single parents

(d) Single persons

(e) All income units

A11: Average real disposable income, by private income quantiles:

(a) Married couples without children

(b) Married couples with children

(c) Single parents

(d) Single persons

(e) All income units

A12: Average real private and disposable income per consumption unit, by private income quantile:

(a) Married couples without children

(b) Married couples with children

(c) Single parents

(d) Single persons

A13: Average disposable income as percentage of average private income, by income unit type and private income quantile

A14: Average real income per consumption unit, (CU) by income unit type and private income quantile, Sweden as % of Australia:

(a) Average real private income per CU

(b) Average real disposable income per CU

Married couple income units without children

A15: One employed: average real income by income quantiles:

(a) Private income, units ranked by private income

(b) Disposable income, units ranked by disposable income

A16: Both employed: average real income by income quantiles:

(a) Private income, units ranked by private income

(b) Disposable income, units ranked by disposable income

A17: All units: average real income by income quantiles:

(a) Private income, units ranked by private income

(b) Disposable income, units ranked by disposable income

A18: One employed: average real income by income quantiles:

(a) Private income, units ranked by private income

(b) Disposable income, units ranked by disposable income

A19: Both employed: average real income by income quantiles

(a) Private income, units ranked by private income

(b) Disposable income, units ranked by disposable income

A20: One child: average real income by income quantiles:

(a) Private income, units ranked by private income

(b) Disposable income, units ranked by disposable income

A21: Two childen: average real income by income quantiles:

(a) Private income, units ranked by private income

(b) Disposable income, units ranked by disposable income

A22: Three children: average real income by income quantiles:

(a) Private income, units ranked by private income

(b) Disposable income, units ranked by disposable income

Single parent income units

A23: All units: average real income by income quantiles:

(a) Private income, units ranked by private income

(b) Disposable income, units ranked by disposable income

A24: Parent employed: average real income by income quantiles:

(a) Private income, units ranked by private income

(b) Disposable income, units ranked by disposable income

Single person income units

A25: Person employed: average real income by income quantiles:

(a) Private income, units ranked by private income

(b) Disposable income, units ranked by disposable income

Income units in 18-19 years of age group

A26: All units: Average real income by income quantiles

(a) Private income, units ranked by private income

(b) Disposable income, units ranked by disposable income

Income units in 65+ age group

A27: All units: average real private income, cash transfers and disposable income

A28: All units, average real income by income quintiles:

(a) Private income, units ranked by private income

(b) Disposable income, units ranked by disposable income

Definitions of terms

A29: Terms used in Australia/Sweden comparisons

Table A Distribution of total household income among households: period income from 1981-82 Income and Housing Survey and current income from 1984 Household Expenditure Survey

% of total household income	% of households		Cumulative % of households	
	1981/82 Income and Housing Survey	1984 HES	1981/82 Income and Housing Survey	1984 HES
5	20.6	19.6	20.6	19.6
10	10.7	11.2	31.3	30.9
15	7.7	8.1	39.0	39.0
20	6.6	6.8	45.6	45.8
25	5.8	6.0	51.4	51.8
30	5.3	5.4	56.7	57.2
35	4.9	4.8	61.5	62.0
40	4.5	4.4	66.0	66.4
45	4.2	4.1	70.2	70.6
50	3.9	3.8	74.1	74.4
55	3.6	3.6	77.1	78.0
60	3.4	3.4	81.1	81.4
65	3.2	3.2	84.3	84.5
70	3.0	2.9	87.3	87.5
75	2.8	2.7	90.0	90.2
80	2.5	2.5	92.6	92.7
85	2.3	2.3	94.9	95.0
90	2.1	2.0	97.0	97.0
95	1.8	1.7	98.8	98.7
100	1.2	1.3	100.0	100.0

Table A1 All income units: number, average real private and disposable income, and total real private and disposable income, by age groups

	Number of income units ('000)	Average private income ($A)	Average disposable income ($A)	Total private income ($Am)	Total disposable income ($Am)
Income units in:					
20-64 age group					
Australia	5,115.7	19,170	16,297	98,068	83,371
Sweden	3,131.8	15,501	13,029	48,546	40,804
18-19 age group					
Australia	435.9	6,299	5,999	2,746	2,615
Sweden	230.0	3,556	3,278	818	754
All under 65 age group					
Australia	5,551.6	18,159	15,489	100,814	85,986
Sweden	3,361.8	14,684	12,362	49,364	41,558
65+ age group					
Australia	1,039.2	4,061	8,473	4,220	8,805
Sweden	1,141.0	2,056	8,209	2,346	9,366
Total					
Australia	6,590.8	15,936	14,382	105,034	94,791
Sweden	4,502.8	11,484	11,309	51,710	50,924

Table A2 All income units; persons and employed persons per 100 income units, by private income quantiles

Private income quantile	Number per 100 income units			
	Persons		Employed persons	
	Australia	Sweden	Australia	Sweden
Lowest 5%	175	123	6	5
Lowest 10%	171	127	6	5
Second decile	157	130	7	3
Third decile	167	134	20	6
Fourth decile	175	132	72	62
Fifth decile	176	148	99	100
Sixth decile	214	156	105	108
Seventh decile	232	179	113	114
Eighth decile	279	252	131	152
Ninth decile	292	287	158	185
Highest 10%	308	290	173	193
Highest 5%	315	294	175	191
Highest 2.5%	307	290	168	189
All income units	217	183	88	93

Table A3 All income units: average real private and disposable income by income quantiles

Income quantile	Average annual income $A'000 Australia	Sweden	As % of total Australia	Sweden
(a) Private income, units ranked by private income				
Lowest 5%	0.0	-0.4	0.0	-0.2
Lowest 10%	0.0	-0.2	0.0	-0.1
Second decile	0.1	0.4	0.1	0.4
Third decile	1.4	1.5	0.9	1.3
Fourth decile	6.9	3.8	4.3	3.3
Fifth decile	12.5	7.4	7.9	6.4
Sixth decile	15.8	11.1	9.9	9.7
Seventh decile	19.3	13.9	12.1	12.1
Eighth decile	24.2	17.9	15.2	15.5
Ninth decile	30.9	23.6	19.3	20.5
Highest 10%	48.4	35.4	30.3	30.9
Highest 5%	58.0	41.9	18.1	18.2
Highest 2.5%	68.7	49.1	10.8	10.7
All income units	16.0	11.5	100.0	100.0
Co-efficient of concentration	*0.504*	*0.520*	*0.504*	*0.520*
(b) Disposable income, units ranked by private income				
Lowest 5%	5.4	5.1	1.9	2.2
Lowest 10%	5.2	5.9	3.6	5.2
Second decile	5.3	6.9	3.7	6.1
Third decile	6.9	6.9	4.8	6.1
Fourth decile	8.2	7.0	5.7	6.2
Fifth decile	11.1	8.8	7.7	7.7
Sixth decile	13.4	9.8	9.3	8.6
Seventh decile	16.0	11.3	11.1	10.0
Eighth decile	19.5	14.7	13.5	13.0
Ninth decile	24.1	18.0	16.7	15.9
Highest 10%	34.4	23.8	23.9	21.2
Highest 5%	39.5	26.9	13.7	11.9
Highest 2.5%	44.4	30.2	7.7	6.7
All income units	14.4	11.3	100.0	100.0
Co-efficient of concentration	*0.335*	*0.259*	*0.335*	*0.259*
(c) Disposable income, units ranked by disposable income				
Lowest 5%	1.3	1.5	0.4	0.7
Lowest 10%	2.7	2.8	1.9	2.5
Second decile	5.2	5.3	3.6	4.7
Third decile	7.4	6.5	5.1	5.7
Fourth decile	9.3	7.7	6.5	6.8
Fifth decile	11.4	8.9	7.9	7.9
Sixth decile	13.6	10.4	9.4	9.2
Seventh decile	16.1	12.7	11.2	11.2
Eighth decile	19.5	15.6	13.6	13.8
Ninth decile	24.1	18.5	16.8	16.4
Highest 10%	34.5	24.7	24.0	21.9
Highest 5%	39.7	27.9	13.8	12.3
Highest 2.5%	44.9	31.6	7.8	7.0
All income units	14.4	11.3	100.0	100.0
Co-efficient of concentration	*0.349*	*0.311*	*0.349*	*0.311*

Table A4 number of income units in 20-64 age group, by income unit type and employment status

	Number of income units		% of income unit type		% of all income units 20-64 years	
	Australia ('000)	Sweden ('000)	Australia %	Sweden %	Australia %	Sweden %
Married couple without children						
0 employed	210.1	33.2	18.8	4.9	4.11	1.06
1 employed	347.3	169.9	31.1	25.1	6.79	5.42
2 employed	559.7	474.4	50.1	70.0	10.94	15.15
Total	1,117.1	677.5	100.0	100.0	21.84	21.63
Of which 1+ employed	907.0	644.3	81.2	95.1	17.73	20.57
Married couple with children						
0 employed	151.3	10.7	8.2	1.2	2.96	0.34
1 employed	844.5	137.9	46.0	16.1	16.51	4.40
2 employed	841.9	708.3	45.8	82.7	16.46	22.61
Total	1,837.7	856.9	100.0	100.0	35.92	27.36
Of which 1+ employed	1,686.5	846.2	91.8	98.8	32.97	27.02
Single parent						
Not employed	189.5	29.8	63.7	14.9	3.70	0.95
Employed	108.2	169.6	36.3	85.1	2.12	5.42
Total	297.7	199.4	100.0	100.0	5.82	6.37
Single person						
Not employed	522.7	264.4	28.1	18.9	10.22	8.44
Employed	1,340.4	1,133.6	71.9	81.1	26.20	36.20
Total	1,863.1	1,398.0	100.0	100.0	36.42	44.64
All income units 20-64						
0 employed	1,973.6	338.1	21.0	10.8	20.99	10.80
1+ employed	4,042.1	2,793.7	79.0	89.2	79.01	89.20
Total	5,115.7	3,131.8	100.0	100.0	100.0	100.0

Table A5 Average real private and disposable income of income units in 20-64 age group by income unit type and employment status

	Private income			Disposable income		
	Australia $A	Sweden $A	A/S %	Australia $A	Sweden $A	A/S %
Married couple without children						
0 Employed	4,594	1,278	359.4	9,896	11,431	86.6
1 employed	22,120	13,751	160.9	17,504	14,057	124.5
2 employed	33,484	25,474	131.4	25,609	18,293	140.0
Total	24,519	21,349	114.8	20,135	16,890	119.2
Of which 1+ employed	29,133	22,376	130.2	22,506	17,182	131.0
Married couple with children						
0 employed	2,337	2,986	78.3	10,585	11,418	92.7
1 employed	22,616	14,598	154.9	18,672	14,821	126.0
2 employed	31,396	24,766	126.8	24,764	19,627	126.2
Total	24,969	22,863	109.2	20,797	18,751	110.9
Of which 1+ employed	26,999	23,113	116.8	21,713	18,849	115.2
Single parent						
Not employed	1,297	986	131.5	7,433	9,737	76.3
Employed	15,004	10,251	146.4	14,100	11,959	117.9
Total	6,280	8,876	70.8	9,857	11,626	84.8
Single person						
Not employed	1,448	1,056	137.1	4,843	5,459	112.7
Employed	16,535	10,973	150.7	12,825	8,403	152.6
Total	12,303	9,098	135.2	10,586	7,848	134.9
All income units 20-64						
0 employed	2,162	1,125	192.2	7,098	6,612	107.4
1+ employed	23,687	17,237	137.4	18,740	13,807	135.7
Total	19,170	15,501	123.7	16,297	13,029	125.1

Table A6 Average real private income, cash transfers and disposable income of income units in 20-64 age group, by income unit type

	Private income	Direct benefits received	Direct taxes paid	Net cash transfers	Disposable income	Disposable income as % of private income
	Average annual value ($A)					%
Married couple without children						
Australia	24,519	+1,336	-5,720	-4,384	20,135	82.1
Sweden	21,349	+3,986	-8,445	-4,459	16,890	79.1
Australia as % of Sweden	114.8				119.2	
Married couple with children						
Australia	24,968	+1,576	-5,748	-4,172	20,796	83.3
Sweden	22,863	+3,611	-7,723	-4,112	18,751	82.0
Australia as % of Sweden	109.2				110.9	
Single parents						
Australia	6,280	+4,809	-1,232	+3,577	9,857	157.0
Sweden	8,876	+5,778	-3,028	+2,750	11,626	131.0
Australia as % of Sweden	70.8				84.8	
Single persons without children						
Australia	12,303	+1,124	-2,841	-1,717	10,586	86.0
Sweden	9,098	+2,472	-3,722	-1,250	7,848	86.3
Australia as % of Sweden	135.2				134.9	
All income units in 20-64 age group						
Australia	19,170	+1,547	-4,420	-2,873	16,297	85.0
Sweden	15,501	+3,320	-5,792	-2,472	13,029	84.1
Australia as % of Sweden	123.7				125.1	

Table A7 All income units in 20-64 age group: average real disposable income, by disposable income quantile

	Average disposable income			
Disposable income quantile	Australia ($A'000)	Sweden ($A'000)	Australia as % of total	Sweden as % of total
Lowest 5%	2.1	2.4	0.6	0.9
Lowest 10%	3.3	3.8	2.0	2.9
Second decile	6.7	6.8	4.1	5.2
Third decile	9.6	8.0	5.9	6.1
Fourth decile	11.8	9.1	7.2	7.0
Fifth decile	13.7	10.7	8.4	8.2
Sixth decile	15.8	13.0	9.7	10.0
Seventh decile	18.4	15.4	11.3	11.8
Eighth decile	21.7	17.6	13.3	13.5
Ninth decile	25.9	20.0	15.9	15.4
Highest 10%	36.1	25.9	22.2	19.9
Highest 5%	41.3	29.0	12.7	11.1
Highest 2.5%	46.6	32.6	7.2	6.2
All income units	16.3	13.0	100.0	100.0
Co-efficient of concentration	*0.314*	*0.278*	*0.314*	*0.278*

Table A8 Income units aged 20-64 with no employed adult: average real private and disposable income by income quantiles

Average annual income				
Income quantile	**Australia $A'000**	**Sweden $A'000**	**Australia as % of total**	**Sweden as % of total**
(a) Private income, units ranked by private income				
Lowest 10%	0.0	-0.1	0.0	-1.0
Second decile	0.0	0.0	0.0	0.0
Third decile	0.0	0.0	0.0	0.1
Fourth decile	0.0	0.1	0.0	1.0
Fifth decile	0.0	0.3	0.0	2.7
Sixth decile	0.1	0.8	0.6	6.8
Seventh decile	0.6	1.3	2.9	11.2
Eighth decile	1.7	1.7	7.9	15.3
Ninth decile	4.9	2.3	22.4	20.9
Highest 10%	14.4	4.8	66.2	43.0
Highest 5%	19.1	6.6	44.2	59.0
All income units	2.2	1.1	100.0	100.0
Co-efficient of concentration	***0.802***	***0.638***	***0.802***	***0.638***
(b) Disposable income, units ranked by disposable income				
Lowest 10%	1.5	1.1	2.1	1.6
Second decile	4.0	2.6	5.6	3.9
Third decile	4.5	4.3	6.3	6.4
Fourth decile	5.0	5.4	7.0	8.2
Fifth decile	5.9	6.1	8.3	9.2
Sixth decile	7.0	6.5	9.9	9.9
Seventh decile	8.0	7.3	11.3	11.1
Eighth decile	9.0	8.3	12.7	12.6
Ninth decile	10.6	10.3	14.9	15.5
Highest 10%	15.5	14.3	21.9	21.6
Highest 5%	18.2	16.2	12.8	12.2
All income units	7.1	6.6	100.0	100.0
Co-efficient of concentration	***0.290***	***0.302***	***0.290***	***0.302***

Table A9 Income units in 20-64 age group with at least one employed adult: persons, employed persons and consumption units per 100 income units, by income unit type and private income quantile

Private income	Number per 100 income units					
	Persons		Employed persons		Consumption units	
	Australia	Sweden	Australia	Sweden	Australia	Sweden
(a) Married couples without children						
Lowest 5%	200	200	138	123	100	100
Lowest 10%	200	200	137	124	100	100
Second decile	200	200	122	133	100	100
Third decile	200	200	133	149	100	100
Fourth decile	200	200	141	165	100	100
Fifth decile	200	200	164	184	100	100
Sixth decile	200	200	177	194	100	100
Seventh decile	200	200	186	196	100	100
Eighth decile	200	200	187	199	100	100
Ninth decile	200	200	188	198	100	100
Highest 10%	200	200	182	190	100	100
Highest 5%	200	200	181	188	100	100
Highest 2.5%	200	200	171	186	100	100
All income units	200	200	162	174	100	100
(b) Married couples with children						
Lowest 5%	404	363	146	142	151	141
Lowest 10%	401	385	144	149	150	146
Second decile	417	390	128	151	154	147
Third decile	408	389	121	171	152	147
Fourth decile	397	383	134	187	149	146
Fifth decile	409	370	140	190	152	143
Sixth decile	398	374	150	196	150	144
Seventh decile	393	375	159	198	148	144
Eighth decile	406	367	167	196	151	142
Ninth decile	405	376	176	198	151	144
Highest 10%	413	377	180	197	153	145
Highest 5%	415	383	175	197	154	146
Highest 2.5%	415	389	168	196	154	147
All income units	405	378	150	183	151	145
(c) Single parents						
Lowest 5%	307	253	100	100	112	98
Lowest 10%	282	245	100	100	106	96
Second decile	275	268	100	100	104	102
Third decile	299	239	100	100	110	95
Fourth decile	245	253	100	100	96	98
Fifth decile	253	251	100	100	98	98
Sixth decile	247	225	100	100	97	91
Seventh decile	270	241	100	100	103	95
Eighth decile	292	225	100	100	108	91

Private income	Number per 100 income units					
	Persons		Employed persons		Consumption units	
	Australia	Sweden	Australia	Sweden	Australia	Sweden
Ninth decile	245	225	100	100	96	91
Highest 10%	280	232	100	100	105	93
Highest 5%	299	225	100	100	110	91
Highest 2.5%	286	228	100	100	107	92
All income units	269	241	100	100	102	95
(d) Single persons						
Lowest 5%	100	100	100	100	60	60
Lowest 10%	100	100	100	100	60	60
Second decile	100	100	100	100	60	60
Third decile	100	100	100	100	60	60
Fourth decile	100	100	100	100	60	60
Fifth decile	100	100	100	100	60	60
Sixth decile	100	100	100	100	60	60
Seventh decile	100	100	100	100	60	60
Eighth decile	100	100	100	100	60	60
Ninth decile	100	100	100	100	60	60
Highest 10%	100	100	100	100	60	60
Highest 5%	100	100	100	100	60	60
Highest 2.5%	100	100	100	100	60	60
All income units	100	100	100	100	60	60
(e) All income units						
Lowest 5%	214	154	116	104		
Lowest 10%	213	143	119	104		
Second decile	190	147	112	105		
Third decile	203	156	110	108		
Fourth decile	230	159	111	109		
Fifth decile	239	181	120	114		
Sixth decile	266	223	123	136		
Seventh decile	289	275	144	169		
Eighth decile	290	291	161	184		
Ninth decile	307	284	170	194		
Highest 10%	313	297	178	194		
Highest 5%	320	294	174	191		
Highest 2.5%	313	296	169	189		
All income units	254	215	135	141		

Table A10 Income units aged 20-64 with at least one employed adult: average real private income, by income unit type and private income quantile

Average annual private income				
Private income quantile	Australia ($A'000)	Sweden ($A'000)	Australia % of total	Sweden % of total
(a) Married couples without children				
Lowest 5%	3.4	2.9	0.6	0.7
Lowest 10%	7.2	5.4	2.4	2.4
Second decile	14.9	11.5	5.1	5.1
Third decile	18.4	14.8	6.4	6.6
Fourth decile	22.4	17.6	7.6	7.9
Fifth decile	26.2	20.3	9.0	9.1
Sixth decile	29.4	23.1	10.0	10.3
Seventh decile	32.7	25.5	11.2	11.4
Eighth decile	36.7	27.9	12.6	12.5
Ninth decile	42.6	31.8	14.5	14.2
Highest 10%	61.2	45.8	21.2	20.5
Highest 5%	71.5	53.6	12.4	12.0
Highest 2.5%	82.2	63.5	7.2	7.1
All income units	29.2	22.4	100.0	100.0
Co-efficient of concentration	*0.278*	*0.268*	*0.278*	*0.268*
(b) Married couples with children				
Lowest 5%	3.4	4.9	0.6	1.1
Lowest 10%	7.1	8.1	2.6	3.5
Second decile	14.7	13.9	5.4	6.0
Third decile	17.3	16.7	6.4	7.2
Fourth decile	20.0	19.0	7.4	8.2
Fifth decile	23.0	21.0	8.6	9.1
Sixth decile	26.1	23.2	9.7	10.1
Seventh decile	29.4	25.3	10.9	10.9
Eighth decile	33.3	27.8	12.3	12.0
Ninth decile	39.5	31.8	14.6	13.8
Highest 10%	59.6	44.2	22.1	19.2
Highest 5%	70.8	50.8	13.3	11.0
Highest 2.5%	85.4	58.3	7.9	6.3
All income units	27.0	23.1	100.0	100.0
Co-efficient of concentration	*0.281*	*0.229*	*0.281*	*0.229*
(c) Single parents				
Lowest 5%	0.8	0.9	0.2	0.4
Lowest 10%	1.4	1.9	0.9	1.8
Second decile	3.5	5.0	2.2	4.9
Third decile	6.8	7.0	4.6	6.9
Fourth decile	10.5	8.4	6.8	8.2
Fifth decile	13.6	9.7	9.4	9.5
Sixth decile	16.6	11.0	10.7	10.7
Seventh decile	18.9	11.9	12.2	11.6
Eighth decile	21.2	13.0	14.4	12.7
Ninth decile	24.5	14.7	16.2	14.3
Highest 10%	33.7	20.0	22.6	19.4

Average annual private income				
Private income quantile	**Australia ($A'000)**	**Sweden ($A'000)**	**Australia % of total**	**Sweden % of total**
Highest 5%	37.0	22.8	12.5	11.1
Highest 2.5%	39.4	25.9	6.8	6.3
All income units	15.1	10.3	100.0	100.0
Co-efficient of concentration	*0.360*	*0.265*	*0.360*	*0.265*
(d) Single persons				
Lowest 5%	1.2	1.7	0.3	0.8
Lowest 10%	3.2	2.8	1.9	2.6
Second decile	9.9	5.2	6.0	4.8
Third decile	12.7	7.1	7.6	6.5
Fourth decile	14.0	8.9	8.5	8.1
Fifth decile	15.1	10.5	9.2	9.6
Sixth decile	16.4	11.7	9.9	10.7
Seventh decile	18.0	12.6	10.9	11.4
Eighth decile	19.9	13.9	12.0	12.7
Ninth decile	23.0	15.5	13.8	14.0
Highest 10%	33.2	21.5	20.2	19.6
Highest 5%	38.8	25.0	11.8	11.4
Highest 2.5%	45.6	29.4	7.0	6.7
All income units	16.5	11.0	100.0	100.0
Co-efficient of concentration	*0.249*	*0.259*	*0.249*	*0.259*
(e) All income units				
Lowest 5%	1.9	1.9	0.4	0.6
Lowest 10%	4.9	3.4	2.1	2.0
Second decile	12.3	7.4	5.2	4.3
Third decile	14.8	10.2	6.2	5.9
Fourth decile	16.8	12.1	7.1	7.0
Fifth decile	19.2	13.9	8.1	8.1
Sixth decile	22.2	16.3	9.4	9.4
Seventh decile	25.9	19.3	10.9	11.2
Eighth decile	30.2	23.2	12.8	13.4
Ninth decile	36.1	27.3	15.2	15.8
Highest 10%	54.5	39.2	23.0	22.9
Highest 5%	64.7	45.9	13.7	13.3
Highest 2.5%	76.7	53.3	8.1	7.7
All income units	23.7	17.2	100.0	100.0
Co-efficient of concentration	*0.304*	*0.320*	*0.304*	*0.320*

Table A11 Income units in 20-64 age group with at least one employed adult: average real disposable income, by income unit type and private income quantile

Average annual disposable income				
Private income quantile	Australia $A'000	Sweden $A'000	Australia As % of total	Sweden As % of total
(a) Married couples without children				
Lowest 5%	6.5	10.1	1.4	2.9
Lowest 10%	8.6	11.6	3.8	6.7
Second decile	13.2	12.8	5.9	7.5
Third decile	15.5	13.7	7.0	8.0
Fourth decile	18.2	14.4	8.0	8.4
Fifth decile	20.9	15.5	9.3	9.0
Sixth decile	23.0	16.8	10.2	9.8
Seventh decile	25.4	18.1	11.3	10.5
Eighth decile	28.0	19.7	12.4	11.4
Ninth decile	31.5	21.5	13.8	12.5
Highest 10%	40.9	27.7	18.3	16.2
Highest 5%	45.9	31.6	10.3	9.2
Highest 2.5%	50.2	35.4	5.7	5.2
All income units	22.5	17.2	100.0	100.0
Co-efficient of concentration	*0.224*	*0.145*	*0.224*	*0.145*
(b) Married couples with children				
Lowest 5%	6.0	10.5	1.4	2.8
Lowest 10%	8.6	12.3	4.0	6.5
Second decile	13.9	14.6	6.4	7.8
Third decile	15.5	15.9	7.1	8.4
Fourth decile	17.5	17.0	8.0	9.0
Fifth decile	19.4	17.4	9.0	9.2
Sixth decile	21.4	18.9	9.9	10.0
Seventh decile	23.5	19.9	10.8	10.6
Eighth decile	26.2	21.0	12.1	11.1
Ninth decile	30.2	22.9	13.9	12.3
Highest 10%	40.8	28.4	18.8	15.1
Highest 5%	46.2	31.2	10.8	8.3
Highest 2.5%	52.7	34.7	6.1	4.6
All income units	21.7	18.8	100.0	100.0
Co-efficient of concentration	*0.220*	*0.128*	*0.220*	*0.128*
(c) Single parents				
Lowest 5%	7.4	10.3	2.5	4.3
Lowest 10%	7.9	9.3	5.5	7.8
Second decile	8.0	9.9	5.5	8.3
Third decile	10.0	10.8	7.2	9.1
Fourth decile	11.1	11.2	7.6	9.4

Average annual disposable income				
Private income quantile	Australia $A'000	Sweden $A'000	Australia As % of total	Sweden As % of total
Fifth decile	12.8	11.6	9.5	9.7
Sixth decile	14.3	12.2	9.8	10.2
Seventh decile	16.4	12.4	11.2	10.4
Eighth decile	17.7	12.4	13.0	10.4
Ninth decile	19.1	13.8	13.4	11.3
Highest 10%	24.2	16.0	17.3	13.4
Highest 5%	25.8	16.9	9.3	7.1
Highest 2.5%	26.5	18.3	4.9	3.8
All income units	14.1	12.0	100.0	100.0
Co-efficient of concentration	*0.203*	*0.081*	*0.203*	*0.081*
(d) Single persons				
Lowest 5%	3.1	5.5	1.2	3.3
Lowest 10%	4.2	5.6	3.3	6.6
Second decile	8.4	6.3	6.5	7.6
Third decile	10.3	6.7	8.0	8.0
Fourth decile	11.3	7.6	8.7	9.1
Fifth decile	12.0	7.8	9.4	9.3
Sixth decile	13.0	8.7	10.2	10.4
Seventh decile	14.1	8.6	11.0	10.2
Eighth decile	15.4	9.3	12.0	11.0
Ninth decile	17.2	10.3	13.4	12.3
Highest 10%	22.5	13.1	17.5	15.5
Highest 5%	25.3	14.7	9.9	8.7
Highest 2.5%	28.5	16.6	5.7	4.9
All income units	12.8	8.4	100.0	100.0
Co-efficient of concentration	*0.204*	*0.132*	*0.204*	*0.132*
(e) All income units				
Lowest 5%	4.7	6.5	1.2	2.3
Lowest 10%	6.4	6.8	3.4	4.9
Second decile	10.8	8.5	5.7	6.2
Third decile	12.6	9.3	6.7	6.7
Fourth decile	14.2	10.1	7.6	7.3
Fifth decile	15.9	11.4	8.5	8.2
Sixth decile	18.0	13.3	9.6	9.6
Seventh decile	20.7	15.6	11.0	11.3
Eighth decile	23.6	17.7	12.6	12.8
Ninth decile	27.6	19.9	14.7	14.4
Highest 10%	37.7	25.5	20.2	18.6
Highest 5%	42.7	28.3	11.4	10.3
Highest 2.5%	48.1	31.6	6.4	5.7
All income units	18.8	13.8	100.0	100.0
Co-efficient of concentration	*0.255*	*0.225*	*0.255*	*0.225*

Table A12 Income units in 20-64 age group with at least one employed adult: average real private and disposable income per consumption unit, by income unit type and private income quantile

Average annual income per consumption unit ($A'000)				
Private income quantile	Private income		Disposable income	
	Australia	Sweden	Australia	Sweden
(a) Married couples without children				
Lowest 5%	3.4	2.9	6.5	10.1
Lowest 10%	7.2	5.4	8.6	11.6
Second decile	14.9	11.5	13.2	12.8
Third decile	18.4	14.8	15.5	13.7
Fourth decile	22.4	17.6	18.2	14.4
Fifth decile	26.2	20.3	20.9	15.5
Sixth decile	29.4	23.1	23.0	16.8
Seventh decile	32.7	25.5	25.4	18.1
Eighth decile	36.7	27.9	28.0	19.7
Ninth decile	42.6	31.8	31.5	21.5
Highest 10%	61.2	45.8	40.9	27.7
Highest 5%	71.5	53.6	45.9	31.6
Highest 2.5%	82.2	63.5	50.2	35.4
All income units	29.2	22.4	22.5	17.2
(b) Married couples with children				
Lowest 5%	2.3	3.5	3.9	7.5
Lowest 10%	4.7	5.5	5.7	8.4
Second decile	9.5	9.4	9.0	9.9
Third decile	11.4	11.4	10.2	10.8
Fourth decile	13.4	13.0	11.7	11.6
Fifth decile	15.1	14.7	12.8	12.2
Sixth decile	17.4	16.2	14.3	13.2
Seventh decile	19.8	17.6	15.9	13.8
Eighth decile	22.0	19.6	17.3	14.8
Ninth decile	26.1	22.0	19.9	15.9
Highest 10%	38.9	30.6	26.6	19.7
Highest 5%	46.0	34.9	30.0	21.4
Highest 2.5%	55.6	39.5	34.3	23.5
All income units	17.9	16.0	14.4	13.0
(c) Single parents				
Lowest 5%	0.8	0.9	6.6	10.5
Lowest 10%	1.4	1.9	7.5	9.7
Second decile	3.4	4.9	7.7	9.8
Third decile	6.3	7.4	9.1	11.4

Average annual income per consumption unit ($A'000)				
Private income quantile	Private income		Disposable income	
	Australia	Sweden	Australia	Sweden
Fourth decile	10.9	8.5	11.6	11.4
Fifth decile	13.7	9.9	13.1	11.9
Sixth decile	17.2	12.0	14.1	13.3
Seventh decile	18.3	12.5	16.9	13.0
Eighth decile	19.7	14.3	16.5	13.6
Ninth decile	25.6	16.1	19.9	15.1
Highest 10%	32.0	21.5	23.1	17.2
Highest 5%	33.7	25.0	23.5	18.5
Highest 2.5%	36.9	28.2	24.9	19.9
All income units	14.7	10.8	13.8	12.6
(d) Single persons				
Lowest 5%	1.9	2.8	5.2	9.2
Lowest 10%	5.3	4.7	7.0	9.3
Second decile	16.5	8.7	14.0	10.6
Third decile	21.1	11.9	17.2	11.2
Fourth decile	23.3	14.8	18.8	12.7
Fifth decile	25.1	17.5	20.0	13.1
Sixth decile	27.4	19.6	21.6	14.5
Seventh decile	30.0	20.9	23.5	14.3
Eighth decile	33.2	22.2	25.7	15.6
Ninth decile	38.3	25.8	28.6	17.2
Highest 10%	55.4	35.8	37.5	21.8
Highest 5%	64.7	41.7	42.1	24.4
Highest 2.5%	76.0	48.8	47.5	27.6
All income units	27.6	18.3	21.4	14.0

Table A13 Income units in 20-64 age group with at least one employed adult: average disposable income as % of average private income, by income unit type and private income quantile

Disposable income as % of private income						
Private income quantile		Married couples without children	Married couples with children	Single parents	Single persons	All units
Lowest 5%	Australia	189.7	174.6	925.0	268.7	247.0
	Sweden	346.7	214.2	1,144.0	324.5	342.0
Lowest 10%	Australia	119.8	121.3	564.0	132.3	130.6
	Sweden	214.4	152.2	489.0	197.0	200.4
Second decile	Australia	88.2	94.5	235.0	84.6	87.8
	Sweden	111.5	105.1	198.0	121.2	114.9
Third decile	Australia	84.3	89.8	147.0	81.5	84.9
	Sweden	92.4	95.0	154.2	94.4	91.2
Fourth decile	Australia	81.5	87.3	105.9	80.5	84.3
	Sweden	81.6	89.2	133.4	85.9	83.5
Fifth decile	Australia	79.7	84.4	94.3	80.1	82.9
	Sweden	76.2	82.9	119.5	74.5	81.8
Sixth decile	Australia	78.5	82.1	86.5	79.1	81.3
	Sweden	72.9	81.5	110.7	74.1	81.6
Seventh decile	Australia	78.0	80.1	86.6	78.2	79.7
	Sweden	71.0	78.6	104.4	68.1	80.8
Eighth decile	Australia	76.2	78.7	83.6	77.2	78.0
	Sweden	70.4	75.3	95.2	66.9	76.4
Ninth decile	Australia	73.8	76.4	77.8	74.7	76.4
	Sweden	67.6	72.2	93.7	66.6	72.8
Highest 10%	Australia	66.9	68.5	71.7	67.7	69.1
	Sweden	60.5	64.3	80.2	60.8	65.1
Highest 5%	Australia	64.2	65.2	69.7	65.2	66.0
	Sweden	59.0	61.4	74.2	58.5	61.7
Highest 2.5%	Australia	61.1	61.7	67.4	62.5	62.8
	Sweden	55.8	59.5	70.8	56.6	59.3
All income units	Australia	77.2	80.4	93.3	77.6	79.3
	Sweden	76.8	81.5	116.7	76.6	80.1

Table A14 Income units in 20-64 age group with at least one employed adult: average real private and disposable income per consumption unit (CU) by income unit type and private income quantile, Sweden as % of Australia

Private income quantile	Married couples without children	Married couples with children	Single parents	Single persons
	Sweden as % of Australia			
(a) Average real private income per CU				
Lowest 5%	85.3	152.2	112.5	147.4
Lowest 10%	75.0	117.0	135.7	88.7
Second decile	77.1	99.2	144.1	52.9
Third decile	80.6	99.9	117.5	56.4
Fourth decile	78.7	97.0	78.0	63.5
Fifth decile	77.7	97.4	72.3	69.7
Sixth decile	78.5	92.8	69.9	71.5
Seventh decile	78.3	88.7	68.3	69.8
Eighth decile	76.2	89.2	72.4	66.9
Ninth decile	74.5	84.6	62.9	67.2
Highest 10%	74.8	78.7	67.2	64.6
Highest 5%	74.9	75.8	74.1	64.5
Highest 2.5%	77.3	71.1	76.2	64.2
All income units	76.7	89.4	73.0	66.4
(b) Average real disposable income per CU				
Lowest 5%	155.0	192.3	159.1	178.0
Lowest 10%	134.9	147.4	129.3	132.7
Second decile	97.4	110.4	127.3	75.8
Third decile	88.4	105.7	125.4	65.3
Fourth decile	78.8	99.1	98.0	67.8
Fifth decile	74.3	95.8	90.8	65.2
Sixth decile	72.9	92.0	94.3	67.0
Seventh decile	71.2	87.0	93.4	60.8
Eighth decile	70.4	85.4	82.4	60.7
Ninth decile	68.3	79.8	75.7	59.9
Highest 10%	67.7	73.9	74.3	58.0
Highest 5%	68.9	71.1	78.9	58.0
Highest 2.5%	70.6	68.6	80.1	58.2
All income units	76.3	90.3	91.3	65.5

Table A15 Married couple income units without children, one employed: average real private and disposable income by income quantiles

Income quantile	Average annual income $A'000 Australia	Sweden	As % of total Australia	Sweden
(a) Private income, units ranked by private income				
Lowest 10%	3.9	2.0	1.7	1.6
Second decile	11.5	5.4	5.2	4.1
Third decile	14.5	7.1	6.6	5.5
Fourth decile	16.1	8.9	7.3	6.8
Fifth decile	17.9	10.8	8.0	8.2
Sixth decile	20.3	12.4	9.2	9.5
Seventh decile	23.2	14.1	10.5	10.8
Eighth decile	26.5	16.1	11.8	12.3
Ninth decile	32.0	18.4	14.5	14.1
Highest 10%	55.8	35.3	25.2	27.0
Highest 5%	70.0	48.8	15.7	18.7
All income units	22.2	13.1	100.0	100.0
Co-efficient of concentration	*0.314*	*0.347*	*0.314*	*0.347*
(b) Disposable income, units ranked by disposable income				
Lowest 10%	7.9	6.9	4.4	4.7
Second decile	11.3	10.1	6.4	6.9
Third decile	13.0	11.4	7.2	7.7
Fourth decile	13.9	12.5	7.9	8.5
Fifth decile	15.4	13.5	8.8	9.2
Sixth decile	16.9	14.3	9.4	9.7
Seventh decile	18.6	15.3	10.6	10.4
Eighth decile	20.5	16.4	11.6	11.2
Ninth decile	23.8	17.9	13.4	12.2
Highest 10%	35.6	28.3	20.3	19.3
Highest 5%	42.5	36.3	12.0	12.4
All income units	17.7	14.7	100.0	100.0
Co-efficient concentration	*0.222*	*0.194*	*0.222*	*0.194*

Table A16 Married couple income units without children, both employed: average real private and disposable income by income quantiles

Income quantile	Average annual income			
	$A'000		As % of total	
	Australia	Sweden	Australia	Sweden
(a) Private income, units ranked by private income				
Lowest 10%	8.7	9.6	2.6	3.8
Second decile	19.7	16.3	6.0	6.4
Third decile	25.3	19.1	7.7	7.6
Fourth decile	28.1	21.5	8.4	8.5
Fifth decile	30.8	23.7	9.4	9.4
Sixth decile	33.3	25.5	10.0	10.1
Seventh decile	36.3	27.4	10.9	10.8
Eighth decile	40.2	29.4	12.1	11.6
Ninth decile	45.6	33.6	13.6	13.3
Highest 10%	63.0	47.0	19.3	18.6
Highest 5%	72.0	54.4	10.9	10.7
All income units	33.1	25.3	100.0	100.0
Co-efficient of concentration	*0.234*	*0.208*	*0.234*	*0.208*
(b) Disposable income, units ranked by disposable income				
Lowest 10%	8.9	9.9	3.5	5.4
Second decile	16.6	14.0	6.5	7.7
Third decile	20.6	15.2	8.1	8.3
Fourth decile	22.5	16.4	8.8	9.0
Fifth decile	24.5	17.3	9.7	9.4
Sixth decile	26.1	18.3	10.3	10.0
Seventh decile	28.1	19.3	11.1	10.5
Eighth decile	30.3	20.9	11.9	11.4
Ninth decile	33.7	22.8	13.3	12.5
Highest 10%	42.6	29.0	16.8	15.8
Highest 5%	46.8	32.4	9.2	8.9
All income units	25.4	18.3	100.0	100.0
Co-efficient of concentration	*0.194*	*0.148*	*0.194*	*0.148*

Table A17 Married couple income units with children: average real private and disposable income by income quantile

Income quantile	Average annual income			
	$A'000		% of total	
	Australia	Sweden	Australia	Sweden
(a) Private income, units ranked by private income				
Lowest 10%	0.9	6.7	0.3	2.9
Second decile	10.8	13.6	3.9	5.9
Third decile	15.7	16.5	5.6	7.2
Fourth decile	18.5	18.8	6.6	8.3
Fifth decile	21.6	20.8	7.7	9.1
Sixth decile	24.9	23.1	8.9	10.1
Seventh decile	28.3	25.2	10.1	11.0
Eighth decile	32.4	27.7	11.6	12.1
Ninth decile	38.4	31.6	13.6	13.9
Highest 10%	58.3	44.2	31.7	19.4
Highest 5%	69.5	50.8	13.9	11.1
All income units	25.0	22.8	100.0	100.0
Co-efficient of concentration	*0.393*	*0.239*	*0.393*	*0.239*
(b) Disposable income, units ranked by disposable income				
Lowest 10%	7.2	9.8	3.5	5.2
Second decile	12.1	14.0	5.8	7.5
Third decile	14.6	15.6	7.0	8.3
Fourth decile	16.5	16.7	8.0	9.0
Fifth decile	18.5	17.8	8.9	9.5
Sixth decile	20.6	19.0	9.9	10.1
Seventh decile	22.9	20.1	11.0	10.7
Eighth decile	25.6	21.4	12.3	11.4
Ninth decile	29.5	23.5	14.1	12.6
Highest 10%	40.3	29.5	19.5	15.8
Highest 5%	45.8	32.9	11.0	8.8
All income units	20.8	18.7	100.0	100.0
Co-efficient of concentration	*0.239*	*0.151*	*0.239*	*0.151*

Table A18 Married couple income units with children, one employed: average real private and disposable incomes by income quantiles

Income quantile	Average annual income: $A'000 Australia	$A'000 Sweden	% of total Australia	% of total Sweden
(a) Private income, units ranked by private income				
Lowest 10%	6.6	1.9	2.9	1.3
Second decile	13.9	8.3	6.2	5.7
Third decile	15.9	11.4	7.0	7.8
Fourth decile	17.5	12.7	7.7	8.7
Fifth decile	19.4	13.6	8.6	9.4
Sixth decile	21.7	14.6	9.6	10.1
Seventh decile	24.2	15.8	10.6	10.8
Eighth decile	27.1	17.3	12.0	11.9
Ninth decile	31.7	19.8	14.0	13.6
Highest 10%	48.2	30.0	21.4	20.6
Highest 5%	58.6	36.7	13.0	12.6
All Income Units	22.6	14.5	100.0	100.0
Co-efficient of concentration	*0.256*	*0.257*	*0.256*	*0.257*
(b) Disposable income, units ranked by disposable income				
Lowest 10%	8.5	6.3	4.6	4.2
Second decile	13.1	11.3	7.0	7.6
Third decile	14.6	12.4	7.8	8.4
Fourth decile	15.7	13.4	8.4	9.0
Fifth decile	17.1	14.2	9.1	9.5
Sixth decile	18.5	15.1	9.9	10.1
Seventh decile	19.9	16.0	10.7	10.8
Eighth decile	21.7	17.1	11.4	11.5
Ninth decile	24.4	19.0	13.3	12.8
Highest 10%	33.1	23.8	17.8	16.0
Highest 5%	38.4	26.7	10.3	9.0
All income units	18.7	14.9	100.0	100.0
Co-efficient of concentration	*0.188*	*0.165*	*0.188*	*0.165*

Table A19 Married couple income units with children, both employed: average real private and disposable incomes by income quantiles

Income quantile	Average annual income: In $A'000		% of total	
	Australia	Sweden	Australia	Sweden
(a) Private income, units ranked by private income				
Lowest 10%	7.7	10.6	2.4	4.3
Second decile	16.6	16.4	5.3	6.6
Third decile	21.2	18.9	6.7	7.6
Fourth decile	25.0	20.7	8.0	8.3
Fifth decile	28.1	22.7	9.0	9.2
Sixth decile	31.1	24.5	9.9	9.9
Seventh decile	34.3	26.4	11.0	10.7
Eighth decile	38.6	28.9	12.2	11.7
Ninth decile	45.3	33.0	14.5	13.3
Highest 10%	66.0	45.4	21.0	18.3
Highest 5%	79.1	51.9	12.6	10.5
All income units	31.4	24.8	100.0	100.0
Co-efficient of concentration	*0.269*	*0.202*	*0.269*	*0.202*
(b) Disposable income, units ranked by disposable income				
Lowest 10%	8.4	11.7	3.4	6.0
Second decile	15.2	15.3	6.1	7.8
Third decile	18.4	16.6	7.5	8.4
Fourth decile	21.1	17.5	8.5	8.9
Fifth decile	23.1	18.6	9.3	9.5
Sixth decile	25.1	19.6	10.2	10.0
Seventh decile	27.2	20.7	11.0	10.5
Eighth decile	30.0	22.0	12.1	11.2
Ninth decile	34.1	24.1	13.8	12.3
Highest 10%	44.8	30.1	18.1	15.4
Highest 5%	51.3	33.5	10.4	8.5
All income units	24.7	19.6	100.0	100.0
Co-efficient of concentration	*0.218*	*0.135*	*0.218*	*0.135*

Table A20 Married couple income units with one child: average real private and disposable income by income quantiles

Income quantile	Average annual income: $A'000 Australia	$A'000 Sweden	% of total Australia	% of total Sweden
(a) Private income, units ranked by private income				
Lowest 10%	0.3	5.7	0.1	2.5
Second decile	7.8	13.2	3.3	5.8
Third decile	14.5	16.4	6.0	7.3
Fourth decile	17.9	18.9	7.6	8.4
Fifth decile	20.8	20.8	8.7	9.2
Sixth decile	24.5	22.9	10.2	10.1
Seventh decile	28.1	25.3	11.8	11.2
Eighth decile	32.0	27.8	13.4	12.3
Ninth decile	37.5	31.6	15.7	14.0
Highest 10%	55.5	43.3	23.2	19.2
Highest 5%	65.6	48.9	13.7	10.8
All income units	23.9	22.6	100.0	100.0
Co-efficient of concentration	*0.348*	*0.242*	*0.348*	*0.242*
(b) Disposable income, units ranked by disposable income				
Lowest 10%	6.3	9.4	3.1	5.2
Second decile	10.3	13.6	5.2	7.5
Third decile	13.5	14.9	6.8	8.3
Fourth decile	15.7	16.1	7.9	8.9
Fifth decile	17.7	17.2	9.0	9.5
Sixth decile	20.0	18.3	10.1	10.1
Seventh decile	22.4	19.6	11.3	10.8
Eighth decile	25.1	20.9	12.5	11.5
Ninth decile	28.7	22.9	14.6	12.6
Highest 10%	38.6	28.1	19.5	15.5
Highest 5%	43.4	30.9	10.9	8.5
All income units	19.8	18.1	100.0	100.0
Co-efficient of concentration	*0.253*	*0.152*	*0.253*	*0.152*

Table A21 Married couple income units with two children: average real private and disposable income by income quantiles

Income quantile	Average annual income: $A'000 Australia	$A'000 Sweden	% of total Australia	% of total Sweden
(a) Private income, units ranked by private income				
Lowest 10%	2.9	7.7	1.1	3.3
Second decile	13.3	14.2	5.2	6.1
Third decile	16.3	17.2	6.4	7.4
Fourth decile	19.2	19.6	7.5	8.4
Fifth decile	22.2	21.6	8.7	9.3
Sixth decile	25.2	23.7	9.9	10.2
Seventh decile	28.1	25.4	10.9	10.9
Eighth decile	31.9	28.0	12.5	12.0
Ninth decile	38.2	31.7	15.0	13.7
Highest 10%	58.4	43.4	22.8	18.7
Highest 5%	69.2	49.6	13.5	10.7
All income units	25.6	23.2	100.0	100.0
Co-efficient of concentration	*0.306*	*0.223*	*0.306*	*0.223*
(b) Disposable income, units ranked by disposable income				
Lowest 10%	7.8	9.5	3.7	5.0
Second decile	13.0	14.2	6.2	7.6
Third decile	14.8	15.8	7.1	8.4
Fourth decile	16.8	16.9	8.0	9.0
Fifth decile	18.8	18.0	9.0	9.6
Sixth decile	20.6	19.1	9.9	10.1
Seventh decile	22.7	20.0	10.8	10.7
Eighth decile	25.2	21.4	12.1	11.4
Ninth decile	29.1	23.5	14.0	12.5
Highest 10%	40.1	29.4	19.2	15.7
Highest 5%	45.6	32.9	10.9	8.8
All income units	20.9	18.8	100.0	100.0
Co-efficient of concentration	*0.228*	*0.150*	*0.228*	*0.150*

Table A22 Married couple income units with three children: average real private and disposable income by income quantiles

Income quantile	Average annual income			
	$A'000		% of total	
	Australia	Sweden	Australia	Sweden
(a) Private income, units ranked by private income				
Lowest 10%	1.4	8.4	0.5	3.6
Second decile	12.5	13.5	4.8	5.8
Third decile	16.6	16.4	6.3	7.1
Fourth decile	19.3	17.9	7.2	7.7
Fifth decile	22.6	19.5	8.5	8.4
Sixth decile	25.8	22.3	9.7	9.6
Seventh decile	30.2	24.8	11.6	10.7
Eighth decile	34.3	27.4	12.8	11.8
Ninth decile	40.3	32.2	14.9	13.9
Highest 10%	61.0	49.6	23.7	21.4
Highest 5%	73.2	60.5	13.8	13.0
All income units	26.4	23.2	100.0	100.0
Co-efficient of concentration	*0.327*	*0.251*	*0.327*	*0.251*
(b) Disposable income, units ranked by disposable income				
Lowest 10%	7.7	11.7	3.5	5.8
Second decile	13.1	15.1	6.0	7.5
Third decile	15.6	16.5	7.0	8.1
Fourth decile	17.7	17.7	7.9	8.8
Fifth decile	19.6	18.9	9.0	9.4
Sixth decile	21.7	20.0	9.8	9.9
Seventh decile	24.5	21.2	11.1	10.5
Eighth decile	27.3	22.8	12.3	11.3
Ninth decile	31.1	25.0	14.0	12.4
Highest 10%	42.4	33.0	19.4	16.3
Highest 5%	48.3	38.4	10.9	9.5
All income units	22.1	20.2	100.0	100.0
Co-efficient of concentration	*0.237*	*0.150*	*0.237*	*0.150*

Table A23 All single parent income units: average real private and disposable income by income quantiles

Income quantile	Average annual income			
	$A'000		% of total	
	Australia	Sweden	Australia	Sweden
(a) Private income, units ranked by private income				
Lowest 10%	0.0	0.0	0.0	0.0
Second decile	0.0	1.7	0.0	1.9
Third decile	0.0	4.2	0.0	4.8
Fourth decile	0.1	6.7	0.2	7.6
Fifth decile	1.2	8.4	1.8	9.5
Sixth decile	2.3	10.0	3.4	11.3
Seventh decile	5.3	11.3	8.4	12.8
Eighth decile	10.4	12.5	16.5	14.2
Ninth decile	17.5	14.1	27.0	16.0
Highest 10%	27.1	19.3	42.7	21.9
Highest 5%	31.3	22.1	24.4	12.5
All income units	6.4	8.8	100.0	100.0
Co-efficient of concentration	*0.682*	*0.360*	*0.682*	*0.360*
(b) Disposable income, units ranked by disposable income				
Lowest 10%	4.0	5.8	4.0	5.0
Second decile	6.2	8.5	6.2	7.3
Third decile	6.6	9.8	6.6	8.4
Fourth decile	7.2	10.5	7.2	9.1
Fifth decile	7.9	11.0	8.1	9.5
Sixth decile	8.8	11.7	8.8	10.1
Seventh decile	10.0	12.5	10.1	10.7
Eighth decile	12.1	13.4	12.1	11.6
Ninth decile	15.6	14.8	15.7	12.8
Highest 10%	21.0	17.9	21.2	15.5
Highest 5%	23.2	19.7	11.7	8.5
All income units	9.9	11.6	100.0	100.0
Co-efficient of concentration	*0.257*	*0.154*	*0.257*	*0.154*

Table A24 Single parent income units, parent employed: average real private and disposable income by income quantiles

Income quantile	Average annual income			
	$A'000		% of total	
	Australia	Sweden	Australia	Sweden
(a) Private income, units ranked by private income				
Lowest 10%	1.4	1.8	0.9	1.7
Second decile	3.4	5.0	2.2	4.9
Third decile	6.8	7.0	4.6	6.8
Fourth decile	10.4	8.3	6.7	8.2
Fifth decile	13.5	9.7	9.4	9.5
Sixth decile	16.5	11.0	10.7	10.7
Seventh decile	18.8	12.0	12.1	11.6
Eighth decile	21.1	13.0	14.5	12.7
Ninth decile	24.3	14.7	16.2	14.3
Highest 10%	33.5	19.9	22.7	19.5
Highest 5%	37.0	22.8	12.3	11.1
All income units	15.1	10.2	100.0	100.0
Co-efficient of concentration	*0.360*	*0.268*	*0.360*	*0.268*
(b) Disposable income, units ranked by disposable income				
Lowest 10%	6.1	6.8	4.3	5.7
Second decile	8.8	9.2	6.2	7.7
Third decile	10.1	10.2	6.8	8.5
Fourth decile	11.2	10.8	8.1	9.0
Fifth decile	12.8	11.2	9.3	9.4
Sixth decile	14.6	11.9	10.6	10.0
Seventh decile	16.1	12.6	10.8	10.6
Eighth decile	17.9	13.6	13.2	11.4
Ninth decile	19.2	14.9	13.2	12.5
Highest 10%	24.0	18.1	17.7	15.2
Highest 5%	25.8	20.0	9.1	8.4
All income units	14.1	11.9	100.0	100.0
Co-efficient of concentration	*0.212*	*0.139*	*0.212*	*0.139*

Table A25 Single person income units, person employed: average real private and disposable income by income quantiles

Income quantile	Average annual income			
	$A'000		% of total	
	Australia	Sweden	Australia	Sweden
(a) Private income, units ranked by private income				
Lowest 10%	2.5	2.7	1.6	2.6
Second decile	8.0	4.7	5.3	4.4
Third decile	10.6	6.3	7.0	6.1
Fourth decile	12.6	8.0	8.2	7.6
Fifth decile	14.0	9.7	9.2	9.3
Sixth decile	15.3	11.3	10.1	10.8
Seventh decile	16.9	12.3	11.1	11.7
Eighth decile	18.8	13.6	12.3	13.0
Ninth decile	21.9	15.2	14.3	14.5
Highest 10%	31.9	21.0	20.9	20.0
Highest 5%	37.4	24.4	12.3	11.7
All income units	15.3	10.5	100.0	100.0
Co-efficient of concentration	*0.273*	*0.276*	*0.273*	*0.276*
(b) Disposable income, units ranked by disposable income				
Lowest 10%	3.8	3.5	3.1	4.4
Second decile	7.2	5.3	6.0	6.6
Third decile	8.9	6.6	7.4	8.1
Fourth decile	10.3	7.3	8.5	9.0
Fifth decile	11.3	7.8	9.4	9.7
Sixth decile	12.2	8.3	10.2	10.2
Seventh decile	13.3	8.8	11.1	10.8
Eighth decile	14.7	9.5	12.2	11.7
Ninth decile	16.6	10.4	13.8	12.9
Highest 10%	21.8	13.4	18.3	16.6
Highest 5%	24.6	15.2	10.3	9.4
All income units	12.0	8.1	100.0	100.0
Co-efficient of concentration	*0.223*	*0.178*	*0.223*	*0.178*

Table A26 Income units in 18-19 years of age group: average real private and disposable income by income quantiles

Income quantile	Average annual income $A'000 Australia	$A'000 Sweden	% of total Australia	% of total Sweden
(a) Private income, units ranked by private income				
Lowest 10%	0.0	0.0	0.0	0.0
Second decile	0.0	0.8	0.0	2.1
Third decile	0.0	1.4	0.0	4.0
Fourth decile	0.8	2.0	1.3	5.5
Fifth decile	5.6	2.5	8.9	7.0
Sixth decile	8.2	3.0	13.2	8.5
Seventh decile	9.5	4.0	15.4	11.3
Eighth decile	10.5	4.8	16.7	13.4
Ninth decile	11.7	6.8	19.0	19.0
Highest 10%	15.8	10.4	25.5	29.2
Highest 5%	17.5	12.1	14.2	17.0
All income units	6.2	3.6	100.0	100.0
Co-efficient of concentration	*0.493*	*0.446*	*0.493*	*0.446*
(b) Disposable income, units ranked by disposable income				
Lowest 10%	0.0	0.4	0.0	1.2
Second decile	0.5	1.2	0.8	3.6
Third decile	3.1	1.7	5.1	5.2
Fourth decile	4.2	2.2	6.9	6.8
Fifth decile	6.0	2.7	10.1	8.1
Sixth decile	7.2	3.2	12.1	9.9
Seventh decile	8.1	3.7	13.3	11.2
Eighth decile	8.8	4.4	14.7	13.4
Ninth decile	9.7	5.7	16.0	17.5
Highest 10%	12.5	7.6	21.0	23.1
Highest 5%	13.7	8.3	11.6	12.7
All income units	6.0	3.3	100.0	100.0
Co-efficient of concentration	*0.364*	*0.352*	*0.364*	*0.352*

Table A27 Average real private income, cash transfers and disposable income of income units in 65+ age group

	Private income	Direct benefits received	Direct taxes paid	Net cash transfers	Disposable income	Disposable income as % of private income
	Average annual value ($A)					%
Married couples 65+						
Australia	6,182	+6,389	-1,204	+5,185	11,367	183.9
Sweden	3,506	+12,912	-4,751	+8,161	11,667	332.8
Australia as % of Sweden	*176.3*				*97.4*	
Single persons 65+						
Australia	2,377	+4,339	-558	+3,781	6,158	259.1
Sweden	1,201	+6,896	-1,925	+4,971	6,172	513.9
Australia as % of Sweden	*197.9*				*99.8*	
All income units in 65+ age group						
Australia	4,061	+5,256	-844	+4,402	8,463	208.4
Sweden	2,056	+9,126	-2,973	+6,153	8,209	399.3
Australia as % of Sweden	*162.1*				*103.1*	

Table A28 Income units in 65 years+ age group: average real private and disposable income by income quantiles

Income quantile	Average annual income			
	$A'000		% of total	
	Australia	Sweden	Australia	Sweden
Private income, units ranked by private income				
Lowest 10%	0.0	-0.1	0.0	-0.5
Second decile	0.0	0.0	0.0	0.1
Third decile	0.0	0.2	0.1	0.8
Fourth decile	0.2	0.3	0.4	1.6
Fifth decile	0.4	0.5	1.1	2.6
Sixth decile	0.9	0.9	2.1	4.2
Seventh decile	1.6	1.3	3.8	6.3
Eighth decile	3.0	1.9	7.4	9.5
Ninth decile	8.4	3.5	20.7	17.0
Highest 10%	26.1	12.0	64.4	58.4
Highest 5%	35.4	17.8	43.7	43.2
All income units	4.1	2.1	100.0	100.0
Co-efficient of concentration	*0.772*	*0.708*	*0.772*	*0.708*
Disposable income, units ranked by disposable income				
Lowest 5%	3.3	3.8	2.0	2.3
Lowest 10%	3.9	4.1	4.6	5.0
Second decile	4.7	4.9	5.6	5.9
Third decile	5.0	5.5	5.9	6.6

Fourth decile	5.4	5.9	6.4	7.2
Fifth decile	6.6	6.6	7.8	8.0
Sixth decile	7.9	7.6	9.3	9.2
Seventh decile	8.6	8.8	10.1	10.7
Eighth decile	9.7	10.0	11.5	12.1
Ninth decile	11.7	11.7	13.8	14.2
Highest 10%	21.0	17.2	25.0	21.1
Highest 5%	26.1	20.6	15.7	12.6
Highest 2.5%	31.8	25.4	9.5	7.7
All income units	8.5	8.2	100.0	100.0
Co-efficient of concentration	*0.281*	*0.242*	*0.281*	*0.242*

Table A29 Terms used in Australia/Sweden comparisons

	As used in tables 'Australia and Sweden 1984'	As used in Income Distribution Survey publications of Statistics Sweden
Income concepts	Private income Direct benefits received Direct taxes paid Disposable income	Factor income Positive transfers Negative transfers Disposable income
Income unit (IU)	Income unit *20-64 age group*:Married couple without children Married couple with children Single parents Single persons without children *65+ age group*:Married couple Single persons *18-19 age group*	Family unit *20-64 age group*:Cohabitants without children Cohabitants with children Single person with children Single persons without children *65+ age group*:Cohabitants Single persons *18-19 age group*
	Note: 'Married couple' includes both legal and defacto relationships as identified by survey respondents. 'Children' are persons under 18 years.	
Consumption unit (CU)	Married couple = 1 CU Single person = 0.6 CU Children = 0.25 CU	
Employment status	Income unit with: 0 employed 1 employed 2 employed 1+ employed	Family unit: Economically inactive With 1 economically active With 2 economically active Economically active
Incomes, benefits and taxes	Average weekly values for Australian income units from the ABS Household Expenditure Survey 1984 are converted to annual levels by multiplying by 52. Average annual values for Swedish 'family units', as given in Income Distribution Survey publications for 1984, are converted to $A assuming a PPP ratio of SKr 7.2 = $A1. Note: Employment of children (persons under 18 years) is disregarded in assessing the employment status of income units.	

Attachment B

Australia and United States 1984: List of tables

B: Distribution of total household income among households: period income from combined data from the Annual Housing Survey, the Income Survey Development Program and the Internal Revenue Service, as well as the March 1985 Current Population Survey (CPS) conducted by the Bureau of the Census, and current income from Australian 1984 Household Expenditure Survey.

All households

By household type

B1 Numbers of households, persons and consumption units

B2 Average real income before and after tax per household and consumption unit

By age of household head

B3 Numbers of households and persons

B4 All households: Average real income before and after tax per household and per person

By nature of housing occupancy

B5 Numbers of households and persons, and average real income fefore and after tax

By household gross income deciles

B6 Average real income before and after tax per household and per person

B7 Direct taxes as % of gross incomes, by type of tax

Direct taxes

B8 Direct taxes as % of gross income, by household type, age of household head, nature of housing occupancy and household gross income decile

Definitions of terms

B9 Terms used in Australia/United States comparisons

Table B1 All households: numbers of households, persons and consumption units, by household type

	Australia	United States
Number of households ('000)	**5,039**	**86,789**
Of which –	%	%
Married couples with no children under 18	30.6	29.2
Married couples with children under 18	36.5	28.8
Female householder, no husband present, with children under 18	4.5	7.9
Single person households	19.I	23.7
All other	9.3	10.4
	100.0	100.0
Number of persons in households ('000)	**14,291**	**233,516**
Of which in households consisting of –	%	%
Married couples with no children under 18	24.8	25.8
Married couples with children under 18	54.9	45.2
Female householder, no husband present, with children under 18	4.9	10.0
Single person households	6.7	8.8
All other	8.7	10.2
	100.0	100.0
Number of consumption units in households ('000)	**6,378**	**108,452**
Of which in households consisting of –	%	%
Married couples with no children under 18	28.4	28.7
Married couples with children under 18	47.2	38.5
Female householder, no husband present, with children under 18	4.4	8.8
Single person households	9.0	11.4
All other	10.9	12.6
	100.0	100.0

Table B2 All households: average real income before and after tax per household and consumption unit, by household type

	Australia	United States
Average real income per household before tax:	**$A23,587**	**$A32,683**
Ratio: Average for all households = 100 –		
Married couples with no children under 18	107.0	123.7
Married couples with children under 18	121.0	125.6
Female householder, no husband present, with children under 18	60.2	51.6
Single person households	49.5	55.8
All other	117.5	100.0

	Australia	United States
Average real income per household after tax:	**$A18,617**	**$A5,664**
Ratio: Average for all households = 100 –		
Married couples with no children under 18	107.2	122.7
Married couples with children under 18	119.2	124.5
Female householder, no husband present, with children under 18	67.1	56.8
Single person households	49.7	56.3
All other	119.9	101.0
Average real income per consumption unit before tax:	**$A18,636**	**$A26,157**
Ratio: Average for all households = 100 –		
Married couples with no children under 18	115.1	125.6
Married couples with children under 18	93.5	94.1
Female householder, no husband present, with children under 18	61.4	46.2
Single person households	104.3	116.2
All other	100.6	82.6
Average real income per consumption unit after tax:	**$A14,709**	**$A20,538**
Ratio: Average for all households = 100 –		
Married couples with no children under 18	115.4	124.6
Married couples with children under 18	92.1	93.2
Female householder, no husband present, with children under 18	68.4	50.8
Single persons households	104.9	117.2
All other	**102.7**	**83.5**

Table B3 All households: numbers of households and persons, by age of household head

	Australia	United States
Number of households ('000)	**5,039**	**86,789**
Of which age of household head:	%	%
Under 25 years	6.8	6.3
25-34 years	22.4	23.1
35-44 years	20.8	20.1
45-54 years	15.0	14.5
55-64 years	16.0	15.1
65 years and over	19.0	20.9
	100.0	100.0
Number of persons in households ('000)	**14,291**	**233,516**
Of which in households with head aged:	%	%
Under 25 years	5.5	5.4
25-34 years	24.5	24.5
35-44 years	28.5	25.9
45-54 years	17.2	17.0
55-64 years	12.8	13.4
65 years and over	11.5	13.8
	100.0	100.0

Table B4 All households: average real income before and after tax per household and per person, by age of household head

	Australia	United States
Average real income per household before tax	**$A23,587**	**$A32,683**
Ratio: Average for all households = 100 –		
Under 25 years	94.0	60.6
25-34 years	108.0	95.3
35-44 years	119.3	121.6
45-54 years	134.0	131.1
55-64 years	92.8	111.1
65 years and over	50.6	66.6
Average real income per household after tax	**$A18,617**	**$A25,664**
Ratio: Average for all households = 100 –		
Under 25 years	95.9	63.6
25-34 years	106.3	95.2
35-44 years	116.4	118.7
45-54 years	130.7	127.2
45-64 years	94.8	108.7
65 years and over	56.0	73.0
Average real income per person before tax	**$A8,305**	**$A12,150**
Ratio: Average income per person before tax = 100 –		
Under 25 years	117.4	70.1
25-34 years	99.00	89.6
35-44 years	87.1	94.5
45-54 years	117.0	112.0
55-64 years	115.1	125.5
65 years and over	83.4	101.1
Average real income per person after tax	**$A6,565**	**$A9,541**
Ratio: Average income per person after tax = 100 –		
Under 25 years	119.8	73.6
25-34 years	97.4	89.5
35-44 years	81.1	92.2
45-54 years	114.2	108.7
55-64 years	117.6	122.7
65 years and over	92.4	110.9

Table B5 All households: numbers of households and persons, and average real income before and after tax per household and per person, by nature of housing occupancy

	Australia	United States
Number of households ('000)	**5,039**	**86,789**
Of which –	%	%
Dwelling owned outright or being bought	71.5	64.3
Dwelling rented or occupied rent free	28.5	35.7
	100.0	100.0
Number of persons in households ('000)	**14,291**	**233,516**
Of which –		
Dwelling owned outright or being bought	73.7	68.1
Dwelling rented or occupied rent free	26.3	31.9
	100.0	100.0
	$A	$A
Average real income per household before tax	**$A23,587**	**$A32,683**
Ratio: Average for all households = 100 –		
Households in owned dwellings	105.5	116.7
Households in rented dwellings	86.1	69.8
Average real income per household after tax	**$A86,617**	**$A25,664**
Ratio: Average for all households = 100 –		
Households in owned dwellings	104.8	115.3
Households in rented dwellings	88.1	71.9
Average real income per person before tax	**$A8,305**	**$A12,150**
Ratio: Average before tax income per person = 100 –		
Persons in owned dwellings	102.6	110.3
Persons in rented dwellings	93.4	78.0
Average real income per person after tax	**$A6,565**	**$A9,541**
Ratio: Average after tax income per person = 100 –		
Persons in owned dwellings	101.7	109.0
Persons in rented dwellings	95.3	80.8

Table B6 All households: average real income before and after tax per household and per person, by household gross income deciles

	Australia	United States
Average real income per household before tax	**$A23,587**	**$A32,683**
Ratio: Average for all households = 100 –		
Lowest 10%	19	12
Second decile	32	27
Third decile	44	42
Fourth decile	61	57
Fifth decile	77	73
Sixth decile	94	91
Seventh decile	114	110
Eighth decile	137	136
Ninth decile	167	173
Highest 10%	255	279
Co-efficient of concentration	0.370	0.407
Average real income per household after tax	**$A18,617**	**$A25,664**
Ratio: Average for all households = 100 –		
Lowest 10%	23	14
Second decile	40	33
Third decile	53	48
Fourth decile	68	63
Fifth decile	82	78
Sixth decile	97	94
Seventh decile	114	113
Eighth decile	134	136
Ninth decile	161	168
Highest 10%	228	253
Co-efficient of concentration	0.325	0.370
Average real income per person before tax	**$A8,305**	**$A12,150**
Ratio: Average income before tax per person = 100 –		
Lowest 10%	41	17
Second decile	45	36
Third decile	48	49
Fourth decile	64	64
Fifth decile	72	75
Sixth decile	86	86
Seventh decile	102	100
Eighth decile	212	117
Ninth decile	142	143
Highest 10%	190	223
Average real income per person after tax	**$A6,565**	**$A9,541**
Ratio: Average income after tax per person = 100 –		
Lowest 10%	50	20
Second decile	55	43
Third decile	57	56
Fourth decile	70	70
Fifth decile	77	80
Sixth decile	89	90
Seventh decile	102	102
Eighth decile	119	117
Ninth decile	137	139
Highest 10%	170	202

Table B7 All households: direct taxes as percentage of gross incomes, by type of tax and gross income decile

	Federal income tax	State income taxes	Payroll taxes on households	Property taxes	All direct taxes
	%	%	%	%	%
Lowest 10%					
Australia	0.4	-	-	3.0	3.4
United States	0.3	0.2	1.8	4.8	7.1
Second decile					
Australia	1.7	-	-	1.9	3.6
United States	1.2	0.4	2.5	3.0	7.1
Third decile					
Australia	3.8	-	-	1.5	5.3
United States	3.5	0.9	3.7	2.3	10.4
Fourth decile					
Australia	11.6	-	-	1.1	12.7
United States	5.7	1.3	4.3	2.1	13.4
Fifth decile					
Australia	15.0	-	-	1.1	16.1
United States	7.4	1.7	4.8	1.8	15.7
Sixth decile					
Australia	17.8	-	-	0.9	18.7
United States	9.0	2.1	5.3	1.8	18.2
Seventh decile					
Australia	20.2	-	-	0.8	21.0
United States	10.0	2.6	5.4	1.7	19.7
Eighth decile					
Australia	21.6	-	-	0.8	22.4
United States	11.5	2.8	5.7	1.7	21.7
Ninth decile					
Australia	23.2	-	-	0.7	23.9
United States	13.9	3.2	5.1	1.5	23.7
Highest 10%					
Australia	28.6	-	-	0.5	29.1
United States	18.7	4.0	4.6	1.4	28.7
All households					
Australia	20.2	-	-	0.9	21.1
United States	12.1	2.8	4.9	1.7	21.5

Table B8 All households: direct taxes as % of gross income, by household type, age of household head, nature of housing occupancy and household gross income decile

	Australia %	United States %
Household type:		
Married couple with no children under 18	20.9	22.2
Married couple with children under 18	22.2	22.2
Female householder, no husband present, with children under 18	12.0	13.7
Single person households	20.6	20.8
All other	19.4	20.7
All households	21.1	21.5
Age of household head:		
Under 25 years	19.5	17.5
25-34 years	22.4	21.6
35-44 years	22.9	23.4
45-54 years	23.0	23.8
55-64 years	19.4	23.2
65 years and over	12.6	13.9
All households	21.1	21.5
Nature of housing occupancy:		
Owned outright or being bought	21.7	22.4
Rented or occupied rent free	19.3	19.1
All households	21.1	21.5
Gross income decile:		
Lowest 10%	3.4	7.1
Second decile	3.6	7.1
Third decile	5.3	10.4
Fourth decile	12.7	13.4
Fifth decile	16.1	15.7
Sixth decile	18.7	18.2
Seventh decile	21.0	19.7
Eighth decile	22.4	21.7
Ninth decile	23.9	23.7
Highest 10%	29.1	28.7
All households	21.1	21.5

Table B9 Terms used in Australia/United States comparisons

<table>
<tr><th></th><th>As used in tables 'Australia and United States 1984'</th><th>As used in ABS Household Expenditure Survey 1984: The Effects of Government Benefits and Taxes on Household Income</th></tr>
<tr><td rowspan="2">Income</td><td>Before-tax income
Direct taxes
After tax income</td><td>Gross income
Direct taxes plus expenditure on general rates from HES
Disposable income less expenditure on general rates from HES</td></tr>
<tr></tr>
<tr><td rowspan="2">Household</td><td>Households:
Married couple with no children under 18
Married couple with children under 18
Female householder, no husband present, with children under 18
Single person households
All other</td><td>Households:
Married couple only
Married couple with children under 18
Single parent: female, with children under 18
Single person households
All other (than households Included above)</td></tr>
<tr><td colspan="2">Note: United States Census Bureau estimates, which are for married couples and female householders with no related children under 18, have not been adjusted.
ABS estimates for married couples or single parents with dependent children (see description in The Effects of Government Benefits and Taxes on Household Income: 79) have been adjusted to include all persons under 18 years of age in households.</td></tr>
<tr><td>Consumption unit (CU)</td><td colspan="2">Married couple = 1 CU
Single person = 0.6 CU
Children = 0.25 CU</td></tr>
<tr><td>Incomes, benefits and taxes</td><td colspan="2">Average weekly values for Australian income units from the ABS Household Expenditure Survey 1984 are converted to annual levels by multiplying by 52.
Average annual values for US households, as given in US bureau of the Census After-Tax Money Income Estimates of Households: 1984, are converted to $A assuming a PPP ratio of $US0.84 = $A1.</td></tr>
</table>

21. Living Standards in Sydney and Japanese Cities: A Comparison[1]

Ian Castles[2]

In the *Report on the Economy* (the *Economic White Paper*) for the fiscal year 1988, the Economic Planning Agency of the Japanese Government devoted a chapter to 'Issues for Enriching Livelihood of the People'.[3] After noting that Japan's *per capita* income was the world's highest and that 'In the broad view, it can be said that Japan has achieved affluence', the Report went on:

> However, the people's view diverges somewhat. Even when we account for the people's desire for improvement by always seeking something better, conditions have not reached a state where the people are satisfied and have a sense of adequacy.

The foreword to the same *Report* by the minister responsible for the Agency included the comment that, although Japan was an affluent country

> It cannot be denied...that in our day-to-day living we cannot get the full feeling of the affluence. Much needs to be improved in such areas of daily living as food, housing and working hours.

In Australia's case, much concern has been expressed in recent years that, over the longer term, average living standards have fallen in relation to those in other countries. For example, the following comments were made by three different eminent observers at a symposium in 1984:

> ...Australia has slipped down the international league table of income per head, from equal first a century ago to a position below most of Western Europe and Japan now.
>
> Why then does Australia, once at the top in living standards, now rank only sixteenth?
>
> Australia will have to struggle to recapture that degree of relative affluence that it enjoyed up to the final quarter of the nineteenth century.[4]

---

1 First published in October 1990 as a mimeograph by the Australian Bureau of Statistics. Later published as a chapter in Kyoko Sheridan (ed), 1992, *The Australian Economy in the Japanese Mirror,* University of Queensland Press. Except where otherwise indicated, all figures and tables in this chapter are Castles' own.

2 Australian Statistician, Canberra, October 1990.

3 Japan, Economic Planning Agency, *Report on the Economy FY (1988)*. Toyko: 179.

4 Australia: the Daedalus Symposium, Sydney, (1985). The comments are made in essays by Hugh Stretton (199), Gordon Jackson (255) and Bruce Williams (291).

The comparisons which provide the basis for these comments, and those in the Japanese Economic Planning Agency report, are national accounting estimates of real *per capita* expenditure or product. These estimates are subject to important limitations when used as indicators of living standards, because they are essentially concerned with *market* transactions.

This paper compares the living standards and modes of living in four Japanese prefectures with those in Sydney. The comparisons are based largely, although not entirely, on statistics compiled by the Statistics Bureau, Management and Co-ordination Agency, Japan and by the Australian Bureau of Statistics (ABS).[5] Although the comparisons are restricted to specific geographical areas within the two countries, they are not confined to those aspects of living standards which are measured in the national accounts. They therefore provide a more comprehensive basis for the assessment of relative living standards than the conventional national accounting framework.

The Japanese cities and Sydney

The four Japanese prefectures chosen for the comparison are Tokyo-to, Kanagawa-ken, Kyoto-fu and Osaka-fu.[6] They had a combined population in 1988 of 31 million, or just over one-quarter of the total population of Japan.

The prefecture of Tokyo-to has a population of almost 12 million of which over 70% live in the city (ku-area) of Tokyo. The daytime population of the ku-area is even greater, because of the large numbers of workers who commute to the city from the remainder of the prefecture and the adjoining prefectures.

One of these is Kanagawa-ken, which has a population of almost eight million. Most people in Kanagawa live in the cities of Yokohama and Kawasaki.

Kyoto-fu has a population of more than 2.5 million, most of whom reside in the city (shi) of Kyoto.

Osaka-fu has a population of over 8.5 million, of which about 30 per cent live in Osaka-shi and most of the remainder in densely populated neighbouring areas.

Sydney is Australia's largest city, and the capital of the most populous state, New South Wales. In 1988, the Sydney Statistical Division, which extends beyond the urban area, had a population of 3.6 million. This was over 60 per cent of the

5 The range of collections and the depth of detail in the publication of results by the Japanese Statistics Bureau are most impressive. Japan is perhaps the only country whose published statistics alone would provide support for comparisons at the level of detail attempted in this paper.

6 The suffixes will generally be omitted except where they are necessary to distinguish the prefectures from the cities with the same name.

population of New South Wales and more than 20 per cent of Australia's total population. Although there are some important differences, the standard and modes of living of people in Sydney can be regarded as broadly representative of those in Australia's major urban centres.

Comparisons of population density

One important pointer to an understanding of the vast difference in modes of living between the Japanese cities and Sydney is the fact that, in relation to population, Sydney occupies a far greater area. Details of area, population and population density are summarised in Table 1.

An examination of that Table 1 shows that:

- Although the area of the Sydney Statistical Division is greater than the combined area of the four Japanese prefectures, the population in the division at the 1986 Australian census was only about *one-tenth* of the population in these prefectures at the 1985 census of Japan.
- The population of the ku-area of Tokyo was almost *six times* as great as that of a group of contiguous inner Sydney statistical subdivisions with a combined area only slightly smaller than that of the ku-area of Tokyo.
- The population of a group of contiguous districts within Osaka-shi was almost *five times* as great as that of Sydney's most densely populated statistical subdivision (Eastern suburbs), which has an area almost as great as these districts of Osaka.

The far greater area of land space *per capita* in Sydney, by comparison with the Japanese cities, is both the outcome of different modes of living in the past and the cause of different modes of living in the present. The differences extend to almost all aspects of the way people live – in their homes and workplaces, and how they travel from one to the other; in shops and public buildings, and their immediate environs; and in private and public recreational spaces and the ways in which they are used.

Table 1 Sydney and four Japanese prefectures: area, population and density of population

	Area sq km	Population ('000)	% of Population	Population per sq km
Sydney statistical division				
Inner Sydney	73.04	258.5	7.7	3,540
Eastern Suburbs	58.09	226.5	6.7	3,900
Canterbury-Bankstown	109.99	280.1	8.3	2,546
Inner West	49.48	148.6	4.4	3,004
Central Western	133.29	256.2	7.6	1,922
Lower Northern	98.60	258.2	7.7	2,619
Total selected statistical subdivisions	522.49	1,428.2	42.4	2,733
Total statistical division	12,154.30	3,364.9	100.0	277
Tokyo-to				
Selected Districts	420.92	6,473.1	54.7	15,378
Total Ku-area	597.89	8,354.6	70.6	13,973
Total Tokyo-to	2,162.34	11,829.4	100.0	5,471
Kanagawa-Ken				
Yokohama-shi	430.75	2,992.9	40.3	6,948
Kawasaki-shi	136.47	1,088.6	14.6	7,977
Total Kanagawa-ken	2,402.07	7,432.0	100.0	3,094
Kyoto-fu				
Kyoto-shi	610.61	1,479.2	57.2	2,423
Total Kyoto-fu	4,612.90	2,586.6	100.0	561
Osaka-fu				
Selected districts	59.65	1,081.9	12.5	18,138
Total Osaka-shi	213.08	2.636.2	30.4	12,372
Total Osaka-fu	1,867.86	8,668.1	100.0	4,641

Source: The table shows the 1986 Census populations of Sydney statistical division and of six contiguous statistical subdivisions within the division; and the 1985 Census populations of the four Japanese prefectures, five cities within the ku-area of Tokyo and within Osaka-shi.The selected districts of Tokyo are those numbered 104-120 in *Population of Tokyo-to, 1985 Population Census of Japan, Abridged Report Series No. 2*, and the selected districts of Osaka are those numbered 115-122 in *Population of Osaka-fu* in the same series.

These differences are not readily captured in statistics. One revealing indication is from household expenditure survey results, which show that in 1988 the spending on rents for car parking by households in Tokyo-to and Osaka-shi was considerably greater than their expenditures on petrol. In Sydney, by contrast, household spending on petrol in 1988-89 exceeded that on parking fees by a margin of more than 40 to 1. These comparisons demonstrate the extent to which expenditure patterns can be influenced by the availability and cost of space. They also highlight the limitations of inter-country comparisons of living standards which rely on the conversion of expenditures into a common currency.

Comparisons of the use of time

Another pointer to an understanding of the differences between Sydney and the Japanese cities is in the differing ways in which people use their time.

Statistical information on this subject is available from the *Survey of Time Use and Leisure Activities*[7] in Japan in 1986 (following similar surveys in 1976 and 1981) and from the *Time Use Pilot Survey*[8] conducted by the ABS in Sydney in May-June 1987. Although the relative size of the sample in the Sydney survey was much smaller than in the Japanese prefectures, it was large enough to give a broad indication of the patterns of time use between major types of activities.

The differences in the pattern of time use between Sydney and the Japanese centres are exhibited in Table 2.

Table 2 Sydney and four Japanese prefectures: use of time by all persons aged 15 years and over

	Sydney	Tokyo	Kanagawa	Kyoto	Osaka
	Hours per week				
Primary activities	75.4	73.4	72.1	73.1	72.7
Sleep	*59.9*	*54.2*	*53.3*	*54.5*	*53.9*
Personal care	*4.9*	*7.2*	*7.4*	*7.2*	*7.2*
Meals	*10.6*	*12.0*	*11.4*	*11.4*	*11.6*
Labour force work	**21.1**	**29.8**	**28.4**	**30.9**	**30.7**
Education	3.6	4.2	4.1	4.7	4.2
Commuting	4.0	5.0	6.1	4.0	4.9
Housework	18.3	14.8	16.5	15.6	15.6
Housekeeping	*11.9*	*10.6*	*11.9*	*11.5*	*11.3*
Childcare	*3.3*	*1.4*	*1.7*	*1.6*	*1.6*
Shopping	*3.1*	*2.8*	*2.9*	*2.5*	*2.7*
Tertiary activities	45.6	40.8	40.8	39.7	39.9
Total	168.0	168.0	168.0	168.0	168.0

7 Japan, Statistics Bureau, Management and Co-ordination Agency. T*he Survey on Time and Use and Leisure Activities 1986*.

8 Australian Bureau of Statistics, *Information Paper: Time Use Pilot Survey* (ABS Catalogue 4111.1).

The classification of activities used in Table 2 is based primarily upon that used in the Japanese Survey, which is explained by the Statistics Bureau in the following terms:

> Activities are grouped into 3 broad areas, called 'primary activities', 'secondary activities', and 'tertiary activities'. Primary activities refer to those which are physiologically necessary, and consists of 'sleep', 'meals' and 'personal care'. Secondary activities comprise those which each person is committed to perform as a member of a family or of the society. Included are 'work (for pay or profit)', 'studies and researches (in connection with academic education)', 'commuting to work or school', 'housekeeping', 'child care', and 'shopping'. These activities may be regarded as socially obligatory activities. From another point of view, they represent production activities in a broad sense. Tertiary activities include all other activities such as 'hobbies and amusements', 'sports', etc. Time spent in tertiary activities corresponds to what is usually called 'free time'.[9]

There are three aspects of this classification which need some explanation. Firstly, the boundary between primary and tertiary activities is not always clear-cut. Although it is physiologically necessary that a certain amount of time be devoted to activities such as sleeping and eating, it is not the case that all of the time which people devote to these activities is physiologically necessary. On the contrary, much of the time spent on a leisurely meal, for example, could be regarded as 'free time'.

Secondly, the boundary between secondary and tertiary activities is also not clear-cut. It can be argued, for example, that gardening and home maintenance activities are unpaid household work rather than 'free time' activities. In the Japanese time use survey, however, 'gardening' and 'do it yourself carpenter' are explicitly identified as falling within the 'hobbies and amusements' classification of activities.

Thirdly, some of the apparent differences between Sydney and the Japanese prefectures may arise from variations in the particular form of the questions asked and the guidance given to respondents. For example, the greater number of hours apparently allocated to child care in Sydney may reflect the fact that, in the Sydney survey, 'child care/minding', included any activity 'where it is necessary for the respondent to remain in the vicinity of the child but not necessarily to interact with him/her (e.g. where a child is sleeping or playing in another room while the respondent performs other activities elsewhere)'.[10]

---

9 *The Survey on Time Use..., Whole Japan, Time Spent on Activities (1)*: 18.

10 ABS, *Time Use Pilot Survey* (ABS Catalogue No. 4111.1): 75.

These qualifications having been made, it is obvious from Table 2 that there is a striking difference between Australia and Japan in the amount of time devoted to 'labour force work'. This was higher in the Japanese prefectures than in Sydney by proportions ranging from 35 per cent (Kanagawa) to 46 per cent (Kyoto).

It must be emphasised that the table shows the average weekly hours devoted to various activities by *all* persons aged 15 and over. Thus the average number of hours allocated to labour force work and to commuting by employed persons was much greater than the average for all persons which is shown in the table. Conversely, people who were not in the paid labour force devoted much more time, on average, to housework and tertiary activities.

Another aspect of the comparison deserves special mention. The proportion of children in the total population is significantly higher in Sydney than in the Japanese prefectures. In 1988, the proportion of the population aged under 15 years was 21.4 per cent in Sydney, compared with less than 19 per cent in Kanagawa, Kyoto and Osaka and 16.1 per cent in Tokyo. This means that the difference between Sydney and the Japanese prefectures in the amount of labour force work per head of the total population is even greater than shown in Table 2. Applying the 1988 population figures to the 1986 and 1987 time use survey results, the indicated average hours of labour force work per head of the *total* population (the concept which would be most appropriate in the context of the international comparisons of per capita incomes) was greater than in Sydney by 39 per cent in Kanagawa and by 50 per cent or more in Tokyo, Kyoto and Osaka.

The detailed time use survey results show that the large difference between the two countries in the time devoted to labour force work has several components.

First, the *working day* in Japan is, on average, considerably longer. This is illustrated in Table 3 which shows, for Sydney and the four Japanese prefectures, the proportion of the population at work at specified hours on a weekday. The table shows that at 8am the proportion of people already at work was somewhat greater in Sydney than in the Japanese prefectures. By 10am, however, the proportion of the adult population at work was higher in the Japanese centres by seven to ten percentage points. By 4pm this difference had widened to between 17 and 21 percentage points, and at 6pm and 8pm the proportion of persons who were working was around twice as great as in Sydney.

A second component of the difference in working hours was the far greater amount of labour force work which was undertaken in Japan at *weekends*. Taking an average of all males over 15 years of age, whether working or not, the time spent at work on Saturday in the Japanese prefectures ranged from less than five hours in Kanagawa to almost six hours in Osaka. These working hours on Saturday are comparable with average hours in Sydney on a weekday.

Table 3 Sydney and four Japanese prefectures: labour force work on weekdays

	Sydney	Tokyo	Kanagawa	Kyoto	Osaka
Percentage engaged in labour force work					
Morning					
8am	21.9	15.2	16.6	19.3	20.4
10am	40.4	49.3	47.1	49.8	50.6
Afternoon					
2pm	39.6	50.1	48.0	50.7	50.6
4pm	29.4	48.6	46.7	50.5	48.8
Evening					
6pm	9.8	24.9	21.5	25.1	23.3
8pm	4.7	11.0	9.0	10.7	10.0

Source: The table shows proportion of persons over 15 years of age engaged in labour force work at the specified hours on weekdays.

For the weekend as a whole, males worked an average of 7-8 hours in the Japanese prefectures, compared with 2 hours 20 minutes in Sydney; and females worked an average of 3-4 hours in the Japanese prefectures, compared with only one hour in Sydney.

Finally, the *working life* in Japan is much longer, with far more labour force work being done by people over 60 years of age. This is brought out in some detail in Tables 4 and 5 which show, for males and females respectively, the average hours devoted to each of the main activities in each of five age groups.

Table 4 shows, for example, that males aged 60-64 years worked an average of only about 16 hours in Sydney, compared with 30 hours in Kanagawa, 32 hours in Osaka, 35 hours in Tokyo and 41 hours in Kyoto. On average, males aged 65 and over worked less than one hour per week in Sydney, compared with 12 hours in Kanagawa, 16 hours in Osaka, 17 hours in Tokyo and 21 hours in Kyoto. In relative terms, the differences between Sydney and the Japanese prefectures in the amount of labour force work done by older women was even greater.

Taking men and women together, and using the average hours worked in the 40-59 years age group in each city-prefecture as the 'normal' for adult workers, the estimates of hours worked in the 60-64 years and 65 years and over age groups imply the equivalent of a standard retirement age of around 62 years in Sydney, compared with 66 years in Kanagawa and Osaka, 67 years in Tokyo and 69 years in Kyoto.

A comparison of Tables 4 and 5 reveals other important differences in modes of living between Sydney and the Japanese centres. It shows, for example, that whilst housework (including child care and shopping) occupied far more of women's time than of men's in Sydney, the difference between the sexes was very much greater in the Japanese prefectures.

Table 4 Sydney and four Japanese prefectures: use of time by males

	Sydney	Tokyo	Kanagawa	Kyoto	Osaka
Average hours per week of all males in age group					
Primary activities					
15-24 yrs	76.1	71.1	69.4	70.0	70.1
25-39	72.2	69.6	68.9	70.8	69.9
40-59 yrs	73.9	72.6	70.9	71.5	71.9
60-64 yrs	75.0	76.2	77.0	75.9	75.1
65 yrs & over	83.0	84.2	83.8	82.7	80.8
Labour force work					
15-24 yrs	24.0	21.5	24.1	19.0	24.2
25-39 yrs	36.9	53.7	51.8	53.6	53.2
40-59 yrs	35.8	51.3	49.4	53.5	52.2
60-64 yrs	16.3	35.4	29.9	41.2	32.5
65 yrs & over	0.9	17.0	11.8	21.2	16.3
Education					
15-24 yrs	16.4	19.9	19.8	26.4	21.8
Commuting					
15-24 yrs	6.3	7.8	9.0	6.4	8.0
25-39 yrs	5.8	7.8	9.4	5.6	7.6
40-59 yrs	5.5	6.9	9.5	6.0	6.9
60-64 yrs	3.3	4.3	4.9	4.9	4.0
65 yrs & over	0.2	1.7	1.5	1.7	1.6
Housework					
15-24 yrs	4.2	1.3	1.4	0.8	1.0
25-39 yrs	10.3	1.9	2.3	1.8	1.9
40-59 yrs	8.7	1.6	1.8	1.7	1.5
65 yrs & over	13.8	5.2	5.9	4.0	3.6
Tertiary activities					
15-24 yrs	41.0	46.4	44.3	45.4	42.9
25-39 yrs	42.8	35.0	35.6	36.2	35.4
40-59 yrs	44.1	35.6	36.4	35.3	35.5
60-64 yrs	61.3	49.9	50.4	43.4	52.7
65 yrs & over	70.1	59.9	65.0	58.4	65.7

Table 5 Sydney and four Japanese prefectures: use of time by females

	Sydney	Tokyo	Kanagawa	Kyoto	Osaka
Average hours per week of all females in age group					
Primary activities					
15-24 yrs	77.4	74.3	72.5	72.4	73.4
25-39 years	73.4	72.5	70.5	71.1	72.2
40-59 yrs	75.0	71.8	70.5	71.1	71.5
60-64 yrs	76.7	76.5	77.7	75.1	74.6
65 yrs & over	81.1	82.6	83.8	84.5	83.3
Labour force work					
15-24 yrs	18.2	20.6	18.7	20.8	20.9
25-39 yrs	17.9	20.4	15.6	20.5	19.5
40-59 yrs	14.9	22.4	20.5	28.1	24.6
60-64 yrs	3.0	11.3	10.2	14.9	15.2
65 yrs & over	0.2	5.7	4.1	9.3	3.4
Education					
15-24 yrs	14.6	16.2	18.0	19.6	17.7
Commuting					
15-24 yrs	6.1	8.1	9.6	6.9	7.5
25-39 yrs	2.5	3.1	2.6	2.3	2.4
40-59 yrs	2.5	2.2	2.5	1.8	2.4
60-64 yrs	0.9	1.0	0.9	0.7	0.8
65 yrs & overs	0.0	0.6	0.5	0.5	0.2
Housework					
15-24 yrs	13.0	7.4	7.3	7.2	8.2
25-39 yrs	35.0	36.1	43.1	39.6	39.3
40-59 yrs	31.7	34.0	36.4	33.6	34.4
60-64 yrs	32.3	32.6	34.0	31.6	30.0
65 yrs & overs	26.7	22.9	23.5	22.5	22.2
Tertiary activities					
15-24 yrs	38.7	41.4	41.9	41.1	40.3
25-39 yrs	39.2	35.9	36.2	34.5	34.6
40-59 yrs	43.9	37.6	38.1	33.4	35.1
60-64 yrs	55.1	46.6	45.2	45.7	47.4
65 yrs & over	60.0	56.2	56.1	51.2	58.9

Thus, in the 25-39 years age group housework occupied an average of 35 hours per week for Sydney women and 10 hours per week for Sydney men. In Kanagawa prefecture, the corresponding averages in this age group were 43 hours for women and two hours for men: by comparison with Sydney, housework occupied eight hours per week *more* of the time of women and eight hours per week *less* of the time of men.

A final aspect of the results of the time use survey which deserves some discussion concerns the time which people spend in commuting to and from work or places of study. The estimates in Table 2 reveal that the average commuting time for all persons over 15 years is about four hours per week in Sydney and Kyoto, five hours per week in Tokyo and Osaka and over six hours per week in Kanagawa. Average commuting times in the Japanese prefectures would be greater but for the fact that large numbers of workers do not commute at all. At the 1985 Census, the proportion of employed persons who worked at home was 21.9 per cent in Kyoto, 15.7 per cent in Tokyo, 13.3 per cent in Osaka and 11.2 per cent in Kanagawa.[11] The corresponding proportion in Sydney at the 1986 Census was only 3.3 per cent.

The results of the time use surveys in the two countries, as reported in Tables 2-5, provide a framework for the examination of the relative roles of market and non-market activities.

If the time spent on labour force work is taken as the measure of market activities, and the total time spent on housework and on tertiary activities as the measure of non-market activities, the balance between the two in Sydney and in the four Japanese prefectures can be derived from Table 2.

On this basis, non-market activities absorbed over three times as much time as market activities in Sydney. The corresponding ratio in the Japanese prefectures was 1.8 times in Kyoto and Osaka, 1.9 times in Tokyo and 2.0 times in Kanagawa.

An examination of estimates for age groups in Tables 4 and 5 reveals even more striking differences between Sydney and the Japanese prefectures in this respect. For example, the average ratio of time spent on non-market activities (as defined) to time spent on labour force work by men in Tokyo rises across the life-cycle from around 0.7 in the 25-39 years age group to about 1.5 in the 60-64 age group. By way of contrast, the corresponding ratio for Sydney men is about 1.5 for the 25-39 and 40-59 age groups, rising to 4.5 for the 60-64 years age group.

In sum, the importance of non-market activities, as indicated by the relative allocation of time, is far greater in Sydney than in the Japanese prefectures selected for this study.

Comparisons of command over goods and services

For most people, labour force work is seen primarily as an exchange of time for money. It is done not for its own sake but in order to provide the resources for other aspects of living, including for the purchase of the 'necessities of life'.

The next stage in our comparative assessment of living standards will therefore be to examine how much of the working time of employees is needed in order

11 Japan, Statistics Bureau, *Major Aspects of Population of Japan*, Tokyo, 1986: 160.

to provide the resources required to purchase necessary supplies of certain foodstuffs and electricity. Unlike most other items of household expenditure, the purchase of these items cannot be deferred, or avoided by the purchase of a cheaper alternative: all households must buy, and regularly pay for, certain basic foodstuffs and electric power (at least for lighting and refrigeration).

Estimates of the levels of weekly and hourly earnings in Sydney and in each of the prefectures are given in Table 6.

Table 6 Sydney and four Japanese prefectures: employees, average weekly hours worked and average weekly and hourly earnings 1987

	Sydney	Tokyo	Kanagawa	Kyoto	Osaka
Average weekly hours worked					
Females	29.9	41.4	40.1	41.6	41.4
Persons	34.8	47.4	47.0	47.1	47.5
Males	453.5	88,490	88,510	78,490	78,830
Average weekly earnings					
	$A	Yen	Yen	Yen	Yen
Males	38.5	50.8	50.4	50.3	50.7
Females	308.3	41,490	36,390	35,080	34,800
Persons	392.2	71,670	71,420	62,470	63,560
Average hourly earnings					
	$A	Yen	Yen	Yen	Yen
Males	11.80	1,743	1,756	1,560	1,554
Females	10.31	1,003	907	894	841
Persons	11.26	1,512	1,519	1,326	1,339
	%	%	%	%	%
Females as % of total					
Employees	42.3	35.8	32.8	36.9	34.7
Hours worked	36.3	31.2	28.0	32.6	30.2
Total earnings	33.2	20.7	16.7	20.7	19.0
Female earnings as % of male					
Weekly	68.0	46.9	41.1	44.7	44.1
Hourly	87.4	57.6	51.7	54.0	54.1

Source: The estimates for the Japanese prefectures are derived from Statistics Bureau, *Survey of Employment Status 1987*, and those for Sydney are derived from unpublished results from the ABS labour force survey for August 1987 and from the survey of *Weekly Earnings and Employees, August 1987* (ABS Catalogue no. 6310.0). The estimates of average weekly earnings for both Japan and Australia implied by these surveys are 5-10 per cent lower than the OECD, *National Accounts, Detailed Tables*, Volume II, 1976-88 by covering estimated wages and salaries (Table 8) to a weekly basis and dividing by the number of employees (Table 15). It is usual for estimates of average earnings from household surveys to be somewhat understated.

The estimates are given separately for males and females, and show that average female earnings were a much higher proportion of average male earnings in

Sydney than in the Japanese cities. On an hourly basis, the ratio was 87 per cent in Sydney, 58 per cent in Tokyo, 54 per cent in Osaka and Kyoto and 52 per cent in Kanagawa.

Taking the average hourly earnings of all employees as the measure of the average value of working time, Tables 7 and 8 provide comparisons of the 'cost' of necessities in terms of working time for Sydney, Tokyo and Osaka.

Table 7A Average annual consumption of selected foods by a family of four in Sydney, and costs of purchase expressed in hours of work in Sydney, Tokyo and Osaka 1987

	Quantity consumed in Sydney	Cost of purchase in hours of work		
		Sydney	Tokyo	Osaka
	kg	hours	hours	hours
Cereals				
Bread	121.5	17.91	29.76	38.11
Flour	3.3	0.29	0.45	0.50
Pasta	33.2	6.43	10.49	11.90
Rice	36.1	3.59	11.50	13.45
Biscuits	21.1	9.29	12.78	14.81
		37.51	64.98	78.77
Meat and Fish				
Beef (a)	77.7	35.40	185.22	205.60
Pork	9.6	3.88	8.97	12.02
Ham and bacon	9.6	5.60	13.76	16.01
Chicken	28.8	8.88	18.60	23.64
Sausages	16.1	3.79	16.41	17.05
Delicatessen meat	7.3	3.89	14.08	15.70
Fish	11.3	7.30	14.27	16.65
		68.74	271.31	306.67
Dairy products and eggs				
Fresh milk (litres)	437.3	32.23	57.58	74.78
Butter	6.6	2.11	6.95	8.02
Cheese	20.4	11.23	17.51	20.05
Icecream (litres)	35.7	4.06	15.18	16.85
Eggs	20.8	5.26	3.80	4.38
		54.89	101.02	124.08
Fruit and vegetables				
Oranges	64.5	7.90	20.89	27.26
Lemons	3.4	0.29	0.55	0.61
Apples	89.1	18.52	25.81	31.47

	Quantity consumed in Sydney	Cost of purchase in hours of work		
		Sydney	Tokyo	Osaka
	kg	hours	hours	hours
Bananas	17.5	1.88	2.64	2.98
Canned fruit	9.1	1.30	3.02	3.92
Potatoes	132.9	8.50	20.12	24.71
Onions	10.6	0.94	1.00	1.15
Carrots	20.4	2.07	4.93	5.62
Tomatoes	25.2	4.36	8.31	11.95
Cabbage	32.1	1.60	4.78	5.61
		47.36	92.05	115.28
Other foods				
Margarine	6.9	1.27	3.78	4.18
Sugar	18.6	1.34	3.15	3.42
Chocolate	16.1	11.87	22.79	25.49
Soft drinks (litres)	87.2	9.85	21.22	24.07
Coffee (b)	3.0	12.23	18.72	21.10
		36.56	69.66	78.26
Total selected foods		**245.06**	**599.02**	**703.06**

Source: Estimated quantities of selected foods consumed in Sydney are derived from Australia, *Department of Health, National dietary survey of adults: 1983, No. 1, Foods consumed,* and Australia, Department of Health and Community Services, *National dietary survey of school children (aged 10-15): 1985, Report 1, Foods consumed.* Estimates represent the total annualised intake for a man aged 35-44 years, a woman aged 35-44 years, a girl aged 12 years and a boy aged 10 years. The prices of foods other than meat and fish are for October or November 1987 and are from International Labour Office, *Bulletin of labour statistics, October inquiry results in 1987 and 1988,* Geneva, 1989. Average prices for beef, pork, ham and bacon, chicken and fish in Sydney for the December quarter of 1984 are given in Australian Bureau of Agricultural and Resource Economics, *Household meat consumption in Sydney and Melbourne, Canberra 1988.* These were brought forward to the December quarter of 1987 using published ABS price index and price data. Prices for these items for Tokyo and Osaka are 1987 average unit prices of household consumption as given in Japan, Statistics Bureau, *Annual Report on the Family Income and Expenditure Survey 1987.* The cost of purchase in local currencies was calculated on the assumption that all of the assumed quantity consumed of each item was expended on the purchase of the particular product/specification (or most nearly comparable product/specification) priced in the October 1987 ILO Price Inquiry. The prices in local currencies were then converted into costs in hours worked using the estimates of average hourly earnings of all persons in Table 6.

(a) 'Quantity consumed' includes the 'beef equivalent' of the quantity consumed of mutton and lamb, using the estimated average prices in the December quarter of 1987.

(b) Average consumption of coffee by a family of four is estimated from per capita consumption statistics in the United Nations *Statistical Yearbook 1987.* It is assumed that one-half of the coffee is purchased as instant coffee.

Table 7B Average annual household purchases of selected foods in Tokyo and Osaka, and costs of purchase expressed in hours of work in Sydney, Tokyo and Osaka 1987

	Quantity purchased		Cost of quantity purchased in Tokyo in:		Cost of quantity purchased in Osaka in:	
	Tokyo kg	Osaka kg	Sydney hours	Tokyo hours	Sydney hours	Osaka hours
Cereals						
Bread	40.2	44.8	5.93	9.84	6.60	13.38
Flour	3.2	4.1	0.28	0.43	0.36	0.62
Pasta	31.0	37.7	6.00	9.80	7.30	13.51
Rice	122.2	142.5	12.16	38.94	14.17	53.11
Biscuits	3.9	2.0	1.73	2.38	0.88	1.40
			26.10	61.39	29.31	82.02
Meat and fish						
Beef	9.7	16.7	4.41	23.12	7.61	44.19
Pork	19.5	13.3	7.90	18.26	5.37	16.66
Ham and bacon	5.8	5.4	3.38	8.31	3.15	9.01
Chicken	12.4	13.9	3.82	8.01	4.28	11.41
Sausages	4.6	3.9	1.08	4.69	0.91	4.13
Fish	52.6	56.8	33.96	66.42	36.67	83.70
			54.55	128.81	57.99	169.10
Dairy products, eggs						
Fresh milk	108.1	103.0	7.97	14.23	7.59	17.62
Butter	0.5	0.4	0.16	0.53	0.13	0.49
Cheese	1.9	1.1	1.05	1.63	0.61	1.09
Icecream	11.2	11.4	1.27	4.75	1.30	5.31
Eggs	35.7	45.6	9.03	7.25	11.53	9.60
			19.48	28.39	21.16	34.11
Fruit and vegetables						
Oranges	37.2	34.0	4.56	12.05	4.17	14.37
Lemons	2.0	1.6	0.17	0.33	0.14	0.29
Apples	15.2	15.9	3.16	4.40	3.30	5.62
Bananas	14.1	12.2	1.52	2.13	1.31	2.08
Canned fruit	1.7	1.9	0.31	0.71	0.27	0.81
Potatoes	17.5	21.0	1.12	2.65	1.34	3.91
Onions	18.9	21.9	1.68	1.79	1.94	2.37
Carrots	11.5	8.9	1.16	2.78	0.90	2.45
Tomatoes	19.2	12.4	3.33	6.33	2.15	5.88

	Quantity purchased		Cost of quantity purchased in Tokyo in:		Cost of quantity purchased in Osaka in:	
	Tokyo	Osaka	Sydney hours	Tokyo hours	Sydney hours	Osaka hours
	kg	kg				
Chinese Cabbage	12.5	16.4	1.94	1.61	2.55	2.24
Green Peppers	3.3	2.7	1.35	1.30	1.11	1.17
Eggplants	9.6	9.1	4.25	2.99	4.03	3.43
Sweet Potatoes	6.1	5.2	1.58	1.59	1.34	1.84
			27.24	43.98	25.68	50.44
Other foods						
Margarine	2.7	2.8	0.50	1.48	0.52	1.70
Sugar	8.0	9.5	0.58	1.35	0.68	1.75
Coffee	1.6	1.6	3.04	4.64	3.26	5.62
			4.12	**7.47**	**4.46**	**9.07**
Total, selected foods			**131.49**	**270.04**	**138.60**	**344.74**

Source: Average annual household purchases of the selected foods in Tokyo and Osaka are from Japan, Statistics Bureau, *Annual Report on the Family Income and Expenditure Survey 1987*. The quantities purchased of biscuits, icecream and canned fruit are inferred from average annual family expenditure and the prices in the ILO October 1987 inquiry. For the sources used for prices and the method of calculation of costs in hours worked see the source to Table 7A.

Table 7 is in two parts, Table 7A shows the cost in hours of work in the three cities of a basket of foodstuffs which is representative of the Australian pattern of consumption of the foods concerned (expenditure on which accounts for more than one-half of household food expenditure in Sydney), whilst Table 7B gives corresponding details for baskets of food representative of the Tokyo and Osaka patterns of consumption of the items listed.[12] Both parts of the table show that the number of hours which must be worked in order to earn household food supplies is far greater in Tokyo and Osaka than in Sydney.

The food regimen shown in Table 7A, which is representative of annual consumption of the foods concerned by a four-person family in Sydney, could have been purchased for 245 hours work by the average employee in Sydney in 1987. The cost would have been about 600 hours of work in Tokyo, and 700 hours in Osaka.

---

12 The estimates of quantities in Tables 7A and 7B should not be compared as they are on differing bases. Those in Table 7A are estimates of the quantities of food *consumed* by a family of two adults and two children, whilst those in Table 7B are reported average amounts of foods *purchased* (other than at restaurants, etc) by all households of two or more persons.

As would be expected, the relative differences are somewhat less marked if the comparison is based on consumption patterns in the Japanese cities. However, the costs in hours worked of baskets of goods representative of consumption patterns in Tokyo and Osaka were still far greater in those cities than in Sydney – by a margin of over 2 to 1 in the case of Tokyo and of about 2.5 to 1 in the case of Osaka.

Similar information in relation to purchases of electricity is shown in Table 8. The table shows, for the average usage of electricity by several household types, the cost in hours worked in Sydney, Tokyo and Osaka of purchasing supplies at the general household tariff. Again the costs in hours worked in the Japanese cities were more than twice as great, and in some cases more than three times as great, as in Sydney.

Table 8 Average annual consumption of electricity by households in Sydney by household composition and costs of purchase expressed in hours of work in Sydney, Tokyo and Osaka 1987

	Average consumption in Sydney	Cost of purchase in hours of work		
	kwh	Sydney hours	Tokyo hours	Osaka hours
Single person	3,500	25.0	57.5	64.7
Two adults, no children	5,830	40.3	105.7	120.3
Two adults, one or two children	8,592	58.4	162.9	186.2
Two adults, three or four children	9,924	67.1	190.4	218.0

Source: The average annual consumption of electricity in Sydney by households of the specified types is from Australian Bureau of Statistics, *New South Wales Energy Survey, October 1984: Part 2, Household Energy Consumption* (ABS Catalogue No. 8212.1). The tariffs assumed for the purpose of estimating costs are: Sydney, from January 1, 1987, 10.21 cents for first 800 kwh per annum, 7.309 cents for the remainder; Tokyo, at end 1986, 3120 yen per annum standing charge, 18.98 yen per kwh for first 1440 kwh per annum, 26.23 yen per kwh for next 1560 kwh per annum, 31.28 yen per kwh for the remainder; Osaka at end 1986, 17.33 yen per kwh for first 180 kwh per annum, 20.06 yen per kwh for next 1260 kwh per annum, 27.06 yen per kwh for next 1560 kwh per annum, 31.96 yen per kwh for the remainder. For the method of calculation of costs in hours worked, see Table 7B.

The costs in hours worked of most other goods and services purchased by households would also have been higher in the Japanese cities than in Sydney, but by a considerably narrower margin. This can be inferred from Table 9, which presents OECD estimates for Australia and Japan of the price levels of major components of consumption expenditure in relation to the prices of foods in 1985.

Table 9 Australia and Japan: prices of selected components of household consumption expenditure in relation to prices of food 1985

	Australia	Japan
Food	100	100
Clothing	134	80
Household equipment and operation	127	83
Transport and communications	123	87
Education, recreation and culture	126	82
Miscellaneous goods and services	133	85

Source: The table is derived from OECD, *Purchasing Power Parities and Real Expenditures 1985*, Table 12, which shows the *relative* price levels of each component of final expenditure on GDP in relation to GDP as a whole, at average OECD prices.

The OECD estimates are based on prices of many hundreds of individual goods and services supplied by statistical offices in individual member countries. They imply that, taking the structure of relative prices in the OECD area as a whole as the reference base, average prices of a wide range of consumer goods and services were dearer in Australia and cheaper in Japan *in relation to* the average prices of food. The margins of difference were, however, much smaller than the differences in the costs of food in terms of hours worked shown in Table 7. The estimates are therefore consistent with the proposition that the 'hours of work' costs of these other objects of consumption were on average lower in *absolute* terms in Sydney than in the Japanese cities.

In short, the available evidence indicates that the purchasing power of earnings, as measured by the command over goods and services obtained on average by a given amount of working time, is much greater in Sydney than in the Japanese cities. The margin of advantage in favour of Sydney workers is greater for women than for men, and greater for the 'necessities of life' than for other objects of consumption.

Living standards of low and high income households

The comments about relative living standards which were quoted at the beginning of this paper refer to the per capita income of 'Japan' being the world's highest and to the ranking of 'Australia' in terms of living standards. In fact, of course, it is not countries but people who have high or low incomes or living standards. National accounts-based comparisons of relative real incomes place the emphasis on averages of aggregates, and may not say very much about the experience of individuals, families or households.

This section looks at some measures of the standard or level of living of low and high income households in Sydney and in the four Japanese prefectures in 1984. The details are provided in Table 10, which is in three parts. Table 10A compares the composition of income and expenditure and certain other characteristics of all households of two or more persons in Sydney and each of the prefectures, whilst Tables 10B and 10C provide the same information for households of two or more persons in the lowest and highest income quintile in each region. 'Income quintile groups' are 20 per cent groupings of the population when households (in this case, households of two or more persons) are ranked in ascending order according to each household's total gross weekly income.

Table 10A Sydney and four Japanese prefectures: income, expenditure and selected characteristics of all households (a) 1984

	Sydney	Tokyo	Kanagawa	Kyoto	Osaka
Persons per household (number)	3.26	3.56	3.76	3.77	3.70
Composition of income (%)					
Wages & salaries	76.1	70.4	77.3	68.6	72.9
Own business	7.8	16.2	10.9	18.7	14.8
Pensions/benefits (b)	8.9	4.3	4.3	6.6	4.8
Other income (b)	7.2	9.2	7.6	6.1	7.5
Total income	100.0	100.0	100.0	100.0	100.0
Labour force work					
Earners per household (number)	1.5	1.5	1.5	1.5	1.5
Earned income (c) as % of total income	83.9	86.6	88.2	87.3	87.7
Housing tenure					
Paying rent (%)	24.9	43.2	31.2	20.4	40.4
Rent as % of income (d)	14.2	7.5	5.6	3.9	5.6
Owning dwelling (e) (%)	71.6	61.7	70.6	79.2	60.6
With mortgage (e) (%)	36.4	29.3	39.4	33.4	27.9
Mortgage/income ratio (f)	0.69	1.56	1.34	1.29	1.52
Composition of expenditure (g) (%)					
Cereals	1.5	4.9	5.1	5.1	5.7
Meat & fish	5.1	9.9	10.1	12.1	12.0
Fruit & veges	3.0	7.87	7.5	7.4	7.8
Food (except eating out) (h)	18.0	32.3	32.4	34.3	35.3
Power and water charges	4.0	8.5	8.1	8.2	8.4
Communications	2.0	3.4	3.3	3.3	3.2

	Sydney	Tokyo	Kanagawa	Kyoto	Osaka
Total food & utilities	24.0	44.1	43.8	45.8	47.0
Clothing	9.3	10.1	9.8	10.1	9.4
Household operation	14.3	7.8	8.5	8.6	7.4
Transportation	19.2	8.8	10.6	8.3	8.3
Reading & recreation	14.2	12.6	12.6	11.5	11.7
Eating out	7.5	7.4	6.0	6.1	6.5
Miscellaneous	11.5	9.3	8.7	9.7	9.7
Total other (non-food) expenditure	76.0	55.9	56.2	54.2	53.0
Total expenditure (g)	100.0	100.0	100.0	100.0	100.0

Table 10B Sydney and four Japanese prefectures: income, expenditure and selected characteristics of households (a) in lowest income quintile group 1984

	Sydney	Tokyo	Kanagawa	Kyoto	Osaka
Persons per household (number)	2.59	3.00	3.21	2.97	3.00
Composition of income (%)					
Wages & salaries	4.9	52.3	65.6	40.9	52.8
Own business	6.9	21.6	13.8	27.4	21.0
Pensions/benefits (b)	74.2	15.6	13.2	22.7	16.9
Other income (b)	14.0	10.5	4.8	9.0	9.3
Total income	100.0	100.0	100.0	100.0	100.0
Labour force work					
Earners per household (no.)	0.2	1.3	1.2	1.1	1.1
Earned income (c) as % of total income	11.8	73.9	79.4	68.3	73.8
Housing tenure					
Paying rent (%)	36.9	57.6	52.2	38.9	58.3
Rent as % of income (d)	35.4	16.3	12.2	8.2	11.5
Own dwelling (e) (%)	59.8	47.7	47.8	61.2	42.2
With mortgage (e) (%)	9.0	8.0	14.3	9.5	9.2
Mortgage/income ratio (f)	1.39	2.81	2.40	2.04	2.34
Composition of expenditure (g) (%)					
Cereals	2.3	6.3	6.1	6.4	7.0
Meat & fish	7.0	10.4	10.6	12.8	12.8
Fruit & veges	4.8	9.0	8.4	9.1	9.2
Total food (exc. eating out) (h)	24.8	36.9	36.2	38.8	40.0
Power & water charges	5.2	9.8	9.2	9.7	10.1
Communications	2.4	3.9	3.7	4.0	3.8
Food & utilities	32.4	50.7	49.2	52.4	53.9
Clothing	8.1	7.5	7.5	6.4	6.8
Household operation	14.0	7.6	8.7	8.7	7.5

	Sydney	Tokyo	Kanagawa	Kyoto	Osaka
Transportation	18.2	7.4	8.0	7.9	7.1
Reading & recreation	11.4	10.5	10.9	10.2	9.3
Eating out	4.4	6.2	5.9	4.9	5.8
Miscellaneous	11.5	10.1	9.8	9.5	9.7
Total other (non-food) expenditure	67.6	49.3	50.8	47.6	46.2
Total expenditure (g)	100.0	100.0	100.0	100.0	100.0

Table 10C Sydney and four Japanese prefectures: income, expenditure and selected characteristics of households (a) in highest income quintile group 1984

	Sydney	Tokyo	Kanagawa	Kyoto	Osaka
Persons per household (number)	3.79	4.0	4.19	4.23	4.06
Composition of income (%)					
Wages & salaries	80.5	70.8	73.3	69.0	72.5
Own business	10.4	12.9	13.2	19.4	13.1
Pensions/benefits (b)	1.9	2.6	3.0	3.9	4.0
Other income (b)	7.1	13.7	10.5	7.7	10.4
Total income	100.0	100.0	100.0	100.0	100.0
Labour force work					
Earners per household (no.)	2.5	1.8	2.0	1.9	1.8
Earned income (c) as % of total income	90.9	83.7	86.5	88.4	85.6
Housing tenure					
Paying rent (%)	15.3	26.6	9.9	5.6	16.0
Rent as % of income (d)	10.8	3.6	3.5	1.6	3.2
Owning dwelling (e) (%)	83.0	83.5	94.6	93.4	85.8
With mortgage (e) (%)	49.8	51.4	59.1	52.8	45.3
Mortgage/income ratio (f)	0.38	0.97	0.77	0.87	0.93
Composition of expenditure (g) (%)					
Cereals	1.1	3.9	4.1	4.0	4.4
Meat & fish	3.8	9.6	9.2	10.8	11.0
Fruit & veges	2.4	6.9	6.4	6.2	6.9
Total food (exc. eating out) (h)	14.3	28.1	27.3	28.8	30.0
Power & water charges	3.2	7.5	7.5	6.7	7.1
Communications	1.6	3.2	3.2	3.0	3.0
Food & utilities	19.1`	38.8	38.0	38.5	40.1
Clothing	10.4	12.2	12.8	14.2	11.9
Household operation	15.4	9.2	9.1	9.7	7.8
Transportation	19.1	9.4	11.7	8.0	9.2
Reading & recreation	15.7	13.4	14.1	11.7	13.2
Eating out	9.5	7.4	5.6	6.8	6.6
Miscellaneous	10.9	9.6	8.6	11.1	11.2
Total other (non–food) expenditure	81.0	61.2	61.9	61.5	59.9
Total expenditure (g)	100.0	100.0	100.0	100.0	100.0

The first line of each part of the table shows that the *average household size* in Sydney was significantly smaller than in the Japanese prefectures. This was particularly true of households in the lowest income quintile group. The main reason for this was that, in Sydney, couples without children are much more likely to live as a separate household.

The next sections of each part of the table show the *composition of income* and the numbers of *earners* per household. In these respects, there were marked differences between Sydney and the Japanese prefectures in the lowest income quintile group. The incomes of low-income households in Sydney were derived mainly from social security pensions and benefits, whereas in the Japanese prefectures the incomes of this group were derived predominantly from employment. Reflecting this difference, the average number of earners per household in Sydney households in the lowest income quintile group was only 0.2, compared with an average of more than one earner per household in this group in the Japanese prefectures.

The section on *housing tenure* shows that, in all cities, the proportion of households paying rent was much higher in the lowest income quintile group. The difference in this respect was much greater in the Japanese prefectures than in Sydney.

The next section shows the *composition of expenditure* as revealed by household expenditure surveys conducted in Australia and Japan in 1984. Expenditure on housing, education and health are excluded from the table on the grounds that spending by individual households on these items do not necessarily reflect their relative consumption of the services concerned. Expenditure on other items is divided into two categories of goods and services according to whether demand is inelastic or elastic in relation to income. In the first, 'inelastic' group are 'food and utilities', which includes food (excluding eating out), power and water charges and communications (largely telephone charges). The second 'elastic' group includes clothing, household services and operation, transportation, reading and recreation, eating out, alcohol, tobacco, personal care and other miscellaneous items.

Although, as noted above, the income of low-income households in Sydney is derived mainly from government social security benefits, only 32 per cent of the selected expenditures of the Sydney households in this group was devoted to food and utilities. The corresponding proportion in the Japanese households, whose incomes came mainly from earnings from employment, ranged from 49 per cent in Kanagawa to 54 per cent in Osaka. Even in the highest income quintile group, the proportion of the selected expenditures directed to food and utilities in the Japanese prefectures approached 40 per cent – a far higher proportion than in the *lowest* income quintile group in Sydney.

The table also reveals significant differences in the allocation of expenditures *within* the food group and, in particular, to the relationship of spending on meat and fish to spending on cereals. Higher income groups spent relatively more on meat and fish in all of the cities, but the absolute ratios were lower in Japan. In Tokyo, for example, the ratio of expenditure on meat and fish to expenditure on cereals rose from 1.66 in the lowest income quintile group to 2.45 in the highest; whereas in Sydney the corresponding ratio rose from 3.01 in the lowest group to 3.35 in the highest income quintile group.

Whilst there are substantial differences between income groups in all cities, the statistics in Table 10 suggest that, on average, households in Sydney are more affluent than their Japanese counterparts. In particular, they suggest that Sydney households have more scope for discretionary expenditures.

Comparisons of housing conditions

The comparisons in Table 1 showed that Sydney's population density is far lower than that of the big Japanese cities. This difference is reflected in housing conditions in a number of ways.

Although the majority of Japanese families share the preference of most Australian families for a separate house on its own allotment, most people in the larger Japanese cities live in apartments in multi-unit structures. The proportion of dwellings in Sydney and the Japanese prefectures which were in structures of various types is shown for 1988 in Table 11. The table shows that the proportion of dwellings which were detached houses (including semi-detached houses)[13] was 74 per cent in Sydney, compared with only 35 per cent in Tokyo and 38 per cent in Osaka. Conversely, the proportion of dwellings in structures of more than three stories was only three per cent in Sydney, compared with almost 30 per cent in Tokyo and Osaka.

13 In the *Housing Survey of Japan* a detached house is defined as 'A building which consists of a dwelling unit'.

Table 11 Sydney and four Japanese prefectures: occupied private dwellings by type of structure

	Sydney ('000)	Tokyo ('000)	Kanagawa ('000)	Kyoto ('000)	Osaka ('000)
Number of dwellings	1,110.1	4,266.2	2,444.1	833.3	2,860.9
		Percentage of total			
Detached house (a)	74.4	34.8	50.3	57.8	37.6
Medium density (b)	22.4	35.5	29.4	24.6	33.1
Flats over 3 stories (c)	3.2	29.7	20.3	17.6	29.3
	100.0	100.0	100.0	100.0	100.0

Source: The statistics of Sydney are from the ABS 1988 Housing Survey, and those for the Japanese prefectures are from the Housing Survey 1988. The numbers of dwellings exclude other types of structure.

(a) For Sydney, comprises 'separate house' and 'semi-detached house'.

(b) For Sydney, comprises 'medium density' and 'low rise flat/unit'. For Japanese prefectures, comprises 'tenement houses' and 'apartments' in structures of 1, 2 or 3 stories. The numbers of apartments of 3 stories are estimated by assuming that the proportion of apartments in structures of 3 stories to apartments in structures of 3-5 stories is the same in Tokyo and Kanagawa as in Keihin Major Metropolitan Area, and the proportion in Kyoto and Osaka is the same as in Keihanshin Major or Metropolitan Area.

(c) For Japanese prefectures, apartments in structures of 4-5 stories are estimated by the method described in footnote (b).

Moreover, the minority of dwellings in the large Japanese cities which are detached houses are, for the most part, built on much smaller allotments than houses in Sydney. Table 12 provides indicative figures suggesting that average allotments in Sydney could be as much as four times as large as in the Japanese prefectures.

Table 12 Sydney and four Japanese prefectures: residential land areas and prices 1988

	Allotment size square metre	Land prices (hours of work)	
		per allotment	per square metre
Sydney	591	14,750	25.0
Groups of suburbs			
With smallest allotments (a)	*142*	*9,040*	*63.5*
Other inner (0-6km)	*452*	*24,550*	*54.3*
Middle distance (6-25km)	*636*	*12,060*	*23.6*
Outer (over 25 kms)	*671*	*6,830*	*12.2*
Gosford/Wyong	*738*	*4,980*	*6.7*
Tokyo	151	87,630	580.3
Kanagawa	184	39,570	215.0
Kyoto	163	19,200	117.8
Osaka	129	23,950	185.7

Source: For Sydney, allotment sizes for each group of suburbs and land prices per square metre in A$ were derived as simple averages from the dimensions of representative residential cottage sites and the values of standard serviced allotments as given in *New South Wales, Valuer-General's Department, Real Estate Market 1989*. The number of suburbs in the five groups shown are, respectively, 5, 6, 25, 19 and 3. Estimates for Sydney were derived as simple averages of the 58 suburbs. For the Japanese prefectures, the allotment sizes are the 'building area per dwelling' for detached houses from the 1988 Housing Survey, as given in *Social indicators by prefecture 1989*, page 124. Land prices per square metre in yen are as given in 'Average prices for land transactions: residential quarter' on page 387 of the same publication and land prices per allotment in yen are derived by multiplying the average price per square metre by the 'building area per dwelling'. Land prices in A$ and yen were converted to 'hours of work' using average hourly earnings estimates for 1988 derived from Table 7.

(a) Balmain, Erskineville, Paddington, Redfern and Ultimo.

In the Japanese prefectures, the average allotment size on which separate houses were built ranged from 129 square metres in Osaka to 184 square metres in Kanagawa. The median size of allotments was even smaller, ranging from about 80 square metres in Osaka to about 140 square metres in Kanagawa.

These figures may be compared with the findings of a governmental study in New South Wales in the late 1970s[14] which was directed towards ensuring that required allotments in new developments were not bigger than people required or could afford. The study estimated that the space requirements for the average household's activities included 150 square metres for the home itself, 40 square metres for a carport for two cars, 100 square metres for an outdoor living area, 75 square metres for the front garden, 25 square metres for a vegetable garden and 25 square metres for an outdoor clothes drying area.

14 Quoted in New South Wales, Department of Environment and Planning, Technical Bulletin 15, *Residential Development Standards* 1982: 10.

Table 12 also provides some indication of relative values of residential land in Sydney and the four prefectures. Comparisons should be made with caution for several reasons, including the big difference in allotment sizes. The figures in the table nonetheless suggest that, in a group of inner Sydney suburbs with allotments as small as those in the Japanese cities, the price per allotment in terms of hours of work in 1988 varied from almost one-half (Kyoto) to little more than one-tenth (Tokyo) of allotments in the Japanese prefectures.

Reference has been made to a study in the late 1970s which estimated that the space required for the average household's activities included 150 square metres for the dwelling alone. By the late 1980s the average floor area of new houses being constructed in Sydney was substantially larger than this. Table 13 shows that the average floor space for all new dwellings (including apartments, townhouses etc) commenced in New South Wales[15] during the years 1984 to 1987 was more than twice as great as in Tokyo and almost twice as great as in the other three prefectures.

As well as being far larger, dwellings in Sydney are better equipped. Statistical information on bathroom and toilet facilities in dwellings in Sydney and the Japanese prefectures is presented in Table 14. In 1987, almost 99 per cent of dwellings in Sydney were equipped with one or more toilets and one or more showers.[16] The corresponding proportions in Japanese cities were much lower. The 1988 Housing Survey in Japan also revealed that between nine per cent (Kyoto) and 20 per cent (Kanagawa) of dwellings had two or more flush toilets for the exclusive use of the household. In Sydney, where the average household size is significantly smaller, the proportion of dwellings with two or more toilets was 40 per cent.

---

15 The majority of the commencements were in Sydney and the average floor area of dwellings commenced in Sydney would not have been significantly less than for the state as a whole.

16 Australian Bureau of Statistics, Domestic Water Use, New South Wales (ABS catalogue No. 8719.1): 12.

Table 13 NSW and four Japanese Prefectures: average floor area of new dwellings constructed 1984-87

	NSW (sq.m.)	Tokyo (sq.m.)	Kanagawa (sq.m.)	Kyoto (sq.m.)	Other (sq.m.)
1984	129.8	68.5	84.5	80.4	79.2
1985	139.8	67.7	80.2	80.9	79.1
1986	141.8	64.3	74.3	75.2	79.1
1987	146.2	66.7	74.9	77.7	75.9
Total 1984-87	**138.9**	**66.6**	**77.8**	**78.4**	**78.1**

Source: Statistics for New South Wales are unpublised results from the ABS Building Activity Survey. Those for the Japanese prefectures are from Statistics Bureau, *Social Indicators by Prefecture 1989* and previous issues.

Table 14 Sydney (1987) and four Japanese prefectures (1988): bathroom and toilet facilities in private dwellings

Percentage of dwellings with:	Sydney %	Tokyo %	Kanagawa %	Kyoto %	Osaka %
No flush toilet	1.2	4.8	9.6	28.7	16.9
Flush toilet used jointly	-	5	1.4	3.9	3.2
	1.2	**9.8**	**11**	**32.6**	**20.1**
Flush toilets for exclusive use of household					
At least 1	98.8	90.2	89	67.4	79.9
At least 2	40.2	16.6	20.4	9	9.6
At least 3	16.9	n.a.	n.a.	n.a.	n.a.
No bathroom	n.a.	16.7	7.6	12.6	17.4
No shower	1.2	n.a.	n.a.	n.a.	n.a.
No bathtub	9	n.a.	n.a.	n.a.	n.a.

Source: The statistics for Sydney are from a survey conducted by the ABS in July 1987, the results of which were published in *Domestic Water Use, New South Wales* (ABS Calatogue No.8719). The data for the Japanese prefectures are from the *1988 Housing Survey of Japan: Volume 3: Results for Prefectures.*

More information on household facilities is provided in Table 15. This table shows, for Sydney and the four selected Japanese prefectures, the proportion of all households possessing motor vehicles and various household durable goods. For most items the ownership rate was higher, and for several items far higher, in Sydney.[17]

17 Microwave ovens were an exception, but the ownership rate in Sydney was rising steeply at the time of the survey (1984). In a survey conducted in 1985-86, almost 40 per cent of Australian households possessing a microwave oven had acquired it during the preceding 12 months.

Table 15 Sydney and four Japanese prefectures: possession of motor vehicles and household durable goods (% of all households)

	Sydney %	Tokyo %	Kanagawa %	Kyoto %	Osaka %
Motor vehicles					
At least 1	90	47.4	60.8	63.5	51.3
At least 2	45.4	3.8	5.7	7.9	3.9
At least 3	10.7	0.5	0.8	0.8	0.4
Refrigerators					
At least 1	99.5	92.8	93.6	95.2	94.4
At least 2	21.6	4.5	5.5	8.1	5.3
Washing machines					
All	89.1	88.6	90.6	92.9	92.3
Fully automatic	72.4	24.9	22.8	27.4	24
Clothes dryer	52.5	9.5	6.4	7.2	8.8
Microwave oven	23	38.1	42.2	48.4	52
Other ovens					
Electric	74.2	41.2	42.9	54.5	48.4
Gas	24.8	38.1	23.8	37.9	36.4
Telephone	91.2	85.4	88.6	91.3	88.9

Source: Statistics for Sydney are from the 1986 Census for motor vehicles: interpolated from surveys of household telephone connections in 1983 and 1986 for telephones; and from ABS *New South Wales Energy Survey, October 1984* (ABS Caalogue No.8212.1) for other items. Statistics for the Japanese prefectures are from Statistics Bureau, *1984 National Survey of Family Income and Expenditure*. Estimates for 2 or more person households and 1-person households are published separately and have been combined. In the case of 1-person households, it was assumed that the proportion of households possessing each item in the four individual prefectures bore the same relationship to the proportion for Japan as a whole as the corresponding proportion in respect of households of 2 or more persons.

Land use

Although the available statistical information is limited, undoubtedly Sydney's lower population densities are reflected not only in more spacious housing but in more generous provision of a range of other amenities: wider and less congested roads, larger grounds for schools in relation to student populations, larger grounds for hospitals and nursing homes in relation to patient populations, and more public open spaces and sporting facilities in relation to the total population.

Table 16 Sydney and four Japanese prefectures: public open space and facilities for sport 1982

	Sydney	Tokyo	Kanagawa	Kyoto	Osaka
TOTAL					
Sites					
Number	6,238	3,026	2,732	1,154	2,544
Area (hectares)	13,086	2,572	1,530	678	2,650
Playing fields: Number	1,580	568	162	104	162
Tennis courts: Number	843	178	105	85	112
Netball courts: Number	1,573	n.a.	n.a.	n.a.	n.a.
PER MILLION OF POPULATION					
Sites					
Number	2,041	260	389	454	299
Area (hectares)	4,283	220	215	265	310
Playing fields: Number	517	48	22	40	19
Tennis courts: Number	276	15	14	33	13
Netball courts: Number	515	n.a.	n.a.	n.a.	n.a.

Source: Information for Sydney is from New South Wales, Department of Environment and Planning, Research Study 5, *1982 Open Space Survey: Open Space in the Sydney Region* (1985). The survey covered municipalities with 93% of the population of the Sydney Statistical Division in 1981. Figures for the number and area of open space sites relate to sites of less than 50 hectares only. Information for the Japanese prefectures is from issues of *Social Indicators by Prefecture*, and relates to 1982 for sites and to 1985 for playing fields and tennis courts. For the Japanese prefectures, 'playing fields' are described in the English translation of the text as 'Grounds for exercise', and include exercise grounds with an area of 992 square metres or more.'

Statistical information on this last aspect is presented in Table 16, which compares the number and area of public open space sites and the numbers of playing fields and tennis courts in Sydney and in the four Japanese prefectures in the early 1980s.

The table shows that, in relation to population, Sydney had over four times as many public open space sites as Kyoto and nearly eight times as many as Tokyo. If allowance is made for the greater average size of the Sydney sites, the differences were even greater. Sydney also had a much greater absolute number of public playing fields and public tennis courts than the four Japanese prefectures combined. In relation to population, the number of these facilities in Sydney was 10 to 20 times greater than in the Japanese prefectures.

Conclusion

Japan's rate of economic growth has been much faster than that of other OECD countries for several decades, and this has been reflected in a rapid improvement in the living standards of the Japanese people. The improvement has occurred both in the quantifiable indicators which are drawn together in national accounts aggregates and in the less tangible aspects which are summarised in the phrase 'quality of life'.

Australia's *per capita* growth rate has been much slower, and in the 1980s many commentators asserted that the incomes and living standards of Australians had been surpassed by the Japanese. The statistics presented in this paper do not support this view. Even on the conventional measures, Australians apparently continued to enjoy higher real consumption levels per capita, in respect of virtually every significant category of expenditure. This was true notwithstanding the facts that they worked fewer hours each week, took longer holidays and had shorter working lives.

This paper has argued that the measures commonly used in inter-country comparisons are in any case inadequate. Many aspects of the mode or level of living which most people would regard as important to their own perception of their living standards are omitted from the reckoning. In general, the effect of allowing for these factors would be to reinforce the conclusion that, at the beginning of the 1990s, most people in Australia continued to enjoy higher living standards than their counterparts in Japan.

If Japan maintains a higher rate of economic growth than Australia in the years ahead, the gap in living standards will continue to narrow. If only because of the differing physical characteristics of the two countries, however, it can be expected that it will become increasingly important to recognise that lifestyles in Japan and Australia are very *different*. There is little point in trying to encapsulate the differences in any single measure, or to establish criteria against which the living standards in either country could be assessed as superior.

In both countries, the task will be to use the skills and strengths of their peoples to improve opportunities for the enhancement of their wellbeing in the broadest sense.

Part Four: Climate Change and Limits to Growth

22. Climate Change and Related Issues: Ian Castles' Contributions in Perspective

David Henderson

Preface

Ian Castles was a top Australian civil servant: the last two posts that he held were as Secretary of the Department of Finance and as Australian Statistician. He and I met in 1995, when we were both retired officials; and some years later, as recounted here, we became jointly involved, as close collaborators, on issues relating to climate change.

This chapter tells the story of our collaboration. In doing so, it develops two related themes. First, it brings out Ian's distinctive contributions in three related subject areas: inter-country measures of output and real expenditure; the continuing climate change debate; and - though this deserves a lot more space than I could give it here – what I call global salvationism, i.e., ways of thinking which combine confident over-pessimistic assessments and predictions with collectivist 'solutions'. Second, it offers a perspective on the evolution of the climate change debate over the past decade.

As compared with an earlier version, which has been widely circulated and posted on Andrew Montford's Bishop Hill blog, the text that follows has a few changes. In particular, I have inserted an extra paragraph in the next-to-final section. It takes account of further messages from Ian to me, following our last meeting in Canberra, which came to light after the earlier text had gone out.

First involvement: How it came about

Ian Castles became seriously engaged with climate change issues in the latter part of 2002, and over the rest of his life those issues came to form his main single professional concern. It was through him that I became involved myself, and as with him my involvement has proved to be a close and continuing one. For both of us, life took a new and unexpected course. Within it we acted not only as collaborators, which we already were, but also as joint authors.

This new departure came about in an entirely unplanned and fortuitous way. In April 2002 a contested election took place for the Chair of the Intergovernmental Panel on Climate Change (the IPCC). As a result, Dr RK Pachauri was appointed to the position, which he still holds. In July he came to Canberra on an official visit, and Ian was invited to a meeting that was held for him. Ian used the occasion to tell Pachauri that the Special Report on Emissions Scenarios (SRES), prepared as an input to the IPCC's Third Assessment Report and published in 2000, was technically at fault, most notably in its handling of international comparisons of GDP. Pachauri invited Ian to write to him on the subject; and accordingly, on 6 August, Ian sent off a long and detailed letter. Three weeks later he sent a further supplementary letter, with an annex appended; and at the end of September Pachauri sent him a friendly holding response. Some time afterwards, Ian wrote to me to suggest that I should write a letter of my own to Pachauri to back him up, and on 28 October I duly complied. These actions of ours brought lasting consequences which neither of us had counted on.

An existing alliance

You might ask why it was that Ian wrote specifically to me, a resident of faraway London, to enlist my support for this new initiative on his part. The reason is straightforward. By the time he thus approached me, we had been friends, allies and informal collaborators for seven years or so. We first met in the early part of 1995, after John Stone, a former Secretary of the Australian Treasury, had suggested that I make sure to contact him during a coming visit of mine to Canberra; and it soon became apparent that we were kindred spirits. I was very much on Ian's side in what he described, in his opening letter to Pachauri, as 'my ongoing correspondence about the use and abuse of statistics in public debates about globalisation, poverty and the distribution of incomes both within and between countries'. In 1999 we worked in harness in connection with the ASSA conference of that year. In early 2000 I published a critique of the *Human Development Report 1999,* brought out by the UN Development Program; and in my opening paragraph I said that the article could be 'read in conjunction with a recently-published searching critique of the previous issue, the 1998 *Report,* by Ian Castles'.

Not only were we regularly exchanging emails at this time, but, at the beginning of 2002, shortly before Dr Pachauri came on the scene, we had discussed the idea of writing a book together. The book would have presented a critique of what I had come to call global salvationism, as reflected for example in the proceedings of successive mammoth UN conferences: in a draft outline that I sent to Ian, in March 2002, I used as one of the headings 'False consensus: dark visions and collectivist remedies'. We would have contrasted the history of failed prophecies of doom with the impressive actual record of economic performance, and argued the case for defending and enlarging the domain of competitive markets. We would have been writing as economic liberals, in the continental European sense of the term – 'classical liberals', if you like.

Now in that draft outline of the book, climate change issues went unmentioned; nor did Ian suggest that this was an omission on my part. Up to then, neither of us had taken a serious interest in the subject, nor had it been raised in our meetings or correspondence. This is worth noting, given that the issues had featured prominently on the policy agenda, national and international, since the late 1980s, and were about to feature prominently on the agenda of the 2002 UN Johannesburg summit meeting on sustainable development, which we had been proposing to review. For a period of 15 years or so, therefore, alike as serving officials and as retirees, we had both remained on the sidelines in the climate change debate. It was only in 2002 that this non-involvement on our part was brought to an end.

A precipitating issue

What had aroused Ian's concern, and mine too, was a specific technical issue. A position that we held in common, then and throughout, is to be found in the 1993 System of National Accounts (SNA), prepared by five international agencies and approved by those agencies' member governments. As Australian Statistician Ian had taken a close interest in this report; and its principal author, Peter Hill, had been one of my staff in my own last official role, as Head of what was then the Economics and Statistics Department of the OECD. In paragraph 38 of the opening chapter of the SNA it is laid down that:

> When the objective is to compare the volumes of goods or services produced or consumed per head, data in national currencies must be converted into a common currency by means of purchasing power parities and not exchange rates ... Exchange rate converted data must not ... be interpreted as measures of the relative volumes of goods and services concerned.

In this connection, in the year 2000, Ian had already registered a notable success. Here is the story, as told in paragraph 3 of his first letter to Pachauri:

> Following the release of the UNDP's *Human Development Report 1999*, I made extensive statistical criticisms of the treatment in that report of trends in global poverty and inequality. At the request of the 2000 meeting of the UN Statistical Commission, those criticisms were examined by a group of expert statisticians constituted as the Friends

> of the Chair of the Commission. The report of the group ... upheld my more serious criticisms. In particular, the Friends of the Chair ... held that HDR 1999 had made a "material error" (i.e., one which left the reader with "a fundamentally distorted view of the phenomenon being described") in relying on national aggregates converted into $US at current exchange rates...

In the letter, Ian went on to record that: 'The HDR Office of the UNDP accepted the report, and has made major improvements in statistical presentation and reporting in subsequent issues of the HDR'.

The main single argument of our three letters to Pachauri was that the six scenario teams which had combined to produce the SRES, and the 40 scenarios which had been presented in the Report, had fallen into this same 'material error'. The scenarios offered projections of GDP and emissions over the period from 1990 to 2100, with the world economy divided into country groupings. For 1990, as the base year, they took as a point of departure figures for each group's GDP per head derived from national data which had been converted into a common measure using exchange rates; and the result of this, as with the 1999 HDR, was to overstate greatly the relative poverty of the poor countries. As Ian pointed out, in his second communication to Pachauri: '... average incomes in developing countries [were in reality] three or four times higher than the IPCC assumed'.

In projecting the growth of GDP per head to 2100, the scenarios provided, in varying degrees, for the closure, or substantial reduction, of this greatly overstated initial gap between rich and poor countries. We argued that in consequence these growth projections for poor countries were biased upward; and we inferred from this – though here we were mistaken, which it took us some time to realise – that a corresponding upward bias had entered into the projections of emissions from those countries.[1]

In voicing this criticism, our hope was that, following the encouraging precedent of the Human Development Report, the 'material error' would be recognised as such by the IPCC and its member governments, so that the required 'major improvements' would be made within the IPCC process. This hope, together

---

1 Our mistake arose because of a failure to think through the implications of an important point that Ian had made right from the start. In his second letter to Pachauri, he had noted that seriously underestimating the GDP of poor countries, through the use of exchange-rate-based comparative measures, brought with it a corresponding overestimate of comparative energy intensities: to quote the letter, 'The assumption of a huge margin of difference in energy intensity ... is false'. Hence the resulting SRES projections embodied, in varying degrees, twin errors which were largely offsetting. We were right to argue that, in so far as they built in the closure of an imaginary initial gap between rich and poor countries, projections of GDP growth in the latter group would be biased upward. We failed to note the corollary: that closing an equally imaginary gap in the energy intensity of those countries would damp down the effect of that GDP growth on emissions.

with another aspiration which we formed, and which I will come to later, was doomed to disappointment. In outlining now the story of extended failure on our part, or at best heavily qualified success, I will start with the unexpected sequence of events that directly arose out of our letters to Pachauri.

Developments in 2003–4

Early in January 2003, Ian and I found ourselves, through an invitation which came from the IPCC Secretariat, at a meeting in Amsterdam of the Panel's Technical Group on Climate Impact Assessment. There we were able to meet some of the leading scenario authors, and to have extended discussions with them outside the main meeting; we were introduced to Dr Pachauri; and in the meeting itself, we were both invited – generously, I felt – to make five-minute presentations of our own, despite the fact that what we had to say was unconnected with the meeting's actual agenda. (In my presentation, I noted that, confronted with these two strange old gentlemen, conference participants might find themselves reminded of Jack Lemmon and Walter Matthau). After we had respectively returned to Canberra and London, and in the light of the Amsterdam proceedings, Ian and I both wrote down, again separately, some further personal thoughts.

Between us we had now assembled, and posted on line, a curious swag of documents: three bulky letters to Pachauri; the two texts used as a basis for our respective five-minute presentations in Amsterdam; and twin post-Amsterdam reflections. We each emailed this collection to various friends and associates. Two of my recipients then reacted in ways that I had neither asked for nor expected, and which between them put the firm of Castles and Henderson truly on the map.

The first of these recipients was my friend Clive Crook, who was then Deputy Editor of *The Economist*: he offered to write up the issues on the 'Economics Focus' page of the paper. Of course I accepted with alacrity; and Clive's brilliant column put our arguments better than we had put them ourselves and gave them wide exposure. Moreover, the timing was perfect, since the column appeared in February 2003 during a plenary meeting of the IPCC, at which (as I learned) the complaint against us was made, not without justice, that '*The Economist* is not a peer-reviewed journal'.

I also sent our swag to a journal editor whom at that stage I knew only by name: this was Sonja Boehmer-Christiansen, and her journal was *Energy and Environment*. To my great surprise, she offered to publish our collection, in full and without alteration. After consulting Ian, I replied that she was most welcome to do this, provided that she wrote right away to Dr Pachauri to invite him to arrange for the scenario authors to write a response to our criticisms, a response which she would guarantee to publish. She agreed, Pachauri agreed, and a (rather indignant) article by a group of 15 of the scenario builders duly appeared, alongside the set of miscellaneous documents by Castles and Henderson, in the same issue of the journal.[2] In her 'editor's note' on our collection, Dr Boehmer-Christiansen observed, you might think with some understatement, that 'This is not a standard journal article'. Few editors would have acted as she did.

In later issues of the same journal, there followed a second exchange of papers. Ian and I wrote a formal co-authored piece, while in turn a rather different team of scenario authors (18 in this case) published a further response to our arguments, which appeared in January 2004.[3] Meanwhile Dr Pachauri himself had joined the debate. At the Ninth Conference of the Parties to the UN Framework Convention on Climate Change, in Milan on 8 December 2003, he gave a special press conference, the sole topic and purpose of which was a condemnation of our work. He described us as 'so-called "two independent commentators"', and said that we should be classed as purveyors of disinformation. His text was then posted, in prudently amended form, on the IPCC website.

Thus the scenario authors, and the IPCC directing circle, were far from accepting our critique. What is more, on this occasion, unlike that of the Human Development Report 1999, no support was forthcoming through the agency of the UN Statistical Commission. Looking through my records when preparing this paper, I came across the following email message from Ian, dated 12 June 2003. 'Dennis Trewin [Castles's successor as Australian Statistician] raised the Castles-Henderson issues at the UN Statistical Commission meeting in March, but was unable to win support from other countries'. This time, therefore, no Friends of the Chair were called in. We did win strong support from a former Canadian official statistician, Jacob Ryten, who published in *Energy and Environment* in mid-2004 an article for which I think I provided the title: it was headed 'MERs, PPPs and IPCC: Illusions and Reality'.[4] In this piece he commented (367):

> I cannot help being shocked by the contrasts between the [Scenario] Teams' bold assertions and peremptory dismissal of the arguments advanced by Castles and Henderson, and their manifest ignorance of the conceptual and practical issues involved in developing and using intercountry measures of economic product.

But Ryten was speaking only for himself, and I fear that his article gained little attention.

---

2 *Energy and Environment*, Vol .14, No. 2-3.

3 Our joint paper was entitled 'Economics, Emissions Scenarios and the Work of the 'IPCC', *Energy and Environment*, Vol. 14 No. 4, 2003. 'Emissions Scenarios: A Final Response', by Arnold Grubler and others, appeared in the same journal in Vol. 15 No. 1, 2004.

4 *Energy and Environment*, Vol. 15 No. 3, 2004.

Two fronts and our first misapprehension

During this period and after, Ian and I were campaigning on two fronts. On the first of these, our target was the IPCC process – not just the SRES, but the process more broadly, as shown by the title of our second piece in *Energy and Environment*. Even in his opening letter to Pachauri, Ian had cited flaws in the treatment of international inequality in the 2001 report of the Panel's Working Group III, as well as in the SRES. In his Amsterdam text, as published, he wrote:

> One might ask how many of the multitude of authors and reviewers of both documents, and the anonymous officials involved in the review process for these two reports, were aware of the existence of the SNA...

In that connection, I checked the extensive list of references in the SRES, to find that SNA 1993 made no appearance there: its existence may indeed have been unknown to the 53 members of the writing team and the 89 reviewers who are listed in the SRES. At one point in the report, revealingly, the concept of gross national product was misdefined.

Alongside the article by Ryten that I noted above, in mid-2004, Ian brought out a short piece in which he criticised the way in which, as he saw it, the IPCC process had evolved. He commented there (372) on a recently-published 340-page report of an IPCC Expert Meeting, observing that: 'Most of the papers fall lamentably short of the minimum standards that could reasonably be expected in the publications of a scientific body'; and in the final sentence of this article (373), he referred to 'disturbing signs that the Panel's role in the assessment of climate change has now become subservient to its role in supporting a specific policy agenda'.

Both Ian and I had come to the view that the IPCC's treatment of statistical and economic issues was flawed, and that those responsible for it were not professionally representative. To remedy this situation, we advocated wider official participation. In writing to Pachauri, Ian had argued for the involvement of national statistical offices and the International Statistical Institute in making new emissions projections. In my own letter I wrote – again with the IPCC process as a whole in mind, not just the scenario exercise – that 'the central economic departments of state ... should likewise be taking an active part'. We emphasised this latter point in our first truly joint article, and it was echoed by Clive Crook in a further piece that he wrote in *The Economist* in late 2003.

The other front on which we continued to be engaged was the use of PPP-based comparative data, not just in IPCC documents, but more generally. In early 2005 we published another lengthy co-authored article: it was entitled

'International Comparisons of GDP: Issues of Theory and Practice'.[5] Here we set out the case for PPP-based as opposed to exchange-rate-based figures, and reviewed the treatment of the issue in various places, including a range of international agencies as well as in the IPCC process. From our standpoint, the results of our survey were sobering. Aside from the UNDP, as mentioned above, none of the agencies appeared free from criticism. Further, we noted (82) 'the cases of several leading [economists] whose ... opinions, though not necessarily identical or consistent with one another, are at variance with what is laid down in SNA93'.

In this context, one of Ian's personal targets, with good reason, was the World Bank; and I still have on my files some email exchanges which he initiated, and which do little credit to the Bank staff members concerned. I also have a long letter from Ian to Dr Pachauri, dated 4 July 2004, which begins by saying 'I am awaiting your substantive reply to my letter to you of 20 April'. I believe that this letter, like its predecessor, and together with a successor dated 30 July and a further letter sent in November 1995, all went without response. From early 2004 onwards, Ian was increasingly treated in a number of official circles, not as a serious professional with a distinguished record, but as a tedious nuisance.

By this time, a disturbing reality was being brought home to us. It was increasingly apparent that in relation to the use and rationale of PPP-based cross-country comparisons it was we, rather than the scenario builders and their kind, who were in a minority. Our initial presumption, that SNA 1993 and the position laid down in it were widely known and generally endorsed by economists and other interested professionals, was revealed as a misapprehension. As will appear below, it was not our only misapprehension.

Lord Lawson and the House of Lords Select Committee

Early in 2004 our joint cause acquired a notable ally, when I convinced a former Chancellor of the Exchequer, Nigel (Lord) Lawson, that climate change issues deserved his serious attention. Lawson has been, and continues to be, a leading and influential contributor to the debate. In 2007 he brought out a book on the subject,[6] and in early 2009 he established in London a think-tank called the Global Warming Policy Foundation, the declared object of which is 'to restore balance and trust to the climate change debate'. The Foundation's news service,

5 *World Economics*, Vol. 6 No. 1, 2005.

6 *In Defence of Reason: A Cool look at Global Warming*, Duckworth Overlook. The 2009 paperback edition incorporates some changes, and includes an extended afterword. In a review of the first edition in the *Financial Times* (14 April 2008) Clive Crook described it as a 'splendid book'.

reports and briefing papers have made a solid contribution to that debate, which Ian would have welcomed and supported: he might well have become a GWPF author.

Lawson was (as he still is) a member of the House of Lords Select Committee on Economic Affairs, and early in 2005 the Committee chose as its next subject of inquiry the economics of climate change: its report on the subject appeared in July of that year. Both Ian and I, separately, submitted memoranda of evidence to the Committee. Ian's submission focused on the defects of the scenarios. He wrote:

> In this submission I draw attention to eight further errors in the SRES and/or in the responses of the SRES Teams to our critiques, in addition to those identified in our previous papers. My purpose is to provide additional evidence in support of the view that the IPCC should not be accepted as the authoritative source of information on the economic aspects of climate change.

In its report, the Select Committee expressed 'significant doubts about some aspects of the IPCC's emissions scenario exercise' and 'some concerns about the objectivity of the IPCC process'. They also called for 'much stronger Treasury involvement' in the analysis of mitigation costs. These conclusions were welcome from our point of view, as also was what they said (in paragraph 53 of the report) about the work of Castles and Henderson, *viz.:* 'We consider that they have performed a public service'.[7]

The Select Committee had included five former Cabinet ministers, a former Financial Secretary to the Treasury, a former Governor of the Bank of England, a noted professor of economics, and the distinguished biographer of JM Keynes. Its membership was drawn from all three political parties, as well as from cross-benchers. Its Specialist Adviser for this exercise was one of the world's leading environmental economists, the late David Pearce. Its report was unanimous. In view of these facts, one might have supposed that the report would be taken seriously in British official circles. Any such notion was dispelled when the then government's wholly dismissive response appeared, in November 2005. I wrote of this document, in a published commentary, that it 'is itself an illustration of those features of the IPCC process and milieu which prompted the Committee's concerns'.[8]

---

7 House of Lords Select Committee on Economic Affairs, 2nd Report of Session 2005-06, *The Economics of Climate Change*, Volume I: Report, Volume II: Evidence. The Stationery Office, 2005.

8 *Government Response to the Economics of Climate Change*, printed in November 2005 as an Appendix to the Select Committee's report. My critique of it was published in *Energy and Environment*, Vol. 17 No. 1, 2006.

The two British government departments concerned, the Department of Environment, Food and Rural Affairs (DEFRA) and Her Majesty's Treasury, had submitted a joint memorandum of evidence to the Select Committee. Two matters of detail arising from this document are worth noting here as symptomatic:

- In the memorandum the two departments said that: 'When the debate first emerged we provided the IPCC with funds so that David Henderson could attend a meeting to discuss the issues with IPCC modellers'. Though presumably made in good faith, this was not a truthful statement.
- In August 2005 Ian sent a long email letter to the then Director, Climate Change and Environmental Risk in DEFRA, commenting on a number of mistakes and misapprehensions in the memorandum's references to our work. So far as I know, he received no response.

Wider aspects

Initially, as I have noted, Ian and I had chiefly focused on economic and statistical aspects of work undertaken and published under IPCC auspices. But as time went on, our involvement broadened in ways that we had neither planned nor anticipated. The following quotation, taken from a piece which I wrote in June 2010, fits Ian's case as well as my own:

> Increasingly, and unexpectedly, I have become critical of the way in which issues of climate change have been viewed and treated by governments across the world. In particular, I have become a critic of the *official expert advisory process* which governments have created and continue to rely on, within which the main single element is the work of the IPCC as reflected in its successive Assessment Reports. Over the past 22 years governments everywhere, and a great many outside observers too, have put their trust in the expert advisory process as a whole and the IPCC process in particular. I have come to believe that this widespread trust is unwarranted.[9]

Among the episodes and publications that influenced us in this direction, from the end of 2003 onwards, I would mention in particular the evidence presented, both separately and in concert, by Stephen McIntyre and Ross McKitrick. Their writings, and later those of David Holland, not only placed in question widely accepted and influential results of IPCC-related work in climate science, but also exposed serious professional flaws in the conduct of that work.[10] Ian

9 This is an excerpt from evidence that I submitted to the Inter-Academy Council Review of the IPCC.

10 There is an array of possible references here: Ross McKitrick's website is a good source. Some leading issues, first raised by McIntyre and McKitrick, were well reviewed in David Holland's 2007 article, 'Bias and

became an occasional and respected contributor to McIntyre's well known blog, Climate Audit. The annex to this present paper summarises, from a later and more complete perspective, the grounds for questioning the advisory process that we both came to hold.

This extension of Ian's involvement, well beyond the specific technical issue which had initially brought him into the climate change debate, was not at all surprising: it was very much in character. His participation in that debate has to be seen, not as an isolated and eccentric late-in-life venture, but rather as a further manifestation, an extra dimension, of his established professional views and outlook. In particular, a prominent element in his thinking had long been a rejection of resource and environmental pessimism especially on the part of leading scientists: an example is his published article of 2001 entitled 'Scientists, Statisticians and the Prophets of Doom', where he also criticised what he called 'the enraged reaction' of some scientific reviewers to Bjorn Lomborg's book, *The Skeptical Environmentalist*. The climate change debate provided Ian with a further and continuing series of variations on what were for him the familiar themes of bias, over-presumption and mishandling of economic issues in some scientific circles. In this connection, I feel sure that he would have been greatly impressed, as I have been, by an outstanding soon-to-be published book, entitled *The Age of Global Warming: A History*, by Rupert Darwall.[11]

For both of us, this broadening of our concerns, beyond economic aspects, led to a development which I at any rate had not anticipated, and which for some time I failed to notice or suspect. In becoming increasingly preoccupied with the defects (as we saw them) of the official expert advisory process as a whole, including the treatment of climate science, we unwittingly separated ourselves from the majority of economists, whether in official positions or the academic world, who had come to hold views on climate change issues. The first intimations of this unforeseen divorce from the profession in general made themselves apparent in early 2006. The occasion was the Stern Review.

Reviewing the Stern Review

At the time of the House of Lords Select Committee report, and for a while afterwards, Ian and I kept to and reiterated our key recommendation, that the central economic departments of state – treasuries, finance ministries, and in the US, the Council of Economic Advisers – should become actively involved in

Concealment in the IPCC Process' (*Energy and Environment*, Vol. 18 No. 7-8); and the main single issue forms the subject of Andrew Montford's book, *The Hockey Stick Illusion: Climategate and the Corruption of Science*' (Stacey International, 2010), which is itself extensively referenced.

11 The book is due to be published in London in March 2013 by Quartet Books.

the climate change debate. We noted with satisfaction that the same point was made, in relation to Her Majesty's Treasury, by Nigel Lawson during the Select Committee inquiry, when evidence was being given by the Treasury. He said that:

> In my time at the Treasury as Chancellor it would have been unthinkable for the Treasury not to spend quite a lot of time on a serious economic analysis of an issue as important as this.

Ian and I presumed, and I think that Lawson too expected, that our shared arguments and concerns would gain support in so far as economists in general, and those in official positions in economic ministries and international agencies in particular, became more closely involved. This was our second misapprehension. We were soon to be given a forcible reminder of that well known cautionary advice: 'Be careful what you wish for'.

In July 2005 the then UK Prime Minister (Tony Blair) and Chancellor of the Exchequer (Gordon Brown) commissioned a top Treasury official, Sir Nicholas (now Lord) Stern, to lead a team to prepare a full-scale report on the economics of climate change. One result of this decision was that Ian and I once again became joint authors, in two separate journal articles, though in both cases as members of a larger group.

The Stern Review appeared in October 2006, while the printed volume, with an additional postscript, was published in early 2007.[12] However, as early as January 2006 three interconnected documents had been issued as first fruits of the Review. They comprised a discussion paper entitled 'What Is the Economics of Climate Change?'; a public lecture by Stern with the same title; and a Technical Annex on 'The science of climate change'. The lecture was published in June 2006 as a lead article in *World Economics*; and towards the end of that same issue, the journal carried two related pieces arising from it: first a critique of the lecture and of its two accompanying texts; and second, a response by Stern himself. The critique was authored by a team of nine like-minded economists which I put together, and which included both Ian and Lord Lawson. (The other signatories comprised another member of the House of Lords Select Committee on Economic Affairs, Robert Skidelsky, together with Ian Byatt, Ross McKitrick, Julian Morris, Alan Peacock and Colin Robinson.)[13]

Looking back now, I can see that our short (six-page) article, which I have only once seen referred to, effectively broke new ground. This was because

12 Nicholas Stern and other authors, *The Economics of Climate Change: The Stern Review*, Cambridge University Press. 2007.

13 Nicholas Stern, 'What Is the Economics of Climate Change?'; 'Ian Byatt *et al.*, 'Climate Change: The Stern Review "Oxonia Papers"'; Nicholas Stern, 'Reply to Byatt *et al.*' *World Economics*, Vol. 7 No. 2, 2006.

we authors, economists though we were, did not direct our main critique to economic issues. Our opening thesis was that 'the treatment of scientific aspects in these documents is unbalanced'; and later in the article we held that the treatment by Stern and his associates was also at fault, first, in accepting uncritically both the procedures and the outcomes of the IPCC process, and second, in disregarding published work which had put that process in serious doubt. In our final paragraph we said (150) that:

> By taking as given hypotheses that remain uncertain, assertions that are debatable or mistaken, and processes of inquiry that are at fault, the Review has put itself on a path that can lead to no useful outcome.

In his reply to this piece, Stern began by contesting our opening thesis. He set out reasons for holding (154) that 'The overwhelming body of evidence leaves no doubt that the threat of climate change is real and serious'. Thus the status and interpretation of the scientific evidence emerged, I think for the first time, as an issue on which economists were divided.

When the Review itself appeared, we returned to the fray. I was able to reconvene our economic group, again including Ian; and I also put together, flanking the economists, a separate team of scientists and engineers: it comprised, Robert Carter, Chris de Freitas, Indur Goklany, David Holland and Richard Lindzen. As a result, two linked review articles, one scientific and the other economic, were published in *World Economics* (Vol. 7 No. 4) at the end of 2006, under the heading of 'The Stern Review: A Dual Critique'. In a joint introduction to the two articles, representing all 14 authors, we wrote (166):

> In relation to both scientific and economic issues, we question the accuracy and completeness of the Review's analysis and the objectivity of its treatment.

The economic critique was the last publication in which Ian and I appeared as joint authors, and it featured an annex entitled 'The Stern Review and the IPCC Scenarios' which he had drafted.

Our second misapprehension revealed

The Stern Review was widely acclaimed across the world; and not surprisingly, academic economists were among the many who judged it favourably. For example, it was endorsed on publication by several leading economists including four Nobel prizewinners; and in Australia, the officially-sponsored Garnaut report of 2008 can be seen as a southern hemisphere counterpart of the Review, which it described as 'a landmark contribution'.[14] On the other side of the fence, a number of prominent economists have been strong critics of the Review, as we had been: in that respect, these were allies.[15] However, there was and remains an important element of difference between our position and that of most of our fellow-critics of Stern. Few economists, whatever their views on Stern, have joined with us in emphasising, first, that prevailing scientific opinion in this area should not be taken as established, and second, that the official expert advisory process on climate change has revealed itself as seriously flawed. Most of the critics of Stern (and Garnaut), along with the many supporters, share a common point of departure which is not ours: they endorse, or at any rate take as given and not to be queried, prevailing scientific opinion which they are apt to refer to as 'the science'; and they do not question the official expert advisory process – or give consideration to what its critics have written. For this reason I class these supporters and critics of the Stern Review together, despite their often-profound disagreements, as *upholders* of generally received opinion. We *dissenters,* or non-subscribers to that received opinion, form a minority.

It is important to note that the professional majority here comprises not only academic economists but also an array of counterparts of theirs in the official world. This is to be expected, in so far as the views held by these officials reflect a broadly common position that their respective organisations have long taken on climate change issues: both national governments and the international agencies which are their creation have continued to subscribe to received opinion. Among the agencies, this is true of the IMF, the World Bank, the OECD (including, alas, my former Department), the International Energy Agency, the EBRD and the European Commission, not to mention the UN Secretariat, UNCTAD, the UNDP, the UNFCCC and the UN Environment Program: in all of these, it would be hard to find economists who hold, and are ready to voice, dissenting views.[16] The same applies within those agencies' member governments. What is especially telling is that the treasuries and finance ministries, on which Ian and I had pinned our hopes, have to be classed among the official upholders, as indeed had been the case from the start. Thus our initial expectation of wide and firm support from fellow-economists, and from departments and agencies with economic responsibilities, was in due course exposed as illusory. That situation still pertains today. It remains our second misapprehension.

---

14 The *Garnaut Climate Change Review* of 2008 was followed by *The Garnaut Review 2011,* likewise published by the Cambridge University Press. I commented on the published first draft of the report in a piece entitled 'Climate Change Issues: An Australian Contribution to the Debate' (*World Economics,* Vol. 9 No. 3, 2008).

15 A recent searching critique of the Review, published in 2012 by the Global Warming Policy Foundation, is '*What Is Wrong with Stern?,* by Peter Lilley MP, a former UK cabinet minister.

16 I published a critique of the IMF's treatment of climate change issues, under the heading of 'Over-Presumption and Myopia', in June 2008 (*World Economics,* Vol 9 No 2).

Voicing dissent

After becoming fully attuned to our minority status, I published a long article in *World Economics* in early 2009 entitled ''Economists and Climate Science: A Critique'. In the following year I returned to the theme in the pages of the quarterly *Newsletter* of the Royal Economic Society, where I was able to take account of the so-called 'Climategate' and 'Glaciergate' affairs and their sequel, all of which had provided further evidence of unprofessional conduct in relevant scientific circles.[17]

This latter article appeared only after Ian's death. However, I believe that he would have agreed fully with the following two excerpts from it. I quote them now despite their length, because I feel that here I was speaking for us both.

First excerpt

> In a recent paper, I presented a critique of positions taken by a range of prominent economists of varying shades of green who were upholders of received opinion. I commented there on the Stern Review; on its Australian counterpart, the officially commissioned Garnaut report; on papers by Dieter Helm, William Nordhaus, and Martin Weitzman; and on the treatment of climate change issues by the IMF. (I could now add the World Bank, the International Energy Agency, and the OECD Secretariat). I charge this impressive array of authors and agencies with three interrelated failings: over-presumption, credulity and inadvertence:

- *Over-presumption*, in accepting too readily that received opinion on global warming is firmly grounded on scientific findings which can no longer be seriously questioned. In so doing, they are treating as established facts what should be viewed as no more than working hypotheses which have won considerable expert support;
- *Credulity*, through placing unwarranted trust in a flawed official expert advisory process, and
- *Inadvertence*, in that they have disregarded published evidence, *evidence whichthey are competent to weigh and evaluate*, which puts that process in serious question.

> The latter two aspects, the credulity and the inadvertence, go together. Economist upholders, both in the groves of academe and around the corridors of power, have not woken up to the ways in which the official

17 'Climate Change Issues: New Developments in a 20-Year Context', Royal Economic Society *Newsletter*, October 2010.

expert advisory process, and the IPCC process as its leading element, have been revealed as professionally not up to the mark. Hence there is a missing dimension in their treatment of policy aspects: they have not caught on to the need to strengthen the basis of policy, by making the advisory process more objective and professionally watertight.

Second excerpt

> ... given what is at stake economically, a responsibility, so far unrecognised, rests on the central economic departments of state – on treasuries, ministries of finance and economics and, in the US, the Council of Economic Advisers.
>
> I am myself a former Treasury official; and much later, as head of what was then the Economics and Statistics Department in the OECD Secretariat, I had close dealings over a number of years with the central economic departments in OECD member countries. I have been surprised by the failure of these agencies to go more deeply into the evidence bearing on climate change issues, their uncritical acceptance of the results of a process of inquiry that is so obviously biased and flawed, and their lack of attention to the well-founded criticisms of that process that have been voiced by independent outsiders – criticisms which, I think, they ought to have been making themselves. A similar lack of resource has characterised the Research Department of the IMF and the Economics Department of the OECD... In all these official bodies with economic responsibilities, there has been a conspicuous failure of due diligence.

Wider aspects revisited

These criticisms of many fellow-economists reflected the broader concerns that Ian and I – and others too - had come to hold about the official handling of climate change issues across the world. In that broader context, here is an excerpt from an article of mine which first appeared in late 2011. Here again I believe that I was speaking for Ian as well as myself:

> In relation to climate change issues, governments in general, and the OECD member governments in particular, have locked themselves into a set of procedures, and an associated way of thinking – in short, a *framework* – which both reflects and yields over-presumptive conclusions which are weighted towards alarm. They have done so through a worrying combination – of credulity and inadvertence on the part of responsible lay persons, and of chronic bias and professional underperformance on

the part of trusted experts and expert bodies. In this whole episode, the capacity of human societies today to arrive at well founded conclusions and decisions has been placed in question.[18]

Last contacts

The last time that I saw and talked with Ian was in March 2007, on a visit to Canberra. (During that visit, by the way, I was invited by the Treasury to speak at a well-attended and exceptionally well-organised seminar: it is a pleasure to thank once again those who were responsible for that invitation). In preparing this paper, I found on my files a number of personal emails from Ian which he had sent me after our final Canberra meeting. Most of these took further the issue of PPP-based versus exchange-rate-based cross-country comparisons, where Ian continued to follow attentively developments on the international scene. Two of the emails, dating from 2008, respectively found fault with the way in which the issue was being handled in the IMF and the International Energy Agency.

Of these latter-year messages from Ian, two were prompt and well-crafted responses to requests on my part for comment. As to the first, I had sent him an article of mine which came out in June 2007, where I had quoted, and now drew to his attention, to an excerpt from a speech in the House of Lords by Richard Layard, a well known London School of Economics professor of economics and a member of the House of Lords Select Committee. Layard had referred to the many statements on climate change issues by national scientific academies, and said that he could not 'really see how non-scientists can take a different view unless we want to question their motivation'. Ian concluded his comments on this argument by writing: 'Examination of the contents of statements by national academies confirms your view that the support of these bodies for the IPCC should not be regarded as decisive and is by no means above question'.

The last personal message that I have on file dates from July 2008. It was prompted by my sending Ian a series of arguments against the use of PPP-based comparisons which had been sent to me by an eminent American professor of economics. Ian dealt with each argument in turn in masterly fashion. Reading those pages, it was saddening for me to be reminded that I had lost forever both a true friend and a much-valued continuing source of ideas, information and advice.

18 The piece from which this passage is taken forms a chapter in a volume of essays in honour of the President of the Czech Republic, Vaclav Klaus (*Today's World and Vaclav Klaus*, edited by Jiri Brodsky and published in 2012 by Fragment). The piece first appeared with a different title in the Australian journal *Quadrant*, and in this form President Klaus posted it on his personal website.

A final glimpse

In preparing this present paper, and looking back at our shared thoughts and activities over more than a decade, I asked myself whether in fact Ian counted as, and would have described himself as, an economic liberal. I feel confident that the answer is Yes; but rather than going into the question directly I will end with a quotation from an original and perceptive article, very characteristic of its author, that Ian wrote and sent to me in (I think) the year 2000. The theme of the article, a favourite one of his, was unwarranted pessimism and collectivist prescriptions on the part of eminent scientists and political leaders who unwisely put their trust in such presumed experts. In this case, the pertinent examples he gave were from Britain in the years after World War II. One of the scientists involved was Sir Henry Tizard, then Chief Scientific Adviser to the Ministry of Defence and chairman of an official Advisory Council on Scientific Policy. The final two paragraphs of Ian's paper, as also of this paper of mine today, read as follows:

> ... Tizard told the 1948 British Association meeting that "All social progress, such as spread of education, promotion of health, opportunities for leisure and healthy recreation, must depend on the power of technology to increase the productivity of industry". Economist [Ludwig] Erhard, architect of Germany's "economic miracle", recognised the vital role of another factor: effectively functioning markets. It is difficult to resist the conclusion that much of the difference in the material achievement of the two countries in the early post-war decades can be attributed to the relative influence of these mindsets.
>
> It would be overly simple to extend the comparison, and attribute all of the changes in the relative economic performance of Britain and Germany through the nineteenth and the twentieth centuries solely to the relative strength in each country of liberal ideas, both in the intellectual and the political spheres. But the pervasive influence of such ideas upon "the material foundations of the liberty and welfare of all peoples" should not be underestimated.

Annex: A Flawed Process

(*The following article by David Henderson appeared in* The Australian *on 16 February 2010, under the title 'Climategate is Just the Tip of the Iceberg'.*)

Two recent episodes have given rise to concerns about the quality and reliability of received expert advice on climate change.

First is the unauthorised release of a mass of email exchanges from the server of the Climatic Research Unit at the University of East Anglia: the contents have put in question the conduct of CRU scientists and some of their correspondents.

Second is the discovery that statements made in the fourth and most recent Assessment Report (AR4) from the Intergovernmental Panel on Climate Change (IPCC) were based on sources which should not have been given weight. In relation to what was said about Himalayan glaciers, the IPCC has issued a formal admission of error.

The concerns raised by these episodes are well founded. However, 'Climategate' and 'Glaciergate' are not to be viewed in isolation. They are instances of a more fundamental and deeply entrenched phenomenon.

In relation to climate change issues, the established official expert advisory process, which governments have commissioned and relied on, has shown itself, over many years, to be not professionally up to the mark. The situation is one of unwarranted trust.

The main headings of unprofessional conduct within the process, all identified and documented before the recent revelations, have been:

- Over-reliance on in-group peer review procedures which do not serve as a guarantee of quality and do not ensure due disclosure.
- Serious and continuing failures of disclosure and archiving in relation to peer-reviewed studies, which the IPCC and member governments have drawn on.
- Continuing resistance to disclosure of basic information, which reputable journals insist on as a precondition for acceptance. (In the CRU emails, participants discuss a range of arguments, pretexts and devices that could be used to fend off disclosure, including the deletion of emails containing material that had been sought under FOI requests – requests that were made only because authors had not followed accepted scholarly procedures).
- Basic errors in the handling of data, through failure to consult or involve trained statisticians.
- Failure to take due account of relevant published work which documented the above lapses, while disregarding IPCC criteria for inclusion in the review process.
- Failure to take due note of comments from dissenting critics who took part in the preparation of AR4.
- Resisting the disclosure of professional exchanges within the AR4 drafting process, despite the formal instruction of member governments that the IPCC's proceedings should be 'open and transparent'. And last but not least
- Failure on the part of the IPCC and its directing circle to acknowledge and remedy the above deficiencies.

In the light of 'Glaciergate', one could add to the above list 'reliance on worthless (non-peer-reviewed) sources'. But mere insistence on peer review would leave in place the other basic flaws.

Comprehensive exposure of these flaws has come from a number of independent commentators. Particular mention should be made of two Canadian authors, Stephen McIntyre and Ross McKitrick: both separately and in joint publications, going back to 2003, they have made an outstanding contribution to public debate. Together with a perceptive British critic, David Holland, they are the subject of unfavourable references in the CRU emails. However, their work and that of other informed critics has been disregarded by governments, and by most commentators in academic journals and the media alike.

The glaring defects in the expert advisory process have gone unacknowledged and unremedied by what I call the environmental policy milieu. This high-level failure, as also the defects themselves, have resulted from chronic and pervasive bias. Right from the start, members of the milieu, and of the IPCC's directing circle, have been characterised by what has been well termed 'pre-commitment to the urgency of the climate cause'.

Although the IPCC in particular is now under fire, this is too restricted a focus. It is true that the Panel's work forms the leading element in the official expert advisory process. But the basic problem of unwarranted trust goes further: it extends to the chronically biased treatment of climate change issues by responsible departments and agencies which the Panel reports to, and in nationally based organisations which they finance (such as the CRU).

It is not just the environmental policy milieu that is to blame for the mishandling by governments of climate change issues. As a former Treasury official and international civil servant, I have been surprised by the failure of economic departments in OECD member countries to audit the evidence bearing on climate change issues, their uncritical acceptance of the results of a process of inquiry which is so obviously biased and flawed, and their lack of attention to the criticisms of that process which have been voiced by independent outsiders – criticisms which they ought to have been making themselves. A similar lack of resource has characterised the Research Department of the IMF and the Economics Department of the OECD. In all these departments and agencies, there has been a conspicuous failure of due diligence.

The chief moral to be drawn is simple. In an area of policy where so much is at stake, and so much remains uncertain and unsettled, policies should be evolutionary and adaptive, rather than presumptive as they are now; and their evolution should be linked to a process of inquiry and review which is more thorough, balanced, open and objective than has so far been the case.

23. Addressing Wellbeing in the Long-Term: a Review of Intergenerational Equity and Discount Rates in Climate Change Analysis

Mark Harrison

Discounting and climate change

Most government policies give rise to a stream of costs and benefits over time. To evaluate them requires us to compare costs and benefits received in different time periods. That requires choosing a discount rate, which determines the value of future costs and benefits relative to current ones.

The choice of discount rate can make a significant difference to whether the present value of a project is positive, and to the relative desirability of alternative projects, especially when costs and benefits accrue at different times and over long periods.

A typical project involves upfront costs, with the benefits coming later. If so, the lower the discount rate, the more attractive is the project (the higher its net present value). If the discount rate is set too high, desirable projects may be rejected. If it is set too low, undesirable projects may be approved. The size of the discount rate makes a huge difference to policies where benefits occur in the distant future, such as many environmental policies.

It was a lower discount rate that drove the differences between the policy conclusions of the Stern report and the consensus view of previous cost-benefit analyses of global warming. Stern's cost-benefit analysis of global warming assumed a real discount rate of 1.4 per cent and concluded there was a case for strong action to reduce carbon emissions, recommending an immediate imposition of a high carbon price. Nordhaus assumed a 5.5 per cent discount rate, and favoured a modest carbon price (one-tenth the level of Stern's), increasing over time. The recommended polices differed because of the discount rate assumptions. When Nordhaus ran his computer model using Stern's discount rates, he got similar results to Stern.[1]

1 See Nordhaus (2007: 694, 698-700); Baker *et al* (2008: 63-64) and Weisbach and Sunstein (2008: 11).

The difference is not surprising because most of the effects of global warming take place decades in the future. At Stern's discount rate of 1.4 per cent a year, $1 grows into $4 in 100 years and $16 in 200 years. At Nordhaus's 5.5 per cent, it would grow to $211 in 100 years and $44,719 in 200 years. Put differently, the present value of $1 of damages in 100 years with Stern's discount rate is 25 cents, more than 50 times greater than with Nordhaus's. A dollar in 200 years is valued at 6 cents now, almost 2,800 times more than Nordhaus's value.

The Garnaut Report used discount rates of 1.35 per cent and 2.65 per cent.[2] Yet the average real return on government bonds (both short and long term, nominal and indexed) in Australia was 3-4 per cent over the past 25-40 years. The market return on capital averages 6-10 per cent.[3]

The mitigation policy to prevent climate change can be viewed as an exhaustible resource problem, which means the discount rate determines the entire path of optimal climate change mitigation. If the objective is to limit atmospheric concentrations of greenhouse gases at some future date, say to 650 CO_2 equivalent ppm, the difference between the limit 650 and current levels (around 390) is an exhaustible resource. The efficient solution is for the marginal costs of emissions reduction and the marginal value of a unit of emissions to rise at the rate of interest used to discount future environmental costs plus the rate at which atmospheric greenhouse gases are re-absorbed. Then the marginal benefit from the emission of a unit to current users is equated to the marginal costs imposed on future generations.

If an ideal carbon price, or cap and trade system, were imposed, the incremental cost of eliminating a unit of emissions and the value of a unit of emissions will be equated to the carbon price, which rises at this rate.[4]

For example, Table 1 shows the price path (ignoring re-aborption) for the carbon price at different discount rates, where the objective is a price of $300 per tonne CO_2 in a hundred years, say because at $300, backstop technology that takes greenhouse gases from the atmosphere for recycling or permanent sequestration becomes viable. In practice, the discount rate will affect the time at which we want the price to reach $300.

2 Garnaut (2008: 19).

3 See Harrison (2010) appendix G.

4 This is derived formally in Becker, Murphy and Topel (2010).

Table 1 Carbon price at different discount rates to reach $300 per tonne CO_2 in 100 years

		Discount rate			
Year	**Years in the future**	**1.35%**	**2.65%**	**4%**	**6%**
2012	0	$78.48	$21.94	$5.94	$0.88
2032	20	$102.62	$37.02	$13.02	$2.84
2052	40	$134.18	$62.46	$28.52	$9.09
2062	50	$153.44	$81.13	$42.21	$16.29
2072	60	$175.46	$105.38	$62.49	$29.17
2092	80	$229.43	$177.80	$136.92	$93.54
2112	100	$300.00	$300.00	$300.00	$300.00

Source: Author's own work.

If the discount rate is high, it pays to wait and ramp up policy over time. The discount rate makes a huge difference. At the low rates chosen by Garnaut and Stern, the current carbon price is $78. At Garnaut's higher rate of 2.65 per cent (which Stern now wishes he had chosen) it is less than one-third of that. At four per cent it is less than one-thirteenth. The case for immediate drastic action to mitigate depends crucially on the discount rate chosen. With a six per cent discount rate (a reasonable estimate of the market return) it takes more than 60 years for the carbon price to reach $30.

The same logic applies in reverse – if the carbon price is set at $23 and grows at four per cent (as Garnaut recommends), then it would reach $1,162 in 100 years, or only take 66 years to reach $300.

Of course this assumes a global carbon price – a partial scheme (such as unilateral action) would reduce the demand for existing fuel sources, bidding their prices down and encouraging greater consumption of existing fuels by those outside the scheme. The net result could be an increase in total emissions if the elasticity of supply of the fuels is low enough (can we prevent existing oil being used?).[5]

Another complication is that for large, non-marginal changes, the interest rate is endogenous. With compounding over long periods, what seem like small amounts can become large. Further, climate change may involve non-marginal effects on productivity and consumption. Policies will involve different paths of interest rates and welfare must be calculated by integrating along each path and comparing the present value of welfare for each policy, using the discount rates consistent with each path. The current rate is the starting point in each case.

The size of the discount rate is a crucial determinant of optimal greenhouse mitigation policy. Those who call for strong immediate action rely on low

5 Murphy (2008).

discount rates to justify their policy conclusions – much lower than standard rates used in cost benefit analysis. These low rates rely on strong, controversial assumptions and value judgements, often imposed in a hidden way.

To understand how climate policy modellers derive their low discount rates, we need to consider the fundamentals of economic policy analysis. Often they abandon the traditional cost benefit approach. Instead, climate policy modellers use a social welfare function approach.

The social welfare function approach to policy evaluation

Virtually all public policies involve gainers and losers, affecting lots of people in different ways. Figuring out what changes are desirable when everyone's interests are taken into account is a very complicated problem. Judging whether a change is good or bad requires comparing one person's welfare to another's, a step that requires normative value judgements to be made. Yet any policy decision involves a judgement of its desirability.

One procedure economists use to evaluate outcomes is to use a social welfare function to determine whether social welfare increases. The social welfare function, which Mishan describes as 'that grandiose but ineffectual excrescence on the body of welfare economics'[6] represents some ethical judgement about the appropriate distribution of welfare across people affected by a policy change. Just as a utility function shows how a person ranks different combinations of consumption goods, the social welfare function represents a value judgement of how society should rank different distributions of utility across people. A social welfare function gives the welfare of the whole society as a function of the utilities of individuals, just as the utility function gives the welfare of the individual as a function of the quantities of goods the individual consumes. To bring other factors in is to say social welfare depends on things no one cares about.

As the social welfare function is based on individual utilities, it requires that those functions be measurable and comparable – or cardinal and interpersonally comparable (otherwise the whole notion of going from individual preferences to a ranking of social states flounders on Arrow's impossibility theorem). Many economists would baulk at that step – utility cannot be measured, and interpersonal comparisons are difficult to make. Consumer choice theory does not require measurable utility. Utility functions are not unique, any monotonic transformation can be used to describe the same behaviour. Which do we pick? It is somewhat arbitrary.

6 Mishan (1981: 47).

If there are N individuals in the relevant society, then a simple social welfare function is: $W = w(u(c_1), u(c_2), \ldots, u(c_N))$ where c_n is the consumption of person n.

This simple form assumes all individuals have the same utility function (u), which depends only on consumption of a composite commodity (c), representing all goods and services consumed. All are usual, but strong, assumptions that can be generalised (for example, for many environmental problems it would be useful to have utility also depending on an environmental commodity). The utility function is assumed to be concave (declining marginal utility of income). Social welfare is a concave function (w) of individual utilities.

If the social welfare function is, $W = w(u(c_1), u(c_2), \ldots, u(c_N))$ the marginal change in social welfare from a change in individual i's consumption is $\frac{\partial W}{\partial c_i} = \frac{\partial w}{\partial u}\frac{\partial u}{\partial c_i}$ which depends on the w and u functions and the level of c_i. Adding up all the changes in social welfare from the changes in each individual's consumption caused by a policy gives the welfare effects of that policy.

The result is the distributional weights approach. Dollars to low-income people count more highly for social welfare than dollars to high-income people. The change in social welfare for an increase in individual i's consumption decreases as c_i increases for two reasons: because marginal utility declines as consumption increases (concavity of the utility function decreases $\frac{\partial u}{\partial c_i}$) and because the social weight declines as utility increases.

The key point is how social welfare depends on consumption: the analyst must specify both the *w* function (how social welfare varies with the utility of each generation) and the *u* function (how utility of each generation varies with consumption).[7] If a generation has its consumption increased, the effect on social welfare depends on how that increase affects its utility and then how that affects social welfare. The problem is to maximise w given the individuals are maximising *u*. The *w* function is ethical and the u function is empirical. A utility function can be deduced from observing the choices an individual actually makes. But a social welfare function cannot be observed; it must be specified according to a particular ethical view.

As the social welfare function represents some ethical judgement, there is no agreement on the appropriate w function. Economists have no advantage in making ethical judgements, but the social welfare function is useful for making inter-personal utility comparisons explicit and seeing the implications of different value judgements. It allows normative judgements to be introduced in a systematic way.

7 This point is strongly made by Kaplow, Moyer and Weisbach (2011).

Comparing the welfare of different generations

Evaluating costs and benefits received in the far future involves valuing the effects of policies on future generations, raising ethical issues. For example, the current generation can adopt policies which harm future generations – not only a different group of people, but one that is not around to defend its interests. Evaluating benefits in the distant future requires deriving the appropriate discount rate. The usual approach is to explicitly compare the welfare of different generations with some form of the following social welfare function (based on growth theory models of a representative, infinitely lived household):[8]

$$W = u(c_0) + \frac{(1+p)^{(1-\varepsilon)}}{(1+\theta)} u(c_1) + \frac{(1+p)^{2(1-\varepsilon)}}{(1+\theta)^2} u(c_2) + \ldots = \sum_{n=0}^{\infty} \frac{(1+p)^{n(1-\varepsilon)}}{(1+\theta)^n} u(c_n)$$

where each term represents a different generation and c_i is the per person value of lifetime consumption of a typical member of generation i. Note it is assumed each generation can be represented by one utility function and that all generations have the same utility function.

The population grows at the exogenous rate p and θ is the pure social rate of time preference, which is used to discount the utility of future generations (the term 'pure' is used for the rate used to discount utility, it is part of the rate used to discount consumption). A positive parameter means less weight is put on the utility of future generations. One reason for a positive θ is the chance of some catastrophic event eliminating human life on earth. More consumption for future generations is worth less if there is some chance they will not exist. The probability of extinction is usually considered quite low. For example, Stern sets it at 0.1 per cent a year (that is an annual probability of one in a thousand).

(1-ε) is the weighting the social welfare function gives to the number of people in each generation. For example, if ε=1, then $W = \sum_{n=0}^{\infty} \frac{u(c_n)}{(1+\theta)^n}$ and social welfare depends only on the average consumption of a generation and the number of descendants does not affect the social welfare.[9] Alternatively, a constant population (p=0) would give the same result, and now models each generation as a constant population of identical individuals with the same utility function.

If ε=0, then $W = \sum_{n=0}^{\infty} \frac{(1+p)^n}{(1+\theta)^n} u(c_n)$. This is the 'Benthamite' formulation, where the social welfare function maximises the present value of the total utility of all current and future people. Because social welfare depends on both the average utility and number of descendants, when the population is growing,

8 See, for example, McCallum (1996).

9 For example, Blanchard and Fischer (1989: 38-39) use this case.

the future is more valuable than when only average utility matters (an increase in future consumption per person has a larger effect on social welfare) and social welfare is lower.

Both extremes can give 'repugnant conclusions'. For example, maximising total utility implies for any population consisting of very good lives there is a better population consisting of a much larger number of people with lives that are barely worth living. Maximising average utility implies for any population consisting of very good lives there is a better population consisting of just one person leading a life at a slightly higher level of wellbeing. More dramatically, the principle also implies that for a population consisting of just one person leading a life at a very negative level of wellbeing, e.g. a life of constant torture, there is another population that is better even though it contains millions of lives at just a slightly less negative level of wellbeing.[10] An intermediate value of ε could avoid these problems.

The standard approach is to assume each generation has the same power utility function $u(c_n) = \frac{c_n^{1-\eta}}{1-\eta}$ with $\eta > 0$, which gives $u(c_j) = ln\ (c_j)$ for $\eta = 1$. Power utility has a constant elasticity of marginal utility with respect to consumption, $\eta = -c_j u''(c_j)/u'(c_j)$ (which is also the co-efficient of relative risk aversion).

The production side of the model is assumed to be a standard neo-classical Solow growth model, with exogenous technical progress at rate g. Then, as derived in Appendix 1, if consumption in each generation is chosen to maximise social welfare, in the steady state the equilibrium interest rate is $r = y'(k) - d = (1+\theta)(1+p)^{\varepsilon}(1+g)^{\eta} - 1$ where $y'(k) - d$ is the net return on capital and so the rate at which consumption can be transferred from period to period through investing in capital. Consumption per person grows at rate g.

Or approximately (exactly true when expressed as continuously compounded rates, see Appendix 1 for details):

$$r = \theta + \varepsilon p + \eta g$$

This is the Ramsey formula for the social discount rate, accounting for population growth: where θ is the pure social rate of time preference used to discount utility and ε depends on how changes in the population are valued and determines the effect of population growth (p) on the discount rate. Consumption per person grows at rate g and η is the (absolute value of the) elasticity of the marginal utility of consumption.

The interest rate r is the appropriate rate to discount consumption. The consumption discount rate (r) is higher than the utility discount rate (θ) because

10 Partridge (2001), Arrhenius, Ryberg, and Tännsjö (2010).

the growth in per head consumption means the marginal utility of future consumption is less than current consumption (and η shows the rate at which it falls). Future generations have a lower marginal utility of consumption and get less utility from a unit of consumption than earlier generations, the so-called concavity of the utility function. A dollar to a future generation adds less to wellbeing than a present dollar.

If the marginal rate of return on investment were greater than the Ramsey rate, social welfare would be improved by increasing the capital stock until the equilibrium condition holds.

A positive θ means utility to future generations counts less than utility to the current generation. Some authors argue that, on ethical grounds, θ should be set to zero (or almost zero, with a tiny allowance for the chance of extinction) so that all generations count equally. For example, Stern argues that it is ethical to give the same weight to the utility of different generations. Individuals often discount their own future utility because of impatience and the chance of death. Cowen points out that utility is not 'productive' over time as is invested capital and that impatience is not relevant in an inter-generational setting because future generations are not impatient to be born – and they do not experience a disutility of waiting to be born.[11] Further, future generations do not face the risk of death before they are born.

When $\theta = 0$ and $p = 0$ (constant population) the social welfare function has the additive form: $W = u(c_1) + u(c_2) + \cdots + u(c_N)$ where social welfare is simply the sum of the individual utilities. This social welfare function is often described as utilitarian, representing Bentham's philosophy that 'the greatest happiness of the greatest number is the foundation of morals and legislation'. [12] Figure 1 illustrates the iso-social welfare curves, analogous to indifference curves, for this social welfare function for a society with two members. An iso-welfare curve shows all the distributions of utility that give the same level of social welfare. The utilitarian social welfare function only considers total utility, and is not concerned with the distribution of utility between people. It requires comparability of changes in utility.

11 Cowen (2001: 5-6).

12 Introduction to the Principles of Morals and Legislation (1789).

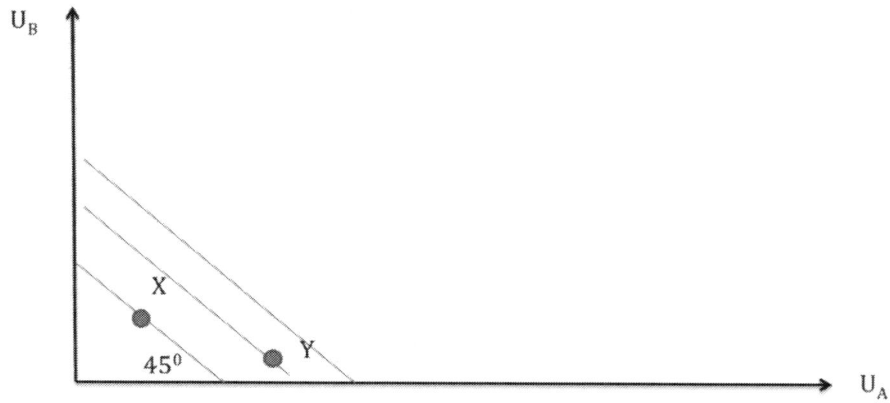

Figure 1 Utilitarian social welfare

Source: Author's own work.

There is fierce debate about whether utilitarianism is an appropriate guide to social welfare. An attractive approach for determining the social welfare function is that individuals should (as an ethical principle) assume they have an equal chance of being each of the people affected by the decision. They will then be in a position to decide objectively whether a policy is in the social interest. For example, in considering what society should look like, consider what society you would like if you were a foetus who did not know your abilities or which part of society you are to be born into (i.e. choosing behind what Rawls, called the 'veil of ignorance' or the original position). Harsanyi (1955) showed that if society's income were fixed and if a person behind the veil of ignorance maximised expected utility, he would want to be born into a society that used a utilitarian social welfare function to determine the distribution of income.

On the other hand, utilitarianism would redistribute income towards 'utility monsters' who derive a great deal of utility and away from people who don't get much enjoyment out of income.

Utilitarianism implies social welfare increases when total utility is increased, no matter who gets it, so the movement from X to Y on Figure 1 increases social welfare, even though it impoverishes person B.

A more general form of the social welfare function, which values both equality and high total social utility, would be: $W = \sum_{n=1}^{N} \frac{u(c_n)^{1-\phi}}{(1-\phi)}$, where $\varphi \geq 0$ is the coefficient of social aversion to relative inequality in utility (a normative concept), assumed constant in this formulation of the social welfare function (which expresses social welfare as a function of individual utilities in a way analogous to the power utility function). The higher is φ, the greater the aversion to inequality in utilities. $\varphi = 0$ corresponds to the utilitarian assumption and as $\varphi \rightarrow \infty$, we approach the 'perfect egalitarian' Rawlsian social welfare function, after philosopher John Rawls where social wellbeing is judged by the welfare of the worst-off member. If $\varphi = 1$ then the social welfare function is log linear – or Cobb Douglas. This is the Nash bargaining outcome.

But even this general form is controversial. Buchanan and Hartley (2000: 135-37) argue that its homotheticity is not appropriate – and the social welfare function should be positively skewed to reflect compassion rather than envy.

How climate change modellers determine the discount rate

The climate change literature uses the reduced form version of the standard social welfare function, expressing social welfare directly in terms of consumption in each generation:

$$W = \sum_{n=0}^{\infty} \frac{c_n^{1-\mu}}{(1+\theta)^n (1-\mu)}$$

where μ is the coefficient of social aversion to relative inequality in consumption, assumed to be constant.[13] The higher is μ, the greater the aversion to inequality in consumption.

If consumption in each generation is chosen to maximise this social welfare function, in the steady state the equilibrium interest rate is: $r = \theta + \mu g$. The usual approach of climate policy modellers is to determine the discount rate for consumption through specifying these parameters, which are normally expressed in annual terms.

This approach makes strong, often concealed, assumptions.

Most authors ignore the effect of population growth on the discount rate – assuming either constant population (p=0) or a Benthamite social welfare function (ε=0). This (usually implicit) assumption gives a lower discount rate (when population growth is positive).

Kaplow, Moyer and Weisbach (2011) point out that the climate modellers approach mixes ethical and empirical parameters and that the determination of the discount rate in climate change models 'usually proceeds without attention

13 See Garnaut (2008) and Smith (2009) for Australian examples.

to the difference between utility functions and the social welfare function and, relatedly, between empirical and ethical discounting'.[14] For example, Stern (2007), Arrow et al (1996), Dasgupta (2008), Nordhaus (2008), Garnaut (2008), Smith (2011) and Quiggin (2006) all use the $r = \theta + \mu g$ formula from the reduced form social welfare function to determine the discount rate for future consumption. But this 'combines empirical facts and ethical views in an opaque and unintuitive manner'.[15]

The climate change writers cited above all use the reduced form social welfare function $W = \sum_{n=0}^{\infty} \frac{c_n^{1-\mu}}{(1+\theta)^n (1-\mu)}$ and set $\theta = 0$ on ethical grounds (except Nordhouse, who sets it equal to 1.5 per cent). That makes social welfare the additive form where social welfare is simply the sum of the utility of each generation. That is, they assume the social welfare function is utilitarian. But that is an extreme representation of social preferences that is unconcerned with equality between generations. It assumes the coefficient of social aversion to relative inequality in utility is zero (that is, $\varphi = 0$ in the more general social welfare function form).

At 1.5 per cent annual growth, per capita income in one hundred years will be about 4.5 times the current level. At two per cent the multiple is 7.2. Growth rates in developing countries such as China or India are expected to be much higher.

Brennan (2006) argues that the standard approach implies that when people are better off, they should receive a lower weight in the social welfare function on equity grounds (extra utility to the better-off is not worth as much to society as extra utility to someone worse off). If ongoing economic growth is expected to make future generations better off and if the social welfare function values equality in utility, then $\varphi > 0$ or the social rate of pure time preference, θ, should be positive. This does not mean future lives are valued less than current lives. It means that future generations are expected to be better off than the current one, and so extra utility to the future is valued less at the margin than extra utility to the current generation.

Further, as Kaplow, Moyer and Weisbach (2011) point out, some modellers suggest that ethical considerations are involved in choosing μ, the coefficient of social aversion to relative inequality in consumption. But this is inconsistent with the modellers' utilitarian assumption that $\theta = 0$, which means social welfare is just the sum of the generational utility functions, $u(c_n) = \frac{c_n^{1-\eta}}{1-\eta}$. But that means $\mu = \eta$, the elasticity of the marginal utility of consumption, and is entirely an empirical parameter of the utility function.

14 Kaplow, Moyer and Weisbach (2011:9).
15 Kaplow, Moyer and Weisbach (2011:10).

For example, Garnaut supports the 'utilitarian principle … that equal weight should be placed on each person' to reject a positive rate of pure social time preference and then immediately writes:

> The second element in the discount rate [i.e. μ] is the marginal elasticity of utility with respect to consumption. This is a measure of society's concern for equity in income distribution. … There are compelling theoretical reasons for using an elasticity of 1, … Dasgupta (2007) argued that an elasticity of 1 implies that 'distribution of well-being among people doesn't matter much. … The Review uses two alternative parameter values for the marginal elasticity of utility, 1 and 2, a range that accommodates strongly diverging views on how much should be spent now to benefit future, presumably richer, generations.[16]

But if μ is a measure of society's concern for equity in income distribution, that contradicts the claim that it is the marginal elasticity of utility with respect to consumption (which is entirely empirical) and that the social welfare function is utilitarian. Once the ethical decision to make the social welfare function utilitarian is made, the issue becomes how consumption affects utility – which is empirical, and nothing to do with further ethical reflection. The utilitarian assumption places no weight on the distribution of wellbeing, it is only concerned about the total. If we reject placing less weight on future generations through a positive θ, why would we want to do it through adjusting μ? It is not clear what the alternative values of 1 and 2 are supposed to be capturing. One interpretation is that it is changes in predicted behaviour from changes in the utility function, evaluated by a given utilitarian social welfare function. But that is contradicted by the statements that it is about different views on distribution.

The climate policy modellers express the relevant discount rate $r = \theta + \mu g$ in annual terms. As they set $\theta = 0$, the only reason to discount future consumption in their model is because of the declining marginal utility of consumption as generations get richer. A strong implicit assumption has been made, without discussion: the personal pure utility discount rate has been ignored or has been confounded with the social pure utility discount rate, again mixing ethical and empirical parameters.

As the modellers express the discount rate in annual terms, and generations live for more than a year, the model must have overlapping generations. The obvious interpretation is that there is a new generation born each year. Then if $\theta = 0$ and the social welfare function has the additive form: $W = u_1 + u_2 + \cdots + u_N$ each term u_i represents the present value, at birth, of generation i's lifetime utility.

16 Garnaut (2008: 19).

Suppose generation i is born in period i and lives for T periods and maximises the power utility function: $u_i = \sum_{t=i}^{T+i} \frac{c_{i,t}^{1-\eta}}{(1+\delta)^{i-t}(1-\eta)}$ where $c_{i,t}$ is generation i's consumption in period t. Note total consumption in period t is the total of the T generations alive in that period.

$$c_t = \sum_{i=t-T}^{t} c_{i,t}$$

Then the representative individual would use the discount rate $r = \delta + g\eta$ to discount consumption over a lifetime, where δ is the personal pure rate of time preference, used by an individual to discount his own future utility. It arises from impatience and the chance of death. Crucially, it is empirical, and different from θ, the pure social rate of time preference – which is an ethical concept in a social welfare function used when aggregating different generations' utilities. Empirically, δ is usually estimated at around 1-2 per cent.[17]

δ and θ are different concepts and there is no necessary connection between them. It is consistent to believe δ is positive and θ should be set to 0 on the ethical view that all generations should be weighted equally. A person may strongly prefer current to future consumption (high δ) and place a high weight on future generations' consumption (low θ). It would also be consistent to value your own future utility the same as current utility ($\delta = 0$) and not care about affects on future generations after you die (high θ).

The climate policy modellers either ignore the personal discount rate or include it in their θ, used in the reduced form social welfare function and resulting Ramsey formula, and then (without discussion) set it to zero. If so, they mix up the personal and social rate of time preference and their θ 'embodies both empirical and ethical components and cannot be set based solely on either empirical measurements or ethical reflection'.[18]

Quiggin (2012) recognises that generations overlap, that θ and δ (using our notation) are distinct parameters and confirms that utilitarianism means $\theta = 0$ – that the utility to all generations counts equally. But he does not consider the appropriate social discount rate and so does not recognise that it may include the personal rate of time preference, and that setting $\theta = 0$ on ethical grounds does not imply that $r = g\eta$.

Quiggin points out that

> by the nature of overlapping generations, there is no point at which a coherent distinction between current and future generations can be drawn. In the absence of some general catastrophe, many children alive

---

17 See Zhuang *et al* (2007: Table 1: 6).

18 Kaplow, Moyer and Weisbach (2011: 10).

> today will still be alive in 2100, at which time people already alive will reasonably be able to anticipate the possibility of survival well into the 22nd century.[19]

Mishan establishes that if two generations overlap and each receives costs or benefits from a project, then we should discount the costs and benefits with the personal consumption discount rate, $r = \delta + g\eta$.[20]

For example, assume income is constant over time ($g = 0$) and everyone has a personal pure rate of time preference $\delta = 2$ per cent. Note that the value of an asset with a two per cent return doubles every 35 years, increasing four-fold in 70 years.

The climate policy modeller would not discount future consumption at all, presuming that (with the same utility functions and constant income), $1 of consumption gives the same utility no matter when it occurs. But if generations receiving the costs and benefits overlap, then a two per cent discount rate should be used. For example, imagine a project in which person A bears a cost of $100 in 2012. That person dies in 2062. The project gives a benefit of $500 in 2082 (70 years later) to person B born in 2032. The costs and benefits of the project accrue to generations who overlap (from 2032 to 2062).

Although B has $\delta = 2$ per cent, we cannot say B is indifferent between $500 in 2082 and $125 in 2012, this being 20 years prior to his birth. Likewise, we cannot say A is indifferent between these two payments because the $500 is received 20 years after he dies.

Yet the project should be evaluated with a discount rate of two per cent. For example, evaluate the net value of the project using 2047 (35 years from 2012 and 2082) as our reference year. Person A is indifferent between a payment of $100 in 2012 and $200 in 2047. Person B is indifferent between $500 received in 2082 and $250 in 2047. Therefore the cost benefit ratio of the project in 2047 is $250/$200 = 1.25 > 1 and the project is efficient, increases B's utility more than it decreases A's and raises social welfare. The benefits to B exceed the costs to A, whether measured in utility or willingness to pay. Moreover, the cost benefit ratio would be the same in any other reference year common to both lifetimes, both numerator and denominator are changed proportionately by the same discount factor.

Further, the cost benefit ratio is the same as that resulting from the conventional method of calculating net present value in 2012. If we discount back from 2047 to 2012, we reduce both numerator and denominator by a factor of $1.02^{35} = 2$, which gives 125/100 = 1.25.

19 Quiggin (2012: 274-275).

20 See Mishan (1981: 196-205).

So if there is a common rate of time preference and an overlap in the lifetimes of people affected by the project, then the discount rate should include the personal pure rate of time preference δ. Whether a project increases or decreases social welfare depends on the changes in utility that different generations experience. If an individual has a positive personal pure time preference rate for consumption, then consumption further in the future adds less to utility than consumption now. A project that pays \$500 in 2082 adds less to B's utility than one that pays \$500 in 2047. A utilitarian social welfare function must accept people's utility functions, including their intertemporal preferences.

Using the personal rate of time preference in the discount rate is not saying that future generations are valued less than current generations – $\theta = 0$ and they count the same. It is merely correctly establishing the effect of each project on each generation's utility, which is an empirical issue, not an ethical one.

If income was growing, then for a utilitarian social welfare function, the discount rate would be $r = \delta + g\eta$, to account for the declining marginal utility of income.

The personal rate of time preference δ is an empirical parameter that is usually estimated as positive (0-3 per cent, usually between 1 and 2),[21] for good reason (for example, it reflects the possibility of death). Further, the modellers use empirical estimates of η (the elasticity of the marginal utility of consumption), but these are usually jointly estimated with δ. It is not clear why the estimates of η are used, but the same empirical work's estimates of δ are discarded, or if it is legitimate to assume $\delta = 0$ but to use the estimates of η jointly estimated with a positive δ.

Problems arise when generations receiving the project's costs and benefits do not overlap, so that a direct Pareto comparison of their gains and losses is not possible. Their gains and losses can be compounded forward or discounted back while they are alive, but not beyond and so cannot be compared. Now Quiggin may be correct that for most practical purposes, most of those who receive costs and benefits do overlap (but some project beneficiaries may be born after those who pay the costs die).

If there is a time gap between those affected by a project, a potential Pareto improvement is possible if there is some institutional mechanism between generations – such as government transfers, private investment or bequests – that can transform the project's net benefit stream into some new pattern. Then standard discounting (including the personal rate of time preference) shows whether there is a potential Pareto improvement amongst overlapping generations, even if the project costs and benefits are not directly borne by some intermediate generations.

21 See Zhuang *et al* (2007: Table 1: 6).

It is useful to know whether a project covers its opportunity costs. Efficiency is not everything, and a potential Pareto improvement still needs to be judged on whether it improves social welfare – taking account of equity effects. But the efficiency effects of a project are something worth knowing and it is valuable to separate equity and efficiency effects because they are distinct considerations. There is a lack of agreement on how to judge equity effects and we can never expect to achieve a general consensus about the weight that should be attached to the welfare of different groups. Whether the project increases efficiency gives valuable information about the consequences of various options for helping future generations. Efficiency and equity concerns can be separated because we can redistribute across generations not merely through emissions reductions but in many ways, including simply by saving more. Because we can always invest at the market rate rather than in the project being evaluated, any decision to save for the future by investing in a lower-returning project wastes resources. The opportunity cost of one project is other projects foregone.

If anything, efficiency analysis is more useful in an inter-generational context. If the generations are linked through altruism and transfers (including human capital investment parents make in their children and bequests), efficiency gains can make all generations better off. A low return project will have an opportunity cost given by current market interest rates. Examining the efficiency effects of different government projects allows us to maximise the benefit to future generations for a given resource transfer. Even if it is decided to transfer more resources to future generations, the efficiency of particular methods of doing so is still relevant. Also, mixing equity and efficiency risks ignoring the current generation's (possibly offsetting) response to the government project.

Moreover, if the discount rate is to be determined through specifying parameters in the Ramsey equation $r = \theta + \mu g$ on an ethical basis, the wide range in ethical beliefs means it does not resolve disagreement about the appropriate discount rate. Table 2 summarises different parameters that have been suggested. It should be noted that most of the papers referred to fail to clearly distinguish ethical and empirical parameters (such as θ from δ) and set empirical parameters such as η on an ethical basis.

The parameters differ greatly, resulting in recommended discount rates that range from 1.3 to eight per cent. As the differences reflect different judgements about values as well as about the empirical literature, they cannot be resolved objectively. Further, the Ramsey formula gives this wide range even with an assumed zero pure rate of time preference (both θ and δ equal to zero). Suggested consumption growth rates (g) range from one to two per cent and the co-efficient of relative risk aversion (η) from one to four, which give a discount rate (ηg) of anywhere from one to eight per cent, wide enough to encompass most views on the social discount rate.

Table 2 Different discount rates derived from the Ramsey formula

Source	Pure rate of social time preference, θ	Elasticity of marginal utility of consumption, η	Growth rate in consumption, g	Discount rate $= \theta + \eta g$
	per cent		**per cent**	**per cent**
Stern (2007)	0.1	1	1.3	1.4
Quiggin (2006)	0	1	1.5	1.5
Cline (1993)	0	1.5	1	1.5
Garnaut (2008)	0	1-2	1.3	1.3-2.6
HM Treasury (2003)	1.5	1	2	3.5
Nordhaus (2007)	1.5	2	2	5.5
Weitzman (2007)	2	2	2	6
Arrow (2007)	0	2-3	If 1-2	2-6
Dasgupta (2006)	0	2-4	If 1-2	2-8
Gollier (2006)	0	2-4	If 1.3	2.6-5.2
Empirical evidence	**0–3**	**0.2-4**	**1.2-2.1 (for Australia)**	**0.24-11 (given range)**

Source: Author's own work and edited empirical evidence.

Zhuang *et al* (2007) survey empirical estimates of δ (the personal pure rate of time preference, but they do not distinguish it from the social pure rate of time preference) and η (the elasticity of the marginal utility of consumption or the co-efficient of relative risk aversion). They find that δ ranges from 0 to three per cent a year and η from 0.2 to four (with most between one and two).[22] Average annual per person consumption growth is usually in the range one to two per cent. For example in recent applications, the Treasury has assumed 1.2 per cent, whereas the Productivity Commission has used 1.75 per cent. Annual GDP growth per capita in Australia averaged 2.1 per cent from 1960 to 2007. Peak to peak labour productivity 1969-70 to 2003-04 averaged 1.71 per cent. Using these parameter ranges in the Ramsey formula gives estimates of a risk-free discount rate ranging from 0.24 to 11 per cent.

Specifying the rate at which society is willing to trade present for future consumption is bound to be controversial. 'Society' is not a decision maker (not even the government controls the whole of society). Inevitably, the analyst imposes a specific discount rate (or the parameters that determine it). Yet economists have no particular expertise about how the future should count.

It is not surprising that there is little agreement about the appropriate social welfare function. What is ethical depends on value judgements and there is no way to reconcile the different value judgements that people may possess.

22 See Zhuang *et al* (2007: 6-7).

Equity issues involve trading off the welfare of one group against another's (for example, the present generation's against future generations') and there is no general consensus about the weight that should be attached to the welfare of different groups. The social welfare function approach makes the discount rate a matter of opinion, and provides no basis for determining which opinion is correct.

Further criticisms of the social welfare function approach

There is not even agreement on whether the social welfare function approach is the appropriate way to judge equity issues. The social welfare function approach is a consequentialist moral theory. It says we should judge policies only in terms of their consequences and the only relevant consequences are individuals' gratifications. Further, it makes strong assumptions about the form of individual preferences. There is the problem of what weight to attach to preferences that involve envy and malice towards others. It usually ignores other social goals such as liberty, justice, order and community. Further, social choice may be concerned with means.

The social welfare function approach is one particular view of social choice that may not capture how most people think about social welfare or account for equity. For example, the standard form of social welfare function focuses on equality. But most people would be unconcerned about a transfer of income from a very rich person to a comfortably rich person, yet a standard social welfare function would say it raises social welfare.

Harberger (1978) points out that the distributional weights approach has a number of disquieting implications. It would only be by accident that the optimal excise tax or subsidy would be zero, as the distributional gains of a change in tax from zero would in general be positive (so long as the gainers and losers had different average incomes). It would generally result in a regressive income tax system. And balancing distributional gains against efficiency losses requires acceptance of large efficiency losses for standard social welfare functions.

For example, in the reduced form social welfare function, assuming $\theta = 0$, the contribution to social welfare of a marginal increase in consumption of generation n is c_n^{μ}. If $\mu = 1$ then we have a log social welfare function, which means a one per cent increase in consumption always has the same social value. For example, $200 to someone on $20,000 a year has the same social value as $2,000 to someone on $200,000 a year.

If generation A has k times the consumption of generation B, then the social value of an extra unit of consumption to B is k^{μ} times the value to A. If consumption grows at annual rate g, a generation n years in the future would be $(1+g)^n$ times richer than the current generation and the social value of extra consumption to the current generation is $(1+g)^{n\mu}$ times greater.

The coefficient of aversion to inequality in consumption, μ, determines the amount of inefficiency we are willing to bear to pursue redistribution. If generation A has k times the consumption of generation B, then a redistribution from A to B that wasted $1 - k^{-\mu}$ of the transfer would be marginal.[23]

For example, if $\mu = 1$ a redistribution that took $2,000 from someone on $200,000 a year, wasted 90 per cent of it and gave the remaining $200 to someone on $20,000 would keep social welfare constant. If $\mu = 2$, a transfer that wasted up to 99 per cent would be worthwhile (for example, a transfer that took $2,000 from A and gave $20 to B would be acceptable).

Harberger (1978) argues this implication of the distributional weights approach results in unacceptable outcomes for transfers within a generation. He concludes that the distributional weights approach does not capture how most people think about distributional issues. It does not represent the value system of most citizens and risks economists' peculiar opinions on distributional issues swamping all other considerations, something that is beyond the economist's professional role.[24]

In contrast, Stern (2008) and Dietz and Stern (2008) also argue that most people would consider such levels of waste in redistribution undesirable, but conclude that means a μ higher than two is implausible. Action to mitigate global warming would impose a cost on the current generation and benefit much richer future generations. Garnaut and Stern predict much higher income levels in the future – even if the effects of global warming occur. If per capita consumption grows at 1.3 per cent a year (Stern's base case), those living in 100 years time would be 3.6 times richer than people today. Those living in 200 years would be 13.2 times richer (and if these levels of growth did not occur, the global warming problem would be very much mitigated).

Their logic is that if it makes no sense to take $2,000 off a rich generation to make a poor generation $20 better off, taking $20 off a poor generation to give $2,000 to the rich generation is justified. They assume that the distributional weights approach captures the relevant ethical considerations (although they do agree it is 'a very narrow view of ethics').[25]

---

23 More generally, if $c_i > c_j$ then $SMU_i < SMU_j$ and we transfer from i to j, where SMU is social marginal utility. If making the transfer costs a proportion d of the transfer, we are willing to transfer until $SMU_i = (1 - d)SMU_j$ (i.e. until the loss to i equals the gain to j). That is, we are willing to put up with waste $d = 1 - SMU_i/SMU_j$. $SMU_i = ci^{-\mu}$. So are willing to waste $1 - c_i\text{-}\mu/c_j\mu = 1 - (c_j/c_i)^{\mu}$. Note that $(c_j/c_i) < 1$, so the higher μ, the more you are willing to waste, $(c_j/c_i)^{\mu}$ gets smaller.

24 See Harberger (1978: S118-S119).

25 Dietz and Stern (2008: 104).

As Schelling points out

> the 'optimization' approach is based on the principle that if the material benefits we procure for those future high-income people are large enough to offset their reduced marginal utilities, we should procure those future utilities just as if those utilities were our own. Few citizens who understood this principle would ever vote for it. ... we are not used to thinking about making our own sacrifices, or imposing sacrifices on our contemporaries, for the benefit of people who are substantially better off.[26]

Rather, the willingness to pay current costs to help future generations is associated with potentially catastrophic outcomes of global warming, not from making richer generations even better off.

Harberger suggests that, judging by people's charitable giving and redistributions within their family, most seem to care about alleviating poverty rather than equality. Genuine deprivation – an inability to afford the necessities of life – is what motivates most charity. Further, the altruism we observe is more closely linked to the basic needs of individuals than to their incomes. Most people genuinely believe it is good for the sick to be healed, the homeless sheltered and so on.

Families step in to help fellow members meet basic needs, but seldom redistribute to equalise income (for example, bequests are usually divided equally rather than to offset income differences between children).

Further, the fact that a large proportion of the public participates willingly in lotteries suggests that many people do not value equality. Lotteries increase inequality – many people purchase tickets and make themselves poorer in order to make a few winners rich.

Harberger suggests a basic needs approach.[27] Rather than rely on the differential weighting of the welfare of different individuals, this approach imputes external benefits connected with the improvement in the circumstances of others. But it is not the recipient's utility that enters the donor's utility function but the consumption of particular goods and services (food, education, medical care, housing, etc) or the attainment of certain states (better nourished, better housed, etc) that are closely correlated with the adequate consumption of certain goods and services. The externality comes from the extent to which the basic needs of certain segments of society are met. It seems in practice the altruism we observe is more closely linked to the basic needs of individuals rather than to their

26 Schelling (1995: 398).

27 See Harberger (1984).

utility or entire consumption bundle. Citizens want welfare payments to be spent on food and clothing, not beer and drugs. Gifts in kind are preferred to cash transfers.

The basic needs approach accepts these elements of paternalism as a more accurate reflection of our true values, attitudes and beliefs. It is society's views that count, rather than the analyst's. The basic needs approach follows standard cost benefit analysis techniques:

> our respective individual gratification (and our underlying willingness to pay) at the fact of a poor child being better nourished is something of a public good. The fact I am gratified in no way precludes you from being gratified also. My willingness to pay to help see that this event comes about can thus appropriately be added to yours, in just the same way that conventional cost benefit analysis adds vertically various citizens' willingness to pay for an environmental improvement that subsequently can be freely enjoyed by all[28]

Four myths about discounting and climate change

Myth 1: Market discount rates imply we would sacrifice our grandchildren for a few dollars

The only reference to discount rates in Garnaut's 2011 update to the Climate Change Review is on the first page of the introduction where Garnaut recounts how he was explaining to the Multi-Party Climate Change Committee the importance of discounting and

> then I said something that brought back the prime minister's attention.
>
> 'If we used the share market's discount rate to value the lives of future Australians', I said, 'and if we knew that doing something would give lots of benefits now but would cause the extinction of our species in half a century, the calculations would tell us to do it[29]

Economists have calculated the willingness to pay to avoid a catastrophe that wipes out one per cent of the population. Using a six per cent discount rate and assuming income grows at two per cent a year, a permanent one per cent loss in national income in 50 years is worth 25 per cent of income in 2062, which has a present value of 3.52 per cent of current income.

28 Harberger (1984: 112).

29 Garnaut (2011: ix).

Concave u(c) means that reductions in c have rising marginal cost to those who experience them, so that a given reduction in aggregate income is more costly when it is highly concentrated. The costs of a climate-related catastrophe that reduces future national incomes by one per cent by killing off one per cent of the population, while leaving others unharmed, has a much greater cost than a 'marginal' change that reduces everyone's income proportionally. Instead, a portion of the population loses their life – and consumer surplus.

Becker, Murphy and Topel (2010) use the framework provided by the economic literature on the value of a statistical life (VSL), which measures people's willingness to pay for a reduction in the probability of death that would save one 'statistical life'. For example, if in a population of 10,000 individuals each would be willing to pay $600 a year to reduce the per-annum probability of accidental death by one in 10,000, then VSL = $6 million.[30] Drawing on the empirical literature, the value of a life-year is about six times current income. Growth in income over time means future individuals will be willing to pay more to reduce risks to their life compared with poorer current individuals – in 50 years at two per cent annual growth, incomes are 2.7 times greater. The VSL would grow even faster if the value of life were income elastic. In this case, if the discount rate was equal to the rate of income growth, as Stern and Garnaut recommend, the present value of saving future lives would be greater than the value of saving current lives. Murphy and Topel (2006) find the income elasticity of the value of a life-year exceeds 1.33.[31] On the other hand, a review of sixty studies finds it to be about 0.5 to 0.6.[32]

To keep it simple, assume that the value of lives saved from mitigating future catastrophes is proportional to income (an elasticity of one). Then the present value of an event that kills off one per cent of the population in 50 years is at least 6 x 3.52% = 21.1 per cent of current income. Even using market discount rates, future loss of life has a substantial present value.

Willingness to pay does not work well for certain death, as money is no use to a corpse, but clearly willingness to pay to avoid the extinction of all humans in 50 years would be an enormous sum – and so would the amount needed to compensate the current population for that prospect.

30 Becker, Murphy and Topel (2010: 12).

31 Murphy and Topel (2006: 882).

32 See Viscusi *et al* (2005: 723).

Myth 2: Life should not be discounted

Some economists argue that the value of life should not be discounted, that a life saved in the future is no less valuable than a life saved today. Lives cannot be invested and earn interest.

Cost benefit analysis does not place a value on human life. Instead, it uses the value of statistical life, which values the reduction in statistical deaths arising from small risks. It is based on people's observed willingness to pay for small reductions in the risk of death rather than buying out the risk of certain death.

Most government policies are about small reductions in mortality risk and the value of statistical life is the correct way to value the benefits from risk reduction. That is, we are not discounting lives, but the money value of life-saving measures. Money can be invested and so the money value of costs and benefits received in the future needs to be discounted.

Cost-benefit analysis converts all costs and benefits to money equivalents based on willingness to pay. The project is exactly equivalent to receiving that flow of dollars over time. The benefit estimates represent the sum of money those who would benefit from the policy are willing to pay to receive the benefits. The cost estimates are the amount of money that needs to be paid to compensate for the costs the project imposes.

Life saving has a financial cost, discounting just allows assessment of the value of expenditures at different periods. 'If willingness to pay to reduce risk is the appropriate metric for allocating regulatory resources, discounting merely adjusts that metric to make expenditures comparable through time'.[33]

Once we express the value in dollar terms, we are saying the benefit is worth that many dollars. Then we must discount, because we can invest dollars to grow over time.

If regulators did not discount the value of future lives, then it would never be worth spending to save a life today. Money spent today to save lives could instead be invested to produce a larger lifesaving budget in the future, saving more lives. All the more so if technological progress makes the cost of saving lives fall over time and income growth increases the VSL. If the value of future lives saved is not discounted, then there is a higher marginal productivity in future spending on lifesaving and all lifesaving resources should be channelled towards the future. But the same argument applies each year. Lifesaving expenditures would be delayed indefinitely.

Choices need to be made between expenditures on reducing the risk to future lives and other goods, not the least of which is saving lives in the present.

33 Sunstein and Rowell (2007: 171).

Myth 3: High private sector discount rates are specific to the share market

Garnaut also informed the committee that

> So we had to choose the right discount rate', I said. 'We can't use the discount rates that determine values in the share market, because they take into account risks of a kind that are not relevant here.[34]

The opportunity cost relevant for climate change mitigation is the foregone return on equivalent private sector investment. Direct measurement of these returns shows them to be high. For example, using national accounts data to divide the total income from capital generated in the private sector by an estimate of the private sector capital stock shows real returns to capital to be consistently high, a number of studies showing they average over eight per cent real for decades, and are much more stable than share market returns (with a 95 per cent confidence interval of plus or minus one percentage point, whereas it is plus or minus four percentage points for share market returns). These estimates are consistent with share market returns, which are after company and property taxes. Estimates of the cost of capital in Australia and of the return to human capital investment are also high.[35] Foregone private investment has a high opportunity cost which is not limited to the share market. In fact, capital market imperfections, such as credit rationing, high borrowing rates and imperfect annuity markets, are likely to make the returns to non-listed companies and family investment in human capital higher than for listed companies.

The high private sector returns relative to the risk-free return (usually measured by the return on government bonds) indicate high-risk premiums are not limited to the share market, but seem to reflect broader attitudes to the cost of risk.

The government should only invest in a project if it can reap a better return from it than from investing in a private sector project of equivalent risk. That requires using the private rate of return to capital as the discount rate.

Myth 4: Governments should discount with the risk-free rate of return because of the Arrow and Lind theorem

The climate policy modellers invariably discount with a risk-free rate. For example, they use the Ramsey equation for the equilibrium risk-free return to derive the social discount rate.

34 Garnaut (2011: ix).

35 See Harrison (2010: 37-39, 128-34).

In a widely cited, classic contribution to public sector discounting theory, Arrow and Lind (1970) showed that if a government project was 'small' (in relation to the total wealth of taxpayers) and 'the returns from a given public investment are independent of other components of national income', then the social cost of the risk for project flows that accrue to taxpayers tends to zero as the number of taxpayers tends to infinity.[36] That is, government investments with diversifiable risks spread over many households should be evaluated using the riskless rate to discount expected benefits (that is, with no adjustment for risk).

This result, known as the Arrow-Lind theorem, is consistent with the CAPM approach. If a project contains only diversifiable risk and no aggregate risk, an efficient private sector would spread the risk and would also use the riskless rate to discount expected project returns.

If a project contains aggregate risk, then a risk premium should be used. Aggregate risk is an irreducible social risk that cannot be diversified, even by government. It is caused by shocks such as recessions and variations in the market return. Most government projects involve aggregate risk. As Bailey and Jensen point out:

> the 'private' (and 'social') risk of even a small project which is perfectly correlated with the average returns on all other assets cannot be reduced one iota by transferring it from the private to the public sector.
>
> The question regarding the size and sign of the covariances of returns on prospective projects is an empirical issue. However, some brief consideration of the problem seems to indicate (contrary to Samuelson et al) that the vast majority of government projects will have outcomes correlated with national income. For instance, any government investment that facilitates ordinary commerce will produce more benefits when national income is high than when it is low. Electric power, highways, waterways, airports, and postal service, for example, all have this character.[37]

The government should only price risk differently if it has some advantage that allows it to improve on an imperfect market. The advantage should be specified, because the government cannot correct some market imperfections. Any comparison of how the government and private sector manage risk should take account of how the government in fact operates under the incentives of the political process.

If governments do not spread the risk, then it is borne by individuals and discounting should be done at a rate that reflects the risk premiums they demand for bearing risk. Arrow and Lind conclude

36 Arrow and Lind (1970: 171).

37 Jensen and Bailey (1972: 7).

> some benefits and costs of sizeable magnitudes accrued directly to individuals so that these individuals incurred the attendant costs of risk bearing ... it is appropriate to discount for risk ... As a practical matter, Hirshliefer's suggestion of finding the marginal rate of return on assets with similar payoffs in the private sector, and using this as the rate of discount, appears reasonable for discounting those costs and benefits which accrue privately.[38]

The market price of risk shows the cost of extra non-diversifiable risk to the private sector, whether the market is efficient in handling risk or not.

The evaluation of the benefits from climate change mitigation should take account of the great uncertainty about the future costs and benefits of such policies, such as uncertainties about the distributions and size of climate damage and the payoffs from mitigation. Becker, Murphy and Topel (2010) set out the appropriate framework to do so. For example, the present value of mitigation increases greatly when climate-related damages are unequally distributed, when future lives are at risk, and when we add uncertainty as to when the damaging events might occur (holding constant the expected time of occurrence).

Risk should be taken into account in the standard way – by adjusting the market interest rate used to discount future flows – not by asserting that a risk-free rate should be used. This allows us to compare how policies deal with the risks; some policies become more attractive precisely because they pay off in bad times. By explicitly accounting for risk, we can distinguish between policies that reduce risk and those that don't.

The appropriate adjustment to the discount rate depends on the covariance of the returns to mitigation with m, the marginal rate of substitution between present and future consumption (which depends on both income growth and the state of the environment, falling if income is growing and rising if the environment becomes degraded). If we divide by the variance in m, we get the environmental project's 'beta'.

If the environmental asset offers greater payoff than the market when m is high (say because the environment is degraded), then it reduces risk and the discount rate would be below the market return (beta is less than one).

If the returns were positively correlated with m, then the expected return would be below the risk-free return (beta is negative). If the returns on mitigation investments avert disasters and avoid large reductions in productivity and living standards or save lives, they pay off exactly when other assets do not and when willingness to pay is great. The appropriate discount rate is below

38 Arrow and Lind (1970: 175-76).

the risk-free rate. That is, when climate policies effectively insure against large downside risks, they have low expected return but high market value because they pay off when the mitigation of damage is most valuable.

That is not true for modest climate change – not costly enough to reduce consumption (both Stern and Garnaut predict growing consumption even with climate change). The gains from mitigation against modest climate change are greatest in the highest GDP states and so have a positive beta.[39] For example, where losses are proportional to GDP, the appropriate beta is one and the discount rate should be the market return. Policies that raise future GDP, already 5-8 times higher than current level, by a few per cent are not that valuable.

Adjusting appropriately for risk, rather than pretending it is irrelevant, allows us to judge the best policies – those with the greatest net present value, such as policies that focus on avoiding extreme outcomes that could happen quickly. For example, Becker, Murphy and Topel (2010) emphasise that research and development investments in mitigation technologies that can be scaled up in the event that damages are large, can offer important insurance against looming catastrophe and should not be heavily discounted. Economically useful policies would encourage research and development into finding such scalable technologies. Further, investments in technology that provide future generations with the means to cope with global warming are less reversible and avoid the problem of ensuring future intervening generations commit to the plan.

Conclusions

A number of assumptions and value judgements go into the claim that discount rates of one to two per cent should be used to evaluate mitigation policies. The case for immediate mitigation to prevent climate change depends crucially on the use of low discount rates, yet the climate policy modellers' standard approach jumbles ethical judgements and empirical facts and makes concealed presumptions that many people would disagree with.

Good cost benefit analysis makes clear and transparent the assumptions and judgements made, so that they can be scrutinised and debated. By contrast, the Stern Review did not even reveal its discount rate in the initial report and as Cowen points out 'the relevant caveats don't seem to find their way into his final presentation of the estimates'.[40]

It is important to separate positive analysis from normative beliefs, because there is less agreement about ethical judgements. At the least, it helps clarify the effects of policies to clearly distinguish empirical parameters that determine

39 See Murphy (2008).

40 http://marginalrevolution.com/marginalrevolution/2006/11/the_stern_repor.html.

behaviour from ethical judgements about how to evaluate results. Further, the wide range of ethical beliefs means the social welfare function approach does not even resolve the issue of the appropriate discount rate – but can support a wide range of risk-free social discount rates from one to 11 per cent.

The ten commandments followed when climate policy modellers choose discount rates are, that:

1. The social welfare function approach is the only relevant way to think about the outcomes of climate change policy.
2. The appropriate social welfare function is utilitarian ($\varphi = 0$) and future utility should not be discounted ($\theta = 0$), which presumes equity between generations is irrelevant.
3. The fact that individuals discount their own future utility is irrelevant ($\delta = 0$).
4. We should maximise total utility ($\varepsilon = 0$) so that population growth is irrelevant for the discount rate.
5. The ethical discount rate is relevant and the current population and future generations will support efforts to direct more to generations still further in the future.
6. Efforts to help future generations won't be offset by the current generation's behaviour.
7. The Ramsey rule is the correct positive model of interest rate determination, with no regard to whether the evidence supports it or alternative models.
8. Risk is irrelevant; the risk-free rate should be used.
9. Despite all these assumptions, there is no need to conduct sensitivity analysis on the discount rate.
10. Whether the transfer is efficient is irrelevant.

The most significant presumptions are the departure from well-established and justified cost benefit analysis in the final two commandments, especially the abandonment of standard efficiency based analysis. Instead, climate policy modellers adopt what Nordhaus calls

> the lofty vantage point of the world social planner, perhaps stoking the dying embers of the British Empire, in determining the way the world should combat the dangers of global warming. The world, according to Government House utilitarianism, should use the combination of time discounting and consumption elasticity that the *Review's* authors find persuasive from their ethical vantage point.[41]

41 Nordhaus (2007b: 148–49).

Appendix 1: Deriving the Ramsey rule

The social welfare function is

$$W = u(c_0) + \frac{(1+p)^{(1-\varepsilon)}}{(1+\theta)} u(c_1) + \frac{(1+p)^{2(1-\varepsilon)}}{(1+\theta)^2} u(c_2) + \ldots = \sum_{n=0}^{\infty} \frac{(1+p)^{n(1-\varepsilon)}}{(1+\theta)^n} u(c_n)$$

where each period represents a different generation and cn is the per person consumption of a typical member of generation n. The population grows at the exogenous rate p and $\theta > 0$ is the pure social rate of time preference, which is used to discount the utility of future generations. (1-ε) is the weighting the social welfare function gives to the number of people in each generation.

The production side of the economy is a standard Solow model, with exogenous labour–augmenting (Harrod neutral) technical progress at rate g. Output per household each generation is a constant returns function of per household capital K and efficiency units of labour, L: $Y_j = Y(K_n, L_n)$ where $L_n = (1+g)^n(1+p)^n$. That is, exogenous labour–augmenting (Harrod neutral) technical progress increases the number of efficiency units of labour per head of population at rate g.

Now express the production function in per efficiency unit terms: let $y_n = Y_n/L_n$ and $k_n = K_n/L_n$ and

$$y_n = (1/L)Y(K/L, 1) = y(k).$$

In the steady state, the effective labour supply, real income and the capital stock all grow at rate $g + p + gp$. Therefore Y/K is constant and so is the rate of return on capital, $Y_K = \partial F/\partial K = \partial f/\partial k$.[42] The share of income going to capital, $Y_K K/Y$ is constant. The share going to labour is constant. The distribution of income is steady, which requires Harrod neutral technical progress.[43]

In the steady state, output, consumption, the wage and capital per efficiency unit are constant. But it is people, not efficiency units, who receive income and consume. Population is growing at rate p. Consumption, capital, the wage and output per person grow at rate g, the rate of technical progress.

A steady state with c_t growing at rate g, is possible only if u′ has a constant elasticity with respect to c_n. Assume, therefore, that each representative household has a power utility function: $u(c_n) = \frac{c_j^{1-\eta}}{1-\eta}$ with $\eta > 0$, which gives $u(c_n) = ln\,(c_n)$ for $\eta = 1$. Power utility has a constant elasticity of marginal utility of $-\eta$ (which is also the co-efficient of relative risk aversion). It determines the rate at which an individual's marginal utility falls as income rises.

42 $\partial F/\partial K = \partial(Nf)/\partial K = N(\partial k/\partial K)(\partial f/\partial k) = \partial f/\partial k$.

43 In the case of a Cobb-Douglas production function, Harrod neutral technical progress is also Hicks neutral. $Y = K^{\alpha}[a(t)L]^{1-\alpha} = [a(t)]^{1-\alpha} K^{\alpha} L^{1-\alpha}$

The household's budget constraint is:

$$y(k_n) = c_n + (1+p)k_{n+1} - (1-d)k_n$$

where capital depreciates at rate d.

Choose values of c_n and K_1, K_2,...to maximise social welfare:

$$W = u(c_0) + \frac{(1+p)^{(1-\varepsilon)}}{(1+\theta)}u(c_1) + \frac{(1+p)^{2(1-\varepsilon)}}{(1+\theta)^2}u(c_2) + \ldots = \sum_{n=0}^{\infty} \frac{(1+p)^{n(1-\varepsilon)}}{(1+\theta)^n}u(c_n)$$

subject to the budget constraint and given k_0.

The first order conditions give:

$$(1+\theta)(1+p)^{\varepsilon}(c_j/c_{j+1})^{-\eta} = y'(k_{j+1}) + 1 - d$$

That is the interest rate is:

$$r = y'(k) - d = (1+\theta)(1+p)^{\varepsilon}(1+g)^{\eta} - 1$$

Or approximately (true when expressed as continuously compounded rates):

$$r = y'(k) - d = \theta + \varepsilon p + \eta g$$

If a variable has a growth rate of x per period, then it is 1+x after one period. If it is continuously compounded at rate x*, then it grows to e^{x^*} after one period. So a growth rate of x is equivalent to a continuously compounded rate of x* when $e^{x^*} = 1 + x$. Taking logs gives x* = ln(1+x).

In equilibrium the net return on capital equals the marginal rate of time preference equals the interest rate. As there are no taxes, the consumer equals the investment rate. If the prescriptive approach specifies a Ramsey rate that is below the marginal rate of return on investment, welfare would be improved by increasing the capital stock until the equilibrium condition holds.

References

Arrhenius, Gustaf, Ryberg, Jesper and Tännsjö, Torbjörn, 'The Repugnant Conclusion', *The Stanford Encyclopedia of Philosophy (Fall 2010 Edition)*, Edward N Zalta (ed.), URL = <http://plato.stanford.edu/archives/fall2010/entries/repugnant-conclusion/>.

Arrow, K, M Cropper, G Eads, R Hahn, L Lave, R Noll, P Portney, M Russell, R Schmalensee, V Smith, and R Stavins (1996). *Benefit-Cost Analysis in Environmental, Health, and Safety Regulation* American Enterprise Institute, The Annapolis Center, and Resources for the Future.

Arrow, K and R Lind (1970). 'Uncertainty and the Evaluation of Public Investment Decisions' *American Economic Review*, v.60, no.3: 364–78. Reprinted in Layard and Glaister (eds) (1994): 160–178.

Becker, G, K Murphy and R Topel (2010). 'On the Economics of Climate Policy' *George J Stigler Center for the Study of the Economy and the State Working Paper no.234,* June.

Blanchard, O, and S Fischer (1989). *Lectures on Macroeconomics.* Cambridge, Mass.: MIT Press.

Brennan, G (2006). 'Discounting the future, yet again' seminar paper for the Research Triangle Ethics Circle. http://www.unc.edu/~gsmunc/EthicsGroup/Brennan%20--%20Discounting%20the%20Future.pdf

Cowen, T (2001). 'What is the Correct Intergenerational Discount Rate?' Mimeo. Department of Economics, George Mason University.

Dasgupta, P (2006). 'Comments on the Stern Review's Economics of Climate Change' December 12. Seminar on the Stern Review's Economics of Climate Change, organised by the Foundation for Science and Technology at the Royal Society, London,

Dietz, S and N Stern (2008). 'Why Economic Analysis Supports Strong Action on Climate Change: A Response to the Stern Review's Critics' *Review of Environmental Economics and Policy*, vol.2, no.1, Winter: 94-113.

Garnaut, R (2011). *The Garnaut Review 2011, Australia in the Global Response to Climate Change* Cambridge University Press.

_____ (2008). *The Garnaut Climate Change Review.* Final report. Cambridge University Press.

Harberger, A (1984). 'Basic needs versus distributional weights in social cost–benefit analysis', *Economic Development and Cultural Change*, vol 32, no 3 (April): 455–474.

____ (1978). 'On the Use of Distributional Weights in Social Cost-Benefit Analysis' *Journal of Political Economy*, vol.86, no.2, part 2, April: S87-S120

Harrison, M (2010). 'Valuing the Future: the social discount rate in cost-benefit analysis' *Visiting Researcher Paper, Productivity Commission*, Canberra. http://www.pc.gov.au/research/visiting-researcher/cost-benefit-discount

Harsanyi, J (1955). 'Cardinal Welfare, Individualistic Ethics, and Interpersonal Comparisons of Utility' *Journal of Political Economy,* v.63, no. 4, August: 309-321.

Jensen, M and M Bailey (1972). 'Risk and the Discount Rate for Public Investment' in *Studies in the Theory of Capital Markets,* M. Jensen, (Ed), Praeger Publishers. http://papers.ssrn.com/abstract=390110.

Kaplow, L (2006). 'Discounting Dollars, Discounting Lives: Intergenerational Distributive Justice and Efficiency' *Prepared for the University of Chicago Conference on Intergenerational Equity and Discounting*, April 10.

Kaplow, L, E Moyer and D Weisbach (2011). 'The Social Evaluation on Intergenerational Policies and Its Application to Integrated Assessment Models of Climate Change' *John M Olin Law & Economics Working Paper No. 565, The Law School, The University Of Chicago,* July

_____ (2003). 'Concavity of Utility, Concavity of Welfare, and Redistribution of Income' *Harvard Law School John M Olin Center for Law, Economics and Business Discussion Paper Series,* Paper 437.

McCallum, B (1996). 'Neoclassical vs. Endogenous Growth Analysis: An Overview' *Federal Reserve Bank of Richmond Economic Quarterly*, Vol. 82, no.4 Fall: 41–71.

Mishan, E (1981). *Economic Efficiency and Social Welfare*, George Allen and Unwin, London.

Murphy, K 'Some simple economics of climate change' Presentation to Mont Pelerin Society 60 the Anniversary Conference, Tokoyo, September 7.

Murphy, K and R Topel (2006). 'The Value of Health and Longevity' *Journal of Political Economy,* 2006, vol. 114, no. 5: 871-904.

Nordhaus, W (2007). 'A Review of the Stern Review on the Economics of Climate Change' *Journal of Economic Literature*, Vol. XLV (September 2007): 686–702.

_____ (2007b). *The Challenge of Global Warming: Economic Models and Environmental Policy.*

Partridge, E (2001). 'Future Generations' from *A Companion to Environmental Ethics,*

Edited by Dale Jamieson, Blackwell. http://gadfly.igc.org/papers/futgens.htm

Portney, P and J Weyant (1999). 'Introduction': 1-11 in Portney and Weyant (1999a).

Quiggin, J (2006). 'Stern and the critics on discounting'.

____ (2012). 'Equity between overlapping generations' *Journal of Public Economic Theory,* 14 (2): 273–283.

Schelling, T (1995). 'Intergenerational discounting' *Energy Policy,* v.23, no. 4/5: 395-401.

Smith, K (2011). 'Discounting, risk and uncertainty in economic appraisals of climate change policy: comparing Nordhaus, Garnaut and Stern' Department of Climate Change and Energy Efficiency, 3 February.

Stern, N (2008). 'The Economics of Climate Change' *American Economic Review: Papers & Proceedings,* vol.98, no.2, May: 1–37.

_____ (2007). *The Economics of Climate Change: The Stern Review,* Cabinet Office – HM Treasury, Cambridge University Press, UK.

Viscusi, W, J Harrington and J Vernon (2005). *Economics of regulation and anti-trust.* MIT Press.

Weisbach, D and C Sunstein (2008). 'Climate Change and Discounting the Future: A guide for the Perplexed' *Reg-Markets Center Working Paper no.08-19, University of Harvard Public Law Working Paper no.08-20.*

Zhuang, J, Z Liang, T Lin, and F De Guzman (2007). 'Theory and Practice in the Choice of Social Discount Rate for Cost–benefit Analysis: A Survey' *ERD Working Paper No. 94,* Asia Development Bank, May.

24. Limits to Growth ... Again[1]

Jeff Bennett

The numerous definitions of sustainability that appear in the economics, ecology and policy literature all focus on the key societal goal of self-preservation. No society wants to see itself reduced in stature with the passage of time just as most of the individuals who comprise society want to see their descendants enjoy a quality of life that is at least as good as their own.

The constant and apparently accelerating rate of change in the factors that determine the wellbeing of society make the goal of sustainability increasingly 'top-of-mind' for individuals and society's decision makers. For example, concerns that we are 'running out' of scarce natural resources are exacerbated when people see the world's population exceeding seven billion along with increasing standards of living (and hence rates of resource use) in populous countries like China and India. The fear is that future generations will not be able to access the bounty of natural resources that has made their parents well off.

As well as this 'economic' element of the sustainability concern, there is the environmental dimension. The fast pace of changing circumstances is feared to involve increasing environmental degradation. This takes the form of more pollution (the 'brown' side) as well as less biodiversity (the 'green' side). So one of the natural resources feared to be in increasingly short supply into the future is 'the environment'.

The third part of the sustainability trifecta (or 'triple bottom line') is broadly defined as the social dimension. Concern is expressed for the integrity of social systems as communities fracture under the pressures of fast-paced change. For instance, greater employment mobility within the population makes it increasingly difficult to establish stable social networks. This, in turn, is feared to have negative consequences for communities facing more change in that people's resilience to change is diminished.[2]

All of these concerns orbit around the issue of society's ability to adapt to change. With the growth of information technology and burgeoning population levels, the current pace of change certainly appears faster than anything ever experienced by humanity; the concerns summarised by the term 'sustainability' are not new.

---

1 Paper presented at 'Economic Growth and Wellbeing: A symposium in honour of Ian Castles AO'. Much of this paper is drawn from material assembled in Bennett, J (2012).

2 This contentious hypothesis (given the increased social 'connectivity' provided by lower costs of transport and electronic communication) is proposed by Albrecht (2010).

Thomas Malthus conceived of the concept if not the terminology in 1798 in his 'An essay on the principle of population'. Malthus forecast an unsustainable world in which poverty and starvation would prevail. The dire prediction was based on a comparison between the perceived rate of growth of population (a geometrical progression) and the rate of growth of food production that was deemed possible at that time (an arithmetic progression). The same theme was picked up by Meadows, et al (1972) in their 'Club of Rome' sponsored analysis of resource use rates and known resource stocks entitled *The Limits to Growth*. Numerous non-renewable natural resources were shown in the analysis to have stocks that would be exhausted by current use rates within two to three decades. Furthermore the 'peak' phenomena (Peak Oil, Peak Phosphate, etc) is an expression of sustainability fears: For example, hitting 'peak oil' means that the rate of extraction begins to fall over time as the available reserves are no longer sufficient to maintain production. The implication is that we are 'running out' and the next generations will no longer be able to enjoy the largess of readily available oil.

All of these analyses focus on the changing circumstances faced by humanity and the potential for those changes to make people worse off. The analogy is to the boxer standing still with gloves lowered as his opponent winds up a big right hook. In the reality of the ring, the boxer ducks and weaves not only to avoid the right hook but also to ready himself to deliver a left jab. So too for society: with change underway and more forecast, societies set up mechanisms to adjust and adapt. In doing so, people work to avoid the negative consequences of changes and to take advantage of opportunities to make themselves better off that are presented by change.

A primary adaptive mechanism that society has evolved over time is the market. Competitive trading in well-defined and well-defended property rights to resources between self-interested individuals and entities has been consistently demonstrated to offer the capacity to deliver improved societal wellbeing, particularly when changing circumstances prevail. The process of arbitrage and its consequential wealth creation capacity has ensured, for example, that the dire predictions of the Club of Rome have not eventuated over the past 40 years. Where increasing relative scarcity of a resource has emerged, the increasing price generated by market exchange has signaled to people that they should economise on their use of that resource and search for alternatives. Producers of the resource have also responded by investing in more exploration or technological developments to increase the efficiency of resource extraction. Similarly, the higher price encourages entrepreneurs to develop substitutes. Markets thus facilitate the process of adaptation to change with prices performing the role of 'signaling' emerging patterns of resource relative scarcity and abundance.

With these market-driven adaptation processes in place, resource exhaustion – epitomised by 'peak oil' – continues to be postponed. The number of years of crude oil supplies that are available given current rates of use has stayed stubbornly at around 42 for a number of decades. Alternative energy sources ranging from natural gas through to photovoltaic cells have become increasingly competitive and consistent improvements in oil use efficiency have been achieved. Most significantly, oil exploration has pushed geographical boundaries so that new fields have been discovered as old oil fields go out of production. Technological advances in energy supply – including the development of 'fracking' for natural gas extraction – have effectively matched expansions in demand.

Of specific importance in refuting the Malthusian concerns regarding the potential starvation of humanity as population growth outstripped food production has been agricultural adaptation. Agricultural productivity has increased dramatically over time with major technological advances in crop and livestock breeding, insect and weed control, mechanisation and irrigation. Markets have, by and large, provided efficient signals to farmers as well as the suppliers of farm inputs that have facilitated this productivity response.

But it is not only the decentralised market mechanism that reacts to change. Collective decision making processes also adapt. Most notably, governments have instituted policies that have been directed toward increasing agricultural productivity through research and development,[3] lessening the pollution loads imposed on open access resources such as air and water and increasing the supply of environmental public goods such as biodiversity. These policies have been introduced in response to political demands from the citizenry. In well-functioning democratic societies, governments that ignore calls for change in response to declining environmental conditions (such as pollution and species extinction) face electoral retribution.

Even Malthus saw that doom was not inevitable. His prescient analysis called for the protection of the rule of law, the education of the citizenry, democracy and a free press as the key foundations of a society that is able to respond and adapt to change. And those foundations underpin both the effectiveness of the market and the capacity of governments to achieve this adaptation. Without the rule of law, markets are unable to operate. Without a well-informed community of voters in a democracy, who are alerted to contexts and government actions (or lack there-of) by an independent press, welfare improving collective adaptation through government policy is also unlikely to be delivered.

The process of adaptation to change, and the generation of gains in social welfare through change are reflected in the concept of the Environmental Kuznets Curve

3 See Alston and Pardey (1996) for a rationale for government involvement in agricultural R&D.

(EKC).[4] The underpinning notion of the EKC is that as economic development proceeds and financial wealth grows, the condition of the environment initially declines but eventually improves. In turn, this relationship between wealth and environmental condition is determined by both demand and supply responses. The (eventual) improvement in the condition of the environment comes about because increased wealth is associated with greater education and hence increased demand for improved environmental conditions. And as wealth increases, the capacity of societies to meet that demand is enhanced. Technologies are developed to lessen environmental damage. Society can afford to set aside resources from the development process for dedication to the supply of biodiversity reserves.

But the EKC processes should not be seen as automatically ensuring that environmental protection and improvement flows from the development of increased wealth. The important link between the two (wealth and the environment) that must be present is an institutional framework that facilitates adaptation. Institutions are the rules of social coordination and can be internal or external.[5]

Internal institutions, such as honesty, punctuality and trust, come from within a society and are developed in an evolutionary manner through time. External institutions, such as codified law, are imposed on society by organisations such as parliament and the courts that originate from within society but which are external to it.

Markets are formed as a result of complex mixtures of internal and external institutions. People trade with each other on the basis of trust and honesty but do so within a regime of property law established and enforced by exogenous organisations. Markets however, can largely be characterised as decentralised instruments of social coordination. In contrast, government policies emerge as exogenous institutions but sit within a context of the endogenous institutions of each society. They therefore are centralised collective instruments.

Market adaptation and policy adaptation to change are fundamentally different but both represent mechanisms whereby the links between increased wealth and environmental improvements can be achieved.

Markets are driven by individual self-interest and their decentralised nature enables fast response to change that is tailored to individual circumstances. Individuals choose to adapt only if it is in their best interests to do so. But through the competitive exchange process whereby both buyer and seller are made better off, reallocations of resources are achieved that are societally beneficial

4 See Yandle, Vijayaraghavan and Bhattarai M (2000).

5 See Kasper, Streit and Boettke (2012).

as well as in the best interests of the individual. Adaptation through markets is therefore fast, efficient and responsive to the preferences of individuals and involves low transaction costs.

In contrast, the collective response is likely to be slow and broad-brushed. It is also likely to come with far higher transaction costs, given the expense of both forming policy and enforcing it as well as the costs of those who are affected by it.

The incentives for policy reform are also more complex. Politicians may respond to voters' demands for change but the political process runs the risk of capture by vested interest groups. By promising to deliver votes in marginal electorates that are critical for political success, an interest group may be able to secure a policy shift that generates returns for itself at the expense of the wider community. If that expense can be spread sufficiently thinly so as not to be 'vote changing', the policy shift can be very attractive to the politician despite its net negative impact on society. Such are the risks where collective action is imposed on the individual. In particular, there are risks that vested interests collude with those genuinely seeking environmental improvement. The analogy is to the prohibition era when the 'baptists' sought to improve social conditions by having alcohol banned and the 'bootleggers' provided support for the cause in order to improve their financial positions.[6]

Yet the collective, external institution route to adaptation may be important in the development of the EKC link between wealth and environmental improvement because the public good characteristics of the environmental goods and services may cause the transaction costs of markets to rise to the point where trade will not take place. The critical aspect of the policy response in that case is to ensure that a 'brake' is in place to stop the actions of rent-seekers from hi-jacking the adaptive process. Put simply, policy initiatives must be safeguarded against the vested interest groups. Admittedly, this slows the collective adaptation process down even further but it would ensure that only welfare improving policies are introduced.

The policy vetting process should involve the use of benefit cost analysis, applied by politically independent analysts. The fundamental process that underpinned the Regulatory Impact Statement (RIS) requirement for new legislation in both federal and state jurisdictions is consistent with this approach.[7] With the results of such analyses transparently available to the press and the voting public, politicians need to establish sound (alternative) logic to argue for the introduction of policies that are not – according to benefit cost analysis – in

6 See Yandle (1983).

7 http://www.finance.gov.au/obpr/ris/gov-ris.html.

society's best interest. Making sure that institutions such as the RIS requirement are in place, and once in place are not diluted to the point where their impact is neutered, is a matter of consistent political vigilance.[8]

Without that vigilance, the prospect is that policy becomes a 'limit to growth' and thus a circumvention of the EKC link between wealth and environmental improvement. For instance, policies that install subsidies on 'green' production or place restrictions on 'brown' competitors diminish competitive pressures. Instead of adaptation taking place, the lack of competition can cause complacency. Cost padding is another potential factor that detracts from the wealth creating process. The process of 'picking green winners' in the policy process can shift the incentive away from adaptation to changing external conditions to one that involves more lobbying for further protection. In this sense, policy acts as a limit to both growth and achieving a more sustainable society.[9]

The policy response to the issue of climate change illustrates these prospects. Concerns regarding the impacts of anthropogenic greenhouse gas (GHG) emissions on the state of the world's climate have given rise to national and international policy measures. The lack of well-defined and well- defended property rights to the use of the atmosphere for the disposal of GHG emissions has provided a conceptual foundation for the introduction of these policies: without those rights, markets will not form to ensure efficient use of the atmosphere as a waste disposal site. Over use is predicted by conventional economic analysis.

The question that remains is whether or not the policies that have been instituted are welfare improving and thus worthwhile contributions to securing the EKC link between wealth and environmental condition.

It is first worth noting that the analyses offered by Stern (2011) and Garnaut (2006) in support of policy measures did not correctly address the welfare impact question. Their logic was that in the absence of any measure to control GHG emissions, the predictions were of climate change consequences that would be very costly to society. In comparison, they argued that the costs of policy action were low. This analysis is incomplete in that it ignores the impact that the policy measure may or may not have on the climate and hence the costs caused by climate change. Put simply, the correct comparison in terms of welfare impacts is between the climate change costs that policy measures will avoid and the costs of implementing the policy. The assumption made by Stern and Garnaut is that the policy measure implemented will be 100 per cent effective in reaching

8 Exemption from RIS examination on the grounds of projects being of 'national significance' is an example in Australia of a breakdown of this vigilance.

9 The introduction in Australia of 'renewable energy certificates' to facilitate the achievement of the 20 per cent of energy use being generated from renewable sources by 2020 is an example of such policies: http://www.energymatters.com.au/carbon-trading/recs/.

a given atmospheric concentration of greenhouse gases. This is unrealistic both at a national and an international level. Furthermore, both Garnaut and Stern implicitly assume that the costs of climate change fall on countries in a way that would encourage those who are being asked to pay for mitigation to agree to act. In fact the costs do not fall in this way making the reaching of international agreements to mitigate carbon emissions almost impossible.

Given this oversight, it is useful first to consider the benefits and costs of policy measures in place and then to investigate the political economy of the policy development process.

The establishment of a price for carbon dioxide emissions (an example of a 'Pigovian pollution tax') in Australia will certainly be costly to the economy in so far as it will encourage the substitution away from lower cost carbon-based fuel sources and toward more expensive renewable energy. If this were not the case, the point of the tax would be lost.

But what of the benefits – the avoided costs of climate change? There are numerous factors that indicate these benefits will be relatively small if not zero. They range from the small proportional impact an Australian change would make on the world's climatic regime (consistent with difficulties in reaching international agreement on GHG reduction targets) through to the offsetting impacts created by compensatory measures introduced along with the carbon tax legislation to 'ease the pain' of higher energy costs and even to the probability that the climate science predicting catastrophic impacts turns out to be wrong.

The conclusion to be drawn then is that the policies being instituted are not welfare improving. Why then have they been introduced? What coalitions of vested interest groups have been formed to ensure that policies contrary to the general public's best interests have been introduced through the political process?

There are many groups within society that are made better off by climate change policies. These betterments often have nothing to do with avoiding the costs of predicted climate change. No doubt there are the proverbial 'baptists' in society that are genuinely concerned about future climate change consequences and want to use the political process to make others in society who do not share their concerns conform to a pattern of behaviour they advocate. But there are also plenty of proverbial 'bootleggers'. They range from 'carbon accountants' who have a new income creating job estimating the extent of GHG emissions from businesses through to the carbon 'brokers' who start new businesses arranging carbon offset schemes to reduce clients' tax incidences. They are researchers who secure lucrative grants to investigate more and more aspects of the social, environmental and economic impacts of climate change as well as the manufacturers – and their work force – of (protected, subsidised) renewable energy sources. That is to say nothing of the army of bureaucrats and diplomats at both national and international levels who find themselves in well-paying 'important' jobs.

There are also gains to be made by the government from the collection of another source of tax revenue. The funds raised from the tax can be distributed in ways that secure the support of wavering voters be it in the form of direct compensation payments or investments in assets that benefit specific groups of people.

Along the way, these redistributive policies cause impacts on the wealth creation process. They may even have unintended consequences in terms of environmental and social impacts. An example is the US and Brazilian governments' policies that subsidise the production of bio-fuels as a substitute for petroleum. First, biofuels (ethanol from corn in the US and sugar in Brazil) are more costly to produce than petroleum. If they weren't, there would be no need for the subsidy payments. Second, the increased demand for corn and sugar has increased their prices and the prices of a wide range of other food stuffs (grains, meat, milk that either compete with the subsidised crops for land and labour or use those crops as inputs). The food price spikes in 2008 and 2011 caused by (amongst other factors such as droughts in the US and Russia) biofuel subsidies sent shock waves around the world.[10] Finally, the subsidies on ethanol have not reduced GHG emissions. The expansion in biofuel crop growing caused increased fuel and fertilizer consumption as well as the clearing of vegetation such that CO_2 emissions increased.[11]

So while such climate change policies are likely to have very little impact on the world's climate they are already having a decidedly negative impact on the functioning of the world's economy to generate wealth that in turn has the capacity to allow the smooth adaptation to climate changes that may arise.

Furthermore, it is important to recognise that while these climate change policies are directing scarce resources to the pursuit of a goal that isn't being achieved, other potential uses for those scarce resources are being neglected. Those alternatives may be improved health for developing country people, increased educational opportunities, more reserves for endangered species, etc. etc. These are the unseen opportunity costs of climate change policies.

10 http://www.fao.org/worldfoodsituation/wfs-home/foodpricesindex/en/.

11 See Timilsina, Beghin, Mensbrugghe and Mevel (2012).

In conclusion, it is clear that change, and adaptation to change, has been and will be a continuing feature of our society. The caution expressed in this paper is that collective action to assist in the adaptation process needs to be carefully vetted to ensure that policy is not the most pressing limit to growth.

References

Albrecht, G (2010). 'Solastalgia and the Creation of New Ways of Living' in *Nature and Culture: Rebuilding Lost Connections*, Earthscan: 217-234.

Alston JM and Pardey PG (1996). *Making Science Pay: the economics of Agricultural R&D Policy*, The AEI Press, Washington DC.

Bennett J (2012). *Little Green Lies,* Melbourne: Connor Court Publishing.

Garnaut R (2011). *The Garnaut Review 2011: Australia in the Global Response to Climate Change,*

Cambridge: Cambridge University Press.

Kasper W, Streit M and Boettke P (2012). *Institutional Economics: Property, competition and policies,* 2nd ed. Cheltenham: Edward Elgar.

Malthus, T (1798). *An essay on the principle of population,* Oxford World Classics reprint. Meadows D, Meadows G, Randers J and Behrens III W (1972). *The Limits to Growth.* New York: Universe Books.

Stern N (2006). *Stern Review on the Economics of Climate Change,* London: HM Treasury.

Timilsina G, Beghin J, van der Mensbrugghe D and Mevel S (2012). 'The Impacts of Biofuel Targets on Land-Use Change and Food Supply: A Global CGE Assessment', *Agriculture Economics,* (43): 315-332.

Yandle B (1983). 'Baptists and Bootleggers: The education of a regulatory economist'. *Regulation* 7(3): 12.

Yandle B, Vijayaraghavan M and Bhattarai M (2000). *The Environmental Kuznets Curve: A Primer.* Bozeman: The Property and Environment Research Center.

25. Scientists, Statisticians and the Prophets of Doom[1]

Ian Castles

In the *Unnatural Nature of Science* (1992), Lewis Wolpert, FRS, Professor of Biology at University College, London, concluded that 'Science is one of humankind's greatest and most beautiful achievements and for its continuation, free and critical discussion, with no political interference, is as essential today as it was in Ionia'.[2]

In principle, the international science community accepts the vital importance of such 'free and critical discussion', and asserts the need for these values of science to be applied to the world's problems. The most recent such proclamation came from 63 academies of science after a meeting in Tokyo in May 2000:

> Science is, in a very fundamental sense, the process of seeking the truth. The values of the scientific enterprise – openness, community, quality and respect for evidence – are of great importance and application to the search for sustainability. The scientific community must be involved in the broad interactive process of establishing societal priorities...and in fostering the public understanding and the political will to ensure that progress moves in directions that correspond to those priorities.[3]

Regrettably, however, there are many in the science community who are more strongly committed to implementing *their* priorities than to the values of the scientific enterprise. This has recently been demonstrated in their enraged reaction to *The Skeptical Environmentalist* by Bjorn Lomborg,[4] a book that takes issue with the claim that the pursuit of economic progress inevitably leads to an ever-deteriorating environment. Lewis Wolpert, for one, has found it convincing:

> At last a book that gives the environment the scientific analysis it deserves, and provides understanding of the problems, the risks and the solutions. Essential Reading.[5]

---

1 This article was first published as 'The Skeptical Environmentalist and his Critics' in *Dialogue* (3/2001), the journal of the Academy of the Social Sciences in Australia.

2 Wolpert, Lewis (1992). *The Unnatural Nature of Science*: 128.

3 InterAcademy Panel (2000). *Transition to Sustainability in the 21st Century: the Contribution of Science and Technology* [A statement of the World's Scientific Academies (May)] (http://interacademics.net/intracad/tokyo2000.nsf).

4 Lomborg, Bjorn (2001). *'The Skeptical Environmentalist: Measuring the Real State of the World'*, Cambridge University Press, Cambridge.

5 *Ibid:* back cover.

But many other scientists are unhappy at the attention that is being given to an alternative view, as James Woodford revealed in his review of the book for the *Sydney Morning Herald:*

> For 350 pages, backed up by nearly 3000 footnotes, the Danish statistician critically examines the slogans and arguments that have galvanised much of the developed world into environmental action. It is a book that the green movement would love to see pulped; several people I have spoken to about the text have asked me not to give Lomborg any more publicity.[6]

Three of Lomborg's critics confronted him on the *Earthbeat* program on ABC Radio on 13 October. Alexandra de Blas introduced the segment with the comment that the new book 'has environmentalists and scientists from around the world fuming'[7] – and she introduced Tom Burke, environmental adviser to Rio Tinto and BHP, as the author of what she called a 'damning paper' on the book.

This was the pamphlet *Ten Pinches of Salt,*[8] which was released by the UK Green Alliance on the same day as Lomborg's book was published by Cambridge University Press. At the launch, Burke labelled *The Skeptical Environmentalist* 'a dishonest and discreditable smear on the many millions of professionals and volunteers working to improve the environment', and claimed that the positions that Lomborg had attacked 'a caricature of his own invention which bear no resemblance to the arguments currently deployed by environmentalists'.[9]

On *Earthbeat,* Alexandra de Blas asked Burke to outline his main concerns with the publication. He began his response by challenging Lomborg's credentials. He (Burke) had 'actually talked to Greenpeace, and they are very clear that they have no record of Bjorn Lomborg...as an activist member'. When Lomborg responded that he had 'never been out in a rubber boat' but was 'a suburban kind of Greenpeace member', Burke replied:

> That doesn't make you an environmentalist, Bjorn. I mean that would make me a statistician because I've done some calculations.[10]

Tom Burke is certainly not a statistician, and it is not possible to identify his area of expertise either from his pamphlet or his comments on *Earthbeat.* In the former, he acknowledged that the Club of Rome had been wrong to argue

6 Woodford, James (2001). 'A load of hot air' in the *Sydney Morning Herald,* 29-30 September: Spectrum: 4-5.

7 ABC (2001). 'Skeptical Environmentalist Debates Critics', *Earthbeat,* Radio National Home, http://www.abc.net.au/rn/science/earth/stories/s394496.htm.

8 Burke, Tom (2001). *Ten Pinches of Salt: A Reply to Bjorn Lomborg,* http:/www.green-alliance.org.uk.

9 Green Alliance (2001). 'What's New', 29 August, http://www.green-alliance.org.uk/WhatsNew.htm.

10 ABC (2001). *Op cit:* 2-3.

that 'natural resources are running out', and that 'Paul Erlich [sic] did make and lose, his famous wager with Julian Simon'. But he asserted that, as of now, 'Environmentalists do not believe that natural resources are running out', and questioned 'what is gained in 2001 by resurrecting a long dead argument only to kill it all over again?'.[11]

Far from being 'long dead', the argument is alive and well in the scientific community: it is just that it is now presented in a somewhat more sophisticated guise than the simplistic models, made notorious by the Club of Rome and the writings and lectures of Ehrlich (Professor of Biological Sciences at Stanford). For example, the statement in May 2000 by 63 academies of science declared that human consumption reduces 'the future availability of materials and energy', and that 'if current trends in ...consumption of energy and materials...persist, many human needs will not be met and the numbers of hungry and poor will increase'.[12]

Perhaps the academies do not realise it, but this assertion effectively implies that 'natural resources are running out'. If they are not, why would growth in the usage of such resources work against the satisfaction of human needs, and lead to increases in the numbers of hungry and poor?

Burke recognises that 'Professor Erlich [sic] did predict in his book *The Population Bomb,* published 23 years ago, that 'In the course of the 1970s the world will experience starvation of tragic proportions – hundreds of millions of people will stave [sic] to death'. And he even goes on to argue that Ehrlich

> was, as we all too often witnessed from the comfort of our living rooms, right...but I cannot recall, and Professor Lomborg does not cite, another occasion on which he made this prediction.[13]

This is wrong on a number of counts. First, Lomborg *does* cite another occasion – an article in *The New Scientist* in which Ehrlich urged the US to announce 'that we will not longer send emergency aid to India where sober analysis shows a hopeless imbalance between food and population'.[14] Second, there were many more such occasions: in 1969, a *New York Times* correspondent reported that the Stanford biologist 'turns out a *steady stream* of popular articles and books warning of unimaginable famine, nuclear destruction and plague if something isn't done quickly about rising population'.[15] Thirdly, no one denies that there

11 Burke, Tom (2001). *Op cit*: 6.
12 InterAcademy Panel (2000). *Op cit*.
13 Burke, Tom (2001). *Op cit*: 6 - 7.
14 Lomborg, Bjorn (2001). *Op cit*: 350.
15 *New York Times* (1969). 'Foe of Pollution Sees Lack of Time', August 10: 53 (emphasis added).

are and always have been starving people in the world, including in the 1970s: images on television screens can only testify to that tragic fact, not to the existence of 'unimaginable famine'.

But, finally, and most importantly, Burke is apparently unaware that the spectre of the imminent deaths of hundreds of millions raised by Paul Ehrlich in his 1968 book was not a 'prediction': it was the most *optimistic* of three 'scenarios' that he offered as a description of the 'kinds of disasters that will occur as mankind slips into the famine decades' – and he challenged his readers to create a more optimistic one.

Paul Ehrlich was explicit that his scenario presuming 'the death by starvation of perhaps as many as half a billion people' was a 'cheerful' one with 'considerably more appeal than the others'. His fear was that it involved 'a maturity of outlook and behaviour in the United States that seems unlikely to develop in the near future'. For example, it would require the suspension of food shipments to 'India, Egypt and some other countries which [the US] considers beyond hope'; the imposition of 'a moderate food rationing program' in the US itself; and the development of a plan to contain the world's population to two billion in 2025 and 1.5 billion in 2100.

The scenarios that Ehrlich considered more likely envisaged either an early global war induced by pressures on food supplies, with more than 100 million Americans dying from the fallout from Chinese thermonuclear devices 'transported in submarines [and] detonated in the sea off our West Coast'; or famines, plagues and anarchy leading to 'a general thermonuclear war' in the 1980s, making the entire globe uninhabitable by humans. The most intelligent creatures ultimately surviving this catastrophe would be cockroaches.[16]

Understandably, Tom Burke and the millions he believes to have been smeared by Lomborg's analysis would prefer these false prophecies of doom to be forgotten. They would like to anathematise Matt Ridley, author of *Genome*, for his advice to every environmentalist to read Lomborg's book 'so that the appalling errors of fact the environmental movement has made in the past are not repeated'.[17]

Under the sarcastic heading 'Simon says', Burke alleges that Lomborg dismisses the issue of waste by leaning heavily 'on data from his mentor, Julian Simon', and claims that *The Skeptical Environmentalist* 'fails to mention toxic or hazardous wastes'.[18] To a lay person, this does not appear to be so. For example, Lomborg cites US statistics showing decreases between 1986 and 1995 in the concentrations of pollutants in mussels of '28 percent for cadmium, 36 percent

16 Ehrlich, Paul R (1968). *The Population Bomb*, New York: 72-80.
17 Lomborg, Bjorn (2001). *Op cit*: back cover.
18 Burke, Tom (2001). *Op cit*: 8.

DDT, 48 percent polychlorinated biphenyl (PCB), 56 percent dieldrin, 62 percent polycyclic aromatic hydrocarbons (PAH) and 86 percent butyl tin'; and Danish statistics showing 'declines of DDT and PCB in saltwater fish of more than 90 percent since 1973'. And he quotes from the latest US *State of the Coastal Environment* report the statement that 'most pollutant concentrations are decreasing and none is increasing'.[19]

Burke goes on to give the following summary of Lomborg's account of the relationship between air pollution and income levels in developing countries:

> Air pollution in the rest of the world, where two-thirds of humanity lives, need not be *considered*, in Professor Lomborg's view, because this will *cease automatically* as they get richer. This confuses cause and correlation, not a mistake you would expect from a statistician.[20]

But Lomborg *does* consider air pollution in developing countries and *does not* claim that it will cease automatically as they get richer. Indeed he recognises that the tendency is for air pollution to continue to rise in developing countries until incomes reach medium levels. Beyond those medium income levels, however, he argues that the tendency is for air pollution to fall (not 'automatically', but as a result of public preferences and political decisions) to 'the level [those countries] had before they started developing'.

Lomborg assembles the evidence for these propositions in the form of charts showing the connection between GDP per capita and particle and SO_2 pollution for 48 cities in 31 countries, for each of the years 1972 and 1986. The analysis includes cities in the developed world and in China, India, Thailand, the Philippines, Korea, Brazil, Chile, Colombia and Venezuela. It shows that, between these two years, both types of pollution fell for all nations at all levels of wealth. Lomborg concludes that 'developing countries can not only achieve both economic growth and a better environment, but over time will get even better environment for a given amount of wealth':

> this is because developing countries can buy progressively cheaper, cleaner technology from the West. The key factor here is that technology makes it possible to achieve growth as well as a better environment.[21]

Many scientists have become so accustomed to thinking of growth and the environment as opposites that they are unable to accept the clear message of the empirical evidence on this fundamental point. Thus Ian Lowe, Emeritus

19 Lomborg, Bjorn (2001). *Op cit*: 195.
20 Burke, Tom (2001). *Op cit*: 9 (emphases added).
21 Lomborg, Bjorn (2001). *Op cit*: 176-7.

Professor of Science, Technology and Society at Griffith University – another critic of *The Skeptical Environmentalist* on the ABC *Earthbeat* segment – claimed that

> ...to say the problems [of the environment] will be solved by greater wealth and private property rights is economic dogma...not science. There's no convincing evidence that greater wealth *necessarily* leads to environmental improvement. Even Bjorn's figures show that in some cases greater wealth makes the environment better, in others it clearly makes it worse. It all depends on the starting point and what options people have.[22]

Again, this is a distortion of Lomborg's argument. It is the *denial* of the proposition that problems of the environment can be solved by greater wealth that represents dogma, not science. Of course it is possible, with ill-considered policies, for the average wealth of medium income countries to increase and for the environment to deteriorate: this was demonstrated by the experience of the Warsaw Pact countries in the 1950s and 1960s. But Lomborg provides strong evidence that in mixed market economies with democratic institutions, the growth of income above a medium level (a level that much of the developing world has either achieved or can be expected to achieve in the not-so-distant future) will lead to environmental improvement and not the reverse.

A major reason for this, as Lomborg points out, is that advancing technology facilitates both growth in average incomes and improvements in the environment. Ian Lowe cannot see this because his conceptual schema puts technology and 'wealth' into separate boxes, and assigns the interest in 'wealth' to a discipline whose practitioners are supposed to have no understanding of technology:

> One particular problem in Australia is that much of the advice reaching government comes from economists who have no understanding of technology...(K)ey areas of the Commonwealth Public Service are thickly infested with economists, carrying with them the *bizarrely simplistic view that technological change is predominantly an economic activity.* There is every reason to argue that technological literacy should be more widespread; in a modern society it could almost be argued to be a prerequisite for positions of responsibility to understand the general principles of technology.[23]

On the *Earthbeat* program on 13 October, the third of the invited contributors, Stephen Schneider, responded as follows to Alexandra de Blas' inquiry as to why he was so 'red hot under the collar' about Lomborg's book:

---

22 ABC (2001). *Op cit*: 8 (emphasis added).

23 Lowe, Ian (1988), 'The Mushroom Treatment', Australian Society, 12-13 November, (emphasis added).

> Well, for those of us who in my case have spent about three decades working with thousands of scientists and policy analysts and others, trying to figure out something about...the future we face...we end up with a maddening degree of uncertainty...We fight amongst ourselves... and have virtually no agreement and now all of a sudden I see in *The Skeptical Environmentalist* the sub-title *'Measuring the Real State of the World'*, and the person who's a non-contributor to the debate has selected largely out of context the happier news.[24]

Schneider, who is Professor of Environmental Biology and Global Change at Stanford, was 'angry' at CUP for publishing Lomborg's book. Asked by de Blas whether this was 'just a case of the old boys' club getting their noses out of joint because there's a new voice with a very different message', Schneider responded:

> It was published from the social and political science part of the shop, yet this book requires a tremendous amount of natural science, physical and biological sciences, upon which a lot of these conclusions about social science are based. And what Cambridge should have done... and I've held them...quite derelict for this, [was] have reviewers across all three of the groups...so they could have found out whether the grounding in other disciplines was a balanced treatment...and I think had they done that, they would have made a very different conclusion about publishing the book.[25]

It is not clear that this is so: Lewis Wolpert, for one, would presumably have advised Cambridge to publish the book if his opinion had been sought. And many of the 'thousands of scientists and policy analysts and others' to whom Schneider refers might not agree that an intelligent and persuasive voice should be denied a hearing for the reasons he gives.

It is perhaps fortunate for Stephen Schneider that Bjorn Lomborg did not review Schneider's contributions to the debate on global climate change and associated issues during the past 30 years. Some of these are worth recording here – not for the purpose of casting doubt on Schneider's distinction as a scientist, but in order to show that the stones he throws at Lomborg come from the occupant of a glass house. Here is Schneider's assessment of the prospective direction of global climate change from a book published in 1976:

> I have cited many examples of recent climatic variability and repeated the warnings of several well-known climatologists that a cooling trend

24 ABC (2001). *Op cit*: 3.

25 *Ibid*: 8.

> has set in – perhaps one akin to the Little Ice Age – and that climatic variability, which is the bane of reliable food production, can be expected to increase along with the cooling.[26]

In 1989, by which time Schneider was calling for immediate action to check the prospect of global *warming*, he gave his view of the way scientists should contribute to the debate:

> ...like most people [we scientists] would like to see the world a better place, which in this context translates into our working to reduce the risk of potentially disastrous climatic change. To do this we need to get some broad-based support, to capture the public's imagination. That, of course, entails getting loads of media coverage. So we have to offer up scary scenarios, make simplified dramatic statements, and make little mention of any doubts we might have. This 'double ethical bind' we find ourselves in cannot be solved by any formula. Each of us has to decide what the right balance is between being effective and being honest. I hope that means being both.[27]

In a recent lecture in India, Deepak Lal, Professor of International Development Studies at UCLA, recalled how he became involved in debates on the environment when he was preparing the 1990 Wincott Lecture:

> Having read the scientific literature I was appalled at how the scientists – like Stephen Schneider – openly admitted they were creating alarm for a phenomenon they themselves recognised as highly speculative. My lecture not surprisingly ended up as an attack on this scientific attempt to bamboozle the public.[28]

While Schneider sees himself as justified in making 'little mention' of his doubts, he condemned Lomborg on the *Earthbeat* program for having 'a confidence that's not based on any significant analysis by him, or any properly balanced citation from the literature'.[29] As the preceding discussion shows, Lomborg's analysis cannot be so lightly dismissed. As a professor of statistics in a school of political science, he is better equipped to assess the relevant evidence, and to understand the processes by which societal priorities are determined, than many of his critics.

At the conclusion of the *Earthbeat* segment on ABC Radio on 13 October, Lomborg summed up his position as follows:

---

26 Schneider, Stephen (1976). *The Genesis Strategy,* New York: 90.

27 Quoted by Jonathan Schell (1989). 'Our Fragile Earth', *Discover,* October: 47.

28 Lal, Deepak (2000). 'The New Cultural Imperialism: the Greens and Economic Development', The Inaugural Julian Simon Memorial Lecture, Liberty Institute, New Delhi, 9 December: 3.

29 ABC (2001). *Op cit*: 3.

> Yes, I'm a political scientist, economist, statistician. Yes, we do actually look at things in a different way. I asked the question which is fundamental to democracy and to our prioritisation process: 'So overall, how are things going?' A lot of these people would like to sit on the debate and say 'We have the right answer'. Well, no, they have the right understanding in many of these models, but the basic question of what should we do, how things are basically going, needs also to come out there, and that I think has not been coming out from science. But certainly we need to get that overview of the world and that is what I've tried to provide.[30]

Lomborg has made an outstanding contribution to the discussion of some of the most vital issues of our time. If parts of his analysis are unsound on scientific grounds, it should not be beyond the capacity of scientists to demonstrate this in free, critical and civil discussion. Those who have chosen instead to distort or suppress his message, or to engage in ill-tempered abuse, are doing a disservice to themselves, their disciplines and scientific enterprise.

30 *Ibid*: 8.

26. Global Warming and the 'Scientific Consensus' 1939–2001[1]

Ian Castles

The probability that human activities are producing significant changes in the earth's climate is increasingly being seen as one of the world's major problems. Yet in 1939, within the lifetime of many of us, one of the world's leading scientists urged governments to take deliberate action to bring about global warming.

JD Bernal advocates a warming globe (1939)...

In *The Social Function of Science,* one of the most influential books of the century, the British physicist JD Bernal, FRS argued that in 'a fully organised world society' it should 'no longer be a question of adapting man to the world but the world to man'. In that context, Professor Bernal lauded 'the work of the Soviet Union in the conquest of the Arctic':

> ... the present Arctic with its wastes of tundra, glacier and sea-ice is a legacy of the geological accident of the Ice Age. It will disappear in time, leaving the world a much pleasanter place, but there is no reason why man should not hasten the process. By an intelligent diversion of warm ocean-currents together with some means of colouring snow so that the sun could melt it, it might be possible to keep the Arctic ice-free for one summer, and that one year might tip the balance and permanently change the climate of the northern hemisphere.[2]

... and dismisses concerns that the Arctic ice cap may melt (1951)

In 1951, Bernal told a London audience about a massive hydro-electric and irrigation scheme in the Soviet Union ('two to three hundred times the size of the Tennessee Valley Authority scheme'), which would divert the northern rivers and make the deserts bloom:

1 First published in *Dialogue* 20, 1/2001.

2 Bernal JD (1939). *The Social Function of Science*: 379-80.

> Its effect will be to convert every river into a series of lakes separated by dams with power stations; there will be no flowing Volga any more, but sea-going ships will go from lake to lake through automatically operated locks... [B]ig dams have been built on the Pechora and Vychegda, which used to flow into the Arctic; these are now being damned [*sic*] up so as to fall back into the tributaries of the Volga. It is possible that no water will ultimately go to the Arctic, where water is of little value; all the water will be turned back into the Black Sea, the Caspian Sea or the Aral Depression ...[3]

In response to a questioner who suggested 'that if the northern waters are deflected from the Arctic it will become saltier and will not freeze so easily, and ... this will reduce the polar ice', Professor Bernal said that 'there would be some such effect', but that 'this is a very long-term matter, and he did not think we should live to see the effect'.[4]

Meanwhile, Bernal was confident that the plan to build the 800-mile long Turkmen canal, based on twenty years of research by 650 Soviet scientists, would turn the Kara-Kum desert into 'one of the wealthiest agricultural districts'.[5] He believed that 'it would be possible to carry out a good deal of blasting in the desert areas with atomic bombs', and 'As the projects are long-term ones the radio-activity problem will be overcome'.[6] And the conversion of the major part of the Turkmen republic from desert into fertile land would help to stabilise the climate of the area:

> Only 60% of the flow of the Amu Darya is being taken for irrigation purposes, and the rest is going into the Aral Sea. The level of the Aral has been rising and this has brought about a change in climate. It is expected that the present level can be kept constant. One questioner says that a lot of water will be required if it is intended to irrigate an area equal to Egypt, but a lot of water is available. Actually the irrigation system of Egypt is very inefficient. Most of the Nile water flows uselessly into the Mediterranean ...[7]

3 Bernal, JD (1951). 'The Developments of Soviet Science' in *Anglo-Soviet Journal*, Autumn: 10.
4 *Ibid*: 14.
5 *Ibid*: 11.
6 *Ibid*: 14.
7 *Ibid*: 14..

Climate Change 2001 International science, politics and climate change

Untenable as these views have now become, they were put forward in all seriousness by a scholar whom CP Snow thought to be 'the most learned scientist of his time, perhaps the last of whom it will be said, with meaning, that he knew science'.[8] Many scientists regarded him as exceptionally knowledgeable: in the *Dictionary of National Biography 1971-1980*, John Kendrew wrote that Bernal

> had an extraordinarily wide knowledge of many branches of science, and of many fields outside science; if anyone in this century deserved the name polymath, it was he. Even as an undergraduate he was given the nickname Sage which stuck to him for the rest of his life... In 1939 he published *The Social Function of Science*. Today almost everything in the book seems obvious; in its time it had an immense influence.[9]

The benefits of hastening the melting of the Arctic ice cap were far from obvious in 1986, when this biographical essay appeared. Its author would have been well aware of this, because he was at this time President of the International Council of Science (ICSU). And in the previous year representatives of ICSU, the World Meteorological Organization (WMO) and the United Nations Environmental Program (UNEP) met to plan the institutional arrangements that the world now knows as the Framework Convention on Climate Change (FCCC) and the Intergovernmental Panel on Climate Change (IPCC).

Aynsley Kellow, then of the Faculty of Environmental Science at Griffith University, told the story at the National Academies Forum (NAF) conference *The Challenge for Australia on Global Climate Change* in Canberra in 1997:

> Representatives of WMO, UNEP and ICSU met in Villach, Austria in October 1985. The conference statement recommended that UNEP, WMO and ICSU take action to initiate, if deemed necessary, consideration of a global convention. This statement influenced the WCED to initiate the formation of the IPCC, which was established on 6 December 1988 by the General Assembly as a joint venture of WMO and UNEP, but it had evolved between 1985 and 1987 largely as the creation of governments, which could significantly influence membership and nominations.[10]

---

8 Snow, CP (1964). 'JD Bernal, A Personal Portrait' in Goldsmith, Maurice and Alan Mackay, *The Science of Science: Society in the Technological Age*, 1964: 24.

9 Kendrew, John C (1986). 'Bernal, JD' in *Dictionary of National Biography 1971-1980*: 53-4.

10 Kellow, Aynsley (1997). 'The Politics of Climate Change: Problem Definition, Precaution, and the International Policy Process' in National Academies Forum, *The Challenge for Australia on Global Climate Change*: 86.

Dr Kellow went on to refer to claims that there were 'indications that a small number of governments with strong research interests in atmospheric modelling and space technology (USA, Canada, Sweden, Germany, UK, Australia) used intergovernmental organisations, especially WMO and UNEP, to keep a check on the research agenda emerging from the US dominated ICSU'.

Climate Change 2001: The IPCC Third Assessment Report

On 17 January 2001, delegations of 99 member countries of the IPCC met in Shanghai to participate in the Eighth Session of the Panel's Working Group 1 (WG1).

After considering the contribution of WG1 to the IPCC's Third Assessment Report and undertaking a line-by-line consideration of the 'Summary for Policymakers', the governments unanimously approved this Summary and accepted the full report *Climate Change 2001: The Scientific Basis.*

This full report, which runs to over 1000 pages, had been over three years in production and was the work of 122 Co-ordinating Lead Authors and Lead Authors, 516 Contributing Authors, 21 Review Editors and 337 Expert Reviewers. The reports of the other two IPCC Working Groups, which are comparable to the Report of WG1 in their length, period of gestation and the number of contributing authors and editors, were considered and accepted at IPCC meetings in Geneva (in mid-February) and Accra (in early March). The Summary for Policymakers of each of the three reports is available on the IPCC's website at www.ipcc.ch.

All three of the full reports are to be formally accepted by a meeting of the full IPCC Plenary in Nairobi, Kenya from 4-6 April, and a 'Synthesis Report', addressing nine specific policy relevant questions that require input from all three Working Group reports, will be adopted at a meeting in London from 24-29 September.

The WG1 Report: critique of the 'Summary for Policymakers'

The assessment by WG1 of the state of the Arctic ice cap that Bernal wanted to melt appears in the 'Summary for Policymakers' of the Working Group's report, which was unanimously approved by governments on 20 January. It appears under the sub-heading 'Snow cover and ice extent have decreased', and reads as follows:

- Satellite data show that there are very likely [i.e. 90-99% chance] to have been decreases of about 10% in the extent of snow cover since the late 1960s, and ground-based observations show that there is very likely [i.e. 90-99% chance] to have been a reduction of about two weeks in the annual duration of lake and river ice cover in the mid- and high latitudes of the *Northern Hemisphere*, over the 20th century...
- *Northern Hemisphere* spring and summer sea-ice extent has decreased by about 10 to 15% since the 1950s. It is likely [i.e. 66-90% chance] that there has been about a 40% decline in *Arctic* sea-ice thickness during late summer to early autumn in recent decades and a considerably slower decline in winter sea-ice thickness (emphases added).

Although the sub-heading states without qualification that 'Snow cover and ice extent *have* decreased' (emphasis added), the references in the text are explicitly stated to relate only to the northern hemisphere and the Arctic.

In order to discover what has happened to the state of the Antarctic ice cap, the policymaker must turn to the final section under the general heading 'An increasing body of observations gives a collective picture of a warming world and other changes in the climate system'. In this section, the following statement is made under the sub-heading 'Some important aspects of climate *appear* [emphasis added] not to have changed':

- No significant trends of Antarctic sea-ice extent are apparent since 1978, the period of reliable satellite measurements.

The projections by WG1 of future changes in the global ice caps appear in a later section of the 'Summary for Policymakers'. Under the heading 'Global average temperature and sea level are projected to rise under all IPCC scenarios' and the sub-heading 'Snow and ice', the summary of the WG1 report presents the prospective changes in the northern and southern hemispheres as follows:

- Northern Hemisphere snow cover and sea-ice extent are projected to decrease further ...
- The Antarctic ice sheet is likely [i.e. 66-90% chance] to gain mass because of greater precipitation, while the Greenland ice sheet is likely to lose mass because the increase in runoff will exceed the precipitation increase.
- Concerns have been expressed about the stability of the West Antarctic ice sheet because it is grounded below sea level. However, loss of grounded ice leading to substantial sea level rise from this source is now widely agreed to be very unlikely [i.e. 1-10% chance] during the 21st century ...

NGOs, the media and greenhouse science

In his paper to the NAF conference in 1997, Aynsley Kellow provided some relevant background information relating to these 'concerns ... about the stability of the West Antarctic ice sheet':

> The problem is even worse when NGOs produce their own 'scientific evidence'. For example, in February 1997 Greenpeace researchers reported to the mass media massive cracks in Antarctic sea ice. Their report simultaneously linked this to the climate change issue, stating that the cracks were evidence of global warming. Indeed, Greenpeace had dispatched its research team to the area precisely to look for ways to highlight global warming to the public, and was able to provide dramatic video footage to a hungry media. The event might or might not be related to climate change, but the point is that this was not peer-reviewed science but a media event supporting a political campaign. (In contrast, the rebuttal of the claim by glaciologists a few days later – pointing out that warming would affect rate of melting, whereas cracking was a natural phenomenon... – received a few mundane column centimetres in the print media).[11]

Dr Kellow also criticised the Policymakers' Summary of the IPCC Second Assessment Report (1995) for ignoring

> the fact that satellite data – the only truly global measurements – which have been available since 1979, show no warming at all, but a slight cooling of 0.05°C per decade (although this is compatible with a zero trend).

The satellite data from 1979 to 2000 are reported in the 'Summary for Policymakers' of the Third Assessment Report (2001) in the following terms:

> Since the start of the satellite record in 1979, both satellite and weather balloon measurements show that the global average temperature of the lowest 8 kilometres of the atmosphere has changed by +0.05-0.10°C per decade ...

It is notable that, while Aynsley Kellow explicitly acknowledged that the observed 'slight cooling of 0.05°C per decade' up to 1995 was compatible with a zero trend, there is no comparable acknowledgement in the 2001 Summary that the observed increase of 0.05°C per decade since 1979 is also compatible with a zero trend. On the contrary, the Summary approved by governments

11 *Ibid*: 82.

last January reports the satellite and weather balloon measurements since 1979 under the sub-heading 'Temperatures have risen during the past four decades in the lowest 8 kilometres of the atmosphere'.

Under the headline 'Global warming rate rings alarm bells', *The Age* (Melbourne) of 23 January 2001 carried a report from its China correspondent on the release of the report of WG1. The 'Key findings of the global warming report' were presented in a box headed 'Climate change hots up'. The list included the WG1 findings about the decline in northern hemisphere snow cover and in Arctic sea-ice thickness, but omitted the finding that there had been no significant change in Antarctic sea-ice extent since reliable measurements began. It included the finding that the atmospheric concentration of carbon dioxide has increased by 31 per cent since 1750, but omitted the finding that the atmospheric concentration of methane had increased by 151 per cent over the same 250-year period. (According to Aynsley Kellow's paper, methane production is highly concentrated in developing countries, with rice paddies contributing 29 per cent, ruminant animals 20 per cent, fossil fuels 21 per cent, biomass burning 15 per cent and landfills 15 per cent of the total methane emissions).[12] And it included the findings that the 1990s were the warmest decade and 1998 the warmest year in the instrumental record since 1861, but omitted the fact (see previous paragraph) that satellite data, which are the only truly global measurements of average temperatures, are compatible with a zero trend since records began in 1978.

UN officials, national governments and the 'scientific consensus'

The text of *The Age* report on the WG1 conclusions gave extensive coverage to warnings by United Nations officials that governments needed to act urgently on greenhouse gas emissions. 'The scientific findings being reported today should convince governments of the need to take constructive steps towards resuming the climate change talks that stalled last November in The Hague', said Michael Zammit Cutzjar, executive secretary of the UN Climate Change Convention. And UNEP executive director Klaus Topfer said that

> The scientific consensus presented in this comprehensive report about human-induced climate change should sound alarm bells in every national capital and in every local community. We must move ahead boldly with clean energy technologies, and we should start preparing ourselves now for the rising sea levels, changing rain patterns and other impacts of global warming.

12 *Ibid*: 84.

In his NAF paper, Aynsley Kellow questioned the insistence of the IPCC on developing a 'scientific consensus', which he 'thought had not been too popular in scientific circles after Galileo'.[13] He challenged the notion that the science of IPCC was as reliable as peer-reviewed science, and argued that 'the greenhouse bandwagon is rolling along a path which is likely to lead to failure *even if the IPCC predictions prove accurate*'.[14] And he drew attention to suggestions

> that global warming might *cause* higher levels of atmospheric carbon, since there is 52 times more carbon dissolved in the oceans than present in the atmosphere, and less would remain dissolved at higher temperatures. This directionality even better accounts for evidence of association in the ice core data than the 'global warming as a result of industrial society' scenario, and some have claimed support for this from statistical analysis.[15]

Perhaps there is an answer to these suggestions somewhere in the 1000 page report from the IPCC's WG1. But there is no answer that policymakers will be able to understand in the 'Summary for Policymakers': all of the argument appears to the lay reader to *assume* that the direction of causality is from GHG concentrations to global warming rather than the other way around.

Climate change science and the international comparison project

The world's governments provide substantial funds to support climate change science: Aynsley Kellow reports an estimate that the United States alone was spending $2.1 billion annually in the mid-1990s.[16] They spend large sums supporting IPCC meetings, such as the conferences that have already taken place this year in Shanghai, Geneva and Accra (not to mention the meetings soon to be held in Nairobi and London). And they devote scarce human as well as financial resources to the negotiation of intergovernmental agreements such as the Kyoto Protocol and 'the climate change talks that stalled last November in The Hague'.

Such expenditures would be justified if they were successful in devising more effective strategies to limit GHG emissions or assisting governments to communicate to their constituencies the importance of achieving effective strategies to this end. But it is not clear that either of these objectives is being achieved.

13 *Ibid*: 85.
14 *Ibid*: 80 (Emphasis in original).
15 *Ibid*: 83 (Emphasis in original).
16 *Ibid*: 82.

For example, in their contribution to a Special Issue of *The Energy Journal* in 1999 which incorporated a series of analyses of the economic and energy sector impacts of the Kyoto Protocol on Climate Change, economists William Nordhaus and Joseph Boyer concluded that the emissions strategy to which the Protocol seeks to give effect 'is highly cost-ineffective, with the global temperature reduction achieved at a cost almost 8 times the cost of a strategy which is cost-effective in terms of "where" and "when" efficiency'.[17] The failure of governments and intergovernmental organisations to maintain support for the United Nations/World Bank International Comparison Program (ICP) provides a sobering contrast to the generous support afforded to the science and politics of climate change. Last year's meeting of the United Nations Statistical Commission (UNSC) 'noted the support of many countries and international agencies for a viable ICP program, but in the light of the serious reservations ... regarding the quality, timeliness, credibility and transparency of the ICP as identified in the Castles and Ryten reports, recommended that the start of the next round of the global ICP be postponed by at least one year so that the following steps could be taken: (i) Securing of adequate funding for the program ...' The World Bank has now reported to the March 2001 meeting of the UNSC that 'Without renewed commitment from the international community, the ICP faces a near certain death in developing countries, where a reliable information base for International Development Goals and poverty alleviation policy is badly needed'.

The entire annual cost of the ICP amounts to about $US3 million: less than the United States alone spends on climate change science each day. A rational world would recognise the need for a viable program to facilitate international comparisons of prices and of the output of nations if only for its potential contribution to the design and implementation of effective policies to meet the challenge of global climate change. But, as the World Bank's statement to the 2001 meeting of the UNSC makes clear, the output of the ICP has many uses. Among the most important is that of supporting the information needs of programs to alleviate poverty in developing countries.

Thanks to the evidence provided by the ICP, we know that average incomes in Turkmenistan are now only about one tenth of those in Japan. Far from being 'one of the wealthiest agricultural districts', the Kara-Kum desert remains a poverty-stricken area. The Turkmen canal ('the most exciting of all' of the massive Soviet construction projects,[18] according to JD Bernal in 1951) has been the cause of an environmental catastrophe since its completion in 1967. Water lost through irrigation and evaporation from the canal has contributed to a

17 Nordhaus, William and Joseph Boyer (1999). 'Requiem for Kyoto: An Economic Analysis' in *The Energy Journal, Special Issue: The Costs of the Kyoto Protocol: A Multi-Model Evaluation*: 93-130.

18 Bernal (1951), *op cit*: 11.

'disastrous decline in the Amu Darya's outflow' and this, together with 'soil and water salinization resulting from the desiccation and shrinking of the Aral Sea... threatens to ruin the Amu Darya delta as an agricultural producer...'[19]

It is not surprising that today's scientific consensus does not share Bernal's enthusiasm for 'adapting...the world to man'.

19 Encyclopedia Brittanica online: 'Turkmenistan'.

27. Ian Castles and the IPCC – Selected Letters

The following are selected letters from Ian Castles to Dr Rajendra Pachauri, Chairman of the Intergovernmental Panel on Climate Change, between 2002 and 2004. Some attachments to the letters are not included, nor are some web references which may no longer be available.[1] To the best of our knowledge, Dr Pachauri never replied substantively to these well researched and carefully crafted letters despite their implications for the vilidity of the IPCC work.

The letters illustrate Castles' original criticisms of the IPCC scenarios and the methodologies involved based upon statistical and economic considerations as distinct from climate science factors. While Castles' criticisms were not properly addressed by the IPCC during this period, some have subsequently been taken into account. Castles remained, however, deeply concerned about the IPCC's work, particularly its long-term scenarios, the lack of careful assessment of their likelihood and the balancing of current costs of action against benefits far into the future.

Andrew Podger, Dennis Trewin

Letter of 6 August 2002 from Ian Castles to Dr Rajendra Pachauri

Dr Rajendra Pachauri,

Chairman,

Intergovernmental Panel on Climate Change

Dear Dr Pachauri,

1. Thank you for your interest in my criticisms of the IPCC *Special Report on Emissions Scenarios* (SRES), and for inviting me to put my concerns in writing. I am taking the liberty of sending copies of this letter to others who joined in discussions on climate change issues with you in Canberra on 23 and 24 July, and also to a 'mailing list' of my colleagues in the international statistical community, government agencies and universities who follow my ongoing correspondence about the use and abuse of statistics in public debates about

1 Except where otherwise indicated, all figures and tables in this chapter are Castles' own.

globalisation, poverty and the distribution of incomes both within and between countries. I will of course forward any comments that you or the SRES authors may have on my criticisms to all of those to whom I am copying this letter.

Credentials

2. As mentioned in our discussions, I was formerly the Australian Statistician (1986 to 1994) and head of the Australian Department of Finance (1979-86). I am a former President of the International Association of Official Statistics (IAOS), a section of the International Statistical Institute (ISI), and have been a consultant to several national statistical offices and international organisations on a range of statistical issues.

Statistics of global poverty and inequality

3. Following the release of the UNDP's *Human Development Report 1999* (HDR 1999), I made extensive statistical criticisms of the treatment in that report of trends in global poverty and inequality. At the request of the 2000 meeting of the UN Statistical Commission (UNSC), those criticisms were examined by a group of expert statisticians constituted as the Friends of the Chair of the Commission. The report of the group upheld my more serious criticisms. In particular, the Friends of the Chair of the UNSC held that HDR 1999 had made a 'material error' (i.e. one which left the reader with 'a fundamentally distorted view of the phenomenon being described') in relying on national accounting aggregates converted into $US at current exchange rates to compare living standards between countries.

4. The HDR Office of the UNDP accepted the report, and has made major improvements in statistical presentation and reporting in subsequent issues of the HDR.

5. Both the SRES and the Contribution of IPCC Working Group III (WG III) to the Third Assessment Report (*Climate Change 2001: Mitigation*) cite incorrect statements from pre-2000 issues of the HDR in support of claims about the international distribution of incomes. Some of these statements involve exactly the same 'material error' as that referred to in paragraph 3 above. Thus the WG III Contribution includes the following:

> The distributional dimension of global poverty was illustrated vividly by the *Human Development Report 1989* (*sic* – the first HDR was published in 1990), in the form that came to be known as the champagne glass [reproduced as Figure 1.4 in the IPCC Report]. This representation of global income distribution shows that in 1988 the richest fifth of the world's population received 82.7% of the global income, which is nearly 60 times the share of the income received by the poorest fifth (1.4%).

More recent statistics indicate that inequality has widened further since then and that in 1999 the richest quintile received 80 times the income earned by the poorest quintile (UNDP 1999) (section 1.3.1).

6. Another paragraph in the same section of the Contribution of WG III cites statements in the World Bank's *World Development Report 2000* in support of similar claims about high and rising global inequality. The Australian Treasury has published a detailed critique of this analysis by the Bank, and has cited statements included in this analysis as examples of 'material errors in the use of statistics' ('Global poverty and inequality in the 20th century: turning the corner', 2001: 24-26, 34-40, available in pdf on the Treasury website at www.treasury.gov.au).

7. The SRES cites the UNDP's HDR 1993 in support of the proposition that 'The poorest 20% of Bangladesh's population ... earn per capita incomes that are a factor of 700 lower than that of the 20% richest Swiss population' (section 4.4.4.1). This comparison is invalid, because it is based on the assumption that the poor Bangladeshi family has converted the whole of its income into foreign currency, and spent it on goods and services at average world prices rather than Bangladeshi prices.

8. The same false assumption underlies the claim that 'When measured across the four SRES regions in 1990, income per capita differences are nearly 40 to 1 (between ASIA and OECD90)' (SRES, section 4.4.4.1). The difference in average incomes between these two regions, properly measured, was less than 10 to 1 in 1990, and has since contracted significantly. Thus the projected growth of real average incomes in the ASIA region (i.e. developing Asia) between 1990 and 2100 that is assumed in the A1 scenarios (an increase by a factor of about 140 to 1) and the B1 scenarios (an increase by a factor of more than 70 to 1) would take incomes in that region to far higher levels than the present OECD90 average, and possibly to higher levels than the OECD90 average in 2100. (This latter comparison is more problematic, because of the difficulty of allowing for the 'Gerschenkron effect').

9. The rates of growth in global GDP presented in the SRES significantly understate the true increases in GDP that underlie the emissions projections. This is because the regions that are expected, by assumption, to achieve the highest rates of economic growth in the twenty-first century are significantly underweighted in the calculations of global GDP. An indication of the possible extent of understatement can be derived by comparing the IMF's estimate of the average annual rate of growth in world GDP between 1994 and 2003 at market exchange rates (2.8 per cent) with the corresponding estimate of this growth measured on the correct basis using purchasing power parities (3.6 per cent). In per capita terms, calculation of the growth rate on the discredited exchange rate-based method used in the SRES yields an average annual increase over this

decade of only 1.4 per cent, compared with an increase of 2.2 per cent on the correct purchasing power-corrected basis (IMF, *World Economic Outlook*, May 2002: 157).

10. On the basis of estimates by Angus Maddison which are used in the SRES itself in other contexts, average real incomes in the United States increased by a factor of perhaps 5 to 1 in the nineteenth century, and average real incomes in Japan increased by a factor of almost 20 to 1 in the twentieth century. Thus the historical record gives no support to projections that in the course of the twenty-first century there could be increases in average incomes in the entire continent of Asia by a factor of 140 to 1 – or even of 70 to 1, which is the assumption underlying the scenario yielding the *lowest* projected level of emissions. Yet it is upon such fantastic assumptions that the IPCC's projections of emissions, and therefore of temperatures, are predicated.

The B1 IMAGE projections

11. The B1 IMAGE projection is of particular interest, because this is the marker projection that yields the lowest increase in temperature between 1990 and 2100 – between 1.4 degrees C. and 2.5 degrees C. for the seven climate models, with a projected increase averaged over those seven models of 1.98 degrees C. from 1990 and of 1.82 degrees C. from 2000 (*Climate Change 2001: The Scientific Basis,* Appendix II, Table II. 4).

12. According to the SRES Terms of Reference (SRES, Appendix I), the process for developing the scenarios was to be: 'First, key input assumptions would be provided to modelers', and 'Second, modelers would be asked to construct emissions scenarios based on the input assumptions provided'.

13. In this case, the opposite process was followed. The B1 IMAGE modelers (1) *assumed* an extraordinarily rapid growth in annual global emissions of carbon dioxide from the burning of fossil fuels (an increase of 1.6 billion tonnes between 2000 and 2010, and a further increase of 1.5 billion tonnes between 2010 and 2020, compared with increases of only 0.8 billion tonnes in the 1980s and of 0.7 billion tonnes in the 1990s); (2) allocated the whole of the very large increases in these emissions in both decades to developing countries; and (3) used the model to estimate the levels of income, energy use and emissions of other greenhouse gases and aerosols that might be associated with the assumed levels of fossil carbon dioxide emissions.

14. In the current decade, for example, the results of the B1 IMAGE model are predicated upon *assumed* increases in emissions of exactly 0.8 billion tonnes both in the ASIA and the ALM (Africa, Latin America and the Middle East) regions. In other words, the modelers assumed that increases in emissions in

each of the SRES developing regions (ASIA and ALM) would be greater in the current decade than the increase for the world as a whole between 1990 and 2000.

15. These assumptions are patently unrealistic, even for a 'high emissions scenario'. They translate into increases in per capita emissions of fossil carbon dioxide of 24 per cent in ASIA and of 46 per cent in ALM. On this basis, the output of the B1 IMAGE model suggests that GDP per head could rise by around 50 per cent in both regions.

16. In the case of the ALM region, it is already certain that such a growth in incomes will not occur. In the IMF's *World Economic Outlook May 2002*, it is estimated that real GDP per head declined in this region in 2001 and that there will be a further decline in 2002 (p. 163). Even if the IMF's rather optimistic 'world medium-term baseline scenario' for the years 2003 to 2007 were to be realised (p. 224), it would require a further increase of no less than 40 per cent in real GDP in 'ALM' in the succeeding three years to achieve the increase in decadal GDP projected in the B1 IMAGE scenario. If the modelers had followed the procedure laid down in the SRES terms of reference, they would have 'fed in' a much lower rate of growth in GDP as a 'key output assumption'. They could then have concluded that fossil carbon emissions in this region will not increase by anything like 0.9 billion tonnes.

17. The projected growth in Asian GDP in the current decade may well be realised, but with a far slower growth in carbon dioxide emissions than is assumed in the B1 IMAGE projection. There is no obvious reason why the rapid decline in 'emissions intensity' in ASIA in the 1990s should not be maintained during the current decade. Again, if the procedure for scenario development laid down in the SRES terms of reference (paragraph 11 above) had been followed, a fast rate of decline in emissions intensity in this region would have been a 'key input assumption'. The output of the model would then have revealed that carbon emissions would not need to increase by anything like 0.8 billion tonnes.

18. In short, the B1 IMAGE projection, which belongs to the 'storyline and scenario family' that features 'rapid change in economic structures toward a service and information economy', 'reductions in material intensity', 'the introduction of clean and resource-efficient technologies' and 'global solutions to economic, social and environmental sustainability', is itself a 'high emissions scenario' – at least in the early decades of the century. It assumes that there will be a sharp reversal in the downward trend in global fossil fuel emissions per head that occurred in the last two decades of the twentieth century. This seems unlikely: under the 'reference' scenario in the World Energy Council Commission Report *Energy for Tomorrow's World* (1993), global carbon dioxide emissions per head were projected to *decrease* by seven per cent between 1990 and 2020. It is significant that the WEC study, unlike the SRES, was based on purchasing power parity estimates of GDP.

Recommendations

19. I believe that it is important that governments be advised as soon as possible that the economic projections used in the IPCC emissions scenarios are technically unsound, having been derived by converting national GDPs in nominal values into a common currency using exchange rates. This procedure is not permissible under the internationally-recognised *System of National Accounts,* and was recently rejected by an expert group in a report to the UN Statistical Commission. The practice of using exchange rate conversion is especially inappropriate in relation to projections of physical phenomena such as emissions of greenhouse gases and aerosols.

20. In the introduction to the first edition of his book *Global Warming: The Complete Briefing* (1994), Sir John Houghton, then Co-Chairman of the Scientific Assessment Working Group of the IPCC, said that 'scientists have a responsibility to communicate the best possible information about the likely magnitude of climate change, along with clear statements of the assumptions made and the level of uncertainty in the estimates'. As there was no clear statement of the assumptions underlying the projections of the likely magnitude of climate change in the IPCC's Third Assessment Report, I consider it vital that governments be advised that the *lowest* of the SRES projections assumed that GDP per capita would increase to more than 70 times its 1990 level in Asia (excluding Japan) and to nearly 30 times its 1990 level in Africa, Latin America and the Middle East, by the end of the century. Contrary to statements made in the SRES, these projections imply that real incomes in the whole of the developing world will be many times greater than those in the richest countries in the world today.

21. As I mentioned in our discussions, it would also be desirable to seek the involvement of national statistical offices and of the International Statistical Institute in the new emissions projections that I understand are to be prepared for the IPCC's Fourth Assessment Report.

22. I hope that these comments are helpful to you. I repeat my congratulations to you on your appointment as Chairman of the IPCC, and wish you well in your difficult but important task.

Sincerely,

Ian Castles

National Centre for Development Studies

Australian National University

Letter of 29 August 2002 from Ian Castles to Dr Rajendra Pachauri

Dr Rajendra Pachauri,

Chairman,

Intergovernmental Panel on Climate Change

Dear Dr Pachauri,

In my letter to you of 6 August, I said that I believed that it was 'important that governments be advised as soon as possible that the economic projections used in the IPCC emissions scenarios are technically unsound, having been derived by converting national GDPs in nominal values into a common currency using exchange rates'.

The pernicious consequences of using this false method of measuring output are apparent in the analysis of greenhouse issues in the *World Development Report 2003*, released by the World Bank last week.

For example, the Bank argues that 'non-OECD countries use ... 3.8 times as much energy per dollar of GDP [as OECD countries]', and claims that 'This disparity suggests looking for ways that developing and transition countries can increase efficiency and reduce fuel costs – with reduced GHG emissions as a welcome side-benefit ...' The Bank goes on to wonder 'why these apparent "win-win" situations are so elusive', and decides that the answer lies in two types of institutional failure: 'distortions in energy policy [which] benefit special interests', and the neglect by firms and households of profitable ways of saving energy 'because it is simply too much trouble to pursue them' (p. 177).

There is a simpler answer to the question that the Bank poses. The assumption of a huge margin of difference in energy intensity between OECD and non-OECD countries which the Bank is seeking to explain is false. The ratio of use of energy per unit of GDP in non-OECD countries to that in OECD countries, calculated using PPPs rather than the spurious exchange-rate conversion basis favoured by the Bank (and the IPCC), is not 3.8:1 but 1.2:1.

On the same page of *WDR 2003*, the Bank wonders what will happen when people 'aspire to the current lifestyle of a prosperous country', and puts forward some 'simple arithmetic' to show why the Bank supposes this to be impossible:

> Among the prosperous countries, Norway has one of the lowest rates of CO_2 emissions per capita from energy, owing in part to ample use Wof hydro-power. Yet if the global population of 2050 emitted CO_2 on average at this rate, the total would be about 2.5 times current global emissions, which would greatly exceed the planet's absorptive capacity.

The argument is grossly misleading for a number of reasons. But the key point that it illustrates is the Bank's failure to understand the basis of the IPCC emissions projections, the lowest of which assumes that developing countries will not only aspire to but will in fact achieve far higher living standards than those of the most prosperous countries today.

Pasted below is the text of an article which appears under my name in this morning's *Canberra Times,* under the heading 'Greenhouse emissions calculations quite wrong'. It puts the view that the IPCC should base its climate projections on realistic assessments of future greenhouse emissions, based in turn on realistic projections of the future of the world economy, rather than on the quantification of fantastic 'storylines'.

With best wishes,

Ian Castles

Canberra Times article text

In January last year the Intergovernmental Panel on Climate Change (IPCC) released its latest projections of prospective global warming. The key finding was that "globally averaged mean surface temperature is projected to increase by 1.4 to 5.8°C over the period 1990 to 2100".

The statement led to widespread alarm. Most commentators, including many scientists, interpreted the IPCC's new projected range as a forecast of massive rises in global temperatures, but the IPCC made projections, not predictions, by feeding hypothetical levels of future greenhouse emissions into climate models. The output of such models cannot be better than the input assumptions upon which they are based.

The simulated temperature increases in the IPCC's lowest emissions scenario ranged from 1.4 to 2.5°C. Some assumptions incorporated in this scenario were conservative, but it also assumed an extraordinarily high rate of economic growth in the developing world.

Specifically, the IPCC assumed that the volume of goods and services produced per head in 2100 would be more than 70 times 1990 levels in developing countries in Asia, and nearly 30 times 1990 levels in other developing countries. Far from marking the lower bound of likely outcomes, such astronomic increases are extremely improbable.

The reasoning that produced these assumptions was as follows. Productivity in the rich countries is likely to continue to increase.

In 1990, average incomes in these countries, on the exchange rate-converted basis used in the IPCC projections, were 40 times higher than in Asian developing countries and 12 times higher than the average of developing countries elsewhere. If this gap is to be substantially closed by 2100 on these assumptions, this century must be an era of unprecedented growth.

In fact, average incomes in developing countries are three or four times higher than the IPCC assumed. By adopting the long-discredited method of converting incomes into a common currency using current exchange rates, the IPCC modellers greatly overstated the size of the development gap, but there are two more fundamental objections to the modellers' argument.

First, living standards in the developing countries in 2100 will depend on their actual economic growth during the coming century. No significant country has ever achieved a 20-fold increase in output per head in a century, let alone the 30-fold or 70-fold increases projected by the IPCC for most of the world's population.

Secondly, and paradoxically, the IPCC's model-builders are hostile to wealth per se. They are obsessed by the belief that growth in productivity and affluence inevitably leads to unacceptable growth in greenhouse emissions. For example, they argue that "if governments support the development of rapid-growth sectors, the tendency may be to promote long-term economic growth, increase household income and consumption, and hence increase GHG emissions".

They even claim that "protectionist policies may ... reduce national economic efficiency, which dampens economic growth and tends to restrict growth in GHG emissions".

These concerns are misplaced. Economic growth maximises the output of goods and services for a minimum expenditure of scarce resources. Conversely, reductions in economic efficiency tend to increase the volume of resources required to produce a given volume of final output, and therefore raise the level of GHG emissions.

In Britain, the first developed economy, average carbon dioxide emissions exceeded 2.5 tonnes of carbon per head of the population in 1880, before the motor age began.

Now Britain produces at least five times the volume of goods and services per head as in 1880, but per capita emissions of carbon dioxide have not increased at all.

According to economic historian Angus Maddison, average incomes in China are now higher than in Britain in 1880, but China's carbon emissions are only 0.6 tonnes of carbon per head---less than a quarter of the levels in late-Victorian Britain.

And China's emissions per unit of output are less than half their levels of twenty years ago.

Global carbon dioxide emissions per head from the burning of fossil fuels reached a peak of over 1.2 tonnes per head of population in 1979. They have since declined by nearly 10 per cent.

It is not true that the per capita emissions of rich countries will necessarily increase as they become still richer. No country in western Europe today emits the 3.2 tonnes of carbon per head that Britons emitted in 1913, and per capita emissions in the United States, Canada, Germany, France, the Netherlands, Belgium and Sweden are now lower than the peak levels reached in the 1970s or earlier.

None of the high-income countries of the Organisation for Economic Co-operation and Development now emits the volume of carbon per head that the failing Communist regime in East Germany was emitting in the late 1980s, and poverty-stricken Communist North Korea emits more carbon dioxide per head than South Korea (and most other OECD countries).

It is true that per capita emissions in most developing countries will increase as the world's poor get richer, but this will be happening in a world in which emissions in many rich countries will continue to decline.

Sadly, there is a serious risk that poverty will escalate in many of the poorest countries, especially in sub-Saharan Africa. The real problem is that the people of these countries may remain very poor, not the impact on the world's climate if they and the rest of the developing world become very rich.

The IPCC should base its climate projections on realistic assessments of future greenhouse emissions, not on the quantification of improbable 'storylines' that assume that all of the world's problems except climate change will be magically overcome.

Ian Castles

National Centre for Development Studies

Australian National University

Letter of 4 July 2004 from Ian Castles to Dr Rajendra Pachauri

Dr R K Pachauri

Chairman

Intergovernmental Panel on Climate Change

Dear Dr Pachauri,

1. I am awaiting your substantive reply to my letter to you of 20 April, in which I requested that the IPCC provide users of its website with access to papers relating to the Castles and Henderson critique of the Panel's economic and statistical work. My letter was written during the week before the session of the IPCC Bureau on 28-30 April, in the hope that you would have discussed my request with your colleagues at that meeting. I am now writing again to reiterate and extend my request, in the expectation that the scoping meeting for the AR4 Synthesis Report which begins tomorrow may provide a further opportunity for consideration of this matter.

The IPCC emissions scenarios are unsuitable for use in AR4

2. When I wrote to you nearly two years ago to set down my concerns about the IPCC scenarios, I thought that it was common ground that these scenarios (at least in the form in which they were published in 2000) were unsuitable for use in AR4. This assumption was reflected in the title of the session of the IPCC expert meeting at which Professor Henderson and I made our presentations in January 2003 ('Assessing importance of updating SRES on the basis of new trends and insights').

3. The explanatory text accompanying the agenda for the meeting recognised that 'A common and shared basis for research will enhance the consistency of future analyses, but may require additional efforts to make the SRES and derived research more readily available; that 'Additional information, not developed earlier, may have to be presented'; and that 'Research since the completion of the TAR suggests a variety of issues need to be addressed in order to facilitate use of the SRES as the continuing basis for analysis'. Among the issues mentioned in this connection were the need to consider 'a variety of additional emissions of either global or regional significance to radiative forcing' and 'whether it is important to provide additional information on the initial years of the SRES scenarios so that they are consistent with actual values for 2000.' The conclusion was that 'These and other issues strongly imply that a careful consideration of

how best to use the SRES scenarios will substantially improve the coherence and completeness of the analysis and will ease the eventual integration of work on many different questions by many different groups.'

4. In the event, the IPCC decided that the SRES scenarios in their original form *do* provide 'a credible and sound set of projections, appropriate for use in the AR4' ('Emissions Scenario for Use by the IPCC', Note submitted by the Chairman to meeting of the IPCC in Vienna, November 2003). The proceedings of the expert meeting in Amsterdam have not been published and the second expert meeting on the use of the SRES scenarios that had been foreshadowed at that time was abandoned.

Need for expert meeting on emissions scenarios

5. It was also agreed at the Panel's plenary session in November 2003 that 'an IPCC expert meeting [on emissions scenarios] will be organised in 2004, bringing together a wide variety of experts in the field, including experts from the fields of development economics and statistics' (IPCC, November 2003, Draft report of 21st session, Annex 5, Recommendation 3). The calendar of events for the remainder of 2004 on the IPCC's website does not yet include any notice of this meeting. (Professor Henderson offered suggestions as to venue, subject matter and possible speakers at a meeting of this kind in a short paper attached to his letter to you of 16 January 2003. This paper was subsequently published by *The Economist*).

6. The need for such a meeting has now become urgent, not least because (as I point out below) differing combinations of the original SRES scenarios are being used in 'work on many different questions by many different groups'. Whether or not this meeting is held, it is becoming increasingly difficult to see how the various strands of work by different groups will eventually be drawn together into a policy relevant Report (see paragraph 10 below).

WGCM climate simulation panel exercise and Global Environmental Change assessments

7. The Working Group on Climate Models (WGCM) Climate Simulation Panel of the World Climate Research Program (WCRP) has recently called for expressions of interest from climate modelling groups to participate in 'an unprecedented set of coordinated...climate change experiments'. The announcement (available at http://www-pcmdi.llnl.gov/cmip/subproject_announcement.pdf) states that there will be an international process to collect, compile and analyse output from this multi-model dataset 'for direct input into the IPCC's Fourth Assessment Report (AR4)'; that *'Any person or group can participate in this multi-model*

analysis activity'; and that 'This is a way for anyone to become involved with the IPCC AR4 process'. The 'runs being performed by modelling groups for the AR4' include simulations of three SRES market scenarios: A1B, B1 and A2.

8. The April 2004 issue of the journal *Global Environmental Change: Human and Policy Dimensions* (which is edited by Professor Martin Parry, Co-Chair of IPCC Working Group II) consists of a series of assessments of impacts under the SRES scenarios. These assessments (dealing, respectively, with projected impacts of climate change on natural ecosystems, water resources, food production, sea level rises and exposure to malaria) are based on analyses of four SRES climate and socio-economic scenarios: the A2, B1 and B2 marker scenarios and the 'high carbon' A1F1 illustrative scenario. In his introductory comment, Professor Parry states that 'This is the first global assessment of impacts under SRES scenarios, but many regional impact assessments are now underway, and will be published within the next 2 years'. He also says that these assessments 'will form a valuable background for the Fourth Assessment Report of the IPCC, due to be completed in 2007'.

9. Thus the projects described in the two preceding paragraphs are both envisaged as providing input to AR4. But the project described in paragraph 6 calls for modelers to perform runs on the AB1 scenario but not the A1F1 scenario; whereas the project described in paragraph 7 used the A1F1 scenario but not the A1B scenario, and this will presumably be true also of the 'many regional impact assessments [which] are now underway'.

10. The data provided on projected greenhouse gas concentrations in the simple model 'SRES Tables' (Appendix II of the WGI contribution to the Third Assessment Report) show that emissions profiles vary greatly between scenarios. This underlines the difficulty of producing a coherent assessment from the work of different groups that have chosen different combinations of SRES scenarios (leaving aside other concerns about the scenarios – relating to plausibility, consistency and statistical methodology – that have been raised by a number of economists and statisticians).

11. In relation to atmospheric concentrations of *carbon dioxide*, for example, the projected increase between 2000 and 2100 in the A1F1 scenario (to be used in analyses of impacts, but not in the proposed climate change simulations) is 162 per cent. The corresponding increase in the A1B scenario (to be used in the climate change simulations, but not in analyses of impacts) is 94 per cent. The increase in the A2 and B1 scenarios to be used in both types of studies) are, respectively, 132 per cent and 49 per cent. And the increase for the century in the Hansen alternative scenario (not proposed to be used in either the WGI or WGII studies) is 28 per cent.

12. Similarly, the projected increase in atmospheric concentrations of *methane* between 2000 and 2100 is 94 per cent in the A1F1 scenario (to be used in analyses of impacts, but not in climate change simulations), compared with 12 per cent in the A1B scenario (to be used in climate change simulations, but not in analyses of impacts). The changes in the A2 and B1 scenarios (to be used in both types of studies) are, respectively, an increase of 112 per cent and a decrease of 11 per cent. And the projected change in the Hansen alternative scenario (not proposed to be used in either type of study) is a decrease of 28 per cent.

13. During the four years to 2003, atmospheric methane concentrations were virtually unchanged: the average annual rate of growth was less than 0.1 per cent. This implies that *emissions* of methane have been declining. Yet *all* of the 40 SRES scenarios projected that global methane emissions would continue to increase for decades. The possibility that these emissions were already declining and might continue to decline seems not to have been recognised ('Results from the 40 SRES scenarios indicate that uncertainties surrounding future CH4 emission levels are likely to increase over time. By 2050 the range across all scenarios is between 359 and 671 MtCH4...': SRES: 255 – even the lower end of this range implies a substantial increase on the level in 2000).

14. A body whose main activity is to 'prepare in regular intervals comprehensive and *up-to-date* assessments of policy relevant...information' (emphasis added) should now be *reassessing* projections that were made in the late 1990s and published in 2000 – not using them uncritically in 2004-05 for a Report that is to be published in 2007 and that will still be presented as containing the 'most up-to-date' assessment until at least 2012.

15. Apart from being obsolete and conceptually unsound, all three of the SRES scenarios that are to be modelled in the simulation exercise being sponsored by the WGCM are highly improbable. The two 'convergence' scenarios (A1B and B1) have been recognised by a 'larger part of the SRES authors' themselves as 'highly unlikely' (Nakicenovic *et al,* 2003, 'IPCC SRES Revisited: A Response' *Energy & Environment,* vol. 14, nos. 2 & 3: 196). And the third scenario included in the exercise – the A2 Scenario – assumes a global population exceeding 15 billion by 2100, with a projected population in mid-century which is well in excess of the 'high variant' of the UN Population Division's projections released in 2002. Such an outcome becomes more and more improbable with every passing year. (The UNPD's medium variant for China assumes that the total fertility rate for the entire period between 2000 and 2050 will be about 1.85 children per woman, whereas the estimated actual rate in 2001 was 1.14 children per woman – UNDP, *World Fertility Report 2003:* 70).

Need for greater transparency in IPCC processes

16. I believe that it would assist the many researchers around the world who are using the SRES scenarios if the IPCC facilitated access to the papers incorporating

the Castles and Henderson critique of the economic and statistical work of the Panel, as well as the SRES teams' responses. These papers were published in three issues of *Energy & Environment* (E&E) in 2003 and 2004.

17. The report of the 29th session of the IPCC Bureau in Paris on 18 February 2003 records that you 'noted that Dr Nakicenovic would shortly publish, in a leading international journal, an article that responds to the substance of the [Castles and Henderson] criticism' (paragraph 3.2.3). This article was prepared following a proposal made by David Henderson and me that the editor of *E&E* write to you to invite the IPCC to prepare a response for publication in the journal. We said in our 'authors' preface' to our first article that 'We are glad that an article by SRES authors is to appear alongside our own contribution' (see Castles and Henderson, 2003, *E&E*, vol. 14, nos. 2 & 3: 161).

18. I find it surprising that the IPCC does not now appear to want to assist researchers to gain access to our papers or to the responses from the IPCC teams. In fact, the Castles and Henderson critique and the SRES teams' responses do not rate a mention in the recent issue of *Global Environmental Change* which is devoted entirely to reporting a series of impact assessments based on four SRES scenarios (see paragraph 8 above). All of this research was funded by the UK Department of the Environment, Food and Rural Affairs (DEFRA), but the assessments have an international audience. If the IPCC wishes to disprove the recent claim by Lord Lawson (former UK Chancellor of the Exchequer) that it is 'an environmentalist closed shop', it should be active in alerting researchers to the continuing controversy over the soundness of the SRES scenarios and other aspects of the Panel's economic and statistical work.

19. In this connection, I attach the texts of two papers that are to be published in the forthcoming issue of *E&E* (vol. 15, no. 3) [Ed: not attached here]:

- 'Can the IPCC SRES be improved?' by the Australian economist Warwick McKibbin, David Pearce and Alison Stegman, This is a much condensed version of the paper 'Long run projections for climate change scenarios' which Professor McKibbin and his co-authors prepared for a workshop convened by the Stanford Energy Modeling Forum in February.
- MERs, PPPs and IPCC: Illusions and Reality' by Jacob Ryten, an eminent expert in the field of economic statistics.

20. The forthcoming issue of *E&E* will also include a paper authored by me which has been published in the Australian electronic journal 'On Line Opinion'. In its press release in Milan on 8 December last, the IPCC drew attention to comments which I made in an article published in this journal three years ago. I welcome the Panel's interest in my remarks on the international distribution of income (which are soundly based, unlike many statements on this subject in the SRES

and in other IPCC reports), but repeat my request that the IPCC also provide a link with my more recent article in the same journal, which is more directly related to climate change issues.

21. I also attach three files containing charts [charts only shown below] which provide graphic comparisons of selected SRES scenarios with scenarios from other sources:

- Figure 1 compares concentrations of greenhouse gases from 2000-2100 under the three SRES scenarios included in the WGCM-sponsored simulations (see paragraph 7 above) with the 'Hansen 1% scenario'. Figure 2 provides a similar comparison between the four SRES scenarios included in the *Global Environmental Change* assessments (paragraph 8 above) with the 'Hansen 1% scenario'. The indexes for each scenario are based on 2000=100, and represent the total concentration in CO_2 equivalent of three major greenhouse gases (carbon dioxide, methane and nitrous oxide) aggregated using the 'Global Warming Potential' technique described in the Glossary of the SRES (592).
- Figures 3 and 4 show, respectively, the growth rate and the level of GHG concentrations for the period 2000-2050, for the three SRES scenarios in the WGCM-sponsored simulations and the 'Hansen 1% scenario'. Figure 1 also includes corresponding data for the period 1960-2000. Further details are given in the 'Sources' notes which follow the figures.
- Figure 5 compares an average carbon emissions per capita of Non Annex 1 countries under two SRES scenarios (A1 ASF and B1 image) for the period 2000-2030 with corresponding projections of average emissions for some alternative scenarios. The alternatives include the simulations of projections using MER and PPP by Professor Manne and Dr Richels to which reference was made in the IPCC press release of 8 December 2003, using data provided to me by Dr Richels. I attached this chart to my letter of 9 January last to the Australian Minister for the Environment and Heritage, Dr David Kemp (copy of which I sent to you). I also sent a copy of the message and attached chart to Dr Richels, for any comments that he might have. As he has not responded, I assume that my charts correctly present the results that he supplied to me.

22. I am sending copies of this message and its attachments to the list of interested persons to whom I sent my earlier correspondence with you, and to some others who have subsequently asked to be added to my list. I would welcome comments, including corrections to the charts. If the projections of emissions and concentrations of greenhouse gases in the various scenarios are correctly plotted in these charts, I do urge the Panel to arrange for further work on long-run projections for climate scenarios to be undertaken for AR4, along the lines canvassed in the conclusion of the paper by McKibbin *et al* (see paragraph 19 above).

23. I also request that the IPCC make publicly available the reports of the 30th and 31st sessions of the Bureau of the IPCC held in, respectively, Vienna (early November 2003) and Geneva (28-30 April 2004). The most recent report of an IPCC Bureau meeting on the IPCC website relates to the session in Paris on 18 February 2003. I do not believe that the Bureau is able to provide adequate support to the AR4 process if summary reports of its meetings are not accessible to the thousands of participants in the process.

Publication by WWF: 'A way forward for Australia'

24. I conclude by stressing that there is an urgent need for a re-evaluation of the IPCC and alternative emissions scenarios, and for scientists and governments to be informed of the results. Many scientists have a poor understanding of the significance of the SRES projections. Only today, WWF Australia has released a publication entitled 'A way forward for Australia', the authors of which include a number of Australia's leading climate change scientists. Under the heading of 'Set a national target of 60% reduction in greenhouse gas emissions by 2050', the authors claim that

> To avoid a high level of climate-change damage, Australia must cut emissions by at least 60% below current levels, as must the rest of the world.

25. This assertion may be based on the same misinterpretation of the IPCC Third Assessment Report as that made in a recent publication of the New South Wales (NSW) Greenhouse Office (to which I referred in my letter of 8 June to Dr Greg Ayers of CSIRO, copy of which I sent you). An extract from my letter to Dr Ayers follows:

> The IPCC indicate that a 60 per cent reduction in emissions will be required by mid-century, to stabilise atmospheric carbon dioxide levels and limit global average temperature to an increase of around 2 degrees C.' The [NSW Greenhouse] Office sources this claim to the 'IPCC 2001 Third Assessment Report – Synthesis Report, pp.10-11, scenario B1'. But it is clear from the relevant chart in this Report (Figure (b): 10) that under scenario B1 (the green line), CO_2 emissions go on *rising* up to about 2050: see http:/www.grida.no/climate/ipcc_tar/vol14/english/fig3-1a.htm. Far from requiring a 60% reduction in emissions by mid-century, the IPCC's B1 scenario assumes a *growth* of 70% in fossil CO_2 emissions over this period.

26. Under the latter scenario, the projected increase in global temperatures in the 21st century, on a 'simple model' average of seven climate models, is less than two degrees C. The increase in some other scenarios in the SRES B1 family would be lower than this, but *all* SRES scenarios assume substantially *higher*

levels of CO_2 emissions in 2150 than in 2100. Thus the IPCC Third Assessment Report does not provide any projections of future climate that are based on an assumption of stable levels of global emissions in the current half century, let alone an assumption that emissions will be reduced by 60 per cent by mid-century.

27. The Hansen alternative scenario requires the growth rate in CO_2 concentrations 'to average about the same in the next 50 years as it did in the past 20 years, which was 1.5ppm per year'. According to Dr Hansen, 'This means, to first approximation, that CO_2 emissions from fossil fuel use would need to remain about the same as today or begin to decline slightly' (see James Hansen's 'Open letter' of 26 October 2000 to 'Natural Science'.

28. The Goddard Institute of Space Studies (GISS) model projections using this emissions profile are for a maximum rise in global temperatures of slightly more than one degree C, which occurs between 2125 and 2150. Presumably the eventual increase in temperatures projected by the GISS model for a 60 per cent reduction of projected emissions, as called for by the authors of the Australian WWF study, would be substantially lower than this. The lowest of the 40 SRES scenarios projects a global level of CO_2 emissions in 2150 which is three times as great as the level to which these emissions must be reduced according to the WWF study. And the lowest of the SRES scenarios that have been or will be used in the studies described in paragraphs 7 and 8 above (the B1 image scenario) projects global CO_2 emissions at over four times the level to which they must be reduced, according to the WWF publication.

29. McKibbin *et al* argue that 'it is crucial to understand the drivers of emissions projections and their sensitivity to key assumptions', but stress that 'this understanding cannot be gleaned from the SRES in its current form' (see attached paper 'Can the IPCC SRES be improved': 13 [not attached]). It follows that the SRES and other IPCC Reports do not provide support for the claim by the authors of the Australian WWF study that global emissions must be reduced by 60 per cent by mid-century if dangerous climate change is to be averted. None of these authors was involved in the SRES and, so far as I know, the socio-economic and climatic implications of a '60% reduction by 2050' scenario have not been subjected to scientific assessment.

With best wishes

Ian Castles

Visiting Fellow

Asia Pacific School of Economics and Government

The Australian National University

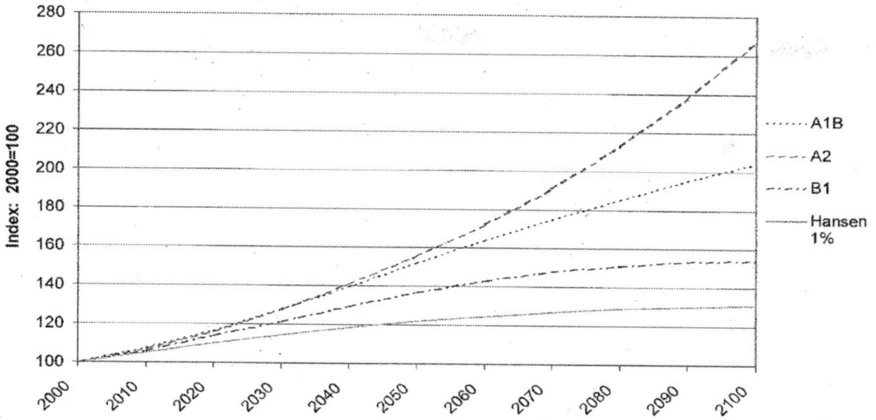

Figure 1 Concentrations of three greenhouse gases. SRES Scenarios from WGCM Climate Simulation Panel Project and Hansen Alternative Scenario

Source: Author's own work.

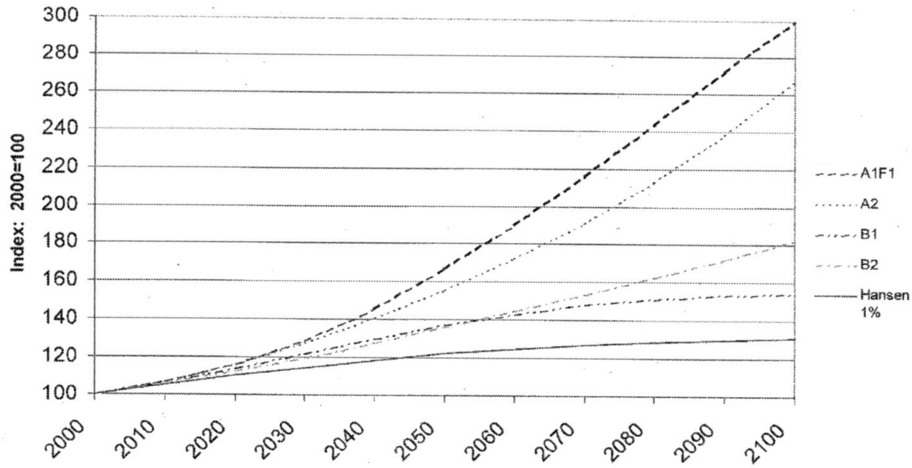

Figure 2 Concentrations of three greenhouse gases. SRES Scenarios from Global Environmental Changes Assessment and Hansen Alternative Scenario

Source: Author's own work.

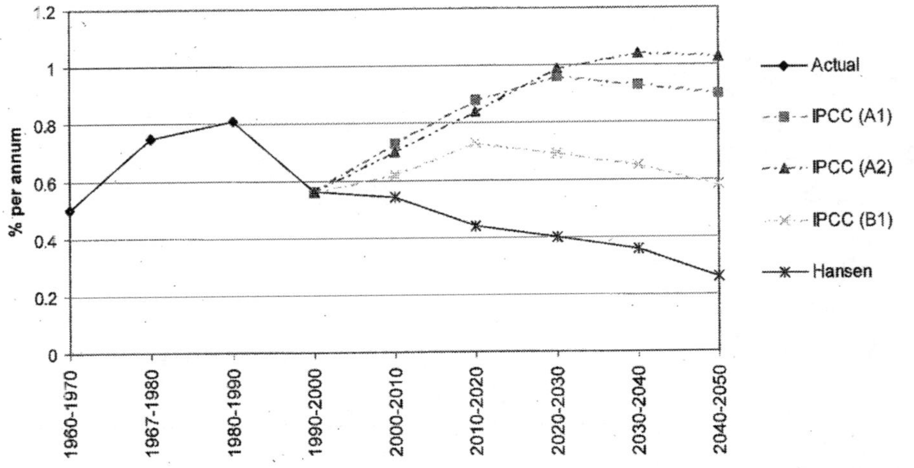

Figure 3 Growth rate in greenhouse gas concentrations 1960-2050: three IPCC Scenarios and Hansen Alternative Scenario[2]

Source: Author's own work.

2 The data represent the growth rate in GHG concentrations measured in equivalent CO2 which the IPCC defines as 'The concentration of CO2 that would cause the same amount of radiative forcing as the given mixture of CO2 and other green-house gases' (IPCC, 1997. *An Introduction to Simple Climate Models Used in the IPCC Second Assessment Report*. John T Houghten *et al* Technical Paper 2).

1960-2000 – Hansen, James and Makiko Sato (2000). *Data for Well Mixed Greenhouse Gases*. (The trends are shown in finer detail in Bjorn Lomborg (2001). *The Skeptical Environmentalist,* Figure 148: 279.

2000-2050 – IPCC Scenarios: IPCC (2001). *Climate Change 2001: The Scientific Basis,* Appendix II: SRES Tables. Hansen Alternative Scenario: Hansen, JM and 27 others (2002). 'Climate Forcings in S12000 Simulations, *Journal of Geographical Research,* 187 (D18), ACI2, Table 1.

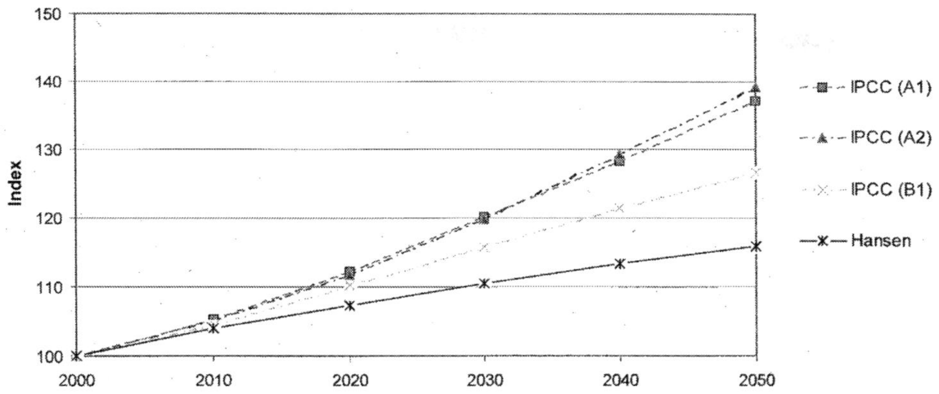

Figure 4 Atmospheric concentrations of major greenhouse gases: three IPCC cenarios and Hansen Alternative Scenario[3]

Source: Author's own work.

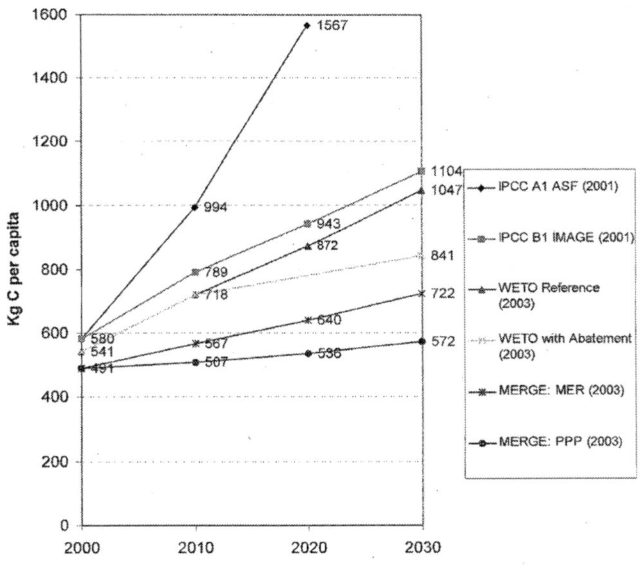

Figure 5 Carbon emissions of Non-Annex 1 Countries 2000-2030 per capita

Source: Author's own work.

3 As for Figure 1 (2000-2050 data). The concentrations of greenhouse gases have been aggregated using the Global Warming Potential factors over a 100-year time horizon adopted by the IPCC: 1 unit CO2 = 21 units CH4 = 310 units N20. Note: The trends relate to the well mixed greenhouse gases CO2, CH4, N20 and CFCs. For the 2000-2050 period, CFCs have not been included (the changes in the CO2 equivalent atmospheric cocentrations of these gases in recent years have been very small).

Letter of 30 July 2004 from Ian Castles to Dr Rajendra Pachauri

Dr R K Pachauri

Chairman

Intergovernmental Panel on Climate Change

Dear Dr Pachauri

1. In its most recent press statement (issued on 8 December 2003), the IPCC dismissed the Castles and Henderson critique of its emissions scenarios on the grounds *inter alia,* that 'over a long period of time as poorer countries increase their incomes, PPP [purchasing power parity] and MEX [market exchange rate] income data tend to converge'. The Panel argued that 'In the IPCC-SRES scenarios exercise (over a 100 year period) it would not matter much what unit is used'.

2. Of course it *does* matter if inter-country differences in output are not properly measured in emissions scenarios, irrespective of whether or not the erroneous estimates affect projections of emissions. One effect of the use of flawed GDP numbers based on market exchange rates is to distort measures of energy and emissions intensities. For example, I pointed out in my letter to you of 29 August 2002 that it is not the case that energy use per unit of GDP is nearly four times as great in non-OECD countries as in OECD countries, as is implied in analyses relying on exchange rate conversions. On the contrary, energy use per unit of GDP is not greatly different between these two groups of countries. This is a point of the highest importance for policy, which is not well understood and continues to remain obscure because of the practice of the IPCC and many other bodies of measuring energy intensities in relation to GDP at market exchange.

3. An important element of the Castles and Henderson critique of the economic and statistical work of the IPCC was our claim that the mistaken use of MER-based comparisons had not only led to misleading conclusions about relative energy and emissions intensities between rich countries and poor but that, taken together with questionable assumptions about 'closing the gap', had imparted an upward bias to projections of economic growth in developing countries – hence to projections of total world emissions.

4. As an example of the potential importance of this apparent upward bias, we roughly reworked the GDP projections for the B1 IMAGE scenario – the IPCC scenario with the lowest cumulative emissions during the twenty-first century. Our conclusion was that '*the prima facie effect of taking a PPP-based gap as a point of departure at the beginning of this century is to reduce prospective world GDP in 2100 in this scenario by over one-quarter*'. And we drew corresponding

conclusions for projected emissions, inferring that 'even the scenarios that show the lowest cumulative emissions over the present century do not present lower limits' (Ian Castles and David Henderson, 2003, 'Economics, Emissions Scenarios and the Work of the IPCC', *Energy & Environment*, vol. 14, no. 4: 425-27, emphasis in original.)

5. In a recent article in the *Australian Financial Review* (AFR), one of Australia's leading economists, Warwick McKibbin, says that it is 'surprising that the IPCC has dismissed the Castles and Henderson critique'. Professor McKibbin argues that the PPP v MER issue is 'potentially important' in at least one of the leading global climate models, and gives the results of simulations using this model which show an upward bias in emissions that is comparable in magnitude to that inferred in the extract of our paper which is quoted in paragraph 4 above:

> Using the G-Cubed multi-country model, one of the major global economic models used for climate change policy evaluation, we show that emission projections based on convergence assumptions using market exchange rates can be 40 per cent higher by 2100 than emissions generated using purchasing power parities (*AFR*, 24-25 July 2004: 62).

6. The full text of the article ('Flaws in climate-change research need fixing') is attached [Ed: not attached here]).

7. In an accompanying editorial, the *AFR* states:

> Professor McKibbin...is one of Australia's leading macro-economists, sits on the board of the Reserve Bank of Australia and is a non-resident senior fellow, in climate change, at Washington's Brookings Institution... Professor McKibbin and his colleagues have...estimated that market exchange rates can inflate carbon emissions by up to 40 per cent by 2100...In the context of a debate about man-made global warming, a 40 per cent increase in carbon emissions can have enormous consequences. You would think that the IPCC would want to clear this up but it has been breathtakingly slow to do so.

8. The IPCC's press release of 8 December asserted that 'The claim of [Castles and Henderson]...that there is an upward bias in the SRES scenarios is totally unfounded'. The findings of Professor McKibbin and his colleagues imply that it may well be the case that it is the IPCC's *rejection* of our claim that is 'totally unfounded'.

Assessing the probability of the IPCC scenarios

9. It is important to stress that the indicative measures of upward bias in the SRES scenarios which are cited in paragraphs 4 and 5 above relate *solely* to the technical error that is introduced in 'convergence' scenarios if the initial gap in

incomes per capita is overstated as a result of the use of market exchange rates to convert values in national currencies into a common unit. The measures attempt to quantify the consequences of this mis-specification of the initial values, but do not say anything about the likelihood that other assumptions underlying the scenario storylines will be realised.

10. For example, the A1 scenarios assume a world 'in which regional average income per capita converge – current distinctions between 'poor' and 'rich' eventually dissolve' (SRES: 179). This convergence occurs at levels of average income which are several times higher than those of the richest countries in the world today. The authors of the IPCC scenarios themselves do not believe that such a scenario is likely to be realised:

> Mr Castles and Mr Henderson obviously consider scenarios of a long term closure of the North-South income gap *highly unlikely*, and many (including a large part of the SRES authors) would agree with them (Nakicenovic *et al*, 2003 'IPCC SRES Revisited: A Response', *Energy & Environment*, vol. 14, nos 2 & 3: 196, emphasis added).

11. Many of the IPCC scenarios assume rates of growth in average incomes in the whole of the developing world in the 21st century which exceed the highest rates that have ever been sustained for such a long period in the past, even by the most successful countries. According to the SRES Team:

> ...in A1 scenarios per capita income in *Asia* increases by a factor of 143.8 between 1990 and 2100 when measured in MER..., but only by a factor of 37.8 when measured in PPP (Nakivenovic *et al*, *ibid*: 194, emphases added).

12. In the past, no individual country has increased its average income level by a factor of about 40 in a century or so, let alone by a factor of 140. Scenario storylines that embody such assumptions for the entire region of *Asia* (with more than half of the world's population) are, literally, 'fantastic': they are the product of a fantasy. It was in relation to projections such as these that David Henderson and I commented:

> it is a dubious procedure to project a specific sequence of future outcomes and events, not on the basis of argument and evidence, but on the grounds that the world would be a better place if it occurred (Castle and Henderson, 2003, *op cit*: 424, emphasis in original).

13. In justification of the modelling of storylines such as the A1 scenarios, the SRES team asked the rhetorical question:

> [Is] it illegitimate to explore in a 'what if...then' scenario exercise the implications in terms of GHG emissions if indeed such developments were to take place...? (Nakicenovic *et al, op cit:* 196).

14. The answer is, of course, that it is legitimate to *explore* these implications, but that there is little point in doing so in the absence of any assessment of the likelihood of the 'developments tak[ing] place'. As Warwick McKibbin writes in his article in the *AFR*:

> Another problem with the methodology of the SRES...is that it follows a 'storyline approach' in which there is no assessment of the likelihood of alternative scenarios. For each scenario, a set of assumptions about economic, social and political conditions over the next century is created and emission outcomes projected from a range of models. This means users such as policymakers, and advocates for either the 'take extreme action' or 'do nothing' approaches can choose from a range of possible futures to suit their own agenda.

15. An obvious example of a user choosing a 'future that suits their own agenda' was the decision to choose the 'very high growth fossil intensive' A1F1 scenario (in preference to the 'very high growth balanced energy sources' A1B scenario or the 'very high growth with high technology' A1T scenario) as one of the 'scenario futures' whose projected impacts are reported in the suite of studies included in the April 2004 'theme issue' of the journal *Global Environmental Change* (the characteristics of the scenarios are taken from SRES, Table 4-2: 178). This journal is edited by IPCC co-chairman Professor Martin Parry and the studies reported in the special issue were funded by the UK Department for the Environment, Food and Rural Affairs (DEFRA).

16. On 21 April last, the Minister responsible for DEFRA said in reply to a question in the UK House of Lords that 'The implications of the rate of change to our planet are so serious that the Government are committed to continuing to be very cautious about listening to those...who say that we are taking the matter too seriously and assuming the worst'. It is reasonable to infer from these comments that the decision to choose the A1 scenario that 'assumes the worst' was probably made on political grounds, and is not based on any informed assessment that it is likely, or even conceivable, that an unimaginably wealthy world would continue to choose to rely mainly on fossil fuels for its energy supplies.

17. A starting point for such an assessment is Box 4-9 of the SRES (216-220), which provides *inter alia,* minimum and maximum projections of the unit costs of, and quantity of energy supplied from, each of 22 different energy technologies for each of seven scenarios for each of the years 1990, 2050 and 2100. All of the

technologies included in the table had already been demonstrated to function on a prototype scale at the time that the SRES was finalised (see fourth paragraph of accompanying text).

18. The table shows, for example, that under the A1T scenario the projected global output of energy from hydrogen fuel cells in 2100 is comparable to the entire global output of energy from all sources in 1990. The accompanying commentary notes that 'the revolutionary change may well be less the hydrogen-powered fuel cell car itself, but rather that it could generate electricity when parked, dispensing entirely the need for centralized power plants and utilities.' According to the A1T projections, unit costs of energy from most sources, expressed as a proportion of average incomes, will be infinitesimal by comparison with those today.

19. By way of contrast, the A1FI scenario projects that by 2100 the per capita use of energy derived from fossil fuels will increase more than fourfold, and that the per capita carbon dioxide emissions from the burning of these fuels will increase almost fourfold, by comparison with present levels. No one can assert that these developments are impossible, nor can it be established with certainty that the massive increases in per capita output and real incomes that are projected in all of the A1 scenarios are incapable of realisation. But there is nothing in the April 2004 theme issue of *GEC* to indicate that the decision to use the A1FI scenario in preference to the A1B and A1T scenarios in the impact studies was informed by any expert assessment of their relative probabilities. It is possible that the A1FI scenario was chosen precisely because it 'assumes the worst' (so far as emissions of greenhouse gases are concerned).

Conclusion

20. Professor McKibbin concludes his article in last weekend's *AFR* with a plea that the problems with the SRES be openly addressed:

> It is critical that the technical analyses used to inform policy decisions, and which drive other research on the impacts of climate change, be thoroughly understood, properly debated and, wherever possible, improved. The problems with the [Special Report on Emissions Scenarios] that have been identified by many different people should be openly addressed before using this body of research as the basis for the next round of assessment.

21. Regrettably, it is clear from the Report of the 'IPCC Expert Meeting on the Science to Address UNFCCC Article 2 including Key Vulnerabilities', which was held in Buenos Aires on 18-20 May, that research using the flawed SRES projections is proceeding apace.

22. It is stated in the first paragraph of this Report that 'Consistent with the principles of the IPCC, this [Fourth Assessment] will be carried out in a comprehensive, objective, open and transparent manner'. In the interest of ensuring that the Assessment will indeed be carried out in this way, I join with Warwick McKibbin in urging that the problems that David Henderson and I (and others) have identified in the SRES be openly addressed as soon as possible.

With best wishes

Ian Castles

28. The Stern Review: A Dual Critique[1]

Alan Peacock, Colin Robinson, CR de Freitas, David Holland, David Henderson, Ian Byatt, Ian Castles, Indur M Goklany, Julian Morris, Nigel Lawson, Robert M Carter, Richard S Lindzen, Ross McKitrick, and Robert Skidelsky

This chapter presents a critique in two parts of the Stern Review on *The Economics of Climate Change*. Part I focuses on scientific issues and their treatment in the Review. It forms the point of departure for Part II, which deals with economic aspects.

Part I: The Science

Robert M Carter, CR de Freitas, Indur M Goklany, David Holland and Richard S Lindzen

Foreword

The Stern Review was commissioned in July 2005 by the UK's Chancellor of the Exchequer, Gordon Brown. It was conducted under the joint auspices of the Cabinet Office and the Treasury, and the final text was delivered to the Chancellor and the Prime Minister who both spoke at its launching at the end of October 2006. Sir Nicholas Stern is Head of the Government Economic Service in the UK and Adviser to the British government on the economics of climate change. Although the Review was commissioned and financed by Her Majesty's Government, and largely drafted by British officials, it is described as 'independent'.

The Review is a formidable document. Its main text comprises over 550 pages, and covers or refers to a vast range of issues. It reflects the work of a team of over 20 officials under the direction of Sir Nicholas, backed by a substantial number

1 This paper was first published in *World Economics* in 2006. The idea of a dual critique, with twin papers authored respectively by scientists and economists, originated with David Henderson, who played the leading part in bringing it to fruition.

of consultants. It draws on an array of already published studies and papers, as well as on a substantial number of specially commissioned outside contributions. In dealing with the economic aspects which form its main concern, it develops a closely constructed argument of its own. On the basis of what it takes to be established science, together with its own distinctive analysis of the economic issues, it draws strong and confident conclusions for policy.

The Review has been widely hailed as an authoritative guide to thinking and policy. It is seen as providing an accurate account of generally agreed and increasingly disturbing scientific conclusions, and as building on these, through solid economic reasoning, an unassailable case for far-reaching and immediate collective action to limit and reduce emissions of 'greenhouse gases' in general and CO_2 in particular. To quote the British Prime Minister, at the launch of the Review,

> ... what is not in doubt is that the scientific evidence of global warming caused by greenhouse gas emissions is now overwhelming... [and] ... that if the science is right, the consequences for our planet are literally disastrous... what the Stern Review shows is how the economic benefits of strong early action easily outweigh any costs.

In what follows, we take issue with such assured and unqualified verdicts. In relation to both scientific and economic issues, we question the accuracy and completeness of the Review's analysis and the objectivity of its treatment. We thus present a critique of the Review, rather than a full assessment of the argument as a whole.

The subject of the Review is the economics of climate change, and its terms of reference did not require it to cover scientific aspects. However, the text carries substantial sections on these; and it is on the basis of what scientific inquiry is taken to have established that the Review adopts as its starting point for the economic analysis that 'climate change... is the greatest and widest-ranging market failure ever seen'. The credibility of the Review as a whole thus depends in large part on what it says or presumes about 'the science'. Hence this critique, though it appears in an economic journal, has a scientific as well as an economic dimension.

The analysis that we present below, and the views that we express, are ours alone: they should not be attributed to any of the various institutions that we are affiliated with. We represent no interests, and we have neither sought nor received any financial or institutional support for our work. We write as independent commentators.

Introduction

The Stern Review includes an introductory chapter that summarises the present state of climate science and, in Part II, an analysis of the physical and environmental impacts of prospective future paths of climate change. The credibility of the document as a whole thus rests in large part on how far the material presented under these two science headings is accurate and balanced.

Two distinct aspects are relevant here. First, there is the question of whether it can indeed be said, as the Review asserts in its opening sentence, that

> The scientific evidence is now overwhelming: climate change presents very serious global risks, and it demands an urgent global response.

Second, there is the related issue of how far the Stern Review, in the sections that it devotes to them, gives an accurate account of the scientific issues.

We consider that the Review is doubly deficient. The scientific evidence for dangerous change is, in fact, far from overwhelming, and the Review presents a picture of the scientific debate that is neither accurate nor objective.

We present our argument under three main headings. In Section 1 we consider the Review's treatment of basic issues of climate science, and its over-confident conclusions about the prospective course of 'greenhouse gas' concentrations and global warming. In Section 2 we turn to what the Review says about the prospective impacts of the climate changes that it envisages as possible or likely. Under both headings, we note two interrelated features of the Review: first, that it greatly understates the extent of uncertainty, for there are strict limits to what can be said with assurance about the evolution of complex systems that are not well understood. Second, that its treatment of sources and evidence is selective and biased. These twin features combine to make the Stern Review a vehicle for alarmism.

Section 3 is concerned with fundamental issues of scientific conduct and procedure that the Review fails to consider. Professional contributions to the climate change debate very largely take the form of published peer-reviewed articles and studies. It is widely assumed, in particular by governments and the Intergovernmental Panel on Climate Change (IPCC), that the peer review process provides a guarantee of quality and objectivity. This is not so. We note that the process as applied to climate science has tolerated gross failures in due disclosure and archiving, and that peer review is both too inbred and insufficiently thorough to serve any audit purpose, which we believe is now essential for science studies that are to be used to drive trillion-dollar policies.

Besides these three main sections and our summary conclusions in Section 4, we comment in an annex on some aspects of the mishandling of data in the Stern Review. Overall, our conclusion is that the Review is flawed to a degree that makes it unsuitable, if not unwise, for use in setting policy.

1. Flaws in the alarmist paradigm

The alarmist view of climate science

Sir Nicholas Stern made a revealing comment in his OXONIA lecture of January 2006: 'in August or July of last year, [he] had an idea what the greenhouse effect was but wasn't really sure'.[2] It seems that, starting from a position of little knowledge of the issues, he has swiftly espoused the official view of the Hadley Centre for Climate Prediction and Research, on whose advice the Review relies heavily. But this Hadley Centre picture of reality, though broadly in line with that of the IPCC, is by no means universally held. Many of the specific claims that are endorsed in the Review have been seriously challenged in the scientific literature, while the text plays down the great uncertainties that remain.

The Hadley message, as reflected in the Review, is an alarmist one. It presumes without question that moderate further increases in atmospheric CO_2 levels will give rise to major climatic changes and that these are likely to be seriously damaging; that the climatic changes observed over recent decades can be reliably blamed on emissions of 'greenhouse gases' in general, and CO_2 in particular; and that climate model projections and forecasts present a sufficiently accurate view of the future at relevant geographic and temporal scales to form a basis for major policy decisions.

The Stern Review itself fails to take proper account of the profound uncertainties and major gaps in knowledge of climate science, and neither does it address the many continuing debates regarding climate change mechanisms and impact assessments. Like its sources, the Review gives unwarranted credence to model projections over firmly established data and findings. By exaggerating climate alarm it focuses on implausible rather than likely outcomes, and thereby fails to provide a sound basis for policy.

Mishandling of uncertainty

The Review states on page 10 that: 'The analysis of climate change requires, by its nature, that we look out over 50, 100, 200 years and more. Any such modeling

2 http://www.hmtreasury.gov.uk/media/695/8C/OXONIA_Oxford_31012006.pdf.

requires caution and humility, and the results are specific to the model and its assumptions. They should not be endowed with a precision and certainty that is simply impossible to achieve'.

Yet in this respect the Review repeatedly fails to heed its own warning. The tone is set by the Executive Summary, which announces without qualification that 'These concentrations [of greenhouse gases] have already caused the world to warm by more than half a degree Celsius and will lead to at least a further half degree warming over the next few decades, because of the inertia in the climate system'. This is only the first of dozens of unqualified Review statements that attribute causality or state what 'will' happen to climate or the biosphere.

A prime element of this unwarranted certainty is the Review's confidence in computer model outputs. Indeed, the Review gives these outputs even more credence than the IPCC, which warned in its Third Assessment Report (TAR) of 2001 that:

> In climate research and modeling, we should recognize that we are dealing with a coupled non-linear chaotic system, and therefore that *the long-term prediction of future climate states is not possible*. The most we can expect to achieve is the prediction of the probability distribution of the system's future possible states by the generation of ensembles of model solutions.[3]

The IPCC has highlighted the 'process whereby uncertainty accumulates throughout the process of climate change prediction and impact assessment [which] has been variously described as a "*cascade of uncertainty*" (Schneider, 1983) or the "*uncertainty explosion*" (Henderson-Sellers, 1993)'.[4] There are many levels of cascaded uncertainty, each one contributing to the overall uncertainty. These cascades of uncertainty extend from estimates of relevant location-specific climatic changes to their biophysical and socioeconomic impacts.

The Review attempts to deal with these uncertainties by comparing thousands of model runs under varying assumptions. The model parameterisation chosen takes no account of the possibility that carbon dioxide emissions may have minor or benign effects, and is slanted towards emphasis on larger impacts, feedbacks and damages than even the IPCC has implied to date.

In arguing that the Review has misread the state of the science, we shall challenge some of its specific assertions on climatic mechanisms. In doing so, we do not deny the possibility of future climate risks, especially from natural

3 IPCC TAR, Working Group I report, Chapter 14.2.2.2. (Emphasis added.).

4 'Uncertainties in the IPCC TAR: Recommendations to Lead Authors for More Consistent Assessment and Reporting,' cf. http://stephenschneider.stanford.edu/Publications/PDF_Papers/UncertaintiesGuidanceFinal2.pdf. (Emphasis added.)

climate change; nor do we argue that models should only be used if they are able to meet an unrealistic standard of perfection, for their main value is heuristic, not predictive. But we do assert that it is misleading of the Review to draw so predominantly from the upper end of risk distributions and then present these as representative of the range of credible outcomes.

Climate prediction: is it a mature or a new science?

Some of the unjustified confidence in the Review appears to derive from a perception that climate prediction is a mature branch of science with a pedigree of unchallenged research dating back to work by Fourier in 1827.[5] This is not so. The reality is that climate prediction, far from being a mature science, is a new area that has emerged from the science of weather forecasting, aided by the dramatic increase in power and availability of computers in the last three decades.

In its last Assessment Report, the IPCC still rated the 'level of scientific understanding' of nine out of twelve identified climate forcings as 'low' or 'very low,[6] highlighted the limitations and short history of climate models,[7] and recognised large uncertainties about how clouds react to climate forcing.[8] Since then, major scientific papers have claimed, among other things, that the forcing of methane has been underestimated by almost half,[9] that half the warming over the twentieth century might be explained by solar changes,[10] that cosmic rays could have a large effect on climate,[11] and that the role of aerosols is more important than that of greenhouse gases.[12] Generally speaking, none of these suggestions is included in current climate models though, as mentioned later, aerosols are used, without any proper or rigorous basis, to cancel greenhouse warming which would otherwise be far in excess of what we have experienced.

Moreover, given that the estimated temperature change over the late twentieth century amounted to only a few tenths of a degree, there must be significant doubt as to whether model simulations of external forcings are even required as an explanation. Such minor fluctuations may rather be due to natural,

---

5 Review: 7.

6 IPCC, TAR, Working Group 1, Technical Summary: 37.

7 *Ibid*: 48–9.

8 *Ibid*: 49ff.

9 Shindell, D T, G Faluvegi, N Bell, and G A Schmidt (2005). 'An emissions-based view of climate forcing by methane and tropospheric ozone', *Geophysical Research Letters,* 32, L04803, DOI:10.1029/2004GL021900.

10 Scafetta, N, and B J West (2006). 'Phenomenological solar contribution to the 1900–2000 global surface warming', *Geophysical Research Letters*. DOI: 1029/2005GL025539.

11 Henrik Svensmark, Jens Olaf P Pedersen, Nigel D Marsh, Martin B Enghoff, and Ulrik I Uggerhøj (2006). 'Experimental evidence for the role of ions in particle nucleation under atmospheric conditions', *Proceedings of the Royal Society A: Mathematical, Physical and Engineering Sciences*. DOI: 10.1098/rspa.2006.1773.

12 Kilcik, Ali (2005), 'Regional sun-climate interaction', *Journal of Atmospheric and Solar-Terrestrial Physics,* 67 (16): 1573–1579, November 2005.

internal, unforced variability. The primary sources of this natural variability are oceans that are never in equilibrium with the surface (because of irregular and poorly understood exchanges between the huge abyssal heat reservoir and the thermocline), together with a turbulent and heterogeneous atmosphere where changing circulation deposits heat in regions with differing infrared opacity. It may be many decades before models can account for this level of complexity, if indeed that ever proves possible.

Exaggerating warming trends

Early in the OXONIA Technical Annex, it was said with unjustified certainty that 'The rate and scale of 20th century warming has been unprecedented for at least the past 1,000 years'. While the Review backtracks somewhat,[13] the claim raises the issue of context. We have at most a 50-year span of accurate global measurements of temperature and greenhouse gases. Meaningful judgements about climate change and, in particular, natural variations, cannot be made based on such a trivially short time span; even 1000 years is short on the climatic time scale.

The only genuinely global records of measured temperature come from weather balloon radiosonde measurements (since 1958) and satellite microwave sounding units (since 1978). These data, for what they are worth over such short time periods, indicate a gentle warming trend of about 0.1-0.2 degrees C/decade.[14] On a century scale this is at the low end of the trends the Review considers. Moreover, much of the increase in the balloon data is associated with a single step-like event in 1976–77. In the post-1979 interval, the most recently revised satellite data show little change, especially in the tropics and Southern Hemisphere.[15] The trend, such as it is, is at least in part an artifact caused by irregularities such as volcanic eruptions and El Nino events,[16] and anyway – *prima facie* – it is unalarming in both rate and magnitude. Nor is there any sign of acceleration either in surface or tropospheric data, calling into question the Review's emphasis on outcomes involving decadal trends of 0.3-0.6 degrees C. Despite the accumulation of CO_2 in the Earth's atmosphere since 1900, and especially since 1950, no global temperature databases exhibit temperature trends of such magnitude. The rates of modern temperature change observed fall well within the rates of minor warmings and coolings inferred for the Holocene in, e.g. the GRIP ice core.[17]

13 'Recent research, for example from the Ad hoc detection and attribution group (IDAG), uses a wider range of proxy data to support the broad conclusion that the rate and scale of 20th century warming is greater than in the past 1000 years (at least for the Northern Hemisphere).' Review: 6.

14 'Temperature trends in the lower atmosphere: Steps for understanding and reconciling differences', (2006). US Climate Change Science Program.

15 http://vortex.nsstc.uah.edu/public/msu/t2lt/tltglhmam_5.2.

16 Gray, V (2006). 'Temperature trends in the lower atmosphere', *Energy and Environment*, 17: 707–714.

17 Davis, J C, and G C Bohling (2001). 'The search for patterns in ice-core temperature curves', in: Gerhard, L C *et al* (eds), Geological Perspectives of Global Climate Change, American Association of Petroleum Geologists, *Studies in Geology*, 47: 213–229.

If comparison is made with the 'global average temperature' statistics since 1860 that is computed from near-surface thermometer measurements,[18] then the *late twentieth-century warming is similar in both amount and rate to an earlier (natural) warming between 1905 and 1940*. Comparisons over longer and more climatically relevant time spans have to be made using local proxy datasets. The best such datasets come from ocean seabed and polar ice cap drill cores. For example, the oxygen isotope (proxy air temperature) record from the Greenland GRIP drilling project shows that the late twentieth-century warming represents an intermittent high on a sinusoidal, millennial temperature pattern[19] of possible solar origin.[20] *This record shows that recent warming occurred at a similar rate, but was of lesser magnitude, than the earlier, millennial warmings associated with the Mediaeval, Roman and Minoan warm periods.*

Thus the Review's apodictic claim that 'An overwhelming body of scientific evidence indicates that the Earth's climate is rapidly changing, predominantly as a result of increases in greenhouse gases caused by human activities,[21] is without foundation.

Reinventing climate history

Public and governmental concerns over anthropogenic global warming (AGW) soared with the intense and, until recently, continuous media use of a single graph from the IPCC's Third Assessment Report of 2001. This diagram, originally taken from papers in 1998 and 1999 by Mann *et al*,[22] showed nine centuries of near constant global temperatures followed by a dramatic rise in the twentieth century correlating with the rise in CO_2 concentrations. The Mediaeval Warm Period (MWP), previously believed significantly warmer than now, and the much colder Little Ice Age (LIA) did not appear on this graph, which was dubbed the 'hockey stick' (owing to the shape of its curve) soon after its publication and became the basis of claims that natural climatic variation had been very small for a thousand years.

Other scientists have undertaken temperature reconstructions that are claimed in the Review to corroborate the 'hockey stick', but overlap in the proxies and methods used in these reconstructions casts doubt on their independence. For

---

18 *Review*, Figure 1.3: 5.

19 Grootes, P M, M Stuiver, J W C White, S Johnsen, and J Jouzel (1993). 'Comparison of oxygen isotope records from the GISP2 and GRIP Greenland ice cores', *Nature*, 366: 552–554.

20 Bond, G, B Kromer, J Beer, R Muscheler, M N Evans, W Showers, S Hoffmann, R Lotti-Bond, I Hajdas, and G Bonani (2001). 'Persistent solar influence on North Atlantic climate during the Holocene', *Science*, 294: 2130–2136.

21 *Review*: 3.

22 Mann, ME, RS Bradley, and MK Hughes (1998). 'Global-scale temperature patterns and climate forcing over the past six centuries', *Nature*, 392: 779–787; Mann, ME, RS Bradley, and MK Hughes (1999). 'Northern hemisphere temperatures during the past millennium: Inferences, uncertainties, and limitations', *Geophysical Research Letters*, 26: 759–762.

many, from various disciplines, from the outset the implications of the 'hockey stick' appeared unlikely. Historians and other scientists had documented the LIA, with its frozen Thames, and the flowering of civilizations in the MWP. Taken at face value, these lines of evidence[23] suggest that natural factors played a far more significant role in climate changes than the 'hockey stick' reconstruction suggested. They put in question claims that recent warmth can only be explained by human-induced increases in greenhouse gases.

Despite implying that the debate on the science of climate change is now settled, the Review had no choice but to admit that major doubts exist over the 'hockey stick'. Two recent US reports, one by the National Research Council (NRC) and one by Edward Wegman, Chair of the National Academy of Sciences Committee on Applied and Theoretical Statistics, have invalidated the 'hockey stick' conclusion.[24] These reports have confirmed earlier findings that the hockey-stick shape is an artifact resulting from a combination of defective statistical methods and inclusion of data on bristlecone pine tree-rings, which have been demonstrated to be unreliable as temperature proxies.[25]

While previously the 'hockey stick' study was represented as proof of human-induced climate change, the Review now says in Box 1.1 (our emphasis) 'Climate change arguments do not rest on 'proving' that the warming trend is unprecedented over the past Millennium. *Whether or not this debate is now settled,* this is only one in a number of lines of evidence for human induced climate change'. However, page 6 then adds that (our emphasis) 'Much of the debate over the attribution of climate change *has now been settled* as new evidence has emerged to reconcile outstanding issues'. The Review fails to specify this 'new evidence' but in any case, attribution studies can never be 'evidence': they are heuristic thought experiments designed to explore possibilities, not provide definitive explanations. Some further problems with such studies are discussed below.

---

23 The Medieval Warm Period Project summarises scores of scientific papers on this subject and sets out the resulting temperature histories: see www.co2science.org/scripts/CO2ScienceB2C/data/mwp/mwpp.jsp. The Project's analysis suggests that about 80 per cent of areal studies estimate that peak MWP temperatures exceeded recent warmth.

24 Wegman concludes that 'Overall, our committee believes that Mann's assessments that the decade of the 1990s was the hottest decade of the millennium and that 1998 was the hottest year of the millennium cannot be supported by his analysis'. http://energycommerce.house.gov/108/home/07142006_Wegman_Report.pdf. The NRC panel concluded that 'uncertainties of the published reconstructions have been underestimated', and confirmed flaws in Mann's methodology: see http://www.house.gov/science/hot/climate%20dispute/NAS%20full%20report.pdf.

25 McIntyre, S, and R McKitrick (2003). 'Corrections to the Mann et al (1998) Proxy Data Base and Northern Hemisphere Average Temperature Series', *Environment and Energy,* 14 (6): 751-771; McIntyre, S, and R McKitrick (2005). 'The M&M critique of the MBH98 Northern Hemisphere Climate Index: update and implications', *Energy and Environment,* 16 (1): 69-100.

While earlier Stern Review documents cited the 'hockey stick' as valid evidence[26] – which it is not – the Review now treats it as irrelevant. But this also is not a tenable position. Climate models are tuned to the low estimate of natural climate variability put forward by the IPCC in 2001. Were it proved that the world was much warmer in mediaeval times, the models could not replicate this without giving more weight to natural variability and, perforce, their ability to identify anthropogenic forcing would be decreased.

Attribution studies: circular reasoning

The Review's confidence that greenhouse gases are likely to give rise to major, deleterious climate change appears to be based in large measure on the results of a single Hadley Centre paper prominently used in the IPCC WGI Third Assessment Report.[27] However, as can be seen from the Assessment Report, in order to simulate observed trends in global mean surface temperature, the Hadley Centre had to eliminate about two-thirds of the anthropogenic greenhouse forcing with countervailing aerosols (the net result being referred to as anthropogenic forcing). That is to say, the model – like others of its kind – exaggerates the actual warming which was only a few tenths of a degree. Further, as leading researchers in aerosol science reported in *Science*,[28] the aerosol forcing is so poorly known that they felt that calculating how much aerosol forcing is needed to cancel greenhouse forcing is as good a way of estimating the aerosol forcing as any. At the same time, the IPCC's use of this level of uncertainty to claim that the model had simulated observations is self-evidently circular. In actuality, even the sign of aerosol forcing is unknown. In a more rational and less politicised environment, one would at least entertain the simplest resolution of the problem: namely, that the models are exaggerating the response to anthropogenic greenhouse forcing.

The circular reasoning that characterises attribution studies based on deterministic modeling of presumed forcings undermines claims that they

---

26 'So I should say while I had temperature in the previous slide starting in the 19th century, if you send that one a long way back as far as we know, if you send it back another 8 or 9 hundred years it would look pretty flat with oscillations around the level. So that's what has been happening to the stock of carbon dioxide and you can see that it is very suggestive in relation to the story of the temperature and of the science. The relation to human activity: this is the stock of carbon dioxide, this is the flow of carbon dioxide simply from the burning of the fossil fuels, so that is the direct link with the human activity.' OXONIA Lecture, *op cit*. .

27 See Figure A1 in the OXONIA Technical Annex available at www.hm-treasury.gov.uk/media/695/0E/OXONIA_Technical_Annex_FINAL.pdf, where the source is given only as 'Hadley Centre (as reported in IPCC 2001)'. The original paper was Stott PA, SFB Tett, GS Jones, M R Allen, JFB Mitchell, and GJ Jenkins (2000). 'External control of twentieth century temperature by natural and anthropogenic forcings', *Science*, 290: 2133–2137.

28 Anderson, TL, RJ Charlson, SE Schwartz, R Knutti, O Bucher, H Rhode, and J Heitzenberg (2003). 'Climate forcing by aerosols–a hazy picture', *Science*, 300: 1103–1104.

prove warming could only be caused by those forcings. The former Director of Research at the Royal Netherlands Meteorological Institute, Dr Hendrik Tennekes[29] recently pointed out that:

> [T]hose that advocate the idea that the response of the real climate to radiative forcing is adequately represented in climate models *have an obligation to prove that they have not overlooked a single nonlinear, possibly chaotic feedback mechanism that Nature itself employs*... [T]he task of finding all nonlinear feedback mechanisms in the microstructure of the radiation balance probably is at least as daunting as the task of finding the proverbial needle in the haystack.

Even the IPCC cautioned in relation to the Hadley attribution study that 'these results show that the forcings included are sufficient to explain the observed changes, *but do not exclude the possibility that other forcings may also have contributed*'.[30] The Review, however, disregards these warnings and flatly asserts that 'more than a decade of research and discussion...has reached the conclusion there is *no other plausible* explanation for the observed warming for at least the past 50 years'.[31]

Though the Review neither mentions nor discusses them, several other plausible explanations of recent warming have been advanced in the professional literature. One line of research has correlated recent temperature trends with local heating caused by urbanisation and industrialisation.[32] Other studies using longer-term geological evidence also suggest minimal impacts from greenhouse gas forcing. One of these concludes that:

> ...the global warming observed during the latest 150 years is just a short episode in the geologic history. The current global warming is most likely a combined effect of increased solar and tectonic activities and *cannot be attributed to the increased anthropogenic impact on the atmosphere*. Humans may be responsible for less than 0.01°C (of approximately 0.56°C total average atmospheric heating during the last century).[33]

---

29 Published on the Roger Pielke, Sr Research Group Weblog at: http://climatesci.atmos.colostate.edu/2006/01/06/guest-weblog-reflections-of-a-climate-skeptic-henk-tennekes/. Dr Hendrik Tennekes, prior to retirement has been Director of Research, Royal Netherlands Meteorological Institute; Professor of Aerospace Engineering at Pennsylvania State University; and Professor of Meteorology at the Free University, Amsterdam. (Emphasis added.)

30 IPCC, TAR, Working Group 1, Summary for Policymakers: 10. (Emphasis added.)

31 *Review*: 3. (Emphasis added.)

32 de Laat, ATJ and AN Maurellis (2004). 'Industrial CO_2 emissions as a proxy for anthropogenic influence on lower tropospheric temperature trends', *Geophysical Research Letters*, 31, L05204, DOI:10.1029/2003GL019024; Kalnay, E and M Cai (2003). 'Impact of urbanization and land use change on climate', *Nature*, 423: 528–531; Hale, RC, KP Gallo, TW Owen, and TR Loveland (2006). 'Land use/land cover change effects on temperature trends at U.S. Climate Normals stations', *Geophysical Research Letters*, 33, L11703.

33 Khilyuk, LF, and GV Chilingar (2006). 'On global forces of nature driving the Earth's climate. Are humans involved?', *Environmental Geology*, 50: 899–910. (Emphasis added.)

The Review fails to refer to any of this research, the very existence of which contradicts claims that the science is settled or that GHG forcing is needed to explain current warming. It also fails to notice that models trained to emulate climate using both the instrumental record and long-term geological evidence – e.g. the last 140 years of surface temperature measurements,[34] the last 5,000 years of proxy climate data from a Caribbean marine core and a South African speleothem,[35] or the 100,000 year-long GRIP ice core[36] – are not only successful in 'predicting' the current warming phase, but also suggest cooling over the next few decades. This conclusion has also recently been strengthened on a more analytical basis by NASA and the Russian Academy of Sciences, both of which have issued predictions that cooling will occur early in the twenty-first century as solar activity decreases.

Carbon dioxide in perspective

It is important to distinguish CO_2 emission levels, CO_2 concentrations in the atmosphere, and climate forcing. It is the last that is directly relevant to the purported problem of warming. Emission reductions proposed by the Kyoto Protocol would have only a minuscule effect on atmospheric concentrations, while increments in these concentrations would anyway have a diminishing impact on climate forcing. A doubling of CO_2 is used as a benchmark for climate sensitivity and represents a forcing of about 3.7 Watts per square metre. Since anthropogenic greenhouse forcing is already estimated at about 2.7 Watts per square metre – a little over half due to CO_2, with about half of the rest to methane – then in terms of climate forcing, we are already about three quarters of the way to an effective doubling of CO_2, yet we have experienced much less warming than such forcing would suggest. *The Review assumes, against all empirical evidence and physical reasoning, that future increments of CO_2 will have substantially greater effects than those in the past.*

Changes in the CO_2 concentration are not well correlated with the 0.6 degree C increase exhibited by the surface thermometer 'global average temperature' estimates during the twentieth century. First, the phase of temperature increase between 1905 and 1940 occurred before any greatly increased industrial emissions of CO_2. Second, the rapid post-1940 increase in CO_2 emissions was accompanied by a falling temperature between 1945 and 1965. The hockey-stick curve had the striking property that its heavy smoothing and axis-scaling

34 Klyashtorin, LB and AA Lyubushin (2003). 'On the coherence between dynamics of the world fuel consumption and global temperature anomaly', *Energy and Environment,* 14: 733-782.

35 Loehle, C (2004). 'Climate change: detection and attribution of trends from long-term geologic data', *Ecological Modelling,* 171: 433–450.

36 Kotov, SR (2001). 'Near-term climate prediction using ice-core data from Greenland', in: Gerhard, LC *et al* (eds), Geological Perspectives of Global Climate Change, American Association of Petroleum Geologists, *Studies in Geology,* 47: 305-315.

visually diminished these matching problems, and led to a much more plausible-looking match between the alleged temperature changes and actual CO_2 curves. Even the direction of causality is open to question. Data from ice cores indicate that, during ancient climate changes, increases in temperature preceded parallel increases in CO_2 by at least hundreds of years.[37]

This brings us to the matter of feedbacks. It is generally calculated that a doubling of CO_2 would, other factors kept constant, result in a global mean warming of about one degree C. Alarming predictions all require that water vapour and clouds act so as to greatly amplify the impact of CO_2. But it is freely acknowledged, including by the IPCC, that water vapour and especially clouds are poorly modeled, while the underlying physics for determining their behaviour is missing or even unknown. The governing equations of fluid dynamics (Navier-Stokes) have resisted solution for over 100 years; indeed the Clay Institute is offering a $1 million prize to anyone who can merely prove a solution exists. The Review's glib treatment of this fundamental issue again spotlights its failure to grasp the uncertainty of climate research.

The Review's only substantive remarks on water vapour feedback[38] turn out to be irrelevant. These relate to Lindzen's 1990 suggestion for a mechanism whereby a warmer surface might lead to a drier tropopause region, even though it has long been shown that changes in water vapour at these levels would have marginal impact on climate.[39] To be sure, water vapour near the surface (where the bulk of the atmosphere's water vapour is found) is also relatively unimportant. Rather, it turns out that water vapour near the middle of the troposphere dominates this feedback. Thus, the 2005 Soden reanalysis of trends in upper atmosphere water vapour,[40] which the Review advances as a definitive refutation of Lindzen's 1990 suggestion, does not relate to any important feedback. More important, it has long been noted that the water vapour and the related cirrus cloud distribution are extremely spatially heterogeneous with distinct moist/cloudy and dry/clear regions. The restriction to clear regions (as is, in fact, done in Soden's study) is

---

37 Mudelsee, M (2001). 'The phase relations among atmospheric CO2 content, temperature and global ice volume over the past 420 ka. quaternary', *Science Reviews*, 20: 583-589; Siegenthaler, U, T Stocker, E Monnin, D Luthi, J Schwander, B Stauffer, D Raynaud, J-M Barnola, H Fischer, V Masson-Delmotte, and J Jouzel (2005). 'Stable carbon cycle–climate relationship during the late Pleistocene', *Science*, 310: 1313-1317.

38 *Review*: 7, footnote 17. This misidentifies Lindzen's paper as 'Lindzen 2005'. The references section misidentifies it as Lindzen's 2001 paper on the Iris Effect. The actual suggestion addressed by Soden's analysis was contained in Lindzen, RS (1990). 'Some coolness concerning global warming', *Bull. Am. Met. Soc.*, 71: 288-299.

39 See, for example, Shine, KP, and A Sinha (1991). 'Sensitivity of the Earth's climate to height dependent changes in the water vapor mixing ratio', *Nature*, 354: 382-384; and Sun, D-Z, and RS Lindzen (1993). 'Distribution of tropical tropospheric water vapor', *Journal of Atmospheric Science*, 50: 1643-1660.

40 Soden, BJ, DL Jackson, V Ramaswamy, MD Schwarzkopf, and X Huang (2005). 'The radiative signature of upper troposphere moistening', *Science*, 310 (5749): 841-844.

unlikely to be meaningful on this count either. For some time now it has been recognised that the real feedback in the atmosphere likely consists in simply changing the relative areas of moist/cloudy and dry/clear regions.[41]

Much recent work supports the existence of such a mechanism, the strength of such a mechanism, and the failure of current models to replicate the data from which such conclusions emerge.[42] Much new research is currently in progress. The process (sometimes referred to as the Iris Effect), it should be noted, would reduce sensitivity to a doubling of CO_2 to less than 0.5 degrees C – rather more consistent with observations.

The Review is too confident and unqualified in assigning an over-riding role to greenhouse gases in determining climate. Its approach ignores observational facts and cherry-picks among papers that promote alarm.

2. Overstating climate impacts

The same pattern of alarmism is apparent in the Review's treatment of climate impacts, for these impacts are made to appear dire by the introduction of two systematic biases. The first is the choice of scenarios. The studies of impacts used in the Review are based largely on four of the 40 scenarios developed by the IPCC.[43] They thus omit two of the six 'illustrative' scenarios chosen by the IPCC as 'equally sound'.[44] The missing scenarios are both from the A1 'very high growth' family: A1B (Balanced) and A1T (predominantly non-fossil fuels). The only A1 scenario used by the Review is the extreme A1FI (fossil fuel intensive) scenario,[45] which yields a central estimate of warming in the twenty-first century of 4.33°C, compared to 2.79°C for scenario A1B and 2.38°C for A1T.[46]

In addition to focusing on the highest of three emissions scenarios that assume rapid global economic growth and ignoring the other 'very high' economic growth scenarios that yield much lower warming projections, the Review selects

---

41 Udelhofen, PM, and DL Hartmann (1995). 'Influence of tropical cloud systems on the relative humidity in the upper troposphere', *J. Geophys. Res.*, 100: 7423-7440; Lindzen, RS (1997). 'Can increasing atmospheric CO2 affect global climate?', *Proc. Natl Acad. Sci. USA*, 94: 8335–8342; Lindzen, RS, M-D Chou, and AY Hou (2001). 'Does the Earth have an adaptive infrared iris?', *Bull. Amer. Met. Soc.*, 82: 417–432.

42 Clement, AC, and B Soden (2005). 'The sensitivity of the tropical-mean radiation budget', *J. Clim.*, 18: 3189–3203; Choi, Yong-Sang, and Chang-Hoi Ho (2006), 'Radiative effect of cirrus with different optical properties over the tropics in MODIS and CERES observations', *Geophys. Res. Ltrs.*, in press; Chou, M-D., and RS Lindzen (2005). 'Comments on "Examination of the Decadal Tropical Mean ERBS Nonscanner Radiation Data for the Iris Hypothesis"', *Journal of Climatology*, 18: 2123–2127.

43 IPCC Special Report on Emissions Scenarios, 2000; summary available at www.ipcc.ch/pub/sres-e.pdf.

44 *Ibid*: 4.

45 *Review*: 61.

46 IPCC WG1 TAR: 552, available here: www.grida.no/climate/ipcc_tar/wg1/552.htm.

IPCC scenario A2 as its base case.[47] This scenario projects global population in 2100 at 15 billion.[48] But according to the International Institute for Applied Systems Analysis, there is only a 2.5 per cent probability that world population will exceed 14.4 billion in 2100.[49] Thus, the A2 population projection is considered highly unlikely by the research institute that prepared it. This is not surprising, since the A2 estimate for 2100 is more than 50 per cent above the UN's latest medium population scenario and seven per cent above its high scenario.[50] This inflated population estimate inflates emissions and, more important, the numbers at risk for each of the climate-sensitive hazards examined in the Review, and hence the consequences and costs of dealing with them.

A second systematic bias in the Review's consideration of climate impacts is its reliance on papers that assume either that human beings will take no countermeasures to combat adverse impacts of climate change, or that any measures they do take will utilise existing technologies. In fact, we can confidently expect improved technologies in the wealthier and more technologically advanced worlds that will eventuate, and are indeed depicted by IPCC's scenarios.

In these and other ways, the Review's consideration of various climate impacts is biased towards damaging or disastrous outcomes. Some specific examples follow.

Hunger and agricultural productivity

The studies cited by the Review under this heading can be traced mainly to a paper by Parry *et al.*[51] This study allows for some adaptations and increased use of existing technology that would improve productivity. But it explicitly excludes any technologies that may be developed specifically to cope with negative impacts of climate change.[52] This is not a sound procedure. The potential for future technologies, including biotechnology, to cope with climate change is large even in developing countries, especially given the prospective continuing increases in their per capita income. Thus, the abrupt declines in yields predicted by the Review once certain temperature thresholds are reached are unlikely given appropriate breeding, crop switching and other

47 *Review*, Box 6.1: 154.

48 *Review*, Box 3.2: 61.

49 See http://www.iiasa.ac.at/Research/POP/proj01/index.html?sb=5; Lutz, W, WC Sanderson and S Scherbov (eds) (2004). *The End of World Population Growth in the 21st Century: New Challenges for Human Capital Formation and Sustainable Development* (London: Earthscan).

50 UN Population Division (2004). *World Population to 2300* (New York: United Nations).

51 Parry, ML, C Rosenzweig, I Iglesias, M Livermore and G Fischer (2004). 'Effects of climate change on global food production under SRES emissions and socio–economic scenarios', *Global Environmental Change*, 14 (1): 53–67.

52 *Ibid*: 57.

adaptations in the decades during which temperature might be rising towards these thresholds.[53] Most other threats to agriculture and food supply, e.g. waterlogging, drought, and salinity, have also to be weighed in the light of the obvious possibilities for adaptation.

The approach used in Parry *et al* to estimate the impacts of climate change decades from now is, in essence, tantamount to estimating today's level of hunger (and agricultural production) based on the technology of fifty years ago. Past prognostications made along these lines have proven to be spectacularly wrong precisely because they omitted from consideration developments in agricultural technology that occurred in subsequent decades.[54]

Another source of the Review's overestimates of future levels of hunger is its treatment of the prospective fertilisation of crops by additional carbon dioxide. The Review says that, following Parry, it assumes that carbon fertilisation is 'weak' and 'smaller than previously thought'.[55] Close scrutiny of the Review's footnotes is required to descry the fact that the actual assumption is not weak fertilisation but *'no fertilisation effect'*.[56] The basis for this assumption, which flies in the face of numerous papers on the reality of carbon fertilisation, is a recent paper (Long *et al*: 2006), which suggests only that under field conditions, carbon fertilisation may be a third to less than half of what is suggested by experiments using growth chambers.[57] The Review's effective assumption of no carbon fertilisation, which is wholly unrealistic, allows it to make a headline projection that '250-550 million additional people may be at risk'[58] of hunger, whereas, on its own figures, an assumption of strong fertilisation would have suggested declining numbers of hungry people, even for a temperature increase of up to 3.5 degrees C.[59]

Ecosystems and extinction risks

The Review acknowledges that much of the 'information' furnished with regard to impacts on ecosystems and extinction risks that it quotes originates with Thomas *et al* (2004) and concedes that there is a 'great deal of uncertainty

53 See Goklany, IM (2001). The Precautionary Principle: A Critical Appraisal of Environmental Risk Assessment (Washington, DC: Cato Institute).

54 Recall, for example, the inaccuracy of the catastrophic warnings in Paul Ehrlich's *The Population Bomb* (1968).

55 *Review*: 67–8; Box 3.4: 70. Figure 3.6: 73 shows the huge impact of this assumption of weak fertilisation on projected numbers of hungry people. The numbers under the A2 scenario, used by the *Review* as a base case, are also far higher than under any other scenario.

56 *Review*: 72, footnote 43.

57 *Review*: 67, footnote 35; Long, SP, EA Ainsworth, ADB Leakey, *et al* (2006). 'Food for thought: lower-than-expected crop yield stimulation with rising CO_2 concentrations', *Science*, 312: 1918–1921.

58 *Review*: 72.

59 Figure 3.6: 73.

inherent in such estimates'.[60] This acknowledgement, however, is offered only several pages after the results of the Thomas *et al* study have been highlighted in the Executive Summary, and in Key Messages for Part II and Chapter 3. Moreover, the Review uses these estimates repeatedly and often without any qualification. For example, Figure 2 of the Executive Summary notes 'Many species face risk (20-50% in one study)', but it fails to note the uncertainties associated with that 'one study'. Similarly, the Executive Summary states that 'Ecosystems will be particularly vulnerable to climate change, with around 15-40% of species potentially facing extinction after only 2°C of warming'.[61] Here, as elsewhere, the reader is not warned that this statement is based on a single study, which, moreover, is fraught with uncertainties.[62]

After finally acknowledging the substantial uncertainty associated with the Thomas *et al* (2004) study, the Review attempts to justify its use by saying that 'other studies looking at climate suitability also predict high levels of extinction'.[63] But many of the problems inherent in the Thomas *et al* study are also endemic to these other studies. A basic issue is whether such climate suitability studies are even able to predict extinction risks under different climatic regimes. For each such regime, atmospheric concentrations of CO_2, rates of plant growth, water use efficiency, the energy requirements of species and their predator-prey relationships would all be different from what they are today.[64] As noted by Schwartz *et al* (2006), 'the efficacy of using bioclimatic models to assess the possible extinction potential of climate change, particularly among species with small distributions, requires empirical assessment', while claiming that climate change puts a particular endemic species at risk of extinction 'requires a detailed understanding of the responsiveness to climate of the target species, as well as that of species with which it is likely to interact'.[65]

The Review also ignores what has been written about the likelihood that carbon fertilisation, and other factors likely to extend secular increases in agricultural productivity, will reduce habitat loss and increase water use efficiency of plants, thereby reducing pressures on ecosystems and biodiversity.[66] Lower habitat loss would also conserve migration corridors, something that has been advanced

60 *Review*: 80, footnote 79.

61 *Review*: vi.

62 For other notable examples in the Review of failure to identify the single-study basis of these conclusions, see the cover page and Key Messages of Part II (55 and 56), and Table 3.1: 57.

63 *Review*: 80, footnote 79.

64 See Pearson RG, and TP Dawson (2003). 'Predicting the impacts of climate change on the distribution of species: Are bioclimatic envelope models useful?', *Global Ecology and Biogeography*, 12: 361–371; Guisan, A, and W Thuiller (2005). 'Predicting species distributions: Offering more than simple habitat models', *Ecology Letters*, 8: 993-1009.

65 Schwartz, MW, LR Iverson, AM Prasad, SN Matthews and RJ O'Connor (2006). 'Predicting extinctions as a result of climate change', *Ecology*, 87: 1611–1615.

66 Idso, SB, and AJ Brazel (1984). 'Rising atmospheric carbon dioxide concentrations may increase streamflow', *Nature*, 312: 51–53; Gedney, N, PM Cox, RA Betts, O Boucher, C Huntingford and PA Stott

as a mechanism to aid species adaption to changed circumstances. Changes in forest productivity (because of higher CO_2 concentrations, for instance) would similarly promote biodiversity. Thus it is conceivable, indeed probable, that at low to moderate levels of climate change, the overall pressure on biodiversity, ecosystems and species would on balance be lower.[67] In sum, the Review's assessment of ecosystem and extinction risks are a worse-than-worst-case scenario, based on a naïve and one-sided appeal to the literature.

Water availability and water shortages

With respect to water supplies and water availability, the Review's information is based mainly on Arnell's studies which indicate that although aggregate populations under water stress through the 2080s – the period considered – may decline, people in some regions could have greater water shortages, while others may have too much water during the rainy season which could lead to both flooding and water shortages during other seasons.[68]

But the magnitude of these adverse outcomes is exaggerated, since Arnell's papers ignore even the adaptation possible with existing technologies, let alone possibilities from new and improved technologies.[69] No account is taken of the fact that human beings have had a long, and mainly successful, history of combating floods as well as dealing with erratic water flows through a variety of supply and demand side adaptations.[70]

Melting ice sheets

The Review's comments concerning Greenland ice melt are similarly slanted. The text repeatedly emphasises 'significant melting and an acceleration of ice flows near the coast'[71] and hammers the possibility of 'irreversible' melting

(2006). 'Detection of a direct carbon dioxide effect in continental river runoff records', *Nature*, 439: 835–838; Goklany, IM (1998). 'Saving habitat and conserving biodiversity on a crowded planet', *BioScience*, 48: 941–953.

67 Goklany, IM (2001). *The Precautionary Principle: A Critical Appraisal of Environmental Risk Assessment* (Washington, DC: Cato Institute); Goklany, IM (2003). 'Relative contributions of global warming to various climate sensitive risks, and their implications for adaptation and mitigation', *Energy & Environment*, 14: 797–822.

68 Arnell, NW (2004). 'Climate change and global water resources: SRES emissions and socio-economic scenarios', *Global Environmental Change*, 14 (1): 31–52; Arnell, NW (2006). 'Climate change and water resources: A global perspective', in: Schellnhuber, HJ, *et al*, *Avoiding Dangerous Climate Change* (Cambridge: Cambridge University Press: 167–175).

69 Page 16 in: Warren, R, N Arnell, R Nicholls, P Levy and J Price (2006). 'Understanding the regional impacts of climate change', research report prepared for the Stern Review, Tyndall Centre Working Paper 90 (Norwich, UK: Tyndall Centre, available from http://www.tyndall.ac.uk/publications/working_papers/twp90.pdf).

70 Goklany, IM (2003). 'Relative contributions of global warming to various climate sensitive risks, and their implications for adaptation and mitigation', *Energy and Environment*, 14: 797–822; Tol, RSJ (2005). 'Adaptation and mitigation: trade-offs in substance and methods', *Environmental Science and Policy*, 8: 572–578.

71 *Review*: 16; also v, 2, 14, 56, 57, 59, 81, 82, 84, etc.

of the Greenland ice sheet.[72] Yet, of the four papers relied on, two, based on satellite altimetry, show a slight net gain in the mass of the Greenland ice sheet (over 1992–2002 and 1992–2003), since although the ice margins of Greenland are shrinking, ice is building up inland due to higher snowfall.[73] A third paper, using data from 1996 to 2005, indicates a net loss of ice mass.[74] The fourth study, which uses meteorological models to estimate the overall mass balance of the ice sheet, finds no significant trend from 1961 to 2003.[75] None of these data has been gathered for a sufficiently long period to enable us to discern whether they constitute short-term fluctuations or long-term trends, let alone for us to identify their causes. We note, however, that papers based on longer data series have found that the temperature around the Greenland coast, while it may have risen just in the last few years, is still lower than it was around 1940,[76] and little changed from the very first instrumental measurements in the 1780s.[77]

The Review also fails to mention that temperatures in the Arctic as a whole are only as warm now as they were in the 1930s,[78] or that the much larger Antarctic ice sheet is growing.[79] A continual build-up of snow and ice on the continent will have a tendency to lower mean global sea level.

General health impacts

The estimates presented in the Review for the present day health impacts of climate change and increases in such impacts through 2030 due to a one degree C increase in temperature[80] can be traced directly, or indirectly through Patz *et al* (2005), to McMichael *et al* (2004).

---

72 *Review*: v, 81, 82, etc.

73 Zwally, HJ, MB Giovanetto, J Li, HG Cornejo, MA Beckley, AC Brenner, JL Saba and D Yi (2005). 'Mass changes of the Greenland and Antarctic ice sheets and shelves and contributions to sea-level rise: 1992–2002', *Journal of Glaciology*, 51 (175): 590–527; Johannssen, OM, K Khvorostovsky, MW Miles, and LP Bobylev (2005). 'Recent ice-sheet growth in the interior of Greenland', *Sciencexpress*: www.sciencexpress.org, 20 October 2005.

74 Rignot, E, and P Kanagaratnam (2005). 'Changes in the velocity structure of the Greenland Ice Sheet', *Science*, 311: 986–990.

75 Hanna, E, P Huybrechts, I Janssens, J Cappelin, K Steffen and A Stephens (2005). *Journal of Geophysical Research*, 110: 10.1029/2004JD005641.

76 See, for example, Chylek P, JE Box and G Lesins (2004). 'Global warming and the Greenland ice sheet', *Climatic Change*, 63: 201–221.

77 Vinther, BM, KK Andersen, PD Jones, KR Briffa and J Cappelen (2006). 'Extending Greenland temperature records into the late eighteenth century', *Journal of Geophysical Research*, 111, 10.1029/2005JD006810.

78 Polyakov, IV, GV Alekseev, RV Bekryaev, U Bhatt, RL Colony, MA Johnson, VP Karklin, AP Makshtas, D Walsh and AV Yulin (2002) 'Observationally based assessment of polar amplification of global warming', *Geophysical Research Letters*, 29: 10.1029/2001GL011111.

79 Wingham, DJ, A Shepherd, A Muir and GJ Marshall (2006). 'Mass balance of the Antarctic ice sheet', *Philosophical Transactions of the Royal Society-A*, 364: 1627–1635; Van de Berg, WJ, MR van den Broeke, CH Reijmer and E van Meijgaard (2006). 'Reassessment of the Antarctic surface mass balance using calibrated output of a regional atmospheric climate model', *Journal of Geophysical Research*, 111: 10.1029/2005JD006495; Vaughn, DG (2005). 'How does the Antarctic ice sheet affect sea level rise?', *Science*, 308: 1877–1878.

80 *Review*: 75–6.

Evidence of bias can be seen in McMichael's explanation of his method:

> ...climate change occurs against a background of substantial natural climate variability, and its health effects are confounded by simultaneous changes in many other influences on population health... Empirical observation of the health consequences of long-term climate change, followed by formulation, testing and then modification of hypotheses would therefore require long time-series (probably several decades) of careful monitoring. *While this process may accord with the canons of empirical science, it would not provide the timely information needed to inform current policy decisions on GHG emission abatement*, so as to offset possible health consequences in the future. *Nor would it allow early implementation of policies for adaptation to climate changes.*[81]

In other words, the estimates in this paper are based not on robust science but on a desire to be policy-relevant. The unquestioning use of the McMichael, Patz and WHO studies that have explicit policy concerns is further evidence of partiality and bias.

Malaria and dengue fever

Most of the Review's disease projections are based on Tanser *et al* (2003), van Lieshout *et al* (2004) and Hales (2002). Importantly, none of these authors takes account of future changes in technology and increases in adaptive capacities of developing nations as they become richer.[82] Van Lieshout *et al*, for instance, factor in adaptive capacity as it was in 1990 but they do not allow for improvements in adaptive capacity that can be expected to occur between 1990 and 2085.[83] Notably, Tol and Dowlatabadi (2001) estimate that malaria is functionally eliminated in a society once annual per capita income reaches $3,100, which is substantially below the average that has been projected in the future for today's developing countries under the poorest (A2) scenario.[84] This is consistent with the basic fact that techniques to eradicate these diseases have been available for decades, so that they are now diseases of poverty, not of climate or climate change.[85]

---

81 McMichael, A, et al (2004). 'Global climate change', in: *Comparative Quantification of Health Risks: Global and Regional Burden of Disease due to Selected Major Risk Factors* (World Health Organization, Geneva: 1546). (Emphases added.)

82 Goklany, IM (2003). 'Relative contributions of global warming to various climate sensitive risks, and their implications for adaptation and mitigation', *Energy and Environment*, 14: 797–822; Tol, RSJ (2005). 'Adaptation and mitigation: trade-offs in substance and methods', *Environmental Science and Policy*, 8: 572–578.

83 Van Lieshout, M, RS Kovats, MTJ Livermore and P Marten (2004). 'Climate change and malaria: analysis of the SRES climate and socio-economic scenarios', *Global Environmental Change*, 14 (1): 87–99.

84 Tol, RSJ and H Dowlatabadi (2001). 'Vector borne diseases, development and climate change', *Integrated Assessment*, 2: 173–181.

85 For an extensive and insightful discussion of the chronic overemphasis of the climate factor in these diseases in IPCC Reports, see the written evidence submitted by Professor Paul Reiter of the Institut Pasteur to the House of Lords Select Committee on Economic Affairs, available at http://www.publications.parliament.uk/pa/ld200506/ldselect/ldeconaf/12/12we21.htm.

Extreme weather

In his earlier response to critics in this journal,[86] Sir Nicholas Stern stated that many uncertainties had been resolved in favour of alarm, but that 'one remaining controversy' existed about the 'attribution of current weather events to human-induced climate change'. He was wrong on both counts, since while significant uncertainty remains in many areas of climate science, it is very broadly agreed that specific weather events cannot be ascribed to global climate changes, let alone to their hypothesised human-induced component. His response, however, gave the opposite impression by selective citation and claiming, without evidence, that 'The world has been experiencing more extreme weather events'.[87] The latter statement is vague (no base period was stated for the comparison), and contradicts the statements in the last IPCC report that there was:

> ...no compelling evidence that the characteristics of tropical and extra-tropical storms have changed... [and that]...Recent analyses of changes in severe local weather (e.g. tornadoes, thunderstorm days, and hail) in a few selected regions do not provide compelling evidence to suggest long-term changes. In general, trends in severe weather events are notoriously difficult to detect because of their relatively rare occurrence and large spatial variability.[88]

Several studies since the last IPCC report have re-confirmed these statements. For example, to evaluate projections of increased floods and droughts as a result of AGW, Svensson *et al* (2005) examined river flow data from the Global Runoff Data Centre in Koblenz, Germany with individual record lengths from stations of between 44 to 100 years.[89] The results of this research showed no general pattern of increasing or decreasing numbers or magnitudes of floods. Andreadis and Lettenmaier (2006) examined trends in drought over the continental United States for the period 1925 to 2003 and found that 'droughts have, for the most part, become shorter, less frequent, less severe, and cover a smaller portion of the country'.[90] The June, 2003, issue of the scientific journal *Natural Hazards* was devoted to assessing whether extreme weather can be attributed to AGW. The editors concluded that most studies find no such connection.

Indeed, elementary considerations of meteorology lead to the conclusion that a warmer world would have less extra-tropical storminess and variability,[91]

---

86 Stern, N (2006). 'Reply to Byatt et al', *World Economics*, 7 (2): 153–157.

87 *Ibid*: 154.

88 Both citations from IPCC WG1 TAR, Technical Summary: 33.

89 Svensson, C, ZW Kundzewicz, and T Maurer (2005). 'Trend detection in river flow series: 2. Flood and low-flow index series', *Hydrological Sciences Journal*, 50: 811–824.

90 Andreadis, K and D Lettenmaier (2006). 'Trends in 20th century drought over the continental United States', *Geophysical Research Letters*, 33, 2006GL025711.

91 The relevant process, baroclinic instability, is shown in all textbooks on dynamic meteorology to be proportional to the north–south temperature difference. viz Holton, JR (2004). *An Introduction to Dynamic Meteorology*, Volume 88, Fourth Edition (International Geophysics) (Hardcover).

while the suggestion of Sir John Houghton that storminess would be abetted by increased evaporation and precipitation (considerations that might be more relevant in the tropics) is inconsistent with the observation that there has been no discernible increase in precipitation since the beginning of satellite measurements.[92]

We note in passing that, contrary to virtually all projections, the 2006 hurricane season in the North Atlantic was relatively mild, underscoring the poor knowledge the climatological community has about the processes that drive storms and extreme weather events, and the folly of giving too much credence to longer-term forecasts based on current knowledge even when forecasting tools have been 'trained' intensely using past information.

To sum up, the Review's analysis of the prospective impacts of possible global warming is consistently biased and selective – and heavily tilted towards unwarranted alarm.

3. The issue of professional standards

The scandal of non-disclosure and poor archiving

Given the global impact of the 'hockey stick', referred to earlier, and similar papers based upon the statistical manipulation of proxy temperature data, one might have expected that governments would by now be insisting that due diligence be applied to all papers concerned with AGW. With the importance now attached to climate prediction, researchers should be required to follow the most stringent professional standards of archiving and disclosure, but with commendable exceptions they do not. Poor disclosure, verification, and media reporting in climate prediction are widespread and a scandal.

The volume of data involved in climate research makes verification of climate prediction impossible without the cooperation of the original workers. The 1998 Mann *et al* 'hockey stick' paper was soon questioned, but so poor is the archiving of its data and computer programs that it took almost eight years and direct action from the US House of Representatives for its statistical flaws and lack of robustness to be exposed. By refusing to release data or computer programs, researchers can effectively prevent verification (which, in science, is the normal route to acceptance) and thereby argue that their thesis has not been falsified.

---

92 Smith, TM, X Yin and A Gruber (2006). 'Variations in annual global precipitation (1979–2004), based on the Global Precipitation Project 2.5° analysis', *Geophysical Research Letters*, 33, 2005GL025393.

Some climate scientists who receive generous public funding appear to be determined to maintain self-regulation solely through peer review, and they have been supported in this aim by the British Government and the IPCC.

The contemporary global temperature series as used by the IPCC plays as central a role in climatology as the Consumer Price Index plays in national economic research. The Review shows it as Figure 1.3. Yet it is not produced by a proper statistical agency working under transparent and rigorous protocols. Instead, it is produced by a small, secretive group of researchers at the Climatic Research Unit (CRU) at the University of East Anglia, an organisation closely affiliated with the Hadley Centre. The CRU has an explicit policy of refusing to allow external examination of how they produce their global temperature series. In response to a request to examine the underlying data and methods, Dr Phil Jones of the CRU stated: 'Why should I make the data available to you, when your aim is to try and find something wrong with it?' Since scepticism and efforts to falsify hypotheses are fundamental elements of scientific method, we find this statement remarkable. The request came from Australian researcher Warwick Hughes, who wished to examine possible Urban Heat Island (UHI) effects and other bias in the CRU instrumental temperature series. Dr Jones repeated his statement to German climatologist Professor Hans von Storch,[93] who, in a presentation to the US National Academy of Sciences on March 2, 2006, made clear his astonishment and contempt towards this attitude.

This is by no means an isolated instance. It would be unimaginable for national statistical agencies to take a secretive position regarding the national accounts and price index data they prepare, yet the same situation is regarded as perfectly acceptable within climate science. In a *Wall Street Journal* interview,[94] asked why he would not cooperate with researchers attempting to replicate his 'hockey stick' diagram, Mann said that he would not be 'intimidated' into releasing his computer program. When US Congressman Barton later asked for this program he replied, 'It also bears emphasis that my computer program is a private piece of intellectual property'.[95] This episode triggered a chorus of indignation from climate prediction scientists – not at Mann's attempt to block verification of his publicly funded paper, but at Congressman Barton's request![96] This, however, raises the question as to whether potentially costly public policies should be based, even in part, on private pieces of intellectual property that, moreover, have not been thoroughly evaluated and replicated.

93 Slide 4, http://meteo.lcd.lu/globalwarming/von_Storch/reconstruction_of_historical_temp_060302.ppt.

94 *Wall Street Journal*, Feb. 14, 2005.

95 http://www.realclimate.org/Mann_response_to_Barton.pdf.

96 This included a letter from the European Geosciences Union pleading to retain self-regulation. See http://pubs.acs.org/subscribe/journals/esthag-w/2005/jul/policy/figures/EGSstatement.pdf.

The full disclosure of all data, statistical techniques and computer code should be a requirement for science used in climate policy formulation, and the Review should have rejected any advice, or publications, for which such disclosure has not been made. The Review should also have advised the UK government to require that full disclosure be made for any future climate science advice that it receives, in line with the recommendations of both the NRC and Wegman panels, and so that the scientific process can function unimpeded by secrecy. The presently permitted secrecy is not only inconsistent with the process of science, but also retards scientific understanding and slows the search for rational policies to address climate change.

Inadequacies of peer review

Policymakers place far too much confidence in the peer review system used by journals, because they misunderstand its purpose and the process. 'Throughout history, most scientists published their views without formal review and peers published their criticisms openly.'[97] The peer review system was developed comparatively recently by editors of publications to maintain the quality of their journals. But while peer review aims to ensure that papers are well-framed and advance hypotheses worthy of consideration by the scientific community, it was never intended to provide a guarantee that hypotheses or recommendations advanced in papers were correct or unchallengeable. In particular, it is no safeguard against dubious assumptions, arguments and conclusions if the peers are largely drawn from the same restricted professional milieu as the authors. Moreover, as the examples above show, peer review does not even ensure that data and methods are open to scrutiny or that results are reproducible.

Bias in science is not usually intentional or even conscious, but it is especially prone to occur when consensus views are sought or expressed. Professor von Storch, who is review editor of the 'Regional Climate Projections' chapter of the IPCC's forthcoming assessment report, recently warned[98] that 'exaggerat[ed] claims pass the internal quality checks of science relatively easily, whereas more reasoned and scientifically accurate claims find an unwelcome audience among scientists'. He went on to argue that 'The practice of scientists exaggerating threatening perspectives of anthropogenic climate change and its implications serves not only the purpose of supporting a policy perceived as "good" but also personal agendas of career and public visibility.'

97 Maciej Henneberg, Peer review: the Holy Office of modern science, *Natural Science*, http://naturalscience.com/ns/articles/01-02/ns_mh.html.

98 von Storch, H, 'Tragedy of the Commons and Sustainability of Climate Science', presentation at the Institute for the Study of Society and Environment, Boulder, Colorado, 8 July 2005. http://w3g.gkss.de/staff/storch/ABSTRACTS/050708.boulder.pdf.

A recent example of how easily flawed papers supporting the alarmist view can pass peer review is that of Chuine *et al,*[99] who claimed that they could derive the summer temperature in Burgundy for any year back to 1370 from the dates of grape harvests. The paper concluded that 2003 was the warmest year since 1370, a dramatic conclusion which helped it gain acceptance in *Nature* and wide attention for the authors. A statistician, Douglas J Keenan,[100] engaged in a long effort to obtain the authors' data, and eventually was able to show that while the Chuine *et al* model treated moderate summers well, it was without statistical merit for estimating exceptionally warm years. The problem for the use of this type of science in the public arena is that far more lay people will have seen or heard media reports of the original paper than hear of its rebuttal.

Keenan says on his web page (our emphasis), 'What is important here is not the truth or falsity of the assertion of Chuine *et al* about Burgundy temperatures. Rather, what is important is that *a paper on what is arguably the world's most important scientific topic [global warming] was published in the world's most prestigious scientific journal with essentially no checking of the work prior to publication'*.

Few papers in climate science are independently verified, often because of the difficulties in getting the original data as reported above.

When the few papers that are critical of the consensus view are published they are often met with a chorus of criticism for their lack of, or inferior, peer review, which stifles discussion of the disputed issues. The dispute over the Mann *et al* paper is an object lesson both as to why those papers based upon large data sets and advanced statistical techniques should be verified, and why peer review alone is inadequate. From what has now been disclosed, and thoroughly investigated, we know that the criticisms of the Mann *et al* paper that were rebuffed by many, including the British government, by repeated reference to peer review, were accurate. Those including the British government who continued to defend the 'hockey stick' work because it had been peer reviewed simply missed the point. Based on this experience, the IPCC peer review process provides no safeguard against dubious assumptions, arguments and conclusions. This is particularly so as, over time, dissenting panellists[101] have withdrawn from the IPCC process, thereby reducing it to a restricted professional milieu within which close colleagues frequently review their own work or that of close colleagues.

---

99 Chuine I, P Yiou, N Viovy, B Seguin, V Daux and E Le Roy Ladurie (2004). 'Grape ripening as a past climate indicator', *Nature*, 432: 289–290. DOI: 10.1038/432289a.

100 Keenan, DJ (2007). 'Grape harvest dates are poor indicators of summer warmth', *Theor. Appl. Climatol.*, 87: 255–256.

101 In an open letter, Dr Chris Landsea explains his reasons for leaving the IPCC AR4 team: http://www.lavoisier.com.au/papers/articles/landsea.html. In written evidence on his work with the IPCC TAR, Professor Paul Reiter of the Institut Pasteur explains why he left the project: http://www.publications.parliament.uk/pa/ld200506/ldselect/ldeconaf/12/12we21.htm.

Conclusion

We conclude that the Stern Review is biased and alarmist in its reading of the science. In particular, it displays:

- a failure to acknowledge the scope and scale of the knowledge gaps and uncertainties in climate science
- credulous acceptance of hypothetical, model-based explanations of the causality of climate phenomena
- massive overestimation of climate impacts through an implausible population scenario and one-sided treatment of the impacts literature, including reliance on agenda-driven advocacy documents
- lack of due diligence in evaluating many pivotal research studies despite the scandalous lack of disclosure of data and methods in these studies
- lack of concern for the defects and inadequacies of the peer review process as a guarantor of quality or truth.

These and other related problems arise because the Review has relied for advice almost exclusively on a small number of people and organisations that have a long history of unbalanced alarmism on the global warming issue. Most of the research cited by the Review does not, on inspection, make a convincing case that greenhouse warming constitutes a major threat that justifies an immediate and radical policy response. Contrary research is consistently ignored, as are basic observational facts showing that alarm is unwarranted.

The Review fails to present an accurate picture of scientific understanding of climate change issues, and will reinforce ill-informed alarm about climate change among the general public, the bureaucracy and the body politic. HM Government will need to look elsewhere for a balanced, impartial and authoritative review of the current climate change debate.

Part II: Economic Aspects

Ian Byatt, Ian Castles, Indur M Goklany, David Henderson, Nigel Lawson, Ross McKitrick, Julian Morris, Alan Peacock, Colin Robinson and Robert Skidelsky

The starting point of the Stern Review is that 'The scientific evidence is now overwhelming: climate change is a serious global threat...'. For reasons that are set out in Part I above, we believe that this assertion is not correct, and that the Review's treatment of scientific issues is open to serious question. Here we go on to question its treatment of economic issues.

This is no straightforward task, because of the lack of clarity which characterises much of the Review's analysis. This has been noted by others: in the article of theirs that follows, and which likewise comments on the Review, Richard Tol and Gary Yohe make the point that 'It is impossible for a reader to understand precisely what is in the calculations that underlie' the Review; and in the same vein, William Nordhaus has written that 'It is virtually impossible for mortals outside the group that did the modeling to understand the detailed results of the Review'. In an after-the-event attempt to clarify matters, a Postscript to the Review, accompanied by a Technical Annex on modeling issues, was published just before this article went to press. But much remains unclear, placing an undue burden on readers to excavate the actual structure of the Review's argument.

Our treatment below falls under six headings. We start in Section 1 by considering the Review's valuation of the possible *impacts* of global warming. Here our point of departure is Section 2 of Part I above, where our scientific colleagues have assessed what the Stern Review says about prospective biophysical impacts. With their conclusions as a basis, we move on to consider, and to put in question, the figures that the Review derives for the prospective costs of these various impacts, and hence for the benefits that would supposedly flow from policies to reduce emissions.

From the projected benefits of mitigation, we turn in Section 2 to consider the prospective costs involved. We think that the Stern Review has understated these, probably by a wide margin. The combination of projected benefits that are pitched too high and projected costs that are pitched too low has led to a seriously unbalanced presentation of policy alternatives.

In Section 3, we consider the central issue of discounting the future. Here again we give reasons to question the Review's treatment. Critical issues are not fully explored, the bias towards immediate and far-reaching actions to reduce emissions is reinforced, and the risks and problems that would arise from following the Review's prescriptions for policy are not faced.

Under all these headings, a recurrent theme is that the Review positions itself well outside the mainstream of published economic writings on these subjects: in relation to the professional debate, it appears as an outlier.

In Section 4, we consider the choice of policy instruments in the context of climate change, and comment on the treatment of these issues in the Review. Section 5 deals with further major omissions from the Review – issues, and contributions to the subject, which the document fails to consider. Some of the points that we make here form a counterpart and extension of the argument in Section 3 of Part I above: we draw attention, as our scientific colleagues have done, to an established and officially approved process of inquiry which is not professionally up to the mark. Section 6 summarises our conclusions.

The Review shows serious weaknesses in its treatment and presentation of basic data. The Annex to Part I (Annex A) comments on one aspect of this failing, namely, the mishandling of basic observational data relating to climate change and the factors that bear on it. Here we present a counterpart annex of a similar kind (Annex B). It deals with the Review's faulty handling of sources which are themselves flawed. The sources in question are the emissions scenarios which form the starting point for the Third Assessment Report of the Intergovernmental Panel on Climate Change (IPCC).

1. Valuing possible impacts

Biased alarmism

The Review presents a dark and dramatic picture of the possible consequences of global warming. The main message is conveyed in the following excerpts, already much quoted by commentators, from the Summary of Conclusions (vi):

> Using the results from formal economic models, the Review estimates that if we don't act, the overall costs and risks of climate change will be equivalent to losing at least 5% of global GDP each year, now and forever. If a wider range of risks and impacts is taken into account, the estimates of damage could rise to 20% of GDP or more.
>
> Our actions now and over the coming decades could create risks of major disruption to economic and social activity, on a scale similar to those associated with the great wars and the economic depression of the first half of the 20th century.

Such conjectures – for they are no more than that – are built up in two stages: first, the possible biophysical impacts over time are listed and reviewed; and second, values are attached to these in order to derive measures of their possible effect on human wellbeing, as in the numbers just quoted.

For both stages, the results presented in the Review refer to possible future developments *over a period of two centuries or more*. This fact alone gives grounds for caution. Both theory and past experience suggest that 'results from formal economic models' are a highly unreliable guide to what may happen so far ahead, while similar doubts can be entertained about the scientific inputs which in this instance form the point of departure for the models.

The Review's treatment of projected biophysical impacts of global warming has been analysed above in Part I. Drawing on a wide range of published sources, the authors review the evidence relating to hunger and agricultural productivity; ecosystems and extinction risks; water availability and shortages; melting ice sheets; general health impacts; malaria and dengue fever; and extreme weather events. They demonstrate that 'the Review's analysis of the prospective impacts of possible global warming is consistently biased and selective – and heavily tilted towards unwarranted alarm'. This conclusion bears on the dramatic claims that the Review makes about the prospective *values* to be attached to these impacts, which consequently appear as greatly overstated.

The arguments set out in Part I are not confined to purely biophysical outcomes: the two aspects, scientific and economic, are partly overlapping. The authors rightly note that the studies which the Review relies on take inadequate account, or no account at all, of the fact that people, enterprises and institutions generally can be expected to adapt their conduct, and the forms which their investment for the future takes, in response to both the experience and the prospect of global warming: now as in the past, they would not just be passive and helpless spectators of climate change. The Review also downplays the possibilities for adaptation arising from future technical progress, the more so since (1[102]) the emergence or prospect of global warming as a problem would increase the incentive for such progress to be directed towards ways of adapting to it, and (2) the time horizon under review is so extended. To disregard or underplay both adaptive behaviour and technical progress is not an acceptable way of defining 'business as usual'.[103]

In weighing the prospects for adaptation, the Review presents a picture of the prospects for developing countries in particular which is in part misleading. It emphasises that adaptation is harder in countries with low levels of GDP per head. But it takes no account of the fact that, in the scenarios that it quotes from the Special Report on Emissions Scenarios (SRES) which point towards high levels of global warming, the projections of GDP per head yield the result that developing countries in general are no longer poor by absolute standards by the time that seriously damaging impacts from warming are seen as emerging.[104] Given such projections of their long-term growth, and the possibilities for resourceful action that this increasing prosperity would help to open up, it is not reasonable to portray the developing countries over the longer term as hapless victims of change.[105]

In this connection, a point worth noting is that in industrial economies climate has little effect on economic activity. Most of the world's economic activity today

102 Numbers in brackets with no other attribution are references to page numbers in the Stern Review.

103 Elsewhere, the Review is ready to make heroic assumptions about the extent to which technological innovation will reduce or eliminate costs of reducing emissions in the future.

104 The SRES, published in 2000, produced emissions projections over the period 1990-2100. These formed the point of departure not only for the IPCC's Third Assessment Report, but also for its successor. For the 'OECD 90' group of countries, the SRES gives a figure of $19,100 for GDP per head in 1990. In all but one of the six 'illustrative' scenarios that it focuses on, the GDP per head in developing countries in 2100 substantially or greatly exceeds this figure.

105 In deploying an argument similar to that of these two last paragraphs, Tol and Yohe write that in the Review, 'vulnerability is assumed to be constant over… two or more centuries'.

takes place indoors: generally speaking, the outputs of both manufacturing and services are unaffected by outdoor conditions. Again, resource extraction also carries on under widely varying climatic conditions, since its location is determined by the resource deposit. In developed countries, only agriculture and forestry can realistically be considered vulnerable to climate change, while for the mid-latitudes, available projections suggest that warming may in fact be beneficial. Only in those lower-latitude countries where the primary sector occupies a large fraction of GDP, and in particular poor tropical countries, does warming as such appear as a possibly significant direct threat to the conduct of economic activity. While the Review rather grudgingly admits that this is the case, it does not make the point that on generally accepted projections of future growth in GDP per head, which it does not put in doubt, the share of these vulnerable sectors can be expected to decline to a relatively low level.

Model-based speculations

The Review spends considerable time discussing Integrated Assessment Model results from the economics literature. Figure 6.2 in the Review shows, for what they are worth, long-term projections of the economic costs associated with global warming scenarios from zero to about six degrees C, as computed by some of the most prominent authors in the field. As noted in Part I, the situation as currently understood points to modest warming trends at most. Up to the 2C level, the model simulations as presented suggest zero or negative expected net costs from climate change. Beyond 2C, two of the three models show moderate global costs of less than two per cent of GDP; and furthermore, they indicate that the costs level off quickly, even out to a 6C warming scenario. Only the Nordhaus and Boyer analysis appears to suggest increasing marginal costs. But this property of their model arises from the same kind of methodological departure that features in the Stern Review – namely, adding in very speculative non-economic costs with little empirical guidance. The Review acknowledges (152) that, in the Nordhaus–Boyer model, the conventional direct economic costs are only one-tenth of those shown in Figure 6.2, the remainder being speculative 'multiplier effects' operating through investment; and even then, as the Review notes, policy analysis based on the Nordhaus model does not support aggressive emission reductions (see Section 4 below).

Thus, looking at the economics information presented in the Review itself, neither the Integrated Assessment Models nor the IPCC scenarios provide a credible basis for expecting dramatic economic damages from global warming. This can fairly be described as the consensus position in the economics literature. Yet the Review summarily sets it aside. Instead, beginning on page 149, it appeals to new insights of its own:

> Existing estimates of the monetary cost of climate change, although very useful, leave many questions unanswered and omit potentially very important impacts. Taking omitted impacts into account will increase cost estimates, and probably strongly.

The Review then positions itself as an outlier by referring to two working papers (cited as Watkiss 2005; Warren *et al* 2006) as the basis for dramatically ramping up estimates of damages due to extreme weather, 'social and political instability', and 'knock-on effects'. Of these three, the Review's treatment of extreme weather is questioned in Part I; some experts in the field are more severe in their criticism.[106] The latter two influences are not at all clearly defined: the reader can consult the Review (151–152) to try to make headway. Later they are grouped into 'non-market impact' and 'risk of catastrophe' effects, though with little further definition provided. According to the Review, they account for some 80–90 per cent of the projected damages due to global warming, and yet everybody else seems to have missed them.

These speculations have two effects: they bump up the projected climate warming outcomes (see Box 6.1: 154), and they add (massively) to the expected costs in the model runs from the PAGE 2002 model on which the Review places heavy reliance. Table 6.1 (163) shows that from the PAGE model one obtains a span of economic costs from the business-as-usual climate change simulation, 90 per cent of which fall between 0.3 and 7.5 per cent (of total current consumption), depending on whether the regular model or the 'high climate' amplified version is used. This is already high compared to the mainstream distribution, but the Review is only getting started – and the later Technical Annex serves to amplify the effects even further. Once the vaguely defined 'non-market impacts' and 'risk of catastrophe' categories are added in, the economic costs come to span 2.2 to 32.6 per cent of total consumption. These additional elements thus amplify the impacts by factors ranging from 4.3 to nine.

To sum up: from 80 to 90 per cent of the impacts of climate change estimated by the Review comprise novel and conjectural cost categories that are not used by the large majority of experts who have studied this issue up to now; that rely on arbitrary amplifications to regular climate model processes; and which have not received proper critical attention in the peer-reviewed economics literature.

This is not an acceptable procedure. It might have been defensible to include such speculative extensions in a second round of estimates, after having first presented results based on the existing published assessments of economic

106 For example,http://sciencepolicy.colorado.edu/prometheus/archives/climate_change/index.html#000973.

damages as recognised in the economics literature to date. But to present these novel, outlier concepts as the central results of the Review betrays a lack of balance.

From projected physical impacts to the figures quoted above, of damages which amount to 'at least 5% of global GDP' and possibly '20% or more', 'now and forever', there is in fact a sequence of argument by which, to take over a phrase from Nordhaus, 'a few more gloomy ingredients are stirred in'. It is via this poorly explained and highly coloured process of accretion that the Review finally derives its startlingly high conjectural figures for the damages that it sees as resulting from the continued pursuit of what it misleadingly portrays as 'business as usual'. Since the treatment of projected damages and disasters is so flawed, these final results cannot be taken at face value: they reflect a bias towards speculative alarmism.

Behind the high damage estimates are emissions estimates that seem themselves to be pessimistic as regards economic pressures for conservation. As relative costs and prices change, new technologies will be adopted because they are profitable: energy saving is an obvious example. As the Review notes, there has been a very big improvement in the fuel efficiency of electricity generation over time; and indeed there is a long history in most developed countries of decline in the energy intensity of GDP. Experience after the 'oil shocks' of the 1970s and early 1980s demonstrated the responsiveness of energy consumption to energy price increases. The elasticity of energy demand with respect to price is low in the short run because the presence of an inherited stock of energy using equipment limits the extent of switching and conservation (Robinson, 1988). But the Review takes a very long view, and in the medium and long terms, the elasticity is much higher as the stock changes in response to changes in the price of energy relative to other goods and the relative prices of different energy sources. World energy consumption, which had increased at a compound rate of over five per cent per annum between 1950 and 1973, continued to rise for a few years after the first oil shock in 1973–74 but then stopped increasing in the first half of the 1980s (BP, 2006). Recent increases in oil and other energy prices are also likely, after a time lag, to bring about a similar response.

In other words, a realistic 'business as usual' (BAU) scenario is itself likely to contain significant energy saving technological advances that will reduce carbon emissions. This is a further reason why the damage resulting from carbon emissions under BAU may well be significantly less than the Review projects.

2. The estimated costs of mitigation

Downward bias

Just as the Review exaggerates damages, so it produces surprisingly low estimates of the costs of abatement. Since it is not clear what the extent of carbon reductions would be under BAU, trying to estimate the costs of further reductions beyond this unknown base becomes a highly speculative exercise. There is a long history of 'appraisal optimism' in attempts to estimate the costs of energy sources which would not come to market without some form of government subsidisation or other form of promotion. The massive underestimation of future costs in Britain's successive government-promoted nuclear power programs from the 1950s onwards is the example nearest to home (Helm, 2003), but there has been a general tendency to underestimate the costs of energy sources that might replace fossil fuels.

One reason why mitigation costs appear low relative to damage costs is because the Review applies its own relatively low rate of interest in discounting projected future costs and benefits: we consider this aspect in Section 3 below. However, other influences also enter into the result.

In chapter 9 of the Review, an analysis of technologies that would help reduce carbon emissions, and their possible costs, results in mitigation cost estimates of -1 per cent to +3.5 per cent of GDP by 2050, with an average of around one per cent. The list of carbon-reducing technologies is one about which there is some consensus among energy specialists (though that is not to say that it will turn out correct, since technological forecasting has a very poor record). But there is considerable doubt about the cost of forcing the adoption of such technologies over and above what would occur without such forcing.

Chapter 9 gives some indication of the uncertainty surrounding its mitigation cost estimates. These depend to a large extent on the work of Dennis Anderson, who has drawn on a number of studies, often by official bodies. Anderson puts the average cost of carbon abatement in 2005 at £225/tonC; but this figure is projected to fall, as a result of incentives, innovation and technical progress to £145 by 2015, £85 by 2020 and £60 by 2050.[107] The Review (231, Figure 9.5) translates the £225/tonC into \$100/CO_2, which exceeds Stern's own estimate, of (\$85/tonCO_2e), which itself is high in comparison with other studies.

107 Stern Review support papers: *Costs and Financing of Abating Carbon Emissions in the Energy Sector*, 20 October 2006: 28.

The Review estimates (233) a technology uncertainty of 4.3 per cent of world GDP, far bigger than the energy price uncertainty of 2.2 per cent (both by 2050). When writing about carbon capture, Anderson says: 'even in the near to medium term, the uncertainties are very large.' Two examples that he gives are:

> [carbon capture and storage] (CCS) is expected to play a crucial role...the range of cost estimates will be narrow when CCS technologies have been demonstrated but, until this occurs, the estimates remain speculative.
>
> The costs of carbon abatement are expected to decline by half over the next 20 years, and then by a third further by 2050. But the longer term estimates of shifting to a low-carbon energy system span a very broad range as indicated...and may even be broader than estimated here.

Anderson also makes the important point that in optimisation models, the results change kaleidoscopally with small changes in relative cost assumptions.

This emphasis on uncertainty is appropriate. However, here as in other parts of the Review, the qualifications made in the body of the document receive little attention when conclusions are drawn. By the end of chapter 9, it is concluded that mitigation costs are likely to be 1 ± 2.5 per cent of annual GDP – which seems a very small range compared with the highly speculative nature of the estimates; and the Executive Summary (xiii) removes all reference to a range of uncertainty, giving the 'upper bound' for the annual cost of emission reductions as one per cent of GDP.

Chapter 10 of the Review goes on to discuss mitigation cost estimates derived from macro-economic modeling exercises, with supporting discussion in Chapter 12. The Chapter 10 estimates are generally consistent with those in Chapter 9, concluding that estimates of mitigation costs in 2050 centre on one per cent of GDP, with a range of -2 to +5 per cent of GDP. While reference is made to the work of many mainstream analysts, heavy reliance is placed on a single meta analysis (cited in the Review as Barker *et al* 2006).

The Review's Table 10.1 summarises the span of surveyed cost estimates for mitigation policy packages adequate to cap atmospheric CO2 at 450 ppm. The basic cost is 3.4 per cent of global output. This is then whittled away by invoking a number of assumptions, until the 3.4 per cent cost of mitigation becomes a 3.9 per cent economic gain – a very large free lunch.

The revenue-cycling aspect

The largest single cost reduction (1.9 per cent of global output) is arrived at by assuming 'active revenue recycling'. Revenue recycling refers to the fact that some emission pricing policies (taxes, auctioned permits) generate revenue for the government, and this added revenue could be used to finance a cut in other tax rates. In order to model the effects of revenue recycling, however, the cost estimation must be done in a model that includes a full treatment of the tax system. Table 10.1 applies a large cost reduction to all the models surveyed, but notes in a footnote (fn. 4: 243) that revenue recycling was a feature only of one model examined.

There is a problem with arbitrarily deducting the benefits of revenue recycling from mitigation cost estimates computed in models without a full treatment of the tax system. The problem is that adding in a proper treatment of the system increases the estimated mitigation costs through 'tax interaction' effects. In studies that have examined this issue, tax interaction costs are typically as large as or larger than revenue recycling effects, so that it is invalid to assume that revenue recycling can be counted against the cost estimates shown in Table 10.1.

Numerous well-known studies, not mentioned in the Review, have concluded that in order to measure the recycling benefit in a theoretically sound way, tax interaction costs must also be modeled (e.g. Bovenberg and de Mooij 1994; Fullerton 1997). Tax interaction effects arise from consideration of the conventional deadweight costs of taxation. A tax drives a wedge between the buyer price and the seller price, destroying more consumer and producer surplus than the tax revenue created. This 'excess burden' is a function of the tax rates and the parameters of demand and supply in the market affected. The cross-price effects of introducing a new tax in one market will affect the excess burden in other markets; and in specific circumstances they will increase that burden in related markets. Empirical examination by economists (e.g. Parry 1995; Bovenberg and Goulder 1996) has shown that emissions taxes will typically interact with factor markets (labour and capital) in such a way as to increase the pre-existing excess burdens, generating positive costs due to tax interaction effects. These effects grow in step with – and indeed slightly faster than – the potential benefits from revenue recycling. This result confirms an early theoretical argument by Agnar Sandmo (1975). Rather than this item bringing a net reduction to modeled costs, therefore, it should be viewed as tending to increase them.

There is also a time dimension here. Insofar as carbon taxes are progressively effective in reducing emissions, their revenue yield will fall accordingly, and this will limit the possibilities for revenue recycling. The Review relies on a model without a tax system and hence does not take into account the changing public finance aspects over time.

The domain of conjecture

Besides the questionable gains from 'recycling', Table 10.1 in the Review also allows for arbitrary, free lunch-style 'induced technology' benefits, and for gains due to ancillary reductions in conventional pollution. These influences, which are far from well defined, bring down the projected costs by a further 0.5 per cent of global GDP. They are elaborated in Chapter 12, where, however, the cited literature is notably heavy on unpublished NGO discussion papers and industry promotional brochures. Another significant effect (0.4 per cent) comes under the heading of 'climate benefit', which however remains undefined.

This whole analysis largely relates to a conjectural future: little attention is given to actual past experience. Measures and programs to reduce CO_2 emissions have been in place for some years, in Britain and elsewhere. The costs and effects of these could have been reviewed, with an eye to the evidence they provide and the lessons to be drawn from them. Such a survey, impartially conducted, would have been a useful contribution to knowledge. Four of us (Byatt, Henderson, Peacock and Robinson) made this point in submitting evidence at the outset of the Review: we suggested that the costs of British mitigation policies, current and prospective, should be identified and documented. This suggestion was not acted on: here as elsewhere, the Review appears as more focused on hypothetical futures than on the evidence and experience of the past.

Much depends on the kinds of measures that are adopted by way of mitigation. Insofar as reliance is placed on regulatory instruments, costs are likely to be appreciably higher. (Here again there may already be useful lessons to be drawn from actual experience to date). Concerned about 'market imperfections', the Review questions the capacity of market-led technological change to adapt to the climate change 'threat'. On the other hand, it seems remarkably optimistic, in the face of past evidence, about the ability of governments to pick technological 'winners' and bring them successfully into the market.

Weighing costs and benefits

The treatment of costs and benefits in the Stern Review is deeply flawed. First, the Review either overlooks or sets aside important elements of the professional literature in favour of its own views, which read as outliers by comparison. Second, whereas the Review is biased towards technological pessimism when assessing the costs of climate change, it is equally (and inconsistently) biased towards technological optimism concerning large-scale mitigation efforts, alternate energy, and so forth. Its treatment of the issues is neither balanced nor credible.

3. Discounting and intergenerational equity

Discounting the future

The comparison of early costs with longer-term benefits is crucial to the conclusion that there is a strong economic case for immediate action on the scale recommended. The Review's conclusions largely derive from the use of social time preference theory, which suggests a discount rate based on (1) pure intergenerational time preference, (2) an assumption as to the future growth of consumption, and (3) a figure for the elasticity of marginal utility with respect to consumption. The numbers chosen by the Review are all open to question and, as the later Technical Annex shows, the results are not robust. What is more, the Review takes no account of the opportunity cost of crowding out other forms of future-directed expenditure.

Welfare economists have treated the issue of allocating consumption across generations using a discount rate that separates into three components, in such a way as to allow the welfare of those now living to be compared with that of future generations, taking into account the fact that because of consumption growth the latter can be expected to be more prosperous. The Review goes over the standard discount rate decomposition, which yields:

$$\rho=\eta\ \dot{C}/C+\delta$$

where C is consumption per head, $\dot{C}/C$ is its projected rate of change, δ (delta) is the pure rate of time preference, η(eta) is the rate of change of marginal utility as consumption increases ($C\times\ U''/U'$, where U is the utility function) and ρ is the resulting discount rate to be applied to public sector projects. To derive the appropriate social time preference rate, values thus have to be assigned to all three of the parameters involved.

Choosing parameters

The choice of values depends on assessments and evaluations which are inherently open to debate. Differing views can be held about the future growth of consumption per head, and different positions can be taken as to the ethical considerations that bear on the values assigned to the other two parameters. Since the issues here are both inescapable and unsettled, no short cuts are permissible. A serious treatment should be both balanced and transparent; and it should explore, through careful sensitivity analysis, the implications of taking different combinations of values. It is against this background that the treatment in the Review has to be weighed.

For the parameter delta, the Review explicitly adopts a value of 0.1 per cent per annum, which is of course a very low figure. To say this is not to reject it. The choice of a low pure time preference rate, as with other parameter values, could be defended if presented as illustrative and plausible, rather than definitive, and if the reader was shown, through the medium of a sensitivity analysis, the implications of other possible choices.

As to the other two parameters, the Review does not specify the values that it has taken, so that its recommended social time reference rate likewise remains undisclosed. This is not a transparent procedure. Further, the Review *provides no sensitivity analysis*. These twin omissions add up to a serious lapse.[108]

Since the appearance of the Review, some progress has been made in making good these deficiencies. First, it has been revealed that the Review sets the value for eta at unity, and that it takes the growth rate of world consumption per head over the next three centuries to be, respectively, 2.0, 1.8, and 1.3 per cent per annum. (The latter rate is assumed to hold perpetually thereafter).[109] Allowing for pure time preference, this implies discount rates, century by century, of 2.1, 1.9, and 1.4 per cent per annum.

The Review argues that the presence of uncertainty should reduce the discount rate used. However, many would argue that, because our knowledge of future events becomes more uncertain as the time horizon is extended, discount rates should if anything increase rather than diminish with time.

The Review's failure to provide sensitivity analysis has been partially remedied in the later Technical Annex. Different values have been run there, through the PAGE 2002 model, for the pure time discount rate (delta) and for the elasticity of the marginal utility of consumption (eta). However, these variations have been treated separately and not in conjunction, while no complementary sensitivity analysis has been performed with respect to the growth rate of consumption per head. Further, the Annex obscures the discount rate sensitivity analysis by simultaneously increasing the damage function parameter: it offers a wholly implausible set of simulations in which the already exaggerated damage costs are further amplified. Its procedures are neither thorough nor transparent, and appear designed to persuade the reader that sensitivity analysis leaves intact the Review's alarmist projections.

Despite its limitations, this belated sensitivity analysis yields some illuminating results. First, the pure time preference rate. In Table PA-3 of the Annex, the average monetary cost of what is taken as a 'business as usual' scenario falls by nearly three-quarters, from five per cent of global GDP to 1.4 per cent, when the

108 Where other models are discussed – e.g. in Table 13.3 – the rates are given and the effect of varying the discount rate is explored.

109 These values were obtained by Christopher Monckton, in a personal communication from HM Treasury.

Review's preferred rate of 0.1 per cent per annum is replaced by 1.5 per cent, thus raising the recommended discount rate from 2.1 per cent per annum to 3.5 per cent which cannot be viewed as an especially high figure.[110]

Second, in the case of eta, the Annex analyses the result of taking a value of 1.5 rather than 1.0: such a figure would not be inconsistent with the distributional concerns in the Review.[111] Here the effect is to reduce prospective damage (as defined above) from five per cent of global GDP to 2.9 per cent. In combination with the 0.1 per cent pure time preference rate, this value of 1.5 yields a discount rate of 3.1 per cent per annum.

Unfortunately, the two sensitivities are not combined in the Annex; and we still await a proper sensitivity analysis on all three parameters, possibly in the form of the Monte Carlo analysis used elsewhere in the Review. Nevertheless, the scale of the potential effect on damage projections, as already revealed by this incomplete sensitivity analysis, shows that when different values are assigned very different results emerge, pointing to very different policy conclusions.

Weighing the present against the future

This is not the place to consider the much-debated issue of just how the welfare of those living today is to be weighed and assessed in relation to that of future generations.[112] But it should be noted that the particular combination of values that the Review favours, of 0.1 per cent for delta and unity for eta, and the low rate of discount which goes with them, point to very high rates of saving for the current generation.

This fact is brought out in a paper by Partha Dasgupta commenting on the Stern Review. He notes that 'in a deterministic economy where the social rate of return on investment is, say, 4% a year', building in the above values for delta and eta leads to the conclusion that '*the current generation in that model economy ought to save a full 97.5% of its GDP for the future!*' (italics in the original). The Review briefly alludes (47) to the argument that low values of eta yield implausibly high implied savings rates, but waves away Arrow's well-known exposure of the problem by saying that it is not convincing. This is not a serious treatment of the issue.

To prescribe such high rates of current saving appears to give too little weight to the interests of the world's poor today and in the near to medium future. The

---

110 It is in fact the rate recommended for public sector projects in the British Treasury's Green Book – which (it is worth noting) stresses the need to conduct full sensitivity analysis.

111 A value of 1.5 implies that we value the utility per head of future generations, who are expected to be many times wealthier than we are, at half the rate of our own. It is the figure suggested as appropriate in the Treasury's Green Book.

112 Some of us would question whether this should be for scholars to decide, with little reference to what people in general want, believe, and are ready to accept.

Review makes much of the need to transfer resources now from developed to developing countries. But this concern with poverty today is not easy to square with the use of such a low discount rate, which *inter alia* implies that the present generation of poor people ought to transfer, via a much higher savings rate than now, a substantially greater part of its income to future generations who will be, on the Review's own assumptions, much wealthier. A way of meeting this objection is to prescribe that the extra burden of reduced consumption and higher savings today should be borne by the rich countries alone; and this seems to be the position that the Review takes. It does not, however, consider how far the imposition of such a considerable extra burden on these countries would be consistent with its surprisingly low estimate of the costs of mitigation.

It is a peculiar feature of the Review that while forecasting that people in the future will be vastly richer than today, it also proposes that the present generation should make substantial new sacrifices on behalf of these more prosperous generations. It is as though, looking back two hundred years (a period comparable to the one the Review purports to cover), we claimed that people living in the early days of industrialisation ought to have made sacrifices on behalf of those living today, even though we are rich beyond the dreams of anyone in those distant times.

The problem of dual standards

The recommendation of the Review is that all future-directed expenditures which are oriented towards reducing future emissions, often if not always with effects that are seen as long term or remote in time, should be evaluated at the real (social time preference) rates of discount that were quoted above. The highest of these, for the whole of this century, is 2.1 per cent per annum. The Review does not dwell on the fact that, everywhere in the world, such relatively low real rates of return are not now characteristic of other investments. While it is true that the minimum acceptable rates of return for investment projects across the world are not known with any precision, and may well differ considerably, there is no doubt that they are typically much higher in the private sector; and even for public sector projects, most public enterprises and governments would probably look for higher real returns on expenditure than 2.1 per cent. The British Treasury, as noted above, recommends using a rate of 3.5 per cent with a full sensitivity analysis. This figure appears as low in relation to the practice of other OECD member countries for which evidence is available, as also of international lending agencies.[113]

113 The issues and evidence are reviewed in Spackman (2001). Figures quoted there for OECD member countries range from 4 per cent to 10 per cent. The author derives (238) suggested lower and upper limits for a social time preference rate of discount. For an assumed growth rate of per capita consumption of 2 per cent per annum, the range would be from 3.1 to 5.1 per cent. Both the World Bank and the Asian Development Bank appear to have standard appraisal rates of 10 to 12 per cent: these are not social time preference rates.

When the marginal rate of return on investments exceeds some officially specified social time preference rate of discount, as in this case, there is a strong argument for using in public expenditure projects the higher of the two rates, since the use of dual criteria opens up the possibility that investments with relatively low returns will crowd out others that would be more beneficial. The risk is all the greater if, as is the case with the Stern Review's recommended course of action, the specially favoured measures, projects and programs are worldwide and large scale.

This problem of dual criteria has been recognised by William Cline, in a study which is in many ways a precursor of the Review. Like the Review, he advocates a low social time preference rate of discount for evaluating climate-change-related expenditures; but unlike the Review, he faces up to the issue of crowding out. His solution is to apply a 'shadow price of capital', so that insofar as mitigation expenditures are thought to displace higher-yielding investments, their initial costs are adjusted upwards: he suggests a mark-up of 60 per cent.[114] Any such procedure, if accepted as valid, would of course serve to push up significantly the true estimated costs of mitigation. Although such a result is arguably implied by its own advocacy of dual expenditure criteria, it is not mentioned in the Review.

4. The choice of policy instruments

The Review raises a great many issues of policy, one of which we have just referred to. Here we focus mainly on the choice of policy instruments, an aspect which the Review considers at length. We end the section with a brief comment on what one might term the policy orientation of the Review.

Prices versus quantities

Moving the discussion to means, rather than ends, brings up another example in which the Review positions itself as an implausible outlier against the specialist literature. Section 14.4 ('Efficiency under uncertainty') presents a standard treatment of the question of instrument choice in the presence of uncertainty over damages and abatement costs. The Report correctly points out that, for the case of carbon dioxide, the marginal damages curve is relatively flat and

---

114 Cline's original study, entitled *The Economics of Global Warming*, was published in 1992. It is not referred to in the Stern Review – a strange omission indeed – but gets a belated mention in the subsequent Technical Annex. Cline returned to the subject in Chapter 1 of *Global Crises, Global Solutions*, edited by Bjørn Lomborg and published in 2004, where his arguments are followed by interesting expert comments. This book is likewise not referred to in the Review (or the Annex).

the marginal abatement cost curve is relatively steep, and the Weitzman-type analysis indicates that emissions pricing yields a smaller expected welfare loss than tradeable quotas.

Combined with the literature on the low monetary value of damages, the available expert literature therefore implies that the optimal carbon policy would be, at most, a small charge on each unit of CO_2 emissions. This in turn would imply a small initial but progressively increasing reduction in emissions below the business-as-usual case. When the second-order costs and benefits ('active revenue recycling') associated with factor market distortions induced by the new carbon tax are also taken into account, even small departures from business-as-usual carbon emissions appear as welfare-reducing (Parry, Williams and Goulder 1999; Bovenberg and Goulder 1996).

These arguments would lead to the conclusion that picking a carbon price is economically more sensible than picking a quantity, and that such a price would initially be likely to be relatively low. Such a conclusion, however – and bearing in mind the difficulty in achieving international agreement on carbon taxation – is not compatible with the 'need to take strong action now' asserted in the first sentence of the Review, and the implication that regulators should set a hard cap on emissions well below current levels.

Perhaps aware that the logic leads away from emission caps, the Review mounts a novel argument, based on a single, recently published conjecture that, in the future, what is currently believed about the relative slopes of the marginal damage and marginal abatement cost curves will be reversed. Figure B in Box 14.1 asserts that while marginal costs of emission reductions will become very low, marginal damages due to carbon dioxide emissions will suddenly become very steep. The Review defends the idea that marginal costs will radically decline by invoking a vague notion that technology will change. The argument that the marginal damages curve will become steep is not defended: instead, on page 314 the reader is referred to Chapter 13 for the discussion. In that chapter (293) there is a list of conjectured horrors – hundreds of millions dead, social upheaval, etc – leading on to the assertion that

> The expected impacts of climate change on wellbeing in the broadest sense are likely to accelerate as the stock of greenhouse gases increases, as argued in Chapter 3. The expected benefits of extra mitigation will therefore increase with the stabilisation level.

Yet the footnote here contains text which goes against the point being made:

> One characteristic of the climate physics works in the opposite direction: the expected rise in temperature is a function of the *proportional* increase in the stock of greenhouse gases, not its *absolute* increase.

In other words, additional units of CO_2 in the atmosphere have an effect that goes with the logarithm of the level of CO_2, so that constant increments of CO_2 have diminishing marginal effect. This in turn implies that annual emissions have diminishing marginal impact, even in the long run.

We conclude, therefore, that the premise of the policy conclusions in Chapter 14 is false even on the Review's own reading of the evidence. The Review conjectures that the relative slopes of the marginal damages and marginal abatement cost curves will reverse, even while acknowledging that this is at odds with the available evidence. We would add that if the Review is correct, that foreseeable technologies will radically reduce the cost of carbon emission abatement in the near future, this is an argument for *delaying* abatement, not hurrying into it.

The Review appears to favour carbon trading, in part because it could involve transfers to developing counties. But very little account has been taken of the practical problems of implementing satisfactory systems, in particular setting up auctions or dealing properly with the initial allocation of emissions caps. These problems would be particularly acute at international level.

In principle, there is a place for 'market instruments' such as carbon taxes or carbon trading. Carbon taxes, for example, are transparent. It is relatively easy to ensure that they are levied widely – on individuals as well as companies. They have the merit that levels can be changed in response to improved knowledge. Their initial level would inevitably be arbitrary, but they could be introduced at a relatively low rate and raised as knowledge of carbon damage and the effectiveness of taxes accrues. Provided that proper explanations are given for changes, appropriate expectations can be created. And as noted in Section 2 above, carbon taxes would provide revenue for the public finances and make it possible to reduce other taxes or, say, to provide resources for other 'green' policies.

There could well be political resistance to carbon taxes – such as the blockages and motorway 'go-slows' in France and the UK in 2000; but acceptance or not of such taxes is a proper test of the willingness of people to support the policies that would lead to lower emissions.

Carbon trading likewise requires initial arbitrary decisions – in its case, on the 'desirable' levels of emissions to be achieved and their allocation to emitters. It is one thing to apply limits to a relatively small level of emitters, say large carbon using companies, and is another to apply them to all emitters, including the personal sector. Yet if limits are applied arbitrarily or unevenly, much of the benefit of using an economic instrument is lost.

Both rules and administrative mechanisms need to be devised for the working of any market for trading permits; and if there is to be international trading, all the governments concerned need to act objectively and fairly, and to be seen to be acting objectively and fairly.

Trading today is very far from being universal: it is being applied only to a limited number of emitters. For example, the EU Emissions Trading Scheme, in its phase one, covers less than 40 per cent of relevant emissions. In the present state of knowledge, there is no way of setting the right levels, at either the national or the European level – and if they are subsequently changed, this creates uncertainty about arrangements that work only because of their longer-term incentives.

Furthermore, until governments start to auction or otherwise charge for the initial level, allocations will typically involve presenting substantial benefits to existing emitters or their suppliers. The Review advocates the use of auctions to allocate the 'desirable' amount of emissions, but the design of an auction for a large number of emitters would be complex and contentious. Until auctions are in place, carbon trading scores badly on transparency. The overall economic costs may be high, albeit disguised. Or the allocations may be so generous that costs are low, but so are the overall reductions in emissions after taking account of the gains that individuals may make by trading what is allocated to them.

There is some empirical evidence on the performance of trading schemes. In relation to the UK Emissions Trading Scheme, the world's first large-scale greenhouse gas trading scheme, that began in 2002, Smith and Swierzbinski (2006) argue that the initial setting of targets for emissions can be the Achilles' heel of emissions trading. The authorities are at an informational disadvantage and the price of making trading arrangements acceptable is to start in generous mode, giving substantial benefits to existing high emitters. They further conclude that adjustment of initial error is both difficult and potentially costly. Efficient functioning of the market requires stability and confidence about current and future property rights, and the repurchasing of rights once allocated can be costly.

The optimal policy target

In Section 13.7 of the Review, the issue is raised of identifying an optimal concentration of 'greenhouse gases'. The Review cites a group of studies (by Nordhaus and Boyer; Tol; and Manne and Richels) and concedes (298) that they all lead to the same conclusion:

> These studies recommend that greenhouse gas emissions be reduced below business-as-usual forecasts, but the reductions suggested have been modest.

But once again, the expert literature is promptly set aside on the basis of the Review's own contrary opinion (298):

> However, the optimal amount of mitigation may in fact be greater than these studies have suggested.

In this context, as elsewhere, conjectural grounds are given as to why the experts who have studied the issue hitherto have all missed the salient features to which only the Review is privy, and which yield an entirely different conclusion, namely that deep emissions cuts are optimal. But the peer-reviewed literature, even that portion surveyed in the Review, suggests that an emissions charge equal to marginal damages – at most, say of US$10 per ton of carbon – is the most aggressive aggregate emissions control policy that could be justified. Because of the steepness of the marginal abatement cost curve, this implies that most countries implementing such a policy would initially reduce emissions only slightly – although the cumulative effect over the longer term would be much greater. Of course, if the path of abatement costs is not as steep as is currently thought, a small CO_2 tax might actually induce large emission reductions. However, to propose deep emissions cuts on that conjecture alone would be to make the mistake associated with the prices-versus-quantities analysis described above. In the case of carbon emissions, the social costs associated with policy uncertainty are minimised by choosing an emissions price and letting the market determine the quantity.

The role of government

While the Review makes many allusions to imperfections and failures in markets, it makes no mention even of the possibility of government failure: in this connection, no reference is made to the arguments and findings of public choice theory. The consequence of ignoring the limits and failings of political action is serious, because the Review points to the need for such action to be undertaken on a grand scale, both nationally and internationally.

While prescribing a greatly expanded role for governments, the Review has failed to think through what could be the considerable problems of defining that role and carrying it into effect. A leading instance is to be found in its recommendation, noted above, that a special and much lower rate of discount should be used for mitigation projects alone. A possible consequence of using such low discount rates, relative to those used in the private sector, is that governments would find themselves faced with an array of potential investments that arguably 'should' be undertaken but which the private sector would not find worthwhile. In such situations, ensuring that the investments were made would require heavy state involvement. Governments would be compelled either to assign to public authorities the responsibility of carrying out the projects in question or to assume the task of designing and putting in place the necessary incentives for private businesses to undertake them; and both these courses of action would involve an expansion of the public sector. The problems that could arise from the adoption of a dual discount rate are not faced in the Review.

5. Missing elements

Despite its considerable bulk, the Stern Review is far from being a complete and well-rounded survey of its subject. The main reason for this is the pervasive bias which we and our scientific colleagues have both noted, and which has led to the disregard or undervaluing of sources which suggest a different view of those aspects of its subject matter that the Review considers. But a further limitation of the Review is that there are aspects which it fails to cover, or even to recognise as pertinent. One such aspect, just noted, is that it does not face up to the problems that may arise from 'government failure'. But this is by no means the only instance where relevant topics and concerns are passed over.

A serious omission concerns an issue which goes beyond economics, and has been raised and discussed in Part I above. Our scientific colleagues have noted there the failures of due disclosure, still unacknowledged and unremedied, that have characterised published and peer-reviewed work which the IPCC and its member governments have drawn on. Neither the failures themselves nor the publications which have exposed them are mentioned in the Review: it simply turns a blind eye to evidence that might put in question any elements of 'the science'.[115] The procedural flaws which it thus disregards put in question the IPCC process as a whole, and further undermine any claim that 'the scientific evidence is now overwhelming'.

A further respect in which the IPCC process is open to question is the treatment within it of economic issues. In this connection, two of us (Castles and Henderson) have pointed to flaws both in the SRES and more broadly. These arguments receive only passing and misleading mention in the Review. Contrary to what is said or implied in the text (182 and 188), this critique of the SRES is by no means confined to the emissions projections made in the report, while what it says about the IPCC – as also the United Nations Environment Program, which is one of the IPCC's two parent agencies – extends well beyond the scenarios. Further – and here again there is a link with Part I – these authors have made the point, in the context of the IPCC process, that peer review offers no safeguard against

115 In particular, no reference is made to the work of McIntyre and McKitrick (2003, 2005, and 2006), nor to the important Wegman report of July 2006 to the Energy and Commerce Committee of the US House of Representatives. The latter document is referred to in footnote 23 of Part I above, and briefly summarised in an annex to Henderson (2006).

dubious assumptions, arguments and conclusions if the peers are largely drawn from the same restricted professional milieu. This aspect also is not touched on in the Review. An article in which the whole of this particular debate was reviewed and taken further (Henderson 2005) is not mentioned in the Review or included in its list of references.[116]

Both these topics – the question of disclosure, and the treatment of economic issues within the IPCC process – were considered in the wide-ranging report, likewise entitled 'The economics of climate change', which was prepared by the House of Lords Select Committee on Economic Affairs and published in July 2005.[117] The report was accompanied by a separate and substantial volume containing the written and oral evidence submitted to the Committee. Despite its having treated the identical subject at length, and in a way that evoked widespread attention, the Select Committee report does not find a place among the 1100 or so references that are listed in the Review. This is an extraordinary omission.

A notable feature of the Select Committee report was the concerns that it expressed about the IPCC. Given the general credibility which the Panel has acquired, it is remarkable that a group of eminent, experienced and responsible persons, drawn from a national legislative body and spanning the political spectrum, with the help of an internationally recognised expert adviser, and after taking and weighing evidence, should have published a considered and unanimous report in which such concerns are prominently voiced.

The Stern Review makes no reference to the issues thus raised. It takes the established official process of inquiry and assessment, including the contribution of the IPCC, as given and fully trustworthy. The possibility that the process could be improved is not entertained. This missing dimension severely limits the usefulness of the Review as a guide to policy. Its uncritical acceptance of officially sponsored sources helps to explain its strong and pervasive bias, since much the same areas and instances of bias, though often in less extreme and unqualified form, are to be seen on the part of its mentors.

---

116 One of the issues raised by Castles and Henderson was the faulty procedure, used in the SRES and elsewhere in IPCC-related documents, by which cross-country comparisons of real GDP were made using market exchange rates rather than on the basis of purchasing power parity (PPP) comparisons. Box 7.2 of the Review, where this issue is taken up, makes two basic errors. First, it says that PPP converters '[compare] the ability to purchase a standard basket of goods and services', when in fact the comparisons extend in principle to all goods and services that enter into GDP. Second, it refers to 'PPP exchange rates', when in fact PPP converters are price index numbers: except in the minds of some modellers, there is no such thing as a 'PPP exchange rate'.

117 The Select Committee included four former cabinet ministers, two of whom had been Chancellors of the Exchequer; two other members with ministerial experience; a former Governor of the Bank of England; and two noted professors. Its Special Adviser was an outstanding British environmental economist.

We believe – and our scientific colleagues concur – that the House of Lords Select Committee was right to raise these questions, and the Stern Review is wrong to ignore them. There is a serious problem here. Although it provides for substantial, well organised and worldwide expert participation, the IPCC process is far from being a model of rigour, inclusiveness and impartiality: it is in fact deeply flawed. Its member governments either fail to notice the flaws or view them with a tolerant eye. There is an urgent need today to build up a sounder basis than now exists for reviewing and assessing issues relating to climate change.[118]

6. Conclusions

Our main conclusions coincide with, and serve to confirm and reinforce, those reached by our scientific colleagues in Part I above. Like them, we would emphasise in particular two inter-related features of the Stern Review:

- it greatly understates the extent of uncertainty as to possible developments, in highly complex systems that are not well understood, over a period of two centuries or more
- its treatment of sources and evidence is persistently selective and biased.

These twin features have combined to make the Review a vehicle for speculative alarmism.

We also endorse, from our own analysis, the judgement of our colleagues that the Review:

- mishandles data;
- gives too little attention to actual observation and evidence, as distinct from the results of model-based exercises;
- takes no account of the failures of due disclosure, and the chronic limitations of peer reviewing, that have been characteristic of work relating to climate change which governments have commissioned and drawn on.

As to specifically economic aspects, we have noted among other weaknesses that the Review:

- systematically overstates projected costs of climate change, partly though by no means wholly as a result of its failure to acknowledge the scope for long-term adaptation to possible global warming;
- underestimates the likely cost – including to the world's poor – of the drastic global mitigation program that it calls for;

118 This subject is further explored in Henderson (2006).

- proposes worldwide adoption of a specially low rate of interest for discounting the costs and benefits of mitigation, on the basis of inadequate analysis and without regard for the problems and risks that would result.

So far from being an authoritative guide to the economics of climate change, the Review is deeply flawed. It does not provide a basis for informed and responsible policies.

Annex A: The Stern Review's mishandling of basic observational data

The Review's presentations of data on the key parameters of the greenhouse equation – emissions, concentrations, and forcing – are inconsistent and unreliable. For example, the Review puts the worst possible face on emission trends:

> Emissions of CO_2, which accounts for the largest share of greenhouse gases, grew at an average annual rate of around 2.5 per cent between 1950 and 2000.[119]

The statement is only true if one ignores all natural emissions, which the Review does persistently and carelessly.[120] At the same time, however, the statement obscures the more important point that the rate of emissions growth fell throughout the period, as Figure 1 shows.

---

119 *Review*: 169.

120 Page 170 of the Review states that 'Total greenhouse-gas emissions were 42 $GtCO_2e$ in 2000', but this ignores natural sources, as does the statement on the same page that '57% of emissions are from burning fossil fuels in power, transport, buildings and industry', and the remark on page 171 that 'A quarter of all global greenhouse-gas emissions come from the generation of power and heat'. Figure 7.1 and Figures A and B in Chapter 7 all omit natural GHG emissions (which comprise 95 per cent of the total for carbon dioxide and are substantial for both methane and nitrous oxide). There is no mention of 'natural emissions' or 'natural sources' of GHGs in Chapter 7.

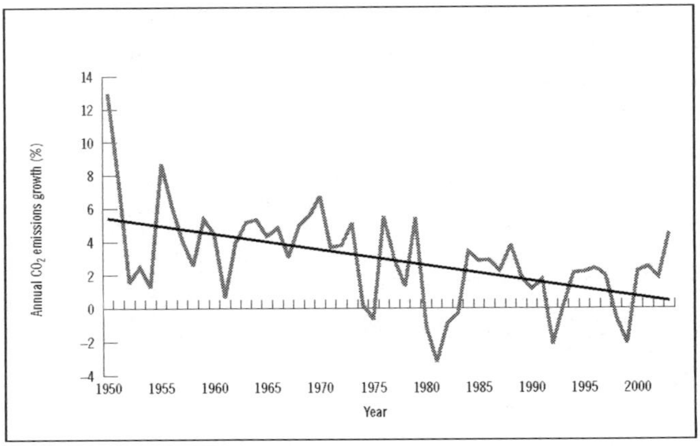

Figure 1 Annual growth of anthropogenic CO_2 emissions 1950-2003

Source: Marland, G, TA Boden and RJ Andres (2006). 'Global, regional, and national CO_2 emissions', in: *Trends: A Compendium of Data on Global Change* (Carbon Dioxide Information Analysis Center, Oak Ridge National Laboratory, US Department of Energy, Oak Ridge, Tenn., USA; available at http://cdiac.ornl.gov/trends/emis/tre_glob.htm).

The Review's handling of current CO_2 equivalent (CO_2e) levels is incompetent. Its first mention of the concept is the following:

> The warming effect due to all (Kyoto) greenhouse gases emitted by human activities is now equivalent to around 430 ppm of carbon dioxide.[121]

This is wrong. If the current CO_2e level is 430 ppm, then the warming effect due to all (Kyoto) greenhouse gases emitted by human activities is actually equivalent to only 150 ppm of carbon dioxide, since 280 ppm of carbon dioxide was already in the atmosphere in the pre-industrial era.[122]

Note, however, that even with this correction, the statement still glides too easily over the difference between emissions from human activities and concentrations. CO_2e levels are concentrations, and concentrations do not simply increase by the amount of emissions from human activities. In fact, most GHGs emitted by human activities have been either reabsorbed by the biosphere (this is the case for about 60 per cent of total man-made CO_2 emissions to date) or destroyed by chemical reactions in the atmosphere (as is the case for methane, nitrous oxide, etc.).

The Review also quotes inconsistent figures for CO_2e levels. The OXONIA Lecture gives 425 ppm. The Review generally quotes 430 ppm, but this excludes

121 *Review*: 3.

122 The Review plainly misunderstands the meaning of CO_2e levels. What these actually express is current CO_2 levels plus the amount of extra CO_2 that would have the same radiative effect as total observed *increases* in other GHGs. Thus, CO_2e figures do not reflect the total warming effect of GHGs, since they do not include the warming effect of pre-industrial concentrations of non-CO_2 gases. Nor do they reflect the relative warming effect of increases in GHGs since pre-industrial times, since they include the pre-industrial level of CO_2.

CFCs solely because they are regulated by the Montreal Protocol rather than the Kyoto Protocol. Including the CFCs, the Review states the figure would be 445 ppm.[123] Yet Box 8.2 on page 202 gives a current level of 450 ppm for Kyoto gases only, implying a total, including CFCs, of ~465 ppm. The true figure may be higher still, as recent papers suggest that the radiative forcing of methane has been underestimated.[124]

The Review says that 'The rate of annual increase in greenhouse gas levels is variable year-on-year, but is increasing.'[125] This is not true, as examination of the data behind the graph presented to back this statement shows.[126] There has been a clear fall in the rate of increase of total GHGs (including CFCs) since the mid-1980s. The fall would have been clearer still if the graph had been on a logarithmic scale, which it should have been in order to reflect the true increase in forcing.

This skews the treatment of *likely future increases in GHGs* towards a worst-case scenario. Page 176 of the Review says, 'Emissions are rising. But suppose they continue to add to GHG concentrations by only 3 ppm a year...' This implies both that 3 ppm is the current rate, and that it is a reasonable minimum rate for the future. Neither proposition is true. Other parts of the Review give the current rate of increase at 'about 2.7 ppm CO_2e per year',[127] 'roughly 2.5 ppm every year',[128] and 'around 2.3 ppm per year'.[129] In fact, over the last 10 years it only averaged 2.2 ppm, and the trend seems downwards, with 1.7 ppm the likely outcome for 2006.[130] Taking 3 ppm as a minimum future value is thus excessively pessimistic. Yet the Review goes even further when it proposes that 'In a plausible "business as usual" scenario, they [concentrations] will reach 550 ppm CO_2e by 2035.[131] As this is based on the Review's assumption that current concentrations are only 430 ppm, it requires an increase of 120 ppm in 30 years, an average of 4 ppm per year. This is unrealistic: it is double the current rate and higher even than the record average level achieved in the peak years of 1976-1988.

---

123 *Review*: 4.

124 For example, Shindell, DT, G Faluvegi, N Bell and GA Schmidt (2005). 'An emissions-based view of climate forcing by methane and tropospheric ozone', *Geophys. Res. Lett.*, 32, L04803, DOI: 10.1029/2004GL021900, observes that 'The emissions-based view indicates that methane emissions have contributed a forcing of ~0.8–0.9 W/m^2, nearly double the abundance-based value'.

125 *Review*: 176.

126 Figure 1.1, *Review*: 4. For a clearer graph of the growth rate, see NASA's *Growth Rates of Greenhouse Gas Forcing (5–year mean)*, available at http://www.giss.nasa.gov/data/simodel/ghgases/. The accumulation rate has fallen further since 2003; the latest data are available at http://www.cmdl.noaa.gov/ccgg/iadv/index.php.

127 *Review*: 169.

128 *Review*: 193.

129 *Review*: 3.

130 As of early November, 2006, Mauna Loa, Cape Grim and the South Pole are all showing trend increases for 2006 implying an annual rise of ~1.65 ppm. The contribution of other GHGs will be negligible. For the latest data, see http://www.cmdl.noaa.gov/ccgg/iadv/index.php.

131 *Review*: 169.

The excessive projections derive from ignoring hard data on concentration trends, and instead using carbon cycle models to predict concentrations from projected emissions. A good test of the reliability of this approach is to compare model predictions for methane with actual observations. Since methane has a shorter atmospheric lifetime than CO_2, it shows the reliability of modeling more quickly. As Figure 2 illustrates, modeling concentrations from emissions is still a very inexact science.

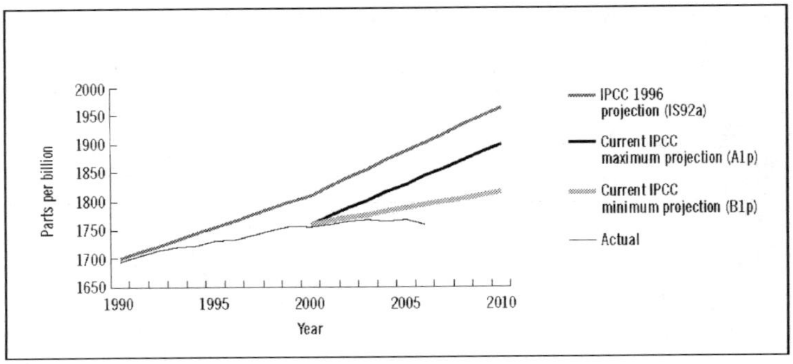

Figure 2 Atmospheric abundance of methane

Source: Note, for example, that in the case of CO_2, the difference in the two estimates quoted by the IPCC for the rate of absorption by tropical forests alone is greater than total estimated global fossil-fuel emissions. See IPCC TAR, Working Group 1: 99, Table 3.2; and Marland, *op cit*.

The real, observed concentration of methane has not increased for the last seven years, contrary to all IPCC modeling and scenarios.[132] While the first chapter of the Review mentions methane more than 20 times and repeatedly emphasises the possibilities for massive escape of the gas from thawing permafrost or ocean hydrates, it fails to observe this important change in atmospheric forcing, let alone discuss possible explanations.[133]

The Review correctly states that 'the warming effect of carbon dioxide rises approximately logarithmically with its concentration in the atmosphere', but then immediately adds, wrongly, that *methane and nitrous oxide concentrations*

132 Methane trends at measuring sites around the world are shown here: http://cdiac.esd.ornl.gov/trends/atm_meth/csiro/csiro_gaslabch4.html. Provisional data indicate that, as at October 2006, the trend level of methane at the benchmark site at Mauna Loa, Hawaii, had fallen by 10 parts per billion from its peak in late 2003. These data are continuously updated at http://www.cmdl.noaa.gov/ccgg/iadv/index.php. The chief compiler of these data, Dlugokencky, recently observed that 'even as the reduction was happening, people doing emission scenarios weren't accounting for it'. (http://www.americanscientist.org/template/AssetDetail/assetid/54097).

133 One recent paper suggests that it may be a temporary phenomenon resulting from reduced precipitation in some wetlands – which had not, however, been predicted by models. See Bousquet *et al* (2006). 'Contribution of anthropogenic and natural sources to atmospheric methane variability', *Nature*, 443: 439–43.

have a linear relationship to radiative forcing.[134] In fact, forcing declines with concentration increments, as shown in Figure 3 for methane using the IPCC formula.[135]

Leaving aside the Review's mistake in describing CO_2e levels, all its misstatements of data on emissions, concentrations and forcing follow a consistent pattern. In each case, total change to date – which has been substantial, but harmless – is minimised. By contrast, present and likely future rates of change – which are presented as having dire consequences – are exaggerated. The Review's data distortions are systematically biased towards alarm.

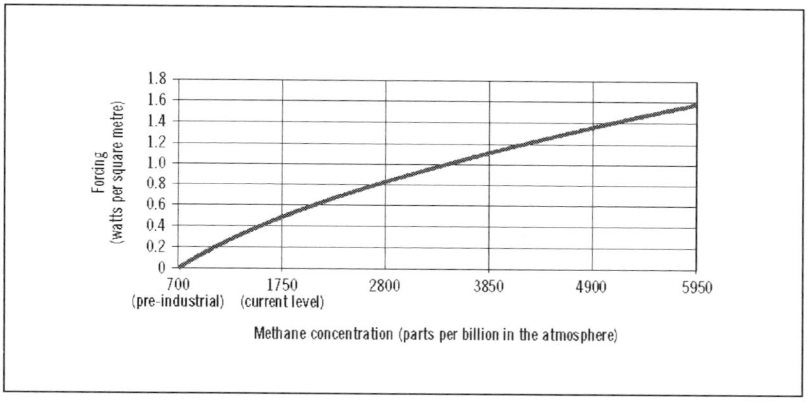

Figure 3 The radiative forcing of methanes

Source: IPCC Third Assessment Report formula, relative to the pre-industrial level.

Annex B: the Stern Review and the IPCC Scenarios

In this Annex, we (the authors of Part 2) examine the Stern Review's uncritical use of the IPCC's scenarios of future emissions of greenhouse gases, as published in the Panel's *Special Report on Emissions Scenarios* (SRES).

The detailed analysis in the Review's assessments of the potential impacts of climate change relies upon 'a series of papers prepared by Professor Martin

134 'Note that other greenhouse gases, such as methane and nitrous oxide, have a linear relationship.' Review: 7, footnote 16.

135 The formula is given in Section 6.3.5 of IPCC Working Group 1 TAR, available here: http://www.grida.no/climate/ipcc_tar/wg1/222.htm#635.

Parry and colleagues ('FastTrack')' which, according to the Review, represents 'one of the few that clearly sets out the assumptions used and explores different sources of uncertainty' (61).

In choosing to use only four of the SRES scenarios in their analysis, Professor Parry and his colleagues disregarded one of the most important sources of uncertainty in the assessment of climate change impacts: the differing possibilities for the developments of energy technologies. The need to take these alternatives into account had been stressed in the Summary for Policymakers of the SRES:

> The *six* scenario groups – the three scenario families A2, B1, and B2, plus three groups within the A1 scenario family, A1B, A1FI, and A1T – and four cumulative emissions categories were developed as *the smallest subsets of SRES scenarios that capture the range of uncertainties* associated with driving forces and emissions. (SRES: 11, emphases added.)

Both the 'FastTrack' exercise and the Stern Review ignore two of the three groups within the A1 scenario family, and present the A1FI scenario as *the* emissions scenario in that family: see, for example, the tabulation of the demographic and economic data relating to the A1 scenario in Box 3.2 (61) of the Review, and the presentation of more than 200 additional millions as at risk of hunger under a hypothetical temperature increase for 'A1' of over 4°C in Figure 3.6 (b) on page 73. If the A1T scenario had been used instead of the A1FI scenario, the temperature increase on the horizontal scale and the 'additional millions at risk' on the vertical scale would both have been much smaller.

Importantly, the Terms of Reference of the SRES required that '*none* of the scenarios in the set includes any future policies that explicitly address additional climate change initiatives', so that 'For example, no scenarios are included that explicitly assume implementation of the emissions targets in the UNFCCC and the Kyoto Protocol' (SRES: 23, emphasis in original).

By choosing to analyse the impacts of the 'very high' economic growth scenario using only the A1FI (fossil fuel intensive) scenario, and disregarding other scenarios that share similar economic growth assumptions but have much lower levels of emissions, the 'FastTrack' studies and the Stern Review present a fundamentally distorted view of the prospective impacts of climate change in the absence of mitigation policies.

This can be seen most readily by noting that the omitted A1T emissions scenario assumes a higher rate of economic growth, and a higher level of global GDP in 2100, than any of the four scenarios used in the 'FastTrack' studies; but that the cumulative level of emissions under this scenario, and the projected increase in global-mean temperatures that goes with it, are *lower* than under the B2 scenario – even though the latter scenario assumes the lowest rate of economic growth, and the lowest global GDP in 2100, of the four scenarios that are used in the 'FastTrack' analyses.[136] By relying entirely upon the A1FI variant of the A1 scenario family and ignoring the A1T variant of the same family, the Stern Review presents it as inevitable that, if rapid economic growth continues, emissions will continue to escalate in the absence of climate policies.

This view does not sit easily with the following statement in the SRES Summary for Policymakers:

> [T]here are scenarios with high per capita incomes in all regions that lead to high CO_2 emissions (e.g. in the high-growth, fossil fuel intensive scenario group A1FI)... [And] there are scenarios with high per capita incomes that lead to low emissions (e.g. the A1T scenario group or the B1 scenario family). (11)

Further, the Review's interpretation is certainly inconsistent with the argument by 15 members of the SRES writing team in their initial response to the Castles and Henderson critique:

> The fact that 17 out of the 40 SRES scenarios explore alternative technological development pathways under a high growth ... scenario family A1 does not constitute a statement that such scenarios should be considered more likely than others with a less dynamic technological and economic development outlook, nor that a similar large number of technological 'bifurcation' scenarios would not be possible in any of the other three scenario families ... The special value of the criticized A1 and B1 scenarios resides precisely in the insight that such an income gap closure [between average incomes in developing and developed countries] might not necessarily be associated with extremely high GHG emissions *but could also evolve even in the absence of climate policies with comparatively low emissions* (as for instance in the technologically optimistic A1T and B1T scenarios). (Nakicenovic *et al*, 2003, 'IPCC SRES Revisited: A Response', *Energy and Environment*, 14 (2 & 3): 195–96, emphasis added.)

It follows that the Review's claim that 'All but one SRES *storyline* envisage a concentration level [of greenhouse gases] well in excess of 650 ppm CO_2e by [the end of the century]' (177, emphasis added) reveals a fundamental misreading of

136 Cumulative projected levels of global CO2 emissions under the A1T MESSAGE illustrative scenario are given on page 446 of the SRES, and the corresponding total under the B2 MESSAGE marker scenario is given on page 561. The projected increases in global-mean-temperatures under the two scenarios are given in IPCC, *Climate Change 2001: The Scientific Basis*, Appendix II, Table II.4 at http://www.grida.no/climate/ipcc_tar/wg1/552.htm.

the SRES. The storylines presented in the Report do not in themselves envisage specific concentration levels at particular times in the future: these levels are also a function of the assumed technological development pathway.[137]

By focusing on the fossil fuel intensive variant of the A1 scenario, and ignoring the technologically optimistic variants or possible variants of the other scenario families, the Review fails to consider the possibility that continuing growth in global emissions is not inevitable, even in the absence of climate policies.

The Review asserts that 'the likelihood of economic growth slowing sufficiently to reverse emissions growth by itself is small' (182). This again reveals a misunderstanding of the SRES scenarios, all of which are presented as 'equally valid with no assigned probabilities of occurrence' (SRES, Box SPM-1: 4). Many of the scenarios project a reversal in emissions growth in the course of the century.

Besides presenting a distorted view, the Review is slipshod in its reporting of the SRES results. For example, the statement that the growth in world GDP under the SRES scenarios is projected 'to continue at between 2 and 3% per year' (182 of the Review) cannot be reconciled with the growth rate of '3.5% p.a.' reported for the A1FI scenario in the table in Box 3.2 (61). The difference is not trivial: over the 110-year time span of the SRES projections, growth at an average rate of 3.5 per cent annually yields a GDP level in 2100 which is 70 per cent greater than the level resulting from an average growth rate of 3.0 per cent annually over the same period. The difference between the projected GDP in 2100 under a 3.5 per cent growth rate from 1990 onwards and that resulting from a 3.0 per cent growth rate over the same period is equivalent to nearly 20 times the level of global GDP in the base year of 1990.

The table in the Review's Box 3.2 reports a projected level of world GDP in 2100 under the A1FI scenario of $550 trillion in 1990 US$. The correct figure, as shown by the SRES (436), is $525 trillion.

Finally, all of the estimates and projections of regional and global GDP in the SRES are distorted as a result of the use of exchange-rate-based conversions as if they measured differences in output across countries. The use of these flawed estimates and projections in the 'FastTracks' project raises in itself serious questions about the validity of the assessments of climate change impacts both in that exercise and in the Stern Review.

137 It is worth noting that the specific role of the SRES is to project emissions, not concentrations.

References

Anderson, Dennis (2006). 'Costs and finance of carbon abatement in the energy sector', paper for the Stern Review, available at www.sternreview.org.uk

Barker, T, MS Qureshi and J Kohler (2006). 'The costs of greenhouse gas mitigation with induced technological change: A meta-analysis of estimates in the literature', 4CMR, Cambridge Centre for Climate Change Mitigation Research.

Bovenberg, A Lans and Lawrence H Goulder (1996). 'Optimal environmental taxation in the presence of other taxes: General-equilibrium analyses', *American Economic Review,* 86 (4): 985–1000.

Bovenberg, A Lans and Ruud A de Mooij (1994). 'Environmental levies and distortionary taxation', *American Economic Review,* 84: 1085–9.

British Petroleum (2006). *Statistical Review of World Energy,* June, and www.bp.com/statisticalreview

Castles, Ian and David Henderson (2003). 'The IPCC emissions scenarios: An economic–statistical critique', *Energy & Environment,* 14 (2 & 3): 173.

Cline, William R (1992). *The Economics of Global Warming,* Washington, DC, Institute of International Economics.

Cline, William R (2004). 'Climate change', chapter 1 of Bjørn Lomborg (ed), *Global Crises, Global Solutions,* Cambridge University Press.

Dasgupta, P (2006). 'Comments on the Stern Review's Economics of Climate Change', Presentation at the Foundation for Science and Technology at the Royal Society, London.

Fullerton, Don (1997). 'Environmental levies and distortionary taxation: Comment', *American Economic Review,* 87 (1): 245–251.

Helm, Dieter (2003). *Energy, The State and The Market,* Oxford University Press.

Henderson, David (2005). 'SRES, IPCC, and the treatment of economic issues: What has emerged?', *Energy and Environment,* 16 (3 & 4).

Henderson, David (2006). 'Governments and climate change issues: The case for a new approach', *Energy and Environment,* 17 (4).

House of Lords Select Committee on Economic Affairs (2005). *The Economics of Climate Change,* Volume I: Report; Volume II: Evidence, London, The Stationery Office.

McIntyre, Stephen and Ross McKitrick (2003). 'Corrections to the Mann et al (1998) Proxy Data Base and Northern Hemisphere Average Temperature Series', *Energy and Environment,* 14 (6): 751–771.

McIntyre, Stephen and Ross McKitrick (2005). 'The M&M critique of the MBH98 Northern Hemisphere Climate Index: Update and Implications', *Energy and Environment,* 16 (1): 69–100.

McIntyre, Stephen and Ross McKitrick (2005). 'Hockey sticks, principal components and spurious significance', *Geophysical Research Letters,* 32 (3), L03710 10.1029/2004GL021750, 12 February 2005.

McKitrick, Ross R (2006). 'Bringing balance, disclosure and due diligence into science-based policymaking', in Porter, Jene (ed), *Public Science in Liberal Democracy: The Challenge to Science and Democracy,* University of Toronto Press.

Mann, Michael E; Bradley, Raymond S; Hughes, Malcolm K (1998). 'Global scale temparature patterns and climate forcing over the past six centuries', *Nature,* 392 (6678): 779 – 787.

Manne, A and R Richels (1995),.'The greenhouse debate: Economic efficiency, burden-sharing and hedging strategies', *The Energy Journal,* 16 (4).

Nordhaus, William (2006). 'The *Stern Review* on the Economics of Climate Change', http://nordhaus.econ.yale.edu/SternReviewD2.pdf.

Nordhaus, William and JG Boyer (2000). *Warming the World: The Economics of the Greenhouse Effect,* MIT Press.

Parry, Ian WH (1995). 'Pollution taxes and revenue recycling', *Journal of Environmental Economics and Management,* 29: S64–77.

Parry, Ian, Roberton C Williams III and Lawrence H Goulder (1999). 'When can carbon abatement policies increase welfare? The fundamental role of distorted factor markets', *Journal of Environmental Economics and Management,* 37: 52–84.

Robinson, Colin (1988). 'Britain's energy market', *The Economic Review,* 5 (3), January.

Sandmo, Agnar (1975). 'Optimal taxation in the presence of externalities', *Swedish Journal of Economics,* 77 (1): 86–98.

Smith, Stephen and Joseph Swierzbinski (2006). 'Assessing the performance of the UK emissions trading scheme', revised submission to *Environmental and Resource Economics,* October.

Spackman, Michael (2001). 'Public investment and discounting in European Union member states', published in *OECD Journal on Budgeting*, 1 (2).

Tol, Richard SJ (1997). 'On the optimal control of carbon dioxide emissions: An application of FUND', *Environmental Modelling and Assessment*, 2.

Tol, Richard SJ (2005). 'The marginal damage costs of carbon dioxide emissions: An assessment of the uncertainties', *Energy Policy*, 33.

Tol, Richard SJ and Gary Yohe (2006). 'A Review of the *Stern Review*', *World Economics*, 7 (4), October–December.

Warren, R, et al (2006). 'Spotlighting impacts functions in integrated assessment models', Norwich, Tyndall Centre for Climate Change Research Working Paper 91.

Watkiss, P, et al (2005). 'Methodological approaches for using social cost of carbon estimates in policy assessment', Final Report, AEA Technology Environment, Culham.

The authors

Bob Carter is a palaeontologist, stratigrapher, marine geologist and environmental scientist with degrees from the University of Otago (NZ; BSc Hons) and Cambridge University (UK; PhD). He has held staff positions at the University of Otago (Dunedin) and James Cook University (Townsville), where he was Head of the School of Earth Sciences 1981–1999 and an Adjunct Research Professor thereafter. He has published research papers on climate change, sea-level change, palaeontology and stratigraphy, based on field studies of Cenozoic sediments from the Australasian region and supported by grants from the Australian Research Council (ARC). In 1998, he was Co-Chief Scientist on Ocean Drilling Leg 181, Southwest Pacific Gateways, a cruise that made fundamental contributions to our knowledge of climate change in southern mid-latitudes. He receives no research funding from special interest organisations such as environmental groups, energy companies or government departments.

Chris de Freitas is a climate scientist in the School of Geography, Geology and Environmental Science at the University of Auckland, where he has been Head of Science and Technology at the Tamaki campus and Pro Vice Chancellor. He has Bachelors and Masters degrees from the University of Toronto and a PhD from the University of Queensland as a Commonwealth Scholar. For ten years he was as an editor of the international journal *Climate Research*. He is an advocate of open and well-informed reporting on scientific issues. In recognition of this, he has three times been the recipient of the New Zealand Association of Scientists Science Communicator Award.

Indur M Goklany is a science and technology policy analyst at the US Department of the Interior. In 30-plus years in government, think tanks, and the private sector, he has written three books and over a hundred monographs, book chapters and papers on topics ranging from climate change, human wellbeing, and technological change to biotechnology, sustainable development and adaptation. He represented the US at the Intergovernmental Panel on Climate Change, and at the negotiations leading to the UN Framework Convention on Climate Change. He was the principal author of the Resource Use and Management Subgroup report in the IPCC's First Assessment. In the 1980s, he managed EPA's fledgling emission trading program before that became popular. His degrees are in Electrical Engineering (BTech, Indian Institute of Technology, Bombay; MS, PhD, Michigan State University). Views expressed here do not necessarily reflect those of the US government or any of its units.

David Holland is an engineer, and a member of the Institution of Engineering and Technology. He has followed the scientific debate over the human contribution to global warming for many years and submitted written evidence to the 2005 House of Lords Enquiry into the Economics of Climate Change.

Richard S Lindzen has been the Alfred P Sloan Professor of Atmospheric Sciences at the Massachusetts Institute of Technology since 1983. Prior to his present position, he held professorships at Harvard and the University of Chicago. His AB, SM and PhD are from Harvard. He is a member of the National Academy of Sciences, the Norwegian Academy of Sciences and Letters, and the American Academy of Arts and Sciences. He is also a fellow of the American Meteorological Society and the American Geophysical Union. He is the recipient of various awards, and has served on numerous committees and panels, including service as a lead author for the IPCC Third Assessment Report. He is the author or coauthor of three books and over 200 papers. His current research is on climate sensitivity, atmospheric convection and on the general circulation of the atmosphere.

Sir Ian Byatt is Chairman of the Water Industry Commission for Scotland, a Senior Associate with Frontier Economics and an Honorary Professor at Birmingham University. He was previously Director General of Water Services (OFWAT) and, before that, Deputy Economic Adviser to HM Treasury.

Ian Castles was a former Head of the Australian Bureau of Statistics, and, at the time of writing, he was a Visiting Fellow in the Asia Pacific School of Economics and Government at The Australian National University, Canberra.

David Henderson is a former Head of the Economics and Statistics Department of the OECD, and is currently a Visiting Professor at the Westminster Business School, London.

*Lord Lawson of Blaby** is a former British Chancellor of the Exchequer, and is currently a member of the House of Lords Select Committee on Economic Affairs.

Ross McKitrick is Associate Professor of Economics at Guelph University, Ontario, Canada, and has written extensively on issues relating to climate change. He was one of twelve experts from around the world asked to present evidence to the US National Academy of Sciences Expert Panel on Millennial Paleoclimate Reconstructions. He is the joint author (with Chris Essex) of *Taken By Storm: The Troubled Science, Policy and Politics of Global Warming* (Key Porter Books), the second edition of which will soon be published.

Julian Morris is Executive Director of the International Policy Network in London and a Visiting Professor at the University of Buckingham.

Sir Alan Peacock is Honorary Professor of Public Finance at Heriot-Watt University and a former Chief Economic Adviser to the Department of Trade and Industry.

Colin Robinson is Emeritus Professor of Economics, University of Surrey, and is a recipient of the International Association for Energy Economics award for 'Outstanding Contributions to the Profession of Energy Economics and its Literature'.

*Lord Skidelsky** is Professor of Political Economy at the University of Warwick, and author of the award-winning biography of John Maynard Keynes. He is currently a member of the House of Lords Select Committee on Economic Affairs.

* Lord Lawson and Lord Skidelsky were signatories of the 2005 report from the Select Committee on Economic Affairs of the House of Lords on 'The Economics of Climate Change'. All the rest of the Part II authors submitted evidence to the Select Committee, to the Stern Review in its opening stages, or to both.

Made in the USA
Monee, IL
13 September 2026

62975586R00437